Members of Congress Since 1789

Third Edition

Members of Congress
Since 1789

Third Edition

Congressional Quarterly Inc.
1414 22nd Street, N.W., Washington, D.C. 20037

Congressional Quarterly Inc.

Congressional Quarterly Inc., an editorial research service and publishing company, serves clients in the fields of news, education, business and government. It combines Congressional Quarterly's specific coverage of Congress, government and politics with the more general subject range of an affiliated service, Editorial Research Reports.

Congressional Quarterly was founded in 1945 by Henrietta and Nelson Poynter. Its basic periodical publication was and still is the *Congressional Quarterly Weekly Report,* mailed to clients every Saturday. A cumulative index is published quarterly.

CQ also publishes college political science textbooks, public affairs paperbacks and reference volumes. The latter include the *CQ Almanac,* a compendium of legislation for one session of Congress that is published each spring, and *Congress and the Nation,* a record of government for a presidential term that is published every four years.

The public affairs books are designed as timely reports to keep journalists, scholars and the public abreast of developing issues, events and trends. Recent titles include *Farm Policy: The Politics of Soil, Surpluses, and Subsidies* and *How Congress Works.*

College textbooks, prepared by outside scholars and published under the CQ Press imprint, include such recent titles as *Congress and Its Members, Second Edition, Congress Reconsidered, Third Edition,* and *Studies of Congress.*

In addition, CQ publishes *The Congressional Monitor,* a daily report on current and future activities of congressional committees. This service is supplemented by *The Congressional Record Scanner,* an abstract of each day's *Congressional Record,* and *Congress in Print,* a weekly listing of committee publications. CQ also publishes newsletters including *Congressional Insight,* a weekly analysis of congressional action, and *Campaign Practices Reports,* a semimonthly update on campaign laws and developments.

CQ conducts seminars and conferences on Congress, the legislative process, the federal budget, national elections and politics, and other current issues. CQ Direct Research is a consulting service that performs contract research and maintains a reference library and query desk for clients.

Editorial Research Reports covers subjects beyond the specialized scope of Congressional Quarterly. It publishes reference material on foreign affairs, business, education, cultural affairs, national security, science and other topics of news interest. Service to clients includes a 6,000-word report four times a month, bound and indexed semiannually. Editorial Research Reports publishes paperback books in its field of coverage. Founded in 1923, the service merged with Congressional Quarterly in 1956.

CQ's online Washington Alert Service provides government affairs specialists with details of congressional action on a continually updated basis.

Printed in the United States of America

Library of Congress Cataloging in Publication Data

Main entry under title:

    Members of Congress Since 1789.
    Bibliography: p.
    1. United States.   Congress—Biography.
    2. Legislators—United States—Biography.   I. Congressional
Quarterly, inc.
JK1010.M45   1985   328.73'092'2   [B]   84-27504
ISBN 0-87187-335-4

Editor: Mary Ames Booker
Contributors: Rhodes Cook, Phil Duncan, Alan Ehrenhalt, Pamela Fessler, Rob Gurwitt, Janet Hook, Catherine P. Jaskowiak, Nancy Lammers, John L. Moore
Cover Design: Robert Redding

━━━━━━━━━━━━━━━━━━━━━━━━━━━━━━━━

Congressional Quarterly Inc.

Eugene Patterson *Editor and President*
Wayne P. Kelley *Publisher*
Peter A. Harkness *Deputy Publisher and Executive Editor*
Robert C. Hur *General Manager*
Robert E. Cuthriell *Director, Research and Development*
I. D. Fuller *Production Manager*
Maceo Mayo *Assistant Production Manager*
Sydney E. Garriss *Computer Services Manager*

Book Department

David R. Tarr *Director*
Joanne D. Daniels *Director, CQ Press*
John L. Moore *Assistant Director*
Kathryn C. Suárez *Book Marketing Manager*
Mary W. Cohn *Associate Editor*
Barbara R. de Boinville *Senior Editor, CQ Press*
Nancy Lammers *Senior Editor*
Nola Healy Lynch *Developmental Editor, CQ Press*
Carolyn Goldinger *Project Editor*
Carolyn McGovern *Project Editor*
Patricia M. Russotto *Project Editor*
Judith Aldock *Editorial Assistant*
Mary Ames Booker *Editorial Assistant*
Catherine P. Jaskowiak *Editorial Assistant*
Mark Johnson *Editorial Assistant*
Renée S. Reiner *Editorial Assistant*
Susanna Spencer *Editorial Assistant*
Elizabeth H. Summers *Editorial Assistant*
Maria Voultsides *Secretary*

Table of Contents

Editor's Note. *Members of Congress Since 1789, Third Edition,* provides researchers, in one volume, with basic biographical data on all persons who have served in Congress since the opening of the First Congress in 1789 through the opening of the 99th Congress in 1985. The first section, "Facts on Members of Congress," contains statistics and summary material on the membership of Congress, including information on age, religion, occupations, women and black members, turnover and shifts between chambers. The more than 11,000 thumbnail biographies that follow this section include dates of birth and death, family relationships between members, party affiliation, state, years of congressional service in House and Senate, and major offices held (president, vice president, governor, Cabinet positions, etc.). The final section, "Congressional Statistics," contains data on congressional sessions, party lineup and leadership.

Profile of Congress

The American electorate makes its decision on a new Congress in November of even-numbered years. Early the following January the elected representatives and senators gather at the Capitol to begin their first session. There always are many new members along with the veterans, especially in the House. But there is a certain uniformity as well because the overall composition of Congress changes gradually. The names of persons elected to Congress change more rapidly than the characteristics of members.

A popular textbook of the 1960s, *American Democracy*, described the "average" member of Congress: "He is a little over 50, has served in Congress for a number of years, and has had previous political experience before coming to Congress, such as membership in his state legislature. He has a college degree, is a lawyer by profession, a war veteran, and, before coming to Congress, was a well-known and popular member of the community. He has been reasonably successful in business or the practice of law, although not so successful that he is sacrificing a huge income in giving up his private occupation for a public job. Congress is clearly not an accurate cross section of the American people but neither is it a community of intellectuals and technicians." [1]

The description was accurate, even to the exclusive use of "he." Although the composition has changed some, most members of Congress are male Caucasian and Christian, especially Protestant. Of the 535 members in Congress at the beginning of 1985, 24 were women, 20 were black (including the non-voting delegate from the District of Columbia) and a scattering were of Hispanic, Asian or Middle Eastern heritage.

Apart from these characteristics, it is likely that a senator earlier served in the House but rare that a representative has served in the Senate. Only two former presidents have served in Congress after their terms in the White House: John Quincy Adams and Andrew Johnson. *(Members of Congress Who Became President, p. 2)*

Although the legal profession has long been dominant among members, most other occupations — including banking, business, journalism, farming and education — have been represented. The principal occupational groups that have been underrepresented are the clergy and workingmen. Scientists and physicians also have been underrepresented in Congress. Few blue-collar workers have served in recent decades, although a few members were from this background before coming to Congress.

Only a handful of Protestant ministers have served in Congress, and no Catholic priest had been a full-fledged member until Rep. Robert F. Drinan, D-Mass., a Jesuit, took his House seat in 1971. (Father Gabriel Richard was the non-voting delegate of the Territory of Michigan from 1821 to 1823.) Drinan did not seek a sixth term in 1980 after Pope John Paul II that year ordered priests not to hold public office. The pope's directive also prompted Robert J. Cornell, a Catholic priest and former U.S. House member, to halt his political comeback bid in Wisconsin. Cornell, a Democrat elected in 1974, served two terms before he was defeated in 1978. In 1985 the incoming 99th Congress contained three clergymen, including the non-voting delegate from the District of Columbia.

From the early days of the republic until the present, the American public often has criticized the qualifications of members of Congress. Through the years the House has received more criticism than the Senate, perhaps because senators were not elected by popular vote until 1914.

An early but still familiar critique of Congress was written in the 1830s by Alexis de Tocqueville, the French aristocrat, scholar and astute observer of America. After he had seen both chambers in session, Tocqueville wrote the following in *Democracy in America:*

> On entering the House of Representatives at Washington, one is struck by the vulgar demeanor of that great assembly. Often there is not a distinguished man in the whole number. Its members are almost all obscure individuals, whose names bring no associations to mind. They are mostly village lawyers, men in trade, or even persons belonging to the lower classes of society. In a country in which education is very general, it is said that the representatives of the people do not always know how to write correctly.
>
> At a few yards' distance is the door of the Senate, which contains within a small space a large proportion of the celebrated men of America. Scarcely an individual is to be seen in it who has not had an active and illustrious career: the Senate is composed of eloquent advocates, distinguished generals, wise magistrates, and statesmen of note, whose arguments would do honor to the most remarkable parliamentary debates of Europe. [2]

The modern view of Congress as a whole probably is not much more charitable than Tocqueville's opinion of the

Members of Congress Who Became President

When Gerald R. Ford became president in 1974, he brought to 23 the number of presidents who had previous service in the House of Representatives or the Senate, or both.

Following is a list of these presidents and the chambers in which they served. Three other presidents — George Washington, John Adams and Thomas Jefferson — had served in the Continental Congress, as had two of those listed, James Madison and James Monroe.

James A. Garfield was elected to the Senate in January 1880 for a term beginning March 4, 1881, but declined to accept in December 1880 because he had been elected president. John Quincy Adams served in the House for 17 years after he had been president, and Andrew Johnson returned to the Senate five months before he died.

House Only	*Senate Only*
James Madison	James Monroe
James K. Polk	John Quincy Adams
Millard Fillmore	Martin Van Buren
Abraham Lincoln	Benjamin Harrison
Rutherford B. Hayes	Warren G. Harding
James A. Garfield	Harry S Truman
William McKinley	
Gerald R. Ford	

Both Chambers

Andrew Jackson	Andrew Johnson
William Henry Harrison	John F. Kennedy
John Tyler	Lyndon B. Johnson
Franklin Pierce	Richard Nixon
James Buchanan	

Source: *Biographical Directory of the American Congress, 1774-1971* (Government Printing Office, 1971).

House. Many voters undoubtedly think that Mark Twain was correct when he quipped that "there is no distinctly native American criminal class except Congress." A Gallup Poll taken in August 1983 found that politicians had a poor public image. Forty-three percent of Americans rated the honesty and ethical standards of senators and representatives as average, while 38 percent rated them as low or very low. Less than 20 percent of the people interviewed gave members of Congress a high rating.[3]

One other major characteristic of Congress is worthy of mention: political control. The Democratic Party controlled both houses for most of the five decades beginning in 1933 as the Great Depression realigned political power in the nation. Only twice — in the 80th Congress (1947-49) and the 83rd Congress (1953-55) — did the Republicans have control. In 1980, however, Republicans gained 12 seats in the U.S. Senate, taking control of that chamber for the first time in a quarter century. The 1980 GOP Senate victory ended the longest one-party dominance of the Senate in American history. Also in 1980 Republicans gained 33 seats in the House, the largest increase for the GOP since 1966. In 1982, though, the Republicans suffered the worst loss by any party at the two-year point in 60 years. The Democrats gained 26 seats, which gave them a 101-seat advantage. In the 1984 elections the GOP gained 14 House seats, leaving Democrats in the majority, but retained control of the Senate while losing two seats.

Characteristics of Members

Age

The average age of members of Congress went up substantially between the Civil War period and the 1950s, but it remained fairly constant from then to the mid-1970s. In the 41st Congress (1869-71), the average age of members was 44.6 years; by the 85th Congress (1957-58), the average had increased by more than nine years, to 53.8. Over the next 18 years, the average fluctuated only slightly. But when the 94th Congress met in January 1975 the average dropped to 50.9 years. The difference was made in the House, where 92 freshmen members reduced the average age of representatives to 49.8 years, the first time since World War II that the average in either chamber had fallen below 50 years.

In the 96th Congress (1979-81) the representatives and senators were younger than in any Congress since 1949. The average age was 49.5 years, the first Congress since World War II in which the figure dropped below 50.

When the 97th Congress met in January 1981, the average dropped again, to 49.2 years. The average age in the Senate dropped from 52.7 years to 52.5 years and in the House from 48.8 to 48.4 years. The House had eight members under 30, the most since World War II.

The 98th Congress (1983-85) surpassed previous records and was the youngest in at least 34 years. The average age was 47.0 years. In the House the average age dropped to 45.5 years, but the Senate grew a little older to 53.4 years.

The 99th Congress was somewhat older than its predecessor, reversing a trend that began with the 91st Congress in 1969. The average 1985 age was 50.5 years — 49.7 in the House and 54.2 in the Senate.

Occupations

From the early days of the republic, the legal profession has been the dominant occupational background of members of Congress, a development that has given that profession substantial overrepresentation. From a level of 37 percent of the House members in the First Congress, the proportion of members with a legal background rose to 70 percent in 1840, then declined slightly in subsequent years and remained at a level of 55 to 60 percent from 1950 to the mid-1970s. More than 54 percent of members of the 95th Congress (1977-79) listed law among their occupations.

The first significant decline in lawyer members began with the 96th Congress. In 1979 the 65 lawyers in the Senate represented a slight decline from 1977. But the House figures changed dramatically. For the first time in at least 30 years, lawyers made up less than a majority of the House. The loss of 17 lawyers between 1976 and 1978 marked the steepest decline among members of the legal profession since 1948.

In the 97th Congress 253 members had law degrees — 17 fewer than in the 96th Congress. The House figures were more dramatic. Only 194 representatives were lawyers, a decline of 11 from the previous Congress and a drop of 28 since 1976. Lawyers in the House and Senate were no longer a majority of the members.

The trend reversed in 1983 when 261 members held law degrees — eight more than in the previous Congress. The Senate increased from 59 to 61 lawyers, and the House grew by six to 200 lawyers.

Law was still the largest single profession among members of Congress in 1985, but the overall number of lawyers dropped to 251. The Senate remained at 61, but the House shrank to 190 lawyers.

The next most common profession of members has been business or banking. Businessmen have held increasingly more seats since 1977. The 99th Congress contained 174 members previously involved in business or banking, which ranked them second to lawyers. Other occupations that have been prominently represented in recent Congresses are education, agriculture, journalism and public service or politics. *(Occupations of Members, 99th Congress, p. 6)*

Religion

Among religious groups, Protestants have comprised nearly three-fourths of the membership of both houses in recent years, although Roman Catholic members have become more numerous than members belonging to any single Protestant denomination. Catholics took the lead from Methodists in 1965 and have retained it since.

At the beginning of the 99th Congress, there were 144 Catholics. More than half of the Protestant members were affiliated with four denominations: Methodists led with 78, followed by 65 Episcopalians, 56 Presbyterians and 47 Baptists. There were 38 Jewish members.

Women in Congress

Women, who were not allowed to vote until 1920, always have been underrepresented in Congress. Starting with Rep. Jeannette Rankin, R-Mont., elected in 1916, a total of 115 women had been elected or appointed to Congress by the beginning of 1985. The total included 101 in the House only, 13 in the Senate only, and one — Margaret Chase Smith, R-Maine — who served in both chambers. *(Women Members of Congress, pp. 4, 7)*

Even the total of 115 is misleading. Two women were never sworn in because Congress was not in session between their election and the expiration of their terms. Another sat in the Senate for just one day. Several were appointed or elected to fill unexpired terms and served in Congress for less than a year. Only five women have been elected to full Senate terms.

By the beginning of 1985, 37 percent of the women members had entered Congress after their husbands. Forty-three were married to members who served before them; 40 of these (six senators and 34 representatives) were appointed or elected to fill the unexpired terms of their late husbands. Rep. Charlotte T. Reid, R-Ill., and Rep. Marilyn Lloyd, D-Tenn., became their parties' nominees when their husbands died between the primary and general elections. One woman, Rep. Emily Taft Douglas, D-Ill., was elected to Congress before her husband, Sen. Paul H. Douglas, D-Ill. Another woman, Rep. Martha Keys, D-Kan., married a colleague from a different state, Rep. Andrew Jacobs, D-

Ind., early in 1976. The marriage, the first in congressional history, was thought to jeopardize her re-election chances, but both Keys and Jacobs returned to the 95th Congress. She did lose the following election.

Following the election of Rep. Rankin in 1916, the number of women in Congress increased only slightly until 1928, when nine were elected to the House for the 71st Congress. Women's membership reached a peak of 19 (two senators, 17 representatives) in the 87th Congress (1961-62) and did not match that until 1975, when 19 women served in the House.

The first woman named to the Senate served there only one day. On Oct. 2, 1922, Rebecca L. Felton, Independent-Democrat, Ga., was appointed to fill the vacancy created by the death of Sen. Thomas E. Watson, D-Ga.; Sen. Felton was not sworn in until Nov. 21, however, and on the next day she turned the seat over to Walter F. George, D-Ga., who had been elected to fill the vacancy. In 1931, Hattie W. Caraway, D-Ark., became the second woman in the Senate's history when she was named to fill the vacancy created by the death of her husband, Thaddeus H. Caraway, D-Ark. In 1932 and 1938, she was elected to full six-year-terms. Through the election of 1980, only four other women — Maurine B. Neuberger, D-Ore., Margaret Chase Smith, R-Maine, Nancy Landon Kassebaum, R-Kan., and Paula Hawkins, R-Fla. — had been elected to full Senate terms. Sen. Kassebaum, re-elected in 1984, was the first woman ever elected to the Senate without being preceded in Congress by her husband.

Although many women elected to Congress on the basis of "widow's mandate" have served only the remainder of the husband's term, others have stayed to build strong political reputations for themselves. Both Sen. Smith and Rep. Edith N. Rogers, R-Mass. — who hold the records for

Age Structure of Congress

(Average ages at start of first session)

	House	Senate	Congress
1949	51.0	58.5	53.8
1951	52.0	56.6	53.0
1953	52.0	56.6	53.0
1955	51.4	57.2	52.2
1957	52.9	57.9	53.8
1959	51.7	57.1	52.7
1961	52.2	57.0	53.2
1963	51.7	56.8	52.7
1965	50.5	57.7	51.9
1967	50.8	57.7	52.1
1969	52.2	56.6	53.0
1971	51.9	56.4	52.7
1973	51.1	55.3	52.0
1975	49.8	55.5	50.9
1977	49.3	54.7	50.3
1979	48.8	52.7	49.5
1981	48.4	52.5	49.2
1983	45.5	53.4	47.0
1985	49.7	54.2	50.5

Women Members of Congress . . .

As of the beginning of 1985, a total of 115 women had been elected or appointed to Congress. One hundred and one served in the House only, 13 in the Senate and one — Margaret Chase Smith, R-Maine

—in both chambers. Following is a list of the women members, their parties, states and the years in which they served. In addition, Mary E. Farrrington, R-Hawaii (1954-57), served as a non-voting delegate.

Senate

Rebecca L. Felton (Ind. D Ga.)*	1922
Hattie W. Caraway (D Ark.)	1931-45
Rose McConnell Long (D La.)	1936-37
Dixie Bibb Graves (D Ala.)	1937-38
Gladys Pyle (R S.D.)†	1938-39
Vera C. Bushfield (R S.D.)	1948
Margaret Chase Smith (R Maine)	1949-73
Hazel H. Abel (R Neb.)	1954
Eva K. Bowring (R Neb.)	1954
Maurine B. Neuberger (D Ore.)	1960-67
Elaine S. Edwards (D La.)	1972
Maryon Pittman Allen (D Ala.)	1978
Muriel Buck Humphrey (D Minn.)	1978
Nancy Landon Kassebaum (R Kan.)	1979—
Paula Hawkins (R Fla.)	1981—

House

Jeannette Rankin (R Mont.)	1917-19; 1941-43
Alice M. Robertson (R Okla.)	1921-23
Winnifred S. M. Huck (R Ill.)	1922-23
Mae E. Nolan (R Calif.)	1923-25
Florence P. Kahn (R Calif.)	1925-37
Mary T. Norton (D N.J.)	1925-51
Edith N. Rogers (R Mass.)	1925-60
Katherine G. Langley (R Ky.)	1927-31
Ruth H. McCormick (R Ill.)	1929-31
Pearl P. Oldfield (D Ark.)	1929-31
Ruth B. Owen (D Fla.)	1929-33
Ruth S. B. Pratt (R N.Y.)	1929-33
Effiegene Wingo (D Ark.)	1930-33
Willa M. B. Eslick (D Tenn.)	1932-33
Marian W. Clarke (R N.Y.)	1933-35
Virginia E. Jenckes (D Ind.)	1933-39
Kathryn O'Loughlin McCarthy (D Kan.)	1933-35
Isabella S. Greenway (D Ariz.)	1934-37
Caroline L. G. O'Day (D N.Y.)	1935-43
Nan W. Honeyman (D Ore.)	1937-39
Elizabeth H. Gasque (D S.C.)†	1938-39
Clara G. McMillan (D S.C.)	1939-41
Jessie Sumner (R Ill.)	1939-47
Frances P. Bolton (R Ohio)	1940-69
Florence R. Gibbs (D Ga.)	1940-41
Margaret Chase Smith (R Maine)	1940-49
Katherine E. Byron (D Md.)	1941-43
Veronica G. Boland (D Pa.)	1942-43
Clare Boothe Luce (R Conn.)	1943-47
Winifred C. Stanley (R N.Y.)	1943-45
Willa L. Fulmer (D S.C.)	1944-45
Emily T. Douglas (D Ill.)	1945-47
Helen G. Douglas (D Calif.)	1945-51
Chase G. Woodhouse (D Conn.)	1945-47; 1949-51
Helen D. Mankin (D Ga.)	1946-47
Eliza J. Pratt (D N.C.)	1946-47
Georgia L. Lusk (D N.M.)	1947-49
Katherine P. C. St. George (R N.Y.)	1947-65

the longest service by women in their respective chambers — were elected to the House to fill the unexpired terms of their late husbands. Smith served in the House until 1948, when she won the first of four terms in the Senate. Rogers served in the House for 35 years, from June 1925 until her death in September 1960.

As women have become more active in politics at all levels, the congressional tradition of "widow's mandate" has weakened. Only three of the 24 women in Congress at the beginning of the 99th Congress held the seats of their late husbands, and all had been elected to the positions. Corrine C. "Lindy" (Mrs. Hale) Boggs, D-La., and Cardiss Collins, D-Ill., have served since 1973. Sala Burton, D-Calif., took her husband's seat in June 1983 and was elected to a full term in 1984.

Women have made notable gains in recent congressional elections. In 1981 for the first time in history there were 21 women members in Congress — 19 in the House and two in the Senate. (In July 1982 Rep. Jean Ashbrook, R-Ohio, took her husband's seat, raising the number to 20 in the House.) The trend continued in 1983 when the number rose to 21 women representatives in the House, while the number of women senators remained the same. By the end of the 98th Congress there were 22 congresswomen (Rep. Sala Burton was elected to fill the seat of her husband, Rep. Phillip Burton, upon his death in 1983). Women did not gain any seats in the 1984 elections. As of January 1985, there were 24 women members in Congress — 22 in the House and two in the Senate.

In her book about women who had served in Congress from 1917 through 1972, Hope Chamberlin wrote:

"Most members of this numerically select group were reared in modest economic circumstances; almost all attended college; only a few never married. The majority have been white, Anglo-Saxon, and Protestant. Beyond hard work and the gift of intuition, however, they have had little else in common. The laws of chance, if nothing else, argue against parallels. Their geographical heritage embraces 38 of the 50 states; their precongressional careers, if any, span a broad spectrum: teaching, stenography, journalism, social work, broadcasting, the theater, law — even cowpunching." [4]

...More Than 100 Since 1917

Reva Z. B. Bosone (D Utah)	1949-53
Cecil M. Harden (R Ind.)	1949-59
Edna F. Kelly (D N.Y.)	1949-69
Vera D. Buchanan (D Pa.)	1951-55
Marguerite S. Church (R Ill.)	1951-63
Maude E. Kee (D W. Va.)	1951-65
Ruth Thompson (R Mich.)	1951-57
Gracie B. Pfost (D Idaho)	1953-63
Leonor K. Sullivan (D Mo.)	1953-77
Iris F. Blitch (D Ga.)	1955-63
Edith Green (D Ore.)	1955-74
Martha W. Griffiths (D Mich.)	1955-74
Coya G. Knutson (D Minn.)	1955-59
Kathryn E. Granahan (D Pa.)	1956-63
Florence P. Dwyer (R N.J.)	1957-73
Catherine D. May (R Wash.)	1959-71
Edna O. Simpson (R Ill.)	1959-61
Jessica McC. Weis (R N.Y.)	1959-63
Julia B. Hansen (D Wash.)	1960-74
Catherine D. Norrell (D Ark.)	1961-63
Louise G. Reece (R Tenn.)	1961-63
Corinne B. Riley (D S.C.)	1962-63
Charlotte T. Reid (R Ill.)	1963-71
Irene B. Baker (R Tenn.)	1964-65
Patsy T. Mink (D Hawaii)	1965-77
Lera M. Thomas (D Texas)	1966-67
Margaret M. Heckler (R Mass.)	1967-83
Shirley Chisholm (D N.Y.)	1969-83
Bella S. Abzug (D N.Y.)	1971-77
Ella T. Grasso (D Conn.)	1971-75
Louise Day Hicks (D Mass.)	1971-73
Elizabeth B. Andrews (D Ala.)	1972-73
Yvonne B. Burke (D Calif.)	1973-79
Marjorie S. Holt (R Md.)	1973—
Elizabeth Holtzman (D N.Y.)	1973-81
Barbara C. Jordan (D Texas)	1973-79

Patricia Schroeder (D Colo.)	1973—
Corinne C. Boggs (D La.)	1973—
Cardiss R. Collins (D Ill.)	1973—
Marilyn Lloyd (D Tenn.)	1975—
Millicent Fenwick (R N.J.)	1975-83
Martha E. Keys (D Kan.)	1975-79
Helen S. Meyner (D N.J.)	1975-79
Virginia Smith (R Neb.)	1975—
Gladys N. Spellman (D Md.)	1975-81
Shirley N. Pettis (R Calif.)	1975-79
Barbara A. Mikulski (D Md.)	1977—
Mary Rose Oakar (D Ohio)	1977—
Beverly Barton Butcher Byron (D Md.)	1979—
Geraldine Ferraro (D N.Y.)	1979-85
Olympia Jean Bouchles Snowe (R Maine)	1979—
Bobbi Fiedler (R Calif.)	1981—
Lynn M. Martin (R Ill.)	1981—
Marge Roukema (R N.J.)	1981—
Claudine Schneider (R R.I.)	1981—
Jean Ashbrook (R Ohio)	1982-83
Barbara B. Kennelly (D Conn.)	1982—
Sala Burton (D Calif.)	1983—
Barbara Boxer (D Calif.)	1983—
Katie Hall (D Ind.)	1983-85
Nancy L. Johnson (R Conn.)	1983—
Marcy Kaptur (D Ohio)	1983—
Barbara Vucanovich (R Nev.)	1983—
Helen Delich Bentley (R Md.)	1985—
Jan Meyers (R Kan.)	1985—

* Felton was sworn in Nov. 21, 1922, to fill the vacancy created by the death of Thomas E. Watson, D (1921-22). The next day she gave up her seat to Walter F. George, D (1922-57), the elected candidate for the vacancy.

† Never sworn in because Congress was not in session between election and expiration of term.

Blacks in Congress

At the beginning of 1985, a total of 57 black Americans had served in Congress — three in the Senate and 54 in the House. Almost half had served in the 19th century after the Civil War. All but 16 of the 35 blacks elected in the 20th century were serving in the 99th Congress when it opened. (Black Members of Congress, pp. 7, 8)

The first black elected to Congress was John W. Menard, R-La., who won election in 1868 to an unexpired term in the 40th Congress. Menard's election was disputed, however, and the House denied him his seat. Thus the distinction of being the first black to serve in Congress went to Hiram Revels, R-Miss., who served in the Senate from February 1870 to March 1871. The first black to serve in the House was Joseph H. Rainey, R-S.C., from 1870 to 1879.

In 1874, a second black, Blanche K. Bruce, R-Miss., was elected to the Senate; Bruce was the first black member to serve a full term in the Senate and the last elected to that chamber until Edward W. Brooke, R-Mass., won in 1966. The last black elected to Congress in the 19th century

was George Henry White, R-N.C., who won election in 1896 and 1898 but did not seek renomination in 1900.

For three decades there were no blacks in Congress. In 1928 Rep. Oscar dePriest, R-Ill., became the first black member elected in the 20th century. Only three more blacks were elected during the next 25 years. But with the election of Rep. Charles C. Diggs Jr., D-Mich., in 1954, black membership began to increase. Three new black representatives were elected in the next decade. Sen. Brooke won his first term in 1966. Three more blacks were elected to the House in 1968, five more in 1970, three more in 1972, one in a special election in 1973, and one more in the 1974 general election. No additional blacks were elected to the 95th Congress. Four blacks were elected to the House in 1978 but Sen. Brooke, the only black in the Senate, was defeated. Four more blacks — all in the House — were elected to the 97th and 98th Congresses. No additional black members were elected in 1984.

While black membership increased, several black representatives achieved enough seniority to be named House committee chairmen. William L. Dawson, D-Ill., served as

Members' Occupations, 99th Congress

The chart of occupations of members of the 99th Congress, which began Jan. 3, 1985, was compiled from the records of Congressional Quarterly. Some members listed more than one occupation.

Almost one-half (190) of the 435 representatives and 61 of the 100 senators cited law as a profession. The next most frequently listed professions were in business or banking; more than a third listed occupations in those fields.

Occupation	House D	House R	House Total	Senate D	Senate R	Senate Total	Congress Total
Aeronautics	0	3	3	1	1	2	5
Agriculture	11	13	24	2	5	7	31
Business or banking	68	76	144	12	18	30	174
Clergy	2	0	2	0	1	1	3
Education	24	13	37	3	7	10	47
Engineering	1	3	4	0	1	1	5
Journalism	11	10	21	6	2	8	29
Labor officials	2	0	2	0	0	0	2
Law	121	69	190	32	29	61	251
Law enforcement	6	2	8	0	0	0	8
Medicine	1	2	3	1	0	1	4
Military	0	1	1	0	1	1	2
Professional sports	2	1	3	1	0	1	4
Public service/ Politics	42	23	65	4	7	11	76

chairman of the Government Operations Committee from 1949 until his death in 1970. Adam Clayton Powell Jr., D-N.Y., was chairman of the Education and Labor Committee from 1961 until the House stripped him of the post in 1967 because of alleged misuse of committee funds. Diggs was chairman of the District of Columbia Committee from 1973 until 1979. He voluntarily relinquished his committee chairmanship after being censured by the House on July 31, 1979, for misuse of clerk-hire funds. Diggs resigned from the House June 3, 1980, after he was convicted on 29 felony counts. Robert N. C. Nix, D-Pa., was chairman of the Post Office and Civil Service Committee from 1977 until he was defeated in the 1978 primary election. Since 1980 there have been several more black committee chairmen.

In 1968 Rep. Shirley Chisholm, D-N.Y., became the first black woman to be elected to Congress. She was joined in the House by Yvonne Brathwaite Burke, D-Calif., and Barbara C. Jordan, D-Texas, who both served from 1972 until 1979. In a special election the following year, Cardiss Collins, D-Ill., won the House seat previously held by her late husband, George W. Collins, and became the fourth black woman in Congress. The fifth black woman, Katie Hall, D-Ind., won a special election in November 1982, filling the seat vacated by the death of Adam Benjamin Jr. She lost the seat in the 1984 Indiana primary elections.

Rep. Jordan and Rep. Andrew Young, D-Ga., both elected in 1972, were the first blacks in the 20th century to represent Southern constituencies. After the 1974 election they were joined by Rep. Harold E. Ford, D-Tenn. In 1977, Andrew Young resigned to become U.S. ambassador to the United Nations.

All 22 black members of Congress in the 19th century were Republicans, reflecting the political alignment of the Civil War. But in the 20th century, through early 1985, only two of the 35 black members had been Republicans.

In 1971 a loose alliance of black representatives formally organized the Congressional Black Caucus, calling themselves congressmen-at-large who represented all black citizens. From 1971 through 1985, every black person elected to the House had joined the caucus. Another caucus member was Walter E. Fauntroy, D, non-voting delegate from the District of Columbia, first elected in 1971.

Turnover in Membership

Congress experienced high turnover rates in the 19th and early 20th centuries. Throughout the 19th century, the turnover in the House was greater than in the Senate, primarily because of the exigencies of campaign travel every two years and the tendency of state legislatures to continue re-electing the same men to the Senate. In 1869, for example, only 98 of 243 House members had served in previous Congresses. For several years after the direct election of senators was instituted by the 17th Amendment in 1913, Senate turnover increased, particularly in the larger states.

In the middle of the 20th century, congressional turnover held steady at a relatively low rate. In the quarter century after World War II, each Congress had an average of about 78 new members — 65 in the House and 12.7 in the Senate.

The 92nd Congress opened in 1971 with 67 freshmen — 56 in the House and 11 in the Senate. The 93rd Congress began in 1973 with 82 freshmen — 69 in the House and 13 in the Senate. In the next Congress the number of freshmen jumped dramatically. The 94th Congress convened early in 1975 with 102 new members — 92 representatives and 10 senators — the largest turnover in the House since 1949.

Several factors contributed to the increased turnover. The elections of 1972 and 1974 were affected by redistrict-

Number of Black Members In Congress 1947-1985

Listed below by Congress is the number of black members of the Senate and House of Representatives from the 80th Congress through the opening of the 99th Congress. The figures do not include the nonvoting delegate from the District of Columbia.

Congress	Senate	House
99th 1985-87	0	19
98th 1983-85	0	20
97th 1981-83	0	17
96th 1979-81	0	16
95th 1977-79	1	16
94th 1975-77	1	16
93rd 1973-75	1	15
92nd 1971-73	1	12
91st 1969-71	1	9
90th 1967-69	1	5
89th 1965-67		6
88th 1963-65		5
87th 1961-63		4
86th 1959-61		4
85th 1957-59		4
84th 1955-57		3
83rd 1953-55		2
82nd 1951-53		2
81st 1949-51		2
80th 1947-49		2

Number of Women Members In Congress 1947-1985

Listed below by Congress is the number of women members of the Senate and House of Representatives from the 80th Congress through the beginning of the 99th Congress. The figures include women appointed to office as well as those chosen by voters in general elections and special elections.

Congress	Senate	House
99th 1985-87	2	22
98th 1983-85	2	22
97th 1981-83	2	21
96th 1979-81	1	16
95th 1977-79	2	18
94th 1975-77	0	19
93rd 1973-75	0	16
92nd 1971-73	2	13
91st 1969-71	1	10
90th 1967-69	1	11
89th 1965-67	2	10
88th 1963-65	2	11
87th 1961-63	2	17
86th 1959-61	1	16
85th 1957-59	1	15
84th 1955-57	1	16
83rd 1953-55	3	12
82nd 1951-53	1	10
81st 1949-51	1	9
80th 1947-49	1	7

ing that followed the 1970 Census; many House veterans had retired rather than face strong new opposition. Those two elections also were the first in which 18-year-olds were allowed to vote for members of Congress. In 1974, probably the chief reason for change was the Watergate scandal, which put an end to the Nixon administration and badly damaged the Republican Party. The Democrats gained 43 seats from the Republicans in the House, and 75 of the 92 freshman representatives at the beginning of the 94th Congress were Democrats.

Most of those Democrats managed to hold on to their seats in the 1976 elections. Of the 75 new Democrats elected in 1974 and the four elected since then, 78 sought reelection and 76 succeeded. The 95th Congress opened in 1977 with 85 freshmen.

In contrast to 1974, the upheaval in the 1976 elections came in the Senate. At the opening of the 95th Congress, there were 18 new members in the Senate. This marked the largest turnover in the Senate since 1958. In the 95th Congress, members elected for the first time in either 1972, 1974 or 1976 made up more than one half of the total membership of the House.

In 1978, 20 new senators were elected representing the second largest group of freshman senators since the begin-

ning of popular Senate elections in 1914. The only larger freshman class was the one after the 1946 election — 23 senators. Three major factors accounted for the arrival of so many newcomers. Ten incumbents retired in 1978, more than in any year since World War II. Three incumbents were beaten in primaries, the most in a decade. And seven incumbents were defeated for reelection, the second highest number in 20 years.

With a record 58 open House seats in the 1978 election because of retirement, desire to seek other office, death or primary defeat, the House gained 77 freshmen.

The 97th Congress opened in 1981 with 92 freshmen — 18 in the Senate and 74 in the House. The Republicans won Senate control for the first time since 1952, ending the longest one-party dominance of the Senate in history. They also netted the largest increase in the House since 1966.

The 1982 election broke several records. With only five new senators, the resulting turnover was the smallest in the 68-year history of popular Senate elections. The Senate party ratio remained the same as in the 97th Congress — 54-46 — and 95 of the 100 senators returned.

In contrast, the House had 81 new members, 57 of them Democrats. The Republicans lost 26 seats in the House, half of them were freshmen. Only three other elec-

Black Members of Congress

As of the beginning of 1985, 57 black Americans had served in Congress: three in the Senate and 54 in the House. Following is a list of the black members, their parties and states and the years of service. In addition, John W. Menard, R-La., won a disputed election in 1868 but was not permitted to take his seat in Congress. Walter E. Fauntroy, D- D.C., began serving in 1971 as non-voting delegate from the District of Columbia.

Senate

Hiram R. Revels (R Miss.)	1870-71
Blanche K. Bruce (R Miss.)	1875-81
Edward W. Brooke (R Mass.)	1967-79

House

Joseph H. Rainey (R S.C.)	1870-79
Jefferson F. Long (R Ga.)	1870-71
Robert B. Elliott (R S.C.)	1871-74
Robert C. DeLarge (R S.C.)	1871-73
Benjamin S. Turner (R Ala.)	1871-73
Josiah T. Walls (R Fla.)	1871-76
Richard H. Cain (R S.C.)	1873-75; 1877-79
John R. Lynch (R Miss.)	1873-77; 1882-83
James T. Rapier (R Ala.)	1873-75
Alonzo J. Ransier (R S.C.)	1873-75
Jeremiah Haralson (R Ala.)	1875-77
John A. Hyman (R N.C.)	1875-77
Charles E. Nash (R La.)	1875-77
Robert Smalls (R S.C.)	1875-79; 1882-83; 1884-87
James E. O'Hara (R N.C.)	1883-87
Henry P. Cheatham (R N.C.)	1889-93
John M. Langston (R Va.)	1890-91
Thomas E. Miller (R S.C.)	1890-91
George W. Murray (R S.C.)	1893-95; 1896-97
George H. White (R N.C.)	1897-1901
Oscar De Priest (R Ill.)	1929-35
Arthur W. Mitchell (D Ill.)	1935-43
William L. Dawson (D Ill.)	1943-70
Adam C. Powell Jr. (D N.Y.)	1945-67; 1969-71
Charles C. Diggs Jr. (D Mich.)	1955-80
Robert N.C. Nix (D Pa.)	1958-79
Augustus F. Hawkins (D Calif.)	1963—
John Conyers Jr. (D Mich.)	1965—
Louis Stokes (D Ohio)	1969—
William L. Clay (D Mo.)	1969—
Shirley Chisholm (D N.Y.)	1969-83
George W. Collins (D Ill.)	1970-72
Ronald V. Dellums (D Calif.)	1971—
Ralph H. Metcalfe (D Ill.)	1971-78
Parren J. Mitchell (D Md.)	1971—
Charles B. Rangel (D N.Y.)	1971—
Yvonne B. Burke (D Calif.)	1973-79
Cardiss Collins (D Ill.)	1973—
Barbara C. Jordan (D Texas)	1973-79
Andrew Young (D Ga.)	1973-77
Harold E. Ford (D Tenn.)	1975—
Julian C. Dixon (D Calif.)	1979—
William H. Gray (D Pa.)	1979—
George T. Leland (D Texas)	1979—
Bennett McVey Stewart (D Ill.)	1979-81
George W. Crockett Jr. (D Mich.)	1981—
Mervin M. Dymally (D Calif.)	1981—
Gus Savage (D Ill.)	1981—
Harold Washington (D Ill.)	1981-83
Katie Hall (D Ind.)	1983-85
Charles A. Hayes (D Ill.)	1983—
Major R. Owens (D N.Y.)	1983—
Edolphus Towns (D N.Y.)	1983—
Alan Wheat (D Mo.)	1983—

Sources: Maurine Christopher, *America's Black Congressmen* (Thomas Y. Crowell Co., 1971), 267-69; *Biographical Directory of the American Congress, 1774-1971* (Government Printing Office, 1971).

tions in the past 30 years had brought in so many freshmen Democrats. As in the 1972 and 1974 elections, redistricting played a major part. The 1980 census shifted 17 seats from the Northeast and Midwest to the Sun Belt states of the South and West. The Democrats took 10 of these seats. The 98th Congress opened with 269 Democrats and 166 Republicans in the House.

In the 1984 elections the Republicans had a modest gain of 14 seats in the House. There were few open seats so there were only 43 new House members in the 99th Congress. The Senate had another low turnover with only seven newcomers. On only four previous occasions since 1914 had there been fewer than 10 Senate newcomers. The Democrats picked up two seats in the Senate. The 99th Congress opened January 3, 1985, with 182 Republicans and 252 Democrats in the House, and 53 Republicans and 47 Democrats in the Senate.

Shifts Between Chambers

From the early days of Congress there has been shifting of membership from one chamber to another. The House and the Senate are equal under the law, and representatives tend to bristle when anyone refers to their chamber as the "lower house." But that does not stop them from running for the Senate whenever they see an opening. From 1789 to 1985, a total of 535 former House members had served in the Senate, while only 57 former senators had become representatives.

In recent years few former senators have gone to the House, and those who did usually had been defeated in their efforts to be re-elected to the Senate. From 1962 to 1985, 110 House members tried for a place in the Senate; however, not one person left the Senate to run for the House.

Those representatives who aspire to become senators

are usually taking a risk. Of the 110 representatives who ran for the Senate from 1962 to 1985, only 42 succeeded. Six out of 16 won in 1970, four out of 10 in 1972, one out of six in 1974, five out of 19 in 1976, six out of seven in 1978, six out of eight in 1980, one out of two in 1982, and four out of 12 in 1984. (Two representatives were defeated in the 1984 primary Senate elections.) The risks are higher if the House members are older and have considerable seniority.

In explaining why they have left the House to try for the Senate, former representatives have cited the Senate's greater prestige and publicity, the more stable six-year term, larger staffs and more generous perquisites, their increased effectiveness as legislators in a chamber of 100 members instead of 435, the Senate's greater role in foreign affairs, and the challenge of moving into a new job with a larger constituency.

Shifting of members from one chamber to the other began in the 1790s, when 19 former representatives became senators and three former senators moved to the House. The number of House members who became senators increased over the next several decades, reaching 55 in the years from 1800 to 1820 and 39 in the 1940s alone. The trend continued. Between 1967 and January 1985, 38 former House members assumed Senate seats. By contrast, the greatest number of former senators to become House members in any one decade was nine in the years between 1810 and 1820. From 1900 through 1985, only 11 former senators became members of the House. The only former senator in the House at the convening of the 99th Congress was Claude Pepper, D-Fla., who had served continuously as a representative since 1963. Pepper had been a senator from 1936 through 1951.

Perhaps the most notable shift from the Senate to the House was that of Henry Clay, Democratic-Republican, Ky., who gave up his Senate seat in 1811 to assume a House seat. In his first term in the House, Clay was elected Speaker — an office he used successfully to help push the country into the War of 1812. After five terms in the House, he returned to the Senate in 1823. Another prominent House member who had once been a senator was John Quincy Adams, Whig-Mass., who also was one of only two former presidents to serve in Congress after his term in the White House. Adams, who was known as "Old Man Elo-

quent," was one of the most influential members of the Whig opposition in the House to President Andrew Jackson in the 1830s.

Congressional Service

As of 1985, the record for the longest service in Congress — 56 years — was held by Carl Hayden, D-Ariz., who retired from the Senate in 1969 at the age of 91.

Hayden gave up his job as a county sheriff to become Arizona's first representative in 1912. He was sworn in Feb. 19, 1912, five days after Arizona became a state, and served in the House for 15 years.

In 1927 he moved to the Senate where he served seven six-year terms. When Hayden retired, he was president pro tempore of the Senate and chairman of the Senate Appropriations Committee.

Runner-up to Hayden was Rep. Emanuel Celler, D-N.Y., who served in the House for 25 consecutive terms, 1923-73. Celler was defeated in a Democratic primary election in 1972.

Notes
1. Robert K. Carr, Marver H. Bernstein, Walter F. Murphy, *American Democracy,* 5th ed. (Holt, Rinehart and Winston, 1968), 231.
2. Alexis de Tocqueville, *Democracy in America,* vol. 1 (Vintage Books, 1971), 211-12.
3. *Gallup Opinion Index,* Aug. 4, 1983.
4. Hope Chamberlin, *A Minority of Members: Women in the U.S. Congress* (Praeger, 1973), pp. 3-4.

Members of Congress
Biographical Index 1789-1985

Members of Congress: 1789-1985

The names in this index include, alphabetically, all senators, representatives, resident commissioners and territorial delegates who served in Congress from March 4, 1789 through January 1985 — the First through the beginning of the 99th Congress.

The material is organized as follows: name, relationship to other members and presidents and vice presidents; party, state (of service); date of birth, date of death (if applicable); congressional service, service as president, vice president, member of the Cabinet or Supreme Court, governor, delegate to the Continental Congress, House or Senate majority leader, Speaker of the House, president pro tempore of the Senate and chairman of the Democratic or Republican National Committee. If member changed parties during his congressional service, party designation appearing after the member's name is that which applied at the end of such service and further breakdown is included after dates of congressional service. Party designation is multiple only if member was elected by two or more parties at the same time. Where service date is left open, member was serving in the 99th Congress.

Dates of service are inclusive, starting in year of service and ending when service ends. Under the Constitution, terms of service from 1789 to 1933 were from March 4 to March 3; since 1934, service has been from Jan. 3 to Jan. 3. In actual practice, members often have been sworn in on other dates at the beginning of a Congress. Exact date is shown (where available) if member began or ended his service in mid-term.

The major source for this list was the *Biographical Directory of the American Congress 1774-1971* compiled under the direction of the Joint Committee on Printing. Additional data were obtained from the files of the Joint Committee on Printing, the House Historian, the Senate Historian, the *Congressional Directory*, and Congressional Quarterly's *Almanac, Guide to Congress, Guide to U.S. Elections,* and *Weekly Report.*

Abbreviation	Party
AAD	Adams Anti Democrat
ABD	Anti Broderick Democrat
AD	Anti Democrat
Ad.D	Adams Democrat
AF	Antifederalist
AJD	Anti Jackson Democrat
AL	American Laborite
Alliance D	Alliance Democrat
AM	Anti Monopolist
AMas.	Anti Mason
AMas. D	Anti Mason Democrat
AMD	Anti Monopoly Democrat
AND	Anti Nebraska Democrat
ASP	American Party
AR	Adams Republican
ASW	Anti Slavery Whig
ATD	Anti Tammany Democrat
AW	American Whig
C	Conservative
Cal.D	Calhoun Democrat
Cal.N	Calhoun Nullifier
CassD	Cass Democrat
CD	Clay Democrat
Clinton D	Clinton Democrat
Coal.	Coalitionist
Con.D	Conservative Democrat
Const U	Constitutional Unionist
CR	Conservative Republican
CU	Conservative Unionist
CW	Clay Whig
D	Democrat
DD	Douglas Democrat
DFL	Democrat Farmer Labor
DR	Democratic Republican
E	Emancipationist
F	Federalist
FA	Farmers Alliance
FL	Farmer Laborite
FS	Free-Soiler
FSD	Free Soil Democrat
FSil.	Free Silver
FSil.R	Free Silver Republican
FSW	Free Soil Whig
Fus	Fusionist
Fus.D	Fusionist Democrat

Abbreviation	Party
G	Greenbacker
GD	Greenback Democrat
G-Lab.	Greenback Laborite
G Lab. Ref.	Greenback Labor Reformer
HCW	Henry Clay Whig
HTW	High Tariff Whig
I	Independent
ID	Independent Democrat
IR	Independent Republican
IRad.	Independent Radical
IRef.	Independent Reformer
ISil.R	Independent Silver Republican
IW	Independent Whig
JD	Jackson Democrat
Jeff.D	Jefferson Democrat
JFSt.	Jackson Free Statesman
KN	Know Nothing
L	Liberal
Lab.	Laborite
LD	Liberal Democrat
L&O	Law & Order
L&OW	Law & Order Whig
LR	Liberal Republican
LW	Liberation Whig
MCD	Missouri Compromise Democrat
N	Nullifier
NAD	Native American Democrat
Nat.	Nationalist
Nat.A	National American
Nat.G	National Greenbacker
ND	Nullifier Democrat
New Prog.	New Progressive
Nonpart.	Nonpartisan
Nonpart.R	Nonpartisan Republican
NR	National Republican
P	Populist
PD	Popular Democrat
PP	People's Party
PR	Progressive Republican

Abbreviation	Party
Prog.	Progressive
Prohib.	Prohibitionist
Protect.	Protectionist
Protect.TD	Protective Tariff Democrat
PSD	Popular Sovereignty Democrat
R	Republican
Rad.	Radical
Read	Readjuster
Ref. R	Reform Republican
RG	Republican Greenbacker
R Prog.	Republican Progressive
RR	Radical Republican
Sil.D	Silver Democrat
Sil.R	Silver Republican
Soc.	Socialist
SR	State Rights Party
SRD	State Rights Democrat
SRFT	State Rights Free Trader
SRW	State Rights Whig
SRWD	State Rights War Democrat
T	Temperance Party
TD	Tariff Democrat
Tyler D	Tyler Democrat
U	Unionist
UA	Ultra Abolitionist
UC	Union Conservative
UD	Union Democrat
UL	Union Laborite
UR	Union Republican
UU	Unconditional Unionist
UW	Union Whig
UWar	Union War Party
VBD	Van Buren Democrat
W	Whig
WD	War Democrat

Other Abbreviations

Abbreviation	
P.I.	Philippine Islands
P.R.	Puerto Rico
Rep.	Representative
Res.Comm.	Resident Commissioner
Terr. Del.	Territorial Delegate

Biographical Index

A

AANDAHL, Fred George (R N.D.) April 9, 1897-April 7, 1966; House 1951-53; Gov. 1945-50.

ABBITT, Watkins Moorman (D Va.) May 21, 1908- —; House Feb. 17, 1948-73.

ABBOTT, Amos (W Mass.) Sept. 10, 1786-Nov. 2, 1868; House 1843-49.

ABBOTT, Jo (Joseph) (D Texas) Jan. 15, 1840-Feb. 11, 1908; House 1887-97.

ABBOTT, Joel (D Ga.) March 17, 1776-Nov. 19, 1826; House 1817-25.

ABBOTT, Joseph Carter (R N.C.) July 15, 1825-Oct. 8, 1881; Senate July 14, 1868-71.

ABBOTT, Josiah Gardner (D Mass.) Nov. 1, 1814-June 2, 1891; House July 28, 1876-77.

ABBOTT, Nehemiah (R Maine) March 29, 1804-July 26, 1877; House 1857-59.

ABDNOR, James (R S.D.) Feb. 13, 1923- —; House 1973-81; Senate 1981- —.

ABEL, Hazel Hempell (R Neb.) July 10, 1888-July 30, 1966; Senate Nov. 8, 1954-Dec. 31, 1954.

ABELE, Homer E. (R Ohio) Nov. 21, 1916- —; House 1963-65.

ABERCROMBIE, James (UW Ala.) 1795-July 2, 1861; House 1851-55.

ABERCROMBIE, John William (D Ala.) May 17, 1866-July 2, 1940; House 1913-17.

ABERNETHY, Charles Laban (D N.C.) March 18, 1872-Feb. 23, 1955; House Nov. 7, 1922-35.

ABERNETHY, Thomas Gerstle (D Miss.) May 16, 1903- —; House 1943-73.

ABOUREZK, James George (D S.D.) Feb. 24, 1931- —; House 1971-73; Senate 1973-79.

ABZUG, Bella Savitzky (D N.Y.) July 24, 1920- —; House 1971-77.

ACHESON, Ernest Francis (R Pa.) Sept. 19, 1855-May 16, 1917; House 1895-1909.

ACKER, Ephraim Leister (D Pa.) Jan. 11, 1827-May 12, 1903; House 1871-73.

ACKERMAN, Ernest Robinson (R N.J.) June 17, 1863-Oct. 18, 1931; House 1919-Oct. 18, 1931.

ACKERMAN, Gary L. (D N.Y.) Nov. 19, 1942- —; House March 2, 1983- —.

ACKLEN, Joseph Hayes (D La.) May 20, 1850-Sept. 28, 1938; House Feb. 20, 1878-81.

ADAIR, Edwin Ross (R Ind.) Dec. 14, 1907-May 7, 1983; House 1951-71.

ADAIR, Jackson Leroy (D Ill.) Feb. 23, 1887-Jan. 19, 1956; House 1933-37.

ADAIR, John (D Ky.) Jan. 9, 1757-May 19, 1840; House 1831-33; Senate Nov. 8, 1805-Nov. 18, 1806; Gov. 1820-24.

ADAIR, John Alfred McDowell (D Ind.) Dec. 22, 1864-Oct. 5, 1938; House 1907-17.

ADAMS, Alva Blanchard (D Colo.) Oct. 29, 1875-Dec. 1, 1941; Senate May 17, 1923-Nov. 30, 1924, 1933-Dec. 1, 1941.

ADAMS, Benjamin (F Mass.) Dec. 16, 1764-March 28, 1837; House Dec. 2, 1816-21.

ADAMS, Brockman (Brock) (D Wash.) Jan. 13, 1927- —; House 1965-Jan. 22, 1977; Secy. of Transportation 1977-July 20, 1979.

ADAMS, Charles Francis (son of John Quincy Adams, grandson of President John Adams) (R Mass.) Aug. 18, 1807-Nov. 21, 1886; House 1859-May 1, 1861.

ADAMS, Charles Henry (R N.Y.) April 10, 1824-Dec. 15, 1902; House 1875-77.

ADAMS, George Everett (R Ill.) June 18, 1840-Oct. 5, 1917; House 1883-91.

ADAMS, George Madison (nephew of Green Adams) (D Ky.) Dec. 20, 1837-April 6, 1920; House 1867-75.

ADAMS, Green (uncle of George Madison Adams) (AP Ky.) Aug. 20, 1812-Jan. 18, 1884; House 1847-49, 1859-61 (1847-49 Whig, 1859-61 American Party).

ADAMS, Henry Cullen (R Wis.) Nov. 28, 1850-July 9, 1906; House 1903-July 9, 1906.

ADAMS, John (JD N.Y.) Aug. 26, 1778-Sept. 25, 1854; House March 4-Dec. 26, 1815, 1833-35 (1815 Democrat, 1833-35 Jackson Democrat).

ADAMS, John Joseph (D N.Y.) Sept. 16, 1848-Feb. 16, 1919; House 1883-87.

ADAMS, John Quincy (son of President John Adams, father of Charles Francis Adams) (W Mass.) July 11, 1767-Feb. 23, 1848; Senate 1803-June 8, 1808 (F); House 1831-Feb. 23, 1848 (W); Secy. of State 1817-25; Pres. 1825-29.

ADAMS, Parmenio (— N.Y.) Sept. 9, 1776-Feb. 19, 1832; House Jan. 7, 1824-27.

ADAMS, Robert Jr. (R Pa.) Feb. 26, 1849-June 1, 1906; House Dec. 19, 1893-June 1, 1906.

ADAMS, Robert Huntington (JD Miss.) 1792-July 2, 1830; Senate Jan. 6, 1830-July 2, 1830.

ADAMS, Sherman (R N.H.) Jan. 8, 1899- —; House 1945-47; Gov. 1949-53.

ADAMS, Silas (R Ky.) Feb. 9, 1839-May 5, 1896; House 1893-95.

ADAMS, Stephen (UD Miss.) Oct. 17, 1807-May 11, 1857; House 1845-47 (D); Senate March 17, 1852-1857 (UD).

ADAMS, Wilbur Louis (D Del.) Oct. 23, 1884-Dec. 4, 1937; House 1933-35.

ADAMSON, William Charles (D Ga.) Aug. 13, 1854-Jan. 3, 1929; House 1897-Dec. 18, 1917.

ADDABBO, Joseph P. (D N.Y.) March 17, 1925- —; House 1961- —.

ADDAMS, William (D Pa.) April 11, 1777-May 30, 1858; House 1825-29.

ADDONIZIO, Hugh Joseph (D N.J.) Jan. 31, 1914-Feb. 2, 1981; House 1949-June 30, 1962.

ADGATE, Asa (D N.Y.) Nov. 17, 1767-Feb. 15, 1832; House June 7, 1815-17.

ADKINS, Charles (R Ill.) Feb. 7, 1863-March 31, 1941; House 1925-33.

ADRAIN, Garnett Bowditch (D N.J.) Dec. 15, 1815-Aug. 17, 1878; House 1857-61.

AHL, John Alexander (D Pa.) Aug. 16, 1813-April 25, 1882; House 1857-59.

AIKEN, David Wyatt (father of Wyatt Aiken, cousin of William Aiken) (D S.C.) March 17, 1828-April 6, 1887; House 1877-87.

AIKEN, George David (R Vt.) Aug. 20, 1892-Nov. 19, 1984; Senate Jan. 10, 1941-75; Gov. 1937-41.

AIKEN, William (cousin of David Wyatt Aiken) (D S.C.) Aug. 4, 1806-Sept. 7, 1887; House 1851-57; Gov. 1844-46.

AIKEN, Wyatt (son of David Wyatt Aiken) (D S.C.) Dec. 14, 1863-Feb. 6, 1923; House 1903-17.

AINEY, William David Blakeslee (R Pa.) April 8, 1864-Sept. 4, 1932; House Nov. 7, 1911-15.

AINSLIE, George (D Idaho) Oct. 30, 1838-May 19, 1913; House (Terr. Del.) 1879-83.

AINSWORTH, Lucien Lester (AM Iowa) June 21, 1831-April 19, 1902; House 1875-77.

AITKEN, David Demerest (R Mich.) Sept. 5, 1853-May 26, 1930; House 1893-97.

AKAKA, Daniel K. (D Hawaii) Sept. 11, 1924- —; House 1977- —.

AKERS, Thomas Peter (AP Mo.) Oct. 4, 1828-April 3, 1877; House Aug. 18, 1856-57.

AKIN, Theron (PR N.Y.) May 23, 1855-March 26, 1933; House 1911-13.

ALBAUGH, Walter Hugh (R Ohio) Jan. 2, 1890-Jan. 21, 1942; House Nov. 8, 1938-39.

ALBERT, Carl Bert (D Okla.) May 10, 1908- —; House 1947-77; House majority leader 1962-71; Speaker 1971-77.

ALBERT, William Julian (R Md.) Aug. 4, 1816-March 29, 1879; House 1873-75.

ALBERTSON, Nathaniel (D Ind.) June 10, 1800-Dec. 16, 1863; House 1849-51.

ALBOSTA, Donald Joseph (D Mich.) Dec. 5, 1925- —; House 1979-85.

ALBRIGHT, Charles (R Pa.) Dec. 13, 1830-Sept. 28, 1880; House 1873-75.

ALBRIGHT, Charles Jefferson (R Ohio) May 9, 1816-Oct. 21, 1883; House 1855-57.

ALCORN, James Lusk (R Miss.) Nov. 4, 1816-Dec. 19, 1894; Senate Dec. 1, 1871-77; Gov. 1870-71.

ALDERSON, John Duffy (D W.Va.) Nov. 29, 1854-Dec. 5, 1910; House 1889-95.

ALDRICH, Cyrus (R Minn.) June 18, 1808-Oct. 5, 1871; House 1859-63.

ALDRICH, James Franklin (son of William Aldrich) (R Ill.) April 6, 1853-March 8, 1933; House 1893-97.

ALDRICH, Nelson Wilmarth (father of Richard Steere Aldrich, cousin of William Aldrich) (R R.I.) Nov. 6, 1841-April 16, 1915; House 1879-Oct. 4, 1881; Senate Oct. 5, 1881-1911.

ALDRICH, Richard Steere (son of Nelson Wilmarth Aldrich) (R R.I.) Feb. 29, 1884-Dec. 25, 1941; House 1923-33.

ALDRICH, Truman Heminway (brother of William Farrington Aldrich (R Ala.) Oct. 17, 1848-April 28, 1932; House June 9, 1896-97.

ALDRICH, William (father of James Franklin Aldrich, cousin of Nelson Wilmarth Aldrich) (R Ill.) Jan. 19, 1820-Dec. 3, 1885; House 1877-83.

ALDRICH, William Farrington (brother of Truman Heminway Aldrich) (R Ala.) March 11, 1853-Oct. 30, 1925; House March 13, 1896-97, Feb. 9, 1898-99, March 8, 1900-01.

ALESHIRE, Arthur William (D Ohio) Feb. 15, 1900-March 11, 1940; House 1937-39.

ALEXANDER, Adam Rankin (F Tenn.) ?-?; House 1823-27.

ALEXANDER, Armstead Milton (D Mo.) May 26, 1834-Nov. 7, 1892; House 1883-85.

ALEXANDER, De Alva Stanwood (R N.Y.) July 17, 1846-Jan. 30, 1925; House 1897-1911.

ALEXANDER, Evan Shelby (cousin of Nathaniel Alexander) (— N.C.) about 1767-Oct. 28, 1809; House Feb. 24, 1806-09.

ALEXANDER, Henry Porteous (W N.Y.) Sept. 13, 1801-Feb. 22, 1867; House 1849-51.

ALEXANDER, Hugh Quincy (D N.C.) Aug. 7, 1911-—; House 1953-63.

ALEXANDER, James Jr. (D Ohio) Oct. 17, 1789-Sept. 5, 1846; House 1837-39.

ALEXANDER, John (D Ohio) April 16, 1777-June 28, 1848; House 1813-17.

ALEXANDER, John Grant (R Minn.) July 16, 1893-Dec. 8, 1971; House 1939-41.

ALEXANDER, Joshua Willis (D Mo.) Jan. 22, 1852-Feb. 27, 1936; House 1907-Dec. 15, 1919; Secy. of Commerce 1919-21.

ALEXANDER, Mark (SRD Va.) Feb. 7, 1792-Oct. 7, 1883; House 1819-33.

ALEXANDER, Nathaniel (cousin of Evan Shelby Alexander) (— N.C.) March 5, 1756-March 7, 1808; House 1803-Nov. 1805; Gov. 1805-07.

ALEXANDER, Syndenham Benoni (D N.C.) Dec. 8, 1840-June 14, 1921; House 1891-95.

ALEXANDER, William Vollie Jr. (D Ark.) Jan. 16, 1934-—; House 1969-—.

ALFORD, Julius Caesar (W Ga.) May 10, 1799-Jan. 1, 1863; House Jan. 2-March 3, 1837, 1839-Oct. 1, 1841 (1837 States Rights Whig, 1839-41 Harrison Whig).

ALFORD, Thomas Dale (D Ark.) Jan. 28, 1916-—; House 1959-63.

ALGER, Bruce Reynolds (R Texas) June 12, 1918-—; House 1955-65.

ALGER, Russell Alexander (R Mich.) Feb. 27, 1836-Jan. 24, 1907; Senate Sept. 27, 1902-Jan. 24, 1907; Gov. 1885-87; Secy. of War 1897-99.

ALLAN, Chilton (CD Ky.) April 6, 1786-Sept. 3, 1858; House 1831-37.

ALLEE, James Frank (R Del.) Dec. 2, 1857-Oct. 12, 1938; Senate March 3, 1903-07.

ALLEN, Alfred Gaither (D Ohio) July 23, 1867-Dec. 9, 1932; House 1911-17.

ALLEN, Amos Lawrence (R Maine) March 17, 1837-Feb. 20, 1911; House Nov. 6, 1899-Feb. 20, 1911.

ALLEN, Asa Leonard (D La.) Jan. 5, 1891-Jan. 5, 1969; House 1937-53.

ALLEN, Charles (FS Mass.) Aug. 9, 1797-Aug. 6, 1869; House 1849-53.

ALLEN, Charles Herbert (R Mass.) April 15, 1848-April 20, 1934; House 1885-89.

ALLEN, Clarence Emir (R Utah) Sept. 8, 1852-July 9, 1932; House Jan. 4, 1896-97.

ALLEN, Clifford Robertson (D Tenn.) Jan. 6, 1912-June 18, 1978; House Nov. 25, 1975-June 18, 1978.

ALLEN, Edward Payson (R Mich.) Oct. 28, 1839-Nov. 25, 1909; House 1887-91.

ALLEN, Elisha Hunt (son of Samuel Clesson Allen) (W Maine) Jan. 28, 1804-Jan. 1, 1883; House 1841-43.

ALLEN, Heman (W Vt.) June 14, 1777-Dec. 11, 1844; House 1831-39.

ALLEN, Heman (D Vt.) Feb. 23, 1779-April 7, 1852; House 1817-April 20, 1818.

ALLEN, Henry Crosby (R N.J.) May 13, 1872-March 7, 1942; House 1905-07.

ALLEN, Henry Dixon (D Ky.) June 24, 1854-March 9, 1924; House 1899-1903.

ALLEN, Henry Justin (R Kan.) Sept. 11, 1868-Jan. 17, 1950; Senate April 1, 1929-Nov. 30, 1930; Gov. 1919-23.

ALLEN, James Browning (D Ala.) Dec. 28, 1912-June 1, 1978; Senate 1969-June 1, 1978.

ALLEN, James Cameron (D Ill.) Jan. 29, 1822-Jan. 30, 1912; House 1853-July 18, 1856, Nov. 4, 1856-57, 1863-65.

ALLEN, John (father of John William Allen) (F Conn.) June 12, 1763-July 31, 1812; House 1797-99.

ALLEN, John Beard (R Wash.) May 18, 1845-Jan. 28, 1903; House (Terr. Del.) March 4-Nov. 11, 1889; Senate Nov. 20, 1889-93.

ALLEN, John Clayton (R Ill.) Feb. 14, 1860-Jan. 12, 1939; House 1925-33.

ALLEN, John James (brother of Robert Allen) (W Va.) Sept. 25, 1797-Sept. 18, 1871; House 1833-35.

ALLEN, John Joseph Jr. (R Calif.) Nov. 27, 1899-—; House 1947-59.

ALLEN, John Mills (D Miss.) July 8, 1846-Oct. 30, 1917; House 1885-1901.

ALLEN, John William (son of John Allen) Aug. 2, 1802-Oct. 5, 1887; House 1837-41.

ALLEN, Joseph (F Mass.) Sept. 2, 1749-Sept. 2, 1827; House Oct. 8, 1810-11.

ALLEN, Judson (D N.Y.) April 3, 1797-Aug. 6, 1880; House 1839-41.

ALLEN, Leo Elwood (R Ill.) Oct. 5, 1898-Jan. 19, 1973; House 1933-61.

ALLEN, Maryon Pittman (D Ala.) Nov. 30, 1925-—; Senate June 12, 1978-Nov. 7, 1978.

ALLEN, Nathaniel (father-in-law of Robert Lawson Rose) (— N.Y.) 1780-Dec. 22, 1832; House 1819-21.

ALLEN, Philip (TD R.I.) Sept. 1, 1785-Dec. 16, 1865; Senate July 20, 1853-59; Gov. 1851-53.

ALLEN, Robert (D Tenn.) June 19, 1778-Aug. 19, 1844; House 1819-27.

ALLEN, Robert (brother of John James Allen) (D Va.) July 30, 1794-Dec. 30, 1859; House 1827-33.

ALLEN, Robert Edward Lee (D W.Va.) Nov. 28, 1865-Jan. 28, 1951; House 1923-25.

ALLEN, Robert Gray (D Pa.) Aug. 24, 1902-Aug. 9, 1963; House 1937-41.

ALLEN, Samuel Clesson (father of Elisha Hunt Allen) (— Mass.) Jan. 5, 1772-Feb. 8, 1842; House 1817-29.

ALLEN, Thomas (D Mo.) Aug. 29, 1813-April 8, 1882; House 1881-April 8, 1882.

ALLEN, William (D Ohio) Dec. 27, 1803-July 11, 1879; House 1833-35; Senate 1837-49; Gov. 1874-76.

ALLEN, William (D Ohio) Aug. 13, 1827-July 6, 1881; House 1859-63.

ALLEN, William Franklin (D Del.) Jan. 19, 1883-June 14, 1946; House 1937-39.

ALLEN, William Joshua (son of Willis Allen) (D Ill.) June 9, 1829-Jan. 26, 1901; House June 2, 1862-65.

ALLEN, William Vincent (P Neb.) Jan. 28, 1847-Jan. 2, 1924; Senate 1893-99, Dec. 13, 1899-March 28, 1901.

ALLEN, Willis (father of William Joshua Allen) (D Ill.) Dec. 15, 1806-April 15, 1859; House 1851-55.

ALLEY, John Bassett (R Mass.) Jan. 7, 1817-Jan. 19, 1896; House 1859-67.

ALLGOOD, Miles Clayton (D Ala.) Feb. 22, 1878-March 4, 1977; House 1923-35.

ALLISON, James Jr. (father of John Allison) (W Pa.) Oct. 4, 1772-June 17, 1854; House 1823-25.

ALLISON, John (son of James Allison Jr.) (W Pa.) Aug. 5, 1812-March 23, 1878; House 1851-53, 1855-57.

Biographical Index

ALLISON, Robert (W Pa.) March 10, 1777-Dec. 2, 1840; House 1831-33.

ALLISON, William Boyd (R Iowa) March 2, 1829-Aug. 4, 1908; House 1863-71; Senate 1873-Aug. 4, 1908.

ALLOTT, Gordon Llewellyn (R Colo.) Jan. 2, 1907-—; Senate 1955-73.

ALMON, Edward Berton (D Ala.) April 18, 1860-June 22, 1933; House 1915-June 22, 1933.

ALMOND, James Lindsay Jr. (D Va.) June 15, 1898-—; House Jan. 22, 1946-April 17, 1948; Gov. 1958-62.

ALSTON, Lemuel James (— S.C.) 1760-1836; House 1807-11.

ALSTON, William Jeffreys (W Ala.) Dec. 31, 1800-June 10, 1876; House 1849-51.

ALSTON, Willis (nephew of Nathaniel Macon) (WD N.C.) 1769-April 10, 1837; House 1799-1815, 1825-31.

ALVORD, James Church (W Mass.) April 14, 1808-Sept. 27, 1839; House 1839-Sept. 27, 1839.

AMBLER, Jacob A. (R Ohio) Feb. 18, 1829-Sept. 22, 1906; House 1869-73.

AMBRO, Jerome Anthony Jr. (D N.Y.) June 27, 1928-—; House 1975-81.

AMERMAN, Lemuel (D Pa.) Oct. 29, 1846-Oct. 7, 1897; House 1891-93.

AMES, Adelbert (father of Butler Ames) (R Miss.) Oct. 31, 1835-April 12, 1933; Senate Feb. 23, 1870-Jan. 10, 1874; Gov. 1868-69, 1874-76.

AMES, Butler (son of Adelbert Ames, grandson of Benjamin Franklin Butler) (R Mass.) Aug. 22, 1871-Nov. 6, 1954; House 1903-13.

AMES, Fisher (F Mass.) April 9, 1758-July 4, 1808; House 1789-97.

AMES, Oakes (R Mass.) Jan. 10, 1804-May 8, 1873; House 1863-73.

AMLIE, Thomas Ryum (Prog. Wis.) April 17, 1897-Aug. 22, 1973; House Oct. 13, 1931-33, 1935-39 (1931-33 Republican Progressive, 1935-39 Progressive).

AMMERMAN, Joseph S. (D Pa.) July 14, 1924-—; House 1977-79.

ANCONA, Sydenham Elnathan (D Pa.) Nov. 20, 1824-June 20, 1913; House 1861-67.

ANDERSEN, Herman Carl (R Minn.) Jan. 27, 1897-July 26, 1978; House 1939-63.

ANDERSON, Albert Raney (IR Iowa) Nov. 8, 1837-Nov. 17, 1898; House 1887-89.

ANDERSON, Alexander Outlaw (son of Joseph Anderson) (D Tenn.) Nov. 10, 1794-May 23, 1869; Senate Feb. 26, 1840-41.

ANDERSON, Carl Carey (D Ohio) Dec. 2, 1877-Oct. 1, 1912; House 1909-Oct. 1, 1912.

ANDERSON, Chapman Levy (D Miss.) March 15, 1845-April 27, 1924; House 1887-91.

ANDERSON, Charles Arthur (D Mo.) Sept. 26, 1899-April 26, 1977; House 1937-41.

ANDERSON, Charles Marley (D Ohio) Jan. 5, 1845-Dec. 28, 1908; House 1885-87.

ANDERSON, Clinton Presba (D N.M.) Oct. 23, 1895-Nov. 11, 1975; House 1941-June 30, 1945; Senate 1949-1973; Secy. of Agriculture 1945-48.

ANDERSON, George Alburtus (D Ill.) March 11, 1853-Jan. 31, 1896; House 1887-89.

ANDERSON, George Washington (RR Mo.) May 22, 1832-Feb. 26, 1902; House 1865-69.

ANDERSON, Glenn M. (D Calif.) Feb. 21, 1913-—; House 1969-—.

ANDERSON, Hugh Johnston (D Maine) May 10, 1801-May 31, 1881; House 1837-41; Gov. 1844-47.

ANDERSON, Isaac (Jeff.D Pa.) Nov. 23, 1760-Oct. 27, 1838; House 1803-07.

ANDERSON, James Patton (D Wash.) Feb. 16, 1822-Sept. 20, 1872; House (Terr. Del.) 1855-57.

ANDERSON, John (Jeff.D Maine) July 30, 1792-Aug. 21, 1853; House 1825-33.

ANDERSON, John Alexander (R Kan.) June 26, 1834-May 18, 1892; House 1879-91 (1879-87 Republican, 1887-89 Independent, 1889-91 Republican).

ANDERSON, John B. (R Ill.) Feb. 15, 1922-—; House 1961-81.

ANDERSON, John Zuinglius (R Calif.) March 22, 1904-Feb. 9, 1981; House 1939-53.

ANDERSON, Joseph (father of Alexander Outlaw Anderson) (— Tenn.) Nov. 5, 1757-April 17, 1837; Senate Sept. 26, 1797-1815; Pres. pro tempore Jan. 13, Feb. 28, March 2, 1805.

ANDERSON, Joseph Halstead (D N.Y.) Aug. 25, 1800-June 23, 1870; House 1843-47.

ANDERSON, Josiah McNair (W Tenn.) Nov. 29, 1807-Nov. 8, 1861; House 1849-51.

ANDERSON, LeRoy Hagen (D Mont.) Feb. 2, 1906-—; House 1957-61.

ANDERSON, Lucian (U Ky.) June 23, 1824-Oct. 18, 1898; House 1863-65.

ANDERSON, Richard Clough Jr. (— Ky.) Aug. 4, 1788-July 24, 1826; House 1817-21.

ANDERSON, Samuel (— Pa.) 1773-Jan. 17, 1850; House 1827-29.

ANDERSON, Simeon H. (father of William Clayton Anderson) (W Ky.) March 2, 1802-Aug. 11, 1840; House 1839-Aug. 11, 1840.

ANDERSON, Sydney (R Minn.) Sept. 18, 1881-Oct. 8, 1948; House 1911-25.

ANDERSON, Thomas Lilbourne (ID Mo.) Dec. 8, 1808-March 6, 1885; House 1857-61 (1857-59 American Party, 1859-61 Independent Democrat).

ANDERSON, Wendell Richard (D Minn.) Feb. 1, 1933-—; Senate Dec. 30, 1976-Dec. 29, 1978; Gov. 1971-76.

ANDERSON, William (Jeff.D Pa.) 1762-Dec. 16, 1829; House 1809-15, 1817-19.

ANDERSON, William Black (ID Ill.) April 2, 1830-Aug. 28, 1901; House 1875-77.

ANDERSON, William Clayton (son of Simeon H. Anderson, nephew of Albert Gallatin Talbott) (AP Ky.) Dec. 26, 1826-Dec. 23, 1861; House 1859-61.

ANDERSON, William Coleman (R Tenn.) July 10, 1853-Sept. 8, 1902; House 1895-97.

ANDERSON, William Robert (D Tenn.) June 17, 1921-—; House 1965-73.

ANDRESEN, August Herman (R Minn.) Oct. 11, 1890-Jan. 14, 1958; House 1925-33, 1935-Jan. 14, 1958.

ANDREW, Abram Piatt Jr. (R Mass.) Feb. 12, 1873-June 3, 1936; House Sept. 27, 1921-June 3, 1936.

ANDREW, John Forrester (D Mass.) Nov. 26, 1850-May 30, 1895; House 1889-93.

ANDREWS, Arthur Glenn (R Ala.) Jan. 15, 1909-—; House 1965-67.

ANDREWS, Charles (D Maine) Feb. 11, 1814-April 30, 1852; House 1851-April 30, 1852.

ANDREWS, Charles Oscar (D Fla.) March 7, 1877-Sept. 18, 1946; Senate Nov. 4, 1936-Sept. 18, 1946.

ANDREWS, Elizabeth Bullock (widow of George William Andrews) (D Ala.) Feb. 12, 1911-—; House April 4, 1972-73.

ANDREWS, George Rex (W N.Y.) Sept. 21, 1808-Dec. 5, 1873; House 1849-51.

ANDREWS, George William (D Ala.) Dec. 12, 1906-Dec. 25, 1971; House March 14, 1944-Dec. 25, 1971.

ANDREWS, Ike Franklin (D N.C.) Sept. 2, 1925-—; House 1973-85.

ANDREWS, John Tuttle (D N.Y.) May 29, 1803-June 11, 1894; House 1837-39.

ANDREWS, Landaff Watson (W Ky.) Feb. 12, 1803-Dec. 23, 1887; House 1839-43.

ANDREWS, Mark (R N.D.) May 19, 1926-—; House Oct. 22, 1963-81; Senate 1981-—.

ANDREWS, Michael Allen (D Texas) Feb. 7, 1944-—; House 1983-—.

ANDREWS, Samuel George (R N.Y.) Oct. 16, 1796-June 11, 1863; House 1857-59.

ANDREWS, Sherlock James (W Ohio) Nov. 17, 1801-Feb. 11, 1880; House 1841-43.

ANDREWS, Walter Gresham (R N.Y.) July 16, 1889-March 5, 1949; House 1931-49.

ANDREWS, William Ezekiel (R Neb.) Dec. 17, 1854-Jan. 19, 1942; House 1895-97, 1919-23.

ANDREWS, William Henry (R N.M.) Jan. 14, 1846-Jan. 16, 1919; House (Terr. Del.) 1905-Jan. 7, 1912.

ANDREWS, William Noble (R Md.) Nov. 13, 1876-Dec. 27, 1937; House 1919-21.

ANDRUS, John Emory (R N.Y.) Feb. 16, 1841-Dec. 26, 1934; House 1905-13.

ANFUSO, Victor L'Episcopo (D N.Y.) March 10, 1905-Dec. 28, 1966; House 1951-53, 1955-63.

ANGEL, William G. (JD N.Y.) July 17, 1790-Aug. 13, 1858; House 1825-27, 1829-33 (1825-27 John Quincy Adams Democrat, 1829-33 Jackson Democrat).

ANGELL, Homer Daniel (R Ore.) Jan. 12, 1875-March 31, 1968; House 1939-55.

ANKENY, Levi (R Wash.) Aug. 1, 1844-March 29, 1921; Senate 1903-09.

ANNUNZIO, Frank (D Ill.) Jan. 12, 1915- —; House 1965- —.

ANSBERRY, Timothy Thomas (D Ohio) Dec. 24, 1871-July 5, 1943; House 1907-Jan. 9, 1915.

ANSORGE, Martin Charles (R N.Y.) Jan. 1, 1882-Feb. 4, 1967; House 1921-23.

ANTHONY, Beryl Franklin Jr. (D Ark.) Feb. 21, 1938- —; House 1979- —.

ANTHONY, Daniel Read Jr. (R Kan.) Aug. 22, 1870-Aug. 4, 1931; House May 23, 1907-29.

ANTHONY, Henry Bowen (R R.I.) April 1, 1815-Sept. 2, 1884; Senate 1859-Sept. 2, 1884; Gov. 1850-51; Pres. pro tempore 1869-73.

ANTHONY, Joseph Biles (D Pa.) June 19, 1795-Jan. 10, 1851; House 1833-37.

ANTONY, Edwin Le Roy (D Texas) Jan. 5, 1852-Jan. 16, 1913; House June 14, 1892-93.

APLIN, Henry Harrison (R Mich.) April 15, 1841-July 23, 1910; House Oct. 20, 1901-03.

APPLEBY, Stewart Hoffman (son of Theodore Frank Appleby) (R N.J.) May 17, 1890-Jan. 12, 1964; House Nov. 3, 1925-27.

APPLEBY, Theodore Frank (father of Stewart Hoffman Appleby) (R N.J.) Oct. 10, 1864-Dec. 15, 1924; House 1921-23.

APPLEGATE, Douglas (D Ohio) March 27, 1928- —; House 1977- —.

APPLETON, John (D Maine) Feb. 11, 1815-Aug. 22, 1864; House 1851-53.

APPLETON, Nathan (cousin of William Appleton) (HTW Mass.) Oct. 6, 1779-July 14, 1861; House 1831-33, June 9-Sept. 28, 1842.

APPLETON, William (cousin of Nathan Appleton) (W Mass.) Nov. 16, 1786-Feb. 15, 1862; House 1851-55, March 4-Sept. 27, 1861.

APSLEY, Lewis Dewart (R Mass.) Sept. 29, 1852-April 11, 1925; House 1893-97.

ARCHER, John (father of Stevenson Archer) (D Md.) May 5, 1741-Sept. 28, 1810; House 1801-07.

ARCHER, Stevenson (son of John Archer) (D Md.) Oct. 11, 1786-June 26, 1848; House Oct. 26, 1811-17, 1819-21.

ARCHER, Stevenson (son of Stevenson Archer, grandson of John Archer) (D Md.) Feb. 28, 1827-Aug. 2, 1898; House 1867-75.

ARCHER, William Reynolds Jr. (R Texas) March 22, 1928- —; House 1971- —.

ARCHER, William Segar (nephew of Joseph Eggleston) (W Va.) March 5, 1789-March 28, 1855; House Jan. 3, 1820-35; Senate 1841-47.

ARENDS, Leslie Cornelius (R Ill.) Sept. 27, 1895- —; House 1935-Dec. 31, 1974.

ARENS, Henry (FL Minn.) Nov. 21, 1873-Oct. 6, 1963; House 1933-35.

ARENTZ, Samuel Shaw (Ulysses) (R Nev.) Jan. 8, 1879-June 17, 1934; House 1921-23, 1925-33.

ARMEY, Richard K. (R Texas) July 7, 1940- —; House 1985- —.

ARMFIELD, Robert Franklin (D N.C.) July 9, 1829-Nov. 9, 1898; House 1879-83.

ARMSTRONG, David Hartley (D Mo.) Oct. 21, 1812-March 18, 1893; Senate Sept. 20, 1877-Jan. 26, 1879.

ARMSTRONG, James (brother of John Armstrong) (F Pa.) Aug. 29, 1748-May 6, 1828; House 1793-95.

ARMSTRONG, John (brother of James Armstrong) (— N.Y.) Nov. 25, 1755-April 1, 1843; Senate Nov. 6, 1800-Feb. 5, 1802; Nov. 10, 1803-June 30, 1804; Secy. of War 1813-14.

ARMSTRONG, Moses Kimball (D Dakota) Sept. 19, 1832-Jan. 11, 1906; House (Terr. Del.) 1871-75.

ARMSTRONG, Orland Kay (R Mo.) Oct. 2, 1893- —; House 1951-53.

ARMSTRONG, William (D Va.) Dec. 23, 1782-May 10, 1865; House 1825-33.

ARMSTRONG, William Hepburn (R Pa.) Sept. 7, 1824-May 14, 1919; House 1869-71.

ARMSTRONG, William Lester (R Colo.) March 16, 1937- —; House 1973-79; Senate 1979- —.

ARNELL, Samuel Mayes (R Tenn.) May 3, 1833-July 20, 1903; House July 24, 1866-71.

ARNOLD, Benedict (brother-in-law of Matthias J. Bovee) (— N.Y.) Oct. 5, 1780-March 3, 1849; House 1829-31.

ARNOLD, Isaac Newton (R Ill.) Nov. 30, 1815-April 24, 1884; House 1861-65.

ARNOLD, Laurence Fletcher (D Ill.) June 8, 1891-Dec. 6, 1966; House 1937-43.

ARNOLD, Lemuel Hastings (great-great-uncle of Theodore Francis Green) (LW R.I.) Jan. 29, 1792-June 27, 1852; House 1845-47; Gov. 1831-32.

ARNOLD, Marshall (D Mo.) Oct. 21, 1845-June 12, 1913; House 1891-95.

ARNOLD, Samuel (D Conn.) June 1, 1806-May 5, 1869; House 1857-59.

ARNOLD, Samuel Greene (granduncle of Theodore Francis Green) (R R.I.) April 12, 1821-Feb. 14, 1880; Senate Dec. 1, 1862-63.

ARNOLD, Samuel Washington (R Mo.) Sept. 21, 1879-Dec. 18, 1961; House 1943-49.

ARNOLD, Thomas Dickens (W Tenn.) May 3, 1798-May 26, 1870; House 1831-33, 1841-43.

ARNOLD, Warren Otis (R R.I.) June 3, 1839-April 1, 1910; House 1887-91, 1895-97.

ARNOLD, William Carlile (R Pa.) July 15, 1851-March 20, 1906; House 1895-99.

ARNOLD, William Wright (D Ill.) Oct. 14, 1877-Nov. 23, 1957; House 1923-Sept. 16, 1935.

ARNOT, John Jr. (D N.Y.) March 11, 1831-Nov. 20, 1886; House 1883-Nov. 20, 1886.

ARRINGTON, Archibald Hunter (uncle of Archibald Hunter Arrington Williams) (D N.C.) Nov. 13, 1809-July 20, 1872; House 1841-45.

ARTHUR, William Evans (D Ky.) March 3, 1825-May 18, 1897; House 1871-75.

ASH, Michael Woolston (— Pa.) March 5, 1789-Dec. 14, 1858; House 1835-37.

ASHBROOK, Jean S. (widow of John Milan Ashbrook) (R Ohio) Sept. 21, 1934- —; House July 12, 1982-83.

ASHBROOK, John Milan (son of William Albert Ashbrook) (R Ohio) Sept. 21, 1928-April 4, 1982; House 1961-April 4, 1982.

ASHBROOK, William Albert (father of John Milan Ashbrook) (D Ohio) July 1, 1867-Jan. 1, 1940; House 1907-21, 1935-Jan. 1, 1940.

ASHE, John Baptista (uncle of John Baptista Ashe of Tenn., Thomas Samuel Ashe and William Shepperd Ashe) (F N.C.) 1748-Nov. 27, 1802; House 1789-93; Cont. Cong. 1787.

ASHE, John Baptista (brother of William Shepperd Ashe, nephew of John Baptista Ashe of N.C. and cousin of Thomas Samuel Ashe) (W Tenn.) 1810-Dec. 29, 1857; House 1843-45.

ASHE, Thomas Samuel (nephew of John Baptista Ashe of N.C., cousin of John Baptista Ashe and William Shepperd Ashe) (D N.C.) July 21, 1812-Feb. 4, 1887; House 1873-77 (1873-75 Conservative, 1875-77 Democrat).

ASHE, William Shepperd (brother of John Baptista Ashe of Tenn., nephew of John Baptista Ashe of N.C., cousin of Thomas Samuel Ashe) (D N.C.) Aug. 12, 1813-Sept. 14, 1862; House 1849-55.

ASHLEY, Chester (D Ark.) June 1, 1790-April 29, 1848; Senate Nov. 8, 1844-April 29, 1848.

ASHLEY, Delos Rodeyn (R Nev.) Feb. 19, 1828-July 18, 1873; House 1865-69.

ASHLEY, Henry (— N.Y.) Feb. 19, 1778-Jan. 14, 1829; House 1825-27.

ASHLEY, James Mitchell (great-grandfather of Thomas William Ludlow Ashley) (R Ohio) Nov. 14, 1824-Sept. 16, 1896; House 1859-69; Gov. (Mont. Terr.) 1869-70.

ASHLEY, Thomas William Ludlow (great-grandson of James Mitchell Ashley) (D Ohio) Jan. 11, 1923- —; House 1955-81.

ASHLEY, William Henry (W Mo.) 1778-March 26, 1838; House Oct. 31, 1831-37.

ASHMORE, John Durant (D S.C.) Aug. 18, 1819-Dec. 5, 1871; House 1859-Dec. 21, 1860.

ASHMORE, Robert Thomas (D S.C.) Feb. 22, 1904-—; House June 2, 1953-69.

ASHMUN, Eli Porter (father of George Ashmun) (— Mass.) June 24, 1770-May 10, 1819; Senate June 12, 1816-May 10, 1818.

ASHMUN, George (son of Eli Porter Ashmun) (W Mass.) Dec. 25, 1804-July 16, 1870; House 1845-51.

ASHURST, Henry Fountain (D Ariz.) Sept. 13, 1874-May 31, 1962; Senate March 27, 1912-41.

ASPER, Joel Funk (RR Mo.) April 20, 1822-Oct. 1, 1872; House 1869-71.

ASPIN, Les (D Wis.) July 21, 1938-—; House 1971-—.

ASPINALL, Wayne Norviel (D Colo.) April 3, 1896-Oct. 9, 1983; House 1949-73.

ASWELL, James Benjamin (D La.) Dec. 23, 1869-March 16, 1931; House 1913-March 16, 1931.

ATCHISON, David Rice (W Mo.) Aug. 11, 1807-Jan. 26, 1886; Senate Oct. 14, 1843-55; Pres. pro tempore 1846-49, 1852-54.

ATHERTON, Charles Gordon (son of Charles Humphrey Atherton) (D N.H.) July 4, 1804-Nov. 15, 1853; House 1837-43; Senate 1843-49, 1853-Nov. 15, 1853.

ATHERTON, Charles Humphrey (father of Charles Gordon Atherton) (F N.H.) Aug. 14, 1773-Jan. 8, 1853; House 1815-17.

ATHERTON, Gibson (D Ohio) Jan. 19, 1831-Nov. 10, 1887; House 1879-83.

ATKESON, William Oscar (R Mo.) Aug. 24, 1854-Oct. 16, 1931; House 1921-23.

ATKINS, Chester G. (D Mass.) April 14, 1948-—; House 1985-—.

ATKINS, John DeWitt Clinton (D Tenn.) June 4, 1825-June 2, 1908; House 1857-59, 1873-83.

ATKINSON, Archibald (D Va.) Sept. 15, 1792-Jan. 7, 1872; House 1843-49.

ATKINSON, Eugene Vincent (D Pa.) April 5, 1927-——; House 1979-83 (1979-Oct. 14, 1981 Democrat; Oct. 14, 1981-83 Republican.)

ATKINSON, George Wesley (R W.Va.) June 29, 1845-April 4, 1925; House Feb. 26, 1890-91; Gov. 1897-1901.

ATKINSON, Louis Evans (R Pa.) April 16, 1841-Feb. 5, 1910; House 1883-93.

ATKINSON, Richard Merrill (D Tenn.) Feb. 6, 1894-April 29, 1947; House 1937-39.

ATWATER, John Wilbur (P N.C.) Dec. 27, 1840-July 4, 1910; House 1899-1901.

ATWOOD, David (R Wis.) Dec. 15, 1815-Dec. 11, 1889; House Feb. 23, 1870-71.

ATWOOD, Harrison Henry (R Mass.) Aug. 26, 1863-Oct. 22, 1954; House 1895-97.

AUCHINCLOSS, James Coats (R N.J.) Jan. 19, 1885-Oct. 2, 1976; House 1943-65.

AuCOIN, Les (D Ore.) Oct. 21, 1942-—; House 1975-—.

AUF DER HEIDE, Oscar Louis (D N.J.) Dec. 8, 1874-March 29, 1945; House 1925-35.

AUSTIN, Albert Elmer (stepfather of Clare Boothe Luce) (R Conn.) Nov. 15, 1877-Jan. 26, 1942; House 1939-41.

AUSTIN, Archibald (D Va.) Aug. 11, 1772-Oct. 16, 1837; House 1817-19.

AUSTIN, Richard Wilson (R Tenn.) Aug. 26, 1857-April 20, 1919; House 1909-19.

AUSTIN, Warren Robinson (R Vt.) Nov. 12, 1877-Dec. 25, 1962; Senate April 1, 1931-Aug. 2, 1946.

AVERETT, Thomas Hamlet (D Va.) July 10, 1800-June 30, 1855; House 1849-53.

AVERILL, John Thomas (R Minn.) March 1, 1825-Oct. 3, 1889; House 1871-75.

AVERY, Daniel (D N.Y.) Sept. 18, 1766-Jan. 30, 1842; House 1811-15, Sept. 30, 1816-17.

AVERY, John (R Mich.) Feb. 29, 1824-Jan. 21, 1914; House 1893-97.

AVERY, William Henry (R Kan.) Aug. 11, 1911-—; House 1955-65; Gov. 1965-67.

AVERY, William Tecumsah (D Tenn.) Nov. 11, 1819-May 22, 1880; House 1857-61.

AVIS, Samuel Brashear (R W.Va.) Feb. 19, 1872-June 8, 1924; House 1913-15.

AXTELL, Samuel Beach (D Calif.) Oct. 14, 1819-Aug. 6, 1891; House 1867-71; Gov. Utah Terr.(R) 1874-75; Gov. N.M. Terr. (R) 1875.

AYCRIGG, John Bancker (W N.J.) July 9, 1798-Nov. 8, 1856; House 1837-39, 1841-43.

AYER, Richard Small (R Va.) Oct. 9, 1829-Dec. 14, 1896; House Jan. 31, 1870-71.

AYERS, Roy Elmer (D Mont.) Nov. 9, 1882-May 23, 1955; House 1933-37; Gov. 1937-41.

AYRES, Steven Beckwith (ID N.Y.) Oct. 27, 1861-June 1, 1929; House 1911-13.

AYRES, William Augustus (D Kan.) April 19, 1867-Feb. 17, 1952; House 1915-21, 1923-Aug. 22, 1934.

AYRES, William Hanes (R Ohio) Feb. 5, 1916-—; House 1951-71.

B

BABBITT, Clinton (D Wis.) Nov. 16, 1831-March 11, 1907; House 1891-93.

BABBITT, Elijah (R Pa.) July 29, 1795-Jan. 9, 1887; House 1859-63 (1859-61 Unionist, 1861-63 Republican).

BABCOCK, Alfred (W N.Y.) April 15, 1805-May 16, 1871; House 1841-43.

BABCOCK, Joseph Weeks (grandson of Joseph Weeks) (R Wis.) March 6, 1850-April 27, 1909; House 1893-1907.

BABCOCK, Leander (D N.Y.) March 1, 1811-Aug. 18, 1864; House 1851-53.

BABCOCK, William (— N.Y.) 1785-Oct. 20, 1838; House 1831-33.

BABKA, John Joseph (D Ohio) March 16, 1884-March 22, 1937; House 1919-21.

BACHARACH, Isaac (R N.J.) Jan. 5, 1870-Sept. 5, 1956; House 1915-37.

BACHMAN, Nathan Lynn (D Tenn.) Aug. 2, 1878-April 23, 1937; Senate Feb. 28, 1933-April 23, 1937.

BACHMAN, Reuben Knecht (D Pa.) Aug. 6, 1834-Sept. 19, 1911; House 1879-81.

BACHMANN, Carl George (R W.Va.) May 14, 1890-Jan. 22, 1980; House 1925-33.

BACON, Augustus Octavius (cousin of William Schley Howard) (D Ga.) Oct. 20, 1839-Feb. 14, 1914; Senate 1895-Feb. 14, 1914.

BACON, Ezekiel (son of John Bacon, father of William Johnson Bacon) (D Mass.) Sept. 1, 1776-Oct. 18, 1870; House Sept. 16, 1807-13.

BACON, Henry (D N.Y.) March 14, 1846-March 25, 1915; House Dec. 6, 1886-89, 1891-93.

BACON, John (father of Ezekiel Bacon, grandfather of William Johnson Bacon) (— Mass.) April 5, 1738-Oct. 25, 1820; House 1801-03.

BACON, Mark Reeves (R Mich.) Feb. 29, 1852-Aug. 20, 1941; House March 4-Dec. 13, 1917.

BACON, Robert Low (R N.Y.) July 23, 1884-Sept. 12, 1938; House 1923-Sept. 12, 1938.

BACON, William Johnson (son of Ezekiel Bacon, grandson of John Bacon) (R N.Y.) Feb. 18, 1803-July 3, 1889; House 1877-79.

BADGER, De Witt Clinton (D Ohio) Aug. 7, 1858-May 20, 1926; House 1903-05.

BADGER, George Edmund (W N.C.) April 17, 1795-May 11, 1866; Senate Nov. 25, 1846-55; Secy. of the Navy March 5-Sept. 11, 1841.

BADGER, Luther (— N.Y.) April 10, 1785-1869; House 1825-27.

BADHAM, Robert E. (R Calif.) June 9, 1929-—; House 1977-—.

BADILLO, Herman (D N.Y.) Aug. 21, 1929-—; House 1971-Dec. 31, 1977.

BAER, George Jr. (F Md.) 1763-April 3, 1834; House 1797-1801, 1815-17.

BAER, John Miller (R N.D.) March 29, 1886-Feb. 18, 1970; House July 10, 1917-21 (1917-19 Nonpartisan League, 1919-21 Republican).

BAFALIS, Louis Arthur (R Fla.) Sept. 28, 1929-—; House 1973-83.

BAGBY, Arthur Pendleton (D Ala.) 1794-Sept. 21, 1858; Senate Nov. 24, 1841-June 16, 1848; Gov. 1837-41.

BAGBY, John Courts (D Ill.) Jan. 24, 1819-April 4, 1896; House 1875-77.

BAGLEY, George Augustus (R N.Y.) July 22, 1826-May 12, 1915; House 1875-79.

BAGLEY, John Holroyd Jr. (D N.Y.) Nov. 26, 1832-Oct. 23, 1902; House 1875-77, 1883-85.

BAILEY, Alexander Hamilton (R N.Y.) Aug. 14, 1817-April 20, 1874; House Nov. 30, 1867-71.

BAILEY, Cleveland Monroe (D W.Va.) July 15, 1886-July 13, 1965; House 1945-47, 1949-63.

BAILEY, David Jackson (SRD Ga.) March 11, 1812-June 14, 1897; House 1851-55.

BAILEY, Donald Allen (D Pa.) July 21, 1945-—; House 1979-83.

BAILEY, Goldsmith Fox (R Mass.) July 17, 1823-May 8, 1862; House 1861-May 8, 1862.

BAILEY, James Edmund (D Tenn.) Aug. 15, 1822-Dec. 29, 1885; Senate Jan. 19, 1877-81.

BAILEY, Jeremiah (W Maine) May 1, 1773-July 6, 1853; House 1835-37.

BAILEY, John (— Mass.) 1786-June 26, 1835; House Dec. 13, 1824-31.

BAILEY, John Mosher (R N.Y.) Aug. 24, 1838-Feb. 21, 1916; House Nov. 5, 1878-81.

BAILEY, Joseph (D Pa.) March 18, 1810-Aug. 26, 1885; House 1861-65.

BAILEY, Joseph Weldon (father of Joseph Weldon Bailey Jr.) (D Texas) Oct. 6, 1862-April 13, 1929; House 1891-1901; Senate 1901-Jan. 3, 1913.

BAILEY, Joseph Weldon Jr. (son of Joseph Weldon Bailey) (D Texas) Dec. 15, 1892-July 17, 1943; House 1933-35.

BAILEY, Josiah William (D N.C.) Sept. 14, 1873-Dec. 15, 1946; Senate 1931-Dec. 15, 1946.

BAILEY, Ralph Emerson (R Mo.) July 14, 1878-April 8, 1948; House 1925-27.

BAILEY, Theodorus (D N.Y.) Oct. 12, 1758-Sept. 6, 1828; House 1793-97, 1799-1801, Oct. 6, 1801-03; Senate 1803-Jan. 16, 1804.

BAILEY, Warren Worth (D Pa.) Jan. 8, 1855-Nov. 9, 1928; House 1913-17.

BAILEY, Willis Joshua (R Kan.) Oct. 12, 1854-May 19, 1932; House 1899-1901; Gov. 1903-05.

BAILEY, Wendell (R Mo.) July 31, 1940-—; House 1981-83.

BAIRD, David (father of David Baird Jr.) (R N.J.) April 7, 1839-Feb. 25, 1927; Senate Feb. 23, 1918-19.

BAIRD, David Jr. (son of David Baird) (R N.J.) Oct. 10, 1881-Feb. 28, 1955; Senate Nov. 30, 1929-Dec. 1, 1930.

BAIRD, Joseph Edward (R Ohio) Nov. 12, 1865-June 14, 1942; House 1929-31.

BAIRD, Samuel Thomas (D La.) May 5, 1861-April 22, 1899; House 1897-April 22, 1899.

BAKER, Caleb (— N.Y.) 1762-June 26, 1849; House 1819-21.

BAKER, Charles Simeon (R N.Y.) Feb. 18, 1839-April 21, 1902; House 1885-91.

BAKER, David Jewett (D Ill.) Sept. 7, 1792-Aug. 6, 1869; Senate Nov. 12-Dec. 11, 1830.

BAKER, Edward Dickinson (R Ill., Ore.) Feb. 24, 1811-Oct. 21, 1861; House 1845-Jan. 15, 1847 (W Ill.), 1849-51 (W Ill.); Senate Oct. 2, 1860-Oct. 21, 1861 (R Ore.).

BAKER, Ezra (— N.J.) ?-?; House 1815-17.

BAKER, Henry Moore (R N.H.) Jan. 11, 1841-May 30, 1912; House 1893-97.

BAKER, Howard Henry (husband of Irene B. Baker, father of Howard Henry Baker Jr.) (R Tenn.) Jan. 12, 1902-Jan. 7, 1964; House 1951-Jan. 7, 1964.

BAKER, Howard Henry Jr. (son of Howard Henry Baker and Irene B. Baker, son-in-law of Everett McKinley Dirksen) (R Tenn.) Nov. 15, 1925-—; Senate 1967-85; Senate majority leader 1981-85.

BAKER, Irene B. (widow of Howard Henry Baker, mother of Howard Henry Baker Jr.) (R Tenn.) Nov. 17, 1901-—; House March 10, 1964-65.

BAKER, Jacob Thompson (D N.J.) April 13, 1847-Dec. 7, 1919; House 1913-15.

BAKER, Jehu (Fus. Ill.) Nov. 4, 1822-March 1, 1903; House 1865-69, 1887-89, 1897-99 (1865-69, 1887-89 Republican, 1897-99 Fusionist).

BAKER, John (F Va.) ?-Aug. 18, 1823; House 1811-13.

BAKER, John Harris (R Ind.) Feb. 28, 1832-Oct. 21, 1915; House 1875-81.

BAKER, LaMar (R Tenn.) Dec. 19, 1915-—; House 1971-75.

BAKER, Lucien (R Kan.) June 8, 1846-June 21, 1907; Senate 1895-1901.

BAKER, Osmyn (W Mass.) May 18, 1800-Feb. 9, 1875; House Jan. 14, 1840-45.

BAKER, Robert (D N.Y.) April 1862-June 15, 1943; House 1903-05.

BAKER, Stephen (R N.Y.) Aug. 12, 1819-June 9, 1875; House 1861-63.

BAKER, William (PP Kan.) April 29, 1831-Feb. 11, 1910; House 1891-97.

BAKER, William Benjamin (R Md.) July 22, 1840-May 17, 1911; House 1895-1901.

BAKER, William Henry (R N.Y.) Jan. 17, 1827-Nov. 25, 1911; House 1875-79.

BAKEWELL, Charles Montague (R Conn.) April 24, 1867-Sept. 19, 1957; House 1933-35.

BAKEWELL, Claude Ignatius (R Mo.) Aug. 9, 1912-—; House 1947-49, March 9, 1951-53.

BALDRIDGE, Howard Malcolm (R Neb.) June 23, 1894-Jan. 19, 1985; House 1931-33.

BALDUS, Alvin James (D Wis.) April 27, 1926-—; House 1975-81.

BALDWIN, Abraham (F Ga.) Nov. 2, 1754-March 4, 1807; House 1789-99; Senate 1799-March 4, 1807; Cont. Cong 1785, 1787-89; Pres. pro tempore 1801-02.

BALDWIN, Augustus Carpenter (UD Mich.) Dec. 24, 1817-Jan. 21, 1903; House 1863-65.

BALDWIN, Harry Streett (D Md.) Aug. 21, 1894-Oct. 19, 1952; House 1943-47.

BALDWIN, Henry (F Pa.) Jan. 14, 1780-April 21, 1844; House 1817-May 8, 1822; Assoc. Justice Supreme Court Jan. 6, 1830-April 21, 1844.

BALDWIN, Henry Alexander (R Hawaii) Jan. 12, 1871-Oct. 8, 1946; House (Terr. Del.) March 25, 1922-23.

BALDWIN, Henry Porter (R Mich.) Feb. 22, 1814-Dec. 31, 1892; Senate Nov. 17, 1879-81; Gov. 1869-73.

BALDWIN, John (— Conn.) April 5, 1772-March 27, 1850; House 1825-29.

BALDWIN, John Denison (R Mass.) Sept. 28, 1809-July 8, 1883; House 1863-69.

BALDWIN, John Finley Jr. (R Calif.) June 28, 1915-March 9, 1966; House 1955-March 9, 1966.

BALDWIN, Joseph Clark (R N.Y.) Jan. 11, 1897-Oct. 27, 1957; House March 11, 1941-47.

BALDWIN, Melvin Riley (D Minn.) April 12, 1838-April 15, 1901; House 1893-95.

BALDWIN, Raymond Earl (R Conn.) Aug. 31, 1893-—; Senate Dec. 27, 1946-Dec. 16, 1949; Gov. 1939-41, 1943-46.

BALDWIN, Roger Sherman (son of Simeon Baldwin) (W Conn.) Jan. 4, 1793-Feb. 19, 1863; Senate Nov. 11, 1847-51; Gov. 1844-46.

BALDWIN, Simeon (father of Roger Sherman Baldwin) (F Conn.) Dec. 14, 1761-May 26, 1851; House 1803-05.

BALL, Edward (W Ohio) Nov. 6, 1811-Nov. 22, 1872; House 1853-57.

BALL, Joseph Hurst (R Minn.) Nov. 3, 1905-—; Senate Oct. 14, 1940-Nov. 17, 1942, 1943-49.

BALL, Lewis Heisler (R Del.) Sept. 21, 1861-Oct. 18, 1932; House 1901-03; Senate March 3, 1903-05, 1919-25.

BALL, Thomas Henry (D Texas) Jan. 14, 1859-May 7, 1944; House 1897-Nov. 16, 1903.

BALL, Thomas Raymond (R Conn.) Feb. 12, 1896-June 16, 1943; House 1939-41.

BALL, William Lee (D Va.) Jan. 2, 1781-Feb. 28, 1824; House 1817-Feb. 28, 1824.

BALLENTINE, John Goff (D Tenn.) May 20, 1825-Nov. 23, 1915; House 1883-87.

BALLOU, Latimer Whipple (R R.I.) March 1, 1812-May 9, 1900; House 1875-81.

BALTZ, William Nicolas (D Ill.) Feb. 5, 1860-Aug. 22, 1943; House 1913-15.

BANDSTRA, Bert (D Iowa) Jan. 25, 1922-—; House 1965-67.

BANKHEAD, John Hollis (father of John Hollis Bankhead 2d and William Brockman Bankhead, grandfather of Walter Will Bankhead) (D Ala.) Sept. 13, 1842-March 1, 1920; House 1887-1907; Senate June 18, 1907-March 1, 1920.

Biographical Index

BANKHEAD, John Hollis 2d (son of John Hollis Bankhead, brother of William Brockman Bankhead, father of Walter Will Bankhead) (D Ala.) July 8, 1872-June 12, 1946; Senate 1931-June 12, 1946.

BANKHEAD, Walter Will (son of John Hollis Bankhead 2d, grandson of John Hollis Bankhead, nephew of William Brockman Bankhead) (D Ala.) July 21, 1897- —; House Jan. 3-Feb. 1, 1941.

BANKHEAD, William Brockman (son of John Hollis Bankhead, brother of John Hollis Bankhead 2d, uncle of Walter Will Bankhead) (D Ala.) April 12, 1874-Sept. 15, 1940; House 1917-Sept. 15, 1940; House majority leader 1936; Speaker June 4, 1936-Sept. 15, 1940.

BANKS, John (W Pa.) Oct. 17, 1793-April 3, 1864; House 1831-36.

BANKS, Linn (D Va.) Jan. 23, 1784-Jan. 13, 1842; House April 28, 1838-Dec. 6, 1841.

BANKS, Nathaniel Prentice (R Mass.) Jan. 30, 1816-Sept. 1, 1894; House 1853-Dec. 24, 1857, Dec. 4, 1865-73, 1875-79, 1889-91 (1853-55 Coalition Democrat, 1855-57 American Party, March 4-Dec. 24, 1857 Republican, Dec. 4, 1865-67 Union Republican, 1867-73 Republican, 1875-79 Liberal Republican, 1889-91 Republican); Speaker 1855-57; Gov. 1858-61.

BANNING, Henry Blackstone (D Ohio) Nov. 10, 1836-Dec. 10, 1881; House 1873-79.

BANNON, Henry Towne (R Ohio) June 5, 1867-Sept. 6, 1950; House 1905-09.

BANTA, Parke Monroe (R Mo.) Nov. 21, 1891-May 12, 1970; House 1947-49.

BARBER, Hiram Jr. (R Ill.) March 24, 1835-Aug. 5, 1924; House 1879-81.

BARBER, Isaac Ambrose (R Md.) Jan. 26, 1852-March 1, 1909; House 1897-99.

BARBER, Joel Allen (R Wis.) Jan. 17, 1809-June 17, 1881; House 1871-75.

BARBER, Laird Howard (D Pa.) Oct. 25, 1848-Feb. 16, 1928; House 1899-1901.

BARBER, Levi (— Ohio) Oct. 16, 1777-April 23, 1833; House 1817-19, 1821-23.

BARBER, Noyes (uncle of Edwin Barbour Morgan and Christopher Morgan) (D Conn.) April 28, 1781-Jan. 3, 1844; House 1821-35.

BARBOUR, Henry Ellsworth (R Calif.) March 8, 1877-March 21, 1945; House 1919-33.

BARBOUR, James (brother of Philip Pendleton Barbour, cousin of John Strode Barbour) (AD/SR Va.) June 10, 1775-June 7, 1842; Senate Jan. 2, 1815-March 7, 1825; Pres. pro tempore 1819; Gov. 1812-14; Secy. of War 1825-28.

BARBOUR, John Strode (father of John Strode Barbour, cousin of James Barbour and Philip Pendleton Barbour) (SRD Va.) Aug. 8, 1790-Jan. 12, 1855; House 1823-33.

BARBOUR, John Strode (son of John Strode Barbour) (D Va.) Dec. 29, 1820-May 14, 1892; House 1881-87; Senate 1889-May 14, 1892.

BARBOUR, Lucien (FS/T/KN Ind.) March 4, 1811-July 19, 1880; House 1855-57.

BARBOUR, Philip Pendleton (brother of James Barbour, cousin of John Strode Barbour) (D Va.) May 25, 1783-Feb. 25, 1841; House Sept. 19, 1814-25, 1827-Oct. 15, 1830; Speaker 1821-23; Assoc. Justice Supreme Court 1836-41.

BARBOUR, William Warren (R N.J.) July 3, 1888-Nov. 22, 1943; Senate Dec. 1, 1931-37, Nov. 9, 1938-Nov. 22, 1943.

BARCHFELD, Andrew Jackson (R Pa.) May 18, 1863-Jan. 28, 1922; House 1905-17.

BARCLAY, Charles Frederick (R Pa.) May 9, 1844-March 9, 1914; House 1907-11.

BARCLAY, David (D Pa.) 1823-Sept. 10, 1889; House 1855-57.

BARD, David (— Pa.) 1744-March 12, 1815; House 1795-99, 1803-March 12, 1815.

BARD, Thomas Robert (R Calif.) Dec. 8, 1841-March 5, 1915; Senate Feb. 7, 1900-05.

BARDEN, Graham Arthur (D N.C.) Sept. 25, 1896-Jan. 29, 1967; House 1935-61.

BARHAM, John All (R Calif.) July 17, 1843-Jan. 22, 1926; House 1895-1901.

BARING, Walter Stephan (D Nev.) Sept. 9, 1911-July 13, 1975; House 1949-53, 1957-73.

BARKER, Abraham Andrews (UR Pa.) March 30, 1816-March 18, 1898; House 1865-67.

BARKER, David Jr. (— N.H.) Jan. 8, 1797-April 1, 1834; House 1827-29.

BARKER, Joseph (D Mass.) Oct. 19, 1751-July 5, 1815; House 1805-09.

BARKLEY, Alben William (D Ky.) Nov. 24, 1877-April 30, 1956; House 1913-27; Senate 1927-Jan. 19, 1949, 1955-April 30, 1956; Senate majority leader 1937-47; Vice Pres. 1949-53.

BARKSDALE, Ethelbert (brother of William Barksdale) (D Miss.) Jan. 4, 1824-Feb. 17, 1893; House 1883-87.

BARKSDALE, William (brother of Ethelbert Barksdale) (SRD Miss.) Aug. 21, 1821-July 2, 1863; House 1853-Jan. 12, 1861.

BARLOW, Bradley (NR Vt.) May 12, 1814-Nov. 6, 1889; House 1879-81.

BARLOW, Charles Averill (P/D Calif.) March 17, 1858-Oct. 3, 1927; House 1897-99.

BARLOW, Stephen (D Pa.) June 13, 1779-Aug. 24, 1845; House 1827-29.

BARNARD, D. Douglas Jr. (D Ga.) March 20, 1922- —; House 1977- —.

BARNARD, Daniel Dewey (W N.Y.) July 16, 1797-April 24, 1861; House 1827-29, 1839-45.

BARNARD, Isaac Dutton (F Pa.) July 18, 1791-Feb. 28, 1834; Senate 1827-Dec. 6, 1831.

BARNARD, William Oscar (R Ind.) Oct. 25, 1852-April 8, 1939; House 1909-11.

BARNES, Demas (D N.Y.) April 4, 1827-May 1, 1888; House 1867-69.

BARNES, George Thomas (D Ga.) Aug. 14, 1833-Oct. 24, 1901; House 1885-91.

BARNES, James Martin (D Ill.) Jan. 9, 1899-June 8, 1958; House 1939-43.

BARNES, Lyman Eddy (D Wis.) June 30, 1855-Jan. 16, 1904; House 1893-95.

BARNES, Michael Darr (D Md.) Sept. 3, 1943- —; House 1979- —.

BARNETT, William (SRD Ga.) March 4, 1761-April 1832; House Oct. 5, 1812-15.

BARNEY, John (F Md.) Jan. 18, 1785-Jan. 26, 1857; House 1825-29.

BARNEY, Samuel Stebbins (R Wis.) Jan. 31, 1846-Dec. 31, 1919; House 1895-1903.

BARNHART, Henry A. (D Ind.) Sept. 11, 1858-March 26, 1934; House Nov. 3, 1908-19.

BARNITZ, Charles Augustus (W Pa.) Sept. 11, 1780-Jan. 8, 1850; House 1833-35.

BARNUM, William Henry (D Conn.) Sept. 17, 1818-April 30, 1889; House 1867-May 18, 1876; Senate May 18, 1876-79; Chrmn. Dem. Nat. Comm. 1877-89.

BARNWELL, Robert (father of Robert Woodward Barnwell) (F S.C.) Dec. 21, 1761-Oct. 24, 1814; House 1791-93; Cont. Cong. 1788-89.

BARNWELL, Robert Woodward (son of Robert Barnwell) (D S.C.) Aug. 10, 1801-Nov. 24, 1882; House 1829-33; Senate June 4-Dec. 8, 1850.

BARR, Joseph Walker (D Ind.) Jan. 17, 1918- —; House 1959-61; Secy. of the Treasury 1968-69.

BARR, Samuel Fleming (R Pa.) June 15, 1829-May 29, 1919; House 1881-85.

BARR, Thomas Jefferson (D N.Y.) 1812-March 27, 1881; House Jan. 17, 1859-61.

BARRERE, Granville (nephew of Nelson Barrere) (R Ill.) July 11, 1829-Jan. 13, 1889; House 1873-75.

BARRERE, Nelson (uncle of Granville Barrere) (W Ohio) April 1, 1808-Aug. 20, 1883; House 1851-53.

BARRET, John Richard (D Mo.) Aug. 21, 1825-Nov. 2, 1903; House 1859-June 8, 1860, Dec. 3, 1860-61.

BARRETT, Frank A. (R Wyo.) Nov. 10, 1892-May 30, 1962; House 1943-Dec. 31, 1950; Senate 1953-59; Gov. 1951-53.

BARRETT, William A. (D Pa.) Aug. 14, 1896-April 12, 1976; House 1945-47, 1949-April 12, 1976.

BARRETT, William Emerson (R Mass.) Dec. 29, 1858-Feb. 12, 1906; House 1895-99.

BARRINGER, Daniel Laurens (uncle of Daniel Moreau Barringer) (D N.C.) Oct. 1, 1788-Oct. 16, 1852; House Dec. 4, 1826-35.

BARRINGER, Daniel Moreau (nephew of Daniel Laurens Barringer) (W N.C.) July 30, 1806-Sept. 1, 1873; House 1843-49.

BARROW, Alexander (W La.) March 27, 1801-Dec. 19, 1846; Senate 1841-Dec. 19, 1846.

BARROW, Middleton Pope (great-grandson of Wilson Lumpkin) (D Ga.) Aug. 1, 1839-Dec. 23, 1903; Senate Nov. 15, 1882-83.

BARROW, Washington (W Tenn.) Oct. 5, 1807-Oct. 19, 1866; House 1847-49.

BARROWS, Samuel June (R Mass.) May 26, 1845-April 21, 1909; House 1897-99.

BARRY, Alexander Grant (R Ore.) Aug. 23, 1892-Dec. 28, 1952; Senate Nov. 9, 1938-39.

BARRY, Frederick George (D Miss.) Jan. 12, 1845-May 7, 1909; House 1885-89.

BARRY, Henry W. (R Miss.) April 1840-June 7, 1875; House Feb. 23, 1870-75.

BARRY, Robert Raymond (R N.Y.) May 15, 1915-—; House 1959-65.

BARRY, William Bernard (D N.Y.) July 21, 1902-Oct. 20, 1946; House Nov. 5, 1935-Oct. 20, 1946.

BARRY, William Taylor (D Ky.) Feb. 15, 1784-Aug. 30, 1835; House Aug. 8, 1810-11; Senate Dec. 16, 1814-May 1, 1816; Postmaster Gen. 1829-35.

BARRY, William Taylor Sullivan (D Miss.) Dec. 10, 1821-Jan. 29, 1868; House 1853-55.

BARSTOW, Gamaliel Henry (NR N.Y.) July 20, 1784-March 30, 1865; House 1831-33.

BARSTOW, Gideon (D Mass.) Sept. 7, 1783-March 26, 1852; House 1821-23.

BARTHOLDT, Richard (R Mo.) Nov. 2, 1855-March 19, 1932; House 1893-1915.

BARTINE, Horace Franklin (R Nev.) March 21, 1848-Aug. 27, 1918; House 1889-93.

BARTLETT, Bailey (F Mass.) Jan. 29, 1750-Sept. 9, 1830; House Nov. 27, 1797-1801.

BARTLETT, Charles Lafayette (D Ga.) Jan. 31, 1853-April 21, 1938; House 1895-1915.

BARTLETT, Dewey Follett (R Okla.) March 28, 1919-March 1, 1979; Senate 1973-79; Gov. 1967-71.

BARTLETT, Edward Lewis (Bob) (D Alaska) April 20, 1904-Dec. 11, 1968; House (Terr. Del.) 1945-59; Senate 1959-Dec. 11, 1968.

BARTLETT, Franklin (D N.Y.) Sept. 10, 1847-April 23, 1909; House 1893-97.

BARTLETT, George Arthur (D Nev.) Nov. 30, 1869-June 1, 1951; House 1907-11.

BARTLETT, Ichabod (AD N.H.) July 24, 1786-Oct. 19, 1853; House 1823-29.

BARTLETT, Josiah Jr. (— N.H.) Aug. 29, 1768-April 16, 1838; House 1811-13.

BARTLETT, Steve (R Texas) Sept. 19, 1947-—; House 1983-—.

BARTLETT, Thomas Jr. (D Vt.) June 18, 1808-Sept. 12, 1876; House 1851-53.

BARTLEY, Mordecai (— Ohio) Dec. 16, 1783-Oct. 10, 1870; House 1823-31; Gov. 1844-46.

BARTON, Bruce (R N.Y.) Aug. 5, 1886-July 5, 1967; House Nov. 2, 1937-41.

BARTON, David (— Mo.) Dec. 14, 1783-Sept. 28, 1837; Senate Aug. 10, 1821-31.

BARTON, Joe (R Texas) Sept. 15, 1949-—; House 1985-—.

BARTON, Richard Walker (W Va.) 1800-March 15, 1859; House 1841-43.

BARTON, Samuel (JD N.Y.) July 27, 1785-Jan. 29, 1858; House 1835-37.

BARTON, Silas Reynolds (R Neb.) May 21, 1872-Nov. 7, 1916; House 1913-15.

BARTON, William Edward (cousin of Courtney Walker Hamlin) (D Mo.) April 11, 1868-July 29, 1955; House 1931-33.

BARWIG, Charles (D Wis.) March 19, 1837-Feb. 15, 1912; House 1889-95.

BASHFORD, Coles (I Ariz.) Jan. 24, 1816-April 25, 1878; House (Terr. Del.) 1867-69; Gov. of Wisconsin (Republican) 1855-58.

BASS, Lyman Kidder (R N.Y.) Nov. 13, 1836-May 11, 1889; House 1873-77.

BASS, Perkins (R N.H.) Oct. 6, 1912-—; House 1955-63.

BASS, Ross (D Tenn.) March 17, 1918-—; House 1955-Nov. 3, 1964; Senate Nov. 4, 1964-67.

BASSETT, Burwell (D Va.) March 18, 1764-Feb. 26, 1841; House 1805-13, 1815-19, 1821-29.

BASSETT, Edward Murray (D N.Y.) Feb. 7, 1863-Oct. 27, 1948; House 1903-05.

BASSETT, Richard (grandfather of Richard Henry Bayard and James Asheton Bayard Jr.) (— Del.) April 2, 1745-Aug. 15, 1815; Senate 1789-93; Gov. 1799-1801.

BATE, William Brimage (D Tenn.) Oct. 7, 1826-March 9, 1905; Senate 1887-March 9, 1905; Gov. 1883-87.

BATEMAN, Ephraim (D N.J.) July 9, 1780-Jan. 28, 1829; House 1815-23; Senate Nov. 10, 1826-Jan. 12, 1829.

BATEMAN, Herbert H. (R Va.) Aug. 7, 1928-—; House 1983-—.

BATES, Arthur Laban (nephew of John Milton Thayer) (R Pa.) June 6, 1859-Aug. 26, 1934; House 1901-13.

BATES, Edward (brother of James Woodson Bates) (AAD Mo.) Sept. 4, 1793-March 25, 1869; House 1827-29; Atty. Gen. 1861-64.

BATES, George Joseph (father of William Henry Bates) (R Mass.) Feb. 25, 1891-Nov. 1, 1949; House 1937-Nov. 1, 1949.

BATES, Isaac Chapman (W Mass.) Jan. 23, 1779-March 16, 1845; House 1827-35 (Anti-Jackson); Senate Jan. 13, 1841-March 16, 1845 (Whig).

BATES, James (D Maine) Sept. 24, 1789-Feb. 25, 1882; House 1831-33.

BATES, James Woodson (brother of Edward Bates) (— Ark.) Aug. 25, 1788-Dec. 16, 1846; House (Terr. Del.) Dec. 21, 1819-23.

BATES, Jim (D Calif.) July 21, 1941-—; House 1983-—.

BATES, Joseph Bengal (D Ky.) Oct. 29, 1893-Sept. 10, 1965; House June 4, 1938-53.

BATES, Martin Waltham (D Del.) Feb. 24, 1787-Jan. 1, 1869; Senate Jan. 14, 1857-59.

BATES, William Henry (son of George Joseph Bates) (R Mass.) April 26, 1917-June 22, 1969; House Feb. 14, 1950-June 22, 1969.

BATHRICK, Elsworth Raymond (D Ohio) Jan. 6, 1863-Dec. 23, 1917; House 1911-15, March 4-Dec. 23, 1917.

BATTIN, James F. (R Mont.) Feb. 13, 1925-—; House 1961-Feb. 27, 1969.

BATTLE, Laurie Calvin (D Ala.) May 10, 1912-—; House 1947-55.

BAUCUS, Max Sieben (D Mont.) Dec. 11, 1941-—; House 1975-Dec. 14, 1978; Senate Dec. 15, 1978-—.

BAUMAN, Robert Edmund (R Md.) April 4, 1937-—; House Aug. 21, 1973-81.

BAUMHART, Albert David Jr. (R Ohio) June 15, 1908-—; House 1941-Sept. 2, 1942, 1955-61.

BAXTER, Portus (R Vt.) Dec. 4, 1806-March 4, 1868; House 1861-67.

BAY, William Van Ness (D Mo.) Nov. 23, 1818-Feb. 10, 1894; House 1849-51.

BAYARD, James Asheton Sr. (father of Richard Henry Bayard and James Asheton Bayard Jr., grandfather of Thomas Francis Bayard Sr., great-grandfather of Thomas Francis Bayard Jr.) (F Del.) July 28, 1767-Aug. 6, 1815; House 1797-1803; Senate Nov. 13, 1804-13.

BAYARD, James Asheton Jr. (son of James Asheton Bayard Sr., grandson of Richard Bassett, father of Thomas Francis Bayard Sr., grandfather of Thomas Francis Bayard Jr.) (D Del.) Nov. 15, 1799-June 13, 1880; Senate 1851-Jan. 29, 1864, April 5, 1867-69.

BAYARD, Richard Henry (son of James Asheton Bayard Sr., grandson of Richard Bassett) (W Del.) Sept. 23, 1796-March 4, 1868; Senate June 17, 1836-Sept. 19, 1839, Jan. 12, 1841-45.

BAYARD, Thomas Francis Sr. (son of James Asheton Bayard Jr., father of Thomas Francis Bayard Jr.) (D Del.) Oct. 29, 1828-Sept. 28, 1898; Senate 1869-March 6, 1885; Pres. pro tempore 1881; Secretary of State 1885-89.

BAYARD, Thomas Francis Jr. (son of Thomas Francis Bayard Sr.) (D Del.) June 4, 1868-July 12, 1942; Senate Nov. 8, 1922-29.

BAYH, Birch Evan (D Ind.) Jan. 22, 1928-—; Senate 1963-81.

BAYLIES, Francis (brother of William Baylies) (— Mass.) Oct. 16, 1784-Oct. 28, 1852; House 1821-27.

Biographical Index

BAYLIES, William (brother of Francis Baylies) (WD Mass.) Sept. 15, 1776-Sept. 27, 1865; House March 4-June 28, 1809, 1813-17, 1833-35.

BAYLOR, Robert Emmett Bledsoe (nephew of Jesse Bledsoe) (D Ala.) May 10, 1793-Jan. 6, 1874; House 1829-31.

BAYLY, Thomas (D Md.) Sept. 13, 1775-1829; House 1817-23.

BAYLY, Thomas Henry (son of Thomas Monteagle Bayly) (SRD Va.) Dec. 11, 1810-June 23, 1856; House May 6, 1844-June 23, 1856.

BAYLY, Thomas Monteagle (father of Thomas Henry Bayly) (D Va.) March 26, 1775-Jan. 7, 1834; House 1813-15.

BAYNE, Thomas McKee (R Pa.) June 14, 1836-June 16, 1894; House 1877-91.

BEACH, Clifton Bailey (R Ohio) Sept. 16, 1845-Nov. 15, 1902; House 1895-99.

BEACH, Lewis (D N.Y.) March 30, 1835-Aug. 10, 1886; House 1881-Aug. 10, 1886.

BEAKES, Samuel Willard (D Mich.) Jan. 11, 1861-Feb. 9, 1927; House 1913-March 3, 1917, Dec. 13, 1917-19.

BEALE, Charles Lewis (R N.Y.) March 5, 1824-Jan. 29, 1900; House 1859-61.

BEALE, James Madison Hite (D Va.) Feb. 7, 1786-Aug. 2, 1866; House 1833-37, 1849-53.

BEALE, Joseph Grant (R Pa.) March 26, 1839-May 21, 1915; House 1907-09.

BEALE, Richard Lee Tuberville (D Va.) May 22, 1819-April 21, 1893; House 1847-49, Jan. 23, 1879-81.

BEALES, Cyrus William (R Pa.) Dec. 16, 1877-Nov. 14, 1927; House 1915-17.

BEALL, James Andrew (Jack) (D Texas) Oct. 25, 1866-Feb. 12, 1929; House 1903-15.

BEALL, James Glenn (father of John Glenn Beall Jr.) (R Md.) June 5, 1894-Jan. 14, 1971; House 1943-53; Senate 1953-65.

BEALL, John Glenn Jr. (son of James Glenn Beall) (R Md.) June 19, 1927-—; House 1969-71; Senate 1971-77.

BEALL, Reasin (W Ohio) Dec. 3, 1769-Feb. 20, 1843; House April 20, 1813-June 7, 1814.

BEAM, Harry Peter (D Ill.) Nov. 23, 1892-—; House 1931-Dec. 6, 1942.

BEAMAN, Fernando Cortez (R Mich.) June 28, 1814-Sept. 27, 1882; House 1861-71.

BEAMER, John Valentine (R Ind.) Nov. 17, 1896-Sept. 8, 1964; House 1951-59.

BEAN, Benning Moulton (D N.H.) Jan. 9, 1782-Feb. 6, 1866; House 1833-37.

BEAN, Curtis Coe (R Ariz.) Jan. 4, 1828-Feb. 1, 1904; House (Terr. Del.) 1885-87.

BEARD, Edward Peter (D R.I.) Jan. 20, 1940-—; House 1975-81.

BEARD, Robin Leo Jr. (R Tenn.) Aug. 21, 1939-—; House 1973-83.

BEARDSLEY, Samuel (D N.Y.) Feb. 6, 1790-May 6, 1860; House 1831-March 29, 1836, 1843-Feb. 29, 1844.

BEATTY, John (— N.J.) Dec. 10, 1749-May 30, 1826; House 1793-95; Cont. Cong. Jan. 13-June 3, 1784, Nov. 11, 1784-Nov. 7, 1785.

BEATTY, John (R Ohio) Dec. 16, 1828-Dec. 21, 1914; House Feb. 5, 1868-73.

BEATTY, William (VBD Pa.) 1787-April 12, 1851; House 1837-41.

BEATY, Martin (W Ky.) ?-?; House 1833-35.

BEAUMONT, Andrew (D Pa.) Jan. 24, 1790-Sept. 30, 1853; House 1833-37.

BECK, Erasmus Williams (D Ga.) Oct. 21, 1833-July 22, 1898; House Dec. 2, 1872-73.

BECK, James Burnie (D Ky.) Feb. 13, 1822-May 3, 1890; House 1867-75; Senate 1877-May 3, 1890.

BECK, James Montgomery (R Pa.) July 9, 1861-April 12, 1936; House Nov. 8, 1927-Sept. 30, 1934.

BECK, Joseph David (R Wis.) March 14, 1866-Nov. 8, 1936; House 1921-29.

BECKER, Frank John (R N.Y.) Aug. 27, 1899-Sept. 4, 1981; House 1953-65.

BECKHAM, John Crepps Wickliffe (grandson of Charles Anderson Wickliffe, cousin of Robert Charles Wickliffe) (D Ky.) Aug. 5, 1869-Jan. 9, 1940; Senate 1915-21; Gov. Feb. 3, 1900-07.

BECKNER, William Morgan (D Ky.) June 19, 1841-March 14, 1910; House Dec. 3, 1894-95.

BECKWITH, Charles Dyer (R N.J.) Oct. 22, 1838-March 27, 1921; House 1889-91.

BECKWORTH, Lindley Gary (D Texas) June 30, 1913-March 9, 1984; House 1939-53, 1957-67.

BEDE, James Adam (R Minn.) Jan. 13, 1856-April 11, 1942; House 1903-09.

BEDELL, Berkley Warren (D Iowa) March 5, 1921-—; House 1975-—.

BEDINGER, George Michael (uncle of Henry Bedinger) (— Ky.) Dec. 10, 1756-Dec. 7, 1843; House 1803-07.

BEDINGER, Henry (nephew of George Michael Bedinger) (D Va.) Feb. 3, 1812-Nov. 26, 1858; House 1845-49.

BEE, Carlos (D Texas) July 8, 1867-April 20, 1932; House 1919-21.

BEEBE, George Monroe (D N.Y.) Oct. 28, 1836-March 1, 1927; House 1875-79.

BEECHER, Philemon (F Ohio) 1775-Nov. 30, 1839; House 1817-21, 1823-29.

BEEDY, Carroll Lynwood (R Maine) Aug. 3, 1880-Aug. 30, 1947; House 1921-35.

BEEKMAN, Thomas (— N.Y.) ?-?; House 1829-31.

BEEMAN, Joseph Henry (D Miss.) Nov. 17, 1833-July 31, 1909; House 1891-93.

BEERMANN, Ralph F. (R Neb.) Aug. 13, 1912-Feb. 17, 1977; House 1961-65.

BEERS, Cyrus (D N.Y.) June 21, 1786-June 5, 1850; House Dec. 3, 1838-39.

BEERS, Edward McMath (R Pa.) May 27, 1877-April 21, 1932; House 1923-April 21, 1932.

BEESON, Henry White (D Pa.) Sept. 14, 1791-Oct. 28, 1863; House May 31, 1841-43.

BEGG, James Thomas (R Ohio) Feb. 16, 1877-March 26, 1963; House 1919-29.

BEGICH, Nicholas J. (D Alaska) April 6, 1932-?; House 1971-72. (Disappeared in a plane Oct. 16, 1972 and presumed dead; congressional seat declared vacant Dec. 29, 1972.)

BEGOLE, Josiah Williams (R Mich.) Jan. 20, 1815-June 5, 1896; House 1873-75; Gov. 1883-85.

BEIDLER, Jacob Atlee (R Ohio) Nov. 2, 1852-Sept. 13, 1912; House 1901-07.

BEILENSON, Anthony Charles (D Calif.) Oct. 26, 1932-—; House 1977-—.

BEIRNE, Andrew (VBD Va.) 1771-March 16, 1845; House 1837-41.

BEITER, Alfred Florian (D N.Y.) July 7, 1894-March 11, 1974; House 1933-39, 1941-43.

BELCHER, Hiram (W Maine) Feb. 23, 1790-May 6, 1857; House 1847-49.

BELCHER, Nathan (D Conn.) June 23, 1813-June 2, 1891; House 1853-55.

BELCHER, Page Henry (R Okla.) April 21, 1899-Aug. 2, 1980; House 1951-73.

BELDEN, George Ogilvie (D N.Y.) March 28, 1797-Oct. 9, 1833; House 1827-29.

BELDEN, James Jerome (R N.Y.) Sept. 30, 1825-Jan. 1, 1904; House Nov. 8, 1887-95, 1897-99.

BELFORD, James Burns (cousin of Joseph McCrum Belford) (R Colo.) Sept. 28, 1837-Jan. 10, 1910; House Oct. 3, 1876-Dec. 13, 1877, 1879-85.

BELFORD, Joseph McCrum (cousin of James Burns Belford) (R N.Y.) Aug. 5, 1852-May 3, 1917; House 1897-99.

BELKNAP, Charles Eugene (R Mich.) Oct. 17, 1846-Jan. 16, 1929; House 1889-91, Nov. 3, 1891-93.

BELKNAP, Hugh Reid (R Ill.) Sept. 1, 1860-Nov. 12, 1901; House Dec. 27, 1895-99.

BELL, Alphonzo (R Calif.) Sept. 19, 1914-—; House 1961-77.

BELL, Charles Henry (nephew of Samuel Bell, cousin of James Bell) (R N.H.) Nov. 18, 1823-Nov. 11, 1893; Senate March 13-June 18, 1879; Gov. 1881-83.

BELL, Charles Jasper (D Mo.) Jan. 16, 1885-Jan. 21, 1978; House 1935-49.

BELL, Charles Keith (nephew of Reese Bowen Brabson) (D Texas) April 18, 1853-April 21, 1913; House 1893-97.

BELL, Charles Webster (PR Calif.) June 11, 1857-April 19, 1927; House 1913-15.

BELL, Hiram (W Ohio) April 22, 1808-Dec. 21, 1855; House 1851-53.

BELL, Hiram Parks (D Ga.) Jan. 19, 1827-Aug. 17, 1907; House 1873-75, March 13, 1877-79.

BELL, James (son of Samuel Bell, uncle of Samuel Newell Bell, cousin of Charles Henry Bell) (W N.H.) Nov. 13, 1804-May 26, 1857; Senate July 30, 1855-May 26, 1857.

BELL, James Martin (D Ohio) Oct. 16, 1796-April 4, 1849; House 1833-35.

BELL, John (W Ohio) June 19, 1796-May 4, 1869; House Jan. 7-March 3, 1851.

BELL, John (W Tenn.) Feb. 15, 1797-Sept. 10, 1869; House 1827-41 (1827-29 Democrat, 1829-41 Whig); Senate Nov. 22, 1847-59; Speaker 1834-35; Secretary of War March 5-Sept. 12, 1841.

BELL, John Calhoun (D Colo.) Dec. 11, 1851-Aug. 12, 1933; House 1893-1903.

BELL, John Junior (D Texas) May 15, 1910-Jan. 24, 1963; House 1955-57.

BELL, Joshua Fry (W Ky.) Nov. 26, 1811-Aug. 17, 1870; House 1845-47.

BELL, Peter Hansbrough (D Texas) March 11, 1810-March 8, 1898; House 1853-57; Gov. 1849-53.

BELL, Samuel (father of James Bell, grandfather of Samuel Newell Bell, uncle of Charles Henry Bell) (— N.H.) Feb. 9, 1770-Dec. 23, 1850; Senate 1823-35; Gov. 1819-23.

BELL, Samuel Newell (grandson of Samuel Bell, nephew of James Bell) (D N.H.) March 25, 1829-Feb. 8, 1889; House 1871-73, 1875-77.

BELL, Theodore Arlington (D Calif.) July 25, 1872-Sept. 4, 1922; House 1903-05.

BELL, Thomas Montgomery (D Ga.) March 17, 1861-March 18, 1941; House 1905-31.

BELLAMY, John Dillard (D N.C.) March 24, 1854-Sept. 25, 1942; House 1899-1903.

BELLINGER, Joseph (— S.C.) 1773-Jan. 10, 1830; House 1817-19.

BELLMON, Henry (R Okla.) Sept. 3, 1921-—; Senate 1969-81; Gov. 1963-67.

BELMONT, Oliver Hazard Perry (brother of Perry Belmont) (D N.Y.) Nov. 12, 1858-June 10, 1908; House 1901-03.

BELMONT, Perry (brother of Oliver Hazard Perry Belmont) (D N.Y.) Dec. 28, 1851-May 25, 1947; House 1881-Dec. 1, 1888.

BELSER, James Edwin (D Ala.) Dec. 22, 1805-Jan. 16, 1859; House 1843-45.

BELTZHOOVER, Frank Eckels (D Pa.) Nov. 6, 1841-June 2, 1923; House 1879-83, 1891-95.

BENDER, George Harrison (R Ohio) Sept. 29, 1896-June 18, 1961; House 1939-49, 1951-Dec. 15, 1954; Senate Dec. 16, 1954-57.

BENEDICT, Charles Brewster (D N.Y.) Feb. 7, 1828-Oct. 3, 1901; House 1877-79.

BENEDICT, Cleve (R W. Va.) March 21, 1935-—; House 1981-83.

BENEDICT, Henry Stanley (R Calif.) Feb. 20, 1878-July 10, 1930; House Nov. 7, 1916-17.

BENET, Christie (D S.C.) Dec. 26, 1879-March 30, 1951; Senate July 6-Nov. 5, 1918.

BENHAM, John Samuel (R Ind.) Oct. 24, 1863-Dec. 11, 1935; House 1919-23.

BENITEZ, Jaime (PD P.R.) Oct. 29, 1908-—; House (Res Comm.) 1973-77.

BENJAMIN, Adam Jr. (D Ind.) Aug. 6, 1935-Sept. 7, 1982; House 1977-Sept. 7, 1982.

BENJAMIN, John Forbes (RR Mo.) Jan. 23, 1817-March 8, 1877; House 1865-71.

BENJAMIN, Judah Philip (D La.) Aug. 6, 1811-May 8, 1884; Senate 1853-Feb. 4, 1861 (1853-59 Whig, 1859-Feb. 4, 1861 Democrat).

BENNER, George Jacob (D Pa.) April 13, 1859-Dec. 30, 1930; House 1897-99.

BENNET, Augustus Witschief (son of William Stiles Bennet) (R N.Y.) Oct. 7, 1897-June 5, 1983; House 1945-47.

BENNET, Benjamin (— N.J.) Oct. 31, 1764-Oct. 8, 1840; House 1815-19.

BENNET, Hiram Pitt (CR Colo.) Sept. 2, 1826-Nov. 11, 1914; House (Terr. Del.) Aug. 19, 1861-65.

BENNET, William Stiles (father of Augustus Witschief Bennet) (R N.Y.) Nov. 9, 1870-Dec. 1, 1962; House 1905-11, Nov. 2, 1915-17.

BENNETT, Charles Edward (D Fla.) Dec. 2, 1910-—; House 1949-—.

BENNETT, Charles Goodwin (R N.Y.) Dec. 11, 1863-May 25, 1914; House 1895-99.

BENNETT, David Smith (R N.Y.) May 3, 1811-Nov. 6, 1894; House 1869-71.

BENNETT, Granville Gaylord (R Dakota) Oct. 9, 1833-June 28, 1910; House (Terr. Del.) 1879-81.

BENNETT, Hendley Stone (D Miss.) April 7, 1807-Dec. 15, 1891; House 1855-57.

BENNETT, Henry (R N.Y.) Sept. 29, 1808-May 10, 1868; House 1849-59 (1849-51 Whig, 1851-59 Republican).

BENNETT, John Bonifas (R Mich.) Jan. 10, 1904-Aug. 9, 1964; House 1943-45, 1947-Aug. 9, 1964.

BENNETT, Joseph Bentley (R Ky.) April 21, 1859-Nov. 7, 1923; House 1905-11.

BENNETT, Marion Tinsley (son of Philip Allen Bennett) (R Mo.) June 6, 1914-—; House Jan. 12, 1943-49.

BENNETT, Philip Allen (father of Marion Tinsley Bennett) (R Mo.) March 5, 1881-Dec. 7, 1942; House 1941-Dec. 7, 1942.

BENNETT, Risden Tyler (D N.C.) June 18, 1840-July 21, 1913; House 1883-87.

BENNETT, Thomas Warren (I Idaho) Feb. 16, 1831-Feb. 2, 1893; House (Terr. Del.) 1875-June 23, 1876; Gov. 1871-75.

BENNETT, Wallace Foster (R Utah) Nov. 13, 1898-—; Senate 1951-Dec. 20, 1974.

BENNY, Allan (D N.J.) July 12, 1867-Nov. 6, 1942; House 1903-05.

BENSON, Alfred Washburn (R Kan.) July 15, 1843-Jan. 1, 1916; Senate June 11, 1906-Jan. 23, 1907.

BENSON, Carville Dickinson (D Md.) Aug. 24, 1872-Feb. 8, 1929; House Nov. 5, 1918-21.

BENSON, Egbert (— N.Y.) June 21, 1746-Aug. 24, 1833; House 1789-93, March 4-Aug. 2, 1813; Cont. Cong. 1784-88.

BENSON, Elmer Austin (FL Minn.) Sept. 22, 1895-—; Senate Dec. 27, 1935-Nov. 3, 1936; Gov. 1937-39.

BENSON, Samuel Page (R Maine) Nov. 28, 1804-Aug. 12, 1876; House 1853-57 (1853-55 Whig, 1855-57 Republican).

BENTLEY, Alvin Morell (R Mich.) Aug. 30, 1918-April 10, 1969; House 1953-61.

BENTLEY, Helen Delich (R Md.) Nov. 28, 1923-—; House 1985-—.

BENTLEY, Henry Wilbur (D N.Y.) Sept. 30, 1838-Jan. 27, 1907; House 1891-93.

BENTON, Charles Swan (D N.Y.) July 12, 1810-May 4, 1882; House 1843-47.

BENTON, Jacob (R N.H.) Aug. 19, 1814-Sept. 29, 1892; House 1867-71.

BENTON, Lemuel (great-grandfather of George William Dargan) (D S.C.) 1754-May 18, 1818; House 1793-99.

BENTON, Maecenas Eason (D Mo.) Jan. 29, 1848-April 27, 1924; House 1897-1905.

BENTON, Thomas Hart (MCD Mo.) March 14, 1782-April 10, 1858; Senate Aug. 10, 1821-51; House 1853-55 (Missouri Compromise Democrat).

BENTON, William (D Conn.) April 1, 1900-March 18, 1973; Senate Dec. 17, 1949-53.

BENTSEN, Lloyd Millard Jr. (D Texas) Feb. 11, 1921-—; House Dec. 4, 1948-55; Senate 1971-—.

BEREUTER, Douglas K. (R Neb.) Oct. 6, 1939-—; House 1979-—.

BERGEN, Christopher Augustus (R N.J.) Aug. 2, 1841-Feb. 18, 1905; House 1889-93.

BERGEN, John Teunis (second cousin of Teunis Garret Bergen) (D N.Y.) 1786-March 9, 1855; House 1831-33.

BERGEN, Teunis Garret (second cousin of John Teunis Bergen) (D N.Y.) Oct. 6, 1806-April 24, 1881; House 1865-67.

BERGER, Victor Luitpold (Soc. Wis.) Feb. 28, 1860-Aug. 7, 1929; House 1911-13, 1923-29.

BERGLAND, Bob Selmer (D Minn.) July 22, 1928- —; House 1971-Jan. 22, 1977; Secy. of Agriculture 1977-81.

BERLIN, William Markle (D Pa.) March 29, 1880-Oct. 14, 1962; House 1933-37.

BERMAN, Howard L. (D Calif.) April 15, 1941- —; House 1983- —.

BERNARD, John Toussaint (FL Minn.) March 6, 1893- —; House 1937-39.

BERNHISEL, John Milton (W Utah) July 23, 1799-Sept. 28, 1881; House (Terr. Del.) 1851-59, 1861-63.

BERRIEN, John Macpherson (W Ga.) Aug. 23, 1781-Jan. 1, 1856; Senate 1825-March 9, 1829, 1841-May 1845, Nov. 14, 1845-47, Nov. 13, 1847-May 28, 1852 (1825-29 Democrat, 1841-52 Whig); Atty. Gen. 1829-31.

BERRY, Albert Seaton (D Ky.) May 13, 1836-Jan. 6, 1908; House 1893-1901.

BERRY, Campbell Polson (cousin of James Henderson Berry) (D Calif.) Nov. 7, 1834-Jan. 8, 1901; House 1879-83.

BERRY, Ellis Yarnal (R S.D.) Oct. 6, 1902- —; House 1951-71.

BERRY, George Leonard (D Tenn.) Sept. 12, 1882-Dec. 4, 1948; Senate May 6, 1937-Nov. 8, 1938.

BERRY, James Henderson (cousin of Campbell Polson Berry) (D Ark.) May 15, 1841-Jan. 30, 1913; Senate March 20, 1885-1907; Gov. 1883-85.

BERRY, John (D Ohio) April 26, 1883-May 18, 1879; House 1873-75.

BESHLIN, Earl Hanley (D/Prohib. Pa.) April 28, 1870-July 12, 1971; House Nov. 8, 1917-19.

BETHUNE, Edwin Ruthvin (R Ark.) Dec. 19, 1934- —; House 1979-85.

BETHUNE, Lauchlin (JD N.C.) April 15, 1785-Oct. 10, 1874; House 1831-33.

BETHUNE, Marion (R Ga.) April 8, 1816-Feb. 20, 1895; House Dec. 22, 1870-71.

BETTON, Silas (— N.H.) Aug. 26, 1768-Jan. 22, 1822; House 1803-07.

BETTS, Jackson Edward (R Ohio) May 26, 1904- —; House 1951-73.

BETTS, Samuel Rossiter (D N.Y.) June 8, 1787-Nov. 2, 1868; House 1815-17.

BETTS, Thaddeus (W Conn.) Feb. 4, 1789-April 7, 1840; Senate 1839-April 7, 1840.

BEVERIDGE, Albert Jeremiah (R Ind.) Oct. 6, 1862-April 27, 1927; Senate 1899-1911.

BEVERIDGE, John Lourie (R Ill.) July 6, 1824-May 3, 1910; House Nov. 7, 1871-Jan. 4, 1873; Gov. 1873-77.

BEVILL, Tom (D Ala.) March 27, 1921- —; House 1967- —.

BIAGGI, Mario (D N.Y.) Oct. 26, 1917- —; House 1969- —.

BIBB, George Motier (— Ky.) Oct. 30, 1776-April 14, 1859; Senate 1811-Aug. 23, 1814, 1829-35; Secy. of the Treasury 1844-45.

BIBB, William Wyatt (D Ga.) Oct. 1, 1780-July 9, 1820; House Jan. 26, 1807-Nov. 6, 1813; Senate Nov. 6, 1813-Nov. 9, 1816; Gov. of Ala. 1817-20.

BIBIGHAUS, Thomas Marshal (W Pa.) March 17, 1817-June 18, 1853; House 1851-53.

BIBLE, Alan Harvey (D Nev.) Nov. 20, 1909- —; Senate Dec. 2, 1954-Dec. 17, 1974.

BICKNELL, Bennet (D N.Y.) Nov. 14, 1781-Sept. 15, 1841; House 1837-39.

BICKNELL, George Augustus (D Ind.) Feb. 6, 1815-April 11, 1891; House 1877-81.

BIDDLE, Charles John (nephew of Richard Biddle) (D Pa.) April 30, 1819-Sept. 28, 1873; House July 2, 1861-63.

BIDDLE, John (W Mich.) March 2, 1792-Aug. 25, 1859; House (Terr. Del.) 1829-Feb. 21, 1831.

BIDDLE, Joseph Franklin (R Pa.) Sept. 14, 1871-Dec. 3, 1936; House Nov. 8, 1932-33.

BIDDLE, Richard (uncle of Charles John Biddle) (W Pa.) March 25, 1796-July 6, 1847; House 1837-40.

BIDEN, Joseph Robinette Jr. (D Del.) Nov. 20, 1942- —; Senate 1973- —.

BIDLACK, Benjamin Alden (D Pa.) Sept. 8, 1804-Feb. 6, 1849; House 1841-45.

BIDWELL, Barnabas (— Mass.) Aug. 23, 1763-July 27, 1833; House 1805-July 13, 1807.

BIDWELL, John (U Calif.) Aug. 5, 1819-April 4, 1900; House 1865-67.

BIEMILLER, Andrew John (D Wis.) July 23, 1906-April 3, 1982; House 1945-47, 1949-51.

BIERMANN, Frederick Elliott (D Iowa) March 20, 1884-July 1, 1968; House 1933-39.

BIERY, James Soloman (R Pa.) March 2, 1839-Dec. 3, 1904; House 1873-75.

BIESTER, Edward G. Jr. (R Pa.) Jan. 5, 1931- —; House 1967-77.

BIGBY, John Summerfield (R Ga.) Feb. 13, 1832-March 28, 1898; House 1871-73.

BIGELOW, Abijah (F Mass.) Dec. 5, 1775-April 5, 1860; House Oct. 8, 1810-March 3, 1815.

BIGELOW, Herbert Seely (D Ohio) Jan. 4, 1870-Nov. 11, 1951; House 1937-39.

BIGELOW, Lewis (— Mass.) Aug. 18, 1785-Oct. 2, 1838; House 1821-23.

BIGGS, Asa (D N.C.) Feb. 4, 1811-March 6, 1878; House 1845-47; Senate 1855-May 5, 1858.

BIGGS, Benjamin Thomas (D Del.) Oct. 1, 1821-Dec. 25, 1893; House 1869-73; Gov. 1887-91.

BIGGS, Marion (D Calif.) May 2, 1823-Aug. 2, 1910; House 1887-91.

BIGLER, William (D Pa.) Jan. 1, 1814-Aug. 9, 1880; Senate Jan. 14, 1856-61; Gov. 1852-55.

BILBO, Theodore Gilmore (D Miss.) Oct. 13, 1877-Aug. 21, 1947; Senate 1935-Aug. 21, 1947; Gov. 1916-20, 1928-32.

BILIRAKIS, Michael (R Fla.) July 16, 1930- —; House 1983- —.

BILLINGHURST, Charles (R Wis.) July 27, 1818-Aug. 18, 1865; House 1855-59.

BILLMEYER, Alexander (D Pa.) Jan. 7, 1841-May 24, 1924; House Nov. 4, 1902-03.

BINDERUP, Charles Gustav (D Neb.) March 5, 1873-Aug. 19, 1950; House 1935-39.

BINES, Thomas (D N.J.) ?-April 9, 1826; House Nov. 2, 1814-15.

BINGAMAN, Jeff (D N.M.) Oct. 3, 1943- —; Senate 1983- —.

BINGHAM, Henry Harrison (R Pa.) Dec. 4, 1841-March 22, 1912; House 1879-March 22, 1912.

BINGHAM, Hiram (father of Jonathan Brewster Bingham) (R Conn.) Nov. 19, 1875-June 6, 1956; Senate Dec. 17, 1924-33; Gov. Jan. 7-Jan. 8, 1925.

BINGHAM, John Armor (R Ohio) Jan. 21, 1815-March 19, 1900; House 1855-63, 1865-73.

BINGHAM, Jonathan Brewster (son of Hiram Bingham) (D N.Y.) April 24, 1914- —; House 1965-83.

BINGHAM, Kinsley Scott (R Mich.) Dec. 16, 1808-Oct. 5, 1861; House (Dem.) 1847-51; Senate 1859-Oct. 5, 1861; Gov. 1854-58.

BINGHAM, William (F Pa.) March 8, 1752-Feb. 7, 1804; Senate 1795-1801; Pres. pro tempore 1797; Cont. Cong. 1787-88.

BINNEY, Horace (W Pa.) Jan. 4, 1780-Aug. 12, 1875; House 1833-35.

BIRCH, William Fred (R N.J.) Aug. 30, 1870-Jan. 25, 1946; House Nov. 5, 1918-19.

BIRD, John (D N.Y.) Nov. 22, 1768-Feb. 2, 1806; House 1799-July 25, 1801.

BIRD, John Taylor (D N.J.) Aug. 16, 1829-May 6, 1911; House 1869-73.

BIRD, Richard Ely (R Kan.) Nov. 4, 1878-Jan. 10, 1955; House 1921-23.

BIRDSALL, Ausburn (D N.Y.) ?-July 10, 1903; House 1847-49.

BIRDSALL, Benjamin Pixley (R Iowa) Oct. 26, 1858-May 26, 1917; House 1903-09.

BIRDSALL, James (D N.Y.) 1783-July 20, 1856; House 1815-17.

BIRDSALL, Samuel (D N.Y.) May 14, 1791-Feb. 8, 1872; House 1837-39.

BIRDSEYE, Victory (W N.Y.) Dec. 25, 1782-Sept. 16, 1853; House 1815-17, 1841-43.

BISBEE, Horatio Jr. (R Fla.) May 1, 1839-March 27, 1916; House 1877-Feb. 20, 1879, Jan. 22-March 3, 1881, June 1, 1882-85.

BISHOP, Cecil William (Runt) (R Ill.) June 29, 1890-Sept. 21, 1971; House 1941-55.

BISHOP, James (W N.J.) May 11, 1816-May 10, 1895; House 1855-57.

BISHOP, Phanuel (— Mass.) Sept. 3, 1739-Jan. 6, 1812; House 1799-1807.

BISHOP, Roswell Peter (R Mich.) Jan. 6, 1843-March 4, 1920; House 1895-1907.

BISHOP, William Darius (D Conn.) Sept. 14, 1827-Feb. 4, 1904; House 1857-59.

BISSELL, William Harrison (D Ill.) April 25, 1811-March 18, 1860; House 1849-55; Gov. 1857-60.

BIXLER, Harris Jacob (R Pa.) Sept. 16, 1870-March 29, 1941; House 1921-27.

BLACK, Edward Junius (father of George Robison Black) (D Ga.) Oct. 30, 1806-Sept. 1, 1846; House 1839-41, Jan. 3, 1842-45 (1839-41 State Rights Whig, 1842-45 Democrat).

BLACK, Eugene (D Texas) July 2, 1879-May 22, 1975; House 1915-29.

BLACK, Frank Swett (R N.Y.) March 8, 1853-March 22, 1913; House 1895-Jan. 7, 1897; Gov. 1897-99.

BLACK, George Robison (son of Edward Junius Black) (D Ga.) March 24, 1835-Nov. 3, 1886; House 1881-83.

BLACK, Henry (W Pa.) Feb. 25, 1783-Nov. 28, 1841; House June 28-Nov. 28, 1841.

BLACK, Hugo Lafayette (D Ala.) Feb. 27, 1886-Sept. 25, 1971; Senate 1927-Aug. 19, 1937; Assoc. Justice Supreme Court 1937-Sept. 17, 1971.

BLACK, James (D Pa.) March 6, 1793-June 21, 1872; House Dec. 5, 1836-37, 1843-47.

BLACK, James Augustus (Cal.D S.C.) 1793-April 3, 1848; House 1843-April 3, 1848.

BLACK, James Conquest Cross (D Ga.) May 9, 1842-Oct. 1, 1928; House 1893-March 4, 1895, Oct. 2, 1895-97.

BLACK, John (— Miss.) ?-Aug. 29, 1854; Senate Nov. 12, 1832-March 3, 1833, Nov. 22, 1833-Jan. 22, 1838.

BLACK, John Charles (D Ill.) Jan. 27, 1839-Aug. 17, 1915; House 1893-Jan. 12, 1895.

BLACK, Loring Milton Jr. (D N.Y.) May 17, 1866-May 21, 1956; House 1923-35.

BLACKBURN, Benjamin Bentley (R Ga.) Feb. 14, 1927-—; House 1967-75.

BLACKBURN, Edmond Spencer (R N.C.) Sept. 22, 1868-March 10, 1912; House 1901-03, 1905-07.

BLACKBURN, Joseph Clay Stiles (D Ky.) Oct. 1, 1838-Sept. 12, 1918; House 1875-85; Senate 1885-97, 1901-07.

BLACKBURN, Robert E. Lee (R Ky.) April 9, 1870-Sept. 20, 1935; House 1929-31.

BLACKBURN, William Jasper (R La.) July 24, 1820-Nov. 10, 1899; House July 18, 1868-69.

BLACKLEDGE, William (father of William Salter Blackledge) (D N.C.) ?-Oct. 19, 1828; House 1803-09, 1811-13.

BLACKLEDGE, William Salter (son of William Blackledge) (D N.C.) 1793-March 21, 1857; House Feb. 7, 1821-23.

BLACKMAR, Esbon (W N.Y.) June 19, 1805-Nov. 19, 1857; House Dec. 4, 1848-49.

BLACKMON, Fred Leonard (D Ala.) Sept. 15, 1873-Feb. 8, 1921; House 1911-Feb. 8, 1921.

BLACKNEY, William Wallace (R Mich.) Aug. 28, 1876-March 14, 1963; House 1935-37, 1939-53.

BLACKWELL, Julius W. (VBD Tenn.) ?-?; House 1839-41, 1843-45.

BLAINE, James Gillespie (R Maine) Jan. 31, 1830-Jan. 27, 1893; House 1863-July 10, 1876; Senate July 10, 1876-March 5, 1881; Speaker 1869-75; Secy. of State March 5-Dec. 12, 1881, March 7, 1889-June 4, 1892.

BLAINE, John James (R Wis.) May 4, 1875-April 18, 1934; Senate 1927-33; Gov. 1921-27.

BLAIR, Austin (R Mich.) Feb. 8, 1818-Aug. 6, 1894; House 1867-73; Gov. 1861-65.

BLAIR, Bernard (W N.Y.) May 24, 1801-May 7, 1880; House 1841-43.

BLAIR, Francis Preston Jr. (D Mo.) Feb. 19, 1821-July 8, 1875; House 1857-59 (Free-Soiler), June 8-25, 1860, 1861-July 1862, 1863-June 10, 1864; Senate Jan. 20, 1871-73 (Democrat).

BLAIR, Henry William (R N.H.) Dec. 6, 1834-March 14, 1920; House 1875-79, 1893-95; Senate June 20, 1879-March 3, 1885, March 5, 1885-91.

BLAIR, Jacob Beeson (U Va. and W.Va.) April 11, 1821-Feb. 12, 1901; House Dec. 2, 1861-63 (Va.), Dec. 7, 1863-65 (W.Va.).

BLAIR, James (D S.C.) 1790-April 1, 1834; House 1821-May 8, 1822, 1829-April 1, 1834 (1821-22 Democrat, 1829-31 Union Democrat, 1831-34 Democrat).

BLAIR, James Gorrall (LR Mo.) Jan. 1, 1825-March 1, 1904; House 1871-73.

BLAIR, John (D Tenn.) Sept. 13, 1790-July 9, 1863; House 1823-35.

BLAIR, Samuel Steel (R Pa.) Dec. 5, 1821-Dec. 8, 1890; House 1859-63.

BLAISDELL, Daniel (F N.H.) Jan. 22, 1762-Jan. 10, 1833; House 1809-11.

BLAKE, Harrison Gray Otis (R Ohio) March 17, 1818-April 16, 1876; House Oct. 11, 1859-63.

BLAKE, John Jr. (— N.Y.) Dec. 5, 1762-Jan. 13, 1826; House 1805-09.

BLAKE, John Lauris (R N.J.) March 25, 1831-Oct. 10, 1899; House 1879-81.

BLAKE, Thomas Holdsworth (AR Ind.) June 14, 1792-Nov. 28, 1849; House 1827-29.

BLAKENEY, Albert Alexander (R Md.) Sept. 28, 1850-Oct. 15, 1924; House 1901-03, 1921-23.

BLAKLEY, William Arvis (D Texas) Nov. 17, 1898-Jan. 5, 1976; Senate Jan. 15-April 28, 1957, Jan. 3-June 14, 1961.

BLANCHARD, George Washington (R Wis.) Jan. 26, 1884-Oct. 2, 1964; House 1933-35.

BLANCHARD, James Johnston (D Mich.) Aug. 8, 1942-—; House 1975-83; Gov. 1983-—.

BLANCHARD, John (W Pa.) Sept. 30, 1787-March 9, 1849; House 1845-49.

BLANCHARD, Newton Crain (D La.) Jan. 29, 1849-June 22, 1922; House 1881-March 12, 1894; Senate March 12, 1894-97; Gov. 1904-08.

BLAND, Oscar Edward (R Ind.) Nov. 21, 1877-Aug. 3, 1951; House 1917-23.

BLAND, Richard Parks (D Mo.) Aug. 19, 1835-June 15, 1899; House 1873-95, 1897-June 15, 1899.

BLAND, Schuyler Otis (D Va.) May 4, 1872-Feb. 16, 1950; House July 2, 1918-Feb. 16, 1950.

BLAND, Theodorick (— Va.) March 21, 1742-June 1, 1790; House 1789-June 1, 1790; Cont. Cong. 1780-83.

BLAND, William Thomas (grandson of John George Jackson, cousin of James Monroe Jackson) (D Mo.) Jan. 21, 1861-Jan. 15, 1928; House 1919-21.

BLANTON, Leonard Ray (D Tenn.) April 10, 1930-—; House 1967-73; Gov. 1975-79.

BLANTON, Thomas Lindsay (D Texas) Oct. 25, 1872-Aug. 11, 1957; House 1917-29, May 20, 1930-37.

BLATNIK, John Anton (D Minn.) Aug. 17, 1911-—; House 1947-Dec. 31, 1974.

BLAZ, Vincente "Ben" (R Guam) Feb. 14, 1928-—; House 1985-—.

BLEAKLEY, Orrin Dubbs (R Pa.) May 15, 1854-Dec. 3, 1927; House March 4-April 3, 1917.

BLEASE, Coleman Livingston (D S.C.) Oct. 8, 1868-Jan. 19, 1942; Senate 1925-31; Gov. 1911-15.

BLEDSOE, Jesse (uncle of Robert Emmett Bledsoe Baylor) (— Ky.) April 6, 1776-June 25, 1836; Senate 1813-Dec. 24, 1814.

BLEECKER, Harmanus (F N.Y.) Oct. 9, 1779-July 19, 1849; House 1811-13.

BLILEY, Thomas J. Jr. (R Va.) Jan. 28, 1932-—; House 1981-—.

BLISS, Aaron Thomas (R Mich.) May 22, 1837-Sept. 16, 1906; House 1889-91; Gov. 1901-05.

BLISS, Archibald Meserole (D N.Y.) Jan. 25, 1838-March 19, 1923; House 1875-83, 1885-89.

BLISS, George (D Ohio) Jan. 1, 1813-Oct. 24, 1868; House 1853-55, 1863-65.

BLISS, Philemon (R Ohio) July 28, 1813-Aug. 25, 1889; House 1855-59.

Biographical Index

BLITCH, Iris Faircloth (D Ga.) April 25, 1912-—; House 1955-63.

BLODGETT, Rufus (D N.J.) Oct. 9, 1834-Oct. 3, 1910; Senate 1887-93.

BLOODWORTH, Timothy (— N.C.) 1736-Aug. 24, 1814; House April 6, 1790-91; Senate 1795-1801; Cont. Cong. 1786-Aug. 13, 1787.

BLOOM, Isaac (— N.Y.) 1716-April 26, 1803; House March 4-April 26, 1803.

BLOOM, Sol (D N.Y.) March 9, 1870-March 7, 1949; House 1923-March 7, 1949.

BLOOMFIELD, Joseph (D N.J.) Oct. 5, 1753-Oct. 3, 1823; House 1817-21; Gov. 1801-12.

BLOUIN, Michael Thomas (D Iowa) Nov. 7, 1945-—; House 1975-79.

BLOUNT, James Henderson (D Ga.) Sept. 12, 1837-March 8, 1903; House 1873-93.

BLOUNT, Thomas (brother of William Blount, uncle of William Grainger Blount) (D N.C.) May 10, 1759-Feb. 7, 1812; House 1793-99, 1805-09, 1811-Feb. 7, 1812.

BLOUNT, William (father of William Grainger Blount, brother of Thomas Blount) (— Tenn.) March 26, 1749-March 21, 1800; Senate Aug. 2, 1796-July 8, 1797; Cont. Cong. (N.C.) 1782-83, 1786-87.

BLOUNT, William Grainger (son of William Blount, nephew of Thomas Blount) (D Tenn.) 1784-May 21, 1827; House Dec. 8, 1815-19.

BLOW, Henry Taylor (R Mo.) July 15, 1817-Sept. 11, 1875; House 1863-67.

BLUE, Richard Whiting (R Kan.) Sept. 8, 1841-Jan. 28, 1907; House 1895-97.

BOARDMAN, Elijah (father of William Whiting Boardman) (D Conn.) March 7, 1760-Aug. 18, 1823; Senate 1821-Aug. 18, 1823.

BOARDMAN, William Whiting (son of Elijah Boardman) (W Conn.) Oct. 10, 1794-Aug. 27, 1871; House Dec. 7, 1840-43.

BOARMAN, Alexander (Aleck) (L La.) Dec. 10, 1839-Aug. 30, 1916; House Dec. 3, 1872-73.

BOATNER, Charles Jahleal (D La.) Jan. 23, 1849-March 21, 1903; House 1889-95, June 10, 1896-97.

BOCKEE, Abraham (JD N.Y.) Feb. 3, 1784-June 1, 1865; House 1829-31, 1833-37.

BOCOCK, Thomas Stanhope (D Va.) May 18, 1815-Aug. 5, 1891; House 1847-61.

BODEN, Andrew (— Pa.) ?-Dec. 20, 1835; House 1817-21.

BODINE, Robert Nall (D Mo.) Dec. 17, 1837-March 16, 1914; House 1897-99.

BODLE, Charles (— N.Y.) 1787-Oct. 31, 1835; House 1833-35.

BOEHLERT, Sherwood L. (D N.Y.) June 28, 1936-—; House 1983-—.

BOEHNE, John William (father of John William Boehne Jr.) (D Ind.) Oct. 28, 1856-Dec. 27, 1946; House 1909-13.

BOEHNE, John William Jr. (son of John William Boehne) (D Ind.) March 2, 1895-July 5, 1973; House 1931-43.

BOEN, Haldor Erickson (PP Minn.) Jan. 2, 1851-July 23, 1912; House 1893-95.

BOGGS, Corinne Claiborne (widow of Thomas Hale Boggs Sr.) (D La.) March 13, 1916-—; House March 20, 1973-—.

BOGGS, James Caleb (R Del.) May 15, 1909-—; House 1947-53; Senate 1961-73; Gov. 1953-60.

BOGGS, Thomas Hale Sr. (husband of Corinne Claiborne Boggs) (D La.) Feb. 15, 1914-?; House 1941-43, 1947-73; House majority leader 1971-73. (Missing in a plane Oct. 16, 1972 and presumed dead; congressional seat declared vacant Jan. 3, 1973.)

BOGY, Lewis Vital (D Mo.) April 9, 1813-Sept. 20, 1877; Senate 1873-Sept. 20, 1877.

BOHN, Frank Probasco (R Mich.) July 14, 1866-June 1, 1944; House 1927-33.

BOIES, William Dayton (R Iowa) Jan. 3, 1857-May 31, 1932; House 1919-29.

BOILEAU, Gerald John (Prog. Wis.) Jan. 15, 1900-—; House 1931-39 (1931-35 Republican, 1935-39 Progressive).

BOKEE, David Alexander (W N.Y.) Oct. 6, 1805-March 15, 1860; House 1849-51.

BOLAND, Edward Patrick (D Mass.) Oct. 1, 1911-—; House 1953-—.

BOLAND, Patrick Joseph (husband of Veronica Grace Boland) (D Pa.) Jan. 6, 1880-May 18, 1942; House 1931-May 18, 1924.

BOLAND, Veronica Grace (widow of Patrick Joseph Boland) (D Pa.) March 18, 1899-—; House Nov. 19, 1942-43.

BOLES, Thomas (R Ark.) July 16, 1837-March 13, 1905; House June 22, 1868-71, Feb. 9, 1872-73.

BOLLES, Stephen (R Wis.) June 25, 1866-July 8, 1941; House 1939-July 8, 1941.

BOLLING, Richard Walker (D Mo.) May 17, 1916-—; House 1949-83.

BOLTON, Chester Castle (husband of Frances Payne Bolton, father of Oliver Payne Bolton) (R Ohio) Sept. 5, 1882-Oct. 29, 1939; House 1929-37, Jan. 3-Oct. 29, 1939.

BOLTON, Frances Payne (widow of Chester Castle Bolton, grand-daughter of Henry B. Payne, mother of Oliver Payne Bolton) (R Ohio) March 29, 1885-March 9, 1977; House Feb. 27, 1940-69.

BOLTON, Oliver Payne (son of Chester Castle Bolton and Frances Payne Bolton, great-grandson of Henry B. Payne) (R Ohio) Feb. 22, 1917-Dec. 13, 1972; House 1953-57, 1963-65.

BOLTON, William P. (D Md.) July 2, 1885-Nov. 22, 1964; House 1949-51.

BOND, Charles Grosvenor (nephew of Charles Henry Grosvenor) (R N.Y.) May 29, 1877-Jan. 8, 1974; House 1921-23.

BOND, Shadrack (D Ill.) Nov. 24, 1773-April 12, 1832; House (Terr. Del.) Dec. 3, 1812-Aug. 2, 1813; Gov. 1818-22.

BOND, William Key (W Ohio) Oct. 2, 1792-Feb. 17, 1864; House 1835-41.

BONE, Homer Truett (D Wash.) Jan. 25, 1883-March 11, 1970; Senate 1933-Nov. 13, 1944.

BONER, William Hill (D Tenn.) Feb. 14, 1945-—; House 1979-—.

BONHAM, Milledge Luke (SRD S.C.) Dec. 25, 1813-Aug. 27, 1890; House 1857-Dec. 21, 1860; Gov. 1862-64.

BONIN, Edward John (R Pa.) Dec. 23, 1904-—; House 1953-55.

BONIOR, David Edward (D Mich.) June 6, 1945-—; House 1977-—.

BONKER, Don Leroy (D Wash.) March 7, 1937-—; House 1975-—.

BONNER, Herbert Covington (D N.C.) May 16, 1891-Nov. 7, 1965; House Nov. 5, 1940-Nov. 7, 1965.

BONYNGE, Robert William (R Colo.) Sept. 8, 1863-Sept. 22, 1939; House Feb. 16, 1904-09.

BOODY, Azariah (W N.Y.) April 21, 1815-Nov. 18, 1885; House March 4-October 1853.

BOODY, David Augustus (D N.Y.) Aug. 13, 1837-Jan. 20, 1930; House March 4-Oct. 13, 1891.

BOOHER, Charles Ferris (D Mo.) Jan. 31, 1848-Jan. 21, 1921; House Feb. 19-March 3, 1889, 1907-Jan. 21, 1921.

BOOKER, George William (C Va.) Dec. 5, 1821-June 4, 1883; House Jan. 26, 1870-71.

BOON, Ratliff (JD Ind.) Jan. 18, 1781-Nov. 20, 1844; House 1825-27, 1829-39; Gov. Sept. 12-Dec. 5, 1822.

BOONE, Andrew Rechmond (D Ky.) April 4, 1831-Jan. 26, 1886; House 1875-79.

BOOTH, Newton (AM Calif.) Dec. 25, 1825-July 14, 1892; Senate 1875-81; Gov. 1871-75.

BOOTH, Walter (FS Conn.) Dec. 8, 1791-April 30, 1870; House 1849-51.

BOOTHMAN, Melvin Morella (R Ohio) Oct. 16, 1846-March 5, 1904; House 1887-91.

BOOZE, William Samuel (R Md.) Jan. 9, 1862-Dec. 6, 1933; House 1897-99.

BORAH, William Edgar (R Idaho) June 29, 1865-Jan. 19, 1940; Senate 1907-Jan. 19, 1940.

BORCHERS, Charles Martin (D Ill.) Nov. 18, 1869-Dec. 2, 1946; House 1913-15.

BORDEN, Nathaniel Briggs (W Mass.) April 15, 1801-April 10, 1865; House 1835-39, 1841-43 (1835-39 Van Buren Democrat, 1841-43 Whig).

BOREING, Vincent (R Ky.) Nov. 24, 1839-Sept. 16, 1903; House 1899-Sept. 16, 1903.

BOREMAN, Arthur Inghram (R W.Va.) July 24, 1823-April 19, 1896; Senate 1869-75; Gov. 1863-69.

BOREN, David Lyle (son of Lyle H. Boren) (D Okla.) April 21, 1941- —; Senate 1979- —; Gov. 1975-79.

BOREN, Lyle H. (father of David Lyle Boren) (D Okla.) May 11, 1909- —; House 1937-47.

BORLAND, Charles Jr. (— N.Y.) June 29, 1786-Feb. 23, 1852; House Nov. 8, 1821-23.

BORLAND, Solon (D Ark.) Sept. 21, 1808-Jan. 1, 1864; Senate March 30, 1848-April 3, 1853.

BORLAND, William Patterson (D Mo.) Oct. 14, 1867-Feb. 20, 1919; House 1909-Feb. 20, 1919.

BORSKI, Robert Anthony Jr. (D Pa.) Oct. 20, 1948- —; House 1983- —.

BORST, Peter I. (JD N.Y.) April 24, 1797-Nov. 14, 1848; House 1829-31.

BOSCH, Albert Henry (R N.Y.) Oct. 30, 1908- —; House 1953-Dec. 31, 1960.

BOSCHWITZ, Rudolf Eli (R Minn.) Nov. 7, 1930- —; Senate Dec. 30, 1978- —.

BOSCO, Douglas H. (D Calif.) July 28, 1946- —; House 1983- —.

BOSONE, Reva Zilpha Beck (D Utah) April 2, 1898-July 21, 1983; House 1949-53.

BOSS, John Linscom Jr. (— R.I.) Sept. 7, 1780-Aug. 1, 1819; House 1815-19.

BOSSIER, Pierre Evariste John Baptiste (Cal.D La.) March 22, 1797-April 24, 1844; House 1843-April 24, 1844.

BOTELER, Alexander Robinson (AP Va.) May 16, 1815-May 8, 1892; House 1859-61.

BOTKIN, Jeremiah Dunham (Fus. Kan.) April 24, 1849-Dec. 29, 1921; House 1897-99.

BOTTS, John Minor (HCW Va.) Sept. 16, 1802-Jan. 8, 1869; House 1839-43, 1847-49.

BOTTUM, Joseph H. (R S.D.) Aug. 7, 1903-July 4, 1984; Senate July 11, 1962-63.

BOUCHER, Frederick C. (D Va.) Aug. 1, 1946- —; House 1983- —.

BOUCK, Gabriel (nephew of Joseph Bouck) (D Wis.) Dec. 16, 1828-Feb. 21, 1904; House 1877-81.

BOUCK, Joseph (uncle of Gabriel Bouck) (D N.Y.) July 22, 1788-March 30, 1858; House 1831-33.

BOUDE, Thomas (F Pa.) May 17, 1752-Oct. 24, 1822; House 1801-03.

BOUDINOT, Elias (— N.J.) May 2, 1740-Oct. 24, 1821; House 1789-95; Cont. Cong. 1777-78, 1781-83.

BOULDIN, James Wood (brother of Thomas Tyler Bouldin) (JD Va.) 1792-March 30, 1854; House March 15, 1834-39.

BOULDIN, Thomas Tyler (brother of James Wood Bouldin) (D Va.) 1781-Feb. 11, 1834; House 1829-33, Aug. 26, 1833-Feb. 11, 1834.

BOULIGNY, Charles Joseph Dominique (uncle of John Edward Bouligny) (— La.) Aug. 22, 1773-March 6, 1833; Senate Nov. 19, 1824-29.

BOULIGNY, John Edward (nephew of Charles Joseph Dominique Bouligny) (AP La.) Feb. 5, 1824-Feb. 20, 1864; House 1859-61.

BOULTER, Beau (R Texas) Feb. 23, 1942- —; House 1985- —.

BOUND, Franklin (R Pa.) April 9, 1829-Aug. 8, 1910; House 1885-89.

BOURN, Benjamin (F R.I.) Sept. 9, 1755-Sept. 17, 1808; House Aug. 31, 1790-96.

BOURNE, Jonathan Jr. (R Ore.) Feb. 23, 1855-Sept. 1, 1940; Senate 1907-13.

BOURNE, Shearjasub (— Mass.) June 14, 1746-March 11, 1806; House 1791-95.

BOUTELL, Henry Sherman (R Ill.) March 14, 1856-March 11, 1926; House Nov. 23, 1897-1911.

BOUTELLE, Charles Addison (R Maine) Feb. 9, 1839-May 21, 1901; House 1883-1901.

BOUTWELL, George Sewel (R Mass.) Jan. 28, 1818-Feb. 27, 1905; House 1863-March 12, 1869; Senate March 17, 1873-77; Gov. 1851-53; Secy. of the Treasury March 12, 1869-March 17, 1873.

BOVEE, Matthias Jacob (JD N.Y.) July 24, 1793-Sept. 12, 1872; House 1835-37.

BOW, Frank Townsend (R Ohio) Feb. 20, 1901-Nov. 13, 1972; House 1951-Nov. 13, 1972.

BOWDEN, George Edwin (nephew of Lemuel Jackson Bowden) (R Va.) July 6, 1852-Jan. 22, 1908; House 1887-91.

BOWDEN, Lemuel Jackson (uncle of George Edwin Bowden) (R Va.) Jan. 16, 1815-Jan. 2, 1864; Senate 1863-Jan. 2, 1864.

BOWDLE, Stanley Eyre (D Ohio) Sept. 4, 1868-April 6, 1919; House 1913-15.

BOWDON, Franklin Welsh (uncle of Sydney Johnston Bowie) (D Ala.) Feb. 17, 1817-June 8, 1857; House Dec. 7, 1846-51.

BOWEN, Christopher Columbus (R S.C.) Jan. 5, 1832-June 23, 1880; House July 20, 1868-71.

BOWEN, David Reece (D Miss.) Oct. 21, 1932- —; House 1973-83.

BOWEN, Henry (son of Rees Tate Bowen, nephew of John Warfield Johnston, cousin of William Bowen Campbell) (R Va.) Dec. 26, 1841-April 29, 1915; House 1883-85, 1887-89 (1883-85 Readjuster, 1887-89 Republican).

BOWEN, John Henry (D Tenn.) Sept. 1780-Sept. 25, 1822; House 1813-15.

BOWEN, Rees Tate (father of Henry Bowen) (C Va.) Jan. 10, 1809-Aug. 29, 1879; House 1873-75.

BOWEN, Thomas Mead (R Colo.) Oct. 26, 1835-Dec. 30, 1906; Senate 1883-89; Gov. (Idaho Terr.) 1871.

BOWER, Gustavus Miller (D Va.) Dec. 12, 1790-Nov. 17, 1864; House 1843-45.

BOWER, William Horton (D N.C.) June 6, 1850-May 11, 1910; House 1893-95.

BOWERS, Eaton Jackson (D Miss.) June 17, 1865-Oct. 26, 1939; House 1903-11.

BOWERS, George Meade (R W.Va.) Sept. 13, 1863-Dec. 7, 1925; House May 9, 1916-23.

BOWERS, John Myer (— N.Y.) Sept. 25, 1772-Feb. 24, 1846; House May 26-Dec. 20, 1813.

BOWERS, William Wallace (R Calif.) Oct. 20, 1834-May 2, 1917; House 1891-97.

BOWERSOCK, Justin De Witt (R Kan.) Sept. 19, 1842-Oct. 27, 1922; House 1899-1907.

BOWIE, Richard Johns (W Md.) June 23, 1807-March 12, 1888; House 1849-53.

BOWIE, Sydney Johnston (nephew of Franklin Welsh Bowdon) (D Ala.) July 26, 1865-May 7, 1928; House 1901-07.

BOWIE, Thomas Fielder (grandnephew of Walter Bowie, brother-in-law of Reverdy Johnson) (D Md.) April 7, 1808-Oct. 30, 1869; House 1855-59.

BOWIE, Walter (granduncle of Thomas Fielder Bowie) (D Md.) 1748-Nov. 9, 1810; House March 24, 1802-05.

BOWLER, James Bernard (D Ill.) Feb. 5, 1875-July 18, 1957; House July 7, 1953-July 18, 1957.

BOWLES, Chester Bliss (D Conn.) April 5, 1901- —; House 1959-61; Gov. 1949-51.

BOWLES, Henry Leland (R Mass.) Jan. 6, 1866-May 17, 1932; House Sept. 29, 1925-29.

BOWLIN, James Butler (D Mo.) Jan. 16, 1804-July 19, 1874; House 1843-51.

BOWLING, William Bismarck (D Ala.) Sept. 24, 1870-Dec. 27, 1946; House Dec. 14, 1920-Aug. 16, 1928.

BOWMAN, Charles Calvin (R Pa.) Nov. 14, 1852-July 3, 1941; House 1911-Dec. 12, 1912.

BOWMAN, Frank Llewellyn (R W.Va.) Jan. 21, 1879-Sept. 15, 1936; House 1925-33.

BOWMAN, Selwyn Zadock (R Mass.) May 11, 1840-Sept. 30, 1928; House 1879-83.

BOWMAN, Thomas (D Iowa) May 25, 1848-Dec. 1, 1917; House 1891-93.

BOWNE, Obadiah (W N.Y.) May 19, 1822-April 27, 1874; House 1851-53.

BOWNE, Samuel Smith (VBD N.Y.) April 11, 1800-July 9, 1865; House 1841-43.

BOWRING, Eva Kelly (R Neb.) Jan. 9, 1892- —; Senate April 16-Nov. 7, 1954.

BOX, John Calvin (D Texas) March 28, 1871-May 17, 1941; House 1919-31.

BOXER, Barbara (D Calif.) Nov. 11, 1940- –; House 1983- –.

BOYCE, William Henry (D Del.) Nov. 28, 1855-Feb. 6, 1942; House 1923-25.

BOYCE, William Waters (SRD S.C.) Oct. 24, 1818-Feb. 3, 1890; House 1853-Dec. 21, 1860.

BOYD, Adam (D N.J.) March 21, 1746-Aug. 15, 1835; House 1803-05, March 8, 1808-13.

BOYD, Alexander (W N.Y.) Sept. 14, 1764-April 8, 1857; House 1813-15.

BOYD, John Frank (R Neb.) Aug. 8, 1853-May 28, 1945; House 1907-09.

BOYD, John Huggins (W N.Y.) July 31, 1799-July 2, 1868; House 1851-53.

BOYD, Linn (D Ky.) Nov. 22, 1800-Dec. 17, 1859; House 1835-37, 1839-55; Speaker 1851-55.

BOYD, Sempronius Hamilton (R Mo.) May 28, 1828-June 22, 1894; House 1863-65, 1869-71 (1863-65 Emancipationist, 1869-71 Republican).

BOYD, Thomas Alexander (R Ill.) June 25, 1830-May 28, 1897; House 1877-81.

BOYDEN, Nathaniel (R N.C.) Aug. 16, 1796-Nov. 20, 1873; House 1847-49, July 13, 1868-69 (1847-49 Whig, 1868-69 Republican).

BOYER, Benjamin Markley (D Pa.) Jan. 22, 1823-Aug. 16, 1887; House 1865-69.

BOYER, Lewis Leonard (D Ill.) May 19, 1886-March 12, 1944; House 1937-39.

BOYKIN, Frank William (D Ala.) Feb. 21, 1885-March 12, 1969; House July 30, 1935-63.

BOYLAN, John Joseph (D N.Y.) Sept. 20, 1878-Oct. 5, 1938; House March 4, 1923-Oct. 5, 1938.

BOYLE, Charles Augustus (D Ill.) Aug. 13, 1907-Nov. 4, 1959; House 1955-Nov. 4, 1959.

BOYLE, Charles Edmund (D Pa.) Feb. 4, 1836-Dec. 15, 1888; House 1883-87.

BOYLE, John (D Ky.) Oct. 28, 1774-Feb. 28, 1834; House 1803-09.

BRABSON, Reese Bowen (uncle of Charles Keith Bell) (D Tenn.) Sept. 16, 1817-Aug. 16, 1863; House 1859-61.

BRACE, Jonathan (F Conn.) Nov. 12, 1754-Aug. 26, 1837; House Dec. 3, 1798-1800.

BRACKENRIDGE, Henry Marie (W Pa.) May 11, 1786-Jan. 18, 1871; House Oct. 13, 1840-41.

BRADBURY, George (F Mass.) Oct. 10, 1770-Nov. 7, 1823; House 1813-17.

BRADBURY, James Ware (D Maine) June 10, 1802-Jan. 7, 1901; Senate 1847-53.

BRADBURY, Theophilus (F Mass.) Nov. 13, 1739-Sept. 6, 1803; House 1795-July 24, 1797.

BRADEMAS, John (D Ind.) March 2, 1927- –; House 1959-81.

BRADFORD, Allen Alexander (R Colo.) July 23, 1815-March 12, 1888; House (Terr. Del.) 1865-67, 1869-71.

BRADFORD, Taul (grandson of Micah Taul) (D Ala.) Jan. 20, 1835-Oct. 28, 1883; House 1875-77.

BRADFORD, William (– R.I.) Nov. 4, 1729-July 6, 1808; Senate 1793-Oct. 1797; Pres. pro tempore 1797.

BRADLEY, Edward (D Mich.) April 1808-Aug. 5, 1847; House March 4-Aug. 5, 1847.

BRADLEY, Frederick Van Ness (R Mich.) April 12, 1898-May 24, 1947; House 1939-May 24, 1947.

BRADLEY, Michael Joseph (D Pa.) May 24, 1897-Nov. 27, 1979; House 1937-47.

BRADLEY, Nathan Ball (R Mich.) May 28, 1831-Nov. 8, 1906; House 1873-77.

BRADLEY, Stephen Row (father of William Czar Bradley) (D Vt.) Feb. 20, 1754-Dec. 9, 1830; Senate Oct. 17, 1791-95, Oct. 15, 1801-13; Pres. pro tempore 1802-03, 1808.

BRADLEY, Thomas Joseph (D N.Y.) Jan. 2, 1870-April 1, 1901; House 1897-1901.

BRADLEY, Thomas Wilson (R N.Y.) April 6, 1844-May 30, 1920; House 1903-13.

BRADLEY, William Czar (son of Stephen Row Bradley) (D Vt.) March 23, 1782-March 3, 1867; House 1813-15, 1823-27 (1813-15 War Democrat, 1823-27 Democrat).

BRADLEY, William O'Connell (R Ky.) March 18, 1847-May 23, 1914; Senate 1909-May 23, 1914; Gov. 1895-99.

BRADLEY, William Warren (D N.J.) July 28, 1943- –; Senate 1979- –.

BRADLEY, Willis Winter (R Calif.) June 28, 1884-Aug. 27, 1954; House 1947-49.

BRADSHAW, Samuel Carey (W Pa.) June 10, 1809-June 9, 1872; House 1855-57.

BRADY, James Dennis (R Va.) April 3, 1843-Nov. 30, 1900; House 1885-87.

BRADY, James Henry (R Idaho) June 12, 1862-Jan. 13, 1918; Senate Feb. 6, 1913-Jan. 13, 1918; Gov. 1909-11.

BRADY, Jasper Ewing (W Pa.) March 4, 1797-Jan. 26, 1871; House 1847-49.

BRADY, Nicholas (R N.J.) April 11, 1930- –; Senate April 20, 1982-Dec. 27, 1982.

BRAGG, Edward Stuyvesant (D Wis.) Feb. 20, 1827-June 20, 1912; House 1877-83, 1885-87.

BRAGG, John (SRD Ala.) Jan. 14, 1806-Aug. 10, 1878; House 1851-53.

BRAGG, Thomas (D N.C.) Nov. 10, 1810-Jan. 21, 1872; Senate 1859-March 6, 1861; Gov. 1855-59.

BRAINERD, Lawrence (FS Vt.) March 16, 1794-May 9, 1870; Senate Oct. 14, 1854-55.

BRAINERD, Samuel Myron (R Pa.) Nov. 13, 1842-Nov. 21, 1898; House 1883-85.

BRAMBLETT, Ernest King (R Calif.) April 25, 1901-Dec. 27, 1966; House 1947-55.

BRANCH, John (uncle of Lawrence O'Bryan Branch) (D N.C.) Nov. 4, 1782-Jan. 3, 1863; Senate 1823-March 9, 1829; House May 12, 1831-33; Gov. (N.C.) 1817-20; Gov. (Fla.) 1844-45; Secy. of the Navy 1829-31.

BRANCH, Lawrence O'Bryan (father of William Augustus Blount Branch, nephew of John Branch) (D N.C.) Nov. 28, 1820-Sept. 17, 1862; House 1855-61.

BRANCH, William Augustus Blount (son of Lawrence O'Bryan Branch) (D N.C.) Feb. 26, 1847-Nov. 18, 1910; House 1891-95.

BRAND, Charles (R Ohio) Nov. 1, 1871-May 23, 1966; House 1923-33.

BRAND, Charles Hillyer (D Ga.) April 20, 1861-May 17, 1933; House 1917-May 17, 1933.

BRANDEGEE, Augustus (father of Frank Bosworth Brandegee) (R Conn.) July 15, 1828-Nov. 10, 1904; House 1863-67.

BRANDEGEE, Frank Bosworth (son of Augustus Brandegee) (R Conn.) July 8, 1864-Oct. 14, 1924; House Nov. 5, 1902-May 10, 1905; Senate May 10, 1905-Oct. 14, 1924.

BRANTLEY, William Gordon (D Ga.) Sept. 18, 1860-Sept. 11, 1934; House 1897-1913.

BRASCO, Frank J. (D N.Y.) Oct. 15, 1932- –; House 1967-75.

BRATTON, John (D S.C.) March 7, 1831-Jan. 12, 1898; House Dec. 8, 1884-85.

BRATTON, Robert Franklin (D Md.) May 3, 1845-May 10, 1894; House 1893-May 10, 1894.

BRATTON, Sam Gilbert (D N.M.) Aug. 19, 1888-Sept. 22, 1963; Senate 1925-June 24, 1933.

BRAWLEY, William Huggins (cousin of John James Hemphill, great-uncle of Robert Witherspoon Hemphill) (D S.C.) May 13, 1841-Nov. 15, 1916; House 1891-Feb. 12, 1894.

BRAXTON, Elliott Muse (D Va.) Oct. 8, 1823-Oct. 2, 1891; House 1871-73.

BRAY, William Gilmer (R Ind.) June 17, 1903-June 4 1979; House 1951-75.

BRAYTON, William Daniel (R R.I.) Nov. 6, 1815-June 30, 1887; House 1857-61.

BREAUX, John Berlinger (D La.) March 1, 1944- –; House Sept. 30, 1972- –.

BREAZEALE, Phanor (D La.) Dec. 29, 1858-April 29, 1934; House 1899-1905.

BRECK, Daniel (brother of Samuel Breck) (W Ky.) Feb. 12, 1788-Feb. 4, 1871; House 1849-51.

BRECK, Samuel (brother of Daniel Breck) (F Pa.) July 17, 1771-Aug. 31, 1862; House 1823-25.

BRECKINRIDGE, Clifton Rodes (son of John Cabell Breckinridge, great-grandson of John Breckinridge) (D Ark.) Nov. 22, 1846-Dec. 3, 1932; House 1883-Sept. 5, 1890, Nov. 4, 1890-Aug. 14, 1894.

BRECKINRIDGE, James (brother of John Breckinridge) (F Va.) March 7, 1763-May 13, 1833; House 1809-17.

BRECKINRIDGE, James Douglas (— Ky.) ?-May 6, 1849; House Nov. 21, 1821-23.

BRECKINRIDGE, John (brother of James Breckinridge, grandfather of John Cabell Breckinridge, William Campbell Preston Breckinridge, great-grandfather of Clifton Rodes Breckinridge) (D Ky.) Dec. 2, 1760-Dec. 14, 1806; Senate 1801-Aug. 7, 1805; Atty. Gen. 1805-06.

BRECKINRIDGE, John Bayne (D Ky.) Nov. 29, 1913-July 29, 1979; House 1973-79.

BRECKINRIDGE, John Cabell (grandson of John Breckinridge, father of Clifton Rodes Breckinridge, cousin of Henry Donnel Foster) (D Ky.) Jan. 21, 1821-May 17, 1875; House 1851-55; Senate March 4-Dec. 4, 1861; Vice Pres. 1857-61.

BRECKINRIDGE, William Campbell Preston (grandson of John Breckinridge, uncle of Levin Irving Handy) (D Ky.) Aug. 28, 1837-Nov. 18, 1904; House 1885-95.

BREEDING, James Floyd (D Kan.) Sept. 28, 1901-Oct. 17, 1977; House 1957-63.

BREEN, Edward G. (D Ohio) June 10, 1908-—; House 1949-Oct. 1, 1951.

BREESE, Sidney (D Ill.) July 15, 1800-June 28, 1878; Senate 1843-49.

BREHM, Walter Ellsworth (R Ohio) May 25, 1892-—; House 1943-53.

BREITUNG, Edward (R Mich.) Nov. 10, 1831-March 3, 1887; House 1883-85.

BREMNER, Robert Gunn (D N.J.) Dec. 17, 1874-Feb. 5, 1914; House 1913-Feb. 5, 1914.

BRENGLE, Francis (W Md.) Nov. 26, 1807-Dec. 10, 1846; House 1843-45.

BRENNAN, Martin Adlai (D Ill.) Sept. 21, 1879-July 4, 1941; House 1933-37.

BRENNAN, Vincent Morrison (R Mich.) April 22, 1890-Feb. 4, 1959; House 1921-23.

BRENNER, John Lewis (D Ohio) Feb. 2, 1832-Nov. 1, 1906; House 1897-1901.

BRENT, Richard (uncle of William Leigh Brent, nephew of Daniel Carroll) (— Va.) 1757-Dec. 30, 1814; House 1795-99, 1801-03; Senate 1809-Dec. 30, 1814.

BRENT, William Leigh (nephew of Richard Brent) (— La.) Feb. 20, 1784-July 7, 1848; House 1823-29.

BRENTANO, Lorenzo (R Ill.) Nov. 4, 1813-Sept. 18, 1891; House 1877-79.

BRENTON, Samuel (R Ind.) Nov. 22, 1810-March 29, 1857; House 1851-53, 1855-March 29, 1857 (1851-53 Whig, 1855-57 Republican).

BRENTS, Thomas Hurley (R Wash.) Dec. 24, 1840-Oct. 23, 1916; House (Terr. Del.) 1879-85.

BRETZ, John Lewis (D Ind.) Sept. 21, 1852-Dec. 25, 1920; House 1891-95.

BREVARD, Joseph (W S.C.) July 19, 1766-Oct. 11, 1821; House 1819-21.

BREWER, Francis Beattie (R N.Y.) Oct. 8, 1820-July 29, 1892; House 1883-85.

BREWER, John Hart (R N.J.) March 29, 1844-Dec. 21, 1900; House 1881-85.

BREWER, Mark Spencer (R Mich.) Oct. 22, 1837-March 18, 1901; House 1877-81, 1887-91.

BREWER, Willis (D Ala.) March 15, 1844-Oct. 30, 1912; House 1897-1901.

BREWSTER, Daniel Baugh (D Md.) Nov. 23, 1923-—; House 1959-63; Senate 1963-69.

BREWSTER, David P. (D N.Y.) June 15, 1801-Feb. 20, 1876; House 1839-43.

BREWSTER, Henry Colvin (R N.Y.) Sept. 7, 1845-Jan. 29, 1928; House 1895-99.

BREWSTER, Ralph Owen (R Maine) Feb. 22, 1888-Dec. 25, 1961; House 1935-41; Senate 1941-Dec. 31, 1952; Gov. 1925-29.

BRICE, Calvin Stewart (D Ohio) Sept. 17, 1845-Dec. 15, 1898; Senate 1891-97; Chrmn. Dem. Nat. Comm. 1889-1892.

BRICK, Abraham Lincoln (R Ind.) May 27, 1860-April 7, 1908; House 1899-April 7, 1908.

BRICKER, John William (R Ohio) Sept. 6, 1893-—; Senate 1947-59; Gov. 1939-45.

BRICKNER, George H. (D Wis.) Jan. 21, 1834-Aug. 12, 1904; House 1889-95.

BRIDGES, George Washington (U Tenn.) Oct. 9, 1825-March 16, 1873; House Feb. 25-March 3, 1863.

BRIDGES, Henry Styles (R N.H.) Sept. 9, 1898-Nov. 26, 1961; Senate 1937-Nov. 26, 1961; Pres. pro tempore 1953-55; Gov. 1935-37.

BRIDGES, Samuel Augustus (D Pa.) Jan. 27, 1802-Jan. 14, 1884; House March 6, 1848-49, 1853-55, 1877-79.

BRIGGS, Clay Stone (D Texas) Jan. 8, 1876-April 29, 1933; House 1919-April 29, 1933.

BRIGGS, Frank Obadiah (son of James Frankland Briggs) (R N.J.) Aug. 12, 1851-May 8, 1913; Senate 1907-13.

BRIGGS, Frank Parks (D Mo.) Feb. 25, 1894-—; Senate Jan. 18, 1945-47.

BRIGGS, George (AP N.Y.) May 6, 1805-June 1, 1869; House 1849-53, 1859-61 (1849-53 Whig, 1859-61 American Party).

BRIGGS, George Nixon (W Mass.) April 12, 1796-Sept. 11, 1861; House 1831-43; Gov. 1844-51.

BRIGGS, James Frankland (father of Frank Obadiah Briggs) (R N.H.) Oct. 23, 1827-Jan. 21, 1905; House 1877-83.

BRIGHAM, Elbert Sidney (R Vt.) Oct. 19, 1877-July 5, 1962; House 1925-31.

BRIGHAM, Elijah (F Mass.) July 7, 1751-Feb. 22, 1816; House 1811-Feb. 22, 1816.

BRIGHAM, Lewis Alexander (R N.J.) Jan. 2, 1831-Feb. 19, 1885; House 1879-81.

BRIGHT, Jesse David (D Ind.) Dec. 18, 1812-May 20, 1875; Senate 1845-Feb. 5, 1862; Pres. pro tempore 1854, 1856, 1860.

BRIGHT, John Morgan (D Tenn.) Jan. 20, 1817-Oct. 3, 1911; House 1871-81.

BRINKERHOFF, Henry Roelif (cousin of Jacob Brinkerhoff) (D Ohio) Sept. 23, 1787-April 30, 1844; House 1843-April 30, 1844.

BRINKERHOFF, Jacob (cousin of Henry Roelif Brinkerhoff) (D Ohio) Aug. 31, 1810-July 19, 1880; House 1843-47.

BRINKLEY, Jack Thomas (D Ga.) Dec. 22, 1930-—; House 1967-83.

BRINSON, Samuel Mitchell (D N.C.) March 20, 1870-April 13, 1922; House 1919-April 13, 1922.

BRISBIN, John (W Pa.) July 13, 1818-Feb. 3, 1880; House Jan. 13-March 3, 1851.

BRISTOW, Francis Marion (W Ky.) Aug. 11, 1804-June 10, 1864; House Dec. 4, 1854-55, 1859-61.

BRISTOW, Henry (R N.Y.) June 5, 1840-Oct. 11, 1906; House 1901-03.

BRISTOW, Joseph Little (R Kan.) July 22, 1861-July 14, 1944; Senate 1909-15.

BRITT, Charles Robin (D N.C.) June 29, 1942-—; House 1983-85.

BRITT, James Jefferson (R N.C.) March 4, 1861-Dec. 26, 1939; House 1915-17, March 1-3, 1919.

BRITTEN, Frederick Albert (R Ill.) Nov. 18, 1871-May 4, 1946; House 1913-35.

BROADHEAD, James Overton (D Mo.) May 29, 1819-Aug. 7, 1898; House 1883-85.

BROCK, Lawrence (D Neb.) Aug. 16, 1906-Aug. 28, 1968; House 1959-61.

BROCK, William Emerson (grandfather of William Emerson Brock III) (D Tenn.) March 14, 1872-Aug. 5, 1950; Senate Sept. 2, 1929-31.

BROCK, William Emerson III (grandson of William Emerson Brock) (R Tenn.) Nov. 23, 1930-—; House 1963-71; Senate 1971-77; Chrmn. Rep. Nat. Comm. 1977-81.

BROCKENBROUGH, William Henry (D Fla.) Feb. 23, 1812-Jan. 28, 1850; House Jan. 24, 1846-47.

BROCKSON, Franklin (D Del.) Aug. 6, 1865-March 16, 1942; House 1913-15.

BROCKWAY, John Hall (W Conn.) Jan. 31, 1801-July 29, 1870; House 1839-43.

BRODBECK, Andrew R. (D Pa.) April 11, 1860-Feb. 27, 1937; House 1913-15, 1917-19.

BRODERICK, Case (cousin of David Colbreth Broderick and Andrew Kennedy) (R Kan.) Sept. 23, 1839-April 1, 1920; House 1891-99.

Biographical Index

BRODERICK, David Colbreth (cousin of Andrew Kennedy and Case Broderick) (D Calif.) Feb. 4, 1820-Sept. 16, 1859; Senate 1857-Sept. 16, 1859.

BRODHEAD, John (D N.H.) Oct. 5, 1770-April 7, 1838; House 1829-33.

BRODHEAD, John Curtis (D N.Y.) Oct. 27, 1780-Jan. 2, 1859; House 1831-33, 1837-39.

BRODHEAD, Joseph Davis (son of Richard Brodhead) (D Pa.) Jan. 12, 1859-April 23, 1920; House 1907-09.

BRODHEAD, Richard (father of Joseph Brodhead) (D Pa.) Jan. 5, 1811-Sept. 16, 1863; House 1843-49; Senate 1851-57.

BRODHEAD, William McNulty (D Mich.) Sept. 12, 1941-—; House 1975-83.

BROGDEN, Curtis Hooks (R N.C.) Nov. 6, 1816-Jan. 5, 1901; House 1877-79; Gov. 1874-77.

BROMBERG, Frederick George (LR/D Ala.) June 19, 1837-Sept. 4, 1930; House 1873-75.

BROMWELL, Henry Pelham Holmes (R Ill.) Aug. 26, 1823-Jan. 7, 1903; House 1865-69.

BROMWELL, Jacob Henry (R Ohio) May 11, 1848-June 4, 1924; House Dec. 3, 1894-1903.

BROMWELL, James E. (R Iowa) March 26, 1920-—; House 1961-65.

BRONSON, David (W Maine) Feb. 8, 1800-Nov. 20, 1863; House May 31, 1841-43.

BRONSON, Isaac Hopkins (D N.Y.) Oct. 16, 1802-Aug. 13, 1855; House 1837-39.

BROOCKS, Moses Lycurgus (D Texas) Nov. 1, 1864-May 27, 1908; House 1905-07.

BROOKE, Edward W. (R Mass.) Oct. 26, 1919-—; Senate 1967-79.

BROOKE, Walker (W Miss.) Dec. 25, 1813-Feb. 18, 1869; Senate Feb. 18, 1852-53.

BROOKHART, Smith Wildman (PR Iowa) Feb. 2, 1869-Nov. 15, 1944; Senate Nov. 7, 1922-April 12, 1926, 1927-33.

BROOKS, Charles Wayland (R Ill.) March 8, 1897-Jan. 14, 1957; Senate Nov. 22, 1940-49.

BROOKS, David (— N.Y.) 1756-Aug. 30, 1838; House 1797-99.

BROOKS, Edward Schroeder (R Pa.) June 14, 1867-July 12, 1957; House 1919-23.

BROOKS, Edwin Bruce (cousin of Edmund Howard Hinshaw) (R Ill.) Sept. 20, 1868-Sept. 18, 1933; House 1919-23.

BROOKS, Franklin Eli (R Colo.) Nov. 19, 1860-Feb. 7, 1916; House 1903-07.

BROOKS, George Merrick (R Mass.) July 26, 1824-Sept. 22, 1893; House Nov. 2, 1869-May 3, 1872.

BROOKS, Jack Bascom (D Texas) Dec. 18, 1922-—; House 1953-—.

BROOKS, James (D N.Y.) Nov. 10, 1810-April 30, 1873; House 1849-53, 1863-April 7, 1866; 1867-April 30, 1873 (1849-53 Whig, 1863-66, 1867-73 Democrat).

BROOKS, Joshua Twing (D Pa.) Feb. 27, 1884-Feb. 7, 1956; House 1933-37.

BROOKS, Micah (— N.Y.) May 14, 1775-July 7, 1857; House 1815-17.

BROOKS, Overton (nephew of John Holmes Overton) (D La.) Dec. 21, 1897-Sept. 16, 1961; House 1937-Sept. 16, 1961.

BROOKS, Preston Smith (SRD S.C.) Aug. 5, 1819-Jan. 27, 1857; House 1853-July 15, 1856, Aug. 1, 1856-Jan. 27, 1857.

BROOKSHIRE, Elijah Voorhees (D Ind.) Aug. 15, 1856-April 14, 1936; House 1889-95.

BROOM, Jacob (son of James Madison Broom) (AW Pa.) July 25, 1808-Nov. 28, 1864; House 1855-57.

BROOM, James Madison (father of Jacob Broom) (F Del.) 1776-Jan. 15, 1850; House 1805-07.

BROOMALL, John Martin (R Pa.) Jan. 19, 1816-June 3, 1894; House 1863-69.

BROOMFIELD, William S. (R Mich.) April 28, 1922-—; House 1957-—.

BROPHY, John Charles (R Wis.) Oct. 8, 1901-Dec. 26, 1976; House 1947-49.

BROSIUS, Marriott (R Pa.) March 7, 1843-March 16, 1901; House 1889-March 16, 1901.

BROTZMAN, Donald Glenn (R Colo.) June 28, 1922-—; House 1963-65, 1967-75.

BROUGHTON, Joseph Melville (D N.C.) Nov. 17, 1888-March 6, 1949; Senate Dec. 31, 1948-March 6, 1949; Gov. 1941-45.

BROUSSARD, Edwin Sidney (brother of Robert Foligny Broussard) (D La.) Dec. 4, 1874-Nov. 19, 1934; Senate 1921-33.

BROUSSARD, Robert Foligny (brother of Edwin Sidney Broussard) (D La.) Aug. 17, 1864-April 12, 1918; House 1897-1915; Senate 1915-April 12, 1918.

BROWER, John Morehead (R N.C.) July 19, 1845-Aug. 5, 1913; House 1887-91.

BROWN, Aaron Venable (D Tenn.) Aug. 15, 1795-March 8, 1859; House 1839-45; Gov. 1845-47; Postmaster Gen. 1857-59.

BROWN, Albert Gallatin (D Miss.) May 31, 1813-June 12, 1880; House 1839-41, 1847-53; Senate Jan. 7, 1854-Jan. 12, 1861; Gov. 1844-48.

BROWN, Anson (W N.Y.) 1800-June 14, 1840; House 1839-June 14, 1840.

BROWN, Arthur (R Utah) March 8, 1843-Dec. 12, 1906; Senate Jan. 22, 1896-97.

BROWN, Bedford (D N.C.) June 6, 1795-Dec. 6, 1870; Senate Dec. 9, 1829-Nov. 16, 1840.

BROWN, Benjamin (nephew of John Brown) (— Mass.) Sept. 23, 1756-Sept. 17, 1831; House 1815-17.

BROWN, Benjamin Gratz (grandson of John Brown of Virginia and Kentucky) (D Mo.) May 28, 1826-Dec. 13, 1885; Senate Nov. 13, 1863-67; Gov. 1871-73.

BROWN, Charles (D Pa.) Sept. 23, 1797-Sept. 4, 1883; House 1841-43, 1847-49.

BROWN, Charles Elwood (R Ohio) July 4, 1834-May 22, 1904; House 1885-89.

BROWN, Charles Harrison (D Mo.) Oct. 22, 1920-—; House 1957-61.

BROWN, Clarence J. (father of Clarence J. Brown Jr.) (R Ohio) July 14, 1893-Aug. 23, 1965; House 1939-Aug. 23, 1965.

BROWN, Clarence J. Jr. (son of Clarence J. Brown) (R Ohio) June 18, 1927-—; House Nov. 2, 1965-83.

BROWN, Elias (W Md.) May 9, 1793-July 7, 1857; House 1829-31.

BROWN, Ernest S. (R Nev.) Sept. 25, 1903-July 23, 1965; Senate Oct. 1-Dec. 1, 1954.

BROWN, Ethan Allen (D Ohio) July 4, 1776-Feb. 24, 1852; Senate Jan. 3, 1822-25; Gov. 1818-22.

BROWN, Foster Vincent (father of Joseph Edgar Brown) (R Tenn.) Dec. 24, 1852-March 26, 1937; House 1895-97.

BROWN, Fred Herbert (D N.H.) April 12, 1879-Feb. 3, 1955; Senate 1933-39; Gov. 1923-25.

BROWN, Garry E. (R Mich.) Aug. 12, 1923-—; House 1967-79.

BROWN, George E. Jr. (D Calif.) March 6, 1920-—; House 1963-71, 1973-—.

BROWN, George Houston (W N.J.) Feb. 12, 1810-Aug. 1, 1865; House 1851-53.

BROWN, Hank (R Colo.) Feb. 12, 1940-—; House 1981-—.

BROWN, James (brother of John Brown of Virginia and Kentucky) (— La.) Sept. 11, 1776-April 7, 1835; Senate Feb. 5, 1813-17, 1819-Dec. 10, 1823.

BROWN, James Sproat (D Wis.) Feb. 1, 1824-April 15, 1878; House 1863-65.

BROWN, James W. (son-in-law of Thomas Marshall Howe) (R Pa.) July 14, 1844-Oct. 23, 1909; House 1903-05.

BROWN, Jason Brevoort (D Ind.) Feb. 26, 1839-March 10, 1898; House 1889-95.

BROWN, Jeremiah (W Pa.) April 14, 1785-March 2, 1858; House 1841-45.

BROWN, John (uncle of Benjamin Brown, grandfather of John Brown Francis) (F R.I.) Jan. 27, 1736-Sept. 20, 1803; House 1799-1801.

BROWN, John (D Md.) ?-Dec. 13, 1815; House 1809-10.

BROWN, John (brother of James Brown, grandfather of Benjamin Gratz Brown) (— Va./Ky.) Sept. 12, 1757-Aug. 29, 1837; House 1789-June 1, 1792 (Ky. district of Va.); Senate June 18, 1792-1805 (Ky.); Pres. pro tempore 1803-04; Cont. Cong. (Ky. district of Va.) 1787-88.

BROWN, John (— Pa.) Aug. 12, 1772-Oct. 12, 1845; House 1821-25.

BROWN, John Brewer (D Md.) May 13, 1836-May 16, 1898; House Nov. 8, 1892-93.

BROWN, John Robert (IR Va.) Jan. 14, 1842-Aug. 4, 1927; House 1887-89.

BROWN, John W. (D N.Y.) Oct. 11, 1796-Sept. 6, 1875; House 1833-37.

BROWN, John Young (nephew of Bryan Rust Young and William Singleton Young) (D Ky.) June 28, 1835-Jan. 11, 1904; House 1859-61, 1873-77; Gov. 1891-95.

BROWN, John Young (D Ky.) Feb. 1, 1900- —; House 1933-35.

BROWN, Joseph Edgar (son of Foster Vincent Brown) (R Tenn.) Feb. 11, 1880-June 13, 1939; House 1921-23.

BROWN, Joseph Emerson (D Ga.) April 15, 1821-Nov. 30, 1894; Senate May 26, 1880-91; Gov. 1857-65.

BROWN, Lathrop (D N.Y.) Feb. 26, 1883-Nov. 28, 1959; House 1913-15.

BROWN, Milton (W Tenn.) Feb. 28, 1804-May 15, 1883; House 1841-47.

BROWN, Norris (R Neb.) May 2, 1863-Jan. 5, 1960; Senate 1907-13.

BROWN, Paul (D Ga.) March 31, 1880-Sept. 24, 1961; House July 5, 1933-61.

BROWN, Prentiss Marsh (D Mich.) June 18, 1889-Dec. 19, 1973; House 1933-Nov. 18, 1936; Senate Nov. 19, 1936-43.

BROWN, Robert (D Pa.) Dec. 25, 1744-Feb. 26, 1823; House Dec. 4, 1798-1815.

BROWN, Seth W. (R Ohio) Jan. 4, 1841-Feb. 24, 1923; House 1897-1901.

BROWN, Titus (— N.H.) Feb. 11, 1786-Jan. 29, 1849; House 1825-29.

BROWN, Webster Everett (R Wis.) July 16, 1851-Dec. 14, 1929; House 1901-07.

BROWN, William (— Ky.) April 19, 1779-Oct. 6, 1833; House 1819-21.

BROWN, William Gay (father of William Gay Brown Jr.) (U Va./W.Va.) Sept. 25, 1800-April 19, 1884; House 1845-49, 1861-63, Dec. 7, 1863-65 (1845-49 Democrat, Va., 1861-63 Unionist, Va., 1863-65 Unionist, W.Va.).

BROWN, William Gay Jr. (son of William Gay Brown) (D W.Va.) April 7, 1856-March 9, 1916; House 1911-March 9, 1916.

BROWN, William John (D Ind.) Aug. 15, 1805-March 18, 1857; House 1843-45, 1849-51.

BROWN, William Ripley (R Kan.) July 16, 1840-March 3, 1916; House 1875-77.

BROWN, William Wallace (R Pa.) April 22, 1836-Nov. 4, 1926; House 1883-87.

BROWNE, Charles (D N.J.) Sept. 28, 1875-Aug. 17, 1947; House 1923-25.

BROWNE, Edward Everts (R Wis.) Feb. 16, 1868-Nov. 23, 1945; House 1913-31.

BROWNE, George Huntington (D R.I.) Jan. 6, 1811-Sept. 26, 1885; House 1861-63.

BROWNE, Thomas Henry Bayly (R Va.) Feb. 8, 1844-Aug. 27, 1892; House 1887-91.

BROWNE, Thomas McLelland (R Ind.) April 19, 1829-July 17, 1891; House 1877-91.

BROWNING, Gordon (D Tenn.) Nov. 22, 1889-May 23, 1976; House 1923-35; Gov. 1937-39, 1949-53.

BROWNING, Orville Hickman (R Ill.) Feb. 10, 1806-Aug. 10, 1881; Senate June 26, 1861-Jan. 12, 1863; Secy. of the Interior 1866-69; Atty. Gen. ad interim 1868.

BROWNING, William John (R N.J.) April 11, 1850-March 24, 1920; House Nov. 7, 1911-March 24, 1920.

BROWNLOW, Walter Preston (nephew of William Gannaway Brownlow) (R Tenn.) March 27, 1851-July 8, 1910; House 1897-July 8, 1910.

BROWNLOW, William Gannaway (uncle of Walter Preston Brownlow) (R Tenn.) Aug. 29, 1805-April 29, 1877; Senate 1869-75; Gov. April 5, 1865-Oct. 1867.

BROWNSON, Charles Bruce (R Ind.) Feb. 5, 1914-—; House 1951-59.

BROYHILL, James T. (R N.C.) Aug. 19, 1927-—; House 1963-—.

BROYHILL, Joel Thomas (R Va.) Nov. 4, 1919-—; House 1953-Dec. 31, 1974.

BRUCE, Blanche Kelso (R Miss.) March 1, 1841-March 17, 1898; Senate 1875-81.

BRUCE, Donald Cogley (R Ind.) April 27, 1921-Aug. 31, 1969; House 1961-65.

BRUCE, Phineas (— Mass.) June 7, 1762-Oct. 4, 1809; elected to House 1803, but did not serve.

BRUCE, Terry L. (D Ill.) March 25, 1944-—; House 1985-—.

BRUCE, William Cabell (D Md.) March 12, 1860-May 9, 1946; Senate 1923-29.

BRUCKER, Ferdinand (D Mich.) Jan. 8, 1858-March 3, 1904; House 1897-99.

BRUCKNER, Henry (D N.Y.) June 17, 1871-April 14, 1942; House 1913-Dec. 31, 1917.

BRUMBAUGH, Clement Laird (D Ohio) Feb. 28, 1863-Sept. 28, 1921; House 1913-21.

BRUMBAUGH, David Emmert (R Pa.) Oct. 8, 1894-April 22, 1977; House Nov. 2, 1943-47.

BRUMM, Charles Napoleon (father of George Franklin Brumm) (RG Pa.) June 9, 1838-Jan. 11, 1917; House 1881-89, 1895-99, Nov. 6, 1906-Jan. 4, 1909.

BRUMM, George Franklin (son of Charles Napoleon Brumm) (R Pa.) Jan. 24, 1880-May 29, 1934; House 1923-27, 1929-May 29, 1934.

BRUNDIDGE, Stephen Jr. (D Ark.) Jan. 1, 1857-Jan. 14, 1938; House 1897-1909.

BRUNNER, David B. (D Pa.) March 7, 1835-Nov. 29, 1903; House 1889-93.

BRUNNER, William Frank (D N.Y.) Sept. 15, 1887-April 23, 1965; House 1929-Sept. 27, 1935.

BRUNSDALE, Clarence Norman (R N.D.) July 9, 1891-Jan. 27, 1978; Senate Nov. 19, 1959-Aug. 7, 1960; Gov. 1951-57.

BRUSH, Henry (— Ohio) June 1778-Jan. 19, 1855; House 1819-21.

BRUYN, Andrew DeWitt (D N.Y.) Nov. 18, 1790-July 27, 1838; House 1837-July 27, 1838.

BRYAN, Guy Morrison (D Texas) Jan. 12, 1821-June 4, 1901; House 1857-59.

BRYAN, Henry H. (— Tenn.) ?-May 7, 1835; House 1819-21, re-elected 1820, but did not serve.

BRYAN, James Wesley (PR Wash.) March 11, 1874-Aug. 26, 1956; House 1913-15.

BRYAN, John Heritage (W N.C.) Nov. 4, 1798-May 19, 1870; House 1825-29.

BRYAN, Joseph (D Ga.) Aug. 18, 1773-Sept. 12, 1812; House 1803-06.

BRYAN, Joseph Hunter (— N.C.) ?-?; House 1815-19.

BRYAN, Nathan (— N.C.) 1748-June 4, 1798; House 1795-June 4, 1798.

BRYAN, Nathan Philemon (brother of William James Bryan) (D Fla.) April 23, 1872-Aug. 8, 1935; Senate 1911-17.

BRYAN, William James (brother of Nathan Philemon Bryan) (D Fla.) Oct. 10, 1876-March 22, 1908; Senate Dec. 26, 1907-March 22, 1908.

BRYAN, William Jennings (father of Ruth Bryan Owen) (D Neb.) March 19, 1860-July 26, 1925; House 1891-95; Secy. of State 1913-15.

BRYANT, John Wiley (D Texas) Feb. 22, 1947-—; House 1983-—.

BRYCE, Lloyd Stephens (D N.Y.) Sept. 20, 1850-April 2, 1917; House 1887-89.

BRYSON, Joseph Raleigh (D S.C.) Jan. 18, 1893-March 10, 1953; House 1939-March 10, 1953.

BUCHANAN, Andrew (D Pa.) April 8, 1780-Dec. 2, 1848; House 1835-39.

BUCHANAN, Frank (D Ill.) June 14, 1862-April 18, 1930; House 1911-17.

BUCHANAN, Frank (husband of Vera Daerr Buchanan) (D Pa.) Dec. 1, 1902-April 27, 1951; House May 21, 1946-April 27, 1951.

BUCHANAN, Hugh (D Ga.) Sept. 15, 1823-June 11, 1890; House 1881-85.

BUCHANAN, James (D Pa.) April 23, 1791-June 1, 1868; House 1821-31; Senate Dec. 6, 1834-March 5, 1845; Secy. of State 1845-49; Pres. 1857-61.

BUCHANAN, James (R N.J.) June 17, 1839-Oct. 30, 1900; House 1885-93.

Biographical Index

BUCHANAN, James Paul (cousin of Edward William Pou) (D Texas) April 30, 1867-Feb. 22, 1937; House April 5, 1913-Feb. 22, 1937.

BUCHANAN, John Alexander (D Va.) Oct. 7, 1843-Sept. 2, 1921; House 1889-93.

BUCHANAN, John Hall Jr. (R Ala.) March 19, 1928- —; House 1965-81.

BUCHANAN, Vera Daerr (widow of Frank Buchanan) (D Pa.) July 20, 1902-Nov. 26, 1955; House July 24, 1951-Nov. 26, 1955.

BUCHER, John Conrad (— Pa.) Dec. 28, 1792-Oct. 15, 1851; House 1831-33.

BUCK, Alfred Eliab (R Ala.) Feb. 7, 1832-Dec. 4, 1902; House 1869-71.

BUCK, Charles Francis (D La.) Nov. 5, 1841-Jan. 19, 1918; House 1895-97.

BUCK, Clayton Douglas (great-grandnephew of John Middleton Clayton) (R Del.) March 21, 1890-Jan. 27, 1965; Senate 1943-49; Gov. 1929-37.

BUCK, Daniel (father of Daniel Azro Ashley Buck) (F Vt.) Nov. 9, 1753-Aug. 16, 1816; House 1795-97.

BUCK, Daniel Azro Ashley (son of Daniel Buck) (D Vt.) April 19, 1789-Dec. 24, 1841; House 1823-25, 1827-29.

BUCK, Ellsworth Brewer (R N.Y.) July 3, 1892-Aug. 14, 1970; House June 6, 1944-49.

BUCK, Frank Henry (D Calif.) Sept. 23, 1887-Sept. 17, 1942; House 1933-Sept. 17, 1942.

BUCK, John Ransom (R Conn.) Dec. 6, 1835-Feb. 6, 1917; House 1881-83, 1885-87.

BUCKALEW, Charles Rollin (D Pa.) Dec. 28, 1821-May 19, 1899; Senate 1863-69; House 1887-91.

BUCKBEE, John Theodore (R Ill.) Aug. 1, 1871-April 23, 1936; House 1927-April 23, 1936.

BUCKINGHAM, William Alfred (R Conn.) May 28, 1804-Feb. 5, 1875; Senate 1869-Feb. 5, 1875; Gov. 1858-66.

BUCKLAND, Ralph Pomeroy (R Ohio) Jan. 20, 1812-May 27, 1892; House 1865-69.

BUCKLER, Richard Thompson (FL Minn.) Oct. 27, 1865-Jan. 23, 1950; House 1935-43.

BUCKLEY, Charles Anthony (D N.Y.) June 23, 1890-Jan. 22, 1967; House 1935-65.

BUCKLEY, Charles Waldron (R Ala.) Feb. 18, 1835-Dec. 4, 1906; House July 21, 1868-73.

BUCKLEY, James Lane (C/R N.Y.) March 9, 1923- —; Senate 1971-77.

BUCKLEY, James Richard (D Ill.) Nov. 18, 1870-June 22, 1945; House 1923-25.

BUCKLEY, James Vincent (D Ill.) May 15, 1894-July 30, 1954; House 1949-51.

BUCKMAN, Clarence Bennett (R Minn.) April 1, 1851-March 1, 1917; House 1903-07.

BUCKNER, Alexander (— Mo.) 1785-June 6, 1833; Senate 1831-June 6, 1833.

BUCKNER, Aylett (son of Richard Aylett Buckner) (W Ky.) July 21, 1806-July 3, 1869; House 1847-49.

BUCKNER, Aylett Hawes (nephew of Aylett Hawes, cousin of Richard Hawes and Albert Gallatin Hawes) (D Mo.) Dec. 14, 1816-Feb. 5, 1894; House 1873-85.

BUCKNER, Richard Aylett (father of Aylett Buckner) (AD Ky.) July 16, 1763-Dec. 8, 1847; House 1823-29.

BUDD, James Herbert (D Calif.) May 18, 1851-July 30, 1908; House 1883-85; Gov. 1895-99.

BUDGE, Hamer Harold (R Idaho) Nov. 21, 1910- —; House 1951-61.

BUEL, Alexander Woodruff (D Mich.) Dec. 13, 1813-April 19, 1868; House 1849-51.

BUELL, Alexander Hamilton (D N.Y.) July 14, 1801-Jan. 29, 1853; House 1851-Jan. 29, 1853.

BUFFETT, Howard Homan (R Neb.) Aug. 13, 1903-April 30, 1964; House 1943-49, 1951-53.

BUFFIN(G)TON, James (R Mass.) March 16, 1817-March 7, 1875; House 1855-63, 1869-March 7, 1875.

BUFFINGTON, Joseph (W Pa.) Nov. 17, 1803-Feb. 3, 1872; House 1843-47.

BUFFUM, Joseph Jr. (D N.H.) Sept. 23, 1784-Feb. 24, 1874; House 1819-21.

BUGG, Robert Malone (W Tenn.) Jan. 20, 1805-Feb. 18, 1887; House 1853-55.

BULKELEY, Morgan Gardner (cousin of Edwin Dennison Morgan) (R Conn.) Dec. 26, 1837-Nov. 6, 1922; Senate 1905-11; Gov. 1889-93.

BULKLEY, Robert Johns (D Ohio) Oct. 8, 1880-July 21, 1965; House 1911-15; Senate Dec. 1, 1930-39.

BULL, John (W Mo.) 1803-Feb. 1863; House 1833-35.

BULL, Melville (R R.I.) Sept. 29, 1854-July 5, 1909; House 1895-1903.

BULLARD, Henry Adams (W La.) Sept. 9, 1788-April 17, 1851; House 1831-Jan. 4, 1834, Dec. 5, 1850-51.

BULLOCH, William Bellinger (D Ga.) 1777-May 6, 1852; Senate April 8-Nov. 6, 1813.

BULLOCK, Robert (D Fla.) Dec. 8, 1828-July 27, 1905; House 1889-93.

BULLOCK, Stephen (F Mass.) Oct. 10, 1735-Feb. 2, 1816; House 1797-99.

BULLOCK, Wingfield (— Ky.) ?-Oct. 13, 1821; House 1821-Oct. 13, 1821.

BULOW, William John (D S.D.) Jan. 13, 1869-Feb. 26, 1960; Senate 1931-43; Gov. 1927-31.

BULWINKLE, Alfred Lee (D N.C.) April 21, 1883-Aug. 31, 1950; House 1921-29, 1931-Aug. 31, 1950.

BUMPERS, Dale (D Ark.) Aug. 12, 1925- —; Senate 1975- —; Gov. 1971-75.

BUNCH, Samuel (W Tenn.) Dec. 4, 1786-Sept. 5, 1849; House 1833-37.

BUNDY, Hezekiah Sanford (R Ohio) Aug. 15, 1817-Dec. 12, 1895; House 1865-67, 1873-75, Dec. 4, 1893-95.

BUNDY, Solomon (R N.Y.) May 22, 1823-Jan. 13, 1889; House 1877-79.

BUNKER, Berkeley Lloyd (D Nev.) Aug. 12, 1906- —; Senate Nov. 27, 1940-Dec. 6, 1942; House 1945-47.

BUNN, Benjamin Hickman (D N.C.) Oct. 19, 1844-Aug. 25, 1907; House 1889-95.

BUNNELL, Frank Charles (R Pa.) March 19, 1842-Sept. 11, 1911; House Dec. 24, 1872-73, 1885-89.

BUNNER, Rudolph (AD N.Y.) Aug. 17, 1779-July 16, 1837; House 1827-29.

BUNTING, Thomas Lathrop (D N.Y.) April 24, 1844-Dec. 27, 1898; House 1891-93.

BURCH, John Chilton (D Calif.) Feb. 1, 1826-Aug. 31, 1885; House 1859-61.

BURCH, Thomas Granville (D Va.) July 3, 1869-March 20, 1951; House 1931-May 31, 1946; Senate May 31-Nov. 5, 1946.

BURCHARD, Horatio Chapin (R Ill.) Sept. 22, 1825-May 14, 1908; House Dec. 6, 1869-79.

BURCHARD, Samuel Dickinson (D Wis.) July 17, 1836-Sept. 1, 1901; House 1875-77.

BURCHILL, Thomas Francis (D N.Y.) Aug. 3, 1882-March 28, 1960; House 1943-45.

BURD, George (— Pa.) 1793-Jan. 13, 1844; House 1831-35.

BURDETT, Samuel Swinfin (R Mo.) Feb. 21, 1836-Sept. 24, 1914; House 1869-73.

BURDICK, Clark (R R.I.) Jan. 13, 1868-Aug. 27, 1948; House 1919-33.

BURDICK, Quentin Northrop (son of Usher Lloyd Burdick, brother-in-law of Robert Woodrow Levering) (D N.D.) June 19, 1908- —; House 1959-Aug. 8, 1960; Senate Aug. 8, 1960- —.

BURDICK, Theodore Weld (R Iowa) Oct. 7, 1836-July 16, 1898; House 1877-79.

BURDICK, Usher Lloyd (father of Quentin Northrop Burdick, father-in-law of Robert Woodrow Levering) (R N.D.) Feb. 21, 1879-Aug. 19, 1960; House 1935-45, 1949-59.

BURGENER, Clair Walter (R Calif.) Dec. 5, 1921- —; House 1973-83.

BURGES, Dempsey (— N.C.) 1751-Jan. 13, 1800; House 1795-99.

BURGES, Tristam (great-great-uncle of Theodore Francis Green) (— R.I.) Feb. 26, 1770-Oct. 13, 1853; House 1825-35.

BURGESS, George Farmer (D Texas) Sept. 21, 1861-Dec. 31, 1919; House 1901-17.

BURGIN, William Olin (D N.C.) July 28, 1877-April 11, 1946; House 1939-April 11, 1946.

BURK, Henry (R Pa.) Sept. 26, 1850-Dec. 5, 1903; House 1901-Dec. 5, 1903.

BURKE, Aedanus (— S.C.) June 16, 1743-March 30, 1802; House 1789-91.

BURKE, Charles Henry (R S.D.) April 1, 1861-April 7, 1944; House 1899-1907, 1909-15.

BURKE, Edmund (D N.H.) Jan. 23, 1809-Jan. 25, 1882; House 1839-45.

BURKE, Edward Raymond (D Neb.) Nov. 28, 1880-Nov. 4, 1968; House 1933-35; Senate 1935-41.

BURKE, Frank Welsh (D Ky.) June 1, 1920-—; House 1959-63.

BURKE, J. Herbert (R Fla.) Jan. 14, 1913-—; House 1967-79.

BURKE, James Anthony (D Mass.) March 30, 1910-Oct. 13, 1983; House 1959-79.

BURKE, James Francis (R Pa.) Oct. 21, 1867-Aug. 8, 1932; House 1905-15.

BURKE, John Harley (D Calif.) June 2, 1894-May 14, 1951; House 1933-35.

BURKE, Michael Edmund (W Wis.) Oct. 15, 1863-Dec. 12, 1918; House 1911-17.

BURKE, Raymond Hugh (R Ohio) Nov. 4, 1881-Aug. 18, 1954; House 1947-49.

BURKE, Robert Emmet (D Texas) Aug. 1, 1847-June 5, 1901; House 1897-June 5, 1901.

BURKE, Thomas A. (D Ohio) Oct. 30, 1898-Dec. 5, 1971; Senate Nov. 10, 1953-Dec. 2, 1954.

BURKE, Thomas Henry (D Ohio) May 6, 1904-Sept. 12, 1959; House 1949-51.

BURKE, William Joseph (R Pa.) Sept. 25, 1862-Nov. 7, 1925; House 1919-23.

BURKE, Yvonne Brathwaite (D Calif.) Oct. 5, 1932-—; House 1973-79.

BURKETT, Elmer Jacob (R Neb.) Dec. 1, 1867-May 23, 1935; House 1899-March 4, 1905; Senate 1905-11.

BURKHALTER, Everett Glenn (D Calif.) Jan. 19, 1897-May 24, 1975; House 1963-65.

BURLEIGH, Edwin Chick (R Maine) Nov. 27, 1843-June 16, 1916; House June 21, 1897-1911; Senate 1913-June 16, 1916; Gov. 1889-93.

BURLEIGH, Henry Gordon (R N.Y.) June 2, 1832-Aug. 10, 1900; House 1883-87.

BURLEIGH, John Holmes (son of William Burleigh) (R Maine) Oct. 9, 1822-Dec. 5, 1877; House 1873-77.

BURLEIGH, Walter Atwood (R Dakota) Oct. 25, 1820-March 7, 1896; House (Terr. Del.) 1865-69.

BURLEIGH, William (father of John Holmes Burleigh) (AD Maine) Oct. 24, 1785-July 2, 1827; House 1823-July 2, 1827.

BURLESON, Albert Sidney (D Texas) June 7, 1863-Nov. 24, 1937; House 1899-March 6, 1913; Postmaster Gen. 1913-21.

BURLESON, Omar Truman (D Texas) March 19, 1906-—; House 1947-Dec. 31, 1978.

BURLINGAME, Anson (R Mass.) Nov. 14, 1820-Feb. 23, 1870; House 1855-61 (1855-59 American Party, 1859-61 Republican).

BURLISON, Bill Dean (D Mo.) March 15, 1933-—; House 1969-81.

BURNELL, Barker (W Mass.) Jan. 30, 1798-June 15, 1843; House 1841-June 15, 1843.

BURNES, Daniel Dee (D Mo.) Jan. 4, 1851-Nov. 2, 1899; House 1893-95.

BURNES, James Nelson (D Mo.) Aug. 22, 1827-Jan. 23, 1889; House 1883-Jan. 23, 1889.

BURNET, Jacob (F N.J.) Feb. 22, 1770-May 10, 1853; Senate Dec. 10, 1828-31.

BURNETT, Edward (D Mass.) March 16, 1849-Nov. 5, 1925; House 1887-89.

BURNETT, Henry Cornelius (D Ky.) Oct. 5, 1825-Oct. 1, 1866; House 1855-Dec. 3, 1861.

BURNETT, John Lawson (D Ala.) Jan. 20, 1854-May 13, 1919; House 1899-May 13, 1919.

BURNEY, William Evans (D Colo.) Sept. 11, 1893-Jan. 29, 1969; House Nov. 5, 1940-41.

BURNHAM, Alfred Avery (R Conn.) March 8, 1819-April 11, 1879; House 1859-63.

BURNHAM, George (R Calif.) Dec. 28, 1868-June 28, 1939; House 1933-37.

BURNHAM, Henry Eben (R N.H.) Nov. 8, 1844-Feb. 8, 1917; Senate 1901-13.

BURNS, John Anthony (D Hawaii) March 30, 1909-April 5, 1975; House (Terr. Del.) 1957-Aug. 21, 1959; Gov. 1962-74.

BURNS, Joseph (D Ohio) March 11, 1800-May 12, 1875; House 1857-59.

BURNS, Robert (D N.H.) Dec. 12, 1792-June 26, 1866; House 1833-37.

BURNSIDE, Ambrose Everett (R R.I.) May 23, 1824-Sept. 13, 1881; Senate 1875-Sept. 13, 1881; Gov. 1866-69.

BURNSIDE, Maurice Gwinn (D W.Va.) Aug. 23, 1902-—; House 1949-53, 1955-57.

BURNSIDE, Thomas (— Pa.) July 28, 1782-March 25, 1851; House Oct. 10, 1815-April 1816.

BURR, Aaron (cousin of Theodore Dwight) (D N.Y.) Feb. 6, 1756-Sept. 14, 1836; Senate 1791-97; Vice Pres. 1801-05.

BURR, Albert George (D Ill.) Nov. 8, 1829-June 10, 1882; House 1867-71.

BURRELL, Orlando (R Ill.) July 26, 1826-June 7, 1922; House 1895-97.

BURRILL, James Jr. (great-grandfather of Theodore Francis Green) (— R.I.) April 25, 1772-Dec. 25, 1820; Senate 1817-Dec. 25, 1820.

BURROUGHS, Sherman Everett (R N.H.) Feb. 6, 1870-Jan. 27, 1923; House June 7, 1917-Jan. 27, 1923.

BURROUGHS, Silas Mainville (R N.Y.) July 16, 1810-June 3, 1860; House 1857-June 3, 1860.

BURROWS, Daniel (uncle of Lorenzo Burrows) (D Conn.) Oct. 26, 1766-Jan. 23, 1858; House 1821-23.

BURROWS, Joseph Henry (G Mo.) May 15, 1840-April 28, 1914; House 1881-83.

BURROWS, Julius Caesar (R Mich.) Jan. 9, 1837-Nov. 16, 1915; House 1873-75, 1879-83, 1885-Jan. 23, 1895; Senate Jan. 24, 1895-1911.

BURROWS, Lorenzo (nephew of Daniel Burrows) (W N.Y.) March 15, 1805-March 6, 1885; House 1849-53.

BURSUM, Holm Olaf (R N.M.) Feb. 10, 1867-Aug. 7, 1953; Senate March 11, 1921-25.

BURT, Armistead (D S.C.) Nov. 13, 1802-Oct. 30, 1883; House 1843-53.

BURTNESS, Olger Burton (R N.D.) March 14, 1884-Jan. 20, 1960; House 1921-33.

BURTON, Charles Germman (R Mo.) April 4, 1846-Feb. 25, 1926; House 1895-97.

BURTON, Clarence Godber (D Va.) Dec. 14, 1886-Jan. 18, 1982; House Nov. 2, 1948-53.

BURTON, Danny Lee (R Ind.) June 21, 1938-—; House 1983-—.

BURTON, Harold Hitz (R Ohio) June 22, 1888-Oct. 28, 1964; Senate 1941-Sept. 30, 1945; Assoc. Justice Supreme Court 1945-58.

BURTON, Hiram Rodney (R Del.) Nov. 13, 1841-June 17, 1927; House 1905-09.

BURTON, Hutchins Gordon (AD N.C.) 1782-April 21, 1836; House Dec. 6, 1819-March 23, 1824; 1824-27.

BURTON, John Lowell (brother of Phillip Burton) (D Calif.) Dec. 15, 1932-—; House June 25, 1974-83.

BURTON, Joseph Ralph (R Kan.) Nov. 16, 1850-Feb. 27, 1923; Senate 1901-June 4, 1906.

BURTON, Laurence Junior (R Utah) Oct. 30, 1926-—; House 1963-71.

BURTON, Phillip (brother of John Lowell Burton) (D Calif.) June 1, 1926-April 10, 1983; House Feb. 18, 1964-April 10, 1983.

BURTON, Sala (widow of Phillip Burton) (D Calif.) April 1, 1925-—; House June 28, 1983-—.

BURTON, Theodore Elijah (R Ohio) Dec. 20, 1851-Oct. 28, 1929; House 1889-91, 1895-1909, 1921-Dec. 15, 1928; Senate 1909-15, Dec. 15, 1928-Oct. 28, 1929.

BURWELL, William Armisted (D Va.) March 15, 1780-Feb. 16, 1821; House Dec. 1, 1806-Feb. 16, 1821.

BUSBEY, Fred Ernst (R Ill.) Feb. 8, 1895-Feb. 11, 1966; House 1943-45, 1947-49, 1951-55.

BUSBY, George Henry (D Ohio) June 10, 1794-Aug. 22, 1869; House 1851-53.

BUSBY, Thomas Jefferson (D Miss.) July 26, 1884-Oct. 18, 1964; House 1923-35.

Biographical Index

BUSEY, Samuel Thompson (D Ill.) Nov. 16, 1835-Aug. 12, 1909; House 1891-93.

BUSH, Alvin Ray (R Pa.) June 4, 1893-Nov. 5, 1959; House 1951-Nov. 5, 1959.

BUSH, George Herbert Walker (son of Prescott Sheldon Bush) (R Texas) June 12, 1924- —; House 1967-71; Chrmn. Rep. Nat. Comm. 1973-74; Vice Pres. 1981- —.

BUSH, Prescott Sheldon (father of George Herbert Walker Bush) (R Conn.) May 15, 1895-Oct. 8, 1972; Senate Nov. 4, 1952-63.

BUSHFIELD, Harlan John (husband of Vera Cahalan Bushfield) (R S.D.) Aug. 6, 1882-Sept. 27, 1948; Senate 1943-Sept. 27, 1948; Gov. 1939-43.

BUSHFIELD, Vera Cahalan (widow of Harlan John Bushfield) (R S.D.) Aug. 9, 1889-April 16, 1976; Senate Oct. 6-Dec. 26, 1948.

BUSHNELL, Allen Ralph (D Wis.) July 18, 1833-March 29, 1909; House 1891-93.

BUSHONG, Robert Grey (grandson of Anthony Ellmaker Roberts) (R Pa.) June 10, 1883-April 6, 1951; House 1927-29.

BUSTAMANTE, Albert G. (D Texas) April 8, 1935- —; House 1985- —.

BUTLER, Andrew Pickens (son of William Butler) (SRD S.C.) Nov. 19, 1796-May 25, 1857; Senate Dec. 4, 1846-May 25, 1857.

BUTLER, Benjamin Franklin (grandfather of Butler Ames) (R Mass.) Nov. 5, 1818-Jan. 11, 1893; House 1867-75, 1877-79; Gov. 1883-84 (Greenback and Democrat).

BUTLER, Chester Pierce (W Pa.) March 21, 1798-Oct. 5, 1850; House 1847-Oct. 5, 1850.

BUTLER, Ezra (D Vt.) Sept. 24, 1763-July 12, 1838; House 1813-15; Gov. 1826-28.

BUTLER, Hugh Alfred (R Neb.) Feb. 28, 1878-July 1, 1954; Senate 1941-July 1, 1954.

BUTLER, James Joseph (D Mo.) Aug. 29, 1862-May 31, 1917; House 1901-June 28, 1902, Nov. 4, 1902-Feb. 26, 1903, 1903-05.

BUTLER, John Cornelius (R N.Y.) July 2, 1887-Aug. 13, 1953; House April 22, 1941-49, 1951-53.

BUTLER, John Marshall (R Md.) July 21, 1897-March 14, 1978; Senate 1951-63.

BUTLER, Josiah (D N.Y.) Dec. 4, 1779-Oct. 27, 1854; House 1817-23.

BUTLER, Manley Caldwell (R Va.) June 2, 1925- —; House Nov. 7, 1972-83.

BUTLER, Marion (P N.C.) May 20, 1863-June 3, 1938; Senate 1895-1901.

BUTLER, Matthew Calbraith (son of William Butler) (D S.C.) March 8, 1836-April 14, 1909; Senate 1877-95.

BUTLER, Mounce Gore (D Tenn.) May 11, 1849-Feb. 13, 1917; House 1905-07.

BUTLER, Pierce (D S.C.) July 11, 1744-Feb. 15, 1822; Senate 1789-Oct. 25, 1796, Nov. 4, 1802-Nov. 21, 1804; Cont. Cong. 1787-88.

BUTLER, Robert Reyburn (grandson of Roderick Random Butler) (R Ore.) Sept. 24, 1881-Jan. 7, 1933; House Nov. 6, 1928-Jan. 7, 1933.

BUTLER, Roderick Random (grandfather of Robert Reyburn Bulter) (R Tenn.) April 9, 1827-Aug. 18, 1902; House 1867-75, 1887-89.

BUTLER, Sampson Hale (D S.C.) Jan. 3, 1803-March 16, 1848; House 1839-Sept. 27, 1842.

BUTLER, Thomas (— La.) April 14, 1785-Aug. 7, 1847; House Nov. 16, 1818-21.

BUTLER, Thomas Belden (W Conn.) Aug. 22, 1806-June 8, 1873; House 1849-51.

BUTLER, Thomas Stalker (R Pa.) Nov. 4, 1855-May 26, 1928; House 1897-May 26, 1928.

BUTLER, Walter Halben (D Iowa) Feb. 13, 1852-April 24, 1931; House 1891-93.

BUTLER, William (father of Andrew Pickens Butler) (AF S.C.) Dec. 17, 1759-Sept. 15, 1821; House 1801-13.

BUTLER, William (son of William Butler, brother of Andrew Pickens Butler, father of Matthew Calbraith Butler) (W S.C.) Feb. 1, 1790-Sept. 25, 1850; House 1841-43.

BUTLER, William Morgan (R Mass.) Jan. 29, 1861-March 29, 1937; Senate Nov. 13, 1924-Dec. 6, 1926; Chrmn. Rep. Nat. Comm. 1924-28.

BUTLER, William Orlando (D Ky.) April 19, 1791-Aug. 6, 1880; House 1839-43.

BUTMAN, Samuel (— Maine) 1788-Oct. 9, 1864; House 1827-31.

BUTTERFIELD, Martin (R N.Y.) Dec. 8, 1790-Aug. 6, 1866; House 1859-61.

BUTTERWORTH, Benjamin (R Ohio) Oct. 22, 1837-Jan. 16, 1898; House 1879-83, 1885-91.

BUTTON, Daniel Evan (R N.Y.) Nov. 1, 1917- —; House 1967-71.

BUTTZ, Charles Wilson (R S.C.) Nov. 16, 1837-July 20, 1913; House Nov. 7, 1876-77.

BYNUM, Jesse Atherton (D N.C.) May 23, 1797-Sept. 23, 1868; House 1833-41.

BYNUM, William Dallas (D Ind.) June 26, 1846-Oct. 21, 1927; House 1885-95.

BYRD, Adam Monroe (D Miss.) July 6, 1859-June 21, 1912; House 1903-11.

BYRD, Harry Flood (father of Harry Flood Byrd Jr., nephew of Henry De La Warr Flood and Joel West Flood) (D Va.) June 10, 1887-Oct. 20, 1966; Senate 1933-Nov. 10, 1965; Gov. 1926-30.

BYRD, Harry Flood Jr. (son of Harry Flood Byrd) (D Va.) Dec. 20, 1914- —; Senate Nov. 12, 1965-83; (1965-71 Democrat, 1971-83 Independent).

BYRD, Robert Carlyle (D W.Va.) Jan. 15, 1918- —; House 1953-59; Senate 1959- —; Senate majority leader 1977-81.

BYRNE, Emmet Francis (R Ill.) Dec. 6, 1896-Sept. 25, 1974; House 1957-59.

BYRNE, James Aloysius (D Pa.) June 22, 1906-Sept. 3, 1980; House 1953-73.

BYRNE, William Thomas (D N.Y.) March 6, 1876-Jan. 27, 1952; House 1937-Jan. 27, 1952.

BYRNES, James Francis (D S.C.) May 2, 1879-April 9, 1972; House 1911-25; Senate 1931-July 8, 1941; Assoc. Justice Supreme Court July 8, 1941-Oct. 3, 1942; Secy. of State 1945-47; Gov. 1951-55.

BYRNES, John William (R Wis.) June 12, 1913-Jan. 12, 1985; House 1945-73.

BYRNS, Joseph Wellington (father of Joseph Wellington Byrns Jr.) (D Tenn.) July 20, 1869-June 4, 1936; House 1909-June 4, 1936; Speaker 1935-June 4, 1936.

BYRNS, Joseph Wellington Jr. (son of Joseph Wellington Byrns) (D Tenn.) Aug. 15, 1903- —; House 1939-41; House majority leader 1933-35.

BYRNS, Samuel (D Mo.) March 4, 1848-July 9, 1914; House 1891-93.

BYRON, Beverly Barton Butcher (widow of Goodloe Edgar Bryon) (D Md.) July 26, 1932- —; House 1979- —.

BYRON, Goodloe Edgar (son of Katharine Edgar Byron and William Devereux Byron, great-grandson of Louis Emory McComas) (D Md.) June 22, 1929-Oct. 11, 1978; House 1971-Oct. 11, 1978.

BYRON, Katharine Edgar (widow of William Devereux Byron, mother of Goodloe Edgar Byron, granddaughter of Louis Emory McComas) (D Md.) Oct. 25, 1903-Dec. 28, 1976; House May 27, 1941-43.

BYRON, William Devereaux (husband of Katharine Edgar Byron, father of Goodloe Edgar Byron) (D Md.) May 15, 1895-Feb. 27, 1941; House 1939-Feb. 27, 1941.

C

CABANISS, Thomas Banks (cousin of Thomas Chipman McRae) (D Ga.) Aug. 31, 1835-Aug. 14, 1915; House 1893-95.

CABELL, Earle (D Texas) Oct. 27, 1906-Sept. 24, 1975; House 1965-73.

CABELL, Edward Carrington (W Fla.) Feb. 5, 1816-Feb. 28, 1896; House Oct. 6, 1845-Jan. 24, 1846, 1847-53.

CABELL, George Craighead (D Va.) Jan. 25, 1836-June 23, 1906; House 1875-87.

CABELL, Samuel Jordan (D Va.) Dec. 15, 1756-Aug. 4, 1818; House 1795-1803.

CABLE, Benjamin Taylor (D Ill.) Aug. 11, 1853-Dec. 13, 1923; House 1891-93.

CABLE, John Levi (great-grandson of Joseph Cable) (R Ohio) April 15, 1884-Sept. 15, 1971; House 1921-25, 1929-33.

CABLE, Joseph (great-grandfather of John Levi Cable) (D Ohio) April 17, 1801-May 1, 1880; House 1849-53.

CABOT, George (great-grandfather of Henry Cabot Lodge) (F Mass.) Dec. 16, 1751-April 18, 1823; Senate 1791-June 9, 1796.

CADMUS, Cornelius Andrew (D N.J.) Oct. 7, 1844-Jan. 20, 1902; House 1891-95.

CADWALADER, John (D Pa.) April 1, 1805-Jan. 26, 1879; House 1855-57.

CADWALADER, Lambert (– N.J.) 1742-Sept. 13, 1823; House 1789-91, 1793-95; Cont. Cong. 1784-87.

CADY, Claude Ernest (D Mich.) May 28, 1878-Nov. 30, 1953; House 1933-35.

CADY, Daniel (uncle of John Watts Cady) (F N.Y.) April 29, 1773-Oct. 31, 1859; House 1815-17.

CADY, John Watts (nephew of Daniel Cady) (W N.Y.) June 28, 1790-Jan. 5, 1854; House 1823-25.

CAFFERY, Donelson (grandfather of Patrick Thomson Caffery) (D La.) Sept. 10, 1835-Dec. 30, 1906; Senate Dec. 31, 1892-1901.

CAFFERY, Patrick Thomson (grandson of Donelson Cafferey) (D La.) July 6, 1932-–; House 1969-73.

CAGE, Harry (– Miss.) ?-1859; House 1833-35.

CAHILL, William Thomas (R N.J.) June 25, 1912-–; House 1959-Jan. 19, 1970; Gov. 1970-74.

CAHOON, William (AMas Vt.) Jan. 12, 1774-May 30, 1833; House 1829-33.

CAIN, Harry Pulliam (R Wash.) Jan. 10, 1906-March 3, 1979; Senate Dec. 26, 1946-53.

CAIN, Richard Harvey (R S.C.) April 12, 1825-Jan. 18, 1887; House 1873-75, 1877-79.

CAINE, John Thomas (PP Utah) Jan. 8, 1829-Sept. 20, 1911; House (Terr. Del.) Nov. 7, 1882-93 (1882-89 Democrat, 1889-93 People's Party).

CAKE, Henry Lutz (R Pa.) Oct. 6, 1827-Aug. 26, 1899; House 1867-71.

CALDER, William Musgrave (R N.Y.) March 3, 1869-March 3, 1945; House 1905-15; Senate 1917-23.

CALDERHEAD, William Alexander (R Kan.) Sept. 26, 1844-Dec. 18, 1928; House 1895-97, 1899-1911.

CALDWELL, Alexander (R Kan.) March 1, 1830-May 19, 1917; Senate 1871-March 24, 1873.

CALDWELL, Andrew Jackson (D Tenn.) July 22, 1837-Nov. 22, 1906; House 1883-87.

CALDWELL, Ben Franklin (D Ill.) Aug. 2, 1848-Dec. 29, 1924; House 1899-1905, 1907-09.

CALDWELL, Charles Pope (D N.Y.) June 18, 1875-July 31, 1940; House 1915-21.

CALDWELL, George Alfred (D Kan.) Oct. 18, 1814-Sept. 17, 1866; House 1843-45, 1849-51.

CALDWELL, Greene Washington (D N.C.) April 13, 1806-July 10, 1864; House 1841-43.

CALDWELL, James (D Ohio) Nov. 30, 1770-May 1838; House 1813-17.

CALDWELL, John Alexander (R Ohio) April 21, 1852-May 24, 1927; House 1889-May 4, 1894.

CALDWELL, John Henry (D Ala.) April 4, 1826-Sept. 4, 1902; House 1873-77.

CALDWELL, John William (D Ky.) Jan. 15, 1837-July 4, 1903; House 1877-83.

CALDWELL, Joseph Pearson (W N.C.) March 5, 1808-June 30, 1853; House 1849-53.

CALDWELL, Millard Fillmore (D Fla.) Feb. 6, 1897-Oct. 23, 1984; House 1933-41; Gov. 1945-49.

CALDWELL, Patrick Calhoun (SRD S.C.) March 10, 1801-Nov. 22, 1855; House 1841-43.

CALDWELL, Robert Porter (D Tenn.) Dec. 16, 1821-March 12, 1885; House 1871-73.

CALDWELL, William Parker (D Tenn.) Nov. 8, 1832-June 7, 1903; House 1875-79.

CALE, Thomas (I Alaska) Sept. 17, 1848-Feb. 3, 1941; House (Terr. Del.) 1907-09.

CALHOON, John (W Ky.) 1797-?; House 1835-39.

CALHOUN, John Caldwell (cousin of John Ewing Colhoun and Joseph Calhoun) (WD S.C.) March 18, 1782-March 31, 1850; House 1811-Nov. 3, 1817; Senate Dec. 29, 1832-March 3, 1843, Nov. 26, 1845-March 31, 1850; Vice Pres. 1825-Dec. 28, 1832; Secy. of War 1817-25; Secy. of State 1844-45.

CALHOUN, Joseph (cousin of John Caldwell Calhoun and John Ewing Colhoun) (D S.C.) Oct. 22, 1750-April 14, 1817; House June 2, 1807-11.

CALHOUN, William Barron (W Mass.) Dec. 29, 1796-Nov. 8, 1865; House 1835-43.

CALKIN, Hervey Chittenden (D N.Y.) March 23, 1828-April 20, 1913; House 1869-71.

CALKINS, William Henry (R Ind.) Feb. 18, 1842-Jan. 29, 1894; House 1877-Oct. 20, 1884.

CALL, Jacob (– Ind.) ?-April 20, 1826; House Dec. 23, 1824-25.

CALL, Richard Keith (uncle of Wilkinson Call) (D Fla.) Oct. 24, 1792-Sept. 14, 1862; House (Terr. Del.) 1823-25; Gov. (Fla. Terr.) 1835-40, 1841-44.

CALL, Wilkinson (nephew of Richard Keith Call, cousin of James David Walker) (D Fla.) Jan. 9, 1834-Aug. 24, 1910; Senate 1879-97.

CALLAHAN, H. L. "Sonny" (R Ala.) Sept. 11, 1932-–; House 1985-–.

CALLAHAN, James Yancy (FSil Okla.) Dec. 19, 1852-May 3, 1935; House (Terr. Del.) 1897-99.

CALLAN, Clair Armstrong (D Neb.) March 20, 1920-–; House 1965-67.

CALLAWAY, Howard Hollis (Bo) (R Ga.) April 2, 1927-–; House 1965-67.

CALLAWAY, Oscar (D Texas) Oct. 2, 1872-Jan. 31, 1947; House 1911-17.

CALLIS, John Benton (R Ala.) Jan. 3, 1828-Sept. 24, 1898; House July 21, 1868-69.

CALVERT, Charles Benedict (UW Md.) Aug. 24, 1808-May 12, 1864; House 1861-63.

CALVIN, Samuel (W Pa.) July 30, 1811-March 12, 1890; House 1849-51.

CAMBRELENG, Churchill Caldom (D N.Y.) Oct. 24, 1786-April 30, 1862; House 1821-39.

CAMDEN, Johnson Newlon (father of Johnson Newlon Camden Jr.) (D W.Va.) March 6, 1828-April 25, 1908; Senate 1881-87, Jan. 25, 1893-95.

CAMDEN, Johnson Newlon Jr. (son of Johnson Newlon Camden) (D Ky.) Jan. 5, 1865-Aug. 16, 1942; Senate June 16, 1914-15.

CAMERON, Angus (R Wis.) July 4, 1826-March 30, 1897; Senate 1875-81, March 14, 1881-85.

CAMERON, James Donald (son of Simon Cameron) (R Pa.) May 14, 1833-Aug. 30, 1918; Senate March 20, 1877-97; Secy. of War 1876-77; Chrmn. Rep. Nat. Comm. 1879-80.

CAMERON, Ralph Henry (R Ariz.) Oct. 21, 1863-Feb. 12, 1953; House (Terr. Del.) 1909-Feb. 18, 1912; Senate 1921-27.

CAMERON, Ronald Brooks (D Calif.) Aug. 16, 1927-–; House 1963-67.

CAMERON, Simon (father of James Donald Cameron) (R Pa.) March 8, 1799-June 26, 1889; Senate March 13, 1845-49, 1857-March 4, 1861, 1867-March 12, 1877 (1845-49 Democrat, 1857-61, 1867-77 Republican); Secy. of War 1861-62.

CAMINETTI, Anthony (D Calif.) July 30, 1854-Nov. 17, 1923; House 1891-95.

CAMP, Albert Sidney (D Ga.) July 26, 1892-July 24, 1954; House Aug. 1, 1939-July 24, 1954.

CAMP, John Henry (R N.Y.) April 4, 1840-Oct. 12, 1892; House 1877-83.

CAMP, John Newbold Happy (R Okla.) May 11, 1908-–; House 1969-75.

CAMPBELL, Albert James (D Mont.) Dec. 12, 1857-Aug. 9, 1907; House 1899-1901.

CAMPBELL, Alexander (– Ohio) 1779-Nov. 5, 1857; Senate Dec. 11, 1809-13.

CAMPBELL, Alexander (I Ill.) Oct. 4, 1814-Aug. 8, 1898; House 1875-77.

CAMPBELL, Brookins (D Tenn.) 1808-Dec. 25, 1853; House March 4-Dec. 25, 1853.

CAMPBELL, Carroll Ashmore Jr. (R S.C.) July 24, 1940-–; House 1979-–.

CAMPBELL, Courtney Warren (D Fla.) April 29, 1895-Dec. 22, 1971; House 1953-55.

CAMPBELL, Ed Hoyt (R Iowa) March 6, 1882-April 26, 1969; House 1929-33.

CAMPBELL, Felix (D N.Y.) Feb. 28, 1829-Nov. 8, 1902; House 1883-91.

Biographical Index

CAMPBELL, George Washington (D Tenn.) Feb. 9, 1769-Feb. 17, 1848; House 1803-09; Senate Oct. 8, 1811-Feb. 11, 1814, Oct. 10, 1815-April 20, 1818; Secy. of the Treasury Feb. 9-Oct. 6, 1814.

CAMPBELL, Guy Edgar (R Pa.) Oct. 9, 1871-Feb. 17, 1940; House 1917-33 (1917-23 Democrat, 1923-33 Republican).

CAMPBELL, Howard Edmond (R Pa.) Jan. 4, 1890-—; House 1945-47.

CAMPBELL, Jacob Miller (R Pa.) Nov. 20, 1821-Sept. 27, 1888; House 1877-79, 1881-87.

CAMPBELL, James Edwin (nephew of Lewis Davis Campbell) (D Ohio) July 7, 1843-Dec. 18, 1924; House June 20, 1884-89; Gov. 1890-92.

CAMPBELL, James Hepburn (W Pa.) Feb. 8, 1820-April 12, 1895; House 1855-57, 1859-63.

CAMPBELL, James Romulus (D Ill.) May 4, 1853-Aug. 12, 1924; House 1897-99.

CAMPBELL, John (F Md.) Sept. 11, 1765-June 23, 1828; House 1801-11.

CAMPBELL, John (brother of Robert Blair Campbell) (SRD S.C.) ?-May 19, 1845; House 1829-31, 1837-45 (1829-31 State Rights Whig, 1837-45 State Rights Democrat).

CAMPBELL, John Goulder (D Ariz.) June 25, 1827-Dec. 22, 1903; House (Terr. Del.) 1879-81.

CAMPBELL, John Hull (W Pa.) Oct. 10, 1800-Jan. 19, 1868; House 1845-47.

CAMPBELL, John Pierce Jr. (AP Ky.) Dec. 8, 1820-Oct. 29, 1888; House 1855-57.

CAMPBELL, John Wilson (D Ohio) Feb. 23, 1782-Sept. 24, 1833; House 1817-27.

CAMPBELL, Lewis Davis (uncle of James Edwin Campbell) (D Ohio) Aug. 9, 1811-Nov. 26, 1882; House 1849-May 25, 1858, 1871-73 (1849-1858 Whig, 1871-73 Democrat).

CAMPBELL, Philip Pitt (R Kan.) April 25, 1862-May 26, 1941; House 1903-23.

CAMPBELL, Robert Blair (brother of John Campbell of South Carolina) (W S.C.) ?-July 12, 1862; House 1823-25, Feb. 27, 1834-37 (1823-25 no party designation, 1834-35 Nullifier, 1835-37 Whig).

CAMPBELL, Samuel (— N.Y.) July 11, 1773-June 2, 1853; House 1821-23.

CAMPBELL, Thomas Jefferson (W Tenn.) 1786-April 13, 1850; House 1841-43.

CAMPBELL, Thompson (D Ill.) 1811-Dec. 6, 1868; House 1851-53.

CAMPBELL, Timothy John (D N.Y.) Jan. 8, 1840-April 7, 1904; House Nov. 3, 1885-89, 1891-95.

CAMPBELL, William Bowen (cousin of Henry Bowen) (D Tenn.) Feb. 1, 1807-Aug. 19, 1867; House 1837-43, July 24, 1866-67 (1837-43 Whig, 1866-67 Democrat); Gov. 1851-53.

CAMPBELL, William W. (AP N.Y.) June 10, 1806-Sept. 7, 1881; House 1845-47.

CAMPBELL, William Wildman (R Ohio) April 2, 1853-Aug. 13, 1927; House 1905-07.

CANBY, Richard Sprigg (W Ohio) Sept. 30, 1808-July 27, 1895; House 1847-49.

CANDLER, Allen Daniel (cousin of Ezekiel Samuel Candler Jr. and Milton Anthony Candler) (D Ga.) Nov. 4, 1834-Oct. 26, 1910; House 1883-91; Gov. 1898-1902.

CANDLER, Ezekiel Samuel Jr. (nephew of Milton Anthony Candle, cousin of Allen Daniel Candler) (D Miss.) Jan. 18, 1862-Dec. 18, 1944; House 1901-21.

CANDLER, John Wilson (R Mass.) Feb. 10, 1828-March 16, 1903; House 1881-83, 1889-91.

CANDLER, Milton Anthony (uncle of Ezekiel Samuel Candler Jr., cousin of Allen Daniel Candler) (D Ga.) Jan. 11, 1837-Aug. 8, 1909; House 1875-79.

CANFIELD, Gordon (R N.J.) April 15, 1898-June 20, 1972; House 1941-61.

CANFIELD, Harry Clifford (D Ind.) Nov. 22, 1875-Feb. 9, 1945; House 1923-33.

CANNON, Arthur Patrick (D Fla.) May 22, 1904-Jan. 23, 1966; House 1939-47.

CANNON, Clarence Andrew (D Mo.) April 11, 1879-May 12, 1964; House 1923-May 12, 1964.

CANNON, Frank Jenne (son of George Quayle Cannon) (R Utah) Jan. 25, 1859-July 25, 1933; House (Terr. Del.) 1895-Jan. 4, 1896; Senate Jan. 22, 1896-99.

CANNON, George Quayle (father of Frank Jenne Cannon) (R Utah) Jan. 11, 1827-April 12, 1901; House (Terr. Del.) 1873-81.

CANNON, Howard Walter (D Nev.) Jan. 26, 1912-—; Senate 1959-83.

CANNON, Joseph Gurney (R Ill.) May 7, 1836-Nov. 12, 1926; House 1873-91, 1893-1913, 1915-23; Speaker 1903-11.

CANNON, Marion (PP/D Calif.) Oct. 30, 1834-Aug. 27, 1920; House 1893-95.

CANNON, Newton (D Tenn.) May 22, 1781-Sept. 16, 1841; House Sept. 16, 1814-17, 1819-23; Gov. 1835-39.

CANNON, Raymond Joseph (D Wis.) Aug. 26, 1894-Nov. 25, 1951; House 1933-39.

CANTOR, Jacob Aaron (D N.Y.) Dec. 6, 1854-July 2, 1921; House Nov. 4, 1913-15.

CANTRILL, James Campbell (D Ky.) July 9, 1870-Sept. 2, 1923; House 1909-Sept. 2, 1923.

CAPEHART, Homer Earl (R Ind.) June 6, 1897-Sept. 3, 1979; Senate 1945-63.

CAPEHART, James (D W.Va.) March 7, 1847-April 28, 1921; House 1891-95.

CAPERTON, Allen Taylor (son of Hugh Caperton) (D W.Va.) Nov. 21, 1810-July 26, 1876; Senate 1875-July 26, 1876.

CAPERTON, Hugh (father of Allen Taylor Caperton) (F Va.) April 17, 1781-Feb. 9, 1847; House 1813-15.

CAPOZZOLI, Louis Joseph (D N.Y.) March 6, 1901-—; House 1941-45.

CAPPER, Arthur (R Kan.) July 14, 1865-Dec. 19, 1951; Senate 1919-49; Gov. 1915-19.

CAPRON, Adin Ballou (R R.I.) Jan. 9, 1841-March 17, 1911; House 1897-1911.

CAPSTICK, John Henry (R N.J.) Sept. 2, 1856-March 17, 1918; House 1915-March 17, 1918.

CAPUTO, Bruce F. (R N.Y.) Aug. 7, 1943-—; House 1977-79.

CARAWAY, Hattie Wyatt (widow of Thaddeus Horatius Caraway) (D Ark.) Feb. 1, 1878-Dec. 21, 1950; Senate Nov. 13, 1931-45.

CARAWAY, Thaddeus Horatius (husband of Hattie Wyatt Caraway) (D Ark.) Oct. 17, 1871-Nov. 6, 1931; House 1913-21; Senate 1921-Nov. 6, 1931.

CARDEN, Cap Robert (D Ky.) Dec. 17, 1866-June 13, 1935; House 1931-June 13, 1935.

CAREW, John Francis (nephew of Thomas Francis Magner) (D N.Y.) April 16, 1873-April 10, 1951; House 1913-Dec. 18, 1929.

CAREY, Hugh Leo (D N.Y.) April 11, 1919-—; House 1961-Dec. 31, 1974; Gov. 1975-83.

CAREY, John (R Ohio) April 5, 1792-March 17, 1875; House 1859-61.

CAREY, Joseph Maull (father of Robert Davis Carey) (R Wyo.) Jan. 19, 1845-Feb. 5, 1924; House (Terr. Del.) 1885-July 10, 1890; Senate Nov. 15, 1890-95; Gov. 1911-15.

CAREY, Robert Davis (son of Joseph Maull Carey) (R Wyo.) Aug. 12, 1878-Jan. 17, 1937; Senate Dec. 1, 1930-37; Gov. 1919-23.

CARLETON, Ezra Child (D Mich.) Sept. 6, 1838-July 24, 1911; House 1883-87.

CARLETON, Peter (D N.H.) Sept. 19, 1755-April 29, 1828; House 1807-09.

CARLEY, Patrick J. (D N.Y.) Feb. 2, 1866-Feb. 25, 1936; House 1927-35.

CARLILE, John Snyder (U Va.) Dec. 16, 1817-Oct. 24, 1878; House 1855-57, March 4-July 9, 1861; Senate July 9, 1861-65 (1855-57, March 4-July 9, 1861 American Party, July 9, 1861-65 Unionist).

CARLIN, Charles Creighton (D Va.) April 8, 1866-Oct. 14, 1938; House Nov. 5, 1907-19.

CARLISLE, John Griffin (D Ky.) Sept. 5, 1835-July 31, 1910; House 1877-May 26, 1890; Senate May 26, 1890-Feb. 4, 1893; Speaker 1883-89; Secy. of the Treasury 1893-97.

CARLSON, Clifford Dale (R Ill.) Dec. 30, 1915-Aug. 28, 1977; House April 4, 1972-73.

CARLSON, Frank (R Kan.) Jan. 23, 1893-—; House 1935-47; Senate Nov. 29, 1950-69; Gov. 1947-50.

CARLTON, Henry Hull (D Ga.) May 14, 1835-Oct. 26, 1905; House 1887-91.

CARLYLE, Frank Ertel (D N.C.) April 7, 1897-Oct. 2, 1960; House 1949-57.

CARMACK, Edward Ward (D Tenn.) Nov. 5, 1858-Nov. 9, 1908; House 1897-1901; Senate 1901-07.

CARMAN, Gregory W. (R N.Y.) Jan. 31, 1937- —; House 1981-83.

CARMICHAEL, Archibald Hill (D Ala.) June 17, 1864-July 15, 1947; House Nov. 14, 1933-37.

CARMICHAEL, Richard Bennett (JD Md.) Dec. 25, 1807-Oct. 21, 1884; House 1833-35.

CARNAHAN, Albert Sidney Johnson (D Mo.) Jan. 9, 1897-March 24, 1968; House 1945-47, 1949-61.

CARNES, Thomas Petters (— Ga.) 1762-May 5, 1822; House 1793-95.

CARNEY, Charles Joseph (D Ohio) April 17, 1913-—; House Nov. 3, 1970-79.

CARNEY, William (R N.Y.) July 1, 1942-—; House 1979-—.

CARPENTER, Cyrus Clay (R Iowa) Nov. 24, 1829-May 29, 1898; House 1879-83; Gov. 1872-76.

CARPENTER, Davis (W N.Y.) Dec. 25, 1799-Oct. 22, 1878; House Nov. 8, 1853-55.

CARPENTER, Edmund Nelson (R Pa.) June 27, 1865-Nov. 4, 1952; House 1925-27.

CARPENTER, Levi D. (D N.Y.) Aug. 21, 1802-Oct. 27, 1856; House Nov. 5, 1844-45.

CARPENTER, Lewis Cass (R S.C.) Feb. 20, 1836-March 6, 1908; House Nov. 3, 1874-75.

CARPENTER, Matthew Hale (R Wis.) Dec. 22, 1824-Feb. 24, 1881; Senate 1869-75, 1879-Feb. 24, 1881; Pres. pro tempore 1873-75.

CARPENTER, Terry McGovern (D Neb.) March 28, 1900-April 27, 1978; House 1933-35.

CARPENTER, William Randolph (D Kan.) April 24, 1894-July 26, 1956; House 1933-37.

CARPER, Thomas Richard (D Del.) Jan. 23, 1947-—; House 1983-—.

CARR, Francis (father of James Carr) (D Mass.) Dec. 6, 1751-Oct. 6, 1821; House April 6, 1812-13.

CARR, James (son of Francis Carr) (— Mass.) Sept. 9, 1777-Aug. 24, 1818; House 1815-17.

CARR, John (D Ind.) April 9, 1793-Jan. 20, 1845; House 1831-37, 1839-41.

CARR, Milton Robert (D Mich.) March 27, 1943-—; House 1975-81, 1983-—.

CARR, Nathan Tracy (D Ind.) Dec. 25, 1833-May 28, 1885; House Dec. 5, 1876-77.

CARR, Wooda Nicholas (D Pa.) Feb. 6, 1871-June 28, 1953; House 1913-15.

CARRIER, Chester Otto (R Ky.) May 5, 1897-—; House Nov. 30, 1943-45.

CARRIGG, Joseph Leonard (R Pa.) Feb. 23, 1901-—; House Nov. 6, 1951-59.

CARROLL, Charles (cousin of Daniel Carroll) (F Md.) Sept. 19, 1737-Nov. 14, 1832; Senate 1789-Nov. 30, 1792; Cont. Cong. 1776-78.

CARROLL, Charles Hobart (CW N.Y.) May 4, 1794-June 8, 1865; House 1843-47.

CARROLL, Daniel (uncle of Richard Brent, cousin of Charles Carroll) (F Md.) July 22, 1730-May 7, 1796; House 1789-91; Cont. Cong. 1780-84.

CARROLL, James (D Md.) Dec. 2, 1791-Jan. 16, 1873; House 1839-41.

CARROLL, John Albert (D Colo.) July 30, 1901-Aug. 31, 1983; House 1947-51; Senate 1957-63.

CARROLL, John Michael (D N.Y.) April 27, 1823-May 8, 1901; House 1871-73.

CARSON, Henderson Haverfield (R Ohio) Oct. 25, 1893-Oct. 5, 1971; House 1943-45, 1947-49.

CARSON, Samuel Price (D N.C.) Jan. 22, 1798-Nov. 2, 1838; House 1825-33.

CARSS, William Leighton (FL Minn.) Feb. 15, 1865-May 31, 1931; House 1919-21, 1925-29 (1919-21 Independent, 1925-29 Farmer Laborite).

CARTER, Albert Edward (R Calif.) July 5, 1881-Aug. 8, 1964; House 1925-45.

CARTER, Charles David (D Okla.) Aug. 16, 1868-April 9, 1929; House Nov. 16, 1907-27.

CARTER, John (— S.C.) Sept. 10, 1792-June 20, 1850; House Dec. 11, 1822-29.

CARTER, Luther Cullen (UR N.Y.) Feb. 25, 1805-Jan. 3, 1875; House 1859-61.

CARTER, Steven V. (D Iowa) Oct. 8, 1915-Nov. 4, 1959; House Jan. 3-Nov. 4, 1959.

CARTER, Thomas Henry (R Mont.) Oct. 30, 1854-Sept. 17, 1911; House (Terr. Del.) March 4-Nov. 7, 1889, (Representative) Nov. 8, 1889-91; Senate 1895-1901, 1905-11; Chrmn. Rep. Nat. Comm. 1892-96.

CARTER, Tim Lee (R Ky.) Sept. 2, 1910-—; House 1965-81.

CARTER, Timothy Jarvis (D Maine) Aug. 18, 1800-March 14, 1838; House Sept. 4, 1837-March 14, 1838.

CARTER, Vincent Michael (R Wyo.) Nov. 6, 1891-Dec. 30, 1972; House 1929-35.

CARTER, William Blount (W Tenn.) Oct. 22, 1792-April 17, 1848; House 1835-41.

CARTER, William Henry (R Mass.) June 15, 1864-April 23, 1955; House 1915-19.

CARTTER, David Kellogg (D Ohio) June 22, 1812-April 16, 1887; House 1849-53.

CARTWRIGHT, Wilburn (D Okla.) Jan. 12, 1892-March 14, 1979; House 1927-43.

CARUTH, Asher Graham (D Ky.) Feb. 7, 1844-Nov. 25, 1907; House 1887-95.

CARUTHERS, Robert Looney (W Tenn.) July 31, 1800-Oct. 2, 1882; House 1841-43.

CARUTHERS, Samuel (D Mo.) Oct. 13, 1820-July 20, 1860; House 1853-59 (1853-57 Whig, 1857-59 Democrat).

CARVILLE, Edward Peter (D Nev.) May 14, 1885-June 27, 1956; Senate July 25, 1945-47; Gov. 1939-45.

CARY, George (— Ga.) Aug. 7, 1789-Sept. 10, 1843; House 1823-27.

CARY, George Booth (D Va.) 1811-March 5, 1850; House 1841-43.

CARY, Glover H. (D Ky.) May 1, 1885-Dec. 5, 1936; House 1931-Dec. 5, 1936.

CARY, Jeremiah Eaton (D N.Y.) April 30, 1803-June 1888; House 1843-45.

CARY, Samuel Fenton (R Ohio) Feb. 18, 1814-Sept. 29, 1900; House Nov. 21, 1867-69.

CARY, Shepard (D Maine) July 3, 1805-Aug. 9, 1866; House May 10, 1844-45.

CARY, William Joseph (R Wis.) March 22, 1865-Jan. 2, 1934; House 1907-19.

CASE, Charles (D Ind.) Dec. 21, 1817-June 30, 1883; House Dec. 7, 1857-61.

CASE, Clifford Philip (R N.J.) April 16, 1904-March 5, 1982; House 1945-Aug. 16, 1953; Senate 1955-79.

CASE, Francis Higbee (R S.D.) Dec. 9, 1896-June 22, 1962; House 1937-51; Senate 1951-June 22, 1962.

CASE, Walter (— N.Y.) 1776-Oct. 7, 1859; House 1819-21.

CASEY, John Joseph (D Pa.) May 26, 1875-May 5, 1929; House 1913-17, 1919-21, 1923-25, 1927-May 5, 1929.

CASEY, Joseph (W Pa.) Dec. 17, 1814-Feb. 10, 1879; House 1849-51.

CASEY, Joseph Edward (D Mass.) Dec. 27, 1898-Sept. 1980; House 1935-43.

CASEY, Levi (— S.C.) about 1752-Feb. 3, 1807; House 1803-Feb. 3, 1807.

CASEY, Lyman Rufus (R N.D.) May 6, 1837-Jan. 26, 1914; Senate Nov. 25, 1889-93.

CASEY, Robert Randolph (Bob) (D Texas) July 17, 1915-—; House 1959-Jan. 22, 1976.

CASEY, Samuel Lewis (R Ky.) Feb. 12, 1821-Aug. 25, 1902; House March 10, 1862-63.

CASEY, Zadoc (JD Ill.) March 7, 1796-Sept. 4, 1862; House 1833-43.

CASKIE, John Samuels (D Va.) Nov. 8, 1821-Dec. 16, 1869; House 1851-59.

CASON, Thomas Jefferson (R Ind.) Sept. 13, 1828-July 10, 1901; House 1873-77.

CASS, Lewis (D Mich.) Oct. 9, 1782-June 17, 1866; Senate 1845-May 29, 1848, 1849-57; Gov. (Mich. Terr.) 1813-31; Secy. of War 1831-36; Pres. pro tempore 1854; Secy. of State 1857-60.

CASSEDY, George (D N.J.) Sept. 16, 1783-Dec. 31, 1842; House 1821-27.

CASSEL, Henry Burd (R Pa.) Oct. 19, 1855-April 28, 1926; House Nov. 5, 1901-09.

Biographical Index

CASSERLY, Eugene (D Calif.) Nov. 13, 1820-June 14, 1883; Senate 1869-Nov. 19, 1873.

CASSIDY, George Williams (D Nev.) April 25, 1836-June 24, 1892; House 1881-85.

CASSIDY, James Henry (R Ohio) Oct. 28, 1869-Aug. 23, 1926; House April 20, 1909-11.

CASSINGHAM, John Wilson (D Ohio) June 22, 1840-March 14, 1930; House 1901-05.

CASTELLOW, Bryant Thomas (D Ga.) July 29, 1876-July 23, 1962; House Nov. 8, 1932-37.

CASTLE, Curtis Harvey (P/D Calif.) Oct. 4, 1848-July 12, 1928; House 1897-99.

CASTLE, James Nathan (D Minn.) May 23, 1836-Jan. 2, 1903; House 1891-93.

CASTOR, George Albert (R Pa.) Aug. 6, 1855-Feb. 19, 1906; House Feb. 16, 1904-Feb. 19, 1906.

CASWELL, Lucien Bonaparte (R Wis.) Nov. 27, 1827-April 26, 1919; House 1875-83, 1885-91.

CATCHINGS, Thomas Clendinen (D Miss.) Jan. 11, 1847-Dec. 24, 1927; House 1885-1901.

CATE, George Washington (IRef. Wis.) Sept. 17, 1825-March 7, 1905; House 1875-77.

CATE, William Henderson (D Ark.) Nov. 11, 1839-Aug. 23, 1899; House 1889-March 5, 1890, 1891-93.

CATHCART, Charles William (D Ind.) July 24, 1809-Aug. 22, 1888; House 1845-49; Senate Dec. 6, 1852-53.

CATLIN, George Smith (D Conn.) Aug. 24, 1808-Dec. 26, 1851; House 1843-45.

CATLIN, Theron Ephron (R Mo.) May 16, 1878-March 19, 1960; House 1911-Aug. 12, 1912.

CATRON, Thomas Benton (R N.M.) Oct. 6, 1840-May 15, 1921; House (Terr. Del.) 1895-97; Senate March 27, 1912-17.

CATTELL, Alexander Gilmore (R N.J.) Feb. 12, 1816-April 8, 1894; Senate Sept. 19, 1866-71.

CAULFIELD, Bernard Gregory (D Ill.) Oct. 18, 1828-Dec. 19, 1887; House Feb. 1, 1875-77.

CAULFIELD, Henry Stewart (R Mo.) Dec. 9, 1873-May 11, 1966; House 1907-09; Gov. 1929-33.

CAUSEY, John Williams (D Del.) Sept. 19, 1841-Oct. 1, 1908; House 1891-95.

CAUSIN, John M. S. (W Md.) 1811-Jan. 30, 1861; House 1843-45.

CAVALCANTE, Anthony (D Pa.) Feb. 6, 1897-Oct. 29, 1966; House 1949-51.

CAVANAUGH, James Michael (D Minn./Mont.) July 4, 1823-Oct. 30, 1879; House May 11, 1858-59 (Minn.), 1867-71 (Terr. Del.- Mont.).

CAVANAUGH, John J. III (D Neb.) Aug. 1, 1945-—; House 1977-81.

CAVICCHIA, Peter Angelo (R N.J.) May 22, 1879-Sept. 11, 1967; House 1931-37.

CEDERBERG, Elford Alfred (R Mich.) March 6, 1918-—; House 1953-Dec. 31, 1978.

CELLER, Emanuel (D N.Y.) May 6, 1888-Jan. 15, 1981; House 1923-73.

CESSNA, John (R Pa.) June 29, 1821-Dec. 13, 1893; House 1869-71, 1873-75.

CHACE, Jonathan (R R.I.) July 22, 1829-June 30, 1917; House 1881-Jan. 26, 1885; Senate Jan. 20, 1885-April 9, 1889.

CHADWICK, E. Wallace (R Pa.) Jan. 17, 1884-Aug. 18, 1969; House 1947-49.

CHAFEE, John Hubbard (R R.I.) Oct. 22, 1922-—; Senate Dec. 29, 1976-—; Gov. 1963-69.

CHAFFEE, Calvin Clifford (AP Mass.) Aug. 28, 1811-Aug. 8, 1896; House 1855-59.

CHAFFEE, Jerome Bunty (R Colo.) April 17, 1825-March 9, 1886; House (Terr. Del.) 1871-75; Senate Nov. 15, 1876-79.

CHALMERS, James Ronald (son of Joseph Williams Chalmers) (I Miss.) Jan. 12, 1831-April 9, 1898; House 1877-April 29, 1882, June 25, 1884-85 (1877-82 Democrat, 1884-85 Independent).

CHALMERS, Joseph Williams (father of James Ronald Chalmers) (D Miss.) Dec. 20, 1806-June 16, 1853; Senate Nov. 3, 1845-47.

CHALMERS, William Wallace (R Ohio) Nov. 1, 1861-Oct. 1, 1944; House 1921-23, 1925-31.

CHAMBERLAIN, Charles Ernest (R Mich.) July 22, 1917-—; House 1957-Dec. 31, 1974.

CHAMBERLAIN, Ebenezer Mattoon (D Ind.) Aug. 20, 1805-March 14, 1861; House 1853-55.

CHAMBERLAIN, George Earle (D Ore.) Jan. 1, 1854-July 9, 1928; Senate 1909-21; Gov. 1903-09.

CHAMBERLAIN, Jacob Payson (R N.Y.) Aug. 1, 1802-Oct. 5, 1878; House 1861-63.

CHAMBERLAIN, John Curtis (F N.H.) June 5, 1772-Dec. 8, 1834; House 1809-11.

CHAMBERLAIN, William (F Vt.) April 27, 1755-Sept. 27, 1828; House 1803-05, 1809-11.

CHAMBERS, David (— Ohio) Nov. 25, 1780-Aug. 8, 1864; House Oct. 9, 1821-23.

CHAMBERS, Ezekiel Forman (W Md.) Feb. 28, 1788-Jan. 30, 1867; Senate Jan. 24, 1826-Dec. 20, 1834.

CHAMBERS, George (W Pa.) Feb. 24, 1786-March 25, 1866; House 1833-37.

CHAMBERS, Henry H. (D Ala.) Oct. 1, 1790-Feb. 24, 1826; Senate 1825-Feb. 24, 1826.

CHAMBERS, John (W Ky.) Oct. 6, 1780-Sept. 21, 1852; House Dec. 1, 1828-29, 1835-39; Gov. (Iowa Terr.) 1841-45.

CHAMPION, Edwin Van Meter (D Ill.) Sept. 18, 1890-Feb. 11, 1976; House 1937-39.

CHAMPION, Epaphroditis (F Conn.) April 6, 1756-Dec. 22, 1834; House 1807-17.

CHAMPLIN, Christopher Grant (— R.I.) April 12, 1768-March 18, 1840; House 1797-1801; Senate June 26, 1809-Oct. 2, 1811.

CHANDLER, Albert Benjamin (D Ky.) July 14, 1898-—; Senate Oct. 10, 1939-Nov. 1, 1945; Gov. 1935-39, 1955-59.

CHANDLER, John (brother of Thomas Chandler, uncle of Zachariah Chandler) (D Mass./Maine) Feb. 1, 1762-Sept. 25, 1841; House (Mass.) 1805-09; Senate (Maine) June 14, 1820-29.

CHANDLER, Joseph Ripley (W Pa.) Aug. 22, 1792-July 10, 1880; House 1849-55.

CHANDLER, Rodney (R Wash.) July 13, 1942-—; House 1983-—.

CHANDLER, Thomas (brother of John Chandler, uncle of Zachariah Chandler) (D N.H.) Aug. 10, 1772-Jan. 28, 1866; House 1829-33.

CHANDLER, Thomas Alberter (R Okla.) July 26, 1871-June 22, 1953; House 1917-19, 1921-23.

CHANDLER, Walter (Clift) (D Tenn.) Oct. 5, 1887-Oct. 1, 1967; House 1935-Jan. 2, 1940.

CHANDLER, Walter Marion (R N.Y.) Dec. 8, 1867-March 16, 1935; House 1912-19, 1921-23 (1912-19 Progressive, 1921-23 Republican).

CHANDLER, William Eaton (R N.H.) Dec. 28, 1835-Nov. 20, 1917; Senate June 14, 1887-March 3, 1889, June 18, 1889-1901; Secy. of the Navy 1882-85.

CHANDLER, Zachariah (nephew of John Chandler and Thomas Chandler, grandfather of Frederick Hale) (R Mich.) Dec. 10, 1813-Nov. 1, 1879; Senate 1857-75, Feb. 22, 1879-Nov. 1, 1879; Secy. of the Interior 1875-77; Chrmn. Rep. Nat. Comm. 1876-79.

CHANEY, John (JD Ohio) Jan. 12, 1790-April 10, 1881; House 1833-39.

CHANEY, John Crawford (R Ind.) Feb. 1, 1853-April 26, 1940; House 1905-09.

CHANLER, John Winthrop (father of William Astor Chanler) (D N.Y.) Sept. 14, 1826-Oct. 19, 1877; House 1863-69.

CHANLER, William Astor (son of John Winthrop Chanler) (D N.Y.) June 11, 1867-March 4, 1934; House 1899-1901.

CHAPIN, Alfred Clark (D N.Y.) March 8, 1848-Oct. 2, 1936; House Nov. 3, 1891-Nov. 16, 1892.

CHAPIN, Chester Williams (D Mass.) Dec. 16, 1798-June 10, 1883; House 1875-77.

CHAPIN, Graham Hurd (D N.Y.) Feb. 10, 1799-Sept. 8, 1843; House 1835-37.

CHAPMAN, Andrew Grant (son of John Grant Chapman) (D Md.) Jan. 17, 1839-Sept. 25, 1892; House 1881-83.

CHAPMAN, Augustus Alexandria (VBD Va.) March 9, 1803-June 7, 1876; House 1843-47.

CHAPMAN, Bird Beers (D Neb.) Aug. 24, 1821-Sept. 21, 1871; House (Terr. Del.) 1855-57.

CHAPMAN, Charles (W Conn.) June 21, 1799-Aug. 7, 1869; House 1851-53.

CHAPMAN, Henry (D Pa.) Feb. 4, 1804-April 11, 1891; House 1857-59.

CHAPMAN, John (F Pa.) Oct. 18, 1740-Jan. 27, 1800; House 1797-99.

CHAPMAN, John Grant (father of Andrew Grant Chapman) (W Md.) July 5, 1798-Dec. 10, 1856; House 1845-49.

CHAPMAN, Pleasant Thomas (R Ill.) Oct. 8, 1854-Jan. 31, 1931; House 1905-11.

CHAPMAN, Reuben (D Ala.) July 15, 1799-May 16, 1882; House 1835-47; Gov. 1847-49.

CHAPMAN, Virgil Munday (D Ky.) March 15, 1895-March 8, 1951; House 1925-29, 1931-49; Senate 1949-March 8, 1951.

CHAPMAN, William Williams (D Iowa) Aug. 11, 1808-Oct. 18, 1892; House (Terr. Del.) Sept. 10, 1838-Oct. 27, 1840.

CHAPPELL, Absalom Harris (cousin of Lucius Quintus Cincinnatus Lamar) (SRW Ga.) Dec. 18, 1801-Dec. 11, 1878; House Oct. 2, 1843-45.

CHAPPELL, John Joel (SRWD S.C.) Jan. 19, 1782-May 23, 1871; House 1813-17.

CHAPPELL, William Venroe Jr. (D Fla.) Feb. 3, 1922-—; House 1969-—.

CHAPPIE, Eugene A. (R Calif.) March 21, 1920-—; House 1981-—.

CHARLES, William Barclay (R N.Y.) April 3, 1861-Nov. 25, 1950; House 1915-17.

CHARLTON, Robert Milledge (— Ga.) Jan. 19, 1807-Jan. 18, 1854; Senate May 31, 1852-53.

CHASE, Dudley (uncle of Salmon Portland Chase and Dudley Chase Denison) (JD Vt.) Dec. 30, 1771-Feb. 23, 1846; Senate 1813-Nov. 3, 1817, 1825-31.

CHASE, George William (W N.Y.) ?-April 17, 1867; House 1853-55.

CHASE, Jackson Burton (R Neb.) Aug. 19, 1890-May 5, 1974; House 1955-57.

CHASE, James Mitchell (R Pa.) Dec. 19, 1891-Jan. 1, 1945; House 1927-33.

CHASE, Lucien Bonaparte (D Tenn.) Dec. 5, 1817-Dec. 4, 1864; House 1845-49.

CHASE, Ray P. (R Minn.) March 12, 1880-Sept. 18, 1948; House 1933-35.

CHASE, Salmon Portland (nephew of Dudley Chase, cousin of Dudley Chase Denison) (R Ohio) Jan. 13, 1808-May 7, 1873; Senate 1849-55, March 4-6, 1861; Gov. 1856-60 (1849-57 Free Soil Democrat, 1857-61 Republican); Secy. of the Treasury 1861-July 1, 1964; Chief Justice Supreme Court 1864-73.

CHASE, Samuel (Ad.D N.Y.) ?-Aug. 3, 1838; House 1827-29.

CHASTAIN, Elijah Webb (UD Ga.) Sept. 25, 1813-April 9, 1874; House 1851-55.

CHATHAM, Richard Thurmond (D N.C.) Aug. 16, 1896-Feb. 5, 1957; House 1949-57.

CHAVES, Jose Francisco (R N.M.) June 27, 1833-Nov. 26, 1904; House (Terr. Del.) 1865-67, Feb. 20, 1869-71.

CHAVEZ, Dennis (D N.M.) April 8, 1888-Nov. 18, 1962; House 1931-35; Senate May 11, 1935-Nov. 18, 1962.

CHEADLE, Joseph Bonaparte (R Ind.) Aug. 14, 1842-May 28, 1904; House 1887-91.

CHEATHAM, Henry Plummer (R N.C.) Dec. 27, 1857-Nov. 29, 1935; House 1889-93.

CHEATHAM, Richard (W Tenn.) Feb. 20, 1799-Sept. 9, 1845; House 1837-39.

CHELF, Frank Leslie (D Ky.) Sept. 22, 1907-Sept. 1, 1982; House 1945-67.

CHENEY, Person Colby (R N.H.) Feb. 25, 1828-June 19, 1901; Senate Nov. 24, 1886-June 14, 1887; Gov. 1875-77.

CHENEY, Richard Bruce (R Wyo.) Jan. 30, 1941-—; House 1979-—.

CHENOWETH, John Edgar (R Colo.) Aug. 17, 1897-—; House 1941-49, 1951-65.

CHESNEY, Chester Anton (D Ill.) March 9, 1916-—; House 1949-51.

CHESNUT, James Jr. (SRD S.C.) Jan. 18, 1815-Feb. 1, 1885; Senate Dec. 3, 1858-Nov. 10, 1860.

CHETWOOD, William (JD N.J.) June 17, 1771-Dec. 17, 1857; House Dec. 5, 1836-37.

CHEVES, Langdon (D S.C.) Sept. 17, 1776-June 26, 1857; House Dec. 31, 1810-15; Speaker 1814-15.

CHICKERING, Charles Addison (R N.Y.) Nov. 26, 1843-Feb. 13, 1900; House 1893-Feb. 13, 1900.

CHILCOTT, George Miles (R Colo.) Jan. 2, 1828-March 6, 1891; House (Terr. Del.) 1867-69; Senate April 17, 1882-Jan. 27, 1883.

CHILD, Thomas Jr. (D N.Y.) March 22, 1818-March 9, 1869; House 1855-57.

CHILDS, Robert Andrew (R Ill.) March 22, 1845-Dec. 19, 1915; House 1893-95.

CHILDS, Timothy (W N.Y.) 1785-Nov. 8, 1847; House 1829-31; 1835-39, 1841-43.

CHILES, Lawton Mainor Jr. (D Fla.) April 3, 1930-—; Senate 1971-—.

CHILTON, Horace (grandson of Thomas Chilton) (D Texas) Dec. 29, 1853-June 12, 1932; Senate June 10, 1891-March 22, 1892, 1895-1901.

CHILTON, Samuel (W Va.) Sept. 7, 1804-Jan. 14, 1867; House 1843-45.

CHILTON, Thomas (grandfather of Horace Chilton) (W Ky.) July 30, 1798-Aug. 15, 1854; House Dec. 22, 1827-31, 1833-35.

CHILTON, William Edwin (D W.Va.) March 17, 1858-Nov. 7, 1939; Senate 1911-17.

CHINDBLOM, Carl Richard (R Ill.) Dec. 21, 1870-Sept. 12, 1956; House 1919-33.

CHINN, Joseph William (D Va.) Nov. 16, 1798-Dec. 5, 1840; House 1831-35.

CHINN, Thomas Withers (cousin of Robert Enoch Withers) (W La.) Nov. 22, 1791-May 22, 1852; House 1839-41.

CHIPERFIELD, Burnett Mitchell (father of Robert Bruce Chiperfield) (R Ill.) June 14, 1870-June 24, 1940; House 1915-17, 1929-33.

CHIPERFIELD, Robert Bruce (son of Burnett Mitchell Chiperfield) (R Ill.) Nov. 20, 1899-April 9, 1971; House 1939-63.

CHIPMAN, Daniel (brother of Nathaniel Chipman) (F Vt.) Oct. 22, 1765-April 23, 1850; House 1815-May 5, 1816.

CHIPMAN, John Logan (grandson of Nathaniel Chipman) (D Mich.) June 5, 1830-Aug. 17, 1893; House 1887-Aug. 17, 1893.

CHIPMAN, John Smith (D Mich.) Aug. 10, 1800 July 27, 1869; House 1845-47.

CHIPMAN, Nathaniel (brother of Daniel Chipman, grandfather of John Logan Chipman) (— Vt.) Nov. 15, 1752-Jan. 15, 1843; Senate Oct. 17, 1797-1803.

CHIPMAN, Norton Parker (R D.C.) March 7, 1836-Feb. 1, 1924; House (Del.) April 21, 1871-75.

CHISHOLM, Shirley Anita (D N.Y.) Nov. 30, 1924-—; House 1969-83.

CHITTENDEN, Martin (— Vt.) March 12, 1763-Sept. 5, 1840; House 1803-13; Gov. 1813-15.

CHITTENDEN, Simeon Baldwin (R N.Y.) March 29, 1814-April 14, 1889; House Nov. 3, 1874-81.

CHITTENDEN, Thomas Cotton (W N.Y.) Aug. 30, 1788-Aug. 22, 1866; House 1839-43.

CHOATE, Rufus (W Mass.) Oct. 1, 1799-July 13, 1859; House 1831-June 30, 1834; Senate Feb. 23, 1841-45.

CHRISMAN, James Stone (D Ky.) Sept. 14, 1818-July 29, 1881; House 1853-55.

CHRISTGAU, Victor (R Minn.) Sept. 20, 1894-—; House 1929-33.

CHRISTIANCY, Isaac Peckham (R Mich.) March 12, 1812-Sept. 8, 1890; Senate 1875-Feb. 10, 1879.

CHRISTIANSON, Theodore (R Minn.) Sept. 12, 1883-Dec. 9, 1948; House 1933-37.

CHRISTIE, Gabriel (— Md.) 1755-April 1, 1808; House 1793-97, 1799-1801.

CHRISTOPHER, George Henry (D Mo.) Dec. 9, 1888-Jan. 23, 1959; House 1949-51, 1955-Jan. 23, 1959.

CHRISTOPHERSON, Charles Andrew (R S.D.) July 23, 1871-Nov. 2, 1951; House 1919-33.

CHUDOFF, Earl (D Pa.) Nov. 16, 1907-—; House 1949-Jan. 5, 1958.

CHURCH, Denver Samuel (D Calif.) Dec. 11, 1862-Feb. 21, 1952; House 1913-19, 1933-35.

CHURCH, Frank Forrester (D Idaho) July 25, 1924-April 7, 1984; Senate 1957-81.

Biographical Index

CHURCH, Marguerite Stitt (widow of Ralph Edwin Church) (R Ill.) Sept. 13, 1892-—; House 1951-63.

CHURCH, Ralph Edwin (husband of Marguerite Stitt Church) (R Ill.) May 5, 1883-March 21, 1950; House 1935-41, 1943-March 21, 1950.

CHURCHILL, George Bosworth (R Mass.) Oct. 24, 1866-July 1, 1925; House March 4-July 1, 1925.

CHURCHILL, John Charles (R N.Y.) Jan. 17, 1821-June 4, 1905; House 1867-71.

CHURCHWELL, William Montgomery (D Tenn.) Feb. 20, 1826-Aug. 18, 1862; House 1851-55.

CILLEY, Bradbury (uncle of Jonathan Cilley and Joseph Cilley) (F N.H.) Feb. 1, 1760-Dec. 17, 1831; House 1813-17.

CILLEY, Jonathan (nephew of Bradbury Cilley, brother of Joseph Cilley) (JD Maine) July 2, 1802-Feb. 24, 1838; House 1837-Feb. 24, 1838.

CILLEY, Joseph (nephew of Bradbury Cilley, brother of Jonathan Cilley) (D N.H.) Jan. 4, 1791-Sept. 12, 1887; Senate June 13, 1846-47.

CITRON, William Michael (D Conn.) Aug. 29, 1896-June 7, 1976; House 1935-39.

CLAFLIN, William (R Mass.) March 6, 1818-Jan. 5, 1905; House 1877-81; Gov. 1869-71; Chrmn. Rep. Nat. Comm. 1868-72.

CLAGETT, Clifton (— N.H.) Dec. 3, 1762-Jan. 25, 1829; House 1803-05, 1817-21.

CLAGETT, William Horace (uncle of Samuel Barrett Pettengill) (R Mont.) Sept. 21, 1838-Aug. 3, 1901; House (Terr. Del.) 1871-73.

CLAGUE, Frank (R Minn.) July 13, 1865-March 25, 1952; House 1921-33.

CLAIBORNE, James Robert (D Mo.) June 22, 1882-Feb. 16, 1944; House 1933-37.

CLAIBORNE, John (son of Thomas Claiborne, brother of Thomas Claiborne Jr.) (— Va.) 1777-Oct. 9, 1808; House 1805-Oct. 9, 1808.

CLAIBORNE, John Francis Hamtramck (nephew of William Charles Cole Claiborne and Nathaniel Herbert Claiborne, great-grandfather of Herbert Claiborne Pell Jr.) (JD Miss.) April 24, 1809-May 17, 1884; House 1835-37, July 18, 1837-Feb. 5, 1838.

CLAIBORNE, Nathaniel Herbert (brother of William Charles Cole Claiborne, uncle of John Francis Hamtramck Claiborne, great-great-granduncle of Herbert Claiborne Pell Jr.) (R Va.) Nov. 14, 1777-Aug. 15, 1859; House 1825-37.

CLAIBORNE, Thomas (father of John Claiborne and Thomas Claiborne Jr.) (— Va.) Feb. 1, 1749-1812; House 1793-99, 1801-05.

CLAIBORNE, Thomas Jr. (son of Thomas Claiborne, brother of John Claiborne) (D Tenn.) May 17, 1780-Jan. 7, 1856; House 1817-19.

CLAIBORNE, William Charles Cole (brother of Nathaniel Herbert Claiborne, uncle of John Francis Hamtramck Claiborne, great-great-

granduncle of Herbert Claiborne Pell Jr.) (Jeff. D Tenn./ D La.) 1775-Nov. 23, 1817; House 1797-1801 (Tenn.); Senate March 4-Nov. 23, 1817 (La.); Gov. (Miss. Terr.) 1801-03; Gov. (Orleans Terr.) 1804-12; Gov. (La.) 1812-16.

CLANCY, Donald D. (R Ohio) July 24, 1921-—; House 1961-77.

CLANCY, John Michael (D N.Y.) May 7, 1837-July 25, 1903; House 1889-95.

CLANCY, John Richard (D N.Y.) March 8, 1859-April 21, 1932; House 1913-15.

CLANCY, Robert Henry (R Mich.) March 14, 1882-April 23, 1962; House 1923-25, 1927-33 (1923-25 Democrat, 1927-33 Republican).

CLAPP, Asa William Henry (D Maine) March 6, 1805-March 22, 1891; House 1847-49.

CLAPP, Moses Edwin (R Minn.) May 21, 1851-March 6, 1929; Senate Jan. 23, 1901-1917.

CLARDY, John Daniel (D Ky.) Aug. 30, 1828-Aug. 20, 1918; House 1895-99.

CLARDY, Kit Francis (R Mich.) June 17, 1892-Sept. 5, 1961; House 1953-55.

CLARDY, Martin Linn (D Mo.) April 26, 1844-July 5, 1914; House 1879-89.

CLARK, Abraham (— N.J.) Feb. 15, 1726-Sept. 15, 1794; House 1791-Sept. 15, 1794; Cont. Cong. 1776-78, 1779-83, 1787-89.

CLARK, Alvah Augustus (cousin of James Nelson Pidcock) (D N.J.) Sept. 13, 1840-Dec. 27, 1912; House 1877-81.

CLARK, Ambrose Williams (R N.Y.) Feb. 19, 1810-Oct. 13, 1887; House 1861-65.

CLARK, Amos Jr. (R N.J.) Nov. 8, 1828-Oct. 31, 1912; House 1873-75.

CLARK, Charles Benjamin (R Wis.) Aug. 24, 1844-Sept. 10, 1891; House 1887-91.

CLARK, Charles Nelson (R Mo.) Aug. 21, 1827-Oct. 4, 1902; House 1895-97.

CLARK, Christopher Henderson (brother of James Clark, uncle of John Bullock Clark) (Jeff. D Va.) 1767-Nov. 21, 1828; House Nov. 5, 1804-July 1, 1806.

CLARK, Clarence Don (R Wyo.) April 16, 1851-Nov. 18, 1930; House Dec. 1, 1890-1893; Senate Jan. 23, 1895-1917.

CLARK, Daniel (— Orleans) about 1766-Aug. 16, 1813; House (Terr. Del.) Dec. 1, 1806-09.

CLARK, Daniel (R N.H.) Oct. 24, 1809-Jan. 2, 1891; Senate June 27, 1857-July 27, 1866; Pres. pro tempore 1864.

CLARK, David Worth (D Idaho) April 2, 1902-June 19, 1955; House 1935-39; Senate 1939-45.

CLARK, Ezra Jr. (AP/R Conn.) Sept. 12, 1813-Sept. 26, 1896; House 1855-59.

CLARK, Frank (D Fla.) March 28, 1860-April 14, 1936; House 1905-25.

CLARK, Frank Monroe (D Pa.) Dec. 24, 1915-—; House 1955-Dec. 31, 1974.

CLARK, Franklin (D Maine) Aug. 2, 1801-Aug. 24, 1874; House 1847-49.

CLARK, Henry Alden (R Pa.) Jan. 7, 1850-Feb. 15, 1944; House 1917-19.

CLARK, Henry Selby (D N.C.) Sept. 9, 1809-Jan. 8, 1869; House 1845-47.

CLARK, Horace Francis (D N.Y.) Nov. 29, 1815-June 19, 1873; House 1857-61.

CLARK, James (brother of Christopher Henderson Clark, uncle of John Bullock Clark) (CD Ky.) Jan. 16, 1770-Sept. 27, 1839; House 1813-16, Aug. 1, 1825-31; Gov. (Whig) 1836-39.

CLARK, James Beauchamp (Champ) (father of Joel Bennett Clark) (D Mo.) March 7, 1850-March 2, 1921; House 1893-95; 1897-March 2, 1921; Speaker 1911-19.

CLARK, James West (D N.C.) Oct. 15, 1779-Dec. 20, 1843; House 1815-17.

CLARK, Jerome Bayard (D N.C.) April 5, 1882-Aug. 26, 1959; House 1929-49.

CLARK, Joel Bennett (Champ) (son of James Beauchamp Clark) Jan. 8, 1890-July 13, 1954; Senate Feb. 4, 1933-45.

CLARK, John Bullock (father of John Bullock Clark Jr., nephew of Christopher Henderson Clark and James Clark) (D Mo.) April 17, 1802-Oct. 29, 1885; House Dec. 7, 1857-July 13, 1861.

CLARK, John Bullock Jr. (son of John Bullock Clark) (D Mo.) Jan. 14, 1831-Sept. 7, 1903; House 1873-83.

CLARK, John Chamberlain (W N.Y.) Jan. 14, 1793-Oct. 25, 1852; House 1827-29, 1837-43 (1827-29, 1837-39 Democrat, 1839-43 Whig).

CLARK, Joseph Sill (D Pa.) Oct. 21, 1901-—; Senate 1957-69.

CLARK, Lincoln (D Iowa) Aug. 9, 1800-Sept. 16, 1886; House 1851-53.

CLARK, Linwood Leon (R Md.) March 21, 1876-Nov. 18, 1965; House 1929-31.

CLARK, Lot (W N.Y.) May 23, 1788-Dec. 18, 1862; House 1823-25.

CLARK, Richard Clarence (D Iowa) Sept. 14, 1929-—; Senate 1973-79.

CLARK, Robert (D N.Y.) June 12, 1777-Oct. 1, 1837; House 1819-21.

CLARK, Rush (R Iowa) Oct. 1, 1834-April 29, 1879; House 1877-April 29, 1879.

CLARK, Samuel (D N.Y./Mich.) Jan. 1800-Oct. 2, 1870; House 1833-35 (N.Y.), 1853-55 (Mich.).

CLARK, Samuel Mercer (R Iowa) Oct. 11, 1842-Aug. 11, 1900; House 1895-99.

CLARK, William (W Pa.) Feb. 18, 1774-March 28, 1851; House 1833-37.

CLARK, William Andrews (D Mont.) Jan. 8, 1839-March 2, 1925; Senate Dec. 4, 1899-May 15, 1900, 1901-07.

CLARK, William Thomas (R Texas) June 29, 1831-Oct. 12, 1905; House March 31, 1870-May 13, 1872.

CLARKE, Archibald Smith (brother of Staley Nichols Clarke) (— N.Y.) 1788-Dec. 4, 1821; House Dec. 2, 1816-17.

CLARKE, Bayard (AW N.Y.) March 17, 1815-June 20, 1884; House 1855-57.

CLARKE, Beverly Leonidas (D Ky.) Feb. 11, 1809-March 17, 1860; House 1847-49.

CLARKE, Charles Ezra (W N.Y.) April 8, 1790-Dec. 29, 1863; House 1849-51.

CLARKE, Frank Gay (R N.H.) Sept. 10, 1850-Jan. 9, 1901; House 1897-Jan. 9, 1901.

CLARKE, Freeman (R N.Y.) March 22, 1809-June 24, 1887; House 1863-65, 1871-75.

CLARKE, James McClure (D N.C.) June 12, 1917-—; House 1983-85.

CLARKE, James Paul (D Ark.) Aug. 18, 1854-Oct. 1, 1916; Senate 1903-Oct. 1, 1916; Pres. pro tempore 1913-16; Gov. 1895-97.

CLARKE, John Blades (D Ky.) April 14, 1833-May 23, 1911; House 1875-79.

CLARKE, John Davenport (husband of Marian Williams Clarke) (R N.Y.) Jan. 15, 1873-Nov. 5, 1933; House 1921-25, 1927-Nov. 5, 1933.

CLARKE, John Hopkins (W R.I.) April 1, 1789-Nov. 23, 1870; Senate 1847-53.

CLARKE, Marian Williams (widow of John Davenport Clarke) (R N.Y.) July 29, 1880-April 8, 1953; House Dec. 28, 1933-35.

CLARKE, Reader Wright (R Ohio) May 18, 1812-May 23, 1872; House 1865-69.

CLARKE, Richard Henry (D Ala.) Feb. 9, 1843-Sept. 26, 1906; House 1889-97.

CLARKE, Sidney (R Kan.) Oct. 16, 1831-June 18, 1909; House 1865-71.

CLARKE, Staley Nichols (brother of Archibald Smith Clarke) (W N.Y.) May 24, 1794-Oct. 14, 1860; House 1841-43.

CLASON, Charles Russell (R Mass.) Sept. 3, 1890-—; House 1937-49.

CLASSON, David Guy (R Wis.) Sept. 27, 1870-Sept. 6, 1930; House 1917-23.

CLAUSEN, Don Holst (R Calif.) April 27, 1923-—; House Jan. 22, 1963-83.

CLAWSON, Delwin (Del) Morgan (R Calif.) Jan. 11, 1914-—; House June 11, 1963-Dec. 31, 1978.

CLAWSON, Isaiah Dunn (W N.J.) March 30, 1822-Oct. 9, 1879; House 1855-59.

CLAY, Alexander Stephens (D Ga.) Sept. 25, 1853-Nov. 13, 1910; Senate 1897-Nov. 13, 1910.

CLAY, Brutus Junius (U Ky.) July 1, 1808-Oct. 11, 1878; House 1863-65.

CLAY, Clement Claiborne Jr. (son of Clement Comer Clay) (D Ala.) Dec. 13, 1816-Jan. 3, 1882; Senate Nov. 29, 1853-Jan. 21, 1861.

CLAY, Clement Comer (father of Clement Claiborne Clay Jr.) (D Ala.) Dec. 17, 1789-Sept. 9, 1866; House 1829-35; Senate June 19, 1837-Nov. 15, 1841; Gov. 1835-37.

CLAY, Henry (father of James Brown Clay) (— Ky.) April 12, 1777-June 29, 1852; Senate Nov. 19, 1806-07, Jan. 4, 1810-11, Nov. 10, 1831-March 31, 1842, 1849-June 29, 1852; House 1811-Jan. 19, 1814, 1815-21, 1823-March 6, 1825; Speaker Nov. 4, 1811-Jan. 19, 1814, Dec. 4, 1815-Oct. 28, 1820, Dec. 1, 1823-25; Secy. of State March 7, 1825-29.

CLAY, James Brown (son of Henry Clay) (D Ky.) Nov. 9, 1817-Jan. 26, 1864; House 1857-59.

CLAY, James Franklin (D Ky.) Oct. 29, 1840-Aug. 17, 1921; House 1883-85.

CLAY, Joseph (— Pa.) July 24, 1769-Aug. 27, 1811; House 1803-08.

CLAY, Matthew (D Va.) March 25, 1754-May 27, 1815; House 1797-1813, March 4-May 27, 1815.

CLAY, William Lacey (D Mo.) April 30, 1931-—; House 1969-—.

CLAYPOOL, Harold Kile (son of Horatio Clifford Claypool, cousin of John Barney Peterson) (D Ohio) June 2, 1886-Aug. 2, 1958; House 1937-43.

CLAYPOOL, Horatio Clifford (father of Harold Kile Claypool, cousin of John Barney Peterson) (D Ohio) Feb. 9, 1859-Jan. 19, 1921; House 1911-15, 1917-19.

CLAYTON, Augustin Smith (SRD Ga.) Nov. 27, 1783-June 21, 1839; House Jan. 21, 1832-35.

CLAYTON, Bertram Tracy (brother of Henry De Lamar Clayton (D N.Y.) Oct. 19, 1862-May 30, 1918; House 1899-1901.

CLAYTON, Charles (R Calif.) Oct. 5, 1825-Oct. 4, 1885; House 1873-75.

CLAYTON, Henry De Lamar (brother of Bertram Tracy Clayton) (D Ala.) Feb. 10, 1857-Dec. 21, 1929; House 1897-May 25, 1914.

CLAYTON, John Middleton (nephew of Joshua Clayton, cousin of Thomas Clayton, great-granduncle of Clayton Douglass Buck) (W Del.) July 24, 1796-Nov. 9, 1856; Senate 1829-Dec. 29, 1836, 1845-Feb. 23, 1849, 1853-Nov. 9, 1856 (1829-36 National Republican, 1845-49, 1853-56 Whig); Secy. of State March 7, 1849-July 22, 1850.

CLAYTON, Joshua (father of Thomas Clayton, uncle of John Middleton Clayton) (— Del.) July 20, 1744-Aug. 11, 1798; Senate Jan. 19, 1798-Aug. 11, 1798; Gov. 1789-96.

CLAYTON, Powell (R Ark.) Aug. 7, 1833-Aug. 25, 1914; Senate 1871-77; Gov. 1868.

CLAYTON, Thomas (son of Joshua Clayton, cousin of John Middleton Clayton) (W Del.) March 9, 1778-Aug. 21, 1854; House 1815-17; Senate Jan. 8, 1824-27, Jan. 9, 1837-47 (1815-17, 1824-27 Federalist, 1837-47 Whig).

CLEARY, William Edward (D N.Y.) July 20, 1849-Dec. 20, 1932; House March 5, 1918-21, 1923-27.

CLEMENS, Jeremiah (D Ala.) Dec. 28, 1814-May 21, 1865; Senate Nov. 30, 1849-53.

CLEMENS, Sherrard (D Va.) April 28, 1820-June 30, 1881; House Dec. 6, 1852-53, 1857-61.

CLEMENTE, Louis Gary (D N.Y.) June 10, 1908-May 13, 1968; House 1949-53.

CLEMENTS, Andrew Jackson (U Tenn.) Dec. 23, 1832-Nov. 7, 1913; House 1861-63.

CLEMENTS, Earle C. (D Ky.) Oct. 22, 1896-—; House 1945-Jan. 6, 1948; Senate Nov. 27, 1950-57; Gov. Jan. 1948-Nov. 1950.

CLEMENTS, Isaac (R Ill.) March 31, 1837-May 31, 1909; House 1873-75.

CLEMENTS, Judson Claudius (D Ga.) Feb. 12, 1846-June 18, 1917; House 1881-91.

CLEMENTS, Newton Nash (— Ala.) Dec. 23, 1837-Feb. 20, 1900; House Dec. 8, 1800-81.

CLENDENIN, David (— Ohio) ? - ?; House Oct. 11, 1814-17.

CLEVELAND, Chauncey Fitch (D Conn.) Feb. 16, 1799-June 6, 1887; House 1849-53; Gov. 1842-44.

CLEVELAND, James Colgate (R N.H.) June 13, 1920-—; House 1963-81.

CLEVELAND, Jesse Franklin (UD Ga.) Oct. 25, 1804-June 22, 1841; House Oct. 5, 1835-39.

CLEVELAND, Orestes (D N.J.) March 2, 1829-March 30, 1896; House 1869-71.

CLEVENGER, Cliff (R Ohio) Aug. 20, 1885-Dec. 13, 1960; House 1939-59.

CLEVENGER, Raymond Francis (D Mich.) June 6, 1926-—; House 1965-67.

CLEVER, Charles P. (D N.M.) Feb. 23, 1830-July 8, 1874; House (Terr. Del.) Sept. 2, 1867-Feb. 20, 1869.

CLIFFORD, Nathan (D Maine) Aug. 18, 1803-July 25, 1881; House 1839-43; Atty. Gen. 1846-48; Assoc. Justice Supreme Court 1858-81.

CLIFT, Joseph Wales (R Ga.) Sept. 30, 1837-May 2, 1908; House July 25, 1868-69.

CLINCH, Duncan Lamont (W Ga.) April 6, 1787-Nov. 27, 1849; House Feb. 15, 1844-45.

CLINE, Cyrus (D Ind.) July 12, 1856-Oct. 5, 1923; House 1909-17.

CLINGER, William Floyd Jr. (R Pa.) April 4, 1929-—; House 1979-—.

CLINGMAN, Thomas Lanier (D N.C.) July 27, 1812-Nov. 3, 1897; House 1843-45, 1847-May 7, 1858 (1843-45 Whig, 1847-58 Democrat); Senate May 7, 1858-March 28, 1861.

CLINTON, De Witt (half brother of James Graham Clinton, cousin of George Clinton) (D N.Y.) March 2, 1769-Feb. 11, 1828; Senate Feb. 9, 1802-Nov. 4, 1803; Gov. 1817-21, 1825-28.

CLINTON, George (cousin of De Witt Clinton, James Graham Clinton) (D N.Y.) June 6, 1771-Sept. 16, 1809; House Feb. 14, 1805-09.

CLINTON, James Graham (half brother of De Witt Clinton, cousin of George Clinton) (D N.Y.) Jan. 2, 1804-May 28, 1849; House 1841-45.

CLIPPINGER, Roy (R Ill.) Jan. 13, 1886-Dec. 24, 1962; House Nov. 6, 1945-49.

CLOPTON, David (SRD Ala.) Sept. 19, 1820-Feb. 5, 1892; House 1859-Jan. 21, 1861.

CLOPTON, John (D Va.) Feb. 7, 1756-Sept. 11, 1816; House 1795-99, 1801-Sept. 11, 1816.

CLOUSE, Wynne F. (R Tenn.) Aug. 29, 1883-Feb. 19, 1944; House 1921-23.

CLOVER, Benjamin Hutchinson (FA Kan.) Dec. 22, 1837-Dec. 30, 1899; House 1891-93.

CLOWNEY, William Kennedy (SRD S.C.) March 21, 1797-March 12, 1851; House 1833-35, 1837-39 (1833-35 Nullifier, 1837-39 State Rights Democrat).

CLUETT, Ernest Harold (R N.Y.) July 13, 1874-Feb. 4, 1954; House 1937-43.

CLUNIE, Thomas Jefferson (D Calif.) March 25, 1852-June 30, 1903; House 1889-91.

CLYMER, George (F Pa.) March 16, 1739-Jan. 23, 1813; House 1789-91; Cont. Cong. 1776-78, 1780-83.

CLYMER, Hiester (nephew of William Hiester, cousin of Isaac Ellmaker Hiester) (D Pa.) Nov. 3, 1827-June 12, 1884; House 1873-81.

COAD, Merwin (D Iowa) Sept. 28, 1924-—; House 1957-63.

COADY, Charles Pearce (D Md.) Feb. 22, 1868-Feb. 16, 1934; House Nov. 4, 1913-21.

COATS, Daniel R. (R Ind.) May 16, 1943-—; House 1981-—.

COBB, Amasa (R Wis.) Sept. 27, 1823-July 5, 1905; House 1863-71.

COBB, Clinton Levering (R N.C.) Aug. 25, 1842-April 30, 1879; House 1860-75.

COBB, David (F Mass.) Sept. 14, 1748-April 17, 1830; House 1793-95.

COBB, George Thomas (D N.J.) Oct. 13, 1813-Aug. 12, 1870; House 1861-63.

COBB, Howell (uncle of Howell Cobb) (— Ga.) Aug. 3, 1772-May 26, 1818; House 1807-12.

COBB, Howell (nephew of the preceding) (D Ga.) Sept. 7, 1815-Oct. 9, 1868; House 1843-51, 1855-57; Speaker 1849-51; Gov. 1851-53; Secy. of the Treasury 1857-60.

COBB, James Edward (— Ala.) Oct. 5, 1835-June 2, 1903; House 1887-April 21, 1896.

COBB, Seth Wallace (D Mo.) Dec. 5, 1838-May 22, 1909; House 1891-97.

COBB, Stephen Alonzo (R Kan.) June 17, 1833-Aug. 24, 1878; House 1873-75.

COBB, Thomas Reed (D Ind.) July 2, 1828-June 23, 1892; House 1877-87.

COBB, Thomas Willis (— Ga.) 1784-Feb. 1, 1830; House 1817-21, 1823-Dec. 6, 1824; Senate Dec. 6, 1824-28.

COBB, Williamson Robert Winfield (D Ala.) June 8, 1807-Nov. 1, 1864; House 1847-Jan. 30, 1861.

COBEY, William Wilfred Jr. (R N.C.) May 13, 1939-—; House 1985-—.

COBLE, Howard (R N.C.) March 18, 1931-—; House 1985-—.

COBURN, Frank Potter (D Wis.) Dec. 6, 1858-Nov. 2, 1932; House 1891-93.

COBURN, John (R Ind.) Oct. 27, 1825-Jan. 28, 1908; House 1867-75.

COBURN, Stephen (R Maine) Nov. 11, 1817-July 4, 1882; House Jan. 2-March 3, 1861.

COCHRAN, Alexander Gilmore (D Pa.) March 20, 1846-May 1, 1928; House 1875-77.

COCHRAN, Charles Fremont (D Mo.) Sept. 27, 1846-Dec. 19, 1906; House 1897-1905.

COCHRAN, James (grandfather of James Cochrane Dobbin) (D N.C.) about 1767-April 7, 1813; House 1809-13.

COCHRAN, James (— N.Y.) Feb. 11, 1769-Nov. 7, 1848; House 1797-99.

COCHRAN, John Joseph (D Mo.) Aug. 11, 1880-March 6, 1947; House Nov. 2, 1926-47.

COCHRAN, Thomas Cunningham (R Pa.) Nov. 30, 1877-Dec. 10, 1957; House 1927-35.

COCHRAN, William Thad (R Miss.) Dec. 7, 1937-—; House 1973-Dec. 26, 1978; Senate Dec. 27, 1978-—.

COCHRANE, Aaron Van Schaick (nephew of Isaac Whitbeck Van Schaick) (R N.Y.) March 14, 1858-Sept. 7, 1943; House 1897-1901.

COCHRANE, Clark Betton (uncle of George Cochrane Hazelton and Gerry Whiting Hazelton) (R N.Y.) May 31, 1815-March 5, 1867; House 1857-61.

COCHRANE, John (SRD N.Y.) Aug. 27, 1813-Feb. 7, 1898; House 1857-61.

COCKE, John (son of William Cocke, uncle of William Michael Cocke) (— Tenn.) 1772-Feb. 16, 1854; House 1819-27.

COCKE, William (father of John Cocke, grandfather of William Michael Cocke) (— Tenn.) 1747-Aug. 22, 1828; Senate Aug. 2, 1796-March 3, 1797, April 22-Sept. 26, 1797, 1799-1805.

COCKE, William Michael (grandson of William Cocke, nephew of John Cocke) (D Tenn.) July 16, 1815-Feb. 6, 1896; House 1845-49.

COCKERILL, Joseph Randolph (D Ohio) Jan. 2, 1818-Oct. 23, 1875; House 1857-59.

COCKRAN, William Bourke (D N.Y.) Feb. 28, 1854-March 1, 1923; House 1887-89, Nov. 3, 1891-95, Feb. 23, 1904-09, 1921-March 1, 1923.

COCKRELL, Francis Marion (brother of Jeremiah Vardaman Cockrell) (D Mo.) Oct. 1, 1834-Dec. 13, 1915; Senate 1875-1905.

COCKRELL, Jeremiah Vardaman (brother of Francis Marion Cockrell) (D Texas) May 7, 1832-March 18, 1915; House 1893-97.

COCKS, William Willets (brother of Frederick Cocks Hicks) (R N.Y.) July 24, 1861-May 24, 1932; House 1905-11.

CODD, George Pierre (R Mich.) Dec. 7, 1869-Feb. 16, 1927; House 1921-23.

CODDING, James Hodge (R Pa.) July 8, 1849-Sept. 12, 1919; House Nov. 5, 1895-99.

COELHO, Anthony Lee (D Calif.) June 15, 1942-—; House 1979-—.

COFFEE, Harry Buffington (D Neb.) March 16, 1890-Oct. 3, 1972; House 1935-43.

COFFEE, John (D Ga.) Dec. 3, 1782-Sept. 25, 1836; House 1833-Sept. 25, 1836.

COFFEE, John Main (D Wash.) Jan. 23, 1897-June 3, 1983; House 1937-47.

COFFEEN, Henry Asa (D Wyo.) Feb. 14, 1841-Dec. 9, 1912; House 1893-95.

COFFEY, Robert Lewis Jr. (D Pa.) Oct. 21, 1918-April 20, 1949; House Jan. 3-April 20, 1949.

COFFIN, Charles Dustin (W Ohio) Sept. 9, 1805-Feb. 28, 1880; House Dec. 20, 1837-39.

COFFIN, Charles Edward (R Md.) July 18, 1841-May 24, 1912; House Nov. 6, 1894-97.

COFFIN, Frank Morey (D Maine) July 11, 1919-—; House 1957-61.

COFFIN, Howard Aldridge (R Mich.) June 11, 1877-Feb. 28, 1956; House 1947-49.

COFFIN, Peleg Jr. (— Mass.) Nov. 3, 1756-March 6, 1805; House 1793-95.

COFFIN, Thomas Chalkley (D Idaho) Oct. 25, 1887-June 8, 1934; House 1933-June 8, 1934.

COFFROTH, Alexander Hamilton (D Pa.) May 18, 1828-Sept. 2, 1906; House 1863-65, Feb. 19-July 18, 1866, 1879-81.

COGHLAN, John Maxwell (R Calif.) Dec. 8, 1835-March 26, 1879; House 1871-73.

COGSWELL, William (R Mass.) Aug. 23, 1838-May 22, 1895; House 1887-May 22, 1895.

COHELAN, Jeffrey (D Calif.) June 24, 1914-—; House 1959-71.

COHEN, John Sanford (D Ga.) Feb. 26, 1870-May 13, 1935; Senate April 25, 1932-Jan. 11, 1933.

COHEN, William Sebastian (R Maine) Aug. 28, 1940-—; House 1973-79; Senate 1979-—.

COHEN, William Wolfe (D N.Y.) Sept. 6, 1874-Oct. 12, 1940; House 1927-29.

COIT, Joshua (F Conn.) Oct. 7, 1758-Sept. 5, 1798; House 1793-Sept. 5, 1798.

COKE, Richard (nephew of Richard Coke Jr.) (D Texas) March 13, 1829-May 14, 1897; Senate 1877-95; Gov. Dec. 1873-Dec. 1, 1877.

COKE, Richard Jr. (uncle of Richard Coke) (JD Va.) Nov. 16, 1790-March 31, 1851; House 1829-33.

COLCOCK, William Ferguson (D S.C.) Nov. 5, 1804-June 13, 1889; House 1849-53.

COLDEN, Cadwallader David (D N.Y.) April 4, 1769-Feb. 7, 1834; House Dec. 12, 1821-23.

COLDEN, Charles J. (D Calif.) Aug. 24, 1870-April 15, 1938; House 1933-April 15, 1938.

COLE, Albert McDonald (R Kan.) Oct. 13, 1901- —; House 1945-53.

COLE, Cornelius (UR Calif.) Sept. 17, 1822-Nov. 3, 1924; House 1863-65; Senate 1867-73.

COLE, Cyrenus (R Iowa) Jan. 13, 1863-Nov. 14, 1939; House July 19, 1921-33.

COLE, George Edward (D Wash.) Dec. 23, 1826-Dec. 3, 1906; House (Terr. Del.) 1863-65; Gov. (Wash. Terr.) Nov. 1866-March 4, 1867.

COLE, Nathan (R Mo.) July 26, 1825-March 4, 1904; House 1877-79.

COLE, Orsamus (W Wis.) Aug. 23, 1819-May 5, 1903; House 1849-51.

COLE, Ralph Dayton (brother of Raymond Clinton Cole) (R Ohio) Nov. 30, 1873-Oct. 15, 1932; House 1905-11.

COLE, Raymond Clinton (brother of Ralph Dayton Cole) (R Ohio) Aug. 21, 1870-Feb. 8, 1957; House 1919-25.

COLE, William Clay (R Mo.) Aug. 29, 1897-Sept. 23, 1965; House 1943-49, 1953-55.

COLE, William Hinson (D Md.) Jan. 11, 1837-July 8, 1886; House 1885-July 8, 1886.

COLE, William Purington Jr. (D Md.) May 11, 1889-Sept. 22, 1957; House 1927-29, 1931-Oct. 26, 1942.

COLE, William Sterling (R N.Y.) April 18, 1904- —; House 1935-Dec. 1, 1957.

COLEMAN, E. Thomas (R Mo.) May 29, 1943- —; House Nov. 2, 1976-—.

COLEMAN, Hamilton Dudley (R La.) May 12, 1845-March 16, 1926; House 1889-91.

COLEMAN, Nicholas Daniel (JD Ky.) April 22, 1800-May 11, 1874; House 1829-31.

COLEMAN, Ronald D. (D Texas) Nov. 29, 1941- —; House 1983-—.

COLEMAN, William Henry (R Pa.) Dec. 28, 1871-June 3, 1943; House 1915-17.

COLERICK, Walpole Gillespie (D Ind.) Aug. 1, 1845-Jan. 11, 1911; House 1879-83.

COLES, Isaac (father of Walter Coles) (— Va.) March 2, 1747-June 3, 1813; House 1789-91, 1793-97.

COLES, Walter (son of Isaac Coles) (D Va.) Dec. 8, 1790-Nov. 9, 1857; House 1835-45.

COLFAX, Schuyler (R Ind.) March 23, 1823-Jan. 13, 1885; House 1855-69; Speaker 1863-69; Vice Pres. 1869-73.

COLHOUN, John Ewing (cousin of John Caldwell Calhoun and Joseph Calhoun) (D S.C.) 1750-Oct. 26, 1802; Senate 1801-Oct. 26, 1802.

COLLAMER, Jacob (R Vt.) Jan. 8, 1792-Nov. 9, 1865; House 1843-49; Senate 1855-Nov. 9, 1865 (1843-49 Whig, 1855-65 Republican); Postmaster Gen. March 7, 1849-July 20, 1850.

COLLIER, Harold Reginald (R Ill.) Dec. 12, 1915- —; House 1957-75.

COLLIER, James William (D Miss.) Sept. 28, 1872-Sept. 28, 1933; House 1909-33.

COLLIER, John Allen (CD N.Y.) Nov. 13, 1787-March 24, 1873; House 1831-33.

COLLIN, John Francis (D N.Y.) April 30, 1802-Sept. 16, 1889; House 1845-47.

COLLINS, Cardiss (widow of George Washington Collins) (D Ill.) Sept. 24, 1931-—; House June 5, 1973-—.

COLLINS, Ela (father of William Collins) (D N.Y.) Feb. 14, 1786-Nov. 23, 1848; House 1823-25.

COLLINS, Francis Dolan (D Pa.) March 5, 1841-Nov. 21, 1891; House 1875-79.

COLLINS, George Washington (husband of Cardiss Collins) (D Ill.) March 5, 1925-Dec. 8, 1972; House Nov. 3, 1970-Dec. 8, 1972.

COLLINS, James M. (R Texas) April 29, 1916-—; House Aug. 24, 1968-83.

COLLINS, Patrick Andrew (D Mass.) March 12, 1844-Sept. 13, 1905; House 1883-89.

COLLINS, Ross Alexander (D Miss.) April 25, 1880-July 14, 1968; House 1921-35, 1937-43.

COLLINS, Samuel LaFort (R Calif.) Aug. 6, 1895-June 26, 1965; House 1933-37.

COLLINS, William (son of Ela Collins) (D N.Y.) Feb. 22, 1818-June 18, 1878; House 1847-49.

COLMER, William Meyers (D Miss.) Feb. 11, 1890-Sept. 9, 1980; House 1933-73.

COLQUITT, Alfred Holt (son of Walter Terry Colquitt) (D Ga.) April 20, 1824-March 26, 1894; House 1853-55; Senate 1883-March 26, 1894; Gov. 1877-82.

COLQUITT, Walter Terry (father of Alfred Holt Colquitt) (VBD Ga.) Dec. 27, 1799-May 7, 1855; House 1839-July 21, 1840, Jan. 3, 1842-43 (1839-40 State Rights Whig, 1842-43 Van Buren Democrat); Senate 1843-Feb. 1848.

COLSON, David Grant (R Ky.) April 1, 1861-Sept. 27, 1904; House 1895-99.

COLSTON, Edward (F Va.) Dec. 25, 1786-April 23, 1852; House 1817-19.

COLT, LeBaron Bradford (R R.I.) June 25, 1846-Aug. 18, 1924; Senate 1913-Aug. 18, 1924.

COLTON, Don Byron (R Utah) Sept. 15, 1876-Aug. 1, 1952; House 1921-33.

COMBEST, Larry Ed (R Texas) March 20, 1945- —; House 1985-—.

COMBS, George Hamilton Jr. (D Mo.) May 2, 1899-Nov. 29, 1977; House 1927-29.

COMBS, Jesse Martin (D Texas) July 7, 1889-Aug. 21, 1953; House 1945-53.

COMEGYS, Joseph Parsons (W Del.) Dec. 29, 1813-Feb. 1, 1893; Senate Nov. 19, 1856-Jan. 14, 1857.

COMER, Braxton Bragg (D Ala.) Nov. 7, 1848-Aug. 15, 1927; Senate March 5-Nov. 2, 1920; Gov. 1907-11.

COMINGO, Abram (D Mo.) Jan. 9, 1820-Nov. 10, 1889; House 1871-75.

COMINS, Linus Bacon (R Mass.) Nov. 29, 1817-Oct. 14, 1892; House 1855-59 (1855-57 American Party, 1857-59 Republican).

COMPTON, Barnes (great-grandson of Philip Key) (D Md.) Nov. 16, 1830-Dec. 4, 1898; House 1885-March 20, 1890, 1891-May 15, 1894.

COMPTON, C. H. Ranulf (R Conn.) Sept. 16, 1878-Jan. 26, 1974; House 1943-45.

COMSTOCK, Charles Carter (Fus. D Mich.) March 5, 1818-Feb. 20, 1900; House 1885-87.

COMSTOCK, Daniel Webster (R Ind.) Dec. 16, 1840-May 19, 1917; House March 4-May 19, 1917.

COMSTOCK, Oliver Cromwell (D N.Y.) March 1, 1780-Jan. 11, 1860; House 1813-19.

COMSTOCK, Solomon Gilman (R Minn.) May 9, 1842-June 3, 1933; House 1889-91.

CONABLE, Barber B. Jr. (R N.Y.) Nov. 2, 1922- —; House 1965-85.

CONARD, John (D Pa.) Nov. 1773-May 9, 1857; House 1813-15.

CONDICT, Lewis (AF N.J.) March 3, 1772-May 26, 1862; House 1811-17, 1821-33.

CONDIT, John (father of Silas Condit) (D N.J.) July 8, 1755-May 4, 1834; House 1799-1803, March 4-Nov. 4, 1819; Senate Sept. 1, 1803-March 3, 1809, March 21, 1809-17.

CONDIT, Silas (son of John Condit) (CD N.J.) Aug. 18, 1778-Nov. 29, 1861; House 1831-33.

CONDON, Francis Bernard (D R.I.) Nov. 11, 1891-Nov. 23, 1965; House Nov. 4, 1930-Jan. 10, 1935.

CONDON, Robert Likens (D Calif.) Nov. 10, 1912-June 3, 1976; House 1953-55.

CONGER, Edwin Hurd (R Iowa) March 7, 1843-May 18, 1907; House 1885-Oct. 3, 1890.

CONGER, Harmon Sweatland (W N.Y.) April 9, 1816-Oct. 22, 1882; House 1847-51.

CONGER, James Lockwood (FSW Mich.) Feb. 18, 1805-April 10, 1876; House 1851-53.

CONGER, Omar Dwight (R Mich.) April 1, 1818-July 11, 1898; House 1869-81; Senate 1881-87.

Biographical Index

CONKLING, Alfred (father of Frederick Augustus Conkling and Roscoe Conkling) (AJD N.Y.) Oct. 12, 1789-Feb. 5, 1874; House 1821-23.

CONKLING, Frederick Augustus (son of Alfred Conlking, brother of Roscoe Conkling) (R N.Y.) Aug. 22, 1816-Sept. 18, 1891; House 1861-63.

CONKLING, Roscoe (son of Alfred Conkling, brother of Frederick Augustus Conkling) (UR N.Y.) Oct. 3, 1829-April 18, 1888; House 1859-63, 1865-March 4, 1867; Senate 1867-May 16, 1881 (1859-63, 1865-March 4, 1867 Republican, 1867-81 Union Republican).

CONLAN, John Bertrand (R Ariz.) Sept. 17, 1930-—; House 1973-77.

CONN, Charles Gerard (D Ind.) Jan. 29, 1844-Jan. 5, 1931; House 1893-95.

CONNALLY, Thomas Terry (Tom) (D Texas) Aug. 19, 1877-Oct. 28, 1963; House 1917-29; Senate 1929-53.

CONNELL, Charles Robert (son of William Connell) (R Pa.) Sept. 22, 1864-Sept. 26, 1922; House 1921-Sept. 26, 1922.

CONNELL, Richard Edward (D N.Y.) Nov. 6, 1857-Oct. 30, 1912; House 1911-Oct. 30, 1912.

CONNELL, William (father of Charles Robert Connell) (R Pa.) Sept. 10, 1827-March 21, 1909; House 1897-1903, Feb. 10, 1904-05.

CONNELL, William James (R Neb.) July 6, 1846-Aug. 16, 1924; House 1889-91.

CONNELLY, John Robert (D Kan.) Feb. 27, 1870-Sept. 9, 1940; House 1913-19.

CONNER, James Perry (R Iowa) Jan. 27, 1851-March 19, 1924; House Dec. 4, 1900-09.

CONNER, John Cogswell (D Texas) Oct. 14, 1842-Dec. 10, 1873; House March 31, 1870-73.

CONNER, Samuel Shepard (— Mass.) about 1783-Dec. 17, 1820; House 1815-17.

CONNERY, Lawrence Joseph (brother of William Patrick Connery Jr.) (D Mass.) Oct. 17, 1895-Oct. 19, 1941; House Sept. 28, 1937-Oct. 19, 1941.

CONNERY, William Patrick Jr. (brother of Lawrence Joseph Connery) (D Mass.) Aug. 24, 1888-June 15, 1937; House 1923-June 15, 1937.

CONNESS, John (UR Calif.) Sept. 22, 1821-Jan. 10, 1909; Senate 1863-69 (elected as a Douglas Democrat).

CONNOLLY, Daniel Ward (D Pa.) April 24, 1847-Dec. 4, 1894; House 1883-85.

CONNOLLY, James Austin (R Ill.) March 8, 1843-Dec. 15, 1914; House 1895-99.

CONNOLLY, James Joseph (R Pa.) Sept. 24, 1881-Dec. 10, 1952; House 1921-35.

CONNOLLY, Maurice (D Iowa) March 13, 1877-May 28, 1921; House 1913-15.

CONNOR, Henry William (D N.C.) Aug. 5, 1793-Jan. 6, 1866; House 1821-41.

CONOVER, Simon Barclay (R Fla.) Sept. 23, 1840-April 19, 1908; Senate 1873-79.

CONOVER, William Sheldrick II (R Pa.) Aug. 27, 1928-—; House April 25, 1972-73.

CONRAD, Charles Mynn (W La.) Dec. 24, 1804-Feb. 11, 1878; Senate April 14, 1842-43; House 1849-August 17, 1850; Secy. of War Aug. 15, 1850-March 7, 1853.

CONRAD, Frederick (F Pa.) 1759-Aug. 3, 1827; House 1803-07.

CONRY, Joseph Aloysius (D Mass.) Sept. 12, 1868-June 22, 1943; House 1901-03.

CONRY, Michael Francis (D N.Y.) April 2, 1870-March 2, 1917; House 1909-March 2, 1917.

CONSTABLE, Albert (D Md.) June 3, 1805-Sept. 18, 1855; House 1845-47.

CONTE, Silvio Otto (R Mass.) Nov. 9, 1921-—; House 1959-—.

CONTEE, Benjamin (uncle of Alexander Contee Hanson, granduncle of Thomas Contee Worthington) (— Md.) 1755-Nov. 30, 1815; House 1789-91; Cont. Cong. 1787-88.

CONVERSE, George Leroy (D Ohio) June 4, 1827-March 30, 1897; House 1879-85.

CONWAY, Henry Wharton (cousin of Ambrose Hundley Sevier) (D Ark.) March 18, 1793-Nov. 9, 1827; House (Terr. Del.) 1823-Nov. 9, 1827.

CONWAY, Martin Franklin (R Kan.) Nov. 19, 1827-Feb. 15, 1882; House Jan. 29, 1861-63.

CONYERS, John Jr. (D Mich.) May 16, 1929-—; House 1965-—.

COOK, Burton Chauncey (R Ill.) May 11, 1819-Aug. 18, 1894; House 1865-Aug. 26, 1871.

COOK, Daniel Pope (— Ill.) 1794-Oct. 16, 1827; House 1819-27.

COOK, George Washington (R Colo.) Nov. 10, 1851-Dec. 18, 1916; House 1907-09.

COOK, Joel (R Pa.) March 20, 1842-Dec. 15, 1910; House Nov. 5, 1907-Dec. 15, 1910.

COOK, John Calhoun (ID Iowa) Dec. 26, 1846-June 7, 1920; House March 3, 1883, Oct. 9, 1883-85.

COOK, John Parsons (W Iowa) Aug. 31, 1817-April 17, 1872; House 1853-55.

COOK, Marlow Webster (R Ky.) July 27, 1926-—; Senate Dec. 17, 1968-Dec. 27, 1974.

COOK, Orchard (— Mass.) March 24, 1763-Aug. 12, 1819; House 1805-11.

COOK, Philip (D Ga.) July 30, 1817-May 24, 1894; House 1873-83.

COOK, Robert Eugene (D Ohio) May 19, 1920-—; House 1959-63.

COOK, Samuel Andrew (R Wis.) Jan. 28, 1849-April 4, 1918; House 1895-97.

COOK, Samuel Ellis (D Ind.) Sept. 30, 1860-Feb. 22, 1946; House 1923-25.

COOK, Zadock (— Ga.) Feb. 18, 1769-Aug. 3, 1863; House Dec. 2, 1816-19.

COOKE, Bates (AMas. N.Y.) Dec. 23, 1787-May 31, 1841; House 1831-33.

COOKE, Edmund Francis (R N.Y.) April 13, 1885-May 13, 1967; House 1929-33.

COOKE, Edward Dean (R Ill.) Oct. 17, 1849-June 24, 1897; House 1895-June 24, 1897.

COOKE, Eleutheros (NR Ohio) Dec. 25, 1787-Dec. 27, 1864; House 1831-33.

COOKE, Thomas Burrage (D N.Y.) Nov. 21, 1778-Nov. 20, 1853; House 1811-13.

COOLEY, Harold Dunbar (D N.C.) July 26, 1897-Jan. 15, 1974; House July 7, 1934-67.

COOLIDGE, Frederick Spaulding (father of Marcus Allen Coolidge) (D Mass.) Dec. 7, 1841-June 8, 1906; House 1891-93.

COOLIDGE, Marcus Allen (son of Frederick Spaulding Coolidge) (D Mass.) Oct. 6, 1865-Jan. 23, 1947; Senate 1931-37.

COOMBS, Frank Leslie (R Calif.) Dec. 27, 1853-Oct. 5, 1934; House 1901-03.

COOMBS, William Jerome (D N.Y.) Dec. 24, 1833-Jan. 12, 1922; House 1891-95.

COON, Samuel Harrison (R Ore.) April 15, 1903-May 8, 1981; House 1953-57.

COONEY, James (D Mo.) July 28, 1848-Nov. 16, 1904; House 1897-1903.

COOPER, Allen Foster (R Pa.) June 16, 1862-April 20, 1917; House 1903-11.

COOPER, Charles Merian (D Fla.) Jan. 16, 1856-Nov. 14, 1923; House 1893-97.

COOPER, Edmund (brother of Henry Cooper) (C Tenn.) Sept. 11, 1821-July 21, 1911; House July 24, 1866-67.

COOPER, Edward (R W.Va.) Feb. 26, 1873-March 1, 1928; House 1915-19.

COOPER, George Byran (D Mich.) June 6, 1808-Aug. 29, 1866; House 1859-May 15, 1860.

COOPER, George William (D Ind.) May 21, 1851-Nov. 27, 1899; House 1889-95.

COOPER, Henry (brother of Edmund Cooper) (D Tenn.) Aug. 22, 1827-Feb. 4, 1884; Senate 1871-77.

COOPER, Henry Allen (R Wis.) Sept. 8, 1850-March 1, 1931; House 1893-1919, 1921-March 1, 1931.

COOPER, James (W Pa.) May 8, 1810-March 28, 1863; House 1839-43; Senate 1849-55.

COOPER, James Haynes Shofner (D Tenn.) June 19, 1954-—; House 1983-—.

COOPER, Jere (D Tenn.) July 20, 1893-Dec. 18, 1957; House 1929-Dec. 18, 1957.

COOPER, John Gordon (R Ohio) April 27, 1872-Jan. 7, 1955; House 1915-37.

COOPER, John Sherman (R Ky.) Aug. 23, 1901- —; Senate Nov. 6, 1946-49, Nov. 5, 1952-55, Nov. 7, 1956-73.

COOPER, Mark Anthony (cousin of Eugenius Aristides Nisbet) (D Ga.) April 20, 1800-March 17, 1885; House 1839-41, Jan. 3, 1842-June 26, 1843 (1839-41, 1842-March 3, 1843 State Rights Whig; March 4-June 26, 1843 Democrat).

COOPER, Richard Matlack (— N.J.) Feb. 29, 1768-March 10, 1843; House 1829-33.

COOPER, Samuel Bronson (D Texas) May 30, 1850-Aug. 21, 1918; House 1893-1905, 1907-09.

COOPER, Thomas (F Del.) 1764-1829; House 1813-17.

COOPER, Thomas Buchecker (D Pa.) Dec. 29, 1823-April 4, 1862; House 1861-April 4, 1862.

COOPER, William (F N.Y.) Dec. 2, 1754-Dec. 22, 1809; House 1795-97, 1799-1801.

COOPER, William Craig (R Ohio) Dec. 18, 1832-Aug. 29, 1902; House 1885-91.

COOPER, William Raworth (D N.J.) Feb. 20, 1793-Sept. 22, 1856; House 1839-41.

COPELAND, Royal Samuel (D N.Y.) Nov. 7, 1868-June 17, 1938; Senate 1923-June 17, 1938.

COPLEY, Ira Clifton (nephew of Richard Henry Whiting) (R Prog. Ill.) Oct. 25, 1864-Nov. 1, 1947; House 1911-23.

CORBETT, Henry Winslow (UR Ore.) Feb. 18, 1827-March 31, 1903; Senate 1867-73.

CORBETT, Robert James (R Pa.) Aug. 25, 1905-April 25, 1971; House 1939-41, 1945-April 25, 1971.

CORCORAN, Thomas J. (R Ill.) May 23, 1939- —; House 1977-85.

CORDON, Guy (R Ore.) April 24, 1890-June 8, 1969; Senate March 4, 1944-55.

CORDOVA, Jorge Luis (New Prog. P.R.) April 20, 1907- —; House (Res. Comm.) 1969-73.

CORKER, Stephen Alfestus (D Ga.) May 7, 1830-Oct. 18, 1879; House Dec. 22, 1870-71.

CORLETT, William Wellington (R Wyo.) April 10, 1842-July 22, 1890; House (Terr. Del.) 1877-79.

CORLEY, Manuel Simeon (R S.C.) Feb. 10, 1823-Nov. 20, 1902; House July 25, 1868-69.

CORLISS, John Blaisdell (R Mich.) June 7, 1851-Dec. 24, 1929; House 1895-1903.

CORMAN, James C. (D Calif.) Oct. 20, 1920- —; House 1961-81.

CORNELL, Robert John (D Wis.) Dec. 16, 1919- —; House 1975-79.

CORNELL, Thomas (R N.Y.) Jan. 27, 1814-March 30, 1890; House 1867-69, 1881-83.

CORNING, Erastus (grandfather of Parker Corning) (D N.Y.) Dec. 14, 1794-April 9, 1872; House 1857-59, 1861-Oct. 5, 1863.

CORNING, Parker (grandson of Erastus Corning) (D N.Y.) Jan. 22, 1874-May 24, 1943; House 1923-37.

CORNISH, Johnston (D N.J.) June 13, 1858-June 26, 1920; House 1893-95.

CORNWELL, David Lance (D Ind.) June 14, 1945- —; House 1977-79.

CORRADA del RIO, Balthazar (New Prog. P.R.) April 10, 1935- —; House (Res. Comm.) 1977-85.

CORWIN, Franklin (nephew of Moses Bledso Corwin and Thomas Corwin) (R Ill.) Jan. 12, 1818-June 15, 1879; House 1873-75.

CORWIN, Moses Bledso (brother of Thomas Corwin, uncle of Franklin Corwin) (W Ohio) Jan. 5, 1790-April 7, 1872; House 1849-51, 1853-55.

CORWIN, Thomas (brother of Moses Bledso Corwin, uncle of Franklin Corwin) (R Ohio) July 29, 1794-Dec. 18, 1865; House 1831-May 30, 1840, 1859-March 12, 1861; Senate 1845-July 20, 1850 (1831-40, 1845-50 Whig, 1859-61 Republican); Gov. 1840-41; Secy. of the Treasury 1850-53.

COSDEN, Jeremiah (— Md.) 1768-Dec. 5, 1824; House 1821-March 19, 1822.

COSGROVE, John (D Mo.) Sept. 12, 1839-Aug. 15, 1925; House 1883-85.

COSTELLO, John Martin (D Calif.) Jan. 15, 1903-Aug. 28, 1976; House 1935-45.

COSTELLO, Peter Edward (R Pa.) June 27, 1854-Oct. 23, 1935; House 1915-21.

COSTIGAN, Edward Prentiss (D Colo.) July 1, 1874-Jan. 17, 1939; Senate 1931-37.

COTHRAN, James Sproull (D S.C.) Aug. 8, 1830-Dec. 5, 1897; House 1887-91.

COTTER, William Ross (D Conn.) July 18, 1926-Sept. 8, 1981; House 1971-Sept. 8, 1981.

COTTMAN, Joseph Stewart (IW Md.) Aug. 16, 1803-Jan. 28, 1863; House 1851-53.

COTTON, Aylett Rains (R Iowa) Nov. 29, 1826-Oct. 30. 1912; House 1871-75.

COTTON, Norris (R N.H.) May 11, 1900- —; House 1947-Nov. 7, 1954; Senate Nov. 8, 1954-Dec. 31, 1974; Aug. 8-Sept. 18, 1975.

COTTRELL, James La Fayette (D Ala.) Aug. 25, 1808-Sept. 7, 1885; House Dec. 7, 1846-47.

COUDERT, Frederick René Jr. (R N.Y.) May 7, 1898-May 21, 1972; House 1947-59.

COUDREY, Harry Marcy (R Mo.) Feb. 28, 1867-July 5, 1930; House June 23, 1906-11.

COUGHLIN, Clarence Dennis (uncle of Robert Lawrence Coughlin) (R Pa.) July 27, 1883-Dec. 15, 1946; House 1921-23.

COUGHLIN, Robert Lawrence (nephew of Clarence Dennis Coughlin) (R Pa.) April 11, 1929- —; House 1969- —.

COULTER, Richard (D Pa.) March 1788-April 21, 1852; House 1827-31, 1831-35 (1827-31 Independent, 1831-35 Democrat).

COURTER, James Andrew (R N.J.) Oct. 14, 1941- —; House 1979- —.

COURTNEY, William Wirt (D Tenn.) Sept. 7, 1889-April 6, 1961; House May 11, 1939-49.

COUSINS, Robert Gordon (R Iowa) Jan. 31, 1859-June 20, 1933; House 1893-1909.

COUZENS, James (R Mich.) Aug. 26, 1872-Oct. 22, 1936; Senate Nov. 29, 1922-Oct. 22, 1936.

COVERT, James Way (D N.Y.) Sept. 2, 1842-May 16, 1910; House 1877-81, 1889-95.

COVINGTON, George Washington (D Md.) Sept. 12, 1838-April 6, 1911; House 1881-85.

COVINGTON, James Harry (D Md.) May 3, 1870-Feb. 4, 1942; House 1909-Sept. 30, 1914.

COVINGTON, Leonard (D Md.) Oct. 30, 1768-Nov. 14, 1813; House 1805-07.

COVODE, John (R Pa.) March 18, 1808-Jan. 11, 1871; House 1855-63, 1867-69, Feb. 9, 1870-Jan. 11, 1871 (1855-57 Anti-Mason Whig, 1857-63, 1867-69, 1870-71 Republican).

COWAN, Edgar (R Pa.) Sept. 19, 1815-Aug. 29, 1885; Senate 1861-67.

COWAN, Jacob Pitzer (D Ohio) March 20, 1823-July 9, 1895; House 1875-77.

COWEN, Benjamin Sprague (W Ohio) Sept. 27, 1793-Sept. 27, 1860; House 1841-43.

COWEN, John Kissig (D Md.) Oct. 28, 1844-April 26, 1904; House 1895-97.

COWGER, William Owen (R Ky.) Jan. 1, 1922-Oct. 2, 1971; House 1967-71.

COWGILL, Calvin (R Ind.) Jan. 7, 1819-Feb. 10, 1903; House 1879-81.

COWHERD, William Strother (D Mo.) Sept. 1, 1860-June 20, 1915; House 1897-1905.

COWLES, Charles Holden (nephew of William Henry Harrison Cowles) (R N.C.) July 16, 1875-Oct. 2, 1957; House 1909-11.

COWLES, George Washington (R N.Y.) Dec. 6, 1823-Jan. 20, 1901; House 1869-71.

COWLES, Henry Booth (— N.Y.) March 18, 1798-May 17, 1873; House 1829-31.

COWLES, William Henry Harrison (uncle of Charles Holden Cowles) (D N.C.) April 22, 1840-Dec. 30, 1901; House 1885-93.

COX, Edward Eugene (D Ga.) April 3, 1880-Dec. 24, 1952; House 1925-Dec. 24, 1952.

COX, Isaac Newton (D N.Y.) Aug. 1, 1846-Sept. 28, 1916; House 1891-93.

COX, Jacob Dolson (R Ohio) Oct. 27, 1828-Aug. 4, 1900; House 1877-79; Gov. 1866-68; Secy. of the Interior 1869-70.

COX, James (D N.J.) June 14, 1753-Sept. 12, 1810; House 1809-Sept. 12, 1810.

COX, James Middleton (D Ohio) March 31, 1870-July 15, 1957; House 1909-Jan. 12, 1913; Gov. 1913-15, 1917-21.

Biographical Index

COX, Leander Martin (AP Ky.) May 7, 1812-March 19, 1865; House 1853-55, 1855-57 (1853-55 Whig, 1855-57 American Party).

COX, Nicholas Nichols (D Tenn.) Jan. 6, 1837-May 2, 1912; House 1891-1901.

COX, Samuel Sullivan (D Ohio/N.Y.) Sept. 30, 1824-Sept. 10, 1889; House (Ohio) 1857-65, (N.Y.) 1869-73, Nov. 4, 1873-May 20, 1885, Nov. 2, 1886-Sept. 10, 1889; Speaker pro tempore 1876.

COX, William Elijah (D Ind.) Sept. 6, 1861-March 11, 1942; House 1907-19.

COX, William Ruffin (D N.C.) March 11, 1831-Dec. 26, 1919; House 1881-87.

COXE, William Jr. (F N.J.) May 3, 1762-Feb. 25, 1831; House 1813-15.

COYLE, William Radford (R Pa.) July 10, 1878-Jan. 30, 1962; House 1925-27, 1929-33.

COYNE, James K. (R Pa.) Nov. 17, 1946- —; House 1981-83.

COYNE, William J. (D Pa.) Aug. 24, 1936- —; House 1981- —.

CRABB, George Whitfield (W Ala.) Feb. 22, 1804-Aug. 15, 1846; House Sept. 4, 1838-41.

CRABB, Jeremiah (D Md.) 1760-1800; House 1795-96.

CRADDOCK, John Durrett (R Ky.) Oct. 26, 1881-May 20, 1942; House 1929-31.

CRADLEBAUGH, John (— Nev.) Feb. 22, 1819-Feb. 22, 1872; House (Terr. Del.) Dec. 2, 1861-1863.

CRAFTS, Samuel Chandler (— Vt.) Oct. 6, 1768-Nov. 19, 1853; House 1817-25; Senate April 23, 1842-43; Gov. 1828-31.

CRAGIN, Aaron Harrison (AP N.H.) Feb. 3, 1821-May 10, 1898; House 1855-59; Senate 1865-77 (1855-57, 1865-77 American Party, 1857-59 Republican).

CRAGO, Thomas Spencer (R Pa.) Aug. 8, 1866-Sept. 12, 1925; House 1911-13, 1915-21, Sept. 20, 1921-23.

CRAIG, Alexander Kerr (D Pa.) Feb. 21, 1828-July 29, 1892; House Feb. 6, 1892-July 29, 1892.

CRAIG, George Henry (R Ala.) Dec. 25, 1845-Jan. 26, 1923; House Jan. 9-March 3, 1885.

CRAIG, Hector (JD N.Y.) 1775-Jan. 31, 1842; House 1823-25, 1829-July 12, 1830.

CRAIG, James (D Mo.) Feb. 28, 1818-Oct. 22, 1888; House 1857-61.

CRAIG, Larry E. (R Idaho) July 20, 1945- —; House 1981- —.

CRAIG, Robert (D Va.) 1792-Nov. 25, 1852; House 1829-33, 1835-41.

CRAIG, Samuel Alfred (R Pa.) Nov. 19, 1839-March 17, 1920; House 1889-91.

CRAIG, William Benjamin (D Ala.) Nov. 2, 1877-Nov. 27, 1925; House 1907-11.

CRAIGE, Francis Burton (D N.C.) March 13, 1811-Dec. 30, 1875; House 1853-61.

CRAIK, William (— Md.) Oct. 31, 1761-prior to 1814; House Dec. 5, 1796-1801.

CRAIL, Joe (R Calif.) Dec. 25, 1877-March 2, 1938; House 1927-33.

CRAIN, William Henry (D Texas) Nov. 25, 1848-Feb. 10, 1896; House 1885-Feb. 10, 1896.

CRALEY, Nathaniel Nieman Jr. (D Pa.) Nov. 17, 1927- —; House 1965-67.

CRAMER, John (D N.Y.) May 17, 1779-June 1, 1870; House 1833-37.

CRAMER, William Cato (R Fla.) Aug. 4, 1922- —; House 1955-71.

CRAMTON, Louis Convers (R Mich.) Dec. 2, 1875-June 23, 1966; House 1913-31.

CRANE, Daniel Bever (brother of Philip Miller Crane) (R Ill.) Jan. 10, 1936- —; House 1979-85.

CRANE, Joseph Halsey (W Ohio) Aug. 31, 1782-Nov. 13, 1851; House 1829-37.

CRANE, Philip Miller (brother of Daniel Bever Crane) (R Ill.) Nov. 3, 1930- —; House Nov. 25, 1969- —.

CRANE, Winthrop Murray (R Mass.) April 23, 1853-Oct. 2, 1920; Senate Oct. 12, 1904-13; Gov. 1900-03.

CRANFORD, John Walter (D Texas) 1862-March 3, 1899; House 1897-March 3, 1899.

CRANSTON, Alan (D Calif.) June 19, 1914- —; Senate 1969- —.

CRANSTON, Henry Young (brother of Robert Bennie Cranston) (W R.I.) Oct. 9, 1789-Feb. 12, 1864; House 1843-47.

CRANSTON, Robert Bennie (brother of Henry Young Cranston) (L&OW R.I.) Jan. 14, 1791-Jan. 27, 1873; House 1837-43, 1847-49 (1837-43 Whig, 1847-49 Law & Order Whig).

CRAPO, William Wallace (R Mass.) May 16, 1830-Feb. 28, 1926; House Nov. 2, 1875-83.

CRARY, Isaac Edwin (D Mich.) Oct. 2, 1804-May 8, 1854; House Jan. 26, 1837-41.

CRAVENS, James Addison (second cousin of James Harrison Cravens) (D Ind.) Nov. 4, 1818-June 20, 1893; House 1861-65.

CRAVENS, James Harrison (second cousin of James Addison Cravens) (W Ind.) Aug. 2, 1802-Dec. 4, 1876; House 1841-43.

CRAVENS, Jordan Edgar (cousin of William Ben Cravens) (D Ark.) Nov. 7, 1830-April 8, 1914; House 1877-83.

CRAVENS, William Ben (father of William Fadjo Cravens, cousin of Jordan Edgar Cravens) (D Ark.) Jan. 17, 1872-Jan. 13, 1939; House 1907-13, 1933-Jan. 13, 1939.

CRAVENS, William Fadjo (son of William Ben Cravens) (D Ark.) Feb. 15, 1889-April 16, 1974; House Sept. 12, 1939-49.

CRAWFORD, Coe Isaac (R S.D.) Jan. 14, 1858-April 25, 1944; Senate 1909-15; Gov. 1907-09.

CRAWFORD, Fred Lewis (R Mich.) May 5, 1888-April 13, 1957; House 1935-53.

CRAWFORD, George Washington (W Ga.) Dec. 22, 1798-July 22, 1872; House Jan. 7-March 3, 1843; Gov. 1843-47; Secy. of War 1849-50.

CRAWFORD, Joel (D Ga.) June 15, 1783-April 5, 1858; House 1817-21.

CRAWFORD, Martin Jenkins (D Ga.) March 17, 1820-July 23, 1883; House 1855-Jan. 23, 1861.

CRAWFORD, Thomas Hartley (JD Pa.) Nov. 14, 1786-Jan. 27, 1863; House 1829-33.

CRAWFORD, William (D Pa.) 1760-Oct. 23, 1823; House 1809-17.

CRAWFORD, William Harris (— Ga.) Feb. 24, 1772-Sept. 15, 1834; Senate Nov. 7, 1807-March 23, 1813; Pres. pro tempore 1812; Secy. of War 1815-16; Secy. of the Treasury 1816-25.

CRAWFORD, William Thomas (D N.C.) June 1, 1856-Nov. 16, 1913; House 1891-95, 1899-May 10, 1900, 1907-09.

CREAGER, Charles Edward (R Okla.) April 28, 1873-Jan. 11, 1964; House 1909-11.

CREAL, Edward Wester (D Ky.) Nov. 20, 1883-Oct. 13, 1943; House Nov. 5, 1935-Oct. 13, 1943.

CREAMER, Thomas James (D N.Y.) May 26, 1843-Aug. 4, 1914; House 1873-75, 1901-03.

CREBS, John Montgomery (D Ill.) April 9, 1830-June 26, 1890; House 1869-73.

CREELY, John Vaudain (R Pa.) Nov. 14, 1839-Sept. 28, 1900; House 1871-73.

CREIGHTON, William Jr. (D Ohio) Oct. 29, 1778-Oct. 8, 1851; House May 4, 1813-17, 1827-28, 1829-33.

CRESWELL, John Andrew Jackson (R Md.) Nov. 18, 1828-Dec. 23, 1891; House 1863-65; Senate March 9, 1865-67; Postmaster Gen. 1869-74.

CRETELLA, Albert William (R Conn.) April 22, 1897-May 24, 1979; House 1953-59.

CRIPPA, Edward David (R Wyo.) April 8, 1899-Oct. 20, 1960; Senate June 24-Nov. 28, 1954.

CRISFELD, John Woodland (UR Md.) Nov. 8, 1806-Jan. 12, 1897; House 1847-49, 1861-63 (1847-49 Whig, 1861-63 Union Republican).

CRISP, Charles Frederick (father of Charles Robert Crisp) (D Ga.) Jan. 29, 1845-Oct. 23, 1896; House 1883-Oct. 23, 1896; Speaker 1891-95.

CRISP, Charles Robert (son of Charles Frederick Crisp) (D Ga.) Oct. 19, 1870-Feb. 7, 1937; House Dec. 19, 1896-97, 1913-Oct. 7, 1932.

CRIST, Henry (— Ky.) Oct. 20, 1764-Aug. 11, 1844; House 1809-11.

CRITCHER, John (C Va.) March 11, 1820-Sept. 27, 1901; House 1871-73.

CRITTENDEN, John Jordan (uncle of Thomas Theodore Crittenden) (U Ky.) Sept. 10, 1787-July 26, 1863; Senate 1817-19, 1835-41, March 31, 1842-June 12, 1848, 1855-61; House 1861-63; Gov. 1848-July 22, 1850; Atty. Gen. March 5-Sept. 13, 1841, July 22, 1850-53.

CRITTENDEN, Thomas Theodore (nephew of John Jordan Crittenden) (D Mo.) Jan. 1, 1832-May 29, 1909; House 1873-75, 1877-79; Gov. 1881-85.

CROCHERON, Henry (brother of Jacob Crocheron) (D N.Y.) Dec. 26, 1772-Nov. 8, 1819; House 1815-17.

CROCHERON, Jacob (brother of Henry Crocheron) (JD N.Y.) Aug. 23, 1774-Dec. 27, 1849; House 1829-31.

CROCKER, Alva (R Mass.) Oct. 14, 1801-Dec. 26, 1874; House Jan. 2, 1872-Dec. 26, 1874.

CROCKER, Samuel Leonard (W Mass.) March 31, 1804-Feb. 10, 1883; House 1853-55.

CROCKETT, David (father of John Wesley Crockett) (W Tenn.) Aug. 17, 1786-March 6, 1836; House 1827-31, 1833-35 (1827-31 Democrat, 1833-35 Whig).

CROCKETT, George W. Jr. (D Mich.) Aug. 10, 1909- —; House Nov. 12, 1980- —.

CROCKETT, John Wesley (son of David Crockett) (W Tenn.) July 10, 1807-Nov. 24, 1852; House 1837-41.

CROFT, George William (father of Theodore Gaillard Croft) (D S.C.) Dec. 20, 1846-March 10, 1904; House 1903-March 10, 1904.

CROFT, Theodore Gaillard (son of George William Croft) (D S.C.) Nov. 26, 1874-March 23, 1920; House May 17, 1904-05.

CROLL, William Martin (D Pa.) April 9, 1866-Oct. 21, 1929; House 1923-25.

CROMER, George Washington (R Ind.) May 13, 1856-Nov. 8, 1936; House 1899-1907.

CRONIN, Paul William (R Mass.) March 14, 1938- —; House 1973-75.

CROOK, Thurman Charles (D Ind.) July 18, 1891-Oct. 23, 1981; House 1949-51.

CROOKE, Philip Schuyler (R N.Y.) March 2, 1810-March 17, 1881; House 1873-75.

CROSBY, Charles Noel (D Pa.) Sept. 29, 1876-Jan. 26, 1951; House 1933-39.

CROSBY, John Crawford (D Mass.) June 15, 1859-Oct. 14, 1943; House 1891-93.

CROSS, Edward (D Ark.) Nov. 11, 1798-April 6, 1887; House 1839-45.

CROSS, Oliver Harian (D Texas) July 13, 1868-April 24, 1960; House 1929-37.

CROSSER, Robert (D Ohio) June 7, 1874-June 3, 1957; House 1913-19, 1923-55.

CROSSLAND, Edward (D Ky.) June 30, 1827-Sept. 11, 1881; House 1871-75.

CROUCH, Edward (D Pa.) Nov. 9, 1764-Feb. 2, 1827; House Oct. 12, 1813-15.

CROUNSE, Lorenzo (R Neb.) Jan. 27, 1834-May 13, 1909; House 1873-77; Gov. 1893-95.

CROUSE, George Washington (R Ohio) Nov. 23, 1832-Jan. 5, 1912; House 1887-89.

CROW, Charles Augustus (R Mo.) March 31, 1873-March 20, 1938; House 1909-11.

CROW, William Evans (father of William Josiah Crow) (R Pa.) March 10, 1870-Aug. 2, 1922; Senate Oct. 24, 1921-Aug. 2, 1922.

CROW, William Josiah (son of William Evans Crow) (R Pa.) Jan. 22, 1902-Oct. 13, 1974; House 1947-49.

CROWE, Eugene Burgess (D Ind.) Jan. 5, 1878-May 12, 1970; House 1931-41.

CROWELL, John (— Ala.) Sept. 18, 1780-June 25, 1846; House (Terr. Del.) Jan. 29, 1818-19; (Rep.) Dec. 14, 1819-21.

CROWELL, John (W Ohio) Sept. 15, 1801-March 8, 1883; House 1847-51.

CROWLEY, Joseph Burns (D Ohio) July 19, 1858-June 25, 1931; House 1899-1905.

CROWLEY, Miles (D Texas) Feb. 22, 1859-Sept. 22, 1921; House 1895-97.

CROWLEY, Richard (R N.Y.) Dec. 14, 1836-July 22, 1908; House 1879-83.

CROWNINSHIELD, Benjamin Williams (brother of Jacob Crowninshield) (D Mass.) Dec. 27, 1772-Feb. 3, 1851; House 1823-31; Secy. of the Navy 1814-18.

CROWNINSHIELD, Jacob (brother of Benjamin Williams Crowninshield) (D Mass.) March 31, 1770-April 15, 1808; House 1803-April 15, 1808.

CROWTHER, Frank (R N.Y.) July 10, 1870-July 20, 1955; House 1919-43.

CROWTHER, George Calhoun (R Mo.) Jan. 26, 1849-March 18, 1914; House 1895-97.

CROXTON, Thomas (D Va.) March 8, 1822-July 3, 1903; House 1885-87.

CROZIER, John Hervey (W Tenn.) Feb. 10, 1812-Oct. 25, 1889; House 1845-49.

CROZIER, Robert (R Kan.) Oct. 13, 1827-Oct. 2, 1895; House Nov. 24, 1873-Feb. 12, 1874.

CRUDUP, Josiah (W N.C.) Jan. 13, 1791-May 20, 1872; House 1821-23.

CRUGER, Daniel (D N.Y.) Dec. 22, 1780-July 12, 1843; House 1817-19.

CRUMP, Edward Hull (D Tenn.) Oct. 2, 1874-Oct. 16, 1954; House 1931-35.

CRUMP, George William (JD Va.) Sept. 26, 1786-Oct. 1, 1848; House Jan. 21, 1826-27.

CRUMP, Rousseau Owen (R Mich.) May 20, 1843-May 1, 1901; House 1895-May 1, 1901.

CRUMPACKER, Edgar Dean (father of Maurice Edgar Crumpacker, cousin of Shepard J. Crumpacker Jr.) (R Ind.) May 27, 1851-May 19, 1930; House 1897-1913.

CRUMPACKER, Maurice Edgar (son of Edgar Dean Crumpacker, cousin of Shepard J. Crumpacker Jr.) (R Ore.) Dec. 19, 1886-July 24, 1927; House 1925-July 24, 1927.

CRUMPACKER, Shepard J. Jr. (cousin of Edgar Dean Crumpacker and Maurice Edgar Crumpacker) (R Ind.) Feb. 13, 1917- —; House 1951-57.

CRUTCHFIELD, William (R Tenn.) Nov. 16, 1824-Jan. 24, 1890; House 1873-75.

CULBERSON, Charles Allen (son of David Browning Culberson) (D Texas) June 10, 1855-March 19, 1925; Senate 1899-1923; Gov. 1895-99.

CULBERSON, David Browning (father of Charles Allen Culberson) (D Texas) Sept. 29, 1830-May 7, 1900; House 1875-97.

CULBERTSON, William Constantine (R Pa.) Nov. 25, 1825-May 24, 1906; House 1889-91.

CULBERTSON, William Wirt (R Ky.) Sept. 22, 1835-Oct. 31, 1911; House 1883-85.

CULBRETH, Thomas (D Md.) April 13, 1786-April 16, 1843; House 1817-21.

CULKIN, Francis Dugan (R N.Y.) Nov. 10, 1874-Aug. 4, 1943; House Nov. 6, 1928-Aug. 4, 1943.

CULLEN, Elisha Dickerson (AP Del.) April 23, 1799-Feb. 8, 1862; House 1855-57.

CULLEN, Thomas Henry (D N.Y.) March 29, 1868-March 1, 1944; House 1919-March 1, 1944.

CULLEN, William (R Ill.) March 4, 1826-Jan. 17, 1914; House 1881-85.

CULLOM, Alvan (brother of William Cullom, uncle of Shelby Moore Cullom) (W Tenn.) June 4, 1810-Dec. 6, 1896; House 1851-55.

CULLOM, Shelby Moore (nephew of Alvan Cullom and William Cullom) (R Ill.) Nov. 22, 1829-Jan. 28, 1914; House 1865-71; Senate 1883-1913; Senate majority leader 1911-13; Gov. Jan. 8, 1877-Feb. 5, 1883.

CULLOM, William (brother of Alvan Cullom, uncle of Shelby Moore Cullom) (W Tenn.) June 4, 1810-Dec. 6, 1896; House 1851-55.

CULLOP, William Allen (D Ind.) March 28, 1853-Oct. 9, 1927; House 1909-17.

CULPEPPER, John (F N.C.) 1761-Jan. 1841; House 1807-Jan. 2, 1808, Feb. 23, 1808-09, 1813-17, 1819-21, 1823-25, 1827-29.

CULVER, Charles Vernon (R Pa.) Sept. 6, 1830-Jan. 10, 1909; House 1865-67.

CULVER, Erastus Dean (W N.Y.) March 15, 1803-Oct. 13, 1889; House 1845-47.

CULVER, John Chester (D Iowa) Aug. 8, 1932- —; House 1965-75; Senate 1975-81.

CUMBACK, William (R Ind.) March 24, 1829-July 31, 1905; House 1855-57.

CUMMING, Thomas William (D N.Y.) 1814 or 1815-Oct. 13, 1855; House 1853-55.

Biographical Index

CUMMINGS, Amos Jay (D N.Y.) May 15, 1841-May 2, 1902; House 1887-89, Nov. 5, 1889-Nov. 21, 1894, Nov. 5, 1895-May 2, 1902.

CUMMINGS, Fred Nelson (D Colo.) Sept. 18, 1864-Nov. 10, 1952; House 1933-41.

CUMMINGS, Henry Johnson Brodhead (R Iowa) May 21, 1831-April 16, 1909; House 1877-79.

CUMMINGS, Herbert Wesley (D Pa.) July 13, 1873-March 4, 1956; House 1923-25.

CUMMINS, Albert Baird (R Iowa) Feb. 15, 1850-July 30, 1926; Senate Nov. 24, 1908-July 30, 1926; Pres. pro tempore 1919-25; Gov. 1902-Nov. 24, 1908.

CUMMINS, John D. (D Ohio) 1791-Sept. 11, 1849; House 1845-49.

CUNNINGHAM, Francis Alanson (D Ohio) Nov. 9, 1804-Aug. 16, 1864; House 1845-47.

CUNNINGHAM, Glenn Clarence (R Neb.) Sept. 10, 1912- —; House 1957-71.

CUNNINGHAM, Paul Harvey (R Iowa) June 15, 1890-July 16, 1961; House 1941-59.

CUNNINGHAM, John Edward III (R Wash.) March 27, 1931- —; House May 23, 1977-Jan. 3, 1979.

CURLEY, Edward Walter (D N.Y.) May 23, 1873-Jan. 6, 1940; House Nov. 5, 1935-Jan. 6, 1940.

CURLEY, James Michael (D Mass.) Nov. 20, 1874-Nov. 12, 1958; House 1911-Feb. 4, 1914, 1943-47; Gov. 1935-37.

CURLIN, William Prather Jr. (D Ky.) Nov. 30, 1933- —; House Dec. 4, 1971-73.

CURRIE, Gilbert Archibald (R Mich.) Sept. 19, 1882-June 5, 1960; House 1917-21.

CURRIER, Frank Dunklee (R N.H.) Oct. 30, 1853-Nov. 25, 1921; House 1901-13.

CURRY, Charles Forrest (father of Charles Forrest Curry Jr.) (R Calif.) March 14, 1858-Oct. 10, 1930; House 1913-Oct. 10, 1930.

CURRY, Charles Forrest Jr. (son of Charles Forrest Curry) (R Calif.) Aug. 13, 1893- —; House 1931-33.

CURRY, George (R N.M.) April 3, 1863-Nov. 27, 1947; House Jan. 8, 1912-13; Gov. (N.M. Terr.) 1907-11.

CURRY, Jabez Lamar Monroe (SRD Ala.) June 5, 1825-Feb. 12, 1903; House 1857-Jan. 21, 1861.

CURTIN, Andrew Gregg (D Pa.) April 22, 1817-Oct. 7, 1894; House 1881-87; Gov. (Republican) 1861-67.

CURTIN, Willard Sevier (R Pa.) Nov. 18, 1905- —; House 1957-67.

CURTIS, Carl Thomas (R Neb.) March 15, 1905- —; House 1939-Dec. 31, 1954; Senate Jan. 1, 1955-79.

CURTIS, Carlton Brandaga (R Pa.) Dec. 17, 1811-March 17, 1883; House 1851-55, 1873-75 (1851-55 Democrat, 1873-75 Republican).

CURTIS, Charles (R Kan.) Jan. 25, 1860-Feb. 8, 1936; House 1893-Jan. 28, 1907; Senate Jan. 29, 1907-13, 1915-29; Pres. pro tempore 1911; Senate majority leader 1924-29; Vice Pres. 1929-33.

CURTIS, Edward (W N.Y.) Oct. 25, 1801-Aug. 2, 1856; House 1837-41.

CURTIS, George Martin (R Iowa) April 1, 1844-Feb. 9, 1921; House 1895-99.

CURTIS, Laurence (R Mass.) Sept. 3, 1893- —; House 1953-63.

CURTIS, Newton Martin (R N.Y.) May 21, 1835-Jan. 8, 1910; House Nov. 3, 1891-97.

CURTIS, Samuel Ryan (R Iowa) Feb. 3, 1805-Dec. 25, 1866; House 1857-Aug. 4, 1861.

CURTIS, Thomas Bradford (R Mo.) May 14, 1911- —; House 1951-69.

CUSACK, Thomas (D Ill.) Oct. 5, 1858-Nov. 19, 1926; House 1899-1901.

CUSHING, Caleb (W Mass.) Jan. 17, 1800-Jan. 2, 1879; House 1835-43; Atty. Gen. 1853-57.

CUSHMAN, Francis Wellington (R Wash.) May 8, 1867-July 6, 1909; House 1899-July 6, 1909.

CUSHMAN, John Paine (— N.Y.) March 8, 1784-Sept. 16, 1848; House 1817-19.

CUSHMAN, Joshua (D Mass./Maine) April 11, 1761-Jan. 27, 1834; House 1819-21 (Mass.), 1821-25 (Maine).

CUSHMAN, Samuel (D N.H.) June 8, 1783-May 20, 1851; House 1835-39.

CUTCHEON, Byron M. (R Mich.) May 11, 1836-April 12, 1908; House 1883-91.

CUTHBERT, Alfred (brother of John Alfred Cuthbert) (D Ga.) Dec. 23, 1785-July 9, 1856; House Dec. 13, 1813-Nov. 9, 1816, 1821-27; Senate Jan. 12, 1835-43.

CUTHBERT, John Alfred (brother of Alfred Cuthbert) (D Ga.) June 3, 1788-Sept. 22, 1881; House 1819-21.

CUTLER, Augustus William (D N.J.) Oct. 22, 1827-Jan. 1, 1897; House 1875-79.

CUTLER, Manasseh (F Mass.) May 13, 1742-July 28, 1823; House 1801-05.

CUTLER, William Parker (R Ohio) July 12, 1812-April 11, 1889; House 1861-63.

CUTTING, Bronson Murray (R N.M.) June 23, 1888-May 6, 1935; Senate Dec. 29, 1927-Dec. 6, 1928, 1929-May 6, 1935.

CUTTING, Francis Brockholst (D N.Y.) Aug. 6, 1804-June 26, 1870; House 1853-55.

CUTTING, John Tyler (R Calif.) Sept. 7, 1844-Nov. 24, 1911; House 1891-93.

CUTTS, Charles (F N.H.) Jan. 31, 1769-Jan. 25, 1846; Senate June 21, 1810-March 3, 1813, April 2-June 10, 1813.

CUTTS, Marsena Edgar (R Iowa) May 22, 1833-Sept. 1, 1883; House 1881-Sept. 1, 1883.

CUTTS, Richard (D Mass.) June 28, 1771-April 7, 1845; House 1801-13.

D

DADDARIO, Emilio Quincy (D Conn.) Sept. 24, 1918- —; House 1959-71.

DAGGETT, David (F Conn.) Dec. 31, 1764-April 12, 1851; Senate May 13, 1813-19.

DAGGETT, Rollin Mallory (R Nev.) Feb. 22, 1831-Nov. 12, 1901; House 1879-81.

DAGUE, Paul Bartram (R Pa.) May 19, 1898-Dec. 2, 1974; House 1947-67.

DAHLE, Herman Bjorn (R Wis.) March 30, 1855-April 25, 1920; House 1899-1903.

DAILY, Samuel Gordon (R Neb.) 1823-Aug. 15, 1866; House (Terr. Del.) May 18, 1860-65.

DALE, Harry Howard (D N.Y.) Dec. 3, 1868-Nov. 17, 1935; House 1913-Jan. 6, 1919.

DALE, Porter Hinman (R Vt.) March 1, 1867-Oct. 6, 1933; House 1915-Aug. 11, 1923; Senate Nov. 7, 1923-Oct. 6, 1933.

DALE, Thomas Henry (R Pa.) June 12, 1846-Aug. 21, 1912; House 1905-07.

D'ALESANDRO, Thomas Jr. (D Md.) Aug. 1, 1903- —; House 1939-May 16, 1947.

DALLAS, George Mifflin (D Pa.) July 10, 1792-Dec. 31, 1864; Senate Dec. 13, 1831-33; Vice Pres. 1845-49.

DALLINGER, Frederick William (R Mass.) Oct. 2, 1871-Sept. 5, 1955; House 1915-25, Nov. 2, 1926-Oct. 1, 1932.

DALTON, Tristram (— Mass.) May 28, 1738-May 30, 1817; Senate 1789-91.

DALY, John Burrwood (D Pa.) Feb. 13, 1872-March 12, 1939; House 1935-March 12, 1939.

DALY, William Davis (D N.J.) June 4, 1851-July 31, 1900; House 1899-July 31, 1900.

DALZELL, John (R Pa.) April 19, 1845-Oct. 2, 1927; House 1887-1913.

D'AMATO, Alfonse M. (R N.Y.) Aug. 1, 1937- —; Senate 1981- —.

D'AMOURS, Norman Edward (D N.H.) Oct. 14, 1937- —; House 1975-85.

DAMRELL, William Shapleigh (R Mass.) Nov. 29, 1809-May 17, 1860; House 1855-57, 1857-59 (1855-57 American Party, 1857-59 Republican).

DANA, Amasa (D N.Y.) Oct. 19, 1792-Dec. 24, 1867; House 1839-41, 1843-45.

DANA, Judah (D Maine) April 25, 1772-Dec. 27, 1845; Senate Dec. 7, 1836-37.

DANA, Samuel (D Mass.) June 26, 1767-Nov. 20, 1835; House Sept. 22, 1814-15.

DANA, Samuel Whittlesey (F Conn.) Feb. 13, 1760-July 21, 1830; House Jan. 3, 1797-May 10, 1810; Senate May 10, 1810-21.

DANAHER, John Anthony (R Conn.) Jan. 9, 1899- —; Senate 1939-45.

DANE, Joseph (F Maine) Oct. 25, 1778-May 1, 1858; House Nov. 6, 1820-23.

DANFORD, Lorenzo (R Ohio) Oct. 18, 1829-June 19, 1899; House 1873-79, 1895-June 19, 1899.

DANFORTH, Henry Gold (R N.Y.) June 14, 1854-April 8, 1918; House 1911-17.

DANFORTH, John Claggett (R Mo.) Sept. 5, 1936-—; Senate Dec. 27, 1976-—.

DANIEL, Charles Ezra (D S.C.) Nov. 11, 1895-Sept. 13, 1964; Senate Sept. 6-Dec. 23, 1954.

DANIEL, Henry (JD Ky.) March 15, 1786-Oct. 5, 1873; House 1827-33.

DANIEL, John Reeves Jones (D N.C.) Jan. 13, 1802-June 22, 1868; House 1841-53.

DANIEL, John Warwick (D Va.) Sept. 5, 1842-June 29, 1910; House 1885-87; Senate 1887-June 29, 1910.

DANIEL, Price Marion (D Texas) Oct. 10, 1910-—; Senate 1953-Jan. 14, 1957; Gov. Jan. 15, 1957-Jan. 15, 1963.

DANIEL, Robert Williams Jr. (R Va.) March 17, 1936-—; House 1973-83.

DANIEL, W. C. (Dan) (D Va.) May 12, 1914-—; House 1969-—.

DANIELL, Warren Fisher (D N.H.) June 26, 1826-July 30, 1913; House 1891-93.

DANIELS, Charles (R N.Y.) March 24, 1825-Dec. 20, 1897; House 1893-97.

DANIELS, Dominick V. (D N.J.) Oct. 18, 1908-—; House 1959-77.

DANIELS, Milton John (R Calif.) April 18, 1838-Dec. 1, 1914; House 1903-05.

DANIELSON, George Elmore (D Calif.) Feb. 20, 1915-—; House 1971-March 9, 1982.

DANNEMEYER, William Edward (R Calif.) Sept. 22, 1929-—; House 1979-—.

DANNER, Joel Buchanan (D Pa.) 1804-July 29, 1885; House Dec. 2, 1850-51.

DARBY, Ezra (D N.J.) June 7, 1768-Jan. 27, 1808; House 1805-Jan. 27, 1808.

DARBY, Harry (R Kan.) Jan. 23, 1895-—; Senate Dec. 2, 1949-Nov. 28, 1950.

DARBY, John Fletcher (W Mo.) Dec. 10, 1803-May 11, 1882; House 1851-53.

DARDEN, Colgate Whitehead Jr. (D Va.) Feb. 11, 1897-June 9, 1981; House 1933-37, 1939-March 1, 1941; Gov. 1942-46.

DARDEN, George (Buddy) (D Ga.) Nov. 22, 1943-—; House Nov. 10, 1983-—.

DARGAN, Edmund Strother (D Ala.) April 15, 1805-Nov. 22, 1879; House 1845-47.

DARGAN, George William (great-grandson of Lemuel Benton) (D S.C.) May 11, 1841-June 29, 1898; House 1883-91.

DARLING, Mason Cook (D Wis.) May 18, 1801-March 12, 1866; House June 9, 1848-49.

DARLING, William Augustus (R N.Y.) Dec. 27, 1817-May 26, 1895; House 1865-67.

DARLINGTON, Edward (cousin of Isaac Darlington and William Darlington) (AMas. Pa.) Sept. 17, 1795-Nov. 21, 1884; House 1833-39 (1833-37 Whig, 1837-39 Anti Mason).

DARLINGTON, Isaac (cousin of Edward Darlington and William Darlington) (F Pa.) Dec. 13, 1781-April 27, 1839; House 1817-19.

DARLINGTON, Smedley (second cousin of Edward Darlington, Isaac Darlington and William Darlington) (R Pa.) Dec. 24, 1827-June 24, 1899; House 1887-91.

DARLINGTON, William (cousin of Edward Darlington and Isaac Darlington) (D Pa.) April 28, 1782-April 23, 1863; House 1815-17, 1819-23.

DARRAGH, Archibald Bard (R Mich.) Dec. 23, 1840-Feb. 21, 1927; House 1901-09.

DARRAGH, Cornelius (W Pa.) 1809-Dec. 22, 1854; House March 26, 1844-47.

DARRALL, Chester Bidwell (R La.) June 24, 1842-Jan. 1, 1908; House 1869-Feb. 20, 1878, 1881-83.

DARROW, George Potter (R Pa.) Feb. 4, 1859-June 7, 1943; House 1915-37, 1939-41.

DASCHLE, Thomas Andrew (D S.D.) Dec. 9, 1947-—; House 1979-—.

DAUB, Harold J. Jr. (R Neb.) April 23, 1941-—; House 1981-—.

DAUGHERTY, James Alexander (D Mo.) Aug. 30, 1847-Jan. 26, 1920; House 1911-13.

DAUGHTON, Ralph Hunter (D Va.) Sept. 23, 1885-Dec. 22, 1958; House Nov. 7, 1944-47.

DAVEE, Thomas (D Maine) Dec. 9, 1797-Dec. 9, 1841; House 1837-41.

DAVENPORT, Franklin (— N.J.) Sept. 1755-July 27, 1832; Senate Dec. 5, 1798-99; House 1799-1801.

DAVENPORT, Frederick Morgan (R N.Y.) Aug. 27, 1866-Dec. 26, 1956; House 1925-33.

DAVENPORT, Harry James (D Pa.) Aug. 28, 1902-Dec. 19, 1977; House 1949-51.

DAVENPORT, Ira (R N.Y.) June 28, 1841-Oct. 6, 1904; House 1885-89.

DAVENPORT, James (brother of John Davenport of Connecticut) (— Conn.) Oct. 12, 1758-Aug. 3, 1797; House Dec. 5, 1796-Aug. 3, 1797.

DAVENPORT, James Sanford (D Okla.) Sept. 21, 1864-Jan. 3, 1940; House Nov. 16, 1907-09, 1911-17.

DAVENPORT, John (brother of James Davenport) (F Conn.) Jan. 16, 1752-Nov. 28, 1830; House 1799-1817.

DAVENPORT, John (— Ohio) Jan. 9, 1788-July 18, 1855; House 1827-29.

DAVENPORT, Samuel Arza (R Pa.) Jan. 15, 1834-Aug. 1, 1911; House 1897-1901.

DAVENPORT, Stanley Woodward (D Pa.) July 21, 1861-Sept. 26, 1921; House 1899-1901.

DAVENPORT, Thomas (F Va.) ?-Nov. 18, 1838; House 1825-35.

DAVEY, Martin Luther (D Ohio) July 25, 1884-March 31, 1946; House Nov. 5, 1918-21, 1923-29; Gov. 1935-39.

DAVEY, Robert Charles (D La.) Oct. 22, 1853-Dec. 26, 1908; House 1893-95, 1897-Dec. 26, 1908.

DAVIDSON, Alexander Caldwell (D Ala.) Dec. 26, 1826-Nov. 6, 1897; House 1885-89.

DAVIDSON, Irwin Delmore (D/L N.Y.) Jan. 2, 1906-—; House 1955-Dec. 31, 1956.

DAVIDSON, James Henry (R Wis.) June 18, 1858-Aug. 6, 1918; House 1897-1913, 1917-Aug. 6, 1918.

DAVIDSON, Robert Hamilton McWhorta (D Fla.) Sept. 23, 1832-Jan. 18, 1908; House 1877-91.

DAVIDSON, Thomas Green (D La.) Aug. 3, 1805-Sept. 11, 1883; House 1855-61.

DAVIDSON, William (F N.C.) Sept. 12, 1778-Sept. 16, 1857; House Dec. 2, 1818-21.

DAVIES, Edward (W Pa.) Nov. 1779-May 18, 1853; House 1837-41.

DAVIES, John Clay (D N.Y.) May 1, 1920-—; House 1949-51.

DAVILA, Felix Cordova (U P.R.) Nov. 20, 1878-Dec. 3, 1938; House (Res. Comm.) Aug. 7, 1917-April 11, 1932.

DAVIS, Alexander Mathews (— Va.) Jan. 17, 1833-Sept. 25, 1889; House 1873-March 5, 1874.

DAVIS, Amos (brother of Garrett Davis) (W Ky.) Aug. 15, 1794-June 11, 1835; House 1833-35.

DAVIS, Charles Russell (R Minn.) Sept. 17, 1849-July 29, 1930; House 1903-25.

DAVIS, Clifford (D Tenn.) Nov. 18, 1897-June 8, 1970; House Feb. 15, 1940-65.

DAVIS, Cushman Kellogg (R Minn.) June 16, 1838-Nov. 27, 1900; Senate 1887-Nov. 27, 1900; Gov. 1874-76.

DAVIS, David (cousin of Henry Winter Davis) (I/D Ill.) March 9, 1815-June 26, 1886; Senate 1877-83; Pres. pro tempore 1881-83; Assoc. Justice Supreme Court 1862-77.

DAVIS, Ewin Lamar (D Tenn.) Feb. 5, 1876-Oct. 23, 1949; House 1919-33.

DAVIS, Garrett (brother of Amos Davis) (D Ky.) Sept. 10, 1801-Sept. 22, 1872; House 1839-47; Senate Dec. 10, 1861-Sept. 22, 1872 (1839-47, Henry Clay Whig, 1861-67 Whig, 1867-72 Democrat).

DAVIS, George Royal (R Ill.) Jan. 3, 1840-Nov. 25, 1899; House 1879-85.

DAVIS, George Thomas (W Mass.) Jan. 12, 1810-June 17, 1877; House 1851-53.

Biographical Index

DAVIS, Glenn Robert (R Wis.) Oct. 28, 1914- -; House April 22, 1947-57, 1965-Dec. 31, 1974.

DAVIS, Henry Gassaway (brother of Thomas Beall Davis, grandfather of Davis Elkins) (D W. Va.) Nov. 16, 1823-March 11, 1916; Senate 1871-83.

DAVIS, Henry Winter (cousin of David Davis) (UU Md.) Aug. 16, 1817-Dec. 30, 1865; House 1855-61, 1863-65 (1855-57 American Party, 1857-61 Republican, 1863-65 Unconditional Unionist).

DAVIS, Horace (R Calif.) March 16, 1831-July 12, 1916; House 1877-81.

DAVIS, Jacob Cunningham (D Ill.) Sept. 16, 1820-Dec. 25, 1883; House Nov. 4, 1856-57.

DAVIS, Jacob Erastus (D Ohio) Oct. 31, 1905- -; House 1941-43.

DAVIS, James Curran (D Ga.) May 17, 1895-Dec. 18, 1981; House 1947-63.

DAVIS, James Harvey (Cyclone) (D Texas) Dec. 24, 1853-Jan. 31, 1940; House 1915-17.

DAVIS, James John (R Pa.) Oct. 27, 1873-Nov. 22, 1947; Senate Dec. 2, 1930-45; Secy. of Labor 1921-30.

DAVIS, Jeff (D Ark.) May 6, 1862-Jan. 3, 1913; Senate 1907-Jan. 3, 1913; Gov. 1901-07.

DAVIS, Jefferson (D Miss.) June 3, 1808-Dec. 6, 1889; House 1845-June 1846; Senate Aug. 10, 1847-Sept. 23, 1851, 1857-Jan. 21, 1861; Secy. of War 1853-57.

DAVIS, John (W Mass.) Jan. 13, 1787-April 19, 1854; House 1825-Jan. 14, 1834; Senate 1835-Jan. 5, 1841, March 24, 1845-53; (1825-34 National Republican, 1835-53 Whig) Gov. 1834-35, 1841-43.

DAVIS, John (D Pa.) Aug. 7, 1788-April 1, 1878; House 1839-41.

DAVIS, John (PP Kan.) Aug. 9, 1826-Aug. 1, 1901; House 1891-95.

DAVIS, John Givan (D Ind.) Oct. 10, 1810-Jan. 18, 1866; House 1851-55, 1857-61.

DAVIS, John James (father of John William Davis of W.Va.) (D W.Va.) May 5, 1835-March 19, 1916; House 1871-75.

DAVIS, John Wesley (D Ind.) April 16, 1799-Aug. 22, 1859; House 1835-37, 1839-41, 1843-47; Speaker 1845-47; Gov. (Oregon Terr.) 1853-54.

DAVIS, John William (son of John James Davis) (D W.Va.) April 13, 1873-March 24, 1955; House 1911-Aug. 29, 1913.

DAVIS, John William (D Ga.) Sept. 12, 1916- -; House 1961-75.

DAVIS, Joseph Jonathan (D N.C.) April 13, 1828-Aug. 7, 1892; House 1875-81.

DAVIS, Lowndes Henry (D Mo.) Dec. 13, 1836-Feb. 4, 1920; House 1879-85.

DAVIS, Mendel Jackson (D S.C.) Oct. 23, 1942- -; House April 27, 1971-81.

DAVIS, Noah (R N.Y.) Sept. 10, 1818-March 20, 1902; House 1869-July 15, 1870.

DAVIS, Reuben (D Miss.) Jan. 18, 1813-Oct. 14, 1890; House 1857-Jan. 12, 1861.

DAVIS, Richard David (D N.Y.) 1799-June 17, 1871; House 1841-45.

DAVIS, Robert Lee (R Pa.) Oct. 29, 1893- -; House Nov. 8, 1932-33.

DAVIS, Robert Thompson (R Mass.) Aug. 28, 1823-Oct. 29, 1906; House 1883-89.

DAVIS, Robert William (R Mich.) July 31, 1932- -; House 1979- -.

DAVIS, Robert Wyche (D Fla.) March 15, 1849-Sept. 15, 1929; House 1897-1905.

DAVIS, Roger (D Pa.) Oct. 2, 1762-Nov. 20, 1815; House 1811-15.

DAVIS, Samuel (F Mass.) 1774-April 20, 1831; House 1813-15.

DAVIS, Thomas (D R.I.) Dec. 18, 1806-July 26, 1895; House 1853-55.

DAVIS, Thomas Beall (brother of Henry Gassaway Davis) (D W.Va.) April 25, 1828-Nov. 26, 1911; House June 6, 1905-07.

DAVIS, Thomas Terry (— Ky.) ?-Nov. 15, 1807; House 1797-1803.

DAVIS, Thomas Treadwell (grandson of Thomas Tredwell) (U N.Y.) Aug. 22, 1810-May 2, 1872; House 1863-67.

DAVIS, Timothy (W Iowa) March 29, 1794-April 27, 1872; House 1857-59.

DAVIS, Timothy (R Mass.) April 12, 1821-Oct. 23, 1888; House 1855-59 (1855-57 American Party, 1857-59 Republican).

DAVIS, Warren Ransom (SRD S.C.) May 8, 1793-Jan. 29, 1835; House 1827-Jan. 29, 1835.

DAVIS, William Morris (R Pa.) Aug. 16, 1815-Aug. 5, 1891; House 1861-63.

DAVISON, George Mosby (R Ky.) March 23, 1855-Dec. 18, 1912; House 1897-99.

DAVY, John Madison (R N.Y.) June 29, 1835-April 21, 1909; House 1875-77.

DAWES, Beman Gates (son of Rufus Dawes, brother of Charles Gates Dawes) (R Ohio) Jan. 14, 1870-May 15, 1953; House 1905-09.

DAWES, Henry Laurens (R Mass.) Oct. 30, 1816-Feb. 5, 1903; House 1857-75; Senate 1875-93.

DAWES, Rufus (father of Charles Gates Dawes and Beman Gates Dawes) (R Ohio) July 4, 1838-Aug. 2, 1899; House 1881-83.

DAWSON, Albert Foster (R Iowa) Jan. 26, 1872-March 9, 1949; House 1905-11.

DAWSON, John (D Va.) 1762-March 31, 1814; House 1797-March 31, 1814; Cont. Cong. 1788-89.

DAWSON, John Bennett (D La.) March 17, 1798-June 26, 1845; House 1841-June 26, 1845.

DAWSON, John Littleton (D Pa.) Feb. 7, 1813-Sept. 18, 1870; House 1851-55, 1863-67.

DAWSON, William (D Mo.) March 17, 1848-Oct. 12, 1929; House 1885-87.

DAWSON, William Adams (R Utah) Nov. 5, 1903- -; House 1947-49, 1953-59.

DAWSON, William Crosby (SRW Ga.) Jan. 4, 1798-May 6, 1856; House Nov. 7, 1836-Nov. 13, 1841; Senate 1849-55.

DAWSON, William Levi (D Ill.) April 26, 1886-Nov. 9, 1970; House 1943-Nov. 9, 1970.

DAY, Rowland (D N.Y.) March 6, 1779-Dec. 23, 1853; House 1823-25, 1833-35.

DAY, Stephen Albion (R Ill.) July 13, 1882-Jan. 5, 1950; House 1941-45.

DAY, Timothy Crane (R Ohio) Jan. 8, 1819-April 15, 1869; House 1855-57.

DAYAN, Charles (D N.Y.) July 8, 1792-Dec. 25, 1877; House 1831-33.

DAYTON, Alston Gordon (R W.Va.) Oct. 18, 1857-July 30, 1920; House 1895-March 16, 1905.

DAYTON, Jonathan (F N.J.) Oct. 16, 1760-Oct. 9, 1824; House 1791-99; Speaker 1795-99; Senate 1799-1805; Cont. Cong. Nov. 6, 1787-89.

DAYTON, William Lewis (W N.J.) Feb. 17, 1807-Dec. 1, 1864; Senate July 2, 1842-51.

DEAL, Joseph Thomas (D Va.) Nov. 19, 1860-March 7, 1942; House 1921-29.

DEAN, Benjamin (D Mass.) Aug. 14, 1824-April 9, 1897; House March 28, 1878-79.

DEAN, Ezra (D Ohio) April 9, 1795-Jan. 25, 1872; House 1841-45.

DEAN, Gilbert (D N.Y.) Aug. 14, 1819-Oct. 12, 1870; House 1851-July 3, 1854.

DEAN, Josiah (D Mass.) March 6, 1748-Oct. 14, 1818; House 1807-09.

DEAN, Sidney (R Conn.) Nov. 16, 1818-Oct. 29, 1901; House 1855-59 (1855-57 American Party, 1857-59 Republican).

DEANE, Charles Bennett (D N.C.) Nov. 1, 1898-Nov. 24, 1969; House 1947-57.

DEAR, Cleveland (D La.) Aug. 22, 1888-Dec. 30, 1950; House 1933-37.

DEARBORN, Henry (father of Henry Alexander Scammell Dearborn) (D Mass.) Feb. 23, 1751-June 6, 1829; House 1793-97; Secy. of War 1801-09.

DEARBORN, Henry Alexander Scammell (son of Henry Dearborn) (— Mass.) March 3, 1783-July 29, 1851; House 1831-33.

DE ARMOND, David Albaugh (D Mo.) March 18, 1844-Nov. 23, 1909; House 1891-Nov. 23, 1909.

DEBERRY, Edmund (W N.C.) Aug. 14, 1787-Dec. 12, 1859; House 1829-31, 1833-45, 1849-51.

DEBOE, William Joseph (R Ky.) June 30, 1849-June 15, 1927; Senate 1897-1903.

DE BOLT, Rezin A. (D Mo.) Jan. 20, 1828-Oct. 30, 1891; House 1875-77.

DECKARD, H. Joel (R Ind.) March 7, 1942-—; House 1979-83.

DECKER, Perl D. (D Mo.) Sept. 10, 1875-Aug. 22, 1934; House 1913-19.

DeCONCINI, Dennis (D Ariz.) May 8, 1937-—; Senate 1977-—.

DEEMER, Elias (R Pa.) Jan. 3, 1838-March 29, 1918; House 1901-07.

DEEN, Braswell Drue (D Ga.) June 28, 1893-Nov. 28, 1981; House 1933-39.

DEERING, Nathaniel Cobb (R Iowa) Sept. 2, 1827-Dec. 11, 1887; House 1877-83.

DE FOREST, Henry Schermerhorn (R N.Y.) Feb. 16, 1847-Feb. 13, 1917; House 1911-13.

DE FOREST, Robert Elliott (D Conn.) Feb. 20, 1845-Oct. 1, 1924; House 1891-95.

DEFREES, Joseph Hutton (R Ind.) May 13, 1812-Dec. 21, 1885; House 1865-67.

DEGENER, Edward (R Texas) Oct. 20, 1809-Sept. 11, 1890; House March 31, 1870-71.

DEGETAU, Frederico (R P.R.) Dec. 5, 1862-Jan. 20, 1914; House (Res. Comm.) 1901-05.

DE GRAFF, John Isaac (D N.Y.) Oct. 2, 1783-July 26, 1848; House 1827-29, 1837-39.

DE GRAFFENREID, Reese Calhoun (D Texas) May 7, 1859-Aug. 29, 1902; House 1897-Aug. 29, 1902.

deGRAFFENRIED, Edward (D Ala.) June 30, 1899-Nov. 5, 1974; House 1949-53.

DE HAVEN, John Jefferson (R Calif.) March 12, 1849-Jan. 26, 1913; House 1889-Oct. 1, 1890.

DEITRICK, Frederick Simpson (D Mass.) April 9, 1875-May 24, 1948; House 1913-15.

DE JARNETTE, Daniel Coleman (D Va.) Oct. 18, 1822-Aug. 20, 1881; House 1859-61.

DE LACY, Emerson Hugh (D Wash.) May 9, 1910-—; House 1945-47.

DE LA GARZA II, Eligio (D Texas) Sept. 22, 1927-—; House 1965-—.

DE LA MATYR, Gilbert (Nat./D Ind.) July 8, 1825-May 17, 1892; House 1879-81.

DE LA MONTANYA, James (D N.Y.) March 20, 1798-April 29, 1849; House 1839-41.

DELANEY, James Joseph (D N.Y.) March 19, 1901-—; House 1945-47, 1949-Dec. 31, 1978.

DELANEY, John Joseph (D N.Y.) Aug. 21, 1878-Nov. 18, 1948; House March 5, 1918-19, 1931-Nov. 18, 1948.

DELANO, Charles (R Mass.) June 24, 1820-Jan. 23, 1883; House 1859-63.

DELANO, Columbus (R Ohio) June 4, 1809-Oct. 23, 1896; House 1845-47, 1865-67, June 3, 1868-69 (1845-47 Whig, 1865-67, 1868-69 Republican); Secy. of the Interior 1870-75.

DE LANO, Milton (R N.Y.) Aug. 11, 1844-Jan. 2, 1922; House 1887-91.

DELAPLAINE, Isaac Clason (Fus. N.Y.) Oct. 27, 1817-July 17, 1866; House 1861-63.

DE LARGE, Robert Carlos (R S.C.) March 15, 1842-Feb. 14, 1874; House 1871-Jan. 24, 1873.

DE LAY, Thomas Dale (R Texas) April 8, 1947-—; House 1985-—.

DELGADO, Francisco Afan (Nat. P.I.) Jan. 25, 1886-Oct. 27, 1964; House (Res. Comm.) 1935-Feb. 14, 1936.

DELLAY, Vincent John (D N.J.) June 23, 1907-—; House 1957-59 (1957 Republican, 1958-59 Democrat).

DELLENBACK, John Richard (R Ore.) Nov. 6, 1918-—; House 1967-75.

DELLET, James (W Ala.) Feb. 18, 1788-Dec. 21, 1848; House 1839-41, 1843-45.

DELLUMS, Ronald V. (D Calif.) Nov. 24, 1935-—; House 1971-—.

DE LUGO, Ron (D V.I.) Aug. 2, 1930-—; House (Terr. Del.) 1973-79, 1981-—.

DEMING, Benjamin F. (W Vt.) 1790-July 11, 1834; House 1833-July 11, 1834.

DEMING, Henry Champion (R Conn.) May 23, 1815-Oct. 8, 1872; House 1863-67.

DE MOTT, John (D N.Y.) Oct. 7, 1790-July 31, 1870; House 1845-47.

DE MOTTE, Mark Lindsey (R Ind.) Dec. 28, 1832-Sept. 23, 1908; House 1881-83.

DEMPSEY, John Joseph (D N.M.) June 22, 1879-March 11, 1958; House 1935-41, 1951-March 11, 1958; Gov. 1943-47.

DEMPSEY, Stephen Wallace (R N.Y.) May 8, 1862-March 1, 1949; House 1915-31.

DE MUTH, Peter Joseph (D Pa.) Jan. 1, 1892-—; House 1937-39.

DeNARDIS, Lawrence J. (R Conn.) March 18, 1938-—; House 1981-83.

DENBY, Edwin (grandson of Graham Newell Fitch) (R Mich.) Feb. 18, 1870-Feb. 8, 1929; House 1905-11; Secy. of the Navy 1921-24.

DENEEN, Charles Samuel (R Ill.) May 4, 1863-Feb. 5, 1940; Senate Feb. 26, 1925-31; Gov. 1905-13.

DENHOLM, Frank E. (D S.D.) Nov. 29, 1923-—; House 1971-75.

DENISON, Charles (nephew of George Denison) (D Pa.) Jan. 23, 1818-June 27, 1867; House 1863-June 27, 1867.

DENISON, Dudley Chase (nephew of Dudley Chase, cousin of Salmon Portland Chase) (R Vt.) Sept. 13, 1819-Feb. 10, 1905; House 1875-79.

DENISON, Edward Everett (R Ill.) Aug. 28, 1873-June 17, 1953; House 1915-31.

DENISON, George (uncle of Charles Denison) (D Pa.) Feb. 22, 1790-Aug. 20, 1831; House 1819-23.

DE NIVERNAIS, Edward James (*See* LIVERNASH, Edward James).

DENNEY, Robert Vernon (R Neb.) April 11, 1916-June 26, 1981; House 1967-71.

DENNING, William (— N.Y.) April 1740-Oct. 30, 1819; House 1809-10.

DENNIS, David Worth (R Ind.) June 7, 1912-—; House 1969-75.

DENNIS, George Robertson (D Md.) April 8, 1822-Aug. 13, 1882; Senate 1873-79.

DENNIS, John (father of John Dennis, uncle of Littleton Purnell Dennis) (F Md.) Dec. 17, 1771-Aug. 17, 1806; House 1797-1805.

DENNIS, John (son of John Dennis) (W Md.) 1807-Nov. 1, 1859; House 1837-41.

DENNIS, Littleton Purnell (nephew of John Dennis) (W Md.) July 21, 1786-April 14, 1834; House 1833-April 14, 1834.

DENNISON, David Short (R Ohio) July 29, 1918-—; House 1957-59.

DENNY, Arthur Armstrong (R Wash.) June 20, 1822-Jan. 9, 1899; House (Terr. Del.) 1865-67.

DENNY, Harmar (great-grandfather of Harmar Denny Jr.) (W Pa.) May 13, 1794-Jan. 29, 1852; House Dec. 15, 1829-37 (1829-35 Anti Mason, 1835-37 Whig).

DENNY, Harmar Denny Jr. (great-grandson of Harmar Denny) (R Pa.) July 2, 1886-Jan. 6, 1966; House 1951-53.

DENNY, James William (D Md.) Nov. 20, 1838-April 12, 1923; House 1899-1901, 1903-05.

DENNY, Walter McKennon (D Miss.) Oct. 28, 1853-Nov. 5, 1926; House 1895-97.

DENOYELLES, Peter (— N.Y.) 1766-May 6, 1829; House 1813-15.

DENSON, William Henry (D Ala.) March 4, 1846-Sept. 26, 1906; House 1893-95.

DENT, George (D Md.) 1756-Dec. 2, 1813; House 1793-1801.

DENT, John Herman (D Pa.) March 10, 1908-—; House Jan. 21, 1958-79.

DENT, Stanley Hubert Jr. (D Ala.) Aug. 16, 1869-Oct. 6, 1938; House 1909-21.

DENT, William Barton Wade (D Ga.) Sept. 8, 1806-Sept. 7, 1855; House 1853-55.

DENTON, George Kirkpatrick (father of Winfield Kirkpatrick Denton) (D Ind.) Nov. 17, 1864-Jan. 4, 1926; House 1917-19.

DENTON, Jeremiah (R Ala.) July 15, 1924-—; Senate 1981-—.

DENTON, Winfield Kirkpatrick (son of George Kirkpatrick Denton) (D Ind.) Oct. 28, 1896-Nov. 2, 1971; House 1949-53, 1955-Dec. 30, 1966.

DENVER, James William (father of Matthew Rombach Denver) (ABD Calif.) Oct. 23, 1817-Aug. 9, 1892; House 1855-57; Gov. (Kansas Terr.) 1857-58.

Biographical Index

DENVER, Matthew Rombach (son of James William Denver) (D Ohio) Dec. 21, 1870-May 13, 1954; House 1907-13.

DEPEW, Chauncey Mitchell (R N.Y.) April 23, 1834-April 5, 1928; Senate 1899-1911.

DE PRIEST, Oscar (R Ill.) March 9, 1871-May 12, 1951; House 1929-35.

DE ROUEN, Rene Louis (D La.) Jan. 7, 1874-March 27, 1942; House Aug. 23, 1927-41.

DEROUNIAN, Steven Boghos (R N.Y.) April 6, 1918- —; House 1953-65.

DERRICK, Butler Carson Jr. (D S.C.) Sept. 30, 1936- —; House 1975- —.

DERSHEM, Franklin Lewis (D Pa.) March 5, 1865-Feb. 14, 1950; House 1913-15.

DERWINSKI, Edward Joseph (R Ill.) Sept. 15, 1926- —; House 1959-83.

DE SAUSSURE, William Ford (D S.C.) Feb. 22, 1792-March 13, 1870; Senate May 10, 1852-53.

DESHA, Joseph (brother of Robert Desha) (D Ky.) Dec. 9, 1768-Oct. 11, 1842; House 1807-19; Gov. 1824-28.

DESHA, Robert (brother of Joseph Desha) (— Tenn.) Jan. 14, 1791-Feb. 6, 1849; House 1827-31.

DESTREHAN, John Noel (— La.) 1780-1824; Senate Sept. 3-Oct. 1, 1812.

DEUSTER, Peter Victor (D Wis.) Feb. 13, 1831-Dec. 31, 1904; House 1879-85.

DEVEREUX, James Patrick Sinnott (R Md.) Feb. 20, 1903- —; House 1951-59.

DE VEYRA, Jaime Carlos (Nat. P.I.) Nov. 4, 1873-March 7, 1963; House (Res. Comm.) 1917-23.

DEVINE, Samuel Leeper (R Ohio) Dec. 21, 1915- —; House 1959-81.

DEVITT, Edward James (R Minn.) May 5, 1911- —; House 1947-49.

DE VRIES, Marion (D Calif.) Aug. 15, 1865-Sept. 11, 1939; House 1897-Aug. 20, 1900.

DEWALT, Arthur Granville (D Pa.) Oct. 11, 1864-Oct. 26, 1931; House 1915-21.

DEWART, Lewis (father of William Lewis Dewart) (JD Pa.) Nov. 14, 1780-April 26, 1852; House 1831-33.

D'EWART, Wesley Abner (R Mont.) Oct. 1, 1889-Sept. 2, 1973; House June 5, 1945-55.

DEWART, William Lewis (son of Lewis Dewart) (D Pa.) June 21, 1821-April 19, 1888; House 1857-59.

DEWEESE, John Thomas (D N.C.) June 4, 1835-July 4, 1906; House July 6, 1868-Feb. 28, 1870.

DEWEY, Charles Schuveldt (R Ill.) Nov. 10, 1880-Dec. 26, 1980; House 1941-45.

DEWEY, Daniel (W Mass.) Jan. 29, 1766-May 26, 1815; House 1813-Feb. 24, 1814.

DeWINE, Michael (R Ohio) Jan. 5, 1947- —; House 1983- —.

DE WITT, Alexander (AP Mass.) April 2, 1798-Jan. 13, 1879; House 1853-57.

DE WITT, Charles Gerrit (JD N.Y.) Nov. 7, 1789-April 12, 1839; House 1829-31.

DE WITT, David Miller (D N.Y.) Nov. 25, 1837-June 23, 1912; House 1873-75.

DE WITT, Francis Byron (R Ohio) March 11, 1849-March 21, 1929; House 1895-97.

DE WITT, Jacob Hasbrouck (Clinton D N.Y.) Oct. 2, 1784-Jan. 30, 1867; House 1819-21.

DE WOLF, James (D R.I.) March 18, 1764-Dec. 21, 1837; Senate 1821-Oct. 31, 1825.

DEXTER, Samuel (F Mass.) May 14, 1761-May 3, 1816; House 1793-95; Senate 1799-May 30, 1880; Secy. of War May 13-Dec. 31, 1800; Secy. of the Treasury Jan. 1-May 6, 1801.

DEZENDORF, John Frederick (R Va.) Aug. 10, 1834-June 22, 1894; House 1881-83.

DIAL, Nathaniel Barksdale (D S.C.) April 24, 1862-Dec. 11, 1940; Senate 1919-25.

DIBBLE, Samuel (D S.C.) Sept. 16, 1837-Sept. 16, 1913; House June 9, 1881-May 31, 1882, 1883-91.

DIBRELL, George Gibbs (D Tenn.) April 12, 1822-May 9, 1888; House 1875-85.

DICK, Charles William Frederick (R Ohio) Nov. 3, 1858-March 13, 1945; House Nov. 8, 1898-March 23, 1904; Senate March 23, 1904-11.

DICK, John (father of Samuel Bernard Dick) (R Pa.) June 17, 1794-May 29, 1872; House 1853-59 (1853-55 Whig, 1855-59 Republican).

DICK, Samuel Bernard (son of John Dick) (R Pa.) Oct. 26, 1836-May 10, 1907; House 1879-81.

DICKENS, Samuel (— N.C.) ?-1840; House Dec. 2, 1816-17.

DICKERMAN, Charles Heber (D Pa.) Feb. 3, 1843-Dec. 17, 1915; House 1903-05.

DICKERSON, Mahlon (brother of Philemon Dickerson) (D N.J.) April 17, 1770-Oct. 5, 1853; Senate 1817-33; Gov. 1815-17; Secy. of the Navy 1834-38.

DICKERSON, Philemon (brother of Mahlon Dickerson) (JD N.J.) Jan. 11, 1788-Dec. 10, 1862; House 1833-Nov. 3, 1836, 1839-41 (1833-36 Democrat, 1839-41 Jackson Democrat); Gov. 1836-37.

DICKERSON, William Worth (D Ky.) Nov. 29, 1851-Jan. 31, 1923; House June 21, 1890-93.

DICKEY, Henry Luther (D Ohio) Oct. 29, 1832-May 23, 1910; House 1877-81.

DICKEY, Jesse Column (W Pa.) Feb. 27, 1808-Feb. 19, 1890; House 1849-51.

DICKEY, John (father of Oliver James Dickey) (W Pa.) June 23, 1794-March 14, 1853; House 1843-45, 1847-49.

DICKEY, Oliver James (son of John Dickey) (R Pa.) April 6, 1823-April 21, 1876; House Dec. 7, 1868-73.

DICKINSON, Clement Cabell (D Mo.) Dec. 6, 1849-Jan. 14, 1938; House Feb. 1, 1910-21, 1923-29, 1931-35.

DICKINSON, Daniel Stevens (D N.Y.) Sept. 11, 1800-April 12, 1866; Senate Nov. 30, 1844-51.

DICKINSON, David W. (nephew of William Hardy Murfree) (W Tenn.) June 10, 1808-April 27, 1845; House 1833-35, 1843-45 (1833-35 Democrat, 1843-45 Whig).

DICKINSON, Edward (W Mass.) Jan. 1, 1803-June 16, 1874; House 1853-55.

DICKINSON, Edward Fenwick (D Ohio) Jan. 21, 1829-Aug. 25, 1891; House 1869-71.

DICKINSON, John Dean (W N.Y.) June 28, 1767-Jan. 28, 1841; House 1819-23, 1827-31 (1819-25 Federalist, 1827-31 Whig).

DICKINSON, Lester Jesse (cousin of Fred Dickinson Letts) (R Iowa) Oct. 29, 1873-June 4, 1968; House 1919-31; Senate 1931-37.

DICKINSON, Philemon (— N.J.) April 5, 1739-Feb. 4, 1809; Senate Nov. 23, 1790-93; Cont. Cong. (Del.) 1782-83.

DICKINSON, Rodolphus (D Ohio) Dec. 28, 1797-March 20, 1849; House 1847-March 20, 1849.

DICKINSON, William Louis (R Ala.) June 5, 1925- —; House 1965- —.

DICKS, Norman Devalois (D Wash.) Dec. 16, 1940- —; House 1977- —.

DICKSON, David (D Miss.) ?-July 31, 1836; House 1835-July 31, 1836.

DICKSON, Frank Stoddard (R Ill.) Oct. 6, 1876-Feb. 24, 1953; House 1905-07.

DICKSON, John (W N.Y.) June 1, 1783-Feb. 22, 1852; House 1831-35.

DICKSON, Joseph (F N.C.) April 1745-April 14, 1825; House 1799-1801.

DICKSON, Samuel (W N.Y.) March 29, 1807-May 3, 1858; House 1855-57.

DICKSON, William (— Tenn.) May 5, 1770-Feb. 1816; House 1801-07.

DICKSON, William Alexander (D Miss.) July 20, 1861-Feb. 25, 1940; House 1909-13.

DICKSTEIN, Samuel (D N.Y.) Feb. 5, 1885-April 22, 1954; House 1923-Dec. 30, 1945.

DIEKEMA, Gerrit John (R Mich.) March 27, 1859-Dec. 20, 1930; House March 17, 1908-11.

DIES, Martin (father of Martin Dies Jr.) (D Texas) March 13, 1870-July 13, 1922; House 1909-19.

DIES, Martin Jr. (son of Martin Dies) (D Texas) Nov. 5, 1900-Nov. 14, 1972; House 1931-45, 1953-59.

DIETERICH, William Henry (D Ill.) March 31, 1876-Oct. 12, 1940; House 1931-33; Senate 1933-39.

DIETRICH, Charles Elmer (D Pa.) July 30, 1889-May 20, 1942; House 1935-37.

DIETRICH, Charles Henry (R Neb.) Nov. 26, 1853-April 10, 1924; Senate March 28, 1901-05; Gov. Jan. 3-May 1, 1901.

DIETZ, William (D N.Y.) June 28, 1778-Aug. 24, 1848; House 1825-27.

DIFFENDERFER, Robert Edward (D Pa.) June 7, 1849-April 27, 1923; House 1911-15.

DIGGS, Charles Coles Jr. (D Mich.) Dec. 2, 1922- —; House 1955-June 3, 1980.

DILL, Clarence Cleveland (D Wash.) Sept. 21, 1884-Jan. 14, 1978; House 1915-19; Senate 1923-35.

DILLINGHAM, Paul Jr. (father of William Paul Dillingham) (D Vt.) Aug. 10, 1799-July 26, 1891; House 1843-47; Gov. 1865-67.

DILLINGHAM, William Paul (son of Paul Dillingham Jr.) (R Vt.) Dec. 12, 1843-July 12, 1923; Senate Oct. 18, 1900-July 12, 1923; Gov. 1888-90.

DILLON, Charles Hall (R S.D.) Dec. 18, 1853-Sept. 15, 1929; House 1913-19.

DILWEG, LaVern Ralph (D Wis.) Nov. 1, 1903-Jan. 2, 1968; House 1943-45.

DIMMICK, Milo Melankthon (brother of William Harrison Dimmick) (D Pa.) Oct. 30, 1811-Nov. 22, 1872; House 1849-53.

DIMMICK, William Harrison (brother of Milo Melankthon Dimmick) (D Pa.) Dec. 20, 1815-Aug. 2, 1861; House 1857-61.

DIMOCK, Davis Jr. (D Pa.) Sept. 17, 1801-Jan. 13, 1842; House 1841-Jan. 13, 1842.

DIMOND, Anthony Joseph (D Alaska) Nov. 30, 1881-May 28, 1953; House (Terr. Del.) 1933-45.

DINGELL, John David (father of John David Dingell Jr.) (D Mich.) Feb. 2, 1894-Sept. 19, 1955; House 1933-Sept. 19, 1955.

DINGELL, John David Jr. (son of John David Dingell) (D Mich.) July 8, 1926- —; House Dec. 13, 1955- —.

DINGLEY, Nelson Jr. (R Maine) Feb. 15, 1832-Jan. 13, 1899; House Sept. 12, 1881-Jan. 13, 1899; Gov. 1874-76.

DINSMOOR, Samuel (WD N.H.) July 1, 1766-March 15, 1835; House 1811-13; Gov. 1831-34.

DINSMORE, Hugh Anderson (D Ark.) Dec. 24, 1850-May 2, 1930; House 1893-1905.

DIO GUARDI, Joseph D. (R N.Y.) Sept. 20, 1940- —; House 1985- —.

DIRKSEN, Everett McKinley (father-in-law of Howard H. Baker Jr.) (R Ill.) Jan. 4, 1896-Sept. 7, 1969; House 1933-49; Senate 1951-Sept. 7, 1969.

DISNEY, David Tiernan (D Ohio) Aug. 25, 1803-March 14, 1857; House 1849-55.

DISNEY, Wesley Ernest (D Okla.) Oct. 31, 1883-March 26, 1961; House 1931-45.

DITTER, John William (R Pa.) Sept. 5, 1888-Nov. 21, 1943; House 1933-Nov. 21, 1943.

DIVEN, Alexander Samuel (R N.Y.) Feb. 10, 1809-June 11, 1896; House 1861-63.

DIX, John Adams (son-in-law of John Jordan Morgan) (D N.Y.) July 24, 1798-April 21, 1879; Senate Jan. 27, 1845-49; Secy. of the Treasury Jan. 11-March 3, 1861; Gov. 1873-75 (Republican).

DIXON, Alan J. (D Ill.) July 7, 1927- —; Senate 1981- —.

DIXON, Archibald (W Ky.) April 2, 1802-April 23, 1876; Senate Sept. 1, 1852-55.

DIXON, Henry Aldous (R Utah) June 29, 1890-Jan. 22, 1967; House 1955-61.

DIXON, James (R Conn.) Aug. 5, 1814-March 27, 1873; House 1845-49; Senate 1857-69 (1845-49 Whig, 1857-69 Republican).

DIXON, Joseph (R N.C.) April 9, 1828-March 3, 1883; House Dec. 5, 1870-71.

DIXON, Joseph Andrew (D Ohio) June 3, 1879-July 4, 1942; House 1937-39.

DIXON, Joseph Moore (R Mont.) July 31, 1867-May 22, 1934; House 1903-07; Senate 1907-13; Gov. 1921-25.

DIXON, Julian Carey (D Calif.) Aug. 8, 1934- —; House 1979- —.

DIXON, Lincoln (D Ind.) Feb. 9, 1860-Sept. 16, 1932; House 1905-19.

DIXON, Nathan Fellows (grandfather of Nathan Fellows Dixon born in 1847, father of the following) (W R.I.) Dec. 13, 1774-Jan. 29, 1842; Senate 1839-Jan. 29, 1842.

DIXON, Nathan Fellows (son of the preceding, father of the following) (R R.I.) May 1, 1812-April 11, 1881; House 1849-51, 1863-71 (1849-51 Whig, 1863-71 Republican).

DIXON, Nathan Fellows (son of the preceding, grandson of Nathan Fellows Dixon born in 1774) (R R.I.) Aug. 28, 1847-Nov. 8, 1897; House Feb. 12-March 3, 1885; Senate April 10, 1889-95.

DIXON, William Wirt (D Mont.) June 3, 1838-Nov. 13, 1910; House 1891-93.

DOAN, Robert Eachus (R Ohio) July 23, 1831-Feb. 24, 1919; House 1891-93.

DOAN, William (D Ohio) April 4, 1792-June 22, 1847; House 1839-43.

DOBBIN, James Cochrane (grandson of James Cochran of North Carolina) (D N.C.) Jan. 17, 1814-Aug. 4, 1857; House 1845-47; Secy. of the Navy 1853-57.

DOBBINS, Donald Claude (D Ill.) March 20, 1878-Feb. 14, 1943; House 1933-37.

DOBBINS, Samuel Atkinson (R N.J.) April 14, 1814-May 26, 1886; House 1873-77.

DOCKERY, Alexander Monroe (D Mo.) Feb. 11, 1845-Dec. 26, 1926; House 1883-99; Gov. 1901-05.

DOCKERY, Alfred (father of Oliver Hart Dockery) (W N.C.) Dec. 11, 1797-Dec. 7, 1875; House 1845-47, 1851-53.

DOCKERY, Oliver Hart (son of Alfred Dockery) (R N.C.) Aug. 12, 1830-March 21, 1906; House July 13, 1868-71.

DOCKWEILER, John Francis (D Calif.) Sept. 19, 1895-Jan. 31, 1943; House 1933-39.

DODD, Christopher John (son of Thomas Joseph Dodd) (D Conn.) May 27, 1944- —; House 1975-81; Senate 1981- —.

DODD, Edward (W N.Y.) Aug. 25, 1805-March 1, 1891; House 1855-59.

DODD, Thomas Joseph (father of Christopher John Dodd) (D Conn.) May 15, 1907-May 24, 1971; House 1953-57; Senate 1959-71.

DODDRIDGE, Philip (— Va.) May 17, 1773-Nov. 19, 1832; House 1829-Nov. 19, 1832.

DODDS, Francis Henry (R Mich.) June 9, 1858-Dec. 23, 1940; House 1909-13.

DODDS, Ozro John (D Ohio) March 22, 1840-April 18, 1882; House Oct. 8, 1872-73.

DODGE, Augustus Caesar (son of Henry Dodge) (D Iowa) Jan. 2, 1812-Nov. 20, 1883; House (Terr. Del.) Oct. 28, 1840-Dec. 28, 1846; Senate Dec. 7, 1848-Feb. 22, 1855.

DODGE, Grenville Mellen (R Iowa) April 12, 1831-Jan. 3, 1916; House 1867-69.

DODGE, Henry (father of Augustus Caesar Dodge) (D Wis.) Oct. 12, 1782-June 19, 1867; House (Terr. Del.) 1841-45; Senate June 8, 1848-57; Gov. (Wis. Terr.) 1836-41, 1845-48.

DODGE, William Earle (R N.Y.) Sept. 4, 1805-Feb. 9, 1883; House April 7, 1866-67.

DOE, Nicholas Bartlett (W N.Y.) June 16, 1786-Dec. 6, 1856; House Dec. 7, 1840-41.

DOIG, Andrew Wheeler (D N.Y.) July 24, 1799-July 11, 1875; House 1839-43.

DOLE, Robert J. (R Kan.) July 22, 1923- —; House 1961-69; Senate 1969- —; Chrmn. Rep. Nat. Comm. 1971-73; Senate majority leader 1985- —.

DOLLINGER, Isidore (D N.Y.) Nov. 13, 1903- —; House 1949-Dec. 31, 1959.

DOLLIVER, James Isaac (nephew of Jonathan Prentiss Dolliver) (R Iowa) Aug. 31, 1894-Dec. 10, 1978; House 1945-57.

DOLLIVER, Jonathan Prentiss (uncle of James Isaac Dolliver) (R Iowa) Feb. 6, 1858-Oct. 15, 1910; House 1889-Aug. 22, 1900; Senate Aug. 22, 1900-Oct. 15, 1910.

DOLPH, Joseph Norton (uncle of Frederick William Mulkey) (R Ore.) Oct. 19, 1835-March 10, 1897; Senate 1883-95.

DOMENGEAUX, James (D La.) Jan. 6, 1907- —; House 1941-April 15, 1944; Nov. 7, 1944-49.

DOMENICI, Pete Vichi (R N.M.) May 7, 1932- —; Senate 1973- —.

DOMINICK, Frederick Haskell (D S.C.) Feb. 20, 1877-March 11, 1960; House 1917-33.

Biographical Index

DOMINICK, Peter Hoyt (nephew of Howard Alexander Smith) (R Colo.) July 7, 1915-March 18, 1981; House 1961-63; Senate 1963-75.

DONAHEY, Alvin Victor (D Ohio) July 7, 1873-April 8, 1946; Senate 1935-41; Gov. 1923-29.

DONDERO, George Anthony (R Mich.) Dec. 16, 1883-Jan. 29, 1968; House 1933-57.

DONLEY, Joseph Benton (R Pa.) Oct. 10, 1838-Jan. 23, 1917; House 1869-71.

DONNAN, William G. (R Iowa) June 30, 1834-Dec. 4, 1908; House 1871-75.

DONNELL, Forrest C. (R Mo.) Aug. 20, 1884-March 3, 1980; Senate 1945-51; Gov. 1941-45.

DONNELL, Richard Spaight (grandson of Richard Dobbs Spaight) (W N.C.) Sept. 20, 1820-June 3, 1867; House 1847-49.

DONNELLY, Brian Joseph (D Mass.) March 2, 1947- —; House 1979- —.

DONNELLY, Ignatius (R Minn.) Nov. 3, 1831-Jan. 1, 1901; House 1863-69

DONOHOE, Michael (D Pa.) Feb. 22, 1864-Jan. 17, 1958; House 1911-15.

DONOHUE, Harold Daniel (D Mass.) June 18, 1901-Nov. 4, 1984; House 1947-Dec. 31, 1974.

DONOVAN, Dennis D. (D Ohio) Jan. 31, 1859-April 21, 1941; House 1891-95.

DONOVAN, James George (D/R/L N.Y.) Dec. 15, 1898- —; House 1951-57.

DONOVAN, Jeremiah (D Conn.) Oct. 18, 1857-April 22, 1935; House 1913-15.

DONOVAN, Jerome Francis (D N.Y.), Feb. 1, 1872-Nov. 2, 1949; House March 5, 1918-21.

DOOLEY, Edwin Benedict (R N.Y.) April 13, 1905-Jan. 25, 1982; House 1957-63.

DOOLING, Peter Joseph (D N.Y.) Feb. 15, 1857-Oct. 18, 1931; House 1913-21.

DOOLITTLE, Dudley (D Kan.) June 21, 1881-Nov. 14, 1957; House 1913-19.

DOOLITTLE, James Rood (R Wis.) Jan. 3, 1815-July 23, 1897; Senate 1857-69.

DOOLITTLE, William Hall (R Wash.) Nov. 6, 1848-Feb. 26, 1914; House 1893-97.

DOREMUS, Frank Ellsworth (D Mich.) Aug. 31, 1865-Sept. 4, 1947; House 1911-21.

DORGAN, Byron L. (D N.D.) May 14, 1942- —; House 1981- —.

DORN, Francis Edwin (R N.Y.) April 18, 1911- —; House 1953-61.

DORN, William Jennings Bryan (D S.C.) April 14, 1916- —; House 1947-49; 1951-75.

DORNAN, Robert Kenneth (R Calif.) April 3, 1933- —; House 1977-83, 1985- —.

DORR, Charles Philips (R W. Va.) Aug. 12, 1852-Oct. 8, 1914; House 1897-99.

DORSEY, Clement (— Md.) 1778-Aug. 6, 1848; House 1825-31.

DORSEY, Frank Joseph Gerard (D Pa.) April 26, 1891-July 13, 1949; House 1935-39.

DORSEY, George Washington Emery (R Neb.) Jan. 25, 1842-June 12, 1911; House 1885-91.

DORSEY, John Lloyd Jr. (D Ky.) Aug. 10, 1891-March 22, 1960; House Nov. 4, 1930-31.

DORSEY, Stephen Wallace (R Ark.) Feb. 28, 1842-March 20, 1916; Senate 1873-79.

DORSHEIMER, William (D N.Y.) Feb. 5, 1832-March 26, 1888; House 1883-85.

DOTY, James Duane (cousin of Morgan Lewis Martin) (FS Wis.) Nov. 5, 1799-June 13, 1865; House Jan. 14, 1839-41 (Terr. Del.) 1849-53 (Rep.) (1839-41, 1849-51 Democrat, 1851-53 Free-Soiler); Gov. (Wis. Terr.) 1841-44, (Utah Terr.) 1863-65.

DOUBLEDAY, Ulysses Freeman (JD N.Y.) Dec. 15, 1792-March 11, 1866; House 1831-33, 1835-37.

DOUGHERTY, Charles (D Fla.) Oct. 15, 1850-Oct. 11, 1915; House 1885-89.

DOUGHERTY, Charles Francis (R Pa.) June 26, 1937- —; House 1979-83.

DOUGHERTY, John (D Mo.) Feb. 25, 1857-Aug. 1, 1905; House 1899-1905.

DOUGHTON, Robert Lee (D N.C.) Nov. 7, 1863-Oct. 1, 1954; House 1911-53.

DOUGLAS, Albert (R Ohio) April 25, 1852-March 14, 1935; House 1907-11.

DOUGLAS, Beverly Browne (D Va.) Dec. 21, 1822-Dec. 22, 1878; House 1875-77, 1877-Dec. 22, 1878 (1875-77 Conservative, 1877-78 Democrat).

DOUGLAS, Emily Taft (wife of Paul H. Douglas) (D Ill.) April 10, 1899- —; House 1945-47.

DOUGLAS, Fred James (R N.Y.) Sept. 14, 1869-Jan. 1, 1949; House 1937-45.

DOUGLAS, Helen Gahagan (D Calif.) Nov. 25, 1900-June 28, 1980; House 1945-51.

DOUGLAS, Lewis Williams (D Ariz.) July 2, 1894-March 7, 1974; House 1927-March 4, 1933.

DOUGLAS, Paul Howard (husband of Emily Taft Douglas) (D Ill.) March 26, 1892-Sept. 24, 1976; Senate 1949-67.

DOUGLAS, Stephen Arnold (PSD Ill.) April 23, 1813-June 3, 1861; House 1843-47; Senate 1847-June 3, 1861 (1847-53 Democrat, 1853-61 Popular Sovereignty Democrat).

DOUGLAS, William Harris (R N.Y.) Dec. 5, 1853-Jan. 27, 1944; House 1901-05.

DOUGLASS, John Joseph (D Mass.) Feb. 9, 1873-April 5, 1939; House 1925-35.

DOUTRICH, Isaac Hoffer (R Pa.) Dec. 19, 1871-May 28, 1941; House 1927-37.

DOVENER, Blackburn Barrett (R W.Va.) April 20, 1842-May 9, 1914; House 1895-1907.

DOW, John Goodchild (D N.Y.) May 6, 1905- —; House 1965-69; 1971-73.

DOWD, Clement (D N.C.) Aug. 27, 1832-April 15, 1898; House 1881-85.

DOWDELL, James Ferguson (SRD Ala.) Nov. 26, 1818-Sept. 6, 1871; House 1853-59.

DOWDNEY, Abraham (D N.Y.) Oct. 31, 1841-Dec. 10, 1886; House 1885-Dec. 10, 1886.

DOWDY, John Vernard (D Texas) Feb. 11, 1912- —; House Sept. 23, 1952-73.

DOWDY, Wayne (D Miss.) July 27, 1943- —; House July 9, 1981- —.

DOWELL, Cassius Clay (R Iowa) Feb. 29, 1864-Feb. 4, 1940; House 1915-35, 1937-Feb. 4, 1940.

DOWNEY, Sheridan (son of Stephen Wheeler Downey) (D Calif.) March 11, 1884-Oct. 25, 1961; Senate 1939-Nov. 30, 1950.

DOWNEY, Stephen Wheeler (father of Sheridan Downey) (R Wyo.) July 25, 1839-Aug. 3, 1902; House (Terr. Del.) 1879-81.

DOWNEY, Thomas Joseph (D N.Y.) Jan. 28, 1949- —; House 1975- —.

DOWNING, Charles (— Fla.) ?-1845; House (Terr. Del.) 1837-41.

DOWNING, Finis Ewing (D Ill. Aug. 24, 1846-March 8, 1936; House 1895-June 5, 1896.

DOWNING, Thomas Nelms (D Va.) Feb. 1, 1919- —; House 1959-77.

DOWNS, Le Roy Donnelly (D Conn.) April 11, 1900-Jan. 18, 1970; House 1941-43.

DOWNS, Solomon Weathersbee (D La.) 1801-Aug. 14, 1854; Senate 1847-53.

DOWSE, Edward (D Mass.) Oct. 22, 1756-Sept. 3, 1828; House 1819-May 26, 1820.

DOX, Peter Myndert (grandson of John Nicholas) (D Ala.) Sept. 11, 1813-April 2, 1891; House 1869-73.

DOXEY, Charles Taylor (R Ind.) July 13, 1841-April 30, 1898; House Jan. 17-March 3, 1883.

DOXEY, Wall (D Miss.) Aug. 8, 1892-March 2, 1962; House 1929-Sept. 28, 1941; Senate Sept. 29, 1941-43.

DOYLE, Clyde Gilman (D Calif.) July 11, 1887-March 14, 1963; House 1945-47, 1949-March 14, 1963.

DOYLE, Thomas Aloysius (D Ill.) Jan. 9, 1886-Jan. 29, 1935; House Nov. 6, 1923-31.

DRAKE, Charles Daniel (R Mo.) April 11, 1811-April 1, 1892; Senate 1867-Dec. 19, 1870.

DRAKE, John Reuben (— N.Y.) Nov. 28, 1782-March 21, 1857; House 1817-19.

DRANE, Herbert Jackson (D Fla.) June 20, 1863-Aug. 11, 1947; House 1917-33.

DRAPER, Joseph (— Va.) Dec. 25, 1794-June 10, 1834; House Dec. 6, 1830-31, Dec. 6, 1832-33.

DRAPER, William Franklin (R Mass.) April 9, 1842-Jan. 28, 1910; House 1893-97.

DRAPER, William Henry (R N.Y.) June 24, 1841-Dec. 7, 1921; House 1901-13.

DRAYTON, William (UD S.C.) Dec. 30, 1776-May 24, 1846; House May 17, 1825-33.

DREIER, David T. (R Calif.) July 5, 1952- —; House 1981- —.

DRESSER, Solomon Robert (R Pa.) Feb. 1, 1842-Jan. 21, 1911; House 1903-07.

DREW, Ira Walton (D Pa.) Aug. 31, 1878-Feb. 12, 1972; House 1937-39.

DREW, Irving Webster (R N.H.) Jan.8, 1845-April 10, 1922; Senate Sept. 2-Nov. 5, 1918.

DREWRY, Patrick Henry (D Va.) May 24, 1875-Dec. 21, 1947; House April 27, 1920-Dec. 21, 1947.

DRIGGS, Edmund Hope (D N.Y.) May 2, 1865-Sept. 27, 1946; House Dec. 6, 1897-1901.

DRIGGS, John Fletcher (R Mich.) March 8, 1813-Dec. 17, 1877; House 1863-69.

DRINAN, Robert Frederick (D Mass.) Nov. 15, 1920- —; House 1971-81.

DRISCOLL, Daniel Angelus (D N.Y.) March 27, 1871-Jan 18, 1958; House 1935-37.

DRISCOLL, Denis Joseph (D Pa.) March 27, 1871-Jan. 18, 1958; House 1935-37.

DRISCOLL, Michael Edward (R N.Y.) Feb. 9, 1851-Jan. 19, 1929; House 1899-1913.

DRIVER, William Joshua (D Ark.) March 2, 1873-Oct. 1, 1948; House 1921-39.

DROMGOOLE, George Coke (uncle of Alexander Dromgoole Sims) (D Va.) May 15, 1797-April 27, 1847; House 1835-41, 1843-April 27, 1847.

DRUKKER, Dow Henry (R N.J.) Feb. 7, 1872-Jan. 11, 1963; House April 7, 1914-19.

DRUM, Augustus (D Pa.) Nov. 26, 1815-Sept. 15, 1858; House 1853-55.

DRYDEN, John Fairfield (R N.J.) Aug. 7, 1839-Nov. 24, 1911; Senate Jan. 29, 1902-07.

DUBOIS, Fred Thomas (D Idaho) May 29, 1851-Feb. 14, 1930; House (Terr. Del.) 1887-July 3, 1890; Senate 1891-97, 1901-07 (1887-97 Republican, 1901 Silver Republican, 1901-07 Democrat).

DU BOSE, Dudley McIver (D Ga.) Oct. 28, 1834-March 2, 1883; House 1871-73.

DUDLEY, Charles Edward (D N.Y.) May 23, 1780-Jan. 23, 1841; Senate Jan. 15, 1829-33.

DUDLEY, Edward Bishop (NR N.C.) Dec. 15, 1769-Oct. 30, 1855; House Nov. 10, 1829-31; Gov. 1837-41.

DUELL, Rodolphus Holland (R N.Y.) Dec. 20, 1824-Feb. 11, 1891; House 1859-63, 1871-75.

DUER, William (W N.Y.) May 25, 1805-Aug. 25, 1879; House 1847-51.

DUFF, James Henderson (R Pa.) Jan. 21, 1883-Dec. 20, 1969; Senate Jan. 16, 1951-57; Gov. 1947-51.

DUFFEY, Warren Joseph (D Ohio) Jan. 24, 1886-July 7, 1936; House 1933-July 7, 1936.

DUFFY, Francis Ryan (D Wis.) June 23, 1888-Aug. 16, 1979; Senate 1933-39.

DUFFY, James Patrick Bernard (D N.Y.) Nov. 25, 1878-Jan. 8, 1969; House 1935-37.

DUGRO, Philip Henry (D N.Y.) Oct. 3, 1855-March 1, 1920; House 1881-83.

DUKE, Richard Thomas Walker (C Va.) June 6, 1822-July 2, 1898; House Nov. 8, 1870-73.

DULLES, John Foster (R N.Y.) Feb. 25, 1888-May 24, 1959; Senate July 7-Nov. 8, 1949; Secy. of State 1953-59.

DULSKI, Thaddeus J. (D N.Y.) Sept. 27, 1915- —; House 1959-75.

DUMONT, Ebenezer (U Ind.) Nov. 23, 1814-April 16, 1871; House 1863-67.

DUNBAR, James Whitson (R Ind.) Oct. 17, 1860-May 19, 1943; House 1919-23, 1929-31.

DUNBAR, William (D La.) 1805-March 18, 1861; House 1853-55.

DUNCAN, Alexander (W Ohio) 1788-March 23, 1853; House 1837-41, 1843-45.

DUNCAN, Daniel (W Ohio) July 22, 1806-May 18, 1849; House 1847-49.

DUNCAN, James (— Pa.) 1756-June 24, 1844; House 1821.

DUNCAN, James Henry (W Mass.) Dec. 5, 1793-Feb. 8, 1869; House 1849-53.

DUNCAN, John J. (R Tenn.) March 24, 1919- —; House 1965- —.

DUNCAN, Joseph (JD Ill.) Feb. 22, 1794-Jan. 15, 1844; House 1827-Sept. 21, 1834; Gov. 1834-38.

DUNCAN, Richard Meloan (D Mo.) Nov. 10, 1889-Aug. 1, 1974; House 1933-43.

DUNCAN, Robert Blackford (D Ore.) Dec. 4, 1920- —; House 1963-67, 1975-81.

DUNCAN, William Addison (D Pa.) Feb. 2, 1836-Nov. 14, 1884; House 1883-Nov. 14, 1884.

DUNCAN, (William) Garnett (W Ky.) March 2, 1800-May 25, 1875; House 1847-49.

DUNGAN, James Irvine (D Ohio) May 29, 1844-Dec. 28, 1931; House 1891-93.

DUNHAM, Cyrus Livingston (D Ind.) Jan. 16, 1817-Nov. 21, 1877; House 1849-55.

DUNHAM, Ransom Williams (R Ill.) March 21, 1838-Aug. 19, 1896; House 1883-89.

DUNLAP, George Washington, (U Ky.) Feb. 22, 1813-June 6, 1880; House 1861-63.

DUNLAP, Robert Pickney (D Maine) Aug. 17, 1794-Oct. 20, 1859; House 1843-47; Gov. 1834-38.

DUNLAP, William Claiborne (D Tenn.) Feb. 25, 1798-Nov. 16, 1872; House 1833-37.

DUNN, Aubert Culberson (D Miss.) Nov. 20, 1896- —; House 1935-37.

DUNN, George Grundy (R Ind.) Dec. 20, 1812-Sept. 4, 1857; House 1847-49, 1855-57 (1847-49 Whig, 1855-57 Republican).

DUNN, George Hedford (W Ind.) Nov. 15, 1794-Jan. 12, 1854; House 1837-39.

DUNN, Jim (R Mich.) July 21, 1943- —; House 1981-83.

DUNN, John Thomas (D N.J.) June 4, 1838-Feb. 22, 1907; House 1893-95.

DUNN, Matthew Anthony (D Pa.) Aug. 15, 1886-Feb. 13, 1942; House 1933-41.

DUNN, Poindexter (D Ark.) Nov. 3, 1834-Oct. 12, 1914; House 1879-89.

DUNN, Thomas Byrne (R N.Y.) March 16, 1853-July 2, 1924; House 1913-23.

DUNN, William McKee (R Ind.) Dec. 12, 1814-July 24, 1887; House 1859-63.

DUNNELL, Mark Hill (R Minn.) July 2, 1823-Aug. 9, 1904; House 1871-83, 1889-91.

DUNPHY, Edward John (D N.Y.) May 12, 1856-July 29, 1926; House 1889-95.

DUNWELL, Charles Tappan (R N.Y.) Feb. 13, 1852-June 12, 1908; House 1903-June 12, 1908.

du PONT, Henry Algernon (cousin of Thomas Coleman du Pont) (R Del.) July 30, 1838-Dec. 31, 1926; Senate June 13, 1906-17.

du PONT, Pierre S. (Pete) IV (R Del.) Jan. 22, 1935- —; House 1971-77; Gov. 1977-85.

du PONT, Thomas Coleman (cousin of Henry Algernon du Pont) (R Del.) Dec. 11, 1863-Nov. 11, 1930; Senate July 7, 1921-Nov. 7, 1922; 1925-Dec. 9, 1928.

DUPRE, Henry Garland (D La.) July 28, 1873-Feb. 21, 1924; House Nov. 8, 1910-Feb. 21, 1924.

DURAND, George Harman (D Mich.) Feb. 21, 1838-June 8, 1903; House 1875-77.

DURBIN, Richard Joseph (D Ill.) Nov. 21, 1944- —; House 1983- —.

DURBOROW, Alan Cathcard Jr. (D Ill.) Nov. 10, 1857-March 10, 1908; House 1891-95.

DURELL, Daniel Meserve (— N.H.) July 20, 1769-April 29, 1841; House 1807-09.

DURENBERGER, David Ferdinand (R Minn.) Aug. 19, 1934- —; Senate Nov. 8, 1978- —.

DUREY, Cyrus (R N.Y.) May 16, 1864-Jan. 4, 1933; House 1907-11.

DURFEE, Job (D R.I.) Sept. 20, 1790-July 26, 1847; House 1821-25 (1821-23 People's Party, 1823-25 Democrat).

DURFEE, Nathaniel Briggs (R R.I.) Sept. 29, 1812-Nov. 9, 1872; House 1855-59 (1855-57 American Party, 1857-59 Republican).

DURGAN, George Richard (D Ind.) Jan. 20, 1872-Jan. 13, 1942; House 1933-35.

DURHAM, Carl Thomas (D N.C.) Aug. 28, 1892-April 29, 1974; House 1939-61.

DURHAM, Milton Jameson (D Ky.) May 16, 1824-Feb. 12, 1911; House 1873-79.

DURKEE, Charles (R Wis.) Dec. 10, 1805-Jan. 14, 1870; House 1849-53; Senate 1855-61; (1849-53 Free-Soiler, 1855-61 Republican) Gov. (Utah Terr.) 1865-69.

DURKIN, John Anthony (D N.H.) March 29, 1936- —; Senate Sept. 18, 1975-Dec. 28, 1980.

DURNO, Edwin R. (R Ore.) Jan. 26, 1899-Nov. 20, 1976; House 1961-63.

DUVAL, Isaac Harding (R W.Va.) Sept. 1, 1824-July 10, 1902; House 1869-71.

DUVAL, William Pope (D Ky.) 1784-March 19, 1854; House 1813-15; Gov. (Fla. Terr.) 1822-34.

DUVALL, Gabriel (D Md.) Dec. 6, 1752-March 6, 1844; House Nov. 11, 1794-March 28, 1796; Assoc. Justice Supreme Court 1812-35.

DWIGHT, Henry Williams (— Mass.) Feb. 26, 1788-Feb. 21, 1845; House 1821-31.

DWIGHT, Jeremiah Wilbur (father of John Wilbur Dwight) (R N.Y.) April 17, 1819-Nov. 26, 1885; House 1877-83.

DWIGHT, John Wilbur (son of Jeremiah Wilbur Dwight) (R N.Y.) May 24, 1859-Jan. 19, 1928; House Nov. 2, 1902-13.

DWIGHT, Theodore (cousin of Aaron Burr) (F Conn.) Dec. 15, 1764-June 12, 1846; House Dec. 1, 1806-07.

DWIGHT, Thomas (F Mass.) Oct. 29, 1758-Jan. 2, 1819; House 1803-05.

DWINELL, Justin (— N.Y.) Oct. 28, 1785-Sept. 17, 1850; House 1823-25.

DWORSHAK, Henry Clarence (R Idaho) Aug. 29, 1894-July 23, 1962; House 1939-Nov. 5, 1946; Senate Nov. 6, 1946-49, Oct. 14, 1949-July 23, 1962.

DWYER, Bernard J. (D N.J.) Jan. 24, 1921- —; House 1981- —.

DWYER, Florence Price (R N.J.) July 4, 1902-Feb. 29, 1976; House 1959-73.

DYAL, Kenneth Warren (D Calif.) July 9, 1910-May 12, 1978; House 1965-67.

DYER, David Patterson (uncle of Leonidas Carstarphen Dyer) (R Mo.) Feb. 12, 1838-April 29, 1924; House 1869-71.

DYER, Leonidas Carstarphen (nephew of David Patterson Dyer) (R Mo.) June 11, 1871-Dec. 15, 1957; House 1911-June 19,1914, 1915-33.

DYMALLY, Mervyn M. (D Calif.) May 12, 1926- —; House 1981- —.

DYSON, Roy (D Md.) Nov. 15, 1948- —; House 1981- —.

E

EAGAN, John Joseph (D N.J.) Jan. 22, 1872-June 13, 1956; House 1913-21, 1923-25.

EAGER, Samuel Watkins (R N.Y.) April 8, 1789-Dec. 23, 1860; House Nov. 2, 1830-31.

EAGLE, Joe Henry (D Texas) Jan. 23, 1870-Jan. 10, 1963; House 1913-21, Jan. 28, 1933-37.

EAGLETON, Thomas F. (D Mo.) Sept. 4, 1929- —; Senate Dec. 28, 1968- —.

EAMES, Benjamin Tucker (R R.I.) June 4, 1818-Oct. 6, 1901; House 1871-79.

EARHART, Daniel Scofield (D Ohio) May 28, 1907-Jan. 2, 1976; House Nov. 3, 1936-37.

EARLE, Elias (uncle of Samuel Earle and John Baylis Earle, great-grandfather of John Laurens Manning Irby and Joseph Haynsworth Earle) (D S.C.) June 19, 1762-May 19, 1823; House 1805-07, 1811-15, 1817-21.

EARLE, John Baylis (nephew of Elias Earle, cousin of Samuel Earle) (— S.C.) Oct. 23, 1766-Feb. 3, 1863; House 1803-05.

EARLE, Joseph Haynsworth (great-grandson of Elias Earle, cousin of John Laurens Manning Irby, nephew of William Lowndes Yancey) (D S.C.) April 30, 1847-May 20, 1897; Senate March 4-May 20, 1897.

EARLE, Samuel (nephew of Elias Earle, cousin of John Baylis Earle) (— S.C.) Nov. 28, 1760-Nov. 24, 1833; House 1795-97.

EARLL, Jonas Jr. (cousin of Nehemiah Hezekiah Earll) (D N.Y.) 1786-Oct. 28, 1846; House 1827-31.

EARLL, Nehemiah Hezekiah (cousin of Jonas Earll Jr.) (D N.Y.) Oct. 5, 1787-Aug. 26, 1872; House 1839-41.

EARLY, Joseph Daniel (D Mass.) Jan. 31, 1933- —; House 1975- —.

EARLY, Peter (— Ga.) June 20, 1773-Aug. 15, 1817; House Jan. 10, 1803-07; Gov. 1813-15.

EARNSHAW, Manuel (I P.I.) Nov. 19, 1862-Feb. 13, 1936; House (Res. Comm.) 1913-17.

EARTHMAN, Harold Henderson (D Tenn.) April 13, 1900- —; House 1945-47.

EAST, John P. (R N.C.) May 5, 1931- —; Senate 1981- —.

EASTLAND, James Oliver (D Miss.) Nov. 28, 1904- —; Senate June 30-Sept. 18, 1941, 1943-Dec. 27, 1978; Pres. pro tempore July 29, 1972-Dec. 27, 1978.

EASTMAN, Ben C. (D Wis.) Oct. 24, 1812-Feb. 2, 1856; House 1851-55.

EASTMAN, Ira Allen (nephew of Nehemiah Eastman) (D N.H.) Jan. 1, 1809-March 21, 1881; House 1839-43.

EASTMAN, Nehemiah (uncle of Ira Allen Eastman) (D N.H.) June 16, 1782-Jan. 11, 1856; House 1825-27.

EASTON, Rufus (D Mo.) May 4, 1774-July 5, 1834; House (Terr. Del.) Sept. 17, 1814-Aug. 5, 1816.

EATON, Charles Aubrey (uncle of William Robb Eaton) (R N.J.) March 29, 1868-Jan. 23, 1953; House 1925-53.

EATON, John Henry (D Tenn.) June 18, 1790-Nov. 17, 1856; Senate Sept. 5, 1818-21, Sept. 27, 1821-March 9, 1829; Secy. of War 1829-31; Gov. (Fla. Terr.) 1834-36.

EATON, Lewis (— N.Y.)?-?; House 1823-25.

EATON, Thomas Marion (R Calif.) Aug. 3, 1896-Sept. 16, 1939; House Jan. 3-Sept. 16, 1939.

EATON, William Robb (nephew of Charles Aubrey Eaton) (R Colo.) Dec. 17, 1877-Dec. 16, 1942; House 1929-33.

EATON, William Wallace (D Conn.) Oct. 11, 1816-Sept. 21, 1898; Senate Feb. 5, 1875-1881; House 1883-85.

EBERHARTER, Herman Peter (D Pa.) April 29, 1892-Sept. 9, 1958; House 1937-Sept. 9, 1958.

ECHOLS, Leonard Sidney (R W.Va.) Oct. 30, 1871-May 9, 1946; House 1919-23.

ECKART, Dennis E. (D Ohio) April 6, 1950- —; House 1981- —.

ECKERT, Charles Richard (D Pa.) Jan. 20, 1868-Oct. 26, 1959; House 1935-39.

ECKERT, Fred J. (R N.Y.) May 6, 1941- —; House 1985- —.

ECKERT, George Nicholas (W Pa.) July 4, 1802-June 28, 1865; House 1847-49.

ECKHARDT, Robert Christian (cousin of Richard Mifflin Kleberg Sr., great-nephew of Rudolph Kleberg, nephew of Harry Mcleary Wurzbach) (D Texas) July 16, 1913- —; House 1967-81.

ECKLEY, Ephraim Ralph (R Ohio) Dec. 9, 1811-March 27, 1908; House 1863-69.

ECTON, Zales Nelson (R Mont.) April 1, 1898-March 3, 1961; Senate 1947-53.

EDDY, Frank Marion (R Minn.) April 1, 1856-Jan. 13, 1929; House 1895-1903.

EDDY, Norman (D Ind.) Dec. 10, 1810-Jan. 28, 1872; House 1853-55.

EDDY, Samuel (D R.I.) March 31, 1769-Feb. 3, 1839; House 1819-25.

EDELSTEIN, Morris Michael (D N.Y.) Feb. 5, 1888-June 4, 1941; House Feb. 6, 1940-June 4, 1941.

EDEN, John Rice (D Ill.) Feb. 1, 1826-June 9, 1909; House 1863-65, 1873-79, 1885-87.

EDGAR, Robert William (D Pa.) May 29, 1943- —; House 1975- —.

EDGE, Walter Evans (R N.J.) Nov. 20, 1873-Oct. 29, 1956; Senate 1919-Nov. 21, 1929; Gov. 1917-19, 1944-47.

EDGERTON, Alfred Peck (brother of Joseph Ketchum Edgerton) (D Ohio) Jan. 11, 1813-May 14, 1897; House 1851-55.

EDGERTON, Alonzo Jay (R Minn.) June 7, 1827-Aug. 9, 1896; Senate March 12-Oct. 30, 1881.

EDGERTON, Joseph Ketchum (brother of Alfred Peck Edgerton) (D Ind.) Feb. 16, 1818-Aug. 25, 1893; House 1863-65.

EDGERTON, Sidney (R Ohio) Aug. 17, 1818-July 19, 1900; House 1859-63; Gov. (Mont. Terr.) 1865-66.

EDIE, John Rufus (W Pa.) Jan. 14, 1814-Aug. 27, 1888; House 1855-59.

EDMANDS, John Wiley (W Mass.) March 1, 1809-Jan. 31, 1877; House 1853-55.

EDMISTON, Andrew (D W.Va.) Nov. 13, 1892-Aug. 28, 1966; House Nov. 28, 1933-43.

EDMOND, William (F Conn.) Sept. 28, 1755-Aug. 1, 1838; House Nov. 13, 1797-1801.

EDMONDS, George Washington (R Pa.) Feb. 22, 1864-Sept. 28, 1939; House 1913-25, 1933-35.

EDMONDSON, Edmond Augustus (brother of James Howard Edmondson) (D Okla.) April 7, 1919--; House 1953-1973.

EDMONDSON, James Howard (brother of Edmond Augustus Edmondson) (D Okla.) Sept. 27, 1925-Nov. 17, 1971; Senate Jan. 9, 1963-Nov. 3, 1964, Gov. 1959-63.

EDMUNDS, George Franklin (R Vt.) Feb. 1, 1828-Feb. 27, 1919; Senate April 3, 1866-Nov. 1, 1891, Pres. pro tempore 1883-85.

EDMUNDS, Paul Carrington (D Va.) Nov. 1, 1836-March 12, 1899; House 1899-95.

EDMUNDSON, Henry Alonzo (D Va.) June 14, 1814-Dec. 16, 1890; House 1849-61.

EDSALL, Joseph E. (D N.J.) 1789-1865; House 1845-49.

EDWARDS, Benjamin (father of Ninian Edwards, grandfather of Benjamin Edwards Grey) (— Md.) Aug. 12, 1753-Nov. 13, 1829; House Jan. 2-March 3, 1795.

EDWARDS, Caldwell, (D/P Mont.) Jan. 8, 1841-July 23, 1922; House 1901-03.

EDWARDS, Charles Gordon (D Ga.) July 2, 1878-July 13, 1931; House 1907-17, 1925-July 13, 1931.

EDWARDS, Don (D Calif.) Jan. 6, 1915--; House 1963--.

EDWARDS, Don Calvin (R Ky.) July 13, 1861-Sept. 19, 1938; House 1905-11.

EDWARDS, Edward Irving (D N.J.) Dec. 1, 1863-Jan. 26, 1931; Senate 1923-29; Gov. 1920-23.

EDWARDS, Edwin Washington (husband of Elaine Schwartzenburg Edwards) (D La.) Aug. 7, 1927--; House Oct. 2, 1965-May 9, 1972; Gov. May 9, 1972-81, 1984--.

EDWARDS, Elaine Schwartzenburg (wife of Edwin Washington Edwards) (D La.) March 8, 1929--; Senate Aug. 1, 1972-Nov. 13, 1972.

EDWARDS, Francis Smith (AP N.Y.) May 28, 1817-May 20, 1899; House 1855-Feb. 28, 1857.

EDWARDS, Henry Waggaman (D Conn.) Oct. 1779-July 22, 1847; House 1819-23; Senate Dec. 1, 1823-27; Gov. 1833, 1835-37.

EDWARDS, Jack (William Jackson) (R Ala.) Sept. 20, 1928--; House 1965-85.

EDWARDS, John (— Ky.) 1748-1837; Senate June 18, 1792-95.

EDWARDS, John (D N.Y.) Aug. 6, 1781-Dec. 28, 1850; House 1837-39.

EDWARDS, John (granduncle of John Edwards Leonard) (W Pa.) 1786-June 26, 1843; House 1839-43.

EDWARDS, John (LR Ark.) Oct. 24, 1805-April 8, 1894; House 1871-Feb. 9, 1872.

EDWARDS, John Cummins (D Mo.) June 24, 1804-Oct. 14, 1888; House 1841-43; Gov. 1844-48.

EDWARDS, Marvin H. (R Okla.) July 12, 1937--; House 1977--.

EDWARDS, Ninian (son of Benjamin Edwards) (D Ill.) March 17, 1775-July 20, 1833; Senate Dec. 3, 1818-24; Gov. 1809-18 (Ill. Terr.), 1826-30 (Ill.).

EDWARDS, Samuel (F Pa.) March 12, 1785-Nov. 21, 1850; House 1819-27.

EDWARDS, Thomas McKey (R N.H.) Dec. 16, 1795-May 1, 1875; House 1859-63.

EDWARDS, Thomas Owen (W Ohio) March 29, 1810-Feb. 5, 1876; House 1847-49.

EDWARDS, Weldon Nathaniel (D N.C.) Jan. 25, 1788-Dec. 18, 1873; House Feb. 7, 1816-27.

EDWARDS, William Posey (R Ga.) Nov. 9, 1835-June 28, 1900; House July 25, 1868-69.

EFNER, Valentine (D N.Y.) May 5, 1776-Nov. 20, 1865; House 1835-37.

EGBERT, Albert Gallatin (D Pa.) April 13, 1828-March 28, 1896; House 1875-77.

EGBERT, Joseph (D N.Y.) April 10, 1807-July 7, 1888; House 1841-43.

EGE, George (— Pa.) March 9, 1748-Dec. 14, 1829; House Dec. 8, 1796-Oct. 1797.

EGGLESTON, Benjamin (R Ohio) Jan. 3, 1816-Feb. 9, 1888; House 1865-69.

EGGLESTON, Joseph (uncle of William Segar Archer) (D Va.) Nov. 24, 1754-Feb. 13, 1811; House Dec. 3, 1798-1801.

EICHER, Edward Clayton (D Iowa) Dec. 16, 1878-Nov. 29, 1944; House 1933-Dec. 2, 1938.

EICKHOFF, Anthony (D N.Y.) Sept. 11, 1827-Nov. 5, 1901; House 1877-79.

EILBERG, Joshua (D Pa.) Feb. 12, 1921--; House 1967-79.

EINSTEIN, Edwin (R N.Y.) Nov. 18, 1842-Jan. 24, 1905; House 1879-81.

EKWALL, William Alexander (R Ore.) June 14, 1887-Oct. 16, 1956; House 1935-37.

ELA, Jacob Hart (R N.H.) July 18, 1820-Aug. 21, 1884; House 1867-71.

ELAM, Joseph Barton (D La.) June 12, 1821-July 4, 1885; House 1877-81.

ELDER, James Walter (D La.) Oct. 5, 1882-Dec. 16, 1941; House 1913-15.

ELDREDGE, Charles Augustus (D Wis.) Feb. 27, 1820-Oct. 26, 1896; House 1863-75.

ELDREDGE, Nathaniel Buel (D Mich.) March 28, 1813-Nov. 27, 1893; House 1883-87.

ELIOT, Samuel Atkins (great-grandfather of Thomas Hopkinson Eliot) (W Mass.) March 5, 1798-Jan. 29, 1862; House Aug. 22, 1850-51.

ELIOT, Thomas Dawes (R Mass.) March 20, 1808-June 14, 1870; House April 17, 1854-1855, 1859-69 (1854-55 Whig, 1859-69 Republican).

ELIOT, Thomas Hopkinson (great-grandson of Samuel Atkins Eliot) (D Mass.) June 14, 1907--; House 1941-43.

ELIZALDE, Joaquin Miguel (— P.I.) Aug. 2, 1896-Feb. 9, 1965; House (Res. Comm.) Sept. 29, 1938-Aug. 9, 1944.

ELKINS, Davis (son of Stephen Benton Elkins, grandson of Henry Gassaway Davis) (R W.Va.) Jan. 24, 1876-Jan. 5, 1959; Senate Jan. 9-Jan. 31, 1911, 1919-25.

ELKINS, Stephen Benton (father of Davis Elkins) (R N.M./W.Va.) Sept. 26, 1841-Jan. 4, 1911; House (Terr. Del. N.M.) 1873-77; Senate (W.Va.) 1895-Jan. 4, 1911; Secy. of War 1891-93.

ELLENBOGEN, Henry (D Pa.) April 3, 1900--; House 1933-Jan. 3, 1938.

ELLENDER, Allen Joseph (D La.) Sept. 24, 1890-July 27, 1972; Senate 1937-July 27, 1972. Pres. pro tempore 1971-July 27, 1972.

ELLERBE, James Edwin (D S.C.) Jan. 12, 1867-Oct. 24, 1917; House 1905-13.

ELLERY, Christopher (D R.I.) Nov. 1, 1768-Dec. 2, 1840; Senate May 6, 1801-05.

ELLETT, Henry Thomas (D Miss.) March 8, 1812-Oct. 15, 1887; House Jan. 26-March 3, 1847.

ELLETT, Tazewell (D Va.) Jan. 1, 1856-May 19, 1914; House 1895-97.

ELLICOTT, Benjamin (D N.Y.) April 17, 1765-Dec. 10, 1827; House 1817-19.

ELLIOTT, Alfred James (D Calif.) June 1, 1895-Jan. 17, 1973; House May 4, 1937-49.

ELLIOTT, Carl Atwood (D Ala.) Dec. 20, 1913--; House 1949-65.

ELLIOTT, Douglas Hemphill (R Pa.) June 3, 1921-June 19, 1960; House April 26-June 19, 1960.

ELLIOTT, James (F Vt.) Aug. 18, 1775-Nov. 10, 1839; House 1803-09.

ELLIOTT, James Thomas (R Ark.) April 22, 1823-July 28, 1875; House Jan. 13-March 3, 1869.

ELLIOTT, John (— Ga.) Oct. 24, 1773-Aug. 9, 1827; Senate 1819-25.

ELLIOTT, John Milton (D Ky.) May 20, 1820-March 26, 1879; House 1853-59.

Biographical Index

ELLIOTT, Mortimer Fitzland (D Pa.) Sept. 24, 1839-Aug. 5, 1920; House 1883-85.

ELLIOTT, Richard Nash (R Ind.) April 25, 1873-March 21, 1948; House June 26, 1917-31.

ELLIOTT, Robert Brown (R S.C.) Aug. 11, 1842-Aug. 9, 1884; House 1871-Nov. 1, 1874.

ELLIOTT, William (D S.C.) Sept. 3, 1838-Dec. 7, 1907; House 1887-Sept. 23, 1890, 1891-93, 1895-June 4, 1896, 1897-1903.

ELLIS, Caleb (— N.H.) April 16, 1767-May 6, 1816; House 1805-07.

ELLIS, Chesselden (D N.Y.) 1808-May 10, 1854; House 1843-45.

ELLIS, Clyde Taylor (D Ark.) Dec. 21, 1908-Feb. 9, 1980; House 1939-43.

ELLIS, Edgar Clarence (R Mo.) Oct. 2, 1854-March 15, 1947; House 1905-09, 1921-23, 1925,27, 1929-31.

ELLIS, Ezekiel John (D La.) Oct. 15, 1840-April 25, 1889; House 1875-85.

ELLIS, Hubert Summers (R W.Va.) July 6, 1887-Dec. 3, 1959; House 1943-49.

ELLIS, Powhatan (D Miss.) Jan. 17, 1790-March 18, 1863; Senate Sept. 28, 1825-Jan. 28, 1826, 1827-July 16, 1832.

ELLIS, William Cox (F Pa.) May 5, 1787-Dec. 13, 1871; House 1821 (Elected 1820 but resigned before Congress assembled), 1823-25.

ELLIS, William Russell (R Ore.) April 23, 1850-Jan. 18, 1915; House 1893-99, 1907-11.

ELLIS, William Thomas (D Ky.) July 24, 1845-Jan. 8, 1925; House 1889-95.

ELLISON, Andrew (D Ohio) 1812-about 1860; House 1853-55.

ELLISON, Daniel (R Md.) Feb. 14, 1886-Aug. 20, 1960; House 1943-45.

ELLMAKER, Amos (— Pa.) Feb. 2, 1787-Nov. 28, 1851; House March 3-July 3, 1815 (elected but did not qualify, resigned before Congress assembled).

ELLSBERRY, William Wallace (D Ohio) Dec. 18, 1833-Sept. 7, 1894; House 1885-87.

ELLSWORTH, Charles Clinton (R Mich.) Jan. 29, 1824-June 25, 1899; House 1877-79.

ELLSWORTH, Franklin Fowler (R Minn.) July 10, 1879-Dec. 23, 1942; House 1915-21.

ELLSWORTH, Matthew Harris (R Ore.) Sept. 17, 1899-—; House 1943-57.

ELLSWORTH, Oliver (father of William Wolcott Ellsworth) (F Conn.) April 29, 1745-Nov. 26, 1807; Senate 1789-March 8, 1796; Cont. Cong. 1777-84; Chief Justice Supreme Court 1796-99.

ELLSWORTH, Robert Fred (R Kan.) June 11, 1926-—; House 1961-67.

ELLSWORTH, Samuel Stewart (D N.Y.) Oct. 13, 1790-June 4, 1863; House 1845-47.

ELLSWORTH, William Wolcott (son of Oliver Ellsworth (W Conn.) Nov. 10, 1791-Jan. 15, 1868; House 1829-July 8, 1834; Gov. 1838-42.

ELLWOOD, Reuben (R Ill.) Feb. 21, 1821-July 1, 1885; House 1883-July 1, 1885.

ELLZEY, Lawrence Russell (D Miss.) March 20, 1891-Dec. 7, 1977; House March 15, 1932-35.

ELMENDORF, Lucas Conrad (D N.Y.) 1758-Aug. 17, 1843; House 1797-1803.

ELMER, Ebenezer (brother of Jonathan Elmer, father of Lucius Quintius Cincinnatus Elmer) (D N.J.) Aug. 23, 1752-Oct. 18, 1843; House 1801-07.

ELMER, Jonathan (brother of Ebenezer Elmer, uncle of Lucius Quintius Cincinnatus Elmer) (F N.J.) Nov. 29, 1745-Sept. 3, 1817; Senate 1789-91; Cont. Cong. 1776-78, 1781-84, 1787-88.

ELMER, Lucius Quintius Cincinnatus (son of Ebenezer Elmer, nephew of Jonathan Elmer) (D N.J.) Feb. 3, 1793-March 11, 1883; House 1843-45.

ELMER, William Price (R Mo.) March 2, 1871-May 11, 1956; House 1943-45.

ELMORE, Franklin Harper (SRD S.C.) Oct. 15, 1799-May 28, 1850; House Dec. 10, 1836-39; Senate April 11-May 28, 1850.

ELSAESSER, Edward Julius (R N.Y.) March 10, 1904-—; House 1945-49.

ELSTON, Charles Henry (R Ohio) Aug. 1, 1891-Sept. 25, 1980; House 1939-53.

ELSTON, John Arthur (PR Calif.) Feb. 10, 1874-Dec. 15, 1921; House 1915-Dec. 15, 1921.

ELTSE, Ralph Roscoe (R Calif.) Sept. 13, 1885-March 18, 1971; House 1933-35.

ELVINS, Politte (R Mo.) March 16, 1878-Jan. 14, 1943; House 1909-11.

ELY, Alfred (R N.Y.0 Feb. 15, 1815-May 18, 1892; House 1859-63.

ELY, Frederick David (R Mass.) Sept. 24, 1838-Aug. 6, 1921; House 1885-87.

ELY, John (D N.Y.) Oct. 8, 1774-Aug. 20, 1849; House 1839-41.

ELY, Smith Jr. (D N.Y.) April 17, 1825-July 1, 1911; House 1871-73, 1875-Dec. 11, 1876.

ELY, William (F Mass.) Aug. 14, 1765-Oct. 9, 1817; House 1805-15.

EMBREE, Elisha (W Ind.) Sept. 28, 1801-Feb. 28, 1863; House 1847-49.

EMERICH, Martin (D Ill.) April 27, 1846-Sept. 27, 1922; House 1903-05.

EMERSON, Henry Ivory (R Ohio) March 15, 1871-Oct. 28, 1953; House 1915-21.

EMERSON, Louis Woodard (R N.Y.) July 25, 1857-June 10, 1924; House 1899-1903.

EMERSON, William (R Mo.) Jan. 1, 1938-—; House 1981-—.

EMERY, David Farnham (R Maine) Sept. 1, 1948-—; House 1975-83.

EMOTT, James (F N.Y.) March 9, 1771-April 7, 1850; House 1809-13.

EMRIE, Jonas Reece (R Ohio) April 25, 1812-June 5, 1869; House 1855-57.

ENGEL, Albert Joseph (R Mich.) Jan. 1, 1888-Dec. 2, 1959; House 1935-51.

ENGLAND, Edward Theodore (R W.Va.) Sept. 29, 1869-Sept. 9, 1934; House 1927-29.

ENGLE, Clair (D Calif.) Sept. 21, 1911-July 30, 1964; House Aug. 31, 1943-59; Senate 1959-July 30, 1964.

ENGLEBRIGHT, Harry Lane (son of William Fellows Englebright) (R Calif.) Jan. 2, 1884-May 13, 1943; House Aug. 31, 1926-May 13, 1943.

ENGLEBRIGHT, William Fellows (father of Harry Lane Englebright) (R Calif.) Nov. 23, 1855-Feb. 10, 1915; House Nov. 6, 1906-11.

ENGLISH, Glenn Lee Jr. (D Okla.) Nov. 30, 1940-—; House 1975-—.

ENGLISH, James Edward (D Conn.) March 13, 1812-March 2, 1890; House 1861-65; Senate Nov. 27, 1875-May 17, 1876; Gov. 1867-69, 1870-71.

ENGLISH, Thomas Dunn (D N.J.) June 29, 1819-April 1, 1902; House 1891-95.

ENGLISH, Warren Barkley (D Calif.) May 1, 1840-Jan. 9, 1913; House April 4, 1894-95.

ENGLISH, William Eastin (son of William Hayden English) (D Ind.) Nov. 3, 1850-April 29, 1926; House May 22, 1884-85.

ENGLISH, William Hayden (father of William Eastin English) (D Ind.) Aug. 27, 1822-Feb. 7, 1896; House 1853-61.

ENLOE, Benjamin Augustine (D Tenn.) Jan. 18, 1848-July 8, 1922; House 1887-95.

ENOCHS, William Henry (R Ohio) March 29, 1842-July 13, 1893; House 1891-July 13, 1893.

EPES, James Fletcher (cousin of Sydney Parham Epes) (D Va.) May 23, 1842-Aug. 24, 1910; House 1891-95.

EPES, Sydney Parham (cousin of James Fletcher Epes) (D Va.) Aug. 20, 1865-March 3, 1900; House 1897-March 23, 1898, 1899-March 3, 1900.

EPPES, John Wayles (D Va.) April 7, 1773-Sept. 13, 1823; House 1803-11, 1813-15; Senate 1817-Dec. 4, 1819.

ERDAHL, Arlen Ingolf (R Minn.) Feb 27, 1931-—; House 1979-83.

ERDMAN, Constantine Jacob (grandson of Jacob Erdman) (D Pa.) Sept. 4, 1846-Jan. 15, 1911; House 1893-97.

ERDMAN, Jacob (grandfather of Constantine Jacob Erdman) (D Pa.) Feb. 22, 1801-July 20, 1867; House 1845-47.

ERDREICH, Ben (D Ala.) Dec. 9, 1938-—; House 1983-—.

ERICKSON, John Edward (D Mont.) March 14, 1863-May 25, 1946; Senate March 13, 1933-Nov. 6, 1934; Gov. 1925-33.

ERK, Edmund Frederick (R Pa.) April 17, 1872-Dec. 14, 1953; House Nov. 4, 1930-33.

ERLENBORN, John Neal (R Ill.) Feb. 8, 1927- —; House 1965-85.

ERMENTROUT, Daniel (D Pa.) Jan. 24, 1837-Sept. 17, 1899; House 1881-89, 1897-Sept. 17, 1899.

ERNST, Richard Pretlow (R Ky.) Feb. 28, 1858-April 13, 1934; Senate 1921-27.

ERRETT, Russell (R Pa.) Nov. 10, 1817-April 7, 1891; House 1877-83.

ERTEL, Allen Edward (D Pa.) Nov. 7, 1936- —; House 1977-83.

ERVIN, James (Protect. S.C.) Oct. 17, 1778-July 7, 1841; House 1817-21.

ERVIN, Joseph Wilson (brother of Samuel James Ervin Jr.) (D N.C.) March 3, 1901-Dec. 25, 1945; House Jan. 3-Dec. 25, 1945.

ERVIN, Samuel James Jr. (brother of Joseph Wilson Ervin) (D N.C.) Sept. 27, 1896- —; House Jan. 22, 1946-47; Senate June 5, 1954-Dec. 31, 1974.

ESCH, John Jacob (R Wis.) March 20, 1861-April 27, 1941; House 1899-1921.

ESCH, Marvin L. (R Mich.) Aug. 4, 1927- —; House 1967-77.

ESHLEMAN, Edwin D. (R Pa.) Dec. 4, 1920-Jan. 12, 1985; House 1967-77.

ESLICK, Edward Everett (husband of Willa McCord Eslick) (D Tenn.) April 19, 1872-June 14, 1932; House 1925-June 14, 1932.

ESLICK, Willa McCord Blake (widow of Edward Everett Eslick) (D Tenn.) Sept. 8, 1878-Feb. 18, 1961; House Aug. 4, 1932-33.

ESSEN, Frederick (R Mo.) April 22, 1863-Aug. 18, 1946; House Nov. 5, 1918-19.

ESTABROOK, Experience (— Neb.) April 30, 1813-March 26, 1894; House (Terr. Del.) 1859-May 18, 1860.

ESTEP, Harry Allison (R Pa.) Feb. 1, 1884-Feb. 28, 1968; House 1927-33.

ESTERLY, Charles Joseph (R Pa.) Feb. 8, 1888-Sept. 3, 1940; House 1925-27, 1929-31.

ESTIL, Benjamin (— Va.) March 13, 1780-July 14, 1853; House 1825-27.

ESTOPINAL, Albert (D La.) Jan. 30, 1845-April 28, 1919; House Nov. 3, 1908-April 28, 1919.

ESTY, Constantine Canaris (R Mass.) Dec. 26, 1824-Dec. 27, 1912; House Dec. 2, 1872-73.

ETHERIDGE, Emerson (W Tenn.) Sept. 28, 1819-Oct. 21, 1902; House 1853-57, 1859-61.

EUSTIS, George Jr. (brother of James Biddle Eustis) (AP La.) Sept. 28, 1828-March 15, 1872; House 1855-59.

EUSTIS, James Biddle (brother of George Eustis Jr.) (D La.) Aug. 27, 1834-Sept. 9, 1899; Senate Jan. 12, 1876-79, 1885-91.

EUSTIS, William (D Mass.) June 10, 1753-Feb. 6, 1825; House 1801-05, Aug. 21, 1820-23; Secy. of War 1809-13; Gov. 1823-25.

EVANS, Alexander (W Md.) Sept. 13, 1818-Dec. 5, 1888; House 1847-53.

EVANS, Alvin (R Pa.) Oct. 4, 1845-June 19, 1906; House 1901-05.

EVANS, Billy Lee (D Ga.) Nov. 10, 1941- —; House 1977-83.

EVANS, Charles Robley (D Nev.) Aug. 9, 1866-Nov. 30, 1954; House 1919-21.

EVANS, Cooper (R Iowa) May 26, 1924- —; House 1981- —.

EVANS, Daniel J. (R Wash.) Oct. 16, 1925- —; House Sept. 12, 1983- —.

EVANS, David Ellicott (D N.Y.) March 19, 1788-May 17, 1850; House March 4-May 2, 1827.

EVANS, David Reid (D S.C.) Feb. 20, 1769-March 8, 1843; House 1813-15.

EVANS, David Walter (D Ind.) Aug. 17, 1946- —; House 1975-83.

EVANS, Frank Edward (D Colo.) Sept. 6, 1923- —; House 1965-79.

EVANS, George (W Maine) Jan. 12, 1797-April 6, 1867; House July 20, 1829-41; Senate 1841-47.

EVANS, Henry Clay (R Tenn.) June 18, 1843-Dec. 12, 1921; House 1889-91.

EVANS, Hiram Kinsman (R Iowa) March 17, 1863-July 9, 1941; House June 4, 1923-25.

EVANS, Isaac Newton (R Pa.) July 29, 1827-Dec. 3, 1901; House 1877-79, 1883-87.

EVANS, James La Fayette (R Ind.) March 27, 1825-May 28, 1903; House 1875-79.

EVANS, John Morgan (D Mont.) Jan. 7, 1863-March 12, 1946; House 1913-21, 1923-33.

EVANS, Joshua Jr. (D Pa.) Jan. 20, 1777-Oct. 2, 1846; House 1829-33.

EVANS, Josiah James (SRD S.C.) Nov. 27, 1786-May 6, 1858; Senate 1853-May 6, 1858.

EVANS, Lane (D Ill.) Aug. 4, 1951- —; House 1983- —.

EVANS, Lemuel Dale (AP Texas) Jan. 8, 1810-July 1, 1877; House 1855-57.

EVANS, Lynden (D Ill.) June 28, 1858-May 6, 1926; House 1911-13.

EVANS, Marcellus Hugh (D N.Y.) Sept. 22, 1884-Nov. 21, 1953; House 1935-41.

EVANS, Melvin Herbert (R V.I.) Aug. 7, 1917- —; House (Terr. Del.) 1979-81.

EVANS, Nathan (W Ohio) June 24, 1804-Sept. 27, 1879; House 1847-51.

EVANS, Robert Emory (R Neb.) July 15, 1856-July 8, 1925; House 1919-23.

EVANS, Thomas (— Va.) ?-?; House 1797-1801.

EVANS, Thomas Beverley Jr. (R Del.) Nov. 5, 1931- —; House 1977-83; Co-Chrmn. Rep. Nat. Comm. 1971-73.

EVANS, Walter (nephew of Burwell Clark Ritter) (R Ky.) Sept. 18, 1842-Dec. 30, 1923; House 1895-99.

EVANS, William Elmer (R Calif.) Dec. 14, 1877-Nov. 12, 1959; House 1927-35.

EVARTS, William Maxwell (grandson of Roger Sherman) (R N.Y.) Feb. 6, 1818-Feb. 28, 1901; Senate 1885-91; Atty. Gen. 1868-69; Secy. of State 1877-81.

EVERETT, Edward (father of William Everett) (NR Mass.) April 11, 1794-Jan. 15, 1865; House 1825-35; Senate 1853-June 1, 1854; Gov. 1836-40; Secy. of State 1852-53.

EVERETT, Horace (W Vt.) July 17, 1779-Jan. 30, 1851; House 1829-43.

EVERETT, Robert Ashton (D Tenn.) Feb. 24, 1915-Jan. 26, 1969; House Feb. 1, 1958-Jan. 26, 1969.

EVERETT, Robert William (D Ga.) March 3, 1839-Feb. 27, 1915; House 1891-93.

EVERETT, William (son of Edward Everett) (D Mass.) Oct. 10, 1839-Feb. 16, 1910; House April 25, 1893-95.

EVERHART, James Bowen (son of William Everhart) (R Pa.) July 26, 1821-Aug. 23, 1888; House 1883-87.

EVERHART, William (father of James Bowen Everhart) (W Pa.) May 17, 1785-Oct. 30, 1868; House 1853-55.

EVINS, John Hamilton (D S.C.) July 18, 1830-Oct. 20, 1884; House 1877-Oct. 20, 1884.

EVINS, Joseph Landon (Joe) (D Tenn.) Oct. 24, 1910-March 31, 1984; House 1947-77.

EWART, Hamilton Glover (R N.C.) Oct. 23, 1849-April 28, 1918; House 1889-91.

EWING, Andrew (brother of Edwin Hickman Ewing) (D Tenn.) June 17, 1813-June 16, 1864; House 1849-51.

EWING, Edwin Hickman (brother of Andrew Ewing) (W Tenn.) Dec. 2, 1809-April 24, 1902; House 1845-47.

EWING, John (W Ind.) May 19, 1789-April 6, 1858; House 1833-35, 1837-39.

EWING, John Hoge (W Pa.) Oct. 5, 1796-June 9, 1887; House 1845-47.

EWING, Presley Underwood (W Ky.) Sept. 1, 1822-Sept. 27, 1854; House 1851-Sept. 27, 1854.

EWING, Thomas (W Ohio) (father of the following) Dec. 28, 1789-Oct. 26, 1871; Senate 1831-37; July 20, 1850-51; Secy. of the Treasury 1841; Secy. of the Interior 1849-50.

EWING, Thomas (son of the preceding) (D Ohio) Aug. 7, 1829-Jan. 21, 1896; House 1877-81.

Biographical Index

EWING, William Lee Davidson (JD Ill.) Aug. 31, 1795-March 25, 1846; Senate Dec. 30, 1835-37; Gov. Nov.-Dec. 1834.

EXON, John James (D Neb.) Aug. 9, 1921- —; Senate 1979- —; Gov. 1971-79.

F

FADDIS, Charles I. (D Pa.) June 13, 1890-April 1, 1972; House 1933-Dec. 4, 1942.

FAIR, James Graham (D Nev.) Dec. 3, 1831-Dec. 28, 1894; Senate 1881-87.

FAIRBANKS, Charles Warren (R Ind.) May 11, 1852-June 4, 1918; Senate 1897-1905; Vice President 1905-09.

FAIRCHILD, Benjamin Lewis (R N.Y.) Jan. 5, 1863-Oct. 25, 1946; House 1895-97, 1917-19, 1921-23, Nov. 6, 1923-27.

FAIRCHILD, George Winthrop (R N.Y.) May 6, 1854-Dec. 31, 1924; House 1907-19.

FAIRFIELD, John (D Maine) Jan. 30, 1797-Dec. 24, 1847; House 1835-Dec. 24, 1838; Senate 1843-Dec. 24, 1847; Gov. 1839-41, 1842-43.

FAIRFIELD, Louis William (R Ind.) Oct. 15, 1858-Feb. 20, 1930; House 1917-25.

FAISON, John Miller (D N.C.) April 17, 1862-April 21, 1915; House 1911-15.

FALCONER, Jacob Alexander (Prog. Wash.) Jan. 26, 1869-July 1, 1928; House 1913-15.

FALL, Albert Bacon (R N.M.) Nov. 26, 1861-Nov. 30, 1944; Senate March 27, 1912-March 4, 1921; Secy. of the Interior 1921-23.

FALLON, George Hyde (D Md.) July 24, 1902-March 21, 1980; House 1945-71.

FANNIN, Paul Jones (R Ariz.) Jan. 29, 1907- —; Senate 1965-77; Gov. 1959-65.

FARAN, James John (D Ohio) Dec. 29, 1808-Dec. 12, 1892; House 1845-49.

FARBSTEIN, Leonard (D N.Y.) Oct. 12, 1902- —; House 1957-71.

FARIS, George Washington (R Ind.) June 9, 1854-April 17, 1914; House 1895-1901.

FARLEE, Isaac Gray (— N.J.) May 18, 1787-Jan. 12, 1855; House 1843-45.

FARLEY, Ephraim Wilder (W Maine) Aug. 29, 1817-April 3, 1880; House 1853-55.

FARLEY, James Indus (D Ind.) Feb. 24, 1871-June 16, 1948; House 1933-39.

FARLEY, James Thompson (D Calif.) Aug. 6, 1829-Jan. 22, 1886; Senate 1879-85.

FARLEY, Michael Francis (D N.Y.) March 1, 1863-Oct. 8, 1921; House 1915-17.

FARLIN, Dudley (D N.Y.) Sept. 2, 1777-Sept. 26, 1837; House 1835-37.

FARNSLEY, Charles Rowland Peaslee (D Ky.) March 28, 1907- —; House 1965-67.

FARNSWORTH, John Franklin (R Ill.) March 27, 1820-July 14, 1897; House 1857-61, 1863-73.

FARNUM, Billie Sunday (D Mich.) April 11, 1916-Nov. 18, 1979; House 1965-67.

FARQUHAR, John Hanson (R Ind.) Dec. 20, 1818-Oct. 1, 1873; House 1865-67.

FARQUHAR, John McCreath (R N.Y.) April 17, 1832-April 24, 1918; House 1885-91.

FARR, Evarts Worcester (R N.H.) Oct. 10, 1840-Nov. 30, 1880; House 1879-Nov. 30, 1880.

FARR, John Richard (R Pa.) July 18, 1857-Dec. 11, 1933; House 1911-19, Feb. 25-March 3, 1921.

FARRELLY, John Wilson (son of Patrick Farrelly) (W Pa.) July 7, 1809-Dec. 20, 1860; House 1847-49.

FARRELLY, Patrick (father of John Wilson Farrelly) (D Pa.) 1770-Jan. 12, 1826; House 1821-Jan. 12, 1826.

FARRINGTON, James (D N.H.) Oct. 1, 1791-Oct. 29, 1859; House 1837-39.

FARRINGTON, Joseph Rider (husband of Mary Elizabeth Pruett Farrington) (R Hawaii) Oct. 15, 1897-June 19, 1954; House (Terr. Del.) 1943-June 19, 1954.

FARRINGTON, Mary Elizabeth Pruett (widow of Joseph Rider Farrington) (R Hawaii) May 30, 1898-July 21, 1984; House (Terr. Del.) July 31, 1954-57.

FARROW, Samuel (WD S.C.) 1759-Nov. 18, 1824; House 1813-15.

FARWELL, Charles Benjamin (R Ill.) July 1, 1823-Sept. 23, 1903; House 1871-May 6, 1876, 1881-83; Senate Jan. 19, 1887-91.

FARWELL, Nathan Allen (cousin of Owen Lovejoy) (R Maine) Feb. 24, 1812-Dec. 9, 1893; Senate Oct. 27, 1864-65.

FARWELL, Sewall Spaulding (R Iowa) April 26, 1834-Sept. 21, 1909; House 1881-83.

FARY, John George (D Ill.) April 11, 1911-June 7, 1984; House July 8, 1975-83.

FASCELL, Dante Bruno (D Fla.) March 9, 1917- —; House 1955- —.

FASSETT, Jacob Sloat (R N.Y.) Nov. 13, 1853-April 21, 1924; House 1905-11.

FAULKNER, Charles James (father of the following) (D Va./W.Va.) July 6, 1806-Nov. 1, 1884; House 1851-59 (Va.), 1875-77 (W.Va.).

FAULKNER, Charles James (son of the preceding) (D W.Va.) Sept. 21, 1847-Jan. 13, 1929; Senate 1887-99.

FAUNTROY, Walter Edward (D D.C.) Feb. 6, 1933- —; House (Delegate) March 23, 1971- —.

FAUST, Charles Lee (R Mo.) April 24, 1879-Dec. 17, 1928; House 1921-Dec. 17, 1928.

FAVROT, George Kent (D La.) Nov. 26, 1868-Dec. 26, 1934; House 1907-09, 1921-25.

FAWELL, Harris Walter (R Ill.) March 25, 1929- —; House 1985- —.

FAY, Francis Ball (W Mass.) June 12, 1793-Oct. 6, 1876; House Dec. 13, 1852-53.

FAY, James Herbert (D N.Y.) April 29, 1899-Sept. 10, 1948; House 1939-41, 1943-45.

FAY, John (D N.Y.) Feb. 10, 1773-June 21, 1855; House 1819-21.

FAZIO, Victor Herbert (D Calif.) Oct. 11, 1942- —; House 1979- —.

FEARING, Paul (F N.W. Terr.) Feb. 28, 1762-Aug. 21, 1822; House (Terr. Del.) 1801-03.

FEATHERSTON, Winfield Scott (D Miss.) Aug. 8, 1820-May 28, 1891; House 1847-51.

FEATHERSTONE, Lewis Porter (UL Ark.) July 28, 1851-March 14, 1922; House March 5, 1890-91.

FEAZEL, William Crosson (D La.) June 10, 1895-March 16, 1965; Senate May 18-Dec. 30, 1948.

FEELY, John Joseph (D Ill.) Aug. 1, 1875-Feb. 15, 1905; House 1901-03.

FEIGHAN, Edward Farrell (nephew of Michael Aloysius Feighan) (D Ohio) Oct. 22, 1947- —; House 1983- —.

FEIGHAN, Michael Aloysius (uncle of Edward Farrell Feighan) (D Ohio) Feb. 16, 1905- —; House 1943-71.

FELCH, Alpheus (D Mich.) Sept. 28, 1804-June 13, 1896; Senate 1847-53; Gov. 1846-47.

FELDER, John Myers (D S.C.) July 7, 1782-Sept. 1, 1851; House 1831-35.

FELLOWS, Frank (R Maine) Nov. 7, 1889-Aug. 27, 1951; House 1941-Aug. 27, 1951.

FELLOWS, John R. (D N.Y.) July 29, 1832-Dec. 7, 1896; House 1891-Dec. 31, 1893.

FELTON, Charles Norton (R Calif.) Jan. 1, 1828-Sept. 13, 1914; House 1885-89; Senate March 19, 1891-93.

FELTON, Rebecca Latimer (widow of William Harrell Felton) (D Ga.) June 10, 1835-Jan. 24, 1930; Senate Oct. 3-Nov. 22, 1922.

FELTON, William Harrell (husband of Rebecca Latimer Felton) (D Ga.) June 1, 1823-Sept. 24, 1909; House 1875-81.

FENERTY, Clare Gerald (R Pa.) July 25, 1895-July 1, 1952; House 1935-37.

FENN, Edward Hart (R Conn.) Sept. 12, 1856-Feb. 23, 1939; House 1921-31.

FENN, Stephen Southmyd (D Idaho) March 28, 1820-April 13, 1892; House (Terr. Del.) June 23, 1876-79.

FENNER, James (D R.I.) Jan. 22, 1771-April 17, 1846; Senate 1805-Sept. 1807; Gov. 1807-11, 1824-31, 1843-45.

FENTON, Ivor David (R Pa.) Aug. 3, 1889- —; House 1939-63.

FENTON, Lucien Jerome (R Ohio) May 7, 1844-June 28, 1922; House 1895-99.

FENTON, Reuben Eaton (R N.Y.) July 4, 1819-Aug. 25, 1885; House 1853-55, 1857-Dec. 20, 1864; Senate 1869-75; Gov. 1865-69.

FENWICK, Millicent Hammond (R N.J.) Feb. 25, 1910- —; House 1975-83.

FERDON, John William (R N.Y.) Dec. 13, 1826-Aug. 5, 1884; House 1879-81.

FERGUSON, Fenner (D Neb.) April 25, 1814-Oct. 11, 1859; House (Terr. Del.) 1857-59.

FERGUSON, Homer (R Mich.) Feb. 25, 1889-Dec. 17, 1982; Senate 1943-55.

FERGUSON, Phillip Colgan (D Okla.) Aug. 15, 1903-Aug. 8, 1978; House 1935-41.

FERGUSSON, Harvey Butler (D N.M.) Sept. 9, 1848-June 10, 1915; House (Terr. Del.) 1897-99; (Rep.) Jan. 8, 1912-15.

FERNALD, Bert Manfred (R Maine) April 3, 1859-Aug. 23, 1926; Senate Sept. 12, 1916-Aug. 23, 1926; Gov. 1909-11.

FERNANDEZ, Antonio Manuel (D N.M.) Jan. 17, 1902-Nov. 7, 1956; House 1943-Nov. 7, 1956.

FERNANDEZ, Joachim Octave (D La.) Aug. 14, 1896-Aug. 8, 1978; House 1931-41.

FERNOS-ISERN, Antonio (PD P.R.) May 10, 1895-Jan. 19, 1974; House (Res. Comm.) Sept. 11, 1946-65.

FERRARO, Geraldine Anne (D N.Y.) Aug. 26, 1935- —; House 1979-85.

FERRELL, Thomas Merrill (D N.J.) June 20, 1844-Oct. 20, 1916; House 1883-85.

FERRIS, Charles Goadsby (JD N.Y.) about 1796-June 4, 1848; House Dec. 1, 1834-35, 1841-43.

FERRIS, Scott (D Okla.) Nov. 3, 1877-June 8, 1945; House Nov. 16, 1907-21.

FERRIS, Woodbridge Nathan (D Mich.) Jan. 6, 1853-March 23, 1928; Senate 1923-March 23, 1928; Gov. 1913-17.

FERRISS, Orange (R N.Y.) Nov. 26, 1814-April 11, 1894; House 1867-71.

FERRY, Orris Sanford (IR/D Conn.) Aug. 15, 1823-Nov. 21, 1875; House 1859-61; Senate 1867-Nov. 21, 1875 (1859-61, 1867-74 Republican, 1874-75 Independent Republican/Democrat).

FERRY, Thomas White (R Mich.) June 10, 1827-Oct. 13, 1896; House 1865-71; Senate 1871-83; Pres. pro tempore 1875, 1877-79.

FESS, Simeon Davison (R Ohio) Dec. 11, 1861-Dec. 23, 1936; House 1913-23; Senate 1923-35; Chrmn. Rep. Nat. Comm. 1930-32.

FESSENDEN, Samuel Clement (brother of Thomas Amory Deblois Fessenden and William Pitt Fessenden) (R Maine) March 7, 1815-April 18, 1882; House 1861-63.

FESSENDEN, Thomas Amory Deblois (brother of Samuel Clement Fessenden and William Pitt Fessenden) (R Maine) Jan. 23, 1826-Sept. 28, 1868; House Dec. 1, 1862-63.

FESSENDEN, William Pitt (brother of Samuel Clement Fessenden and Thomas Amory Deblois Fessenden) (W Maine) Oct. 16, 1806-Sept. 9, 1869; House 1841-43; Senate Feb. 10, 1854-July 1, 1864, 1865-Sept. 9, 1869; Secy. of the Treasury 1864-65.

FEW, William (D Ga.) June 8, 1748-July 16, 1828; Senate 1789-93; Cont. Cong. 1780-88.

FICKLIN, Orlando Bell (D Ill.) Dec. 16, 1808-May 5, 1886; House 1843-49, 1851-53.

FIEDLER, Bobbi (R Calif.) April 22, 1937- —; House 1981- —.

FIEDLER, William Henry Frederick (D N.J.) Aug. 25, 1847-Jan. 1, 1919; House 1883-85.

FIELD, David Dudley (D N.Y.) Feb. 13, 1805-April 13, 1894; House Jan. 11-March 3, 1877.

FIELD, Moses Whelock (R Mich.) Feb. 10, 1828-March 14, 1889; House 1873-75.

FIELD, Richard Stockton (R N.J.) Dec. 31, 1803-May 25, 1870; Senate Nov. 21, 1862-Jan. 14, 1863.

FIELD, Scott (D Texas) Jan. 26, 1847-Dec. 20, 1931; House 1903-07.

FIELD, Walbridge Abner (R Mass.) April 26, 1833-July 15, 1899; House 1877-March 28, 1878, 1879-81.

FIELDER, George Bragg (D N.J.) July 24, 1842-Aug. 14, 1906; House 1893-95.

FIELDS, Jack (R Texas) Feb. 3, 1952- —; House 1981- —.

FIELDS, William Craig (R N.Y.) Feb. 13, 1804-Oct. 27, 1882; House 1867-69.

FIELDS, William Jason (D Ky.) Dec. 29, 1874-Oct. 21, 1954; House 1911-Dec. 11, 1923; Gov. 1923-27.

FIESINGER, William Louis (D Ohio) Oct. 25, 1877-Sept. 11, 1953; House 1931-37.

FILLMORE, Millard (W N.Y.) Jan. 7, 1800-March 8, 1874; House 1833-35, 1837-43; Vice President 1849-July 9, 1850; President July 10, 1850-53.

FINCH, Isaac (D N.Y.) Oct. 13, 1783-June 23, 1845; House 1829-31.

FINCK, William Edward (D Ohio) Sept. 1, 1822-Jan. 25, 1901; House 1863-67, Dec. 7, 1874-75.

FINDLAY, James (brother of John Findlay and William Findlay) (JD Ohio) Oct. 12, 1770-Dec. 28, 1835; House 1825-33.

FINDLAY, John (brother of James Findlay and William Findlay) (D Pa.) March 31, 1766-Nov. 5, 1838; House Oct. 9, 1821-27.

FINDLAY, John Van Lear (D Md.) Dec. 21, 1839-April 19, 1907; House 1883-87.

FINDLAY, William (brother of James Findlay and John Findlay) (D Pa.) June 20, 1768-Nov. 12, 1846; Senate Dec. 10, 1821-27; Gov. 1817-20.

FINDLEY, Paul (R Ill.) June 23, 1921- —; House 1961-83.

FINDLEY, William (D Pa.) 1741 or 1742-April 4, 1821; House 1791-99, 1803-17.

FINE, John (D N.Y.) Aug. 26, 1794-Jan. 4, 1867; House 1839-41.

FINE, Sidney Asher (D N.Y.) Sept. 14, 1903-April 13, 1982; House 1951-Jan. 2, 1956.

FINERTY, John Frederick (ID Ill.) Sept. 10, 1846-June 10, 1908; House 1883-85.

FINKELNBURG, Gustavus Adolphus (LR Mo.) April 6, 1837-May 18, 1908; House 1869-71 1871-73 (1869-71 Republican, 1871-73 Liberal).

FINLEY, Charles (son of Hugh Franklin Finley) (R Ky.) March 26, 1865-March 18, 1941; House Feb. 15, 1930-33.

FINLEY, David Edward (D S.C.) Feb. 28, 1861-Jan. 26, 1917; House 1899-Jan. 26, 1917.

FINLEY, Ebenezer Byron (nephew of Stephen Ross Harris) (D Ohio) July 31, 1833-Aug. 22, 1916; House 1877-81.

FINLEY, Hugh Franklin (father of Charles Finley) (R Ky.) Jan. 18, 1833-Oct. 16, 1909; House 1887-91.

FINLEY, Jesse Johnson (D Fla.) Nov. 18, 1812-Nov. 6, 1904; House April 19, 1876-77, Feb. 20-March 3, 1879, 1881-June 1, 1882.

FINNEGAN, Edward Rowan (D Ill.) June 5, 1905-Feb. 2, 1971; House 1961-Dec. 6, 1964.

FINNEY, Darwin Abel (R Pa.) Aug. 11, 1814-Aug. 25, 1868; House 1867-Aug. 25, 1868.

FINO, Paul Albert (R N.Y.) Dec. 15, 1913- —; House 1953-Dec. 31, 1968.

FISCHER, Israel Frederick (R N.Y.) Aug. 17, 1858-March 16, 1940; House 1895-99.

FISH, Hamilton (father of the following, grandfather of Hamilton Fish Jr. born in 1888, great-grandfather of Hamilton Fish Jr. born in 1926) (W N.Y.) Aug. 3, 1808-Sept. 7, 1893; House 1843-45; Senate 1851-57; Gov. 1849-51; Secy of State 1869-77.

FISH, Hamilton (son of the preceding, father of the following, grandfather of Hamilton Fish Jr.) (R N.Y.) April 17, 1849-Jan. 15, 1936; House 1909-11.

FISH, Hamilton Jr. (son of the preceding, father of the following, grandson of Hamilton Fish) (R N.Y.) Dec. 7, 1888- —; House Nov. 2, 1920-45.

FISH, Hamilton Jr. (son of the preceding, grandson of Hamilton Fish born in 1849, great-grandson of Hamilton Fish born in 1808) (R N.Y.) June 3, 1926- —; House 1969- —.

FISHBURNE, John Wood (cousin of Fontaine Maury Maverick) (D Va.) March 8, 1868-June 24, 1937; House 1931-33.

FISHER, Charles (D N.C.) Oct. 20, 1789-May 7, 1849; House Feb. 11, 1819-21, 1839-41.

FISHER, David (W Ohio) Dec. 3, 1794-May 7, 1886; House 1847-49.

FISHER, George (— N.Y.) March 17, 1788-March 26, 1861; House 1829-Feb. 5, 1830.

FISHER, George Purnell (UR Del.) Oct. 13, 1817-Feb. 10, 1899; House 1861-63.

FISHER, Horatio Gates (R Pa.) April 21, 1838-May 8, 1890; House 1879-83.

Biographical Index

FISHER, Hubert Frederick (D Tenn.) Oct. 6, 1877-June 16, 1941; House 1917-31.

FISHER, John (R N.Y.) March 13, 1806-March 28, 1882; House 1869-71.

FISHER, Joseph Lyman (D Va.) Jan. 11, 1914- —; House 1975-81.

FISHER, Ovie Clark (D Texas) Nov. 22, 1903- —; House 1943-75.

FISHER, Spencer Olive (D Mich.) Feb. 3, 1843-June 1, 1919; House 1885-89.

FISK, James (D Vt.) Oct. 4, 1763-Nov. 17, 1844; House 1805-09, 1811-15; Senate Nov. 4, 1817-Jan. 8, 1818.

FISK, Jonathan (D N.Y.) Sept. 26, 1778-July 13, 1832; House 1809-11, 1813-March 1815.

FITCH, Asa (F N.Y.) Nov. 10, 1765-Aug. 24, 1843; House 1811-13.

FITCH, Ashbel Parmelee (D N.Y.) Oct. 8, 1838-May 4, 1904; House 1887-89, 1889-Dec. 26, 1893 (1887-89 Republican, 1889-93 Democrat).

FITCH, Graham Newell (grandfather of Edwin Denby) (D Ind.) Dec. 5, 1809-Nov. 29, 1892; House 1849-53; Senate Feb. 4, 1857-61.

FITCH, Thomas (R Nev.) Jan. 27, 1838-Nov. 12, 1923; House 1869-71.

FITE, Samuel McClary (D Tenn.) June 12, 1816-Oct. 23, 1875; House March 4-Oct. 23, 1875.

FITHIAN, Floyd James (D Ind.) Nov. 3, 1928- —; House 1975-83.

FITHIAN, George Washington (D Ill.) July 4, 1854-Jan. 21, 1921; House 1889-95.

FITZGERALD, Frank Thomas (D N.Y.) May 4, 1857-Nov. 25, 1907; House March 4-Nov. 4, 1889.

FITZGERALD, John Francis (grandfather of John F. Kennedy, Robert F. Kennedy and Edward M. Kennedy) (D Mass.) Feb. 11, 1863-Oct. 2, 1950; House 1895-1901, March 4-Oct. 23, 1919.

FITZGERALD, John Joseph (D N.Y.) March 10, 1872-May 13, 1952; House 1899-Dec. 31, 1917.

FITZGERALD, Roy Gerald (R Ohio) Aug. 25, 1875-Nov. 16, 1962; House 1921-31.

FITZGERALD, Thomas (D Mich.) April 10, 1796-March 25, 1855; Senate June 8, 1849-49.

FITZGERALD, William (JD Tenn.) Aug. 6, 1799-March 1864; House 1831-33.

FITZGERALD, William Joseph (D Conn.) March 2, 1887-May 6, 1947; House 1937-39, 1941-43.

FITZGERALD, William Thomas (R Ohio) Oct. 13, 1858-Jan. 12, 1939; House 1925-29.

FITZGIBBONS, John (D N.Y.) July 10, 1868-Aug. 4, 1941; House 1933-35.

FITZHENRY, Louis (D Ill.) June 13, 1870-Nov. 18, 1935; House 1913-15.

FITZPATRICK, Benjamin (SRD Ala.) June 30, 1802-Nov. 25, 1869; Senate Nov. 25, 1848-Nov. 30, 1849, Jan. 14, 1853-55, Nov. 26, 1855-Jan. 21, 1861; Pres. pro tempore 1857-61; Gov. 1841-45.

FITZPATRICK, James Martin (D N.Y.) June 27, 1869-April 10, 1949; House 1927-45.

FITZPATRICK, Morgan Cassius (D Tenn.) Oct. 29, 1868-June 25, 1908; House 1903-05.

FITZPATRICK, Thomas Young (D Ky.) Sept. 20, 1850-Jan. 21, 1906; House 1897-1901.

FITZSIMONS, Thomas (F Pa.) 1741-Aug. 26, 1811; House 1789-95; Cont. Cong. 1782-83.

FJARE, Orvin Benonie (R Mont.) April 16, 1918- —; House 1955-57.

FLACK, William Henry (R N.Y.) March 22, 1861-Feb. 2, 1907; House 1903-Feb. 2, 1907.

FLAGLER, Thomas Thorn (W N.Y.) Oct. 12, 1811-Sept. 6, 1897; House 1853-57.

FLAHERTY, Lawrence James (R Calif.) July 4, 1878-June 13, 1926; House 1925-June 13, 1926.

FLAHERTY, Thomas Aloysius (D Mass.) Dec. 21, 1898-April 27, 1965; House Dec. 14, 1937-43.

FLANAGAN, De Witt Clinton (D N.J.) Dec. 28, 1870-Jan. 15, 1946; House June 18, 1902-03.

FLANAGAN, James Winright (R Texas) Sept. 5, 1805-Sept. 28, 1887; Senate March 30, 1870-75.

FLANDERS, Alvan (R Wash.) Aug. 2, 1825-March 14, 1884; House (Terr. Del.) 1867-69; Gov. (Wash. Terr.) 1869-70.

FLANDERS, Benjamin Franklin (U La.) Jan. 26, 1816-March 13, 1896; House Dec. 3, 1862-63; Military Gov. 1867-68.

FLANDERS, Ralph Edward (R Vt.) Sept. 28, 1880-Feb. 19, 1970; Senate Nov. 1, 1946-59.

FLANNAGAN, John William Jr. (D Va.) Feb. 20, 1885-April 27, 1955; House 1931-49.

FLANNERY, John Harold (D Pa.) April 19, 1898-June 3, 1961; House 1937-42.

FLEEGER, George Washington (R Pa.) March 13, 1839-June 25, 1894; House 1885-87.

FLEETWOOD, Frederick Gleed (R Vt.) Sept. 27, 1868-Jan. 28, 1938; House 1923-25.

FLEGER, Anthony Alfred (D Ohio) Oct. 21, 1900-July 16, 1963; House 1937-39.

FLEMING, William Bennett (D Ga.) Oct. 29, 1803-Aug. 19, 1886; House Feb. 10-March 3, 1879.

FLEMING, William Henry (D Ga.) Oct. 18, 1856-June 9, 1944; House 1897-1903.

FLETCHER, Charles Kimball (R Calif.) Dec. 15, 1902- —; House 1947-49.

FLETCHER, Duncan Upshaw (D Fla.) Jan. 6, 1859-June 17, 1936; Senate 1909-June 17, 1936.

FLETCHER, Isaac (AMas. D Vt.) Nov. 22, 1784-Oct. 19, 1842; House 1837-41.

FLETCHER, Loren (R Minn.) April 10, 1833-April 15, 1919; House 1893-1903, 1905-07.

FLETCHER, Richard (W Mass.) Jan. 8, 1788-June 21, 1869; House 1837-39.

FLETCHER, Thomas (— Ky.) Oct. 21, 1779-?; House Dec. 2, 1816-17.

FLETCHER, Thomas Brooks (D Ohio) Oct. 10, 1879-July 1, 1945; House 1925-29, 1933-39.

FLICK, James Patton (R Iowa) Aug. 28, 1845-Feb. 25, 1929; House 1889-93.

FLINT, Frank Putnam (R Calif.) July 15, 1862-Feb. 11, 1929; Senate 1905-11.

FLIPPO, Ronnie G. (D Ala.) Aug. 15, 1937- —; House 1977- —.

FLOOD, Daniel John (D Pa.) Nov. 26, 1903- —; House 1945-47, 1949-53, 1955-Jan. 31, 1980.

FLOOD, Henry De La Warr (half brother of Joel West Flood, uncle of Harry Flood Byrd) (D Va.) Sept. 2, 1865-Dec. 8, 1921; House 1901-Dec. 8, 1921.

FLOOD, Joel West (half brother of Henry De La Warr Flood, uncle of Harry Flood Byrd) (D Va.) Aug. 2, 1894-April 27, 1964; House Nov. 8, 1932-33.

FLOOD, Thomas Schmeck (R N.Y.) April 12, 1844-Oct. 28, 1908; House 1887-91.

FLORENCE, Elias (W Ohio) Feb. 15, 1797-Nov. 21, 1880; House 1843-45.

FLORENCE, Thomas Birch (D Pa.) Jan. 26, 1812-July 3, 1875; House 1851-61.

FLORIO, James Joseph (D N.J.) Aug. 29, 1937- —; House 1975- —.

FLOURNOY, Thomas Stanhope (W Va.) Dec. 15, 1811-March 12, 1883; House 1847-49.

FLOWER, Roswell Pettibone (D N.Y.) Aug. 7, 1835-May 12, 1899; House Nov. 8, 1881-83, 1889-Sept. 16, 1891; Gov. 1892-95.

FLOWERS, Walter (D Ala.) April 12, 1933-April 12, 1984; House 1969-79.

FLOYD, Charles Albert (D N.Y.) 1791-Feb. 20, 1873; House 1841-43.

FLOYD, John (— Ga.) Oct. 3, 1769-June 24, 1839; House 1827-29.

FLOYD, John (D Va.) April 24, 1783-Aug. 17, 1837; House 1817-29; Gov. 1830-34.

FLOYD, John Charles (D Ark.) April 14, 1858-Nov. 4, 1930; House 1905-15.

FLOYD, John Gelston (D N.Y.) Feb. 5, 1806-Oct. 5, 1881; House 1839-43, 1851-53.

FLOYD, William (— N.Y.) Dec. 17, 1734-Aug. 4, 1821; House 1789-91; Cont. Cong. 1774-77, 1778-83.

FLYE, Edwin (R Maine) March 4, 1817-July 12, 1886; Dec. 4, 1876-77.

FLYNN, Dennis Thomas (R Okla.) Feb. 13, 1861-June 19, 1939; House (Terr. Del.) 1893-97, 1899-1903.

FLYNN, Gerald Thomas (D Wis.) Oct. 7, 1910- --; House 1959-61.

FLYNN, Joseph Vincent (D N.Y.) Sept. 2, 1883-Feb. 6, 1940; House 1915-19.

FLYNT, John James Jr. (D Ga.) Nov. 8, 1914- --; House Nov. 2, 1954-79.

FOCHT, Benjamin Kurtz (R Pa.) March 12, 1863-March 27, 1937; House 1907-13, 1915-23, 1933-March 27, 1937.

FOELKER, Otto Godfrey (R N.Y.) Dec. 29, 1875-Jan. 18, 1943; House Nov. 3, 1908-11.

FOERDERER, Robert Herman (R Pa.) May 16, 1860-July 26, 1903; House 1901-July 26, 1903.

FOGARTY, John Edward (D R.I.) March 23, 1913-Jan. 10, 1967; House 1941-Dec. 7, 1944; 1945-Jan. 10, 1967.

FOGG, George Gilman (R N.H.) May 26, 1813-Oct. 5, 1881; Senate Aug. 31, 1866-67.

FOGLIETTA, Thomas M. (Ind. Pa.) Dec. 3, 1928- --; House 1981- --.

FOLEY, James Bradford (D Ind.) Oct. 18, 1807-Dec. 5, 1886; House 1857-59.

FOLEY, John Robert (D Md.) Oct. 16, 1917- --; House 1959-61.

FOLEY, Thomas Stephen (D Wash.) March 6, 1929- --; House 1965- --.

FOLGER, Alonzo Dillard (brother of John Hamlin Folger) (D N.C.) July 9, 1888-April 30, 1941; House 1939-April 30, 1941.

FOLGER, John Hamlin (brother of Alonzo Dillard Folger) (D N.C.) Dec. 18, 1880-July 19, 1963; House June 14, 1941-49.

FOLGER, Walter Jr. (D Mass.) June 12, 1765-Sept. 8, 1849; House 1817-21.

FOLLETT, John Fassett (D Ohio) Feb. 18, 1831-April 15, 1902; House 1883-85.

FONG, Hiram Leong (R Hawaii) Oct. 1, 1907- --; Senate Aug. 21, 1959-77.

FOOT, Solomon (R Vt.) Nov. 19, 1802-March 28, 1866; House 1843-47; Senate 1851-March 28, 1866 (1843-47, 1851-57 Whig, 1857-66 Republican) Pres. pro tempore 1861-64.

FOOTE, Charles Augustus (D N.Y.) April 15, 1785-Aug. 1, 1828; House 1823-25.

FOOTE, Ellsworth Bishop (R Conn.) Jan. 12, 1898-Jan. 18, 1977; House 1947-49.

FOOTE, Henry Stuart (U Miss.) Feb. 28, 1804-May 19, 1880; Senate 1847-Jan. 8, 1852; Gov. 1852-54.

FOOTE, Samuel Augustus (W Conn.) Nov. 8, 1780-Sept. 15, 1846; House 1819-21, 1823-25, 1833-May 9, 1834; Senate 1827-33; Gov. 1834-35.

FOOTE, Wallace Turner Jr. (R N.Y.) April 7, 1864-Dec. 17, 1910; House 1895-99.

FORAKER, Joseph Benson (R Ohio) July 5, 1846-May 10, 1917; Senate 1897-1909; Gov. 1886-90.

FORAN, Martin Ambrose (D Ohio) Nov. 11, 1844-June 28, 1921; House 1883-89.

FORAND, Aime Joseph (D R.I.) May 23, 1895-Jan. 18, 1972; House 1937-39, 1941-61.

FORD, Aaron Lane (D Miss.) Dec. 21, 1903-July 8, 1983; House 1935-43.

FORD, George (D Ind.) Jan. 11, 1846-Aug. 30, 1917; House 1885-87.

FORD, Gerald R. Jr. (R Mich.) July 14, 1913- --; House 1949-Dec. 6, 1973; Vice Pres. Dec. 6, 1973-Aug. 9, 1974; President Aug. 9, 1974-77.

FORD, Harold Eugene (D Tenn.) May 20, 1945- --; House 1975- --.

FORD, James (JD Pa.) May 4, 1783-Aug.18, 1859; House 1829-33.

FORD, Leland Merritt (R Calif.) March 8, 1893-Nov. 27, 1965; House 1939-43.

FORD, Melbourne Haddock (D Mich.) June 30, 1849-April 20, 1891; House 1887-89; March 4-April 20, 1891.

FORD, Nicholas (LR Mo.) June 21, 1833-June 18, 1897; House 1879-83.

FORD, Thomas Francis (D Calif.) Feb. 18, 1873-Dec. 26, 1958; House 1933-45.

FORD, Wendell Hampton (D Ky.) Sept. 8, 1924- --; Senate Dec. 28, 1974- --; Gov. 1971-74.

FORD, William D. (D N.Y.) 1779-Oct. 1, 1833; House 1819-21.

FORD, William David (D Mich.) Aug. 6, 1927- --; House 1965- --.

FORDNEY, Joseph Warren (R Mich.) Nov. 5, 1853-Jan. 8, 1932; House 1899-1923.

FOREMAN, Edgar Franklin (R Texas/N.M.) Dec. 22, 1933- --; House 1963-65 (Texas), 1969-71 (N.M.).

FORESTER, John B. (-- Tenn.) ?-Aug. 31, 1845; House 1833-37.

FORKER, Samuel Carr (D N.J.) March 16, 1821-Feb. 10, 1900; House 1871-73.

FORMAN, William St. John (D Ill.) Jan. 20, 1847-June 10, 1908; House 1889-95.

FORNANCE, Joseph (D Pa.) Oct. 18, 1804-Nov. 24, 1852; House 1839-43.

FORNES, Charles Vincent (D N.Y.) Jan. 22, 1844-May 22, 1929; House 1907-13.

FORNEY, Daniel Munroe (son of Peter Forney) (-- N.C.) May 1784-Oct. 15, 1847; House 1815-18.

FORNEY, Peter (father of Daniel Munroe Forney) (D N.C.) April 21, 1756-Feb. 1, 1834; House 1813-15.

FORNEY, William Henry (grandson of Peter Forney) (D Ala.) Nov. 9, 1823-Jan. 16, 1894; House 1875-93.

FORREST, Thomas (-- Pa.) 1747-March 20, 1825; House 1819-21, Oct. 8, 1822-23.

FORREST, Uriah (F Md.) 1756-July 6, 1805; House 1793-Nov. 8, 1794; Cont. Cong. 1786-87.

FORRESTER, Elijah Lewis (D Ga.) Aug. 16, 1896-March 19, 1970; House 1951-65.

FORSYTH, John (D Ga.) Oct. 22, 1780-Oct. 21, 1841; House 1813-Nov. 23, 1818, 1823-Nov. 7, 1827; Senate Nov. 23, 1818-Feb. 17, 1819, Nov. 9, 1829-June 27, 1834; Secy. of State 1834-41; Gov. 1827-29.

FORSYTHE, Albert Palaska (R Ill.) May 24, 1830-Sept. 2, 1906; House 1879-81.

FORSYTHE, Edwin Bell (R N.J.) Jan. 17, 1916-March 29, 1984; House Nov. 3, 1970-March 29, 1984.

FORT, Franklin William (R N.J.) March 30, 1880-June 20, 1937; House 1925-31.

FORT, Greenbury Lafayette (R Ill.) Oct. 17, 1825-Jan. 13, 1883; House 1873-81.

FORT, Tomlinson (D Ga.) July 14, 1787-May 11, 1859; House 1827-29.

FORWARD, Chauncey (brother of Walter Forward) (D Pa.) Feb. 4, 1793-Oct. 19, 1839; House Dec. 4, 1826-31.

FORWARD, Walter (brother of Chauncey Forward) (D Pa.) Jan. 24, 1783-Nov. 24, 1852; House Oct. 8, 1822-25; Secy. of the Treasury 1841-43.

FOSDICK, Nicoll (W N.Y.) Nov. 9, 1785-May 7, 1868; House 1825-27.

FOSS, Eugene Noble (brother of George Edmund Foss) (D Mass.) Sept. 24, 1858-Sept. 13, 1939; House March 22, 1910-Jan. 4, 1911; Gov. 1911-14.

FOSS, Frank Herbert (R Mass.) Sept. 20, 1865-Feb. 15, 1947; House 1925-35.

FOSS, George Edmund (brother of Eugene Noble Foss) (R Ill.) July 2, 1863-March 15, 1936; House 1895-1913, 1915-19.

FOSTER, A. Lawrence (W N.Y.) ?-?; House 1841-43.

FOSTER, Abiel (-- N.H.) Aug. 8, 1735-Feb. 6, 1806; House 1789-91, 1795-1803; Cont. Cong. 1783-85.

FOSTER, Addison Gardner (R Wash.) Jan. 28, 1837-Jan. 16, 1917; Senate 1899-1905.

FOSTER, Charles (R Ohio) April 12, 1828-Jan. 9, 1904; House 1871-79; Secy. of the Treasury 1891-93; Gov. 1880-84.

FOSTER, David Johnson (R Vt.) June 27, 1857-March 21, 1912; House 1901-March 21, 1912.

FOSTER, Dwight (brother of Theodore Foster) (F Mass.) Dec. 7, 1757-April 29, 1823; House 1793-June 6, 1800; Senate June 6, 1800-March 2, 1803.

FOSTER, Ephraim Hubbard (W Tenn.) Sept. 17, 1794-Sept. 14, 1854; Senate Sept. 17, 1838-1839; Oct. 17, 1843-45.

FOSTER, George Peter (D Ill.) April 3, 1858-Nov. 11, 1928; House 1899-1905.

FOSTER, Henry Allen (D N.Y.) May 7, 1800-May 11, 1889; House 1837-39; Senate Nov. 30, 1844-Jan. 27, 1845.

FOSTER, Henry Donnel (cousin of John Cabell Breckinridge) (D Pa.) Dec. 19, 1808-Oct. 16, 1880; House 1843-37, 1871-73.

FOSTER, Israel Moore (R Ohio) Jan. 12, 1873-June 10, 1950; House 1919-25.

FOSTER, John Hopkins (R Ind.) Jan. 31, 1862-Sept. 5, 1917; House May 16, 1905-09.

FOSTER, Lafayette Sabine (R Conn.) Nov. 22, 1806-Sept. 19, 1880; Senate 1855-67; Pres. pro tempore 1865-67.

FOSTER, Martin David (D Ill.) Sept. 3, 1861-Oct. 20, 1919; House 1907-19.

FOSTER, Murphy James (D La.) Jan. 12, 1849-June 12, 1921; Senate 1901-13; Gov. 1892-1900.

FOSTER, Nathaniel Greene (D Ga.) Aug. 25, 1809-Oct. 19, 1869; House 1855-57 (elected as AP candidate).

FOSTER, Stephen Clark (R Maine) Dec. 24, 1799-Oct. 5, 1872; House 1857-61.

FOSTER, Theodore (brother of Dwight Foster) (L&O R.I.) April 29, 1752-Jan. 13, 1828; Senate June 7, 1790-1803.

FOSTER, Thomas Flournoy (D Ga.) Nov. 23, 1790-Sept. 14, 1848; House 1829-35, 1841-43.

FOSTER, Wilder De Ayr (R Mich.) Jan. 8, 1819-Sept. 20, 1873; House Dec. 4, 1871-Sept. 20, 1873.

FOUKE, Philip Bond (D Ill.) Jan. 23, 1818-Oct. 3, 1876; House 1859-63.

FOULKES, George Ernest (D Mich.) Dec. 25, 1878-Dec. 13, 1960; House 1933-35.

FOULKROD, William Walker (R Pa.) Nov. 22, 1846-Nov. 13, 1910; House 1907-Nov. 13, 1910.

FOUNTAIN, Lawrence H. (D N.C.) April 23, 1913-—; House 1953-83.

FOWLER, Charles Newell (R N.J.) Nov. 2, 1852-May 27, 1932; House 1895-1911.

FOWLER, Hiram Robert (D Ill.) Feb. 7, 1851-Jan. 5, 1926; House 1911-15.

FOWLER, John (— Ky.) 1755-Aug. 22, 1840; House 1797-1807.

FOWLER, John Edgar (P N.C.) Sept. 8, 1866-July 4, 1930; House 1897-99.

FOWLER, Joseph Smith (UR Tenn.) Aug. 31, 1820-April 1, 1902; Senate July 24, 1866-71.

FOWLER, Orin (FSW Mass.) July 19, 1791-Sept. 3, 1852; House 1849-Sept. 3, 1852.

FOWLER, Samuel (grandfather of the following) (JD N.J.) Oct. 30, 1779-Feb. 20, 1844; House 1833-37.

FOWLER, Samuel (grandson of the preceding) (D N.J.) March 22, 1851-March 17, 1919; House 1889-93.

FOWLER, William Wyche Jr. (D Ga.) Oct. 6, 1940-—; House April 6, 1977-—.

FOX, Andrew Fuller (D Miss.) April 26, 1849-Aug. 29, 1926; House 1897-1903.

FOX, John (D N.Y.) June 30, 1835-Jan. 17, 1914; House 1867-71.

FRANCE, Joseph Irvin (R Md.) Oct. 11, 1873-Jan. 26, 1939; Senate 1917-23.

FRANCHOT, Richard (R N.Y.) June 2, 1816-Nov. 23, 1875; House 1861-63.

FRANCIS, George Blinn (R N.Y.) Aug. 12, 1883-May 20, 1967; House 1917-19.

FRANCIS, John Brown (grandson of John Brown of Rhode Island) (L&O R.I.) May 31, 1791-Aug. 9, 1864; Senate Jan. 25, 1844-45; Gov. 1833-38.

FRANCIS, William Bates (D Ohio) Oct. 25, 1860-Dec. 5, 1954; House 1911-15.

FRANK, Augustus (nephew of William Patterson of N.Y.) (R N.Y.) July 17, 1826-April 29, 1895; House 1859-65.

FRANK, Barney (D Mass.) March 31, 1940-—; House 1981-—.

FRANK, Nathan (R/UL Mo.) Feb. 23, 1852-April 5, 1931; House 1889-91.

FRANKHAUSER, William Horace (R Mich.) March 5, 1863-May 9, 1921; House March 4-May 9, 1921.

FRANKLIN, Benjamin Joseph (D Mo.) March 1839-May 18, 1898; House 1875-79; Gov. (Ariz. Terr.) 1896-97.

FRANKLIN, Jesse (brother of Meshack Franklin) (D N.C.) March 24, 1760-Aug. 31, 1823; House 1795-97; Senate 1799-1805, 1807-13; Pres. pro tempore 1804-05; Gov. 1820-21.

FRANKLIN, John Rankin (W Md.) May 6, 1820-Jan. 11, 1878; House 1853-55.

FRANKLIN, Meshack (brother of Jesse Franklin) (D N.C.) 1772-Dec. 18, 1839; House 1807-15.

FRANKLIN, William Webster (R Miss.) Dec. 13, 1941-—; House 1983-—.

FRASER, Donald MacKay (D Minn.) Feb. 20, 1924-—; House 1963-79.

FRAZIER, James Beriah (father of the following) (D Tenn.) Oct. 18, 1856-March 28, 1937; Senate March 21, 1905-11; Gov. 1903-05.

FRAZIER, James Beriah Jr. (son of the preceding) (D Tenn.) June 23, 1890-Oct. 30, 1978; House 1949-63.

FRAZIER, Lynn Joseph (R N.D.) Dec. 21, 1874-Jan. 11, 1947; Senate 1923-41; Gov. 1917-21.

FREAR, James Archibald (R Wis.) Oct. 24, 1861-May 28, 1939; House 1913-35.

FREAR, Joseph Allen Jr. (D Del.) March 7, 1903-—; Senate 1949-61.

FREDERICK, Benjamin Todd (D Iowa) Oct. 5, 1834-Nov. 3, 1903; House March 3, 1885-87.

FREDERICKS, John Donnan (R Calif.) Sept. 10, 1869-Aug. 26, 1945; House May 1, 1923-27.

FREE, Arthur Monroe (R Calif.) Jan. 15, 1879-April 1, 1953; House 1921-33.

FREEDLEY, John (W Pa.) May 22, 1793-Dec. 8, 1851; House 1847-51.

FREEMAN, Chapman (R Pa.) Oct. 8, 1832-March 22, 1904; House 1875-79.

FREEMAN, James Crawford (R Ga.) April 1, 1820-Sept. 3, 1885; House 1873-75.

FREEMAN, John D. (U Miss.) ?-Jan. 17, 1886; House 1851-53.

FREEMAN, Jonathan (uncle of Nathaniel Freeman Jr.) (F N.H.) March 21, 1745-Aug. 20, 1808; House 1797-1801.

FREEMAN, Nathaniel Jr. (nephew of Jonathan Freeman) (— Mass.) May 1, 1766-Aug. 22, 1800; House 1795-99.

FREEMAN, Richard Patrick (R Conn.) April 24, 1869-July 8, 1944; House 1915-33.

FREER, Romeo Hoyt (R W.Va.) Nov. 9, 1846-May 9, 1913; House 1899-1901.

FRELINGHUYSEN, Frederick (father of Theodore Frelinghuysen, great-great-great-grandfather of Peter Hood Ballantine Frelinghuysen Jr.) (F N.J.) April 13, 1753-April 13, 1804; Senate 1793-Nov. 12, 1796; Cont. Cong. 1778-79, 1782-83.

FRELINGHUYSEN, Frederick Theodore (nephew and adopted son of Theodore Frelinghuysen, uncle of Joseph Sherman Frelinghuysen, great-grandfather of Peter Hood Ballantine Frelinghuysen Jr.) (R N.J.) Aug. 4, 1817-May 20, 1885; Senate Nov. 12, 1866-69, 1871-77; Secy. of State 1881-85.

FRELINGHUYSEN, Joseph Sherman (nephew of Frederick Theodore Frelinghuysen, cousin of Peter Hood Ballantine Frelinghuysen Jr.) (R N.J.) March 12, 1869-Feb. 8, 1948; Senate 1917-23.

FRELINGHUYSEN, Peter Hood Ballantine Jr. (cousin of Joseph Sherman Frelinghuysen, great-grandson of Frederick Theodore Frelinghuysen, great-great-great-nephew of Theodore Frelinghuysen, great-great-great-grandson of Frederick Frelinghuysen) (R N.J.) Jan. 17, 1916-—; House 1953-75.

FRELINGHUYSEN, Theodore (son of Frederick Frelinghuysen, great-great-great-uncle of Peter Hood Ballantine Frelinghuysen Jr.) (Ad.D N.J.) March 28, 1787-April 12, 1862; Senate 1829-35.

FREMONT, John Charles (FSD Calif.) Jan. 21, 1813-July 13, 1890; Senate Sept. 9, 1850-51; Gov. (Ariz. Terr.) 1878-81.

FRENCH, Burton Lee (R Idaho) Aug. 1, 1875-Sept. 12, 1954; House 1903-09, 1911-15, 1917-33.

FRENCH, Carlos (D Conn.) Aug. 6, 1835-April 14, 1903; House 1887-89.

FRENCH, Ezra Bartlett (R Maine) Sept. 23, 1810-April 24, 1880; House 1859-61.

FRENCH, John Robert (R N.C.) May 28, 1819-Oct. 2, 1890; House July 6, 1868-69.

FRENCH, Richard (D Ky.) June 20, 1792-May 1, 1854; House 1835-37, 1843-45, 1847-49.

FRENZEL, William E. (R Minn.) July 31, 1928- —; House 1971- —.

FREY, Louis Jr. (R Fla.) Jan. 11, 1934- —; House 1969-79.

FREY, Oliver Walter (D Pa.) Sept. 7, 1887-Aug. 26, 1939, House Nov. 7, 1933-39.

FRICK, Henry (W Pa.) March 17, 1795-March 1, 1844; House 1843-March 1, 1844.

FRIEDEL, Samuel Nathaniel (D Md.) April 18, 1898-March 21, 1979; House 1953-71.

FRIES, Frank William (D Ill.) May 1, 1893- —; House 1937-41.

FRIES, George (D Ohio) 1799-Nov. 13, 1866; House 1845-49.

FROEHLICH, Harold Vernon (R Wis.) May 12, 1932- —; House 1973-75.

FROMENTIN, Eligius (— La.) ?-Oct. 6, 1822; Senate 1813-19.

FROST, Joel (— N.Y.) ?-?; House 1823-25.

FROST, Jonas Martin III (D Texas) Jan. 1, 1942- —; House 1979- —.

FROST, Richard Graham (D Mo.) Dec. 29, 1851-Feb. 1, 1900; House 1879-March 2, 1883.

FROST, Rufus Smith (R Mass.) July 18, 1826-March 6, 1894; House 1875-July 28, 1876.

FROTHINGHAM, Louis Adams (R Mass.) July 13, 1871-Aug. 23, 1928; House 1921-Aug. 23, 1928.

FRY, Jacob Jr. (D Pa.) June 10, 1802-Nov. 28, 1866; House 1835-39.

FRY, Joseph Jr. (D Pa.) Aug. 4, 1781-Aug. 15, 1860; House 1827-31.

FRYE, William Pierce (grandfather of Wallace Humphrey White Jr.) (R Maine) Sept. 2, 1830-Aug. 8, 1911; House 1871-March 17, 1881; Senate March 18, 1881-Aug. 8, 1911, Pres. pro tempore 1896-1911.

FUGATE, Thomas Bacon (D Va.) April 10, 1899-Sept. 22, 1980; House 1949-53.

FULBRIGHT, James Franklin (D Mo.) Jan. 24, 1877-April 5, 1948; House 1923-25, 1927-29, 1931-33.

FULBRIGHT, James William (D Ark.) April 9, 1905- —; House 1943-45; Senate 1945-Dec. 31, 1974.

FULKERSON, Abram (D Va.) May 13, 1834-Dec. 17, 1902; House 1881-83 (elected as a Readjuster).

FULKERSON, Frank Ballard (R Mo.) March 5, 1866-Aug. 30, 1936; House 1905-07.

FULLER, Alvan Tufts (R Mass.) Feb. 27, 1878-April 30, 1958; House 1917-Jan. 5, 1921; Gov. 1925-29.

FULLER, Benoni Stinson (D Ind.) Nov. 13, 1825-April 14, 1903; House 1875-79.

FULLER, Charles Eugene (R Ill.) March 31, 1849-June 25, 1926; House 1903-13, 1915-June 25, 1926.

FULLER, Claude Albert (D Ark.) Jan. 20, 1876-Jan. 8, 1968; House 1929-39.

FULLER, George (D Pa.) Nov. 7, 1802-Nov. 24, 1888; House Dec. 2, 1844-45.

FULLER, Hawden Carlton (R N.Y.) Aug. 28, 1895- —; House Nov. 2, 1943-49.

FULLER, Henry Mills (W Pa.) Jan. 3, 1820-Dec. 26, 1860; House 1851-53, 1855-57.

FULLER, Philo Case (W N.Y.) Aug. 14, 1787-Aug. 16, 1855; House 1833-Sept. 2, 1836.

FULLER, Thomas James Duncan (D Maine) March 17, 1808-Feb. 13, 1876; House 1849-57.

FULLER, Timothy (D Mass.) July 11, 1778-Oct. 1, 1835; House 1817-25.

FULLER, William Elijah (R Iowa) March 30, 1846-April 23, 1918; House 1885-89.

FULLER, William Kendall (D N.Y.) Nov. 24, 1792-Nov. 11, 1883; House 1833-37.

FULLERTON, David (uncle of David Fullerton Robison) (— Pa.) Oct. 4, 1772-Feb. 1, 1843; House 1819-May 15, 1820.

FULMER, Hampton Pitts (husband of Willa Lybrand Fulmer) (D S.C.) June 23, 1875-Oct. 19, 1944; House 1921-Oct. 19, 1944.

FULMER, Willa Lybrand, (widow of Hampton Pitts Fulmer) (D S.C.) Feb. 3, 1884-May 13, 1968; House Nov. 7, 1944-45.

FULTON, Andrew Steele (brother of John Hall Fulton) (W Va.) Sept. 29, 1800-Nov. 22, 1884; House 1847-49.

FULTON, Charles William (brother of Elmer Lincoln Fulton) (R Ore.) Aug. 24, 1853-Jan. 27, 1918; Senate 1903-09.

FULTON, Elmer Lincoln (brother of Charles William Fulton) (D Okla.) April 22, 1865-Oct. 4, 1939; House Nov. 16, 1907-09.

FULTON, James Grove (R Pa.) March 1, 1903-Oct. 6, 1971; House Feb. 2, 1945-Oct. 6, 1971.

FULTON, John Hall (brother of Andrew Steele Fulton) (W Va.) ?-Jan. 28, 1836; House 1833-35.

FULTON, Richard Harmon (D Tenn.) Jan. 27, 1927- —; House 1963-Aug. 14, 1975.

FULTON, William Savin (D Ark.) June 2, 1795-Aug. 15, 1844; Senate Sept. 18, 1836-Aug. 15, 1844; Gov. (Ark. Terr.) 1835-36.

FUNK, Benjamin Franklin (father of Frank Hamilton Funk) (R Ill.) Oct. 17, 1838-Feb. 14, 1909; House 1893-95.

FUNK, Frank Hamilton (son of Benjamin Franklin Funk) (R Ill.) April 5, 1869-Nov. 24, 1940; House 1921-27.

FUNSTON, Edward Hogue (R Kan.) Sept. 16, 1836-Sept. 10, 1911; House March 21, 1884-Aug. 2, 1894.

FUQUA, Don (D Fla.) Aug. 20, 1933- —; House 1963- —.

FURCOLO, Foster (D Mass.) July 29, 1911- —; House 1949-Sept. 30, 1952; Gov. 1957-61.

FURLONG, Robert Grant (D Pa.) Jan. 4, 1886-March 19, 1973; House 1943-45.

FURLOW, Allen John (R Minn.) Nov. 9, 1890-Jan. 29, 1954; House 1925-29.

FUSTER, Jaime (PD P.R.) Jan. 12, 1941- —; House (Res. Comm.) 1985- —.

FYAN, Robert Washington (D Mo.) March 11, 1835-July 28, 1896; House 1883-85, 1891-95.

G

GABALDON, Isauro (Nat. P.I.) Dec. 8, 1875-Dec. 21, 1942; House (Res. Comm.) 1920-July 16, 1928.

GAGE, Joshua (D Mass.) Aug. 7, 1763-Jan. 24, 1831; House 1817-19.

GAHN, Harry Conrad (R Ohio) April 26, 1880-Nov. 2, 1962; House 1921-23.

GAILLARD, John (uncle of Theodore Gaillard Hunt) (D S.C.) Sept. 5, 1765-Feb. 26, 1826; Senate Dec. 6, 1804-Feb. 26, 1826; Pres. pro tempore 1810, 1814-18, 1820-25.

GAINES, John Pollard (W Ky.) Sept. 22, 1795-Dec. 9, 1857; House 1847-49; Gov. (Ore. Terr.) 1850-53.

GAINES, John Wesley (D Tenn.) Aug. 24, 1860-July 4, 1926; House 1897-1909.

GAINES, Joseph Holt (R W.Va.) Sept. 3, 1864-April 12, 1951; House 1901-11.

GAINES, William Embre (R Va.) Aug. 30, 1844-May 4, 1912; House 1887-89.

GAITHER, Nathan (D Ky.) Sept. 15, 1788-Aug. 12, 1862; House 1829-33.

GALBRAITH, John (D Pa.) Aug. 2, 1794-June 15, 1860; House 1833-37, 1839-41.

GALE, George (father of Levin Gale) (— Md.) June 3, 1756-Jan. 2, 1815; House 1789-91.

GALE, Levin (son of George Gale) (— Md.) April 24, 1784-Dec. 18, 1834; House 1827-29.

GALE, Richard Pillsbury (R Minn.) Oct. 30, 1900-Dec. 4, 1973; House 1941-45.

GALIFIANAKIS, Nick (D N.C.) July 22, 1928- —; House 1967-73.

GALLAGHER, Cornelius Edward (D N.J.) March 2, 1921- —; House 1959-73.

GALLAGHER, James A. (R Pa.) Jan. 16, 1869-Dec. 8, 1957; House 1943-45, 1947-49.

GALLAGHER, Thomas (D Ill.) July 6, 1850-Feb. 24, 1930; House 1909-21.

GALLAGHER, William James (D Minn.) May 13, 1875-Aug. 13, 1946; House 1945-Aug. 13, 1946.

Biographical Index

GALLATIN, Albert (D Pa.) Jan. 29, 1761-Aug. 12, 1849; Senate Dec. 2, 1793-Feb. 28, 1794; House 1795-1801; Secy. of the Treasury 1801-14.

GALLEGOS, Jose Manuel (D N.M.) Oct. 30, 1815-April 21, 1875; House (Terr. Del.) 1853-July 23, 1856, 1871-73.

GALLINGER, Jacob Harold (R N.H.) March 28, 1837-Aug. 17, 1918; House 1885-89; Senate 1891-Aug. 17, 1918.

GALLIVAN, James Ambrose (D Mass.) Oct. 22, 1866-April 3, 1928; House April 7, 1914-April 3, 1928.

GALLO, Dean A. (R N.J.) Nov. 23, 1935-—; House 1985-—.

GALLOWAY, Samuel (R Ohio) March 20, 1811-April 5, 1872; House 1855-57.

GALLUP, Albert (D N.Y.) Jan. 30, 1796-Nov. 5, 1851; House 1837-39.

GAMBLE, James (D Pa.) Jan. 28, 1809-Feb. 22, 1883; House 1851-55.

GAMBLE, John Rankin (brother of Robert Jackson Gamble, uncle of Ralph Abernethy Gamble) (R S.D.) Jan. 15, 1848-Aug. 14, 1891; House March 4-Aug. 14, 1891.

GAMBLE, Ralph Abernethy (son of Robert Jackson Gamble, nephew of John Rankin Gamble) (R N.Y.) May 6, 1885-March 4, 1959; House Nov. 2, 1937-57.

GAMBLE, Robert Jackson (brother of John Rankin Gamble, father of Ralph Abernethy Gamble) (R S.D.) Feb. 7, 1851-Sept. 22, 1924; House 1895-97, 1899-1901; Senate 1901-13.

GAMBLE, Roger Lawson (W Ga.) 1787-Dec. 20, 1847; House 1833-35; 1841-43 (1833-35 Democrat, 1841-43 Whig).

GAMBRELL, David Henry (D Ga.) Dec. 20, 1929-—; Senate Feb. 1, 1971-Nov. 7, 1972.

GAMBRILL, Stephen Warfield (D Md.) Oct. 2, 1873-Dec. 19, 1938; House Nov. 4, 1924-Dec. 19, 1938.

GAMMAGE, Robert Alton (D Texas) March 13, 1938-—; House 1977-79.

GANDY, Harry Luther (D S.D.) Aug. 13, 1881-Aug. 15, 1957; House 1915-21.

GANLY, James Vincent (D N.Y.) Sept. 13. 1878-Sept. 7, 1923; House 1919-21, March 4-Sept. 7, 1923.

GANNETT, Barzillai (D Mass.) June 17, 1764-1832; House 1809-12.

GANSON, John (D N.Y.) Jan. 1, 1818-Sept. 28, 1874; House 1863-65.

GANTZ, Martin Kissinger (D Ohio) Jan. 28, 1862-Feb. 10, 1916; House 1891-93.

GARBER, Harvey Cable (D Ohio) July 6, 1866-March 23, 1938; House 1903-07.

GARBER, Jacob Aaron (R Va.) Jan. 25, 1879-Dec. 2, 1953; House 1929-31.

GARBER, Milton Cline (R Okla.) Nov. 30, 1867-Sept. 12, 1948; House 1923-33.

GARCIA, Robert (D N.Y.) Jan. 9, 1933-—; House Feb. 21, 1978-—.

GARD, Warren (D Ohio) July 2, 1873-Nov. 1, 1929; House 1913-21.

GARDENIER, Barent (F N.Y.) ?-Jan. 10, 1822; House 1807-11.

GARDNER, Augustus Peabody (uncle of Henry Cabot Lodge Jr. and John Davis Lodge) (R Mass.) Nov. 5, 1865-Jan. 14, 1918; House Nov. 3, 1902-May 15, 1917.

GARDNER, Edward Joseph (D Ohio) Aug. 7, 1898-Dec. 7, 1950; House 1945-47.

GARDNER, Francis (— N.H.) Dec. 27, 1771-June 25, 1835; House 1807-09.

GARDNER, Frank (D Ind.) May 8, 1872-Feb. 1, 1937; House 1923-29.

GARDNER, Gideon (— Mass.) May 30, 1759-March 22, 1832; House 1809-11.

GARDNER, James Carson (R N.C.) April 8, 1933-—; House 1967-69.

GARDNER, John James (R N.J.) Oct. 17, 1845-Feb. 7, 1921; House 1893-1913.

GARDNER, Mills (R Ohio) Jan. 30, 1830-Feb. 20, 1910; House 1877-79.

GARDNER, Obadiah (D Maine) Sept. 13, 1850-July 24, 1938; Senate Sept. 23, 1911-13.

GARDNER, Washington (R Mich.) Feb. 16, 1845-March 31, 1928; House 1899-1911.

GARFIELD, James Abram (R Ohio) Nov. 19, 1831-Sept. 19, 1881; House 1863-Nov. 8, 1880; President March 4-Sept. 19, 1881.

GARFIELDE, Selucius (R Wash.) Dec. 8, 1822-April 13, 1881; House (Terr. Del.) 1869-73.

GARLAND, Augustus Hill (D Ark.) June 11, 1832-Jan. 26, 1899; Senate 1877-March 6, 1885; Gov. 1874-77; Atty. General 1885-89.

GARLAND, David Shepherd (D Va.) Sept. 27, 1769-Oct. 7, 1841; House Jan. 17, 1810-11.

GARLAND, James (D Va.) June 6, 1791-Aug. 8, 1885; House 1835-41.

GARLAND, Mahlon Morris (R Pa.) May 4, 1856-Nov. 19, 1920; House 1915-Nov. 19, 1920.

GARLAND, Peter Adams (R Maine) June 16, 1923-—; House 1961-63.

GARLAND, Rice (W La.) about 1795-1861; House April 28, 1834-July 21, 1840.

GARMATZ, Edward Alexander (D Md.) Feb. 7, 1903-—; House July 15, 1947-1973.

GARN, Edwin Jacob (R Utah) Oct. 12, 1932-—; Senate Dec. 21, 1974-—.

GARNER, Alfred Buckwalter (R Pa.) March 4, 1873-July 30, 1930; House 1909-11.

GARNER, John Nance (D Texas) Nov. 22, 1868-Nov. 7, 1967; House 1903-33; Speaker 1931-33; Vice Pres. 1933-41.

GARNETT, James Mercer (brother of Robert Selden Garnett, grandfather of Muscoe Russell Hunter Garnett, cousin of Charles Fenton Mercer) (D Va.) June 8, 1770-April 23, 1843; House 1805-09.

GARNETT, Muscoe Russell Hunter (grandson of James Mercer Garnett) (D Va.) July 25, 1821-Feb. 14, 1864; House Dec. 1, 1856-61.

GARNETT, Robert Selden (brother of James Mercer Garnett, cousin of Charles Fenton Mercer) (D Va.) April 26, 1789-Aug. 15, 1840; House 1817-27.

GARNSEY, Daniel Greene (JD N.Y.) June 17, 1779-May 11, 1851; House 1825-29.

GARRETT, Abraham Ellison (D Tenn.) March 6, 1830-Feb. 14, 1907; House 1871-73.

GARRETT, Clyde Leonard (D Texas) Dec. 16, 1885-Dec. 18, 1959; House 1937-41.

GARRETT, Daniel Edward (D Texas) April 28, 1869-Dec. 13, 1932; House 1913-15; 1917-19; 1921-Dec. 13, 1932.

GARRETT, Finis James (D Tenn.) Aug. 26, 1875-May 25, 1956; House 1905-29.

GARRISON, Daniel (D N.J.) April 3, 1782-Feb. 13, 1851; House 1823-27.

GARRISON, George Tankard (D Va.) Jan. 14, 1835-Nov. 14, 1889; House 1881-83; March 20, 1884-85.

GARROW, Nathaniel (D N.Y.) April 25, 1780-March 3, 1841; House 1827-29.

GARTH, William Willis (D Ala.) Oct. 28, 1828-Feb. 25, 1912; House 1877-79.

GARTNER, Fred Christian (R Pa.) March 14, 1896-Sept. 1, 1972; House 1939-41.

GARTRELL, Lucius Jeremiah (uncle of Choice Boswell Randell) (D Ga.) Jan. 7, 1821-April 7, 1891; House 1857-Jan. 23, 1861.

GARVIN, William Swan (D Pa.) July 25, 1806-Feb. 20, 1883; House 1845-47.

GARY, Frank Boyd (D S.C.) March 9, 1860-Dec. 7, 1922; Senate March 6, 1908-09.

GARY, Julian Vaughan (D Va.) Feb. 25, 1892-Sept. 6, 1973; House March 6, 1945-65.

GASQUE, Allard Henry (husband of Elizabeth (Bessie) Hawley Gasque) (D S.C.) March 8, 1873-June 17, 1938; House 1923-June 17, 1938.

GASQUE, Elizabeth (Bessie) Hawley (widow of Allard Henry Gasque — later Mrs. A. J. Van Exem) (D S.C.) ?-—; House Sept. 13, 1938-39.

GASSAWAY, Percy Lee (D Okla.) Aug. 30, 1885-May 15, 1937; House 1935-37.

GASTON, Athelston (D Pa.) April 24, 1838-Sept. 23, 1907; House 1899-1901.

GASTON, William (F N.C.) Sept. 19, 1778-Jan. 23, 1844; House 1813-17.

GATES, Seth Merrill (ASW N.Y.) Oct. 10, 1800-Aug. 24, 1877; House 1839-43.

GATHINGS, Ezekiel Candler (D Ark.) Nov. 10, 1903-May 2, 1979; House 1939-69.

GATLIN, Alfred Moore (— N.C.) April 20, 1790-?; House 1823-25.

GAUSE, Lucien Coatsworth (D Ark.) Dec. 25, 1836-Nov. 5, 1880; House 1875-79.

GAVAGAN, Joseph Andrew (D N.Y.) Aug. 20, 1892-Oct. 18, 1968; House Nov. 5, 1929-Dec. 30, 1943.

GAVIN, Leon Harry (R Pa.) Feb. 25, 1893-Sept. 15, 1963; House 1943-Sept. 15, 1963.

GAY, Edward James (grandfather of the following) (D La.) Feb. 3, 1816-May 30, 1889; House 1885-May 30, 1889.

GAY, Edward James (grandson of the preceding) (D La.) May 5, 1878-Dec. 1, 1952; Senate Nov. 6, 1918-21.

GAYDOS, Joseph M. (D Pa.) July 3, 1926-—; House Nov. 5, 1968-—.

GAYLE, John (W Ala.) Sept. 11, 1792-July 28, 1859; House 1847-49; Gov. 1831-35.

GAYLE, June Ward (D Ky.) Feb. 22, 1865-Aug. 5, 1942; House Jan. 15, 1900-01.

GAYLORD, James Madison (— Ohio) May 29, 1811-June 14, 1874; House 1851-53.

GAZLAY, James William (JFSt. Ohio) July 23, 1784-June 8, 1874; House 1823-25.

GEAR, John Henry (R Iowa) April 7, 1825-July 14, 1900; House 1887-91; 1893-95; Senate 1895-July 14, 1900; Gov. 1878-82.

GEARHART, Bertrand Wesley (R Calif.) May 31, 1890-Oct. 11, 1955; House 1935-49.

GEARIN, John McDermeid (D Ore.) Aug. 15, 1851-Nov. 12, 1930; Senate Dec. 13, 1905-Jan. 23, 1907.

GEARY, Thomas J. (D/AP Calif.) Jan. 18, 1854-July 6, 1929; House Dec. 9, 1890-95.

GEBHARD, John (— N.Y.) Feb. 22, 1782-Jan. 3, 1854; House 1821-23.

GEDDES, George Washington (D Ohio) July 16, 1824-Nov. 9, 1892; House 1879-87.

GEDDES, James (F N.Y.) July 22, 1763-Aug. 19, 1838; House 1813-15.

GEELAN, James Patrick (D Conn.) Aug. 11, 1901-Aug. 10, 1982; House 1945-47.

GEHRMANN, Bernard John (Prog. Wis.) Feb. 13, 1880-July 12, 1958; House 1935-43.

GEISSENHAINER, Jacob Augustus (D N.J.) Aug. 28, 1839-July 20, 1917; House 1889-95.

GEJDENSON, Samuel (D Conn.) May 20, 1948-—; House 1981-—.

GEKAS, George William (R Pa.) April 14, 1930-—; House 1983-—.

GENSMAN, Lorraine Michael (R Okla.) Aug. 26, 1878-May 27, 1954; House 1921-23.

GENTRY, Brady Preston (D Texas) March 25, 1896-Nov. 9, 1966; House 1953-57.

GENTRY, Meredith Poindexter (W Tenn.) Sept. 15, 1809-Nov. 2, 1866; House 1839-43, 1845-53.

GEORGE, Henry Jr. (D N.Y.) Nov. 3, 1862-Nov. 14, 1916; House 1911-15.

GEORGE, James Zachariah (D Miss.) Oct. 20, 1826-Aug. 14, 1897; Senate 1881-Aug. 14, 1897.

GEORGE, Melvin Clark (R Ore.) May 13, 1894-Feb. 22, 1933; House 1881-85.

GEORGE, Myron Virgil (R Kan.) Jan. 6, 1900-April 11, 1972; House Nov. 7, 1950-59.

GEORGE, Newell A. (D Kan.) Sept. 24, 1904-—; House 1959-61.

GEORGE, Walter Franklin (D Ga.) Jan. 29, 1878-Aug. 4, 1957; Senate Nov. 22, 1922-57; Pres. pro tempore 1955-57.

GEPHARDT, Richard Andrew (D Mo.) Jan. 31, 1941-—; House 1977-—.

GERAN, Elmer Hendrickson (D N.J.) Oct. 24, 1875-Jan. 12, 1954; House 1923-25.

GERLACH, Charles Lewis (R Pa.) Sept. 14, 1895-May 5, 1947; House 1939-May 5, 1947.

GERMAN, Obadiah (D N.Y.) April 22, 1766-Sept. 24, 1842; Senate 1809-15.

GERNERD, Fred Benjamin (R Pa.) Nov. 22, 1879-Aug. 7, 1948; House 1921-23.

GERRY, Elbridge (great-grandfather of Peter Goelet Gerry, grandfather of the following) (D Mass.) July 17, 1744-Nov. 23, 1814; House 1789-93; Cont. Cong. 1776-81, 1782-85; Gov. 1810-11, Vice Pres. 1813-Nov. 23, 1814 (1789-93 Anti Federalist; 1810-14 Democrat).

GERRY, Elbridge (grandson of the preceding) (D Maine) Dec. 6, 1813-April 10, 1886; House 1849-51.

GERRY, James (D Pa.) Aug. 14, 1796-July 19, 1873; House 1839-43.

GERRY, Peter Goelet (great-grandson of Elbridge Gerry) (D R.I.) Sept. 18, 1879-Oct. 31, 1957; House 1913-15; Senate 1917-29; 1935-47.

GEST, William Harrison (R Ill.) Jan. 7, 1838-Aug. 9, 1912; House 1887-91.

GETTYS, Thomas Smithwick (D S.C.) June 19, 1912-—; House Nov. 3, 1964-Dec. 31, 1974.

GETZ, James Lawrence (D Pa.) Sept. 14, 1821-Dec. 25, 1891; House 1867-73.

GEYER, Henry Sheffie (D Mo.) Dec. 9, 1790-March 5, 1859; Senate 1851-57.

GEYER, Lee Edward (D Calif.) Sept. 9, 1888-Oct. 11, 1941; 1939-Oct. 11, 1941.

GHOLSON, James Herbert (D Va.) 1798-July 2, 1848; House 1833-35.

GHOLSON, Samuel Jameson (D Miss.) May 19, 1808-Oct. 16, 1883; House Dec. 1, 1836-37; July 18, 1837-Feb. 5, 1838.

GHOLSON, Thomas Jr. (D Va.) ?-July 4, 1816; House Nov. 7, 1808-July 4, 1816.

GIAIMO, Robert Nicholas (D Conn.) Oct. 15, 1919-—; House 1959-81.

GIBBONS, Sam M. (D Fla.) Jan. 20, 1920-—; House 1963-—.

GIBBS, Florence Reville (widow of Willis Benjamin Gibbs) (D Ga.) April 4, 1890-Aug. 19, 1964; House Oct. 1, 1940-41.

GIBBS, Willis Benjamin (husband of Florence Reville Gibbs) (D Ga.) April 15, 1889-Aug. 7, 1940; House 1939-Aug. 7, 1940.

GIBSON, Charles Hopper (cousin of Henry Richard Gibson) (D Md.) Jan. 19, 1842-March 31, 1900; House 1885-91; Senate Nov. 19, 1891-97.

GIBSON, Ernest Willard (father of Ernest William Gibson) (R Vt.) Dec. 29, 1872-June 20, 1940; House Nov. 6, 1923-Oct. 19, 1933; Senate Nov. 21, 1933-June 20, 1940.

GIBSON, Ernest William (son of Ernest Willard Gibson) (R Vt.) March 6, 1901-Nov. 4, 1969; Senate June 24, 1940-41; Gov. 1947-50.

GIBSON, Eustace (D W.Va.) Oct. 4, 1842-Dec. 10, 1900; House 1883-87.

GIBSON, Henry Richard (cousin of Charles Hopper Gibson) (R Tenn.) Dec. 24, 1837-May 25, 1938; House 1895-1905.

GIBSON, James King (D Va.) Feb. 18, 1812-March 30, 1879; House Jan. 28, 1870-71.

GIBSON, John Strickland (D Ga.) Jan. 3, 1893-Oct. 19, 1960; House 1941-47.

GIBSON, Paris (D Mont.) July 1, 1830-Dec. 16, 1920; Senate March 7, 1901-05.

GIBSON, Randall Lee (D La.) Sept. 10, 1832-Dec. 15, 1892; House 1875-83; Senate 1883-Dec. 15, 1892.

GIDDINGS, De Witt Clinton (D Texas) July 18, 1827-Aug. 19, 1903; House May 13, 1872-75; 1877-79.

GIDDINGS, Joshua Reed (ASW Ohio) Oct. 6, 1795-May 27, 1864; House Dec. 3, 1838-March 22, 1842; Dec. 5, 1842-59.

GIDDINGS, Napoleon Bonaparte (D Neb.) Jan. 2, 1816-Aug. 3, 1897; House (Terr. Del.) Jan. 5-March 3, 1855.

GIFFORD, Charles Laceille (R Mass.) March 15, 1871-Aug. 23, 1947; House Nov. 7, 1922-Aug. 23, 1947.

GIFFORD, Oscar Sherman (R S.D.) Oct. 20, 1842-Jan. 16, 1913; House (Terr. Del. Dakota) 1885-89; (Rep.) Nov. 2, 1889-91.

GILBERT, Abijah (R Fla.) June 18, 1806-Nov. 23, 1881; Senate 1869-75.

GILBERT, Edward (D Calif.) about 1819-Aug. 2, 1852; House Sept. 11, 1850-51.

GILBERT, Ezekiel (— N.Y.) March 25, 1756-July 17, 1841; House 1793-97.

GILBERT, George Gilmore (father of Ralph Waldo Emerson Gilbert) (D Ky.) Dec. 24, 1849-Nov. 9, 1909; House 1899-1907.

Biographical Index

GILBERT, Jacob H. (D N.Y.) June 17, 1920-Feb. 27, 1981; House March 8, 1960-1971.

GILBERT, Newton Whiting (R Ind.) May 24, 1862-July 5, 1939; House 1905-Nov. 6, 1906.

GILBERT, Ralph Waldo Emerson (son of George Gilmore Gilbert) (D Ky.) Jan. 17, 1882-July 30, 1939; House 1921-29; 1931-33.

GILBERT, Sylvester (— Conn.) Oct. 20, 1755-Jan. 2, 1846; House Nov. 16, 1818-19.

GILBERT, William Augustus (W N.Y.) Jan. 25, 1815-May 25, 1875; House 1855-Feb. 27, 1857.

GILCHRIST, Fred Cramer (R Iowa) June 2, 1868-March 10, 1950; House 1931-45.

GILDEA, James Hilary (D Pa.) Oct. 21, 1890-—; House 1935-39.

GILES, William Branch (D Va.) Aug. 12, 1762-Dec. 4, 1830; House Dec. 7, 1790-Oct. 2, 1798, 1801-03; Senate Aug. 11, 1804-15 (1790-98 Anti-Federalist, 1801-15 Democrat); Gov. 1827-30.

GILES, William Fell (D Md.) April 8, 1807-March 21, 1879; House 1845-47.

GILFILLAN, Calvin Willard (R Pa.) Feb. 20, 1832-Dec. 2, 1901; House 1869-71.

GILFILLAN, John Bachop (R Minn.) Feb. 11, 1835-Aug. 19, 1924; House 1885-87.

GILHAMS, Clarence Chauncey (R Ind.) April 11, 1860-June 5, 1912; House Nov. 6, 1906-09.

GILL, John Jr. (D Md.) June 9, 1850-Jan. 27, 1918; House 1905-11.

GILL, Joseph John (R Ohio) Sept. 21, 1846-May 22, 1920; House Dec. 4, 1899-Oct. 31, 1903.

GILL, Michael Joseph (D Mo.) Dec. 5, 1864-Nov. 1, 1918; House June 19, 1914-15.

GILL, Patrick Francis (D Mo.) Aug. 16, 1868-May 21, 1923; House 1909-11; Aug. 12, 1912-13.

GILL, Thomas P. (D Hawaii) April 21, 1922-—; House 1963-65.

GILLEN Courtland Craig (D Ind.) July 3, 1880-Sept. 1, 1954; House 1931-33.

GILLESPIE, Dean Milton (R Colo.) May 3, 1884-Feb. 2, 1949; House March 7, 1944-47.

GILLESPIE, Eugene Pierce (D Pa.) Sept. 24, 1852-Dec. 16, 1899; House 1891-93.

GILLESPIE, James (— N.C.) ?-Jan. 11, 1805; House 1793-99, 1803-Jan. 11, 1805.

GILLESPIE, James Frank (D Ill.) April 18, 1869-Nov. 26, 1954; House 1933-35.

GILLESPIE, Oscar William (D Texas) June 20, 1858-Aug. 23, 1927; House 1903-11.

GILLET, Charles William (R N.Y.) Nov. 26, 1840-Dec. 31, 1908; House 1893-1905.

GILLET, Ransom Hooker (D N.Y.) Jan. 27, 1800-Oct. 24, 1876; House 1833-37.

GILLETT, Frederick Huntington (R Mass.) Oct. 16, 1851-July 31, 1935; House 1893-1925; Speaker 1919-25; Senate 1925-31.

GILLETT, James Norris (R Calif.) Sept. 20, 1860-April 20, 1937; House 1903-Nov. 4, 1906; Gov. 1907-11.

GILLETTE, Edward Hooker (son of Francis Gillette) (G Iowa) Oct. 1, 1840-Aug. 14, 1918; House 1879-81.

GILLETTE, Francis (father of Edward Hooker Gillette) (FSW Conn.) Dec. 14, 1807-Sept. 30, 1879; Senate May 24, 1854-55.

GILLETTE, Guy Mark (D Iowa) Feb. 3, 1879-March 3, 1973; House 1933-Nov. 3, 1936; Senate Nov. 4, 1936-45, 1949-55.

GILLETTE, Wilson Darwin (R Pa.) July 1, 1880-Aug. 7, 1951; House Nov. 4, 1941-Aug. 7, 1951.

GILLIE, George W. (R Ind.) Aug. 15, 1880-July 3, 1963; House 1939-49.

GILLIGAN, John J. (D Ohio) March 22, 1921-—; House 1965-67; Gov. 1971-75.

GILLIS, James Lisle (D Pa.) Oct. 2, 1792-July 8, 1881; House 1857-59.

GILLON, Alexander (— S.C.) 1741-Oct. 6, 1794; House 1793-Oct. 6, 1794.

GILMAN, Benjamin Arthur (R N.Y.) Dec. 6, 1922-—; House 1973-—.

GILMAN, Charles Jervis (grandnephew of Nicholas Gilman) (R Maine) Feb. 26, 1824-Feb. 5, 1901; House 1857-59.

GILMAN, Nicholas (granduncle of Charles Jervis Gilman) (D N.H.) Aug. 3, 1755-May 2, 1814; House 1789-97; Senate 1805-May 2, 1814 (1789-97 Federalist, 1805-14 Democrat); Cont. Cong. 1786-88.

GILMER, George Rockingham (D Ga.) April 11, 1790-Nov. 16, 1859; House 1821-23, Oct. 1, 1827-29, 1833-35; Gov. 1829-31, 1837-39.

GILMER, John Adams (AP N.C.) Nov. 4, 1805-May 14, 1868; House 1857-61.

GILMER, Thomas Walker (D Va.) April 6, 1802-Feb. 28, 1844; House 1841-43, 1843-Feb. 16, 1844 (1841-43 Whig, 1843-44 Democrat); Gov. 1840-41; Secy. of the Navy Feb. 15-Feb. 28, 1844.

GILMER, William Franklin (Dixie) (D Okla.) June 7, 1901-June 9, 1954; House 1949-51.

GILMORE, Alfred (son of John Gilmore) (D Pa.) June 9, 1812-June 29, 1890; House 1849-53.

GILMORE, Edward (D Mass.) Jan. 4, 1867-April 10, 1924; House 1913-15.

GILMORE, John (father of Alfred Gilmore) (JD Pa.) Feb. 18, 1780-May 11, 1845; House 1829-33.

GILMORE, Samuel Louis (D La.) July 30, 1859-July 18, 1910; House March 30, 1909-July 18, 1910.

GINGERY, Don (D Pa.) Feb. 19, 1884-Oct. 15, 1961; House 1935-39.

GINGRICH, Newton Leroy (R Ga.) June 17, 1943-—; House 1979-—.

GINN, Ronald Bryan (D Ga.) May 31, 1934-—; House 1973-83.

GIST, Joseph (D S.C.) Jan. 12, 1775-March 8, 1836; House 1821-27.

GITTINS, Robert Henry (D N.Y.) Dec. 14, 1869-Dec. 25, 1957; House 1913-15.

GLASCOCK, John Raglan (D Calif.) Aug. 25, 1845-Nov. 10, 1913; House 1883-85.

GLASCOCK, Thomas (UD Ga.) Oct. 21, 1790-May 19, 1841; House Oct. 5, 1835-39.

GLASGOW, Hugh (— Pa.) Sept. 8, 1769-Jan. 31, 1818; House 1813-17.

GLASS, Carter (D Va.) Jan. 4, 1858-May 28, 1946; House Nov. 4, 1902-Dec. 16, 1918; Senate Feb. 2, 1920-May 28, 1946; Secy. of the Treasury 1918-20; Pres. pro tempore 1941-45.

GLASS, Presley Thornton (D Tenn.) Oct. 18, 1824-Oct. 9, 1902; House 1885-89.

GLATFELTER, Samuel Feiser (D Pa.) April 7, 1858-April 23, 1927; House 1923-25.

GLEN, Henry (— N.Y.) July 13, 1739-Jan. 6, 1814; House 1793-1801.

GLENN, John Herschel Jr. (D Ohio) July 18, 1921-—; Senate Dec. 24, 1974-—.

GLENN, Milton Willits (R N.J.) June 18, 1903-Dec. 14, 1967; House Nov. 5, 1957-65.

GLENN, Otis Ferguson (R Ill.) Aug. 27, 1879-March 11, 1959; Senate Dec. 3, 1928-33.

GLENN, Thomas Louis (P Idaho) Feb. 2, 1847-Nov. 18, 1918; House 1901-03.

GLICKMAN, Daniel Robert (D Kan.) Nov. 24, 1944-—; House 1977-—.

GLONINGER, John (D Pa.) Sept. 19, 1758-Jan. 22, 1836; House March 4-Aug. 2, 1813.

GLOSSBRENNER, Adam John (D Pa.) Aug. 31, 1810-March 1, 1889; House 1865-69.

GLOVER, David Delano (D Ark.) Jan. 18, 1868-April 5, 1952; House 1929-35.

GLOVER, John Milton (nephew of John Montgomery Glover) (D Mo.) June 23, 1852-Oct. 20, 1929; House 1885-89.

GLOVER, John Montgomery (uncle of John Milton Glover) (D Mo.) Sept. 4, 1822-Nov. 15, 1891; House 1873-79.

GLYNN, James Peter (R Conn.) Nov. 12, 1867-March 6, 1930; House 1915-23, 1925-March 6, 1930.

GLYNN, Martin Henry (D N.Y.) Sept. 27, 1871-Dec. 14, 1924; House 1899-1901; Gov. 1913-15.

GODDARD, Calvin (F Conn.) July 17, 1768-May 2, 1842; House May 14, 1801-05.

GODSHALK, William (R Pa.) Oct. 25, 1817-Feb. 6, 1891; House 1879-83.

GODWIN, Hannibal Lafayette (D N.C.) Nov. 3, 1873-June 9, 1929; House 1907-21.

GOEBEL, Herman Philip (R Ohio) April 5, 1853-May 4, 1930; House 1903-11.

GOEKE, John Henry (D Ohio) Oct. 28, 1869-March 25, 1930; House 1911-15.

GOFF, Abe McGregor (R Idaho) Dec. 21, 1899-—; House 1947-49.

GOFF, Guy Despard (son of Nathan Goff, father of Louise Goff Reece) (R W.Va.) Sept. 13, 1866-Jan. 7, 1933; Senate 1925-31.

GOFF, Nathan (father of Guy Despard Goff, grandfather of Louise Goff Reece) (R W.Va.) Feb. 9, 1843-April 24, 1920; House 1883-89; Senate April 1, 1913-19; Secy. of the Navy Jan. 6-March 5, 1881.

GOGGIN, William Leftwich (W.Va.) May 31, 1807-Jan. 3, 1870; House 1839-43; April 25, 1844-45, 1847-49.

GOLD, Thomas Ruggles (F N.Y.) Nov. 4, 1764-Oct. 24, 1827; House 1809-13, 1815-17.

GOLDEN, James Stephen (R Ky.) Sept. 10, 1891-Sept. 6, 1971; House 1949-55.

GOLDER, Benjamin Martin (R Pa.) Dec. 23, 1891-Dec. 30, 1946; House 1925-33.

GOLDFOGLE, Henry Mayer (D N.Y.), May 23, 1856-June 1, 1929; House 1901-15, 1919-21.

GOLDSBOROUGH, Charles (great-grandfather of Thomas Alan Goldsborough and Winder Laird Henry) (F Md.) July 15, 1765-Dec. 13, 1834; House 1805-17; Gov. 1819.

GOLDSBOROUGH, Phillips Lee (R Md.) Aug. 6, 1865-Oct. 22, 1946; Senate 1929-35; Gov. 1912-16.

GOLDSBOROUGH, Robert Henry (great-grandfather of Winder Laird Henry) (W Md.) Jan. 4, 1779-Oct. 5, 1836; Senate May 21, 1813-19; Jan. 13, 1835-Oct. 5, 1836 (1813-19 Federalist, 1835-36 Whig).

GOLDSBOROUGH, Thomas Alan (great-grandson of Charles Goldsborough) (D Md.) Sept. 16, 1877-June 16, 1951; House 1921-April 5, 1939.

GOLDTHWAITE, George Thomas (D Ala.) Dec. 10, 1809-March 18, 1879; Senate 1871-77.

GOLDWATER, Barry Morris (father of Barry Morris Goldwater Jr.) (R Ariz.) Jan. 1, 1909-—; Senate 1953-65, 1969-—.

GOLDWATER, Barry Morris Jr. (son of Barry Morris Goldwater) (R Calif.) July 15, 1938-—; House April 29, 1969-83.

GOLDZIER, Julius (D Ill.) Jan. 20, 1854-Jan. 20, 1925; House 1893-95.

GOLLADAY, Edward Isaac (brother of Jacob Shall Golladay) (D Tenn.) Sept. 9, 1830-July 11, 1897; House 1871-73.

GOLLADAY, Jacob Shall (brother of Edward Isaac Golladay) (D Ky.) Jan. 19, 1819-May 20, 1887; House Dec. 5, 1867-Feb. 28, 1870.

GONZALEZ, Henry B. (D Texas) May 3, 1916-—; House Nov. 4, 1961-—.

GOOCH, Daniel Linn (D Ky.) Oct. 28, 1853-April 12, 1913; House 1901-05.

GOOCH, Daniel Wheelwright (R Mass.) Jan. 8, 1820-Nov. 11, 1891; House Jan. 31, 1858-Sept. 1, 1865, 1873-75.

GOOD, James William (R Iowa) Sept. 24, 1866-Nov. 18, 1929; House 1909-June 15, 1921; Secy. of War March 5-Nov. 18, 1929.

GOODALL, Louis Bertrand (R Maine) Sept. 23, 1851-June 26, 1935; House 1917-21.

GOODE, John Jr. (D Va.) May 27, 1829-July 14, 1909; House 1875-81.

GOODE, Patrick Gaines (W Ohio) May 10, 1798-Oct. 17, 1862; House 1837-43.

GOODE, Samuel (— Va.) March 21, 1756-Nov. 14, 1822; House 1799-1801.

GOODE, William Osborne (D Va.) Sept. 16, 1798-July 3, 1859; House 1841-43, 1853-July 3, 1859.

GOODELL, Charles Ellsworth (R N.Y.) March 16, 1926-—; House May 26, 1959-Sept. 10, 1968; Senate Sept. 10, 1968-71.

GOODENOW, John Milton (JD Ohio) 1782-July 20, 1838; House 1829-April 9, 1830.

GOODENOW, Robert (brother of Rufus King Goodenow) (W Maine) April 19, 1800-May 15, 1874; House 1851-53.

GOODENOW, Rufus King (brother of Robert Goodenow) (W Maine) April 24, 1790-March 24, 1863; House 1849-51.

GOODHUE, Benjamin (— Mass.) Sept. 20, 1748-July 28, 1814; House 1789-June 1796; Senate June 11, 1796-Nov. 8, 1800.

GOODIN, John Randolph (D Kan.) Dec. 14, 1836-Dec. 18, 1885; House 1875-77.

GOODING, Frank Robert (R Idaho) Sept. 16, 1859-June 24, 1928; Senate Jan. 15, 1921-June 24, 1928; Gov. 1905-09.

GOODLING, George Atlee (father of William Franklin Goodling) (R Pa.) Sept. 26, 1896-Oct. 17, 1982; House 1961-65, 1967-75.

GOODLING, William Franklin (son of George Atlee Goodling) (R Pa.) Dec. 5, 1927-—; House 1975-—.

GOODNIGHT, Isaac Herschel (D Ky.) Jan. 31, 1849-July 24, 1901; House 1889-95.

GOODRICH, Chauncey (brother of Elizur Goodrich) (F Conn.) Oct. 20, 1759-Aug. 18, 1815; House 1795-1801; Senate Oct. 25, 1807-May 1813.

GOODRICH, Elizur (brother of Chauncey Goodrich) (F Conn.) March 24, 1761-Nov. 1, 1849; House 1799-1801.

GOODRICH, John Zacheus (W Mass.) Sept. 27, 1804-April 19, 1885; House 1851-55.

GOODRICH, Milo (R N.Y.) Jan. 3, 1814-April 15, 1881; House 1871-73.

GOODWIN, Angier Louis (R Mass.) Jan. 30, 1881-June 20, 1975; House 1943-55.

GOODWIN, Forrest (R Maine) June 14, 1862-May 28, 1913; House March 4-May 28, 1913.

GOODWIN, Godfrey Gummer (R Minn.) Jan. 11, 1873-Feb. 16, 1933; House 1925-Feb. 16, 1933.

GOODWIN, Henry Charles (R N.Y.) June 25, 1824-Nov. 12, 1860; House Nov. 7, 1854-55, 1857-59.

GOODWIN, John Noble (R Maine/Ariz.) Oct. 18, 1824-April 29, 1887; House (Rep. Maine) 1861-63 (Terr. Del. Ariz.) 1865-67; Gov. (Ariz. Terr.) 1863-65.

GOODWIN, Philip Arnold (R N.Y.) Jan. 20, 1882-June 6, 1937; House 1933-June 6, 1937.

GOODWIN, Robert Kingman (R Iowa) May 23, 1905-Feb. 21, 1983; House March 5, 1940-41.

GOODWIN, William Shields (D Ark.) May 2, 1866-Aug. 9, 1937; House 1911-21.

GOODWYN, Albert Taylor (D Ala.) Dec. 17, 1842-July 2, 1931; House April 22, 1896-97.

GOODWYN, Peterson (D Va.) 1745-Feb. 21, 1818; House 1803-Feb. 21, 1818.

GOODYEAR, Charles (D N.Y.) April 26, 1804-April 9, 1876; House 1845-47, 1865-67.

GOODYKOONTZ, Wells (R W.Va.) June 3, 1872-March 2, 1944; House 1919-23.

GORDON, Bart (D Tenn.) Jan. 24, 1949-—; House 1985-—.

GORDON, George Washington (D Tenn.) Oct. 5, 1836-Aug. 9, 1911; House 1907-Aug. 9, 1911.

GORDON, James (F N.Y.) Oct. 31, 1739-Jan. 17, 1810; House 1791-95.

GORDON, James (— Miss.) Dec. 6, 1833-Nov. 28, 1912; Senate Dec. 27, 1909-Feb. 22, 1910.

GORDON, John Brown (D Ga.) Feb. 6, 1832-Jan. 9, 1904; Senate 1873-May 26, 1880, 1891-97; Gov. 1886-90.

GORDON, Robert Bryarly (D Ohio) Aug. 6, 1855-Jan. 3, 1923; House 1899-1903.

GORDON, Samuel (D N.Y.) April 28, 1802-Oct. 28, 1873; House 1841-43, 1845-47.

GORDON, Thomas Sylvy (D Ill.) Dec. 17, 1893-Jan. 22, 1959; House 1943-59.

GORDON, William (— N.H.) April 12, 1763-May 8, 1802; House 1797-June 12, 1800.

GORDON, William (D Ohio) Dec. 15, 1862-Jan. 16, 1942; House 1913-19.

GORDON, William Fitzhugh (D Va.) Jan. 13, 1787-Aug. 28, 1858; House Jan. 25, 1830-35.

GORE, Albert Arnold (father of Albert Arnold Gore Jr.) (D Tenn.) Dec. 26, 1907-—; House 1939-Dec. 4, 1944, 1945-53; Senate 1953-71.

GORE, Albert Arnold Jr. (son of Albert Arnold Gore) (D Tenn.) March 31, 1948-—; House 1977-85; Senate 1985-—.

GORE, Christopher (— Mass.) Sept. 21, 1758-March 1, 1827; Senate May 5, 1813-May 30, 1816; Gov. 1809-10.

GORE, Thomas Pryor (D Okla.) Dec. 10, 1870-March 16, 1949; Senate Dec. 11, 1907-21, 1931-37.

GORHAM, Benjamin (— Mass.) Feb. 13, 1775-Sept. 27, 1855; House Nov. 6, 1820-23, July 23, 1827-31, 1833-35.

Biographical Index

GORMAN, Arthur Pue (D Md.) March 11, 1839-June 4, 1906; Senate 1881-99, 1903-June 4, 1906.

GORMAN, George Edmund (D Ill.) April 13, 1873-Jan. 13, 1935; House 1913-15.

GORMAN, James Sedgwick (D Mich.) Dec. 28, 1850-May 27, 1923; House 1891-95.

GORMAN, John Jerome (R Ill.) June 2, 1883-Feb. 24, 1949; House 1921-23, 1925-27.

GORMAN, Willis Arnold (D Ind.) Jan. 12, 1816-May 20, 1876; House 1849-53; Gov. (Minn. Terr.) 1853-57.

GORSKI, Chester Charles (D N.Y.) June 22, 1906-April 25, 1975; House 1949-51.

GORSKI, Martin (D Ill.) Oct. 30, 1886-Dec. 4, 1949; House 1943-Dec. 4, 1949.

GORTON, Slade (R Wash.) Jan. 8, 1928- —; Senate 1981- —.

GOSS, Edward Wheeler (R Conn.) April 27, 1893- —; House Nov. 4, 1930-35.

GOSS, James Hamilton (R S.C.) Aug. 9, 1820-Oct. 31, 1886; House July 18, 1868-69.

GOSSETT, Charles Clinton (D Idaho) Sept. 2, 1888-Sept. 20, 1974; Senate Nov. 17, 1945-47; Gov. Jan.-Nov. 16, 1945.

GOSSETT, Ed Lee (D Texas) Jan. 27, 1902- —; House 1939-July 31, 1951.

GOTT, Daniel (W N.Y.) July 10, 1794-July 6, 1864; House 1847-51.

GOULD, Arthur Robinson (R Maine) March 16, 1857-July 24, 1946; Senate Nov. 30, 1926-31.

GOULD, Herman Day (W N.Y.) Jan. 16, 1799-Jan. 26, 1852; House 1849-51.

GOULD, Norman Judd (grandson of Norman Buel Judd) (R N.Y.) March 15, 1877-Aug. 20, 1964; House Nov. 2, 1915-23.

GOULD, Samuel Wadsworth (D Maine) Jan. 1, 1852-Dec. 19, 1935; House 1911-13.

GOULDEN, Joseph Aloysius (D N.Y.) Aug. 1, 1844-May 3, 1915; House 1903-11; 1913-May 3, 1915.

GOURDIN, Theodore (D S.C.) March 20, 1764-Jan. 17, 1826; House 1813-15.

GOVAN, Andrew Robison (— S.C.) Jan. 13, 1794-June 27, 1841; House Dec. 4, 1822-27.

GOVE, Samuel Francis (R Ga.) March 9, 1822-Dec. 3, 1900; House June 25, 1868-69.

GRABOWSKI, Bernard F. (D Conn.) June 11, 1923- —; House 1963-67.

GRADISON, Willis David Jr. (R Ohio) Dec. 28, 1928- —; House 1975- —.

GRADY, Benjamin Franklin (D N.C.) Oct. 10, 1831-March 6, 1914; House 1891-95.

GRAFF, Joseph Verdi (R Ill.) July 1, 1854-Nov. 10, 1921; House 1895-1911.

GRAHAM, Frank Porter (D N.C.) Oct. 14, 1886-Feb. 16, 1972: Senate March 29, 1949-Nov. 26, 1950.

GRAHAM, George Scott (R Pa.) Sept. 13, 1850-July 4, 1931; House 1913-July 4, 1931.

GRAHAM, James (brother of William Alexander Graham) (W N.C.) Jan. 7, 1793-Sept. 25, 1851; House 1833-March 29, 1836; Dec. 5, 1836-1843; 1845-47.

GRAHAM, James Harper (R N.Y.) Sept. 18, 1812-June 23, 1881; House 1859-61.

GRAHAM, James McMahon (D Ill.) April 14, 1852-Oct. 23, 1945; House 1909-15.

GRAHAM, John Hugh (D N.Y.) April 1, 1835-July 11, 1895; House 1893-95.

GRAHAM, Louis Edward (R Pa.) Aug. 4, 1880-Nov. 9, 1965; House 1939-55.

GRAHAM, William (W Ind.) March 16, 1782-Aug. 17, 1858; House 1837-39.

GRAHAM, William Alexander (brother of James Graham) (W N.C.) Sept. 5, 1804-Aug. 11, 1875; Senate Nov. 25, 1840-43; Gov. 1845-49; Secy. of the Navy 1850-52.

GRAHAM, William Harrison (R Pa.) Aug. 3, 1844-March 2, 1923; House Nov. 29, 1898-1903, 1905-11.

GRAHAM, William Johnson (R Ill.) Feb. 7, 1872-Nov. 10, 1937; House 1917-June 7, 1924.

GRAMM, William Philip (R Texas) July 8, 1942- —; House 1979-85; Senate 1985- — (1979-Jan. 5, 1983, Democrat, Feb. 22, 1983- — Republican).

GRAMMER, Elijah Sherman (R Wash.) April 3, 1868-Nov. 19, 1936; Senate Nov. 22, 1932-33.

GRANAHAN, Kathryn Elizabeth (widow of William Thomas Granahan) (D Pa.) Dec. 7, 1906-July 10, 1979; House Nov. 6, 1956-63.

GRANAHAN, William Thomas (husband of Kathryn Elizabeth Granahan) (D Pa.) July 26, 1895-May 25, 1956; House 1945-47; 1949-May 25, 1956.

GRANATA, Peter Charles (R Ill.) Oct. 28, 1898- —; House 1931-April 5, 1932.

GRANFIELD, William Joseph (D Mass.) Dec. 18, 1889-May 28, 1959; House Feb. 11, 1930-37.

GRANGER, Amos Phelps (cousin of Francis Granger) (W N.Y.) June 3, 1789-Aug. 20, 1866; House 1855-59.

GRANGER, Bradley Francis (D Mich.) March 12, 1825-Nov. 4, 1882; House 1861-63.

GRANGER, Daniel Larned Davis (D R.I.) May 30, 1852-Feb. 14, 1909; House 1903-Feb. 14, 1909.

GRANGER, Francis (cousin of Amos Phelps Granger) (W N.Y.) Dec. 1, 1792-Aug. 31, 1868; House 1835-37; 1839-March 5, 1841; Nov. 27, 1841-43; Postmaster Gen. March 6-Sept. 18, 1841.

GRANGER, Miles Tobey (D Conn.) Aug. 12, 1817-Oct. 21, 1895; House 1887-89.

GRANGER, Walter Keil (D Utah) Oct. 11, 1888-April 21, 1978; House 1941-53.

GRANT, Abraham Phineas (D N.Y.) April 5, 1804-Dec. 11, 1871; House 1837-39.

GRANT, George McInvale (D Ala.) July 11, 1897-Nov. 3, 1982; House June 14, 1938-65.

GRANT, John Gaston (R N.C.) Jan. 1, 1858-June 21, 1923; House 1909-11.

GRANT, Robert Allen (R Ind.) July 31, 1905- —; House 1939-49.

GRANTLAND, Seaton (U Ga.) June 8, 1782-Oct. 18, 1864; House 1835-39.

GRASSLEY, Charles Ernest (R Iowa) Sept. 17, 1933- —; House 1975-81; Senate 1981- —.

GRASSO, Ella T. (D Conn.) May 10, 1919-Feb. 5, 1981; House 1971-1975; Gov. 1975-Dec. 31, 1980.

GRAVEL, Maurice Robert (D Alaska) May 13, 1930- —; Senate 1969-81.

GRAVELY, Joseph Jackson (R Mo.) Sept. 25, 1828-April 28, 1872; House 1867-69.

GRAVES, Alexander (D Mo.) Aug. 25, 1844-Dec. 23, 1916; House 1883-85.

GRAVES, Dixie Bibb (D Ala.) July 26, 1882-Jan. 21, 1965; Senate Aug. 19, 1937-Jan. 10, 1938.

GRAVES, William Jordan (W Ky.) 1805-Sept. 27, 1848; House 1835-41.

GRAY, Edward Winthrop (R N.J.) Aug. 18, 1870-June 10, 1942; House 1915-19.

GRAY, Edwin (— Va.) July 18, 1743-?; House 1799-1813.

GRAY, Finly Hutchinson (D Ind.) July 21, 1863-May 8, 1947; House 1911-17; 1933-39.

GRAY, George (D Del.) May 4, 1840-Aug. 7, 1925; Senate March 18, 1885-99.

GRAY, Hiram (D N.Y.) July 10, 1801-May 6, 1890; House 1837-39.

GRAY, John Cowper (— Va.) 1783-May 18, 1823; House Aug. 28, 1820-21.

GRAY, Joseph Anthony (D Pa.) Feb. 25, 1884-May 8, 1966; House 1935-39.

GRAY, Kenneth James (D Ill.) Nov. 14, 1924- —; House 1955-Dec. 31, 1974, 1985- —.

GRAY, Oscar Lee (D Ala.) July 2, 1865-Jan. 2, 1936; House 1915-19.

GRAY, William H. III (D Pa.) Aug. 20, 1941- —; House 1979- —.

GRAYSON, William (father of William John Grayson, uncle of Alexander Dalrymple Orr) (— Va.) 1740-March 12, 1790; Senate 1789-March 12, 1790; Cont. Cong. 1784-87.

GRAYSON, William John (son of William Grayson, cousin of Alexander Dalrymple Orr) (W S.C.) Nov. 2, 1788-Oct. 4, 1863; House 1833-37.

GREELEY, Horace (W N.Y.) Feb. 3, 1811-Nov. 29, 1872; House Dec. 4, 1848-49.

GREEN, Bryam (— N.Y.) April 15, 1786-Oct. 18, 1865; House 1843-45.

GREEN, Edith (D Ore.) Jan. 17, 1910- — ; House 1955-Dec. 31, 1974.

GREEN, Frederick William (D Ohio) Feb. 18, 1816-June 18, 1879; House 1851-55.

GREEN, Henry Dickinson (D Pa.) May 3, 1857-Dec. 29, 1929; House Nov. 7, 1899-1903.

GREEN, Innis (D Pa.) Feb. 26, 1776-Aug. 4, 1839; House 1827-31.

GREEN, Isaiah Lewis (— Mass.) Dec. 28, 1761-Dec. 5, 1841; House 1805-09; 1811-13.

GREEN, James Stephen (D Mo.) Feb. 28, 1817-Jan. 19, 1870; House 1847-51; Senate Jan. 12, 1857-61.

GREEN, Robert Alexis (D Fla.) Feb. 10, 1892-Feb. 9, 1973; House 1925-Nov. 25, 1944.

GREEN, Robert Stockton (D N.J.) March 25, 1831-May 7, 1895; House 1885-Jan. 17, 1887; Gov. 1887-90.

GREEN, Sedgwick William (R N.Y.) Oct. 16, 1929- — ; House Feb. 21, 1978- — .

GREEN, Theodore Francis (grandnephew of Samuel Greene Arnold, great-grandnephew of Tristam Burges, great-grandson of James Burrill Jr., great-great-nephew of Lemuel Hastings Arnold) (D R.I.) Oct. 2, 1867-May 19, 1966; Senate 1937-61; Gov. 1933-37.

GREEN, Wharton Jackson (grandson of Jesse Wharton, cousin of Matt Whitaker Ransom) (D N.C.) Feb. 28, 1831-Aug. 6, 1910; House 1883-87.

GREEN, William Joseph Jr. (father of William Joseph Green III) (D Pa.) March 5, 1910-Dec. 21, 1963; House 1945-47; 1949-Dec. 21, 1963.

GREEN, William Joseph III (son of William Joseph Green Jr.) (D Pa.) June 24, 1938- — ; House April 28, 1964-77.

GREEN, William Raymond (R Iowa) Nov. 7, 1856-June 11, 1947; House June 5, 1911-March 31, 1928.

GREEN, Willis (W Ky.) ?-?; House 1839-45.

GREENE, Albert Collins (W R.I.) April 15, 1791-Jan. 8, 1863; Senate 1845-51.

GREENE, Frank Lester (R Vt.) Feb. 10, 1870-Dec. 17, 1930; House July 30, 1912-1923; Senate 1923-Dec. 17, 1930.

GREENE George Woodward (D N.Y.) July 4, 1831-July 21, 1895; House 1869-Feb. 17, 1870.

GREENE, Ray (— R.I.) Feb. 2, 1765-Jan 11, 1829; Senate Nov. 13, 1797-1801.

GREENE, Thomas Marston (— Miss.) Feb. 26, 1758-Feb. 7, 1813; House (Terr. Del.) Dec. 6, 1802-03.

GREENE, William Laury (P Neb.) Oct. 3, 1849-March 11, 1899; House 1897-March 11, 1899.

GREENE, William Stedman (R Mass.) April 28, 1841-Sept. 22, 1924; House May 31, 1898-Sept. 22, 1924.

GREENHALGE, Frederick Thomas (R Mass.) July 19, 1842-March 5, 1896; House 1889-91; Gov. 1894-96.

GREENLEAF, Halbert Stevens (D N.Y.) April 12, 1827-Aug. 25, 1906; House 1883-85; 1891-93.

GREENMAN, Edward Whitford (D N.Y.) Jan. 26, 1840-Aug. 3, 1908; House 1887-89.

GREENUP, Christopher (— Ky.) 1750-April 27, 1818; House Nov. 9, 1792-1797; Gov. 1804-08.

GREENWAY, Isabella Selmes (later Mrs. Harry Orland King) (D Ariz.) March 22, 1886-Dec. 18, 1953; House Oct. 3, 1933-37.

GREENWOOD, Alfred Burton (D Ark.) July 11, 1811-Oct. 4, 1889; House 1853-59.

GREENWOOD, Arthur Herbert (D Ind.) Jan. 31, 1880-April 26, 1963; House 1923-39.

GREENWOOD, Ernest (D N.Y.) Nov. 25, 1884-June 15, 1955; House 1951-53.

GREEVER, Paul Ranous (D Wyo.) Sept. 28, 1891-Feb. 16, 1943; House 1935-39.

GREGG, Alexander White (D Texas) Jan. 31, 1855-April 30, 1919; House 1903-19.

GREGG, Andrew (grandfather of James Xavier McLanahan) (— Pa.) June 10, 1755-May 20, 1835; House 1791-1807; Senate 1807-13; Pres. pro tempore 1809.

GREGG, Curtis Hussey (D Pa.) Aug. 9, 1865-Jan. 18, 1933; House 1911-13.

GREGG, James Madison (D Ind.) June 26, 1806-June 16, 1869; House 1857-59.

GREGG, Judd (R N.H.) Feb. 14, 1947- — ; House 1981- — .

GREGORY, Dudley Sanford (W N.J.) Feb. 5, 1800-Dec. 8, 1874; House 1847-49.

GREGORY, Noble Jones (brother of William Voris Gregory) (D Ky.) Aug. 30, 1897-Sept. 26, 1971; House 1937-59.

GREGORY, William Voris (brother of Noble Jones Gregory (D Ky.) Oct. 21, 1877-Oct. 10, 1936; House 1927-Oct. 10, 1936.

GREIG, John (W N.Y.) Aug. 6, 1779-April 9, 1858; House May 21-Sept. 25, 1841.

GREIGG, Stanley Lloyd (D Iowa) May 7, 1931-— ; House 1965-67.

GRENNELL, George Jr. (— Mass.) Dec. 25, 1786-Nov. 19, 1877; House 1829-39.

GRESHAM, Walter (D Texas) July 22, 1841-Nov. 6, 1920; House 1893-95.

GREY, Benjamin Edwards (grandson of Benjamin Edwards) (W Ky.) ?-?; House 1851-55.

GRIDER, George William (D Tenn.) Oct. 1, 1912-— ; House 1965-67.

GRIDER, Henry (W Ky.) July 16, 1796-Sept. 7, 1866; House 1843-47; 1861-Sept. 7, 1866.

GRIEST, William Walton (R Pa.) Sept. 22, 1858-Dec. 5, 1929; House 1909-Dec. 5, 1929.

GRIFFIN, Anthony Jerome (D N.Y.) April 1, 1866-Jan. 13, 1935; House March 5, 1918-Jan. 13, 1935.

GRIFFIN, Charles Hudson (great-great-grandson of Isaac Griffin) (D Miss.) May 9, 1926-— ; House March 12, 1968-1973.

GRIFFIN, Daniel Joseph (D N.Y.) March 26, 1880-Dec. 11, 1926; House 1913-Dec. 31, 1917.

GRIFFIN, Isaac (great-grandfather of Eugene McLanahan Wilson, great-great-grandfather of Charles Hudson Griffin) (D Pa.) Feb. 27, 1756-Oct. 12, 1827; House Feb. 16, 1813-17.

GRIFFIN, John King (SRW S.C.) Aug. 13, 1789-Aug. 1, 1841; House 1831-41.

GRIFFIN, Levi Thomas (D Mich.) May 23, 1837-March 17, 1906; House Dec. 4, 1893-95.

GRIFFIN, Michael (R Wis.) Sept. 9, 1842-Dec. 29, 1899; House Nov. 5, 1894-99.

GRIFFIN, Robert Paul (R Mich.) Nov. 6, 1923-— ; House 1957-May 10, 1966; Senate May 11, 1966-79.

GRIFFIN, Samuel (— Va.) ?-Nov. 3, 1810; House 1789-95.

GRIFFIN, Thomas (— Va.) 1773-Oct. 7, 1837; House 1803-05.

GRIFFITH, Francis Marion (D Ind.) Aug. 21, 1849-Feb. 8, 1927; House Dec. 6, 1897-1905.

GRIFFITH, John Keller (D La.) Oct. 16, 1882-Sept. 25, 1942; House 1937-41.

GRIFFITH, Samuel (D Pa.) Feb. 14, 1816-Oct. 1, 1893; House 1871-73.

GRIFFITHS, Martha Wright (D Mich.) Jan. 29, 1912-— ; House 1955-Dec. 31, 1974.

GRIFFITHS, Percy Wilfred (R Ohio) March 30, 1893-June 12, 1984; House 1943-49.

GRIGGS, James Mathews (D Ga.) March 29, 1861-Jan. 5, 1910; House 1897-Jan. 5, 1910.

GRIGSBY, George Barnes (D Alaska) Dec. 2, 1874-May 9, 1962; House (Terr. Del.) June 3, 1920-March 1, 1921.

GRIMES, James Wilson (R Iowa) Oct. 20, 1816-Feb. 7, 1872; Senate 1859-Dec. 6, 1869; Gov. 1854-58.

GRIMES, Thomas Wingfield (D Ga.) Dec. 18, 1844-Oct. 28, 1905; House 1887-91.

GRINNELL, Joseph (brother of Moses Hicks Grinnell) (W Mass.) Nov. 17, 1788-Feb. 7, 1885; House Dec. 7, 1843-51.

GRINNELL, Josiah Bushnell (R Iowa) Dec. 22, 1821-March 31, 1891; House 1863-67.

GRINNELL, Moses Hicks (brother of Joseph Grinnell) (W N.Y.) March 3, 1803-Nov. 24, 1877; House 1839-41.

GRISHAM, Wayne Richard (R Calif.) Jan. 10, 1923-— ; House 1979-83.

GRISWOLD, Dwight Palmer (R Neb.) Nov. 27, 1893-April 12, 1954; Senate Nov. 5, 1952-April 12, 1954; Gov. 1941-47.

GRISWOLD, Gaylord (F N.Y.) Dec. 18, 1767-March 1, 1809; House 1803-05.

GRISWOLD, Glenn Hasenfratz (D Ind.) Jan. 20, 1890-Dec. 5, 1940; House 1931-39.

GRISWOLD, Harry Wilbur (R Wis.) May 19, 1886-July 4, 1939; House Jan. 3-July 4, 1939.

GRISWOLD, John Ashley (D N.Y.) Nov. 18, 1822-Feb. 22, 1902; House 1869-71.

GRISWOLD, John Augustus (R N.Y.) Nov. 11, 1822-Oct. 31, 1872; House 1863-69 (1863-65 Democrat, 1865-69 Republican).

GRISWOLD, Matthew (grandson of Roger Griswold) (R Pa.) June 6, 1833-May 19, 1919; House 1891-93; 1895-97.

GRISWOLD, Roger (grandfather of Matthew Griswold) (F Conn.) May 21, 1762-Oct. 25, 1812; House 1795-1805; Gov. 1811-12.

GRISWOLD, Stanley (— Ohio) Nov. 14, 1763-Aug. 21, 1815; Senate May 18-Dec. 11, 1809.

GROESBECK, William Slocum (D Ohio) July 24, 1815-July 7, 1897; House 1857-59.

GRONNA, Asle Jorgenson (R N.D.) Dec. 10, 1858-May 4, 1922; House 1905-Feb. 2, 1911; Senate Feb. 2, 1911-21.

GROOME, James Black (D Md.) April 4, 1838-Oct. 5, 1893; Senate 1879-85; Gov. 1874-76.

GROSS, Chester Heilman (R Pa.) Oct. 13, 1888-Jan. 9, 1973; House 1939-41; 1943-49.

GROSS, Ezra Carter (D N.Y.) July 11, 1787-April 9, 1829; House 1819-21.

GROSS, Harold Royce (R Iowa) June 30, 1899-—; House 1949-1975.

GROSS, Samuel (D Pa.) Nov. 10, 1774-March 19, 1844; House 1819-23.

GROSVENOR, Charles Henry (uncle of Charles Grosvenor Bond) (R Ohio) Sept. 20, 1833-Oct. 30, 1917; House 1885-91; 1893-1907.

GROSVENOR, Thomas Peabody (F N.Y.) Dec. 20, 1778-April 24, 1817; House Jan. 29, 1813-17.

GROTBERG, John E. (R Ill.) March 21, 1925-—; House 1985-—.

GROUT, Jonathan (D Mass.) July 23, 1737-Sept. 8, 1807; House 1789-91.

GROUT, William Wallace (R Vt.) May 24, 1836-Oct. 7, 1902; House 1881-83; 1885-1901.

GROVE, William Barry (F N.C.) Jan. 15, 1764-March 30, 1818; House 1791-1803.

GROVER, Asa Porter (D Ky.) Feb. 18, 1819-July 20, 1887; House 1867-69.

GROVER, James R. Jr. (R N.Y.) March 5, 1919-—; House 1963-1975.

GROVER, La Fayette (D Ore.) Nov. 29, 1823-May 10, 1911; House Feb. 15-March 3, 1859; Senate 1877-83; Gov. 1870-77.

GROVER, Martin (NAD N.Y.) Oct. 20, 1811-Aug. 23, 1875; House 1845-47.

GROW, Galusha Aaron (R Pa.) Aug. 31, 1823-March 31, 1907; House 1851-63; Feb. 26, 1894-1903 (1851-57 Free Soil Democrat, 1857-63, 1894-1903 Republican); Speaker 1861-63.

GRUENING, Ernest (D Alaska) Feb. 6, 1887-June 26, 1974; Senate 1959-69; Gov. (Alaska Terr.) 1939-53.

GRUNDY, Felix (WD Tenn.) Sept. 11, 1777-Dec. 19, 1840; House 1811-14; Senate Oct. 19, 1829-July 4, 1838; Nov. 19, 1839-Dec. 19, 1840; Atty. Gen. 1838-39.

GRUNDY, Joseph Ridgway (R Pa.) Jan. 13, 1863-March 3, 1961; Senate Dec. 11, 1929-Dec. 1, 1930.

GUARINI, Frank Joseph (D N.J.) Aug. 20, 1924-—; House 1979-—.

GUBSER, Charles Samuel (R Calif.) Feb. 1, 1916-—; House 1953-Dec. 31, 1974.

GUDE, Gilbert (R Md.) March 9, 1923-—; House 1967-77.

GUDGER, James Madison Jr. (father of Katherine Gudger Langley) (D N.C.) Oct. 22, 1855-Feb. 29, 1920; House 1903-07; 1911-15.

GUDGER, Lamar (D N.C.) April 30, 1919-—; House 1977-81.

GUENTHER, Richard William (R Wis.) Nov. 30, 1845-April 5, 1913; House 1881-89.

GUERNSEY, Frank Edward (R Maine) Oct. 15, 1866-Jan. 1, 1927; House Nov. 3, 1908-17.

GUEVARA, Pedro (Nat. P.I.) Feb. 23, 1879-Jan. 19, 1937; House (Res. Comm.) 1923-Feb. 14, 1936.

GUFFEY, Joseph F. (D Pa.) Dec. 29, 1870-March 6, 1959; Senate 1935-47.

GUGGENHEIM, Simon (R Colo.) Dec. 30, 1867-Nov. 2, 1941; Senate 1907-13.

GUILL, Ben Hugh (R Texas) Sept. 8, 1909-—; House May 6, 1950-51.

GUION, Walter (D La.) April 3, 1849-Feb. 7, 1927; Senate April 22-Nov. 5, 1918.

GUNCKEL, Lewis B. (R Ohio) Oct. 15, 1826-Oct. 3, 1903; House 1873-75.

GUNDERSON, Steven (R Wis.) May 10, 1951-—; House 1981-—.

GUNN, James (— Ga.) March 13, 1753-July 30, 1801; Senate 1789-1801; Cont. Cong. 1788-89.

GUNN, James (P Idaho) March 6, 1843-Nov. 5, 1911; House 1897-99.

GUNTER, Thomas Montague (D Ark.) Sept. 18, 1826-Jan. 12, 1904; House June 16, 1874-83.

GUNTER, William Dawson Jr. (D Fla.) July 16, 1934-—; House 1973-75.

GURLEY, Henry Hosford (W La.) May 20, 1788-March 16, 1833; House 1823-31.

GURLEY, John Addison (R Ohio) Dec. 9, 1813-Aug. 19, 1863; House 1859-63.

GURNEY, Chan (John Chandler) (R S.D.) May 21, 1896-—; Senate 1939-51.

GURNEY, Edward John (R Fla.) Jan. 12, 1914-—; House 1963-69; Senate 1969-Dec. 31, 1974.

GUSTINE, Amos (D Pa.) 1789-March 3, 1844; House May 4, 1841-43.

GUTHRIE, James (D Ky.) Dec. 5, 1792-March 13, 1869; Senate 1865-Feb. 7, 1868; Secy. of the Treasury 1853-57.

GUYER, Tennyson (R Ohio) Nov. 29, 1913-April 12, 1981; House 1973-April 12, 1981.

GUYER, Ulysses Samuel (R Kan.) Dec. 13, 1868-June 5, 1943; House Nov. 4, 1924-25; 1927-June 5, 1943.

GUYON, James Jr. (F N.Y.) Dec. 24, 1778-March 9, 1846; House Jan. 14, 1820-21.

GWIN, William McKendree (D Miss./Calif.) Oct. 9, 1805-Sept. 3, 1885; House 1841-43 (Miss.); Senate Sept. 9, 1850-55; Jan. 13, 1857-61 (Calif.).

GWINN, Ralph Waldo (R N.Y.) March 29, 1884-Feb. 27, 1962; House 1945-59.

GWYNNE, John William (R Iowa) Oct. 20, 1889-—; House 1935-49.

H

HABERSHAM, Richard Wylly (SRD Ga.) Dec 1786-Dec. 2, 1842; House 1839-Dec. 2, 1842.

HACKETT, Richard Nathaniel (D N.C.) Dec. 4, 1866-Nov. 22, 1923; House 1907-09.

HACKETT, Thomas C. (D Ga.) ?-Oct. 8, 1851; House 1849-51.

HACKLEY, Aaron Jr. (— N.Y.) May 6, 1783-Dec. 28, 1868; House 1819-21.

HACKNEY, Thomas (D Mo.) Dec. ll, 1861-Dec. 24, 1946; House 1907-09.

HADLEY, Lindley Hoag (R Wash.) June 19, 1861-Nov. 1, 1948; House 1915-33.

HADLEY, William Flavius Lester (R Ill.) June 15, 1847-April 25, 1901; House Dec. 2, 1895-97.

HAGAN, G. Elliott (D Ga.) May 24, 1916-—; House 1961-73.

HAGANS, John Marshall (R W. Va.) Aug. 13, 1838-June 17, 1900; House 1873-75.

HAGEDORN, Thomas Michael (R Minn.) Nov. 27, 1943-—; House 1975-83.

HAGEN, Harlan Francis (D Calif.) Oct. 8, 1914-—; House 1953-67.

HAGEN, Harold Christian (R Minn.) Nov. 10, 1901-March 19, 1957; House 1943-55 (1943-45 Farmer Laborite, 1945-55 Republican).

HAGER, Alva Lysander (R Iowa) Oct. 29, 1850-Jan. 29, 1923; House 1893-99.

HAGER, John Sharpenstein (AMD Calif.) March 12, 1818-March 19, 1890; Senate Dec. 23, 1873-75.

HAGGOTT, Warren Armstrong (R Colo.) May 18, 1864-April 29, 1958; House 1907-09.

HAHN, John (D Pa.) Oct. 30, 1776-Dec. 26, 1823; House 1815-17.

HAHN, Michael (R La.) Nov. 24, 1830-March 15, 1886; House Dec. 3, 1862-63; 1885-March 15, 1886 (1862-63 Unionist, 1885-86 Republican).

HAIGHT, Charles (D N.J.) Jan. 4, 1838-Aug. 1, 1891; House 1867-71.

HAIGHT, Edward (D N.Y.) March 26, 1817-Sept. 15, 1885; House 1861-63.

HAILE, William (— Miss.) 1797-March 7, 1837; House July 10, 1826-Sept. 12, 1828.

HAILEY, John (D Idaho) Aug. 29, 1835-April 10, 1921; House (Terr. Del.) 1873-75; 1885-87.

HAINER, Eugene Jerome (R Neb.) Aug. 16, 1851-March 17, 1929; House 1893-97.

HAINES, Charles Delemere (D N.Y.) June 9, 1856-April 11, 1929; House 1893-95.

HAINES, Harry Luther (D Pa.) Feb. 1, 1880-March 29, 1947; House 1931-39; 1941-43.

HALDEMAN, Richard Jacobs (D Pa.) May 19, 1831-Oct. 1, 1886; House 1869-73.

HALE, Artemas (W Mass.) Oct. 20, 1783-Aug. 3, 1882; House 1845-49.

HALE, Eugene (father of Frederick Hale) (R Maine) June 9, 1836-Oct. 28, 1918; House 1869-79; Senate 1881-1911.

HALE, Fletcher (R N.H.) Jan. 22, 1883-Oct. 22, 1931; House 1925-Oct 22, 1931.

HALE, Frederick (son of Eugene Hale, grandson of Zachariah Chandler, cousin of Robert Hale) (R Maine) Oct. 7, 1874-Sept. 28, 1963; Senate 1917-41.

HALE, James Tracy (R Pa.) Oct. 14, 1810-April 6, 1865; House 1859-65.

HALE, John Blackwell (D Mo.) Feb. 27, 1831-Feb. 1, 1905; House 1885-87.

HALE, John Parker (FS N.H.) March 31, 1806-Nov. 19, 1873; House 1843-45; Senate 1847-53, July 30, 1855-1865 (1843-45 Democrat, 1847-53, 1855-65 Free-Soiler).

HALE, Nathan Wesley (R Tenn.) Feb. 11, 1860-Sept. 16, 1941; House 1905-09.

HALE, Robert (cousin of Frederick Hale) (R Maine) Nov. 29, 1889-Nov. 30, 1976; House 1943-59.

HALE, Robert Safford (R N.Y.) Sept. 24, 1822-Dec. 14, 1881; House Dec. 3, 1866-67; 1873-75.

HALE, Salma (D N.H.) March 7, 1787-Nov. 19, 1866; House 1817-19.

HALE, William (F N.H.) Aug. 6, 1765-Nov. 8, 1848; House 1809-11; 1813-17.

HALEY, Elisha (D Conn.) Jan. 21, 1776-Jan. 22, 1860; House 1835-39.

HALEY, James Andrew (D Fla.) Jan. 4, 1899-Aug. 6, 1981; House 1953-77.

HALL, Albert Richardson (R Ind.) Aug. 27, 1884-Nov. 29, 1969; House 1925-31.

HALL, Augustus (D Iowa) April 29, 1814-Feb. 1, 1861; House 1855-57.

HALL, Benton Jay (D Iowa) Jan. 13, 1835-Jan. 5, 1894; House 1885-87.

HALL, Bolling (WD Ga.) Dec. 25, 1767-Feb. 25, 1836; House 1811-17.

HALL, Chapin (R Pa.) July 12, 1816-Sept. 12, 1879; House 1859-61.

HALL, Darwin Scott (R Minn.) Jan. 23, 1844-Feb. 23, 1919; House 1889-91.

HALL, David McKee (D N.C.) May 16, 1918-Jan. 29, 1960; House 1959-Jan. 29, 1960.

HALL, Durward Gorham (R Mo.) Sept. 14, 1910- —; House 1961-73.

HALL, Edwin Arthur (R N.Y.) Feb. 11, 1909- —; House Nov. 7, 1939-53.

HALL, George (D N.Y.) May 12, 1770-March 20, 1840; House 1819-21.

HALL, Hiland (W Vt.) July 20, 1795-Dec. 18, 1885; House Jan. 1, 1833-43; Gov. (Republican) 1858-60.

HALL, Homer William (R Ill.) July 22, 1870-Sept. 22, 1954; House 1927-33.

HALL, James Knox Polk (D Pa.) Sept. 30, 1844-Jan. 5, 1915; House 1899-Nov. 29, 1902.

HALL, Joseph (D Maine) June 26, 1793-Dec. 31, 1859; House 1833-37.

HALL, Joshua Gilman (R N.H.) Nov. 5, 1828-Oct. 31, 1898; House 1879-83.

HALL, Katie Beatrice Green (D Ind.) April 3, 1938- —; House 1983-85.

HALL, Lawrence Washington (D Ohio) 1819-Jan. 18, 1863; House 1857-59.

HALL, Leonard Wood (R N.Y.) Oct. 2, 1900-June 2, 1979; House 1939-Dec. 31, 1952; Chrmn. Rep. Nat. Comm. 1953-57.

HALL, Nathan Kelsey (W N.Y.) March 28, 1810-March 2, 1874; House 1847-49; Postmaster Gen. 1850-52.

HALL, Norman (D Pa.) Nov. 17, 1829-Sept. 29, 1917; House 1887-89.

HALL, Obed (D N.H.) Dec. 23, 1757-April 1, 1828; House 1811-13.

HALL, Osee Matson (D Minn.) Sept. 10, 1847-Nov. 26, 1914; House 1891-95.

HALL, Philo (R S.D.) Dec. 31, 1865-Oct. 7, 1938; House 1907-09.

HALL, Ralph M. (D Texas) May 3, 1923- —; House 1981- —.

HALL, Robert Bernard (R Mass.) Jan. 28, 1812-April 15, 1868; House 1855-57, 1857-59 (1855-57 American Party, 1857-59 Republican).

HALL, Robert Samuel (D Miss.) March 10, 1879-June 10, 1941; House 1929-33.

HALL, Sam Blakeley Jr. (D Texas) Jan. 11, 1924- —; House June 19, 1976- —.

HALL, Thomas (R N.D.) June 6, 1869-Dec. 4, 1958; House Nov. 4, 1924-33.

HALL, Thomas H. (D N.C.) June 1773-June 30, 1853; House 1817-25; 1827-35.

HALL, Tim Lee (D Ill.) June 11, 1925- —; House 1975-77.

HALL, Tony Patrick (D Ohio) Jan. 16, 1942- —; House 1979- —.

HALL, Uriel Sebree (son of William Augustus Hall, nephew of Willard Preble Hall) (D Mo.) April 12, 1852-Dec. 30, 1932; House 1893-97.

HALL, Willard (D Del.) Dec. 24, 1780-May 10, 1875; House 1817-Jan. 22, 1821.

HALL, Willard Preble (brother of William Augustus Hall, uncle of Uriel Sebree Hall) (D Mo.) May 9, 1820-Nov. 2, 1882; House 1847-53; Gov. 1864-65.

HALL, William (D Tenn.) Feb. 11, 1775-Oct. 7, 1856; House 1831-33; Gov. 1829.

HALL, William Augustus (father of Uriel Sebree Hall, brother of Willard Prebe Hall) (D Mo.) Oct. 15, 1815-Dec. 15, 1888; House Jan. 20, 1862-65.

HALL, Wilton Earle (D S.C.) March 11, 1901- —; Senate Nov. 20, 1944-45.

HALLECK, Charles Abraham (R Ind.) Aug. 22, 1900- —; House Jan. 29, 1935-69; House majority leader 1947-49, 1953-55.

HALLOCK, John Jr. (D N.Y.) July 1783-Dec. 6, 1840; House 1825-29.

HALLOWAY, Ransom (W N.Y.) about 1793-April 6, 1851; House 1849-51.

HALLOWELL, Edwin (D Pa.) April 2, 1844-Sept. 13, 1916; House 1891-93.

HALPERN, Seymour (R N.Y.) Nov. 19, 1913- —; House 1959-73.

HALSELL, John Edward (D Ky.) Sept. 11, 1826-Dec. 26, 1899; House 1883-87.

HALSEY, George Armstrong (R N.J.) Dec. 7, 1827-April 1, 1894; House 1867-69; 1871-73.

HALSEY, Jehiel Howell (son of Silas Halsey, brother of Nicoll Halsey) (JD N.Y.) Oct. 7, 1788-Dec. 5, 1867; House 1829-31.

HALSEY, Nicoll (son of Silas Halsey, brother of Jehiel Howell Halsey) (D N.Y.) March 8, 1782-March 3, 1865; House 1833-35.

HALSEY, Silas (father of Jehiel Howell Halsey and Nicoll Halsey) (D N.Y.) Oct. 6, 1743-Nov. 19, 1832; House 1805-07.

HALSEY, Thomas Jefferson (R Mo.) May 4, 1863-March 17, 1951; House 1929-31.

HALSTEAD, William (W N.J.) June 4, 1794-March 4, 1878; House 1837-39; 1841-43.

HALTERMAN, Frederick (R Pa.) Oct. 22, 1831-March 22, 1907; House 1895-97.

HALVORSON, Kittel (FA/Prohib. Minn.) Dec. 15, 1846-July 12, 1936; House 1891-93.

Biographical Index

HAMBLETON, Samuel (D Md.) Jan. 8, 1812-Dec. 9, 1886; House 1869-73.

HAMER, Thomas Lyon (uncle of Thomas Ray Hamer) (D Ohio) July 1800-Dec. 2, 1846; House 1833-39.

HAMER, Thomas Ray (nephew of Thomas Lyon Hamer) (R Idaho) May 4, 1864-Dec. 22, 1950; House 1909-11.

HAMILL, James Alphonsus (D N.J.) March 30, 1877-Dec. 15, 1941; House 1907-21.

HAMILL, Patrick (D Md.) April 28, 1817-Jan. 15, 1895; House 1869-71.

HAMILTON, Andrew Holman (D Ind.) June 7, 1834-May 9, 1895; House 1875-79.

HAMILTON, Andrew Jackson (brother of Morgan Calvin Hamilton) (ID Texas) Jan. 28, 1815-April 11, 1875; House 1859-61; Military Gov. 1862-65; Provisional Gov. 1865-66.

HAMILTON, Charles Mann (R N.Y.) Jan. 23, 1874-Jan. 3, 1942; House 1913-19.

HAMILTON, Charles Memorial (R Fla.) Nov. 1, 1840-Oct. 22, 1875; House July 1, 1868-71.

HAMILTON, Cornelius Springer (R Ohio) Jan. 2, 1821-Dec. 22, 1867; House March 4-Dec. 22, 1867.

HAMILTON, Daniel Webster (D Iowa) Dec. 20, 1861-Aug. 21, 1936; House 1907-09.

HAMILTON, Edward La Rue (R Mich.) Dec. 9, 1857-Nov. 2, 1923; House 1897-1921.

HAMILTON, Finley (D Ky.) June 19, 1886-Jan. 10, 1940; House 1933-35.

HAMILTON, James Jr. (SRFT S.C.) May 8, 1786-Nov. 15, 1857; House Dec. 13, 1822-29; Gov. 1830-32.

HAMILTON, John (D Pa.) Nov. 25, 1754-Aug. 22, 1837; House 1805-07.

HAMILTON, John M. (D W.Va.) March 16, 1855-Dec. 27, 1916; House 1911-13.

HAMILTON, John Taylor (D Iowa) Oct. 16, 1843-Jan. 25, 1925; House 1891-93.

HAMILTON, Lee Herbert (D Ind.) April 20, 1931-—; House 1965-—.

HAMILTON, Morgan Calvin (brother of Andrew Jackson Hamilton) (R Texas) Feb. 25, 1809-Nov. 21, 1893; Senate March 30, 1870-77.

HAMILTON, Norman Rond (D Va.) Nov. 13, 1877-March 26, 1964; House 1937-39.

HAMILTON, Robert (D N.J.) Dec. 9, 1809-March 14, 1878; House 1873-77.

HAMILTON, William Thomas (D Md.) Sept. 8, 1820-Oct. 26, 1888; House 1849-55; Senate 1869-75; Gov. 1880-84.

HAMLIN, Courtney Walker (cousin of William Edward Barton) (D Mo.) Oct. 27, 1858-Feb. 16, 1950; House 1903-05; 1907-19.

HAMLIN, Edward Stowe (W Ohio) July 6, 1808-Nov. 23, 1894; House Oct. 8, 1844-45.

HAMLIN, Hannibal (R Maine) Aug. 27, 1809-July 4, 1891; House 1843-47; Senate June 8, 1848-Jan. 7, 1857, 1857-Jan. 17, 1861, 1869-81 (1843-47, 1848-57 Democrat, 1857-61,1869-81 Republican); Gov. Jan. 8-Feb. 20, 1857; Vice Pres. 1861-65.

HAMLIN, Simon Moulton (D Maine) Aug. 10, 1866-July 27, 1939; House 1935-37.

HAMMER, William Cicero (D N.C.) March 24, 1865-Sept. 26, 1930; House 1921-Sept. 26, 1930.

HAMMERSCHMIDT, John Paul (R Ark.) May 4, 1922-—; House 1967-—.

HAMMETT, William H. (D Miss.) ?-?; House 1843-45.

HAMMOND, Edward (D Md.) March 17, 1812-Oct. 19, 1882; House 1849-53.

HAMMOND, Jabez Delno (D N.Y.) Aug. 2, 1778-Aug. 18, 1855; House 1815-17.

HAMMOND, James Henry (SRD S.C.) Nov. 15, 1807-Nov. 13, 1864; House 1835-Feb. 26, 1836; Senate Dec. 7, 1857-Nov. 11, 1860 (1835-36 State Rights Free Trader, 1857-60 State Rights Democrat); Gov. 1842-44.

HAMMOND, John (R N.Y.) Aug. 17, 1827-May 28, 1889; House 1879-83.

HAMMOND, Nathaniel Job (D Ga.) Dec. 26, 1833-April 20, 1899; House 1879-87.

HAMMOND, Peter Francis (D Ohio) June 30, 1887-April 2, 1971; House Nov. 30, 1936-37.

HAMMOND, Robert Hanna (VBD Pa.) April 28, 1791-June 2, 1847; House 1837-41.

HAMMOND, Samuel (D Ga.) Sept. 21, 1757-Sept. 11, 1842; House 1803-Feb. 2, 1805; Gov. (Upper Louisiana Terr.) 1805-24.

HAMMOND, Thomas (D Ind.) Feb. 27, 1843-Sept. 21, 1909; House 1893-95.

HAMMOND, Winfield Scott (D Minn.) Nov. 17, 1863-Dec. 30, 1915; House 1907-Jan. 6, 1915; Gov. Jan.-Dec. 30, 1915.

HAMMONS, David (D Maine) May 12, 1808-Nov. 7, 1888; House 1847-49.

HAMMONS, Joseph (JD N.H.) March 3, 1787-March 29, 1836; House 1829-33.

HAMPTON, James Giles (W N.J.) June 13, 1814-Sept. 22, 1861; House 1845-49.

HAMPTON, Moses (W Pa.) Oct. 28, 1803-June 27, 1878; House 1847-51.

HAMPTON, Wade (grandfather of the following) (D S.C.) 1752-Feb. 4, 1835; House 1795-97; 1803-05.

HAMPTON, Wade (grandson of the preceding) (D S.C.) March 28, 1818-April 11, 1902; Senate 1879-91; Gov. 1876-79.

HANBACK, Lewis (R Kan.) March 27, 1839-Sept. 7, 1897; House 1883-87.

HANBURY, Harry Alfred (R N.Y.) Jan. 1, 1863-Aug. 22, 1940; House 1901-03.

HANCE, Kent Ronald (D Texas) Nov. 14, 1942-—; House 1979-85.

HANCHETT, Luther (R Wis.) Oct. 25, 1825-Nov. 24, 1862; House 1861-Nov. 24, 1862.

HANCOCK, Clarence Eugene (R N.Y.) Feb. 13, 1885-Jan. 3, 1948; House Nov. 8, 1927-47.

HANCOCK, Franklin Wills Jr. (D N.C.) Nov. 1, 1894-Jan. 23, 1969; House Nov. 4, 1930-39.

HANCOCK, George (D Va.) June 13, 1754-July 18, 1820; House 1793-97.

HANCOCK, John (D Texas) Oct. 24, 1824-July 19, 1893; House 1871-77; 1883-85.

HAND, Augustus Cincinnatus (D N.Y.) Sept. 4, 1803-March 8, 1878; House 1839-41.

HAND, Thomas Millet (R N.J.) July 7, 1902-Dec. 26, 1956; House 1945-Dec. 26, 1956.

HANDLEY, William Anderson (D Ala.) Dec. 15, 1834-June 23, 1909; House 1871-73.

HANDY, Levin Irving (nephew of William Campbell Preston Breckenridge) (D Del.) Dec. 24, 1861-Feb. 3, 1922; House 1897-99.

HANKS, James Millander (D Ark.) Feb. 12, 1833-May 24, 1909; House 1871-73.

HANLEY, James M. (D N.Y.) July 19, 1920-—; House 1965-81.

HANLY, James Franklin (R Ind.) April 4, 1863-Aug. 1, 1920; House 1895-97; Gov. 1905-09.

HANNA, John (R Ind.) Sept. 3, 1827-Oct. 24, 1882; House 1877-79.

HANNA, John Andre (grandfather of Archibald McAllister) (AF Pa.) 1762-July 23, 1805; House 1797-July 23, 1805.

HANNA, Louis Benjamin (R N.D.) Aug. 9, 1861-April 23, 1948; House 1909-Jan. 7, 1913; Gov. 1913-17.

HANNA, Marcus Alonzo (father of Ruth Hanna McCormick) (R Ohio) Sept. 24, 1837-Feb. 15, 1904; Senate March 5, 1897-Feb. 15, 1904; Chrmn. Rep. Nat. Comm. 1896-1904.

HANNA, Richard Thomas (D Calif.) June 9, 1914-—; House 1963-Dec. 31, 1974.

HANNA, Robert (W Ind.) April 6, 1786-Nov. 16, 1858; Senate Aug. 19, 1831-Jan. 3, 1832.

HANNAFORD, Mark Warren (D Calif.) Feb. 7, 1925-—; House 1975-79.

HANNEGAN, Edward Allen (D Ind.) June 25, 1807-Feb. 25, 1859; House 1833-37; Senate 1843-49.

HANRAHAN, Robert Paul (R Ill.) Feb. 25, 1934-—; House 1973-75.

HANSBROUGH, Henry Clay (R N.D.) Jan. 30, 1848-Nov. 16, 1933; House Nov. 2, 1889-1891; Senate 1891-1909.

HANSEN, Clifford Peter (R Wyo.) Oct. 16, 1912-—; Senate 1967-Dec. 31, 1978; Gov. 1963-67.

HANSEN, George Vernon (R Idaho) Sept. 14, 1930-—; House 1965-69, 1975-85.

HANSEN, James V. (R Utah) Aug. 14, 1932- —; House 1981- —.

HANSEN, John Robert (D Iowa) Aug. 24, 1901-Sept. 23, 1974; House 1965-67.

HANSEN, Julia Butler (D Wash.) June 14, 1907- —; House Nov. 8, 1960-Dec. 31, 1974.

HANSEN, Orval Howard (R Idaho) Aug. 3, 1926- —; House 1969-75.

HANSON, Alexander Contee (grandnephew of Benjamin Contee) (F Md.) Feb. 27, 1786-April 23, 1819; House 1813-16; Senate Dec. 20, 1816-April 23, 1819.

HARALSON, Hugh Anderson (D Ga.) Nov. 13, 1805-Sept. 25, 1854; House 1843-51.

HARALSON, Jeremiah (R Ala.) April 1, 1846-about 1916; House 1875-77.

HARD, Gideon (W N.Y.) April 29, 1797-April 27, 1885; House 1833-37.

HARDEMAN, Thomas Jr. (D Ga.) Jan. 12, 1825-March 6, 1891; House 1859-Jan. 23, 1861; 1883-85.

HARDEN, Cecil Murray (R Ind.) Nov. 21, 1894- —; House 1949-59.

HARDENBERGH, Augustus Albert (D N.J.) May 18, 1830-Oct. 5, 1889; House 1875-79; 1881-83.

HARDIN, Benjamin (cousin of Martin Davis Hardin) (W Ky.) Feb. 29, 1784-Sept. 24, 1852; House 1815-17; 1819-23; 1833-37.

HARDIN, John J. (son of Martin Davis Hardin) (W Ill.) Jan. 6, 1810-Feb. 23, 1847; House 1843-45.

HARDIN, Martin Davis (cousin of Benjamin Hardin, father of John J. Hardin) (D Ky.) June 21, 1780-Oct. 8, 1823; Senate Nov. 13, 1816-17.

HARDING, Aaron (UD Ky.) Feb. 20, 1805-Dec. 24, 1875; House 1861-67.

HARDING, Abner Clark (R Ill.) Feb. 10, 1807-July 19, 1874; House 1865-69.

HARDING, Benjamin Franklin (R Ore.) Jan. 4, 1823-June 16, 1899; Senate Sept. 12, 1862-65.

HARDING, John Eugene (R Ohio) June 27, 1877-July 26, 1959; House 1907-09.

HARDING, Ralph R. (D Idaho) Sept. 9, 1929- —; House 1961-65.

HARDING, Warren Gamaliel (R Ohio) Nov. 2, 1865-Aug. 2, 1923; Senate 1915-Jan. 13, 1921; President 1921-Aug. 2, 1923.

HARDWICK, Thomas William (D Ga.) Dec. 9, 1872-Jan. 31, 1944; House 1903-Nov. 2, 1914; Senate Nov. 4, 1914-19; Gov. 1921-23.

HARDY, Alexander Merrill (R Ind.) Dec. 16, 1847-Aug. 31, 1927; House 1895-97.

HARDY, Guy Urban (R Colo.) April 4, 1872-Jan. 26, 1947; House 1919-33.

HARDY, John (D N.Y.) Sept. 19, 1835-Dec. 9, 1913; House Dec. 5, 1881-85.

HARDY, Porter Jr. (D Va.) June 1, 1903- —; House 1947-69.

HARDY, Rufus (D Texas) Dec. 16, 1855-March 13, 1943; House 1907-23.

HARE, Butler Black (father of James Butler Hare) (D S.C.) Nov. 25, 1875-Dec. 30, 1967; House 1925-33; 1939-47.

HARE, Darius Dodge (D Ohio) Jan. 9, 1843-Feb. 10, 1897; House 1891-95.

HARE, James Butler (son of Butler Black Hare) (D S.C.) Sept. 4, 1918-July 16, 1966; House 1949-51.

HARE, Silas (D Texas) Nov. 13, 1827-Nov. 26, 1907; House 1887-91.

HARGIS, Denver David (D Kan.) July 22, 1921- —; House 1959-61.

HARKIN, Thomas Richard (D Iowa) Nov. 19, 1939- —; House 1975-85; Senate 1985- —.

HARLAN, Aaron (cousin of Andrew Jackson Harlan) (W Ohio) Sept. 8, 1802-Jan. 8, 1868; House 1853-59.

HARLAN, Andrew Jackson (cousin of Aaron Harlan) (D Ind.) March 29, 1815-May 19, 1907; House 1849-51; 1853-55.

HARLAN, Byron Berry (D Ohio) Oct. 22, 1886-Nov. 11, 1949; House 1931-39.

HARLAN, James (W Ky.) June 22, 1800-Feb. 18, 1863; House 1835-39.

HARLAN, James (R Iowa) Aug. 26, 1820-Oct. 5, 1899; Senate Dec. 31, 1855-Jan. 12, 1857, Jan. 29, 1857-May 15, 1865, 1867-73 (1855-57 Whig, 1857-65, 1867-73 Republican); Secy. of the Interior May 15, 1865-July 27, 1866.

HARLESS, Richard Fielding (D Ariz.) Aug. 6, 1905-Nov. 24, 1970; House 1943-49.

HARMANSON, John Henry (D La.) Jan. 15, 1803-Oct. 24, 1850; House 1845-Oct. 24, 1850.

HARMER, Alfred Crout (R Pa.) Aug. 8, 1825-March 6, 1900; House 1871-75; 1877-March 6, 1900.

HARMON, Randall S. (D Ind.) July 19, 1903-Aug. 18, 1982; House 1959-61.

HARNESS, Forest Arthur (R Ind.) June 24, 1895-July 29, 1974; House 1939-49.

HARPER, Alexander (W Ohio) Feb. 5, 1786-Dec. 1, 1860; House 1837-39; 1843-47; 1851-53.

HARPER, Francis Jacob (D Pa.) March 5, 1800-March 18, 1837; House March 4-18, 1837.

HARPER, James (W Pa.) March 28, 1780-March 31, 1873; House 1833-37 (1833-35 Clay Democrat, 1835-37 Whig).

HARPER, James Clarence (C N.C.) Dec. 6, 1819-Jan. 8, 1890; House 1871-73.

HARPER, John Adams (WD N.H.) Nov. 2, 1779-June 18, 1816; House 1811-13.

HARPER, Joseph Morrill (D N.H.) June 21, 1787-Jan. 15, 1865; House 1831-35.

HARPER, Robert Goodloe (F S.C./Md.) Jan. 1765-Jan. 14, 1825; House Feb. 5, 1795-1801 (S.C.); Senate Jan. 29-Dec. 6, 1816 (Md.).

HARPER, William (SRD S.C.) Jan. 17, 1790-Oct. 10, 1847; Senate March 8-Nov. 29, 1826.

HARRELD, John William (R Okla.) Jan. 24, 1872-Dec. 26, 1950; House Nov. 8, 1919-21; Senate 1921-27.

HARRIES, William Henry (D Minn.) Jan. 15, 1843-July 23, 1921; House 1891-93.

HARRINGTON, Henry William (D Ind.) Sept. 12, 1825-March 20, 1882; House 1863-65.

HARRINGTON, Michael Joseph (D Mass.) Sept. 2, 1936- —; House Sept. 30, 1969-79.

HARRINGTON, Vincent Francis (D Iowa) May 16, 1903-Nov. 29, 1943; House 1937-Sept. 5, 1942.

HARRIS, Benjamin Gwinn (D Md.) Dec. 13, 1805-April 4, 1895; House 1863-67.

HARRIS, Benjamin Winslow (father of Robert Orr Harris) (R Mass.) Nov. 10, 1823-Feb. 7, 1907; House 1873-83.

HARRIS, Charles Murray (D Ill.) April 10, 1821-Sept. 20, 1896; House 1863-65.

HARRIS, Christopher Columbus (D Ala.) Jan. 28, 1842-Dec. 28, 1935; House May 11, 1914-15.

HARRIS, Fred Roy (D Okla.) Nov. 13, 1930- —; Senate Nov. 4, 1964-Jan. 3, 1973; Chrmn. Dem. Nat. Comm. 1969-70.

HARRIS, George Emrick (R Miss.) Jan. 6, 1827-March 19, 1911; House Feb. 23, 1870-73.

HARRIS, Henry Richard (D Ga.) Feb. 2, 1828-Oct. 15, 1909; House 1873-79; 1885-87.

HARRIS, Henry Schenck (D N.J.) Dec. 27, 1850-May 2, 1902; House 1881-83.

HARRIS, Herbert Eugene II (D Va.) April 14, 1926- —; House 1975-81.

HARRIS, Ira (grandfather of Henry Riggs Rathbone) (R N.Y.) May 31, 1802-Dec. 2, 1875; Senate 1861-67.

HARRIS, Isham Green (D Tenn.) Feb. 10, 1818-July 8, 1897; House 1849-53; Senate 1877-July 8, 1897; Pres. pro tempore 1893-95; Gov. 1857-62.

HARRIS, James Morrison (AP Md.) Nov. 20, 1817-July 16, 1898; House 1855-61.

HARRIS, John (cousin of Robert Harris) (— N.Y.) Sept. 26, 1760-Nov. 1824; House 1807-09.

HARRIS, John Spafford (R La.) Dec. 18, 1825-Jan. 25, 1906; Senate July 9, 1868-71.

HARRIS, John Thomas (cousin of John Hill of Virginia) (D Va.) May 8, 1823-Oct. 14, 1899; House 1859-61; 1871-81.

HARRIS, Mark (— Maine) Jan. 27, 1779-March 2, 1843; House Dec. 2, 1822-23.

HARRIS, Oren (D Ark.) Dec. 20, 1903- —; House 1941-Feb. 2, 1966.

Biographical Index

HARRIS, Robert (cousin of John Harris) (— Pa.) Sept. 5, 1768-Sept. 3, 1851; House 1823-27.

HARRIS, Robert Orr (son of Benjamin Winslow Harris) (R Mass.) Nov. 8, 1854-June 13, 1926; House 1911-13.

HARRIS, Sampson Willis (D Ala.) Feb. 23, 1809-April 1, 1857; House 1847-57.

HARRIS, Stephen Ross (uncle of Ebenezer Byron Finley) (R Ohio) May 22, 1824-Jan. 15, 1905; House 1895-97.

HARRIS, Thomas K. (D Tenn.) ?-March 18, 1816; House 1813-15.

HARRIS, Thomas Langrell (D Ill.) Oct. 29, 1816-Nov. 24, 1858; House 1849-51; 1855-Nov. 24, 1858.

HARRIS, Wiley Pope (D Miss.) Nov. 9, 1818-Dec. 3, 1891; House 1853-55.

HARRIS, William Alexander (father of the following) (D Va.) Aug. 24, 1805-March 28, 1864; House 1841-43.

HARRIS, William Alexander (son of the preceding) (D Kan.) Oct. 29, 1841-Dec. 20, 1909; House 1893-95; Senate 1897-1903 (1893-95 Populist, 1897-1903 Democrat).

HARRIS, William Julius (great-grandson of Charles Hooks) (D Ga.) Feb. 3, 1868-April 18, 1932; Senate 1919-April 18, 1932.

HARRIS, Winder Russell (D Va.) Dec. 3, 1888-Feb. 24, 1973; House April 8, 1941-Sept. 15, 1944.

HARRISON, Albert Galliton (VBD Mo.) June 26, 1800-Sept. 7, 1839; House 1835-39.

HARRISON, Benjamin (grandson of William Henry Harrison, son of John Scott Harrison, grandfather of William Henry Harrison of Wyoming) (R Ind.) Aug. 20, 1833-March 13, 1901; Senate 1881-87; President 1889-93.

HARRISON, Burr Powell (son of Thomas Walter Harrison) (D Va.) July 2, 1904-Dec. 29, 1973; House Nov. 6, 1946-63.

HARRISON, Byron Patton (Pat) (D Miss.) Aug. 29, 1881-June 22, 1941; House 1911-19; Senate 1919-June 22, 1941; Pres. pro tempore 1941.

HARRISON, Carter Bassett (brother of President William Henry Harrison) (— Va.) ?-April 18, 1808; House 1793-99.

HARRISON, Carter Henry (D Ill.) Feb. 15, 1825-Oct. 28, 1893; House 1875-79.

HARRISON, Francis Burton (D N.Y.) Dec. 18, 1873-Nov. 21, 1957; House 1903-05; 1907-Sept. 1, 1913.

HARRISON, Frank (D Pa.) Feb. 2, 1940-—; House 1983-85.

HARRISON, George Paul (D Ala.) March 19, 1841-July 17, 1922; House Nov. 6, 1894-97.

HARRISON, Horace Harrison (R Tenn.) Aug. 7, 1829-Dec. 20, 1885; House 1873-75.

HARRISON, John Scott (son of President William Henry Harrison, father of President Benjamin Harrison) (W Ohio) Oct. 4, 1804-May 25, 1878; House 1853-57.

HARRISON, Richard Almgill (UD Ohio) April 8, 1824-July 30, 1904; House July 4, 1861-63.

HARRISON, Robert Dinsmore (R Neb.) Jan. 26, 1897-June 11, 1977; House Dec. 4, 1951-59.

HARRISON, Samuel Smith (D Pa.) 1780-April 1853; House 1833-37.

HARRISON, Thomas Walter (father of Burr Powell Harrison) (D Va.) Aug. 5, 1856-May 9, 1935; House Nov. 7, 1916-Dec. 15, 1922; 1923-29.

HARRISON, William Henry (father of John Scott Harrison, brother of Carter Basset Harrison, grandfather of Benjamin Harrison, great-great-grandfather of William Henry Harrison of Wyoming) (W Ohio) Feb. 9, 1773-April 4, 1841; House (Terr. Del.) 1799-May 14, 1800; (Rep.) Oct. 8, 1816-19; Senate 1825-May 20, 1828; Gov. (Indiana Terr.) 1801-13; President March 4-April 4, 1841.

HARRISON, William Henry (great-great-grandson of President William Henry Harrison, grandson of President Benjamin Harrison and Alvin Saunders) (R Wyo.) Aug. 10, 1896-—; House 1951-55; 1961-65, 1967-69.

HARSHA, William Howard (R Ohio) Jan. 1, 1921-—; House 1961-81.

HART, Alphonso (R Ohio) July 4, 1830-Dec. 23, 1910; House 1883-85.

HART, Archibald Chapman (D N.J.) Feb. 27, 1873-July 24, 1935; House Nov. 5, 1912-March 3, 1913; July 22, 1913-17.

HART, Edward Joseph (D N.J.) March 25, 1893-April 20, 1961; House 1935-55.

HART, Elizur Kirke (D N.Y.) April 8, 1841-Feb. 18, 1893; House 1877-79.

HART, Emanuel Bernard (D N.Y.) Oct. 27, 1809-Aug. 29, 1897; House 1851-53.

HART, Gary Warren (D Colo.) Nov. 28, 1937-—; Senate 1975-—.

HART, Joseph Johnson (D Pa.) April 18, 1859-July 13, 1926; House 1895-97.

HART, Michael James (D Mich.) July 16, 1877-Feb. 14, 1951; House Nov. 3, 1931-35.

HART, Philip Aloysius (D Mich.) Dec. 10, 1912-Dec. 26, 1976; Senate 1959-Dec. 26, 1976.

HART, Roswell (R N.Y.) Aug. 4, 1824-April 20, 1883; House 1865-67.

HART, Thomas Charles (R Conn.) June 12, 1877-July 4, 1971; Senate Feb. 15, 1945-Nov. 5, 1946.

HARTER, Dow Watters (D Ohio) Jan. 2, 1885-Sept. 4, 1971; House 1933-43.

HARTER, John Francis (R N.Y.) Sept. 1, 1897-Dec. 20, 1947; House 1939-41.

HARTER, Michael Daniel (grandson of Robert Moore) (D Ohio) April 6, 1846-Feb. 22, 1896; House 1891-95.

HARTKE, Rupert Vance (D Ind.) May 31, 1919-—; Senate 1959-77.

HARTLEY, Fred Allan Jr. (R N.J.) Feb. 22, 1902-May 11, 1969; House 1929-49.

HARTLEY, Thomas (— Pa.) Sept. 7, 1748-Dec. 21, 1800; House 1789-Dec. 21, 1800.

HARTMAN, Charles Sampson (SilR. Mont.) March 1, 1861-Aug. 3, 1929; House 1893-99 (1893-97 Republican, 1897-99 Silver Republican).

HARTMAN, Jesse Lee (R Pa.) June 18, 1853-Feb. 17, 1930; House 1911-13.

HARTNETT, Thomas F. (R S.C.) Aug. 7, 1941-—; House 1981-—.

HARTRIDGE, Julian (D Ga.) Sept. 9, 1829-Jan. 8, 1879; House 1875-Jan. 8, 1879.

HARTZELL, William (D Ill.) Feb. 20, 1837-Aug. 14, 1903; House 1875-79.

HARVEY, David Archibald (R Okla.) March 20, 1845-May 24, 1916; House (Terr. Del.) Nov. 4, 1890-93.

HARVEY, James (R Mich.) July 4, 1922-—; House 1961-Jan. 31, 1974.

HARVEY, James Madison (R Kan.) Sept. 21, 1833-April 15, 1894; Senate Feb. 2, 1874-77; Gov. 1869-73.

HARVEY, Jonathan (brother of Matthew Harvey) (— N.H.) Feb. 25, 1780-Aug. 23, 1859; House 1825-31.

HARVEY, Matthew (brother of Jonathan Harvey) (D N.H.) June 21, 1781-April 7, 1866; House 1821-25; Gov. 1830-31.

HARVEY, Ralph (R Ind.) Aug. 9, 1901-—; House Nov. 4, 1947-59; 1961-Dec. 30, 1966.

HASBROUCK, Abraham Bruyn (cousin of Abraham Joseph Hasbrouck) (NR N.Y.) Nov. 29, 1791-Feb. 24, 1879; House 1825-27.

HASBROUCK, Abraham Joseph (cousin of Abraham Bruyn Hasbrouck) (Clinton D N.Y.) Oct. 16, 1773-Jan. 12, 1845; House 1813-15.

HASBROUCK, Josiah (— N.Y.) March 5, 1755-March 19, 1821; House April 28, 1803-05, 1817-19.

HASCALL, Augustus Porter (W N.Y.) June 24, 1800-June 27, 1872; House 1851-53.

HASKELL, Dudley Chase (grandfather of Otis Halbert Holmes) (R Kan.) March 23, 1842-Dec. 16, 1883; House 1877-Dec. 16, 1883.

HASKELL, Floyd Kirk (D Colo.) Feb. 7, 1916-—; Senate 1973-79.

HASKELL, Harry Garner Jr. (R Del.) May 27, 1921-—; House 1957-59.

HASKELL, Reuben Locke (R N.Y.) Oct. 5, 1878-Oct. 2, 1971; House 1915-Dec. 31, 1919.

HASKELL, William T. (nephew of Charles Ready) (W Tenn.) July 21, 1818-March 12, 1859; House 1847-49.

HASKIN, John Bussing (D N.Y.) Aug. 27, 1821-Sept. 18, 1895; House 1857-61.

HASKINS, Kittredge (R Vt.) April 8, 1836-Aug. 7, 1916; House 1901-09.

HASTINGS, Daniel Oren (R Del.) March 5, 1874-May 9, 1966; Senate Dec. 10, 1928-37.

HASTINGS, George (D N.Y.) March 13, 1807-Aug. 29, 1866; House 1853-55.

HASTINGS, James Fred (R N.Y.) April 10, 1926- —; House 1969-Jan. 20, 1976.

HASTINGS, John (JD Ohio) 1778-Dec. 8, 1854; House 1839-43.

HASTINGS, Serranus Clinton (D Iowa) Nov. 14, 1813-Feb. 18, 1893; House Dec. 28, 1846-47.

HASTINGS, Seth (father of William Soden Hastings) (F Mass.) April 8, 1762-Nov. 19, 1831; House Aug. 24, 1801-07.

HASTINGS, William Soden (son of Seth Hastings) (D Mass.) June 3, 1798-June 17, 1842; House 1837-June 17, 1842.

HASTINGS, William Wirt (D Okla.) Dec. 31, 1866-April 8, 1938; House 1915-21; 1923-35.

HATCH, Carl Atwood (D N.M.) Nov. 27, 1889-Sept. 14, 1963; Senate Oct. 10, 1933-49.

HATCH, Herschel Harrison (R Mich.) Feb. 17, 1837-Nov. 30, 1920; House 1883-85.

HATCH, Israel Thompson (D N.Y.) June 30, 1808-Sept. 24, 1875; House 1857-59.

HATCH, Jethro Ayers (R Ind.) June 18, 1837-Aug. 3, 1912; House 1895-97.

HATCH, Orrin Grant (R Utah) March 22, 1934- —; Senate 1977- —.

HATCH, William Henry (D Mo.) Sept. 11, 1833-Dec. 23, 1896; House 1879-95.

HATCHER, Charles F. (D Ga.) July 1, 1939- —; House 1981- —.

HATCHER, Robert Anthony (D Mo.) Feb. 24, 1819-Dec. 4, 1886; House 1873-79.

HATFIELD, Henry Drury (R W.Va.) Sept. 15, 1875-Oct. 23, 1962; Senate 1929-35; Gov. 1913-17.

HATFIELD, Mark Odom (R Ore.) July 12, 1922- —; Senate Jan. 10, 1967- —; Gov. 1959-67.

HATFIELD, Paul Gerhart (D Mont.) April 29, 1928- —; Senate Jan. 23, 1978-Dec. 14, 1978.

HATHAWAY, Samuel Gilbert (D N.Y.) July 18, 1780-May 2, 1867; House 1833-35.

HATHAWAY, William Dodd (D Maine) Feb. 21, 1924- —; House 1965-1973; Senate 1973-79.

HATHORN, Henry Harrison (R N.Y.) Nov. 28, 1813-Feb. 20, 1887; House 1873-77.

HATHORN, John (F N.Y.) Jan. 9, 1749-Feb. 19, 1825; House 1789-91; 1795-97; Cont. Cong. 1788.

HATTON, Robert Hopkins (AP Tenn.) Nov. 2, 1826-May 31, 1862; House 1859-61.

HAUGEN, Gilbert Nelson (R Iowa) April 21, 1859-July 18, 1933; House 1899-1933.

HAUGEN, Nils Pederson (R Wis.) March 9, 1849-April 23, 1931; House 1887-95.

HAUGHEY, Thomas (R Ala.) 1826-Aug. 1869; House July 21, 1868-69.

HAUN, Henry Peter (D Calif.) Jan. 18, 1815-June 6, 1860; Senate Nov. 3, 1859-March 4, 1860.

HAVEN, Nathaniel Appleton (F N.H.) July 19, 1762-March 13, 1831; House 1809-11.

HAVEN, Solomon George (W N.Y.) Nov. 27, 1810-Dec. 24, 1861; House 1851-57.

HAVENNER, Franck Roberts (D Calif.) Sept. 20, 1882-July 24, 1967; House 1937-41, 1945-53 (1937-39 Progressive, 1939-41, 1945-53 Democrat).

HAVENS, Harrison Eugene (R Mo.) Dec. 15, 1837-Aug. 16, 1916; House 1871-75.

HAVENS, James Smith (D N.Y.) May 28, 1859-Feb. 27, 1927; House April 19, 1910-11.

HAVENS, Jonathan Nicoll (D N.Y.) June 18, 1757-Oct. 25, 1799; House 1795-Oct. 25, 1799.

HAWES, Albert Gallatin (brother of Richard Hawes, nephew of Aylett Hawes, granduncle of Harry Bartow Hawes, uncle of Aylett Hawes Buckner) (JD Ky.) April 1, 1804-March 14, 1849; House 1831-37.

HAWES, Aylett (uncle of Richard Hawes, Albert Gallatin Hawes and Aylett Hawes Buckner) (D Va.) April 21, 1768-Aug. 31, 1833; House 1811-17.

HAWES, Harry Bartow (grandnephew of Albert Gallatin Hawes) (D Mo.) Nov. 15, 1869-July 31, 1947; House 1921-Oct. 15, 1926; Senate Dec. 6, 1926-Feb. 3, 1933.

HAWES, Richard (brother of Albert Gallatin Hawes, nephew of Aylett Hawes, cousin of Aylett Hawes Buckner) (W Ky.) Feb. 6, 1797-May 25, 1877; House 1837-41.

HAWK, Robert Moffett Allison (R Ill.) April 23, 1839-June 29, 1882; House 1879-June 29, 1882.

HAWKES, Albert Wahl (R N.J.) Nov. 20, 1878-May 9, 1971; Senate 1943-49.

HAWKES, James (— N.Y.) Dec. 13, 1776-Oct. 2, 1865; House 1821-23.

HAWKINS, Augustus F. (D Calif.) Aug. 31, 1907- —; House 1963- —.

HAWKINS, Benjamin (uncle of Micajah Thomas Hawkins) (F N.C.) Aug. 15, 1754-June 6, 1816; Senate Nov. 27, 1789-95; Cont. Cong. 1781-84, 1786-87.

HAWKINS, George Sydney (D Fla.) 1808-March 15, 1878; House 1857-Jan. 21, 1861.

HAWKINS, Isaac Roberts (R Tenn.) May 16, 1818-Aug. 12, 1880; House July 24, 1866-71.

HAWKINS, Joseph (Ad.D N.Y.) Nov. 14, 1781-April 20, 1832; House 1829-31.

HAWKINS, Joseph H. (F Ky.) ?-1823; House March 29, 1814-15.

HAWKINS, Micajah Thomas (nephew of Benjamin Hawkins and Nathaniel Macon) (D N.C.) May 20, 1790-Dec. 22, 1858; House Dec. 15, 1831-41.

HAWKINS, Paula (R Fla.) Jan. 24, 1927- —; Senate 1981- —.

HAWKS, Charles Jr. (R Wis.) July 7, 1899-Jan. 6, 1960; House 1939-41.

HAWLEY, John Baldwin (R Ill.) Feb. 9, 1831-May 24, 1895; House 1869-75.

HAWLEY, Joseph Roswell (R Conn.) Oct. 31, 1826-March 17, 1905; House Dec. 2, 1872-75, 1879-81; Senate 1881-1905; Gov. 1866-67.

HAWLEY, Robert Bradley (R Texas) Oct. 25, 1849-Nov. 28, 1921; House 1897-1901.

HAWLEY, Willis Chatman (R Ore.) May 5, 1864-July 24, 1941; House 1907-33.

HAWS, John Henry Hobart (W N.Y.) 1809-Jan. 27, 1858; House 1851-53.

HAY, Andrew Kessler (W N.J.) Jan. 19, 1809-Feb. 7, 1881; House 1849-51.

HAY, James (D Va.) Jan. 9, 1856-June 12, 1931; House 1897-Oct. 1, 1916.

HAY, John Breese (R Ill.) Jan. 8, 1834-June 16, 1916; House 1869-73.

HAYAKAWA, Samuel Ichiye (R Calif.) July 18, 1906- —; Senate Jan. 2, 1977-83.

HAYDEN, Carl Trumbull (D Ariz.) Oct. 2, 1877-Jan. 25, 1972; House Feb. 19, 1912-27; Senate 1927-69; Pres. pro tempore 1957-69.

HAYDEN, Edward Daniel (R Mass.) Dec. 27, 1833-Nov. 15, 1908; House 1885-89.

HAYDEN, Moses (— N.Y.) 1786-Feb. 13, 1830; House 1823-27.

HAYES, Charles Arthur (D Ill.) Feb. 17, 1918- —; House Sept. 12, 1983- —.

HAYES, Everis Anson (R Calif.) March 10, 1855-June 3, 1942; House 1905-19.

HAYES, Philip Cornelius (R Ill.) Feb. 3, 1833-July 13, 1916; House 1877-81.

HAYES, Philip Harold (D Ind.) Sept. 1, 1940- —; House 1975-77.

HAYES, Rutherford Birchard (R Ohio) Oct. 4, 1822-Jan. 17, 1893; House 1865-July 20, 1867; President 1877-81; Gov. 1868-72, 1876-77.

HAYES, Walter Ingalls (D Iowa) Dec. 9, 1841-March 14, 1901; House 1887-95.

HAYMOND, Thomas Sherwood (W Va.) Jan. 15, 1794-April 5, 1869; House Nov. 8, 1849-51.

HAYMOND, William Summerville (D/L Ind.) Feb. 20, 1823-Dec. 24, 1885; House 1875-77.

HAYNE, Arthur Peronneau (brother of Robert Young Hayne) (D S.C.) March 12, 1790-Jan. 7, 1867; Senate May 11-Dec. 2, 1858.

HAYNE, Robert Young (brother of Arthur Peronneau Hayne) (TD S.C.) Nov. 10, 1791-Sept. 24, 1839; Senate 1823-Dec. 13, 1832; Gov. 1832-34.

Biographical Index

HAYNES, Charles Eaton (U Ga.) April 15, 1784-Aug. 29, 1841; House 1825-31, 1835-39 (1825-31 Democrat, 1835-39 Unionist).

HAYNES, Martin Alonzo (R N.H.) July 30, 1842-Nov. 28, 1919; House 1883-87.

HAYNES, William Elisha (cousin of George William Palmer) (D Ohio) Oct. 19, 1829-Dec. 5, 1914; House 1889-93.

HAYS, Charles (R Ala.) Feb. 2, 1834-June 24, 1879; House 1869-77.

HAYS, Edward Dixon (R Mo.) April 28, 1872-July 25, 1941; House 1919-23.

HAYS, Edward Retilla (R Iowa) May 26, 1847-Feb. 28, 1896; House Nov. 4, 1890-91.

HAYS, Lawrence Brooks (D Ark.) Aug. 9, 1898-Oct. 12, 1981; House 1943-59.

HAYS, Samuel (D Pa.) Sept. 10, 1783-July 1, 1868; House 1843-45.

HAYS, Samuel Lewis (D Va.) Oct. 20, 1794-March 17, 1871; House 1841-43.

HAYS, Wayne Levere (D Ohio) May 13, 1911- —; House 1949-Sept. 1, 1976.

HAYWARD, Monroe Leland (R Neb.) Dec. 22, 1840-Dec. 5, 1899; Senate March 8-Dec. 5, 1899.

HAYWARD, William Jr. (D Md.) 1787-Oct. 19, 1836; House 1823-25.

HAYWOOD, William Henry Jr. (D N.C.) Oct. 23, 1801-Oct. 7, 1852; Senate 1843-July 25, 1846.

HAYWORTH, Donald (D Mich.) Jan. 13, 1898-Feb. 25, 1982; House 1955-57.

HAZARD, Nathaniel (D R.I.) 1776-Dec. 17, 1820; House 1819-Dec. 17, 1820.

HAZELTINE, Abner (W N.Y.) June 10, 1793-Dec. 20, 1879; House 1833-37.

HAZELTINE, Ira Sherwin (RG Mo.) July 13, 1821-Jan. 13, 1899; House 1881-83.

HAZELTON, George Cochrane (brother of Gerry Whiting Hazelton, nephew of Clark Betton Cochrane) (R Wis.) Jan. 3, 1832-Sept. 4, 1922; House 1877-83.

HAZELTON, Gerry Whiting (brother of George Cochrane Hazelton, nephew of Clark Betton Cochrane) (R Wis.) Feb. 24, 1829-Sept. 19, 1920; House 1871-75.

HAZELTON, John Wright (R N.J.) Dec. 10, 1814-Dec. 20, 1878; House 1871-75.

HAZLETT, James Miller (R Pa.) Oct. 14, 1864-Nov. 8, 1940; House March 4-Oct. 20, 1927.

HEALD, William Henry (R Del.) Aug. 27, 1864-June 3, 1939; House 1909-13.

HEALEY, Arthur Daniel (D Mass.) Dec. 29, 1889-Sept. 16, 1948; House 1933-Aug. 3, 1942.

HEALEY, James Christopher (D N.Y.) Dec. 24, 1909-Dec. 16, 1981; House Feb. 7, 1956-65.

HEALY, Joseph (D N.H.) Aug. 21, 1776-Oct. 10, 1861; House 1825-29.

HEALY, Ned R. (D Calif.) Aug. 9, 1905-Sept. 10, 1977; House 1945-47.

HEARD, John Thaddeus (D Mo.) Oct. 29, 1840-Jan. 27, 1927; House 1885-95.

HEARST, George (father of William Randolph Hearst) (D Calif.) Sept. 3, 1820-Feb. 28, 1891; Senate March 23-Aug. 4, 1886, 1887-Feb. 28, 1891.

HEARST, William Randolph (son of George Hearst) (D N.Y.) April 29, 1863-Aug. 14, 1951; House 1903-07.

HEATH, James P. (D Md.) Dec. 21, 1777-June 12, 1854; House 1833-35.

HEATH, John (R Va.) May 8, 1758-Oct. 13, 1810; House 1793-97.

HEATON, David (R N.C.) March 10, 1823-June 25, 1870; House July 15, 1868-June 25, 1870.

HEATON, Robert Douglas (R Pa.) July 1, 1873-June 11, 1933; House 1915-19.

HEATWOLE, Joel Prescott (R Minn.) Aug. 22, 1856-April 4, 1910; House 1895-1903.

HEBARD, William (W Vt.) Nov. 29, 1800-Oct. 20, 1875; House 1849-53.

HEBERT, Felix (R R.I.) Dec. 11, 1874-Dec. 14, 1969; Senate 1929-35.

HEBERT, Felix Edward (D La.) Oct. 12, 1901-Dec. 29, 1979; House 1941-77.

HECHLER, Ken (D W.Va.) Sept. 20, 1914- —; House 1959-77.

HECHT, Chic (R Nev.) Nov. 30, 1928- —; Senate 1983- —.

HECKLER, Margaret M. (R Mass.) June 21, 1931- —; House 1967-83; Secy. Health and Human Services 1983- —.

HEDGE, Thomas (R Iowa) June 24, 1844-Nov. 28, 1920; 1899-1907.

HEDRICK, Erland Harold (D W.Va.) Aug. 9, 1894-Sept. 20, 1954; House 1945-53.

HEFFERNAN, James Joseph (D N.Y.) Nov. 8, 1888-Jan. 27, 1967; House 1941-53.

HEFLIN, Howell Thomas (D Ala.) June 19, 1921- —; Senate 1979- —.

HEFLIN, James Thomas (nephew of Robert Stell Heflin) (D Ala.) April 9, 1869-April 22, 1951; House May 10, 1904-Nov. 1, 1920; Senate Nov. 3, 1920-31.

HEFLIN, Robert Stell (uncle of James Thomas Heflin) (R Ala.) April 15, 1815-Jan. 24, 1901; House 1869-71.

HEFNER, Willie Gathrel (D N.C.) April 11, 1930- —; House 1975- —.

HEFTEL, Cecil (D Hawaii) Sept. 30, 1924- —; House 1977- —.

HEIDINGER, James Vandaveer (R Ill.) July 17, 1882-March 22, 1945; House 1941-March 22, 1945.

HEILMAN, William (great-grandfather of Charles Marion La Follette) (R Ind.) Oct. 1, 1824-Sept. 22, 1890; House 1879-83.

HEINER, Daniel Brodhead (R Pa.) Dec. 30, 1854-Feb. 14, 1944; House 1893-97.

HEINKE, George Henry (R Neb.) July 22, 1882-Jan. 2, 1940; House 1939-Jan. 2, 1940.

HEINTZ, Victor (R Ohio) Nov. 20, 1876-Dec. 27, 1968; House 1917-19.

HEINZ, Henry John III (R Pa.) Oct. 23, 1938- —; House Nov. 2, 1971-77; Senate 1977- —.

HEISKELL, John Netherland (D Ark.) Nov. 2, 1872-Dec. 28, 1972; Senate Jan. 6-Jan. 29, 1913.

HEITFELD, Henry (P Idaho) Jan. 12, 1859-Oct. 21, 1938; Senate 1897-1903.

HELGESEN, Henry Thomas (R N.D.) June 26, 1857-April 10, 1917; House 1911-April 10, 1917.

HELLER, Louis Benjamin (D N.Y.) Feb. 10, 1905- —; House Feb. 15, 1949-July 21, 1954.

HELM, Harvey (D Ky.) Dec. 2, 1865-March 3, 1919; House 1907-March 3, 1919.

HELMICK, William (R Ohio) Sept. 6, 1817-March 31, 1888; House 1859-61.

HELMS, Jesse Alexander (R N.C.) Oct. 18, 1921- —; Senate 1973- —.

HELMS, William (D N.J.) ?-1813; House 1801-11.

HELSTOSKI, Henry (D N.J.) March 21, 1925- —; House 1965-77.

HELVERING, Guy Tresillian (D Kan.) Jan. 10, 1878-July 4, 1946; House 1913-19.

HEMENWAY, James Alexander (R Ind.) March 8, 1860-Feb. 10, 1923; House 1895-1905; Senate 1905-09.

HEMPHILL, John (uncle of John James Hemphill, great-great-uncle of Robert Witherspoon Hemphill) (SRD Texas) Dec. 18, 1803-Jan. 7, 1862; Senate 1859-July 11, 1861.

HEMPHILL, John James (cousin of William Huggins Brawley, nephew of John Hemphill, great-uncle of Robert Witherspoon Hemphill) (D S.C.) Aug. 25, 1849-May 11, 1912; House 1883-93.

HEMPHILL, Joseph (JD Pa.) Jan. 7, 1770-May 29, 1842; House 1801-03, 1819-26, 1829-31 (1801-03, 1819-26 Federalist, 1829-31 Jackson Democrat).

HEMPHILL, Robert Witherspoon (great-great nephew of John Hemphill, great-nephew of John James Hemphill and William Huggins Brawley, great-great-grandson of Robert Witherspoon) (D S.C.) May 10, 1915-Dec. 25, 1983; House 1957-May 1, 1964.

HEMPSTEAD, Edward (— Mo.) June 3, 1780-Aug. 10, 1817; House (Terr. Del.) Nov. 9, 1812-Sept. 17, 1814.

HENDEE, George Whitman (R Vt.) Nov. 30, 1832-Dec. 6, 1906; House 1873-79.

HENDERSON, Archibald (F N.C.) Aug. 7, 1768-Oct. 21, 1822; House 1799-1803.

HENDERSON, Bennett H. (— Tenn.) Sept. 5, 1784-?; House 1815-17.

HENDERSON, Charles Belknap (D Nev.) June 8, 1873-Nov. 8, 1954; Senate Jan. 12, 1918-21.

HENDERSON, David Bremner (R Iowa) March 14, 1840-Feb. 25, 1906; House 1883-1903; Speaker 1899-1903.

HENDERSON, David Newton (D N.C.) April 16, 1921-—; House 1961-77.

HENDERSON, James Henry Dickey (UR Ore.) July 23, 1810-Dec. 13, 1885; House 1865-67.

HENDERSON, James Pinckney (SRD Texas) March 31, 1808-June 4, 1858; Senate Nov. 9, 1857-June 4, 1858; Gov. 1846-47.

HENDERSON, John (W Miss.) 1795-Sept. 13, 1866; Senate 1839-45.

HENDERSON, John Brooks (D Mo.) Nov. 16, 1826-April 12, 1913; Senate Jan. 17, 1862-69.

HENDERSON, John Earl (R Ohio) Jan. 4, 1917-—; House 1955-61.

HENDERSON, John Steele (D N.C.) Jan. 6, 1846-Oct. 9, 1916; House 1885-95.

HENDERSON, Joseph (— Pa.) Aug. 2, 1791-Dec. 25, 1863; House 1833-37.

HENDERSON, Samuel (R Pa.) Nov. 27, 1764-Nov. 17, 1841; House Oct. 11, 1814-15.

HENDERSON, Thomas (— N.J.) Aug. 15, 1743-Dec. 15, 1824; House 1795-97.

HENDERSON, Thomas Jefferson (R Ill.) Nov. 29, 1824-Feb. 6, 1911; House 1875-95.

HENDON, William A. (R N.C.) Nov. 9, 1944-—; House 1981-83, 1985-—.

HENDRICK, John Kerr (D Ky.) Oct. 10, 1849-June 20, 1921; House 1895-97.

HENDRICKS, Joseph Edward (D Fla.) Sept. 24, 1903-—; House 1937-49.

HENDRICKS, Thomas Andrews (nephew of William Hendricks) (D Ind.) Sept. 7, 1819-Nov. 25, 1885; House 1851-55; Senate 1863-69; Gov. 1873-77; Vice Pres. March 4-Nov. 25, 1885.

HENDRICKS, William (uncle of Thomas Andrews Hendricks) (D Ind.) Nov. 12, 1782-May 16, 1850; House Dec. 11, 1816-July 25, 1822; Senate 1825-37; Gov. 1822-25.

HENDRICKSON, Robert Clymer (R N.J.) Aug. 12, 1898-Dec. 7, 1964; Senate 1949-55.

HENDRIX, Joseph Clifford (D N.Y.) May 25, 1853-Nov. 9, 1904; House 1893-95.

HENKLE, Eli Jones (D Md.) Nov. 24, 1828-Nov. 1, 1893; House 1875-81.

HENLEY, Barclay (son of Thomas Jefferson Henley) (D Calif.) March 17, 1843-Feb. 15, 1914; House 1883-87.

HENLEY, Thomas Jefferson (father of Barclay Henley) (D Ind.) April 2, 1810-Jan. 2, 1865; House 1843-49.

HENN, Bernhart (D Iowa) 1817-Aug. 30, 1865; House 1851-55.

HENNEY, Charles William Francis (D Wis.) Feb. 2, 1884-Nov. 16, 1969; House 1933-35.

HENNINGS, Thomas Carey Jr. (D Mo.) June 25, 1903-Sept. 13, 1960; House 1935-Dec. 31, 1940; Senate 1951-Sept. 13, 1960.

HENRY, Charles Lewis (R Ind.) July 1, 1849-May 2, 1927; House 1895-99.

HENRY, Daniel Maynadier (D Md.) Feb. 19, 1823-Aug. 31, 1899; House 1877-81.

HENRY, Edward Stevens (R Conn.) Feb. 10, 1836-Oct. 10, 1921; House 1895-1913.

HENRY, John (D Md.) Nov. 1750-Dec. 16, 1798; Senate 1789-Dec. 10, 1797; Gov. 1797-98; Cont. Cong. 1778-81, 1784-87.

HENRY, John (W Ill.) Nov. 1, 1800-April 28, 1882; House Feb. 5-March 3, 1847.

HENRY, John Flournoy (— Ky.) Jan. 17, 1793-Nov. 12, 1873; House Dec. 11, 1826-27.

HENRY, Lewis (R N.Y.) June 8, 1885-July 23, 1941; House April 11, 1922-23.

HENRY, Patrick (uncle of the following) (D Miss.) Feb. 12, 1843-May 18, 1930; House 1897-1901.

HENRY, Patrick (nephew of the preceding) (D Miss.) Feb. 15, 1861-Dec. 28, 1933; House 1901-03.

HENRY, Paul B. (R Mich.) July 9, 1942-—; House 1985-—.

HENRY, Robert Kirkland (R Wis.) Feb. 9, 1890-Nov. 20, 1946; House 1945-Nov. 20, 1946.

HENRY, Robert Lee (D Texas) May 12, 1864-July 9, 1931; House 1897-1917.

HENRY, Robert Pryor (CD Ky.) Nov. 24, 1788-Aug. 25, 1826; House 1823-Aug. 25, 1826.

HENRY, Thomas (W Pa.) 1779-July 20, 1849; House 1837-43.

HENRY, William (W Vt.) March 22, 1788-April 16, 1861; House 1847-51.

HENRY, Winder Laird (great-grandson of Charles Goldsborough and Robert Henry Goldsborough) (D Md.) Dec. 20, 1864-July 5, 1940; House Nov. 6, 1894-95.

HENSLEY, Walter Lewis (D Mo.) Sept. 3, 1871-July 18, 1946; House 1911-19.

HEPBURN, William Peters (great-grandson of Matthew Lyon) (R Iowa) Nov. 4, 1833-Feb. 7, 1916; House 1881-87; 1893-1909.

HERBERT, Hilary Abner (D Ala.) March 12, 1834-March 5, 1919; House 1877-93; Secy. of the Navy 1893-97.

HERBERT, John Carlyle (F Md.) Aug. 16, 1775-Sept. 1, 1846; House 1815-19.

HERBERT, Philemon Thomas (D Calif.) Nov. 1, 1825-July 23, 1864; House 1855-57.

HEREFORD, Frank (D W.Va.) July 4, 1825-Dec. 21, 1891; House 1871-Jan. 31, 1877; Senate Jan. 31, 1877-81.

HERKIMER, John (D N.Y.) 1773-June 8, 1848; House 1817-19, 1823-25.

HERLONG, Albert Sydney Jr. (D Fla.) Feb. 14, 1909-—; House 1949-69.

HERMANN, Binger (R Ore.) Feb. 19, 1843-April 15, 1926; House 1885-97, June 1, 1903-07.

HERNANDEZ, Benigno Cardenas (R N.M.) Feb. 13, 1862-Oct. 18, 1954; House 1915-17, 1919-21.

HERNANDEZ, Joseph Marion (— Fla.) Aug. 4, 1793-June 8, 1857; House (Terr. Del.) Sept. 30, 1822-23.

HERNDON, Thomas Hord (D Ala.) July 1, 1828-March 28, 1883; House 1879-March 28, 1883.

HERNDON, William Smith (D Texas) Nov. 27, 1835-Oct. 11, 1903; House 1871-75.

HEROD, William (W Ind.) March 31, 1801-Oct. 20, 1871; House Jan. 25, 1837-39.

HERRICK, Anson (son of Ebenezer Herrick) (D N.Y.) Jan. 21, 1812-Feb. 6, 1868; House 1863-65.

HERRICK, Ebenezer (father of Anson Herrick) (— Maine) Oct. 21, 1785-May 7, 1839; House 1821-27.

HERRICK, Joshua (D Maine) March 18, 1793-Aug. 30, 1874; House 1843-45.

HERRICK, Manuel (R Okla.) Sept. 20, 1876-Feb. 29, 1952; House 1921-23.

HERRICK, Richard Platt (W N.Y.) March 23, 1791-June 20, 1846; House 1845-June 20, 1846.

HERRICK, Samuel (D Ohio) April 14, 1779-June 4, 1852; House 1817-21.

HERRING, Clyde LaVerne (D Iowa) May 3, 1879-Sept. 15, 1945; Senate Jan. 15, 1937-43; Gov. 1933-37.

HERSEY, Ira Greenlief (R Maine) March 31, 1858-May 6, 1943; House 1917-29.

HERSEY, Samuel Freeman (R Maine) April 12, 1812-Feb. 3, 1875; House 1873-Feb. 3, 1875.

HERSMAN, Hugh Steel (D Calif.) July 8, 1872-March 7, 1954; House 1919-21.

HERTEL, Dennis M. (D Mich.) Dec. 7, 1938-—; House 1981-—.

HERTER, Christian Archibald (R Mass.) March 28, 1895-Dec. 30, 1966; House 1943-53; Secy. of State 1959-61; Gov. 1953-57.

HESELTON, John Walter (R Mass.) March 17, 1900-Aug. 19, 1962; House 1945-59.

HESS, William Emil (R Ohio) Feb. 13, 1898-—; House 1929-37, 1939-49, 1951-61.

HEWITT, Abram Stevens (D N.Y.) July 31, 1822-Jan. 18, 1903; House 1875-79, 1881-Dec. 30, 1886; Chrmn. Dem. Nat. Comm. 1876-77.

HEWITT, Goldsmith Whitehouse (D Ala.) Feb. 14, 1834-May 27, 1895; House 1875-79, 1881-85.

Biographical Index

HEYBURN, Wildon Brinton (R Idaho) May 23, 1852-Oct. 17, 1912; Senate 1903-Oct. 17, 1912.

HIBBARD, Ellery Albee (cousin of Harry Hibbard) (D N.H.) July 31, 1826-July 24, 1903; House 1871-73.

HIBBARD, Harry (cousin of Ellery Albee Hibbard) (D N.H.) June 1, 1816-July 28, 1872; House 1849-55.

HIBSHMAN, Jacob (R Pa.) Jan. 31, 1772-May 19, 1852; House 1819-21.

HICKENLOOPER, Bourke Blakemore (R Iowa) July 21, 1896-Sept. 4, 1971; Senate 1945-69; Gov. 1943-45.

HICKEY, Andrew James (R Ind.) Aug. 27, 1872-Aug. 20, 1942; House 1919-31.

HICKEY, John Joseph (D Wyo.) Aug. 22, 1911-Sept. 22, 1970; Senate 1961-Nov. 6, 1962; Gov. 1959-61.

HICKMAN, John (R Pa.) Sept. 11, 1810-March 23, 1875; House 1855-63 (1855-59 Democrat, 1859-61 Douglas Democrat, 1861-63 Republican).

HICKS, Floyd Verne (D Wash.) May 29, 1915- —; House 1965-77.

HICKS, Frederick Cocks (original name: Frederick Hicks Cocks, brother of William Willets Cocks) (R N.Y.) March 6, 1872-Dec. 14, 1925; House 1915-23.

HICKS, Josiah Duane (R Pa.) Aug. 1, 1844-May 9, 1923; House 1893-99.

HICKS, Louise Day (D Mass.) Oct. 16, 1923- —; House 1971-73.

HICKS, Thomas Holliday (R Md.) Sept. 2, 1798-Feb. 14, 1865; Senate Dec. 29, 1862-Feb. 14, 1865; Gov. 1858-62.

HIESTAND, Edgar Willard (R Calif.) Dec. 3, 1888-Aug. 19, 1970; House 1953-63.

HIESTAND, John Andrew (R Pa.) Oct. 2, 1824-Dec. 13, 1890; House 1885-89.

HIESTER, Daniel (brother of John Hiester, cousin of Joseph Hiester, uncle of William Hiester and Daniel Hiester) (— Pa./Md.) June 25, 1747-March 7, 1804; House 1789-July 1, 1796 (Pa.), 1801-March 7, 1804 (Md.).

HIESTER, Daniel (son of John Hiester, nephew of the preceding) (— Pa.) 1774-March 8, 1834; House 1809-11.

HIESTER, Isaac Ellmaker (son of William Hiester, cousin of Hiester Clymer) (W Pa.) May 29, 1824-Feb. 6, 1871; House 1853-55.

HIESTER, John (brother of Daniel Hiester, cousin of Joseph Hiester, uncle of William Hiester) (— Pa.) April 9, 1745-Oct. 15, 1821; House 1807-09.

HIESTER, Joseph (cousin of John Hiester and Daniel Hiester, grandfather of Henry Augustus Muhlenberg) (F Pa.) Nov. 18, 1752-June 10, 1832; House Dec. 1, 1797-1805, 1815-Dec. 1820; Gov. 1820-23.

HIESTER, William (father of Isaac Ellmaker Hiester, uncle of Hiester Clymer, nephew of John Hiester and Daniel Hiester) (W Pa.) Oct. 10, 1790-Oct. 13, 1853; House 1831-37.

HIGBY, William (R Calif.) Aug. 18, 1813-Nov. 27, 1887; House 1863-69.

HIGGINS, Anthony (R Del.) Oct. 1, 1840-June 26, 1912; Senate 1889-95.

HIGGINS, Edwin Werter (R Conn.) July 2, 1874-Sept. 24, 1954; House Oct. 2, 1905-13.

HIGGINS, John Patrick (D Mass.) Feb. 19, 1893-Aug. 2, 1955; House 1935-Sept. 30, 1937.

HIGGINS, William Lincoln (R Conn.) March 8, 1867-Nov. 19, 1951; House 1933-37.

HIGHTOWER, Jack English (D Texas) Sept. 6, 1926- —; House 1975-85.

HILBORN, Samuel Greeley (R Calif.) Dec. 9, 1834-April 19, 1899; House Dec. 5, 1892-April 4, 1894, 1895-99.

HILDEBRANDT, Fred Herman (D S.D.) Aug. 2, 1874-Jan. 26, 1956; House 1933-39.

HILDEBRANT, Charles Quinn (R Ohio) Oct. 17, 1864-March 31, 1953; House 1901-05.

HILER, John P. (R Ind.) April 24, 1953- —; House 1981- —.

HILL, Benjamin Harvey (cousin of Hugh Lawson White Hill) (D Ga.) Sept. 14, 1823-Aug. 16, 1882; House May 5, 1875-77; Senate 1877-Aug. 16, 1882.

HILL, Charles Augustus (R Ill.) Aug. 23, 1833-May 29, 1902; House 1889-91.

HILL, Clement Sidney (ID Ky.) Feb. 13, 1813-Jan. 5, 1892; House 1853-55.

HILL, David Bennett (D N.Y.) Aug. 29, 1843-Oct. 20, 1910; Senate Jan. 7, 1892-97; Gov. 1885-92.

HILL, Ebenezer J. (R Conn.) Aug. 4, 1845-Sept. 27, 1917; House 1895-1913, 1915-Sept. 27, 1917.

HILL, Hugh Lawson White (cousin of Benjamin Harvey Hill) (D Tenn.) March 1, 1810-Jan. 18, 1892; House 1847-49.

HILL, Isaac (D N.H.) April 6, 1788-March 22, 1851; Senate 1831-May 30, 1836; Gov. 1836-39.

HILL, John (D N.C.) April 9, 1797-April 24, 1861; House 1839-41.

HILL, John (cousin of John Thomas Harris) (W Va.) July 18, 1800-April 19, 1880; House 1839-41.

HILL, John (R N.J.) June 10, 1821-July 24, 1884; House 1867-73, 1881-83.

HILL, John Boynton Philip Clayton (R Md.) May 2, 1879-May 23, 1941; House 1921-27.

HILL, Joseph Lister (D Ala.) Dec. 29, 1894-Dec. 20, 1984; House Aug. 14, 1923-Jan. 11, 1938; Senate Jan. 11, 1938-69.

HILL, Joshua (UR Ga.) Jan. 10, 1812-March 6, 1891; House 1857-Jan. 23, 1861; Senate Feb. 1, 1871-73 (1857-61 American Party, 1871-73 Union Republican.).

HILL, Knute (D Wash.) July 31, 1876-Dec. 3, 1963; House 1933-43.

HILL, Mark Langdon (— Mass./Maine) June 30, 1772-Nov. 26, 1842; House 1819-21 (Mass.), 1821-23 (Maine).

HILL, Nathaniel Peter (R Colo.) Feb. 18, 1832-May 22, 1900; Senate 1879-85.

HILL, Ralph (R Ind.) Oct. 12, 1827-Aug. 20, 1899; House 1865-67.

HILL, Robert Potter (D Ill./Okla.) April 18, 1874-Oct. 29, 1937; House 1913-15 (Ill.), Jan. 3-Oct. 29, 1937 (Okla.).

HILL, Samuel Billingsley (D Wash.) April 2, 1875-March 16, 1958; House Sept. 25, 1923-June 25, 1936.

HILL, William David (D Ohio) Oct. 1, 1833-Dec. 26, 1906; House 1879-81, 1883-87.

HILL, William Henry (F N.C.) May 1, 1767-1809; House 1799-1803.

HILL, William Henry (R N.Y.) March 23, 1877-July 24, 1972; House 1919-21.

HILL, William Luther (D Fla.) Oct. 17, 1873-Jan. 5, 1951; Senate July 1-Nov. 3, 1936.

HILL, William Silas (R Colo.) Jan. 20, 1886-Aug. 28, 1972; House 1941-59.

HILL, Wilson Shedric (D Miss.) Jan. 19, 1863-Feb. 14, 1921; House 1903-09.

HILLELSON, Jeffrey Paul (R Mo.) March 9, 1919- —; House 1953-55.

HILLEN, Solomon Jr. (D Md.) July 10, 1810-June 26, 1873; House 1839-41.

HILLHOUSE, James (F Conn.) Oct. 21, 1754-Dec. 29, 1832; House 1791-96; Senate Dec. 6, 1796-June 10, 1810; Pres. pro tempore 1801.

HILLIARD, Benjamin Clark (D Colo.) Jan. 9, 1868-Aug. 7, 1951; House 1915-19.

HILLIARD, Henry Washington (W Ala.) Aug. 4, 1808-Dec. 17, 1892; House 1845-51.

HILLINGS, Patrick Jerome (R Calif.) Feb. 19, 1923- —; House 1951-59.

HILLIS, Elwood Haynes (R Ind.) March 6, 1926- —; House 1971- —.

HILLYER, Junius (D Ga.) April 23, 1807-June 21, 1886; House 1851-55.

HIMES, Joseph Hendrix (R Ohio) Aug. 15, 1885-Sept. 9, 1960; House 1921-23.

HINDMAN, Thomas Carmichael (D Ark.) Jan. 28, 1828-Sept. 27, 1868; House 1859-61.

HINDMAN, William (— Md.) April 1, 1743-Jan. 19, 1822; House Jan. 30, 1793-1799; Senate Dec. 12, 1800-Nov. 19, 1801; Cont. Cong. 1784-88.

HINDS, Asher Crosby (R Maine) Feb. 6, 1863-May 1, 1919; House 1911-17.

HINDS, James (R Ark.) Dec. 5, 1833-Oct. 22, 1868; House June 22-Oct. 22, 1868.

HINDS, Thomas (D Miss.) Jan. 9, 1780-Aug. 23, 1840; House Oct. 21, 1828-31.

HINEBAUGH, William Henry (Prog. Ill.) Dec. 16, 1867-Sept. 22, 1943; House 1913-15.

HINES, Richard (D N.C.) ?-Nov. 20, 1851; House 1825-27.

HINES, William Henry (D Pa.) March 15, 1856-Jan. 17, 1914; House 1893-95.

HINRICHSEN, William Henry (D Ill.) May 27, 1850-Dec. 18, 1907; House 1897-99.

HINSHAW, Andrew Jackson (R Calif.) Aug. 4, 1923- -; House 1973-77.

HINSHAW, Edmund Howard (cousin of Edwin Bruce Brooks) (R Neb.) Dec. 8, 1860-June 15, 1932; House 1903-11.

HINSHAW, John Carl Williams (R Calif.) July 28, 1894-Aug. 5, 1956; House 1939-Aug. 5, 1956.

HINSON, Jon C. (R Miss.) March 16, 1942-April 13, 1981.; House 1979-April 13, 1981.

HIRES, George (R N.J.) Jan. 26, 1835-Feb. 16, 1911; House 1885-89.

HISCOCK, Frank (R N.Y.) Sept. 6, 1834-June 18, 1914; House 1877-87; Senate 1887-93.

HISE, Elijah (D Ky.) July 4, 1802-May 8, 1867; House Dec. 3, 1866-May 8, 1867.

HITCHCOCK, Gilbert Monell (son of Phineas Warren Hitchcock) (D Neb.) Sept. 18, 1859-Feb. 3, 1934; House 1903-05, 1907-11; Senate 1911-23.

HITCHCOCK, Herbert Emery (D S.D.) Aug. 22, 1867-Feb. 17, 1958; Senate Dec. 29, 1936-Nov. 8, 1938.

HITCHCOCK, Peter (— Ohio) Oct. 19, 1781-March 4, 1854; House 1817-19.

HITCHCOCK, Phineas Warren (father of Gilbert Monell Hitchcock) (R Neb.) Nov. 30, 1831-July 10, 1881; House (Terr. Del.) 1865-March 1, 1867; Senate 1871-77.

HITT, Robert Roberts (R Ill.) Jan. 16, 1834-Sept. 19, 1906; House Nov. 7, 1882-Sept. 19, 1906.

HOAG, Truman Harrison (D Ohio) April 9, 1816-Feb. 5, 1870; House 1869-Feb. 5, 1870.

HOAGLAND, Moses (D Ohio) June 19, 1812-April 16, 1865; House 1849-51.

HOAR, Ebenezer Rockwood (son of Samuel Hoar, brother of George Frisbie Hoar, father of Sherman Hoar) (R Mass.) Feb. 21, 1816-Jan. 31, 1895; House 1873-75; Atty. Gen. 1869-70.

HOAR, George Frisbie (son of Samuel Hoar, brother of Ebenezer Rockwood Hoar, father of Rockwood Hoar) (R Mass.) Aug. 29, 1826-Sept. 30, 1904; House 1869-77; Senate 1877-Sept. 30, 1904.

HOAR, Rockwood (son of George Frisbie Hoar) (R Mass.) Aug. 24, 1855-Nov. 1, 1906; House 1905-Nov. 1, 1906.

HOAR, Samuel (father of Ebenezer Rockwood Hoar and George Frisbie Hoar) (W Mass.) May 18, 1778-Nov. 2, 1856; House 1835-37.

HOAR, Sherman (son of Ebenezer Rockwood Hoar) (D Mass.) July 30, 1860-Oct. 7, 1898; House 1891-93.

HOARD, Charles Brooks (R N.Y.) June 5, 1805-Nov. 20, 1886; House 1857-61.

HOBART, Aaron (D Mass.) June 26, 1787-Sept. 19, 1858; House Nov. 24, 1820-27.

HOBART, John Sloss (— N.Y.) May 6, 1738-Feb. 4, 1805; Senate Jan. 11-April 16, 1798.

HOBBIE, Selah Reeve (JD N.Y.) March 10, 1797-March 23, 1854; House 1827-29.

HOBBS, Samuel Francis (Sam) (D Ala.) Oct. 5, 1887-May 31, 1952; House 1935-51.

HOBLITZELL, Fetter Schrier (D Md.) Oct. 7, 1838-May 2, 1900; House 1881-85.

HOBLITZELL, John Dempsey Jr. (R W.Va.) Dec. 30, 1912-Jan. 6, 1962; Senate Jan. 25-Nov. 4, 1958.

HOBSON, Richmond Pearson (D Ala.) Aug. 17, 1870-March 16, 1937; House 1907-15.

HOCH, Daniel Knabb (D Pa.) Jan. 31, 1866-Oct. 11, 1960; House 1943-47.

HOCH, Homer (R Kan.) July 4, 1879-Jan. 30, 1949; House 1919-33.

HODGES, Asa (R Ark.) Jan. 22, 1822-June 6, 1900; House 1873-75.

HODGES, Charles Drury (D Ill.) Feb. 4, 1810-April 1, 1884; House Jan. 4-March 3, 1859.

HODGES, George Tisdale (R Vt.) July 4, 1789-Aug. 9, 1860; House Dec. 1, 1856-57.

HODGES, James Leonard (— Mass.) April 24, 1790-March 8, 1846; House 1827-33.

HODGES, Kaneaster Jr. (D Ark.) Aug. 20, 1938- -; Senate Dec. 10, 1977-Jan. 3, 1979.

HOEPPEL, John Henry (D Calif.) Feb. 10, 1881-Sept. 21, 1976; House 1933-37.

HOEVEN, Charles Bernard (R Iowa) March 30, 1895-Nov. 9, 1980; House 1943-65.

HOEY, Clyde Roark (D N.C.) Dec. 11, 1877-May 12, 1954; House Dec. 16, 1919-21; Senate 1945-May 12, 1954; Gov. 1937-41.

HOFFECKER, John Henry (father of Walter Oakley Hoffecker) (R Del.) Sept. 12, 1827-June 16, 1900; House 1899-June 16, 1900.

HOFFECKER, Walter Oakley (son of John Henry Hoffecker) (R Del.) Sept. 20, 1854-Jan. 23, 1934; House Nov. 6, 1900-01.

HOFFMAN, Carl Henry (R Pa.) Aug. 12, 1896- -; House May 21, 1946-47.

HOFFMAN, Clare Eugene (R Mich.) Sept. 10, 1875-Nov. 3, 1967; House 1935-63.

HOFFMAN, Elmer Joseph (R Ill.) July 7, 1899-June 25, 1976; House 1959-65.

HOFFMAN, Harold Giles (R N.J.) Feb. 7, 1896-June 4, 1954; House 1927-31; Gov. 1935-38.

HOFFMAN, Henry William (AP Md.) Nov. 10, 1825-July 28, 1895; House 1855-57.

HOFFMAN, Josiah Ogden (W N.Y.) May 3, 1793-May 1, 1856; House 1837-41.

HOFFMAN, Michael (D N.Y.) Oct. 11, 1787-Sept. 27, 1848; House 1825-33.

HOFFMAN, Richard William (R Ill.) Dec. 23, 1893-July 6, 1975; House 1949-57.

HOGAN, Earl Lee (D Ind.) March 13, 1920- -; House 1959-61.

HOGAN, John (D Mo.) Jan. 2, 1805-Feb. 5, 1892; House 1865-67.

HOGAN, Lawrence Joseph (R Md.) Sept. 30, 1928- -; House 1969-75.

HOGAN, Michael Joseph (R N.Y.) April 22, 1871-May 7, 1940; House 1921-23.

HOGAN, William (JD N.Y.) July 17, 1792-Nov. 25, 1874; House 1831-33.

HOGE, John (brother of William Hoge) (D Pa.) Sept. 10, 1760-Aug. 4, 1824; House Nov. 2, 1804-05.

HOGE, John Blair (D W.Va.) Feb. 2, 1825-March 1, 1896; House 1881-83.

HOGE, Joseph Pendleton (D Ill.) Dec. 15, 1810-Aug. 14, 1891; House 1843-47.

HOGE, Solomon Lafayette (R S.C.) July 11, 1836-Feb. 23, 1909; House April 8, 1869-71, 1875-77.

HOGE, William (brother of John Hoge) (F Pa.) 1762-Sept. 25, 1814; House 1801-Oct. 15, 1804, 1807-09.

HOGEBOOM, James Lawrence (W N.Y.) Aug. 25, 1766-Dec. 23, 1839; House 1823-25.

HOGG, Charles Edgar (father of Robert Lynn Hogg) (D W.Va.) Dec. 21, 1852-June 14, 1935; House 1887-89.

HOGG, David (R Ind.) Aug. 21, 1886-Oct. 23, 1973; House 1925-33.

HOGG, Herschel Millard (R Colo.) Nov. 21, 1853-Aug. 27, 1934; House 1903-07.

HOGG, Robert Lynn (son of Charles Edgar Hogg) (R W.Va.) Dec. 30, 1893-July 21, 1973; House Nov. 4, 1930-33.

HOGG, Samuel (D Tenn.) April 18, 1783-May 28, 1842; House 1817-19.

HOIDALE, Einar (D Minn.) Aug. 17, 1870-Dec. 5, 1952; House 1933-35.

HOLADAY, William Perry (R Ill.) Dec. 14, 1882-Jan. 29, 1946; House 1923-33.

HOLBROCK, Greg John (D Ohio) June 21, 1906- -; House 1941-43.

HOLBROOK, Edward Dexter (D Idaho) May 6, 1836-June 18, 1870; House (Terr. Del.) 1865-69.

HOLCOMBE, George (D N.J.) March 1786-Jan. 14, 1828; House 1821-Jan. 14, 1828.

Biographical Index

HOLIFIELD, Chester Earl (D Calif.) Dec. 3, 1903--; House 1943-Dec. 31, 1974.

HOLLADAY, Alexander Richmond (D Va.) Sept. 18, 1811-Jan. 29, 1877; House 1849-53.

HOLLAND, Cornelius (D Maine) July 9, 1783-June 2, 1870; House Dec. 6, 1830-33.

HOLLAND, Edward Everett (D Va.) Feb. 26, 1861-Oct. 23, 1941; House 1911-21.

HOLLAND, Elmer Joseph (D Pa.) Jan. 8, 1894-Aug. 9, 1968; House May 19, 1942-43; Jan. 24, 1956-Aug. 9, 1968.

HOLLAND, James (AF N.C.) 1754-May 19, 1823; House 1795-97; 1801-11.

HOLLAND, Kenneth Lamar (D S.C.) Nov. 24, 1934--; House 1975-83.

HOLLAND, Spessard Lindsey (D Fla.) July 10, 1892-Nov. 6, 1971; Senate Sept. 25, 1946-71; Gov. 1941-45.

HOLLEMAN, Joel (VBD Va.) Oct. 1, 1799-Aug. 5, 1844; House 1839-40.

HOLLENBECK, Harold Capistran (R N.J.) Dec. 29, 1938--; House 1977-83.

HOLLEY, John Milton (W N.Y.) Nov. 10, 1802-March 8, 1848; House 1847-March 8, 1848.

HOLLIDAY, Elias Selah (R Ind.) March 5, 1842-March 13, 1936; House 1901-09.

HOLLINGS, Ernest F. (D S.C.) Jan. 1, 1922--; Senate Nov. 9, 1966--; Gov. 1959-63.

HOLLINGSWORTH, David Adams (R Ohio) Nov. 21, 1844-Dec. 3, 1929; House 1909-11, 1915-19.

HOLLIS, Henry French (D N.H.) Aug. 30, 1869-July 7, 1949; Senate March 13, 1913-19.

HOLLISTER, John Baker (R Ohio) Nov. 7, 1890-Jan. 4, 1979; House Nov. 3, 1931-37.

HOLLOWAY, David Pierson (PP Ind.) Dec. 7, 1809-Sept. 9, 1883; House 1855-57.

HOLMAN, Rufus Cecil (R Ore.) Oct. 14, 1877-Nov. 27, 1959; Senate 1939-45.

HOLMAN, William Steele (D Ind.) Sept. 6, 1822-April 22, 1897; House 1859-65, 1867-77, 1881-95, March 4-April 22, 1897.

HOLMES, Adoniram Judson (R Iowa) March 2, 1842-Jan. 21, 1902; House 1883-89.

HOLMES, Charles Horace (R N.Y.) Oct. 24, 1827-Oct. 2, 1874; House Dec. 6, 1870-71.

HOLMES, David (— Va./Miss.) March 10, 1769-Aug. 20, 1832; House 1797-1809 (Va.); Senate Aug. 30, 1820-Sept. 25, 1825 (Miss.); Gov. 1809-17 (Miss. Terr.), 1817-20 (Miss.).

HOLMES, Elias Bellows (W N.Y.) May 22, 1807-July 31, 1866; House 1845-49.

HOLMES, Gabriel (— N.C.) 1769-Sept. 26, 1829; House 1825-Sept. 26, 1829; Gov. 1821-24.

HOLMES, Isaac Edward (D S.C.) April 6, 1796-Feb. 24, 1867; House 1839-51.

HOLMES, John (D Mass./Maine) March 14, 1773-July 7, 1843; House 1817-March 15, 1820 (Mass.); Senate June 13, 1820-27, Jan. 15, 1829-33 (Maine).

HOLMES, Otis Halbert (Hal) (grandson of Dudley Chase Haskell) (R Wash.) Feb. 22, 1902-July 27, 1977; House 1943-59.

HOLMES, Pehr Gustaf (R Mass.) April 9, 1881-Dec. 19, 1952; House 1931-47.

HOLMES, Sidney Tracy (R N.Y.) Aug. 14, 1815-Jan. 16, 1890; House 1865-67.

HOLMES, Uriel (F Conn.) Aug. 26, 1764-May 18, 1827; House 1817-18.

HOLSEY, Hopkins (UD Ga.) Aug. 25, 1779-March 31, 1859; House Oct. 5, 1835-39.

HOLT, Hines (W Ga.) April 27, 1805-Nov. 4, 1865; House Feb. 1-March 3, 1841.

HOLT, Joseph Franklin 3d (R Calif.) July 6, 1924--; House 1953-61.

HOLT, Marjorie Sewell (R Md.) Sept. 17, 1920--; House 1973--.

HOLT, Orrin (D Conn.) March 13, 1792-June 20, 1855; House Dec. 5, 1836-39.

HOLT, Rush Dew (D W.Va.) June 19, 1905-Feb. 8, 1955; Senate June 21, 1935-41.

HOLTEN, Samuel (— Mass.) June 9, 1738-Jan. 2, 1816; House 1793-95; Cont. Cong. 1778-80, 1782-87.

HOLTON, Hart Benton (R Md.) Oct. 13, 1835-Jan. 4, 1907; House 1883-85.

HOLTZMAN, Elizabeth (D N.Y.) Aug. 11, 1941--; House 1973-81.

HOLTZMAN, Lester (D N.Y.) June 1, 1913--; House 1953-Dec. 31, 1961.

HONEYMAN, Nan Wood (D Ore.) July 15, 1881-Dec. 10, 1970; House 1937-39.

HOOD, George Ezekial (D N.C.) Jan. 25, 1875-March 8, 1960; House 1915-19.

HOOK, Enos (D Pa.) Dec. 3, 1804-July 15, 1841; House 1839-April 18, 1841.

HOOK, Frank Eugene (D Mich.) May 26, 1893-June 21, 1982; House 1935-43, 1945-47.

HOOKER, Charles Edward (D Miss.) 1825-Jan. 8, 1914; House 1875-83, 1887-95, 1901-03.

HOOKER, James Murray (D Va.) Oct. 29, 1873-Aug. 6, 1940; House Nov. 8, 1921-25.

HOOKER, Warren Brewster (R N.Y.) Nov. 24, 1856-March 5, 1920; House 1891-Nov. 10, 1898.

HOOKS, Charles (great-grandfather of William Julius Harris) (D N.C.) Feb. 20, 1768-Oct. 18, 1843; House Dec. 2, 1816-17, 1819-25.

HOOPER, Benjamin Stephen (Read. Va.) March 6, 1835-Jan. 17, 1898; House 1883-85.

HOOPER, Joseph Lawrence (R Mich.) Dec. 22, 1877-Feb. 22, 1934; House Aug. 18, 1925-Feb. 22, 1934.

HOOPER, Samuel (R Mass.) Feb. 3, 1808-Feb. 14, 1875; House Dec. 2, 1861-Feb. 14, 1875.

HOOPER, William Henry (D Utah) Dec. 25, 1813-Dec. 30, 1882; House (Terr. Del.) 1859-61; 1865-73.

HOPE, Clifford Ragsdale (R Kan.) June 9, 1893-May 16, 1970; House 1927-57.

HOPKINS, Albert Cole (R Pa.) Sept. 15, 1837-June 9, 1911; House 1891-95.

HOPKINS, Albert Jarvis (R Ill.) Aug. 15, 1846-Aug. 23, 1922; House Dec. 7, 1885-1903; Senate 1903-09.

HOPKINS, Benjamin Franklin (R Wis.) April 22, 1829-Jan. 1, 1870; House 1867-Jan. 1, 1870.

HOPKINS, David William (R Mo.) Oct. 31, 1897-Oct. 14, 1968; House Feb. 5, 1929-33.

HOPKINS, Francis Alexander (Frank) (D Ky.) May 27, 1853-June 5, 1918; House 1903-07.

HOPKINS, George Washington (D Va.) Feb. 22, 1804-March 1, 1861; House 1835-47, 1857-59.

HOPKINS, James Herron (D Pa.) Nov. 3, 1832-June 17, 1904; House 1875-77, 1883-85.

HOPKINS, Larry Jones (R Ky.) Oct. 25, 1933--; House 1979--.

HOPKINS, Nathan Thomas (R Ky.) Oct. 27, 1852-Feb. 11, 1927; House Feb. 18-March 3, 1897.

HOPKINS, Samuel (D Ky.) April 9, 1753-Sept. 16, 1819; House 1813-15.

HOPKINS, Samuel Isaac (D Va.) Dec. 12, 1843-Jan. 15, 1914; House 1887-89.

HOPKINS, Samuel Miles (— N.Y.) May 9, 1772-March 9, 1837; House 1813-15.

HOPKINS, Stephen Tyng (R N.Y.) March 25, 1849-March 3, 1892; House 1887-89.

HOPKINSON, Joseph (F Pa.) Nov. 12, 1770-Jan. 15, 1842; House 1815-19.

HOPWOOD, Robert Freeman (R Pa.) July 24, 1856-March 1, 1940; House 1915-17.

HORAN, Walter Franklin (R Wash.) Oct. 15, 1898-Dec. 19, 1966; House 1943-65.

HORN, Henry (JD Pa.) 1786-Jan. 12, 1862; House 1831-33.

HORNBECK, John Westbrook (W Pa.) Jan. 24, 1804-Jan. 16, 1848; House 1847-Jan. 16, 1848.

HORNOR, Lynn Sedwick (D W.Va.) Nov. 3, 1874-Sept. 23, 1933; House 1931-Sept. 23, 1933.

HORR, Ralph Ashley (R Wash.) Aug. 12, 1884-Jan. 26, 1960; House 1931-33.

HORR, Roswell Gilbert (R Mich.) Nov. 26, 1830-Dec. 19, 1896; House 1879-85.

HORSEY, Outerbridge (F Del.) March 5, 1777-June 9, 1842; Senate Jan. 12, 1810-21.

HORSFORD, Jerediah (W N.Y.) March 8, 1791-Jan. 14, 1875; House 1851-53.

HORTON, Frank Jefferson (R N.Y.) Dec. 12, 1919--; House 1963--.

HORTON, Frank Ogilvie (R Wyo.) Oct. 18, 1882-Aug. 17, 1948; House 1939-41.

HORTON, Thomas Raymond (R N.Y.) April 1822-July 26, 1894; House 1855-57.

HORTON, Valentine Baxter (W Ohio) Jan. 29, 1802-Jan. 14, 1888; House 1855-59, 1861-63.

HOSKINS, George Gilbert (R N.Y.) Dec. 24, 1824-June 12, 1893; House 1873-77.

HOSMER, Craig (R Calif.) May 6, 1915-Oct. 11, 1982; House 1953-Dec. 31, 1974.

HOSMER, Hezekiah Lord (— N.Y.) June 7, 1765-June 9, 1814; House 1797-99.

HOSTETLER, Abraham Jonathan (D Ind.) Nov. 22, 1818-Nov. 24, 1899; House 1879-81.

HOSTETTER, Jacob (D Pa.) May 9, 1754-June 29, 1831; House Nov. 16, 1818-21.

HOTCHKISS, Giles Waldo (R N.Y.) Oct. 25, 1815-July 5, 1878; House 1863-67, 1869-71.

HOTCHKISS, Julius (R Conn.) July 11, 1810-Dec. 23, 1878; House 1867-69.

HOUCK, Jacob Jr. (D N.Y.) Jan. 14, 1801-Oct. 2, 1857; House 1841-43.

HOUGH, David (— N.H.) March 13, 1753-April 18, 1831; House 1803-07.

HOUGH, William Jervis (D N.Y.) March 20, 1795-Oct. 4, 1869; House 1845-47.

HOUGHTON, Alanson Bigelow (R N.Y.) Oct. 10, 1863-Sept. 15, 1941; House 1919-Feb. 28, 1922.

HOUGHTON, Sherman Otis (R Calif.) April 10, 1828-Aug. 31, 1914; House 1871-75.

HOUK, George Washington (D Ohio) Sept. 25, 1825-Feb. 9, 1894; House 1891-Feb. 9, 1894.

HOUK, John Chiles (son of Leonidas Campbell Houk) (R Tenn.) Feb. 26, 1860-June 3, 1923; House Dec. 7, 1891-95.

HOUK, Leonidas Campbell (father of John Chiles Houk) (R Tenn.) June 8, 1836-May 25, 1891; House 1879-May 25, 1891.

HOUSE, John Ford (D Tenn.) Jan. 9, 1827-June 28, 1904; House 1875-83.

HOUSEMAN, Julius (D Mich.) Dec. 8, 1832-Feb. 8, 1891; House 1883-85.

HOUSTON, Andrew Jackson (son of Samuel Houston) (D Texas) June 21, 1854-June 26, 1941; Senate April 21-June 26, 1941.

HOUSTON, George Smith (D Ala.) Jan. 17, 1808-Dec. 31, 1879; House 1841-49, 1851-Jan. 21, 1861; Senate March 4-Dec. 31, 1879; Gov. 1874-78.

HOUSTON, Henry Aydelotte (D Del.) July 10, 1847-April 5, 1925; House 1903-05.

HOUSTON, John Mills (D Kan.) Sept. 15, 1890-April 29, 1975; House 1935-43.

HOUSTON, John Wallace (uncle of Robert Griffith Houston) (W Del.) May 4, 1814-April 26, 1896; House 1845-51.

HOUSTON, Robert Griffith (nephew of John Wallace Houston) (R Del.) Oct. 13, 1867-Jan. 29, 1946; House 1925-33.

HOUSTON, Samuel (father of Andrew Jackson Houston, cousin of David Hubbard) (D Tenn./Texas) March 2, 1793-July 26, 1863; House 1823-27 (Tenn.); Senate Feb. 21, 1846-59 (Texas); Gov. 1827-April 16, 1829 (Tenn.), 1859-61 (Texas).

HOUSTON, Victor Stewart Kaleoaloha (R Hawaii) July 22, 1876-July 31, 1959; House (Terr. Del.) 1927-33.

HOUSTON, William Cannon (D Tenn.) March 17, 1852-Aug. 30, 1931; House 1905-19.

HOVEY, Alvin Peterson (R Ind.) Sept. 6, 1821-Nov. 23, 1891; House 1887-Jan. 17, 1889; Gov. 1889-91.

HOWARD, Benjamin (— Ky.) 1760-Sept. 18, 1814; House 1807-April 10, 1810; Gov. (La. Terr.) 1810-12.

HOWARD, Benjamin Chew (son of John Eager Howard) (D Md.) Nov. 5, 1791-March 6, 1872; House 1829-33, 1835-39.

HOWARD, Edgar (D Neb.) Sept. 16, 1858-July 19, 1951; House 1923-35.

HOWARD, Everette Burgess (D Okla.) Sept. 19, 1873-April 3, 1950; House 1919-21, 1923-25, 1927-29.

HOWARD, Guy Victor (R Minn.) Nov. 28, 1879-Aug. 20, 1954; Senate Nov. 4, 1936-37.

HOWARD, Jacob Merritt (R Mich.) July 10, 1805-April 2, 1871; House 1841-43; Senate Jan. 17, 1862-71 (1841-43 Whig, 1862-71 Republican).

HOWARD, James John (D N.J.) July 24, 1927- —; House 1965- —.

HOWARD, John Eager (father of Benjamin Chew Howard) (F Md.) June 4, 1752-Oct. 12, 1827; Senate Nov. 30, 1796-1803; Pres. pro tempore 1801; Gov. 1789-91; Cont. Cong. 1784-88.

HOWARD, Jonas George (D Ind.) May 22, 1825-Oct. 5, 1911; House 1885-89.

HOWARD, Milford Wriarson (P Ala.) Dec. 18, 1862-Dec. 28, 1937; House 1895-99.

HOWARD, Tilghman Ashurst (D Ind.) Nov. 14, 1797-Aug. 16, 1844; House Aug. 5, 1839-July 1, 1840.

HOWARD, Volney Erskine (D Texas) Oct. 22, 1809-May 14, 1889; House 1849-53.

HOWARD, William (D Ohio) Dec. 31, 1817-June 1, 1891; House 1859-61.

HOWARD, William Alanson (R Mich.) April 8, 1813-April 10, 1880; House 1855-59, May 15, 1860-61; Gov. (Dakota Terr.) 1878-80.

HOWARD, William Marcellus (D Ga.) Dec. 6, 1857-July 5, 1932; House 1897-1911.

HOWARD, William Schley (cousin of Augustus Octavius Bacon) (D Ga.) June 29, 1875-Aug. 1, 1953; House 1911-19.

HOWE, Albert Richards (R Miss.) Jan. 1, 1840-June 1, 1884; House 1873-75.

HOWE, Allan Turner (D Utah) Sept. 6, 1927- —; House 1975-77.

HOWE, James Robinson (R N.Y.) Jan. 27, 1839-Sept. 21, 1914; House 1895-99.

HOWE, John W. (FSW Pa.) 1801-Dec. 1, 1873; House 1849-53.

HOWE, Thomas Marshall (father-in-law of James W. Brown) (W Pa.) April 20, 1808-July 20, 1877; House 1851-55.

HOWE, Thomas Y. Jr. (D N.Y.) 1801-July 15, 1860; House 1851-53.

HOWE, Timothy Otis (UR Wis.) Feb. 24, 1816-March 25, 1883; Senate 1861-79; Postmaster Gen. 1882-83.

HOWELL, Benjamin Franklin (R N.J.) Jan. 27, 1844-Feb. 1, 1933; House 1895-1911.

HOWELL, Charles Robert (D N.J.) April 23, 1904-July 5, 1973; House 1949-55.

HOWELL, Edward (D N.Y.) Oct. 16, 1792-Jan. 30, 1871; House 1833-35.

HOWELL, Elias (father of James Bruen Howell) (W Ohio) 1792-May 1844; House 1835-37.

HOWELL, George (R Pa.) June 28, 1859-Nov. 19, 1913; House 1903-Feb. 10, 1904.

HOWELL, George Evan (R Ill.) Sept. 21, 1905-Jan. 18, 1980; House 1941-Oct. 5, 1947.

HOWELL, James Bruen (son of Elias Howell) (R Iowa) July 4, 1816-June 17, 1880; Senate Jan. 18, 1870-71.

HOWELL, Jeremiah Brown (F R.I.) Aug. 28, 1771-Feb. 5, 1822; Senate 1811-17.

HOWELL, Joseph (R Utah) Feb. 17, 1857-July 18, 1918; House 1903-17.

HOWELL, Nathaniel Woodhull (— N.Y.) Jan. 1, 1770-Oct. 15, 1851; House 1813-15.

HOWELL, Robert Beecher (R Neb.) Jan. 21, 1864-March 11, 1933; Senate 1923-March 11, 1933.

HOWEY, Benjamin Franklin (nephew of Charles Creighton Sratton) (R N.J.) March 17, 1828-Feb. 6, 1895; House 1883-85.

HOWLAND, Benjamin (D R.I.) July 27, 1755-May 1, 1821; Senate Oct. 29, 1804-09.

HOWLAND, Leonard Paul (R Ohio) Dec. 5, 1865-Dec. 23, 1942; House 1907-13.

HOXWORTH, Stephen Arnold (D Ill.) May 1, 1860-Jan. 25, 1930; House 1913-15.

HOYER, Steny (D Md.) June 14, 1939- —; House June 3, 1981- —.

HRUSKA, Roman Lee (R Neb.) Aug. 16, 1904- —; House 1953-Nov. 8, 1954; Senate Nov. 8, 1954-Dec. 27, 1976.

HUBARD, Edmund Wilcox (D Va.) Feb. 20, 1806-Dec. 9, 1878; House 1841-47.

HUBBARD, Asahel Wheeler (father of Elbert Hamilton Hubbard) (R Iowa) Jan. 19, 1819-Sept. 22, 1879; House 1863-69.

Biographical Index

HUBBARD, Carroll Jr. (D Ky.) July 7, 1937- —; House 1975- —.

HUBBARD, Chester Dorman (father of William Pallister Hubbard) (R W.Va.) Nov. 25, 1814-Aug. 23, 1891; House 1865-69.

HUBBARD, David (cousin of Samuel Houston) (SRD Ala.) 1792-Jan. 20, 1874; House 1839-41, 1849-51.

HUBBARD, Demas Jr. (R N.Y.) Jan. 17, 1806-Sept. 2, 1873; House 1865-67.

HUBBARD, Elbert Hamilton (son of Asahel Wheeler Hubbard) (R Iowa) Aug. 19, 1849-June 4, 1912; House 1905-June 4, 1912.

HUBBARD, Henry (D N.H.) May 3, 1784-June 5, 1857; House 1829-35; Senate 1835-41; Gov. 1842-44.

HUBBARD, Joel Douglas (R Mo.) Nov. 6, 1860-May 26, 1919; House 1895-97.

HUBBARD, John Henry (R Conn.) March 24, 1804-July 30, 1872; House 1863-67.

HUBBARD, Jonathan Hatch (F Vt.) May 7, 1768-Sept. 20, 1849; House 1809-11.

HUBBARD, Levi (D Mass.) Dec. 19, 1762-Feb. 18, 1836; House 1813-15.

HUBBARD, Richard Dudley (D Conn.) Sept. 7, 1818-Feb. 28, 1884; House 1867-69; Gov. 1877-79.

HUBBARD, Samuel Dickinson (W Conn.) Aug. 10, 1799-Oct. 8, 1855; House 1845-49; Postmaster Gen. 1852-53.

HUBBARD, Thomas Hill (D N.Y.) Dec. 5, 1781-May 21, 1857; House 1817-19, 1821-23.

HUBBARD, William Pallister (son of Chester Dorman Hubbard) (R W.Va.) Dec. 24, 1843-Dec. 5, 1921; House 1907-11.

HUBBELL, Edwin Nelson (D N.Y.) Aug. 13, 1815-?; House 1865-67.

HUBBELL, James Randolph (R Ohio) July 13, 1824-Nov. 26, 1890; House 1865-67.

HUBBELL, Jay Abel (R Mich.) Sept. 15, 1829-Oct. 13, 1900; House 1873-83.

HUBBELL, William Spring (D N.Y.) Jan. 17, 1801-Nov. 16, 1873; House 1843-45.

HUBBS, Orlando (R N.C.) Feb. 18, 1840-Dec. 5, 1930; House 1881-83.

HUBER, Robert James (R Mich.) Aug. 29, 1922- —; House 1973-75.

HUBER, Walter B. (D Ohio) June 29, 1903-Aug. 8, 1982; House 1945-51.

HUBLEY, Edward Burd (JD Pa.) 1792-Feb. 23, 1856; House 1835-39.

HUCK, Winnifred Sprague Mason (daughter of William Ernest Mason) (R Ill.) Sept. 14, 1882-Aug. 24, 1936; House Nov. 7, 1922-23.

HUCKABY, Thomas Jerry (D La.) July 19, 1941- —; House 1977- —.

HUDD, Thomas Richard (D Wis.) Oct. 2, 1835-June 22, 1896; House March 8, 1886-89.

HUDDLESTON, George (father of George Huddleston Jr.) (D Ala.) Nov. 11, 1869-Feb. 29, 1960; House 1915-37.

HUDDLESTON, George Jr. (son of George Huddleston) (D Ala.) March 19, 1920-Sept. 14, 1971; House 1955-65.

HUDDLESTON, Walter Darlington (D Ky.) April 15, 1926- —; Senate 1973-85.

HUDNUT, William Herbert III (R Ind.) Oct. 17, 1932- —; House 1973-75.

HUDSON, Charles (W Mass.) Nov. 14, 1795-May 4, 1881; House May 3, 1841-49.

HUDSON, Grant Martin (R Mich.) July 23, 1868-Oct. 26, 1955; House 1923-31.

HUDSON, Thomas Jefferson (P Kan.) Oct. 30, 1839-Jan. 4, 1923; House 1893-95.

HUDSPETH, Claude Benton (D Texas) May 12, 1877-March 19, 1941; House 1919-31.

HUFF, George Franklin (R Pa.) July 16, 1842-April 18, 1912; House 1891-93, 1895-97, 1903-11.

HUFFMAN, James Wylie (D Ohio) Sept. 13, 1894- —; Senate Oct. 8, 1945-Nov. 5, 1946.

HUFTY, Jacob (D N.J.) ?-May 20, 1814; House 1808-May 20, 1814.

HUGER, Benjamin (— S.C.) 1768-July 7, 1823; House 1799-1805, 1815-17.

HUGER, Daniel (father of Daniel Elliott Huger) (— S.C.) Feb. 20, 1742-July 6, 1799; House 1789-93; Cont. Cong. 1786-88.

HUGER, Daniel Elliott (son of Daniel Huger) (SRD S.C.) June 28, 1779-Aug. 21, 1854; Senate 1843-45.

HUGHES, Charles (D N.Y.) Feb. 27, 1822-Aug. 10, 1887; House 1853-55.

HUGHES, Charles James Jr. (D Colo.) Feb. 16, 1853-Jan. 11, 1911; Senate 1909-Jan. 11, 1911.

HUGHES, Dudley Mays (D Ga.) Oct. 10, 1848-Jan. 20, 1927; House 1909-17.

HUGHES, George Wurtz (D Md.) Sept. 30, 1806-Sept. 3, 1870; House 1859-61.

HUGHES, Harold Everett (D Iowa) Feb. 10, 1922- —; Senate 1969-75; Gov. 1963-69.

HUGHES, James (D Ind.) Nov. 24, 1823-Oct. 24, 1873; House 1857-59.

HUGHES, James Anthony (R W.Va.) Feb. 27, 1861-March 2, 1930; House 1901-15, 1927-March 2, 1930.

HUGHES, James Frederic (D Wis.) Aug. 7, 1883-Aug. 9, 1940; House 1933-35.

HUGHES, James Hurd (D Del.) Jan. 14, 1867-Aug. 29, 1953; Senate 1937-43.

HUGHES, James Madison (D Mo.) April 7, 1809-Feb. 26, 1861; House 1843-45.

HUGHES, Thomas Hurst (W N.J.) Jan. 10, 1769-Nov. 10, 1839; House 1829-33.

HUGHES, William (D N.J.) April 3, 1872-Jan. 30, 1918; House 1903-05, 1907-Sept. 27, 1912; Senate 1913-Jan. 30, 1918.

HUGHES, William John (D N.J.) Oct. 17, 1932- —; House 1975- —.

HUGHSTON, Jonas Abbott (W N.Y.) 1808-Nov. 10, 1862; House 1855-57.

HUGUNIN, Daniel Jr. (— N.Y.) Feb. 6, 1790-June 21, 1850; House Dec. 15, 1825-27.

HUKRIEDE, Theodore Waldemar (R Mo.) Nov. 9, 1878-April 14, 1945; House 1921-23.

HULBERT, George Murray (D N.Y.) May 14, 1881-April 26, 1950; House 1915-Jan. 1, 1918.

HULBERT, John Whitefield (F Mass.) June 1, 1770-Oct. 19, 1831; House Sept. 26, 1814-17.

HULBURD, Calvin Tilden (R N.Y.) June 5, 1809-Oct. 25, 1897; House 1863-69.

HULICK, George Washington (R Ohio) June 29, 1833-Aug. 13, 1907; House 1893-97.

HULING, James Hall (R W.Va.) March 24, 1844-April 23, 1918; House 1895-97.

HULINGS, Willis James (R Pa.) July 1, 1850-Aug. 8, 1924; House 1913-15, 1919-21 (1913-15 Progressive, 1919-21 Republican).

HULL, Cordell (D Tenn.) Oct. 2, 1871-July 23, 1955; House 1907-21, 1923-31; Senate 1931-March 3, 1933; Secy. of State 1933-44; Chrmn. Dem. Nat. Comm. 1921-24.

HULL, Harry Edward (R Iowa) March 12, 1864-Jan. 16, 1938; House 1915-25.

HULL, John Albert Tiffin (R Iowa) May 1, 1841-Sept. 26, 1928; House 1891-1911.

HULL, Merlin (R Wis.) Dec. 18, 1870-May 17, 1953; House 1929-31, 1935-May 17, 1953 (1929-31 Republican, 1935-47 Progressive, 1947-53 Republican).

HULL, Morton Denison (R Ill.) Jan. 13, 1867-Aug. 20, 1937; House April 3, 1923-33.

HULL, Noble Andrew (D Fla.) March 11, 1827-Jan. 28, 1907; House 1879-Jan. 22, 1881.

HULL, William Edgar (R Ill.) Jan. 13, 1866-May 30, 1942; House 1923-33.

HULL, William Raleigh Jr. (D Mo.) April 17, 1906-Aug. 15, 1977; House 1955-73.

HUMPHREY, Augustin Reed (R Neb.) Feb. 18, 1859-Dec. 10, 1937; House Nov. 7, 1922-23.

HUMPHREY, Charles (D N.Y.) Feb. 14, 1792-April 17, 1850; House 1825-27.

HUMPHREY, Gordon J. (R N.H.) Oct. 7, 1940- —; Senate 1979- —.

HUMPHREY, Herman Leon (R Wis.) March 14, 1830-June 10, 1902; House 1877-83.

HUMPHREY, Hubert Horatio Jr. (husband of Muriel Buck Humphrey) (D Minn.) May 27, 1911-Jan. 13, 1978; Senate 1949-Dec. 29, 1964, 1971-Jan. 13, 1978; Vice Pres. 1965-69.

HUMPHREY, James (R N.Y.) Oct. 9, 1811-June 16, 1866; House 1859-61, 1865-June 16, 1866.

HUMPHREY, James Morgan (D N.Y.) Sept. 21, 1819-Feb. 9, 1899; House 1865-69.

HUMPHREY, Muriel Buck (widow of Hubert Horatio Humphrey Jr.) (D Minn.) Feb. 20, 1912-—; Senate Feb. 6, 1978-Nov. 7, 1978.

HUMPHREY, Reuben (— N.Y.) Sept. 2, 1757-Aug. 12, 1831; House 1807-09.

HUMPHREY, William Ewart (R Wash.) March 31, 1862-Feb. 14, 1934; House 1903-17.

HUMPHREYS, Andrew (D Ind.) March 30, 1821-June 14, 1904; House Dec. 5, 1876-77.

HUMPHREYS, Benjamin Grubb (father of William Yerger Humphreys) (D Miss.) Aug. 17, 1865-Oct. 16, 1923; House 1903-Oct. 16, 1923.

HUMPHREYS, Parry Wayne (D Tenn.) 1778-Feb. 12, 1839; House 1813-15.

HUMPHREYS, Robert (D Ky.) Aug. 20, 1893-Dec. 31, 1977; Senate June 21-Nov. 6, 1956.

HUMPHREYS, William Yerger (son of Benjamin Grubb Humphreys) (D Miss.) Sept. 9, 1890-Feb. 26, 1933; House Nov. 27, 1923-25.

HUNGATE, William Leonard (D Mo.) Dec. 24, 1922-—; House Nov. 3, 1964-77.

HUNGERFORD, John Newton (R N.Y.) Dec. 31, 1825-April 2, 1883; House 1877-79.

HUNGERFORD, John Pratt (D Va.) Jan. 2, 1761-Dec. 21, 1833; House March 4-Nov. 29, 1811, 1813-17.

HUNGERFORD, Orville (D N.Y.) Oct. 29, 1790-April 6, 1851; House 1843-47.

HUNT, Carleton (nephew of Theodore Gaillard Hunt) (D La.) Jan. 1, 1836-Aug. 14, 1921; House 1883-85.

HUNT, Hiram Paine (W N.Y.) May 23, 1796-Aug. 14, 1865; House 1835-37, 1839-43.

HUNT, James Bennett (D Mich.) Aug. 13, 1799-Aug. 15, 1857; House 1843-47.

HUNT, John Edmund (R N.J.) Nov. 25, 1908-—; House 1967-75.

HUNT, John Thomas (D Mo.) Feb. 2, 1860-Nov. 30, 1916; House 1903-07.

HUNT, Jonathan (NR Vt.) Aug. 12, 1787-May 15, 1832; House 1827-May 15, 1832.

HUNT, Lester Callaway (D Wyo.) July 8, 1892-June 19, 1954; Senate 1949-June 19, 1954; Gov. 1943-49.

HUNT, Samuel (— N.H.) July 8, 1765-July 7, 1807; House Dec. 6, 1802-05.

HUNT, Theodore Gaillard (nephew of John Gaillard, uncle of Carleton Hunt) (W La.) Oct. 23, 1805-Nov. 15, 1893; House 1853-55.

HUNT, Washington (W N.Y.) Aug. 5, 1811-Feb. 2, 1867; House 1843-49; Gov. 1851-53.

HUNTER, Allan Oakley (R Calif.) June 15, 1916-—; House 1951-55.

HUNTER, Andrew Jackson (D Ill.) Dec. 17, 1831-Jan. 12, 1913; House 1893-95, 1897-99.

HUNTER, Duncan L. (R Calif.) May 31, 1948-—; House 1981-—.

HUNTER, John (F S.C.) 1732-1802; House 1793-95; Senate Dec. 8, 1796-Nov. 26, 1798.

HUNTER, John Feeney (D Ohio) Oct. 19, 1896-Dec. 19, 1957; House 1937-43.

HUNTER, John Ward (— N.Y.) Oct. 15, 1807-April 16, 1900; House Dec. 4, 1866-67.

HUNTER, Morton Craig (R Ind.) Feb. 5, 1825-Oct. 25, 1896; House 1867-69, 1873-79.

HUNTER, Narsworthy (— Miss.) ?-March 11, 1802; House (Terr. Del.) 1801-March 11, 1802.

HUNTER, Richard Charles (D Neb.) Dec. 3, 1884-Jan. 23, 1941; Senate Nov. 7, 1934-35.

HUNTER, Robert Mercer Taliaferro (D Va.) April 21, 1809-July 18, 1887; House 1837-43, 1845-47; Senate 1847-March 28, 1861; Speaker 1839-41.

HUNTER, Whiteside Godfrey (R Ky.) Dec. 25, 1841-Nov. 2, 1917; House 1887-89, 1895-97, Nov. 10, 1903-05.

HUNTER, William (R Vt.) Jan. 3, 1754-Nov. 30, 1827; House 1817-19.

HUNTER, William (F R.I.) Nov. 26, 1774-Dec. 3, 1849; Senate Oct. 28, 1811-21.

HUNTER, William Forrest (W Ohio) Dec. 10, 1808-March 30, 1874; House 1849-53.

HUNTER, William H. (D Ohio) ?-1842; House 1837-39.

HUNTINGTON, Abel (D N.Y.) Feb. 21, 1777-May 18, 1858; House 1833-37.

HUNTINGTON, Benjamin (— Conn.) April 19, 1736-Oct. 16, 1800; House 1789-91; Cont. Cong. 1780-84, 1787-88.

HUNTINGTON, Ebenezer (W Conn.) Dec. 26, 1754-June 17, 1834; House Oct. 11, 1810-11, 1817-19.

HUNTINGTON, Jabez Williams (W Conn.) Nov. 8, 1788-Nov. 1, 1847; House 1829-Aug. 16, 1834; Senate May 4, 1840-Nov. 1, 1847.

HUNTON, Eppa (D Va.) Sept. 24, 1822-Oct. 11, 1908; House 1873-81; Senate May 28, 1892-95.

HUNTSMAN, Adam (JD Tenn.) ?-?; House 1835-37.

HUOT, Joseph Oliva (D N.H.) Aug. 11, 1917-Aug. 5, 1983; House 1965-67.

HURD, Frank Hunt (D Ohio) Dec. 25, 1840-July 10, 1896; House 1875-77, 1879-81, 1883-85.

HURLBUT, Stephen Augustus (R Ill.) Nov. 29, 1815-March 27, 1882; House 1873-77.

HURLEY, Denis Michael (R N.Y.) March 14, 1843-Feb. 26, 1899; House 1895-Feb. 26, 1899.

HUSTED, James William (R N.Y.) March 16, 1870-Jan. 2, 1925; House 1915-23.

HUSTING, Paul Oscar (D Wis.) April 25, 1866-Oct. 21, 1917; Senate 1915-Oct. 21, 1917.

HUTCHESON, Joseph Chappell (D Texas) May 18, 1842-May 25, 1924; House 1893-97.

HUTCHINS, John (cousin of Wells Andrews Hutchins) (R Ohio) July 25, 1812-Nov. 20, 1891; House 1859-63.

HUTCHINS, Waldo (D N.Y.) Sept. 30, 1822-Feb. 8, 1891; House Nov. 4, 1879-85.

HUTCHINS, Wells Andrews (cousin of John Hutchins) (D Ohio) Oct. 8, 1818-Jan. 25, 1895; House 1863-65.

HUTCHINSON, Edward (R Mich.) Oct. 13, 1914-—; House 1963-77.

HUTCHINSON, Elijah Cubberley (R N.J.) Aug. 7, 1855-June 25, 1932; House 1915-23.

HUTCHINSON, John G. (D W. Va.) Feb. 4, 1935-—; House June 10, 1980-81.

HUTTO, Earl Dewitt (D Fla.) May 12, 1926-—; House 1979-—.

HUTTON, John Edward (D Mo.) March 28, 1828-Dec. 28, 1893; House 1885-89.

HUYLER, John (D N.J.) April 9, 1808-Jan. 9, 1870; House 1857-59.

HYDE, DeWitt Stephen (R Md.) March 21, 1909-—; House 1953-59.

HYDE, Henry John (R Ill.) April 18, 1924-—; House 1975-—.

HYDE, Ira Barnes (R Mo.) Jan. 18, 1838-Dec. 6, 1926; House 1873-75.

HYDE, Samuel Clarence (R Wash.) April 22, 1842-March 7, 1922; House 1895-97.

HYMAN, John Adams (R N.C.) July 23, 1840-Sept. 14, 1891; House 1875-77.

HYNEMAN, John M. (D Pa.) April 25, 1771-April 16, 1816; House 1811-Aug. 2, 1813.

HYNES, William Joseph (Ref. R Ark.) March 31, 1843-April 2, 1915; House 1873-75.

I

ICHORD, Richard H. (D Mo.) June 27, 1926-—; House 1961-81.

IGLESIAS, Santiago (formerly Santiago Iglesias Pantin) (Coal. P.R.) Feb. 22, 1872-Dec. 5, 1939; House (Res. Comm.) 1933-Dec. 5, 1939.

IGOE, James Thomas (D Ill.) Oct. 23, 1883-Dec. 2, 1971; House 1927-33.

IGOE, Michael Lambert (D Ill.) April 16, 1885-Aug. 21, 1967; House Jan. 3-June 2, 1935.

IGOE, William Leo (D Mo.) Oct. 19, 1879-April 20, 1953; House 1913-21.

IHRIE, Peter Jr. (JD Pa.) Feb. 3, 1796-March 29, 1871; House Oct. 13, 1829-33.

IKARD, Frank Neville (D Texas) Jan. 30, 1914-—; House Sept. 8, 1951-Dec. 15, 1961.

Biographical Index

IKIRT, George Pierce (D Ohio) Nov. 3, 1852-Feb. 12, 1927; House 1893-95.

ILSLEY, Daniel (D Mass.) May 30, 1740-May 10, 1813; House 1807-09.

IMHOFF, Lawrence E. (D Ohio) Dec. 28, 1895- —; House 1933-39, 1941-43.

IMLAY, James Henderson (— N.J.) Nov. 26, 1764-March 6, 1823; House 1797-1801.

INGALLS, John James (R Kan.) Dec. 29, 1833-Aug. 16, 1900; Senate 1873-91; Pres. pro tempore 1887-91.

INGE, Samuel Williams (nephew of William Marshall Inge) (D Ala.) Feb. 22, 1817-June 10, 1868; House 1847-51.

INGE, William Marshall (uncle of Samuel Williams Inge) (D Tenn.) 1802-46; House 1833-35.

INGERSOLL, Charles Jared (brother of Joseph Reed Ingersoll) (D Pa.) Oct. 3, 1782-May 14, 1862; House 1813-15, 1841-49.

INGERSOLL, Colin Macrae (son of Ralph Isaacs Ingersoll) (D Conn.) March 11, 1819-Sept. 13, 1903; House 1851-55.

INGERSOLL, Ebon Clark (R Ill.) Dec. 12, 1831-May 31, 1879; House May 20, 1864-71.

INGERSOLL, Joseph Reed (brother of Charles Jared Ingersoll) (W Pa.) June 14, 1786-Feb. 20, 1868; House 1835-37, Oct. 12, 1841-49.

INGERSOLL, Ralph Isaacs (father of Colin Macrae Ingersoll) (D Conn.) Feb. 8, 1789-Aug. 26, 1872; House 1825-33.

INGHAM, Samuel (D Conn.) Sept. 5, 1793-Nov. 10, 1881; House 1835-39.

INGHAM, Samuel Delucenna (Jeff. D Pa.) Sept. 16, 1779-June 5, 1860; House 1813-July 6, 1818, Oct. 8, 1822-29; Secy. of the Treasury 1829-31.

INOUYE, Daniel Ken (D Hawaii) Sept. 7, 1924- —; House Aug. 21, 1959-63; Senate 1963- —.

IRBY, John Laurens Manning (great-grandson of Elias Earle) (D S.C.) Sept. 10, 1854-Dec. 9, 1900; Senate 1891-97.

IREDELL, James (D N.C.) Nov. 2, 1788-April 13, 1853; Senate Dec. 15, 1828-31; Gov. 1827-28.

IRELAND, Andrew P. (R Fla.) Aug. 23, 1930- —; House 1977- — (1977-84, Democrat, July 5, 1984- —, Republican).

IRELAND, Clifford Cady (R Ill.) Feb. 14, 1878-May 24, 1930; House 1917-23.

IRION, Alfred Briggs (D La.) Feb. 18, 1833-May 21, 1903; House 1885-87.

IRVIN, Alexander (W Pa.) Jan. 18, 1800-March 20, 1874; House 1847-49.

IRVIN, James (W Pa.) Feb. 18, 1800-Nov. 28, 1862; House 1841-45.

IRVIN, William W. (D Ohio) 1778-March 28, 1842; House 1829-33.

IRVINE, William (— Pa.) Nov. 3, 1741-July 29, 1804; House 1793-95; Cont. Cong. 1786-88.

IRVINE, William (R N.Y.) Feb. 14, 1820-Nov. 12, 1882; House 1859-61.

IRVING, Theodore Leonard (D Mo.) March 24, 1898-March 8, 1962; House 1949-53.

IRVING, William (D N.Y.) Aug. 15, 1766-Nov. 9, 1821; House Jan. 22, 1814-19.

IRWIN, Donald J. (D Conn.) Sept. 7, 1926- —; House 1959-61, 1965-69.

IRWIN, Edward Michael (R Ill.) April 14, 1869-Jan. 30, 1933; House 1925-31.

IRWIN, Harvey Samuel (R Ky.) Dec. 10, 1844-Sept. 3, 1916; House 1901-03.

IRWIN, Jared (D Pa.) Jan. 19, 1768-?; House 1813-17.

IRWIN, Thomas (D Pa.) Feb. 22, 1785-May 14, 1870; House 1829-31.

IRWIN, William Wallace (W Pa.) 1803-Sept. 15, 1856; House 1841-43.

ISACKS, Jacob C. (— Tenn.) ?-?; House 1823-33.

ISACSON, Leo (AL N.Y.) April 20, 1910- —; House Feb. 17, 1948-49.

ITTNER, Anthony Friday (R Mo.) Oct. 8, 1837-Feb. 22, 1931; House 1877-79.

IVERSON, Alfred Sr. (D Ga.) Dec. 3, 1798-March 5, 1873; House 1847-49; Senate 1855-Jan. 28, 1861.

IVES, Irving McNeil (R N.Y.) Jan. 24, 1896-Feb. 24, 1962; Senate 1947-59.

IVES, Willard (D N.Y.) July 7, 1806-April 19, 1896; House 1851-53.

IZAC, Edouard Victor Michel (D Calif.) Dec. 18, 1891- —; House 1937-47.

IZARD, Ralph (— S.C.) Jan. 23, 1742-May 30, 1804; Senate 1789-95; Pres. pro tempore 1794-95; Cont. Cong. 1782-83.

IZLAR, James Ferdinand (D S.C.) Nov. 25, 1832-May 26, 1912; House April 12, 1894-95.

J

JACK, Summers Melville (R Pa.) July 18, 1852-Sept. 16, 1945; House 1899-1903.

JACK, William (D Pa.) July 19, 1788-Feb. 28, 1852; House 1841-43.

JACKSON, Alfred Metcalf (D Kan.) July 14, 1860-June 11, 1924; House 1901-03.

JACKSON, Amos Henry (R Ohio) May 10, 1846-Aug. 30, 1924; House 1903-05.

JACKSON, Andrew (D Tenn.) March 15, 1767-June 8, 1845; House Dec. 5, 1796-97; Senate Sept. 26, 1797-April 1798, 1823-Oct. 14, 1825; Gov. (Florida Terr.) March 10-July 18, 1821; President 1829-37.

JACKSON, David Sherwood (D N.Y.) 1813-Jan. 20, 1872; House 1847-April 19, 1848.

JACKSON, Donald L. (R Calif.) Jan. 23, 1910-May 27, 1981; House 1947-61.

JACKSON, Ebenezer Jr. (W Conn.) Jan. 31, 1796-Aug. 17, 1874; House Dec. 1, 1834-35.

JACKSON, Edward Brake (son of George Jackson, brother of John George Jackson) (D Va.) Jan. 25, 1793-Sept. 8, 1826; House Oct. 23, 1820-23.

JACKSON, Fred Schuyler (R Kan.) April 19, 1868-Nov. 21, 1931; House 1911-13.

JACKSON, George (father of John George Jackson and Edward Brake Jackson) (— Va.) Jan. 9, 1757-May 17, 1831; House 1795-97, 1799-1803.

JACKSON, Henry Martin (D Wash.) May 31, 1912-Sept. 1, 1983; House 1941-53; Senate 1953-Sept. 1, 1983; Chrmn. Dem. Nat. Comm. 1960-61.

JACKSON, Howell Edmunds (D Tenn.) April 8, 1832-Aug. 8, 1895; Senate 1881-April 14, 1886; Assoc. Justice Supreme Court 1894-95.

JACKSON, Jabez Young (son of Senator James Jackson, uncle of Representative James Jackson) (UD Ga.) July 1790-?; House Oct. 5, 1835-39.

JACKSON, James (father of Jabez Young Jackson, grandfather of the following) (— Ga.) Sept. 21, 1757-March 19, 1806; House 1789-91; Senate 1793-95, 1801-March 19, 1806; Gov. 1798-1801.

JACKSON, James (grandson of the preceding, nephew of Jabez Young Jackson) (D Ga.) Oct. 18, 1819-Jan. 13, 1887; House 1857-Jan. 23, 1861.

JACKSON, James Monroe (cousin of William Thomas Bland) (D W.Va.) Dec. 3, 1825-Feb. 14, 1901; House 1889-Feb. 3, 1890.

JACKSON, James Streshley (U Ky.) Sept. 27, 1823-Oct. 8, 1862; House March 4-Dec. 13, 1861.

JACKSON, John George (son of George Jackson, brother of Edward Brake Jackson, grandfather of William Thomas Bland) (D Va.) Sept. 22, 1777-March 28, 1825; House 1803-Sept. 28, 1810, 1813-17.

JACKSON, Joseph Webber (D Ga.) Dec. 6, 1796-Sept. 29, 1854; House March 4, 1850-53.

JACKSON, Oscar Lawrence (R Pa.) Sept. 2, 1840-Feb. 16, 1920; House 1885-89.

JACKSON, Richard Jr. (F R.I.) July 3, 1764-April 18, 1838; House Nov. 11, 1808-15.

JACKSON, Samuel Dillon (D Ind.) May 28, 1895-March 8, 1951; Senate Jan. 28-Nov. 13, 1944.

JACKSON, Thomas Birdsall (D N.Y.) March 24, 1797-April 23, 1881; House 1837-41.

JACKSON, William (W Mass.) Sept. 2, 1783-Feb. 26, 1855; House 1833-37.

JACKSON, William Humphreys (father of William Purnell Jackson) (R Md.) Oct. 15, 1839-April 3, 1915; House 1901-05, 1907-09.

JACKSON, William Purnell (son of William Humphreys Jackson) (R Md.) Jan. 11, 1868-March 7, 1939; Senate Nov. 29, 1912-Jan. 28, 1914.

JACKSON, William Terry (W N.Y.) Dec. 29, 1794-Sept. 15, 1882; House 1849-51.

JACOBS, Andrew Sr. (father of Andrew Jacobs Jr.) (D Ind.) Feb. 22, 1906-—; House 1949-51.

JACOBS, Andrew Jr. (son of Andrew Jacobs Sr., husband of Martha Elizabeth Keys) (D Ind.) Feb. 24, 1932-—; House 1965-73, 1975-—.

JACOBS, Ferris Jr. (R N.Y.) March 20, 1836-Aug. 30, 1886; House 1881-83.

JACOBS, Israel (— Pa.) June 9, 1726-about Dec. 10, 1796; House 1791-93.

JACOBS, Orange (R Wash.) May 2, 1827-May 21, 1914; House (Terr. Del.) 1875-79.

JACOBSEN, Bernhard Martin (father of William Sebastian Jacobsen) (D Iowa) March 26, 1862-June 30, 1936; House 1931-June 30, 1936.

JACOBSEN, William Sebastian (son of Bernhard Martin Jacobsen) (D Iowa) Jan. 15, 1887-April 10, 1955; House 1937-43.

JACOBSTEIN, Meyer (D N.Y.) Jan. 25, 1880-April 18, 1963; House 1923-29.

JACOWAY, Henderson Madison (D Ark.) Nov. 7, 1870-Aug. 4, 1947; House 1911-23.

JADWIN, Cornelius Comegys (R Pa.) March 27, 1835-Aug. 17, 1913; House 1881-83.

JAMES, Addison Davis (grandfather of John Albert Whitaker) (R Ky.) Feb. 27, 1850-June 10, 1947; House 1907-09.

JAMES, Amaziah Bailey (R N.Y.) July 1, 1812-July 6, 1883; House 1877-81.

JAMES, Benjamin Franklin (R Pa.) Aug. 1, 1885-Jan. 26, 1961; House 1949-59.

JAMES, Charles Tillinghast (Protect.TD R.I.) Sept. 15, 1805-Oct. 17, 1862; Senate 1851-57.

JAMES, Darwin Rush (R N.Y.) May 14, 1834-Nov. 19, 1908; House 1883-87.

JAMES, Francis (W Pa.) April 4, 1799-Jan. 4, 1886; House 1839-41.

JAMES, Hinton (D N.C.) April 24, 1884-Nov. 3, 1948; House Nov. 4, 1930-31.

JAMES, Ollie Murray (D Ky.) July 27, 1871-Aug. 28, 1918; House 1903-13; Senate 1913-Aug. 28, 1918.

JAMES, Rorer Abraham (D Va.) March 1, 1859-Aug. 6, 1921; House June 15, 1920-Aug. 6, 1921.

JAMES, William Francis (Frank) (R Mich.) May 23, 1873-Nov. 17, 1945; House 1915-35.

JAMESON, John (D Mo.) March 6, 1802-Jan. 24, 1857; House Dec. 12, 1839-41, 1843-45, 1847-49.

JAMIESON, William Darius (D Iowa) Nov. 9, 1873-Nov. 18, 1949; House 1909-11.

JANES, Henry Fisk (W/AM Vt.) Oct. 10, 1792-June 6, 1879; House Dec. 2, 1834-37.

JARMAN, John (R Okla.) July 17, 1915-Jan. 15, 1982; House 1951-77 (1951-Jan. 24, 1975 Democrat, Jan. 24, 1975-77 Republican).

JARMAN, Pete (D Ala.) Oct. 31, 1892-Feb. 17, 1955; House 1937-49.

JARNAGIN, Spencer (W Tenn.) 1792-June 25, 1853; Senate Oct. 17, 1843-47.

JARRETT, Benjamin (R Pa.) July 18, 1881-July 20, 1944; House 1937-43.

JARRETT, William Paul (D Hawaii) Aug. 22, 1877-Nov. 10, 1929; House (Terr. Del.) 1923-27.

JARVIS, Leonard (D Maine) Oct. 19, 1781-Oct. 18, 1854; House 1829-37.

JARVIS, Thomas Jordan (D N.C.) Jan. 18, 1836-June 17, 1915; Senate April 19, 1894-Jan. 23, 1895; Gov. 1879-85.

JAVITS, Jacob Koppel (R N.Y.) May 18, 1904-—; House 1947-Dec. 31, 1954; Senate Jan. 9, 1957-81.

JAYNE, William (— Dakota) Oct. 8, 1826-March 20, 1916; House (Terr. Del.) 1863-June 17, 1864; Gov. 1861-63.

JEFFERIS, Albert Webb (R Neb.) Dec. 7, 1868-Sept. 14, 1942; House 1919-23.

JEFFERS, Lamar (D Ala.) April 16, 1888-June 1, 1983; House June 7, 1921-35.

JEFFORDS, Elza (R Miss.) May 23, 1826-March 19, 1885; House 1883-85.

JEFFORDS, James Merrill (R Vt.) May 11, 1934-—; House 1975-—.

JEFFREY, Harry Palmer (R Ohio) Dec. 26, 1901-—; House 1943-45.

JEFFRIES, James Edmund (R Kan.) June 1, 1925-—; House 1979-83.

JEFFRIES, Walter Sooy (R N.J.) Oct. 16, 1893-Oct. 11, 1954; House 1939-41.

JENCKES, Thomas Allen (R R.I.) Nov. 2, 1818-Nov. 4, 1875; House 1863-71.

JENCKES, Virginia Ellis (D Ind.) Nov. 6, 1877-Jan. 9, 1975; House 1933-39.

JENIFER, Daniel (NR Md.) April 15, 1791-Dec. 18, 1855; House 1831-33, 1835-41.

JENISON, Edward Halsey (R Ill.) July 27, 1907-—; House 1947-53.

JENKINS, Albert Gallatin (D Va.) Nov. 10, 1830-May 21, 1864; House 1857-61.

JENKINS, Edgar Lanier (D Ga.) Jan. 4, 1933-—; House 1977-—.

JENKINS, John James (R Wis.) Aug. 24, 1843-June 8, 1911; House 1895-1909.

JENKINS, Lemuel (D N.Y.) Oct. 20, 1789-Aug. 18, 1862; House 1823-25.

JENKINS, Mitchell (R Pa.) Jan. 24, 1896-Sept. 15, 1977; House 1947-49.

JENKINS, Robert (— Pa.) July 10, 1769-April 18, 1848; House 1807-11.

JENKINS, Thomas Albert (R Ohio) Oct. 28, 1880-Dec. 21, 1959; House 1925-59.

JENKINS, Timothy (D N.Y.) Jan. 29, 1799-Dec. 24, 1859; House 1845-49, 1851-53.

JENKS, Arthur Byron (R N.H.) Oct. 15, 1866-Dec. 14, 1947; House 1937-June 9, 1938, 1939-43.

JENKS, George Augustus (D Pa.) March 26, 1836-Feb. 10, 1908; House 1875-77.

JENKS, Michael Hutchinson (W Pa.) May 21, 1795-Oct. 16, 1867; House 1843-45.

JENNER, William Ezra (R Ind.) July 21, 1908-—; Senate Nov. 14, 1944-45, 1947-59.

JENNESS, Benning Wentworth (D N.H.) July 14, 1806-Nov. 16, 1879; Senate Dec. 1, 1845-June 13, 1846.

JENNINGS, David (— Ohio) 1787-1834; House 1825-May 25, 1826.

JENNINGS, John Jr. (R Tenn.) June 6, 1880-Feb. 27, 1956; House Dec. 30, 1939-51.

JENNINGS, Jonathan (D Ind.) 1784-July 26, 1834; House (Terr. Del.) Nov. 27, 1809-Dec. 11, 1816, (Rep.) Dec. 2, 1822-31; Gov. 1816-22.

JENNINGS, William Pat (D Va.) Aug. 20, 1919-—; House 1955-67.

JENRETTE, John Wilson Jr. (D S.C.) May 19, 1936-—; House 1975-Dec. 10, 1980.

JENSEN, Benton Franklin (Ben) (R Iowa) Dec. 16, 1892-Feb. 5, 1970; House 1939-65.

JEPSEN, Roger William (R Iowa) Dec. 23, 1928-—; Senate 1979-85.

JETT, Thomas Marion (D Ill.) May 1, 1862-Jan. 10, 1939; House 1897-1903.

JEWETT, Daniel Tarbox (R Mo.) Sept. 14, 1807-Oct. 7, 1906; Senate Dec. 19, 1870-Jan. 20, 1871.

JEWETT, Freeborn Garrettson (JD N.Y.) Aug. 4, 1791-Jan. 27, 1858; House 1831-33.

JEWETT, Hugh Judge (brother of Joshua Husband Jewett) (D Ohio) July 1, 1817-March 6, 1898; House 1873-June 23, 1874.

JEWETT, Joshua Husband (brother of Hugh Judge Jewett) (D Ky.) Sept. 30, 1815-July 14, 1861; House 1855-59.

JEWETT, Luther (F Vt.) Dec. 24, 1772-March 8, 1860; House 1815-17.

JOELSON, Charles S. (D N.J.) Jan. 27, 1916-—; House 1961-Sept. 4, 1969.

JOHANSEN, August Edgar (R Mich.) July 21, 1905-—; House 1955-65.

JOHNS, Joshua Leroy (R Wis.) Feb. 27, 1881-March 16, 1947; House 1939-43.

JOHNS, Kensey Jr. (F Del.) Dec. 10, 1791-March 28, 1857; House Oct. 2, 1827-31.

JOHNSON, Adna Romulus (R Ohio) Dec. 14, 1860-June 11, 1938; House 1909-11.

JOHNSON, Albert (R Wash.) March 5, 1869-Jan. 17, 1957; House 1913-33.

Biographical Index

JOHNSON, Albert Walter (R Pa.) April 17, 1906- —; House Nov. 5, 1963-77.

JOHNSON, Andrew (R Tenn.) Dec. 29, 1808-July 31, 1875; House 1843-53; Senate Oct. 8, 1857-62, March 4-July 31, 1875; Gov. 1853-57; Vice Pres. March 4-April 15, 1865; President April 15, 1865-69 (1843-62 Democrat, 1865-69 Republican).

JOHNSON, Anton Joseph (R Ill.) Oct. 20, 1878-April 16, 1958; House 1939-49.

JOHNSON, Ben (D Ky.) May 20, 1858-June 4, 1950; House 1907-27.

JOHNSON, Byron Lindberg (D Colo.) Oct. 12, 1917- —; House 1959-61.

JOHNSON, Calvin Dean (R Ill.) Nov. 22, 1898- —; House 1943-45.

JOHNSON, Cave (D Tenn.) Jan. 11, 1793-Nov. 23, 1866; House 1829-37, 1839-45; Postmaster Gen. 1845-49.

JOHNSON, Charles (— N.Y.) ?-July 23, 1802; House 1801-July 23, 1802.

JOHNSON, Charles Fletcher (D Maine) Feb. 14, 1859-Feb. 15, 1930; Senate 1911-17.

JOHNSON, Dewey William (FL Minn.) March 14, 1899-Sept. 18, 1941; House 1937-39.

JOHNSON, Edwin Carl (D Colo.) Jan. 1, 1884-May 30, 1970; Senate 1937-55; Gov. 1933-37, 1955-57.

JOHNSON, Edwin Stockton (D S.D.) Feb. 26, 1857-July 19, 1933; Senate 1915-21.

JOHNSON, Francis (Ad.D Ky.) June 19, 1776-May 16, 1842; House Nov. 13, 1820-27.

JOHNSON, Frederick Avery (— N.Y.) Jan. 2, 1833-July 17, 1893; House 1883-87.

JOHNSON, Fred Gustus (R Neb.) Oct. 16, 1876-April 30, 1951; House 1929-31.

JOHNSON, George William (D W.Va.) Nov. 10, 1869-Feb. 24, 1944; House 1923-25, 1933-43.

JOHNSON, Glen Dale (D Okla.) Sept. 11, 1911-Feb. 10, 1983; House 1947-49.

JOHNSON, Grove Lawrence (father of Hiram Warren Johnson) (R Calif.) March 27, 1841-Feb. 1, 1926; House 1895-97.

JOHNSON, Harold Terry (D Calif.) Dec. 2, 1907- —; House 1959-81.

JOHNSON, Harvey Hull (D Ohio) Sept. 7, 1808-Feb. 4, 1896; House 1853-55.

JOHNSON, Henry (W La.) Sept. 14, 1783-Sept. 4, 1864; Senate Jan. 12, 1818-May 27, 1824, Feb. 12, 1844-49; House Sept. 25, 1834-39; Gov. 1824-28.

JOHNSON, Henry Underwood (R Ind.) Oct. 28, 1850-June 4, 1939; House 1891-99.

JOHNSON, Herschel Vespasian (D Ga.) Sept. 18, 1812-Aug. 16, 1880; Senate Feb. 4, 1848-49; Gov. 1853-57.

JOHNSON, Hiram Warren (son of Grove Lawrence Johnson) (R Calif.) Sept. 2, 1866-Aug. 6, 1945; Senate March 16, 1917-Aug. 6, 1945; Gov. 1911-17.

JOHNSON, Jacob (R Utah) Nov. 1, 1847-Aug. 15, 1925; House 1913-15.

JOHNSON, James (D Va.) ?-Dec. 7, 1825; House 1813-Feb. 1, 1820.

JOHNSON, James (brother of Richard Mentor Johnson and John Telemachus Johnson, uncle of Robert Ward Johnson) (D Ky.) Jan. 1, 1774-Aug. 14, 1826; House 1825-Aug. 14, 1826.

JOHNSON, James (U Ga.) Feb. 12, 1811-Nov. 20, 1891; House 1851-53; Provisional Gov. 1865.

JOHNSON, James Augustus (D Calif.) May 16, 1829-May 11, 1896; House 1867-71.

JOHNSON, James Hutchins (— N.H.) June 3, 1802-Sept. 2, 1887; House 1845-49.

JOHNSON, James Leeper (W Ky.) Oct. 30, 1818-Feb. 12, 1877; House 1849-51.

JOHNSON, James Paul (R Colo.) June 2, 1930- —; House 1973-81.

JOHNSON, Jed Joseph (father of Jed Johnson Jr.) (D Okla.) July 31, 1888-May 8, 1963; House 1927-47.

JOHNSON, Jed Jr. (son of Jed Joseph Johnson) (D Okla.) Dec. 17, 1939- —; House 1965-67.

JOHNSON, Jeromus (D N.Y.) Nov. 2, 1775-Sept. 7, 1846; House 1825-29.

JOHNSON, John (I Ohio) 1805-Feb. 5, 1867; House 1851-53.

JOHNSON, John Telemachus (brother of James Johnson of Kentucky and Richard Mentor Johnson, uncle of Robert Ward Johnson) (JD Ky.) Oct. 5, 1788-Dec. 17, 1856; House 1821-25.

JOHNSON, Joseph (uncle of Waldo Porter Johnson) (D Va.) Dec. 19, 1785-Feb. 27, 1877; House 1823-27, Jan. 21-March 3, 1833, 1835-41, 1845-47; Gov. 1852-56.

JOHNSON, Joseph Travis (D S.C.) Feb. 28, 1858-May 8, 1919; House 1901-April 19, 1915.

JOHNSON, Justin Leroy (R Calif.) April 8, 1888-March 26, 1961; House 1943-57.

JOHNSON, Lester Roland (D Wis.) June 16, 1901-July 24, 1975; House Oct. 13, 1953-65.

JOHNSON, Luther Alexander (D Texas) Oct. 29, 1875-June 6, 1965; House 1923-July 17, 1946.

JOHNSON, Lyndon Baines (D Texas) Aug. 27, 1908-Jan. 22, 1973; House April 10, 1937-49; Senate 1949-61; Senate majority leader 1955-1961; Vice Pres. 1961-Nov. 22, 1963; President Nov. 22, 1963-69.

JOHNSON, Magnus (FL Minn.) Sept. 19, 1871-Sept. 13, 1936; Senate July 16, 1923-25; House 1933-35.

JOHNSON, Martin Nelson (R N.D.) March 3, 1850-Oct. 21, 1909; House 1891-99, Senate March 4-Oct. 21, 1909.

JOHNSON, Nancy Lee (R Conn.) Jan. 5, 1935- —; House 1983- —.

JOHNSON, Noadiah (D N.Y.) 1795-April 4, 1839; House 1833-35.

JOHNSON, Noble Jacob (R Ind.) Aug. 23, 1887-March 17, 1968; House 1925-31, 1939-July 1, 1948.

JOHNSON, Paul Burney (D Miss.) March 23, 1880-Dec. 26, 1943; House 1919-23; Gov. 1940-43.

JOHNSON, Perley Brown (W Ohio) Sept. 8, 1798-Feb. 9, 1870; House 1843-45.

JOHNSON, Philip (R Pa.) Jan. 17, 1818-Jan. 29, 1867; House 1861-Jan. 29, 1867.

JOHNSON, Reverdy (brother-in-law of Thomas Fielder Bowie) (D Md.) May 21, 1796-Feb. 10, 1876; Senate 1845-March 7, 1849, 1863-July 10, 1868 (1845-49 Whig, 1863-68 Democrat); Atty Gen. 1849-50.

JOHNSON, Richard Mentor (brother of James Johnson of Kentucky and John Telemachus Johnson, uncle of Robert Ward Johnson) (D Ky.) Oct. 17, 1781-Nov. 19, 1850; House 1807-19, 1829-37; Senate Dec. 10, 1819-29; Vice Pres. 1837-41 (1807-19 Democrat, 1819-37 Jackson Democrat, 1837-41 Democrat).

JOHNSON, Robert Davis (D Mo.) Aug. 12, 1883-Oct. 23, 1961; House Sept. 29, 1931-33.

JOHNSON, Robert Ward (nephew of James Johnson of Kentucky, John Telemachus Johnson and Richard Mentor Johnson) (D Ark.) July 22, 1814-July 26, 1879; House 1847-53; Senate July 6, 1853-61.

JOHNSON, Royal Cleaves (R S.D.) Oct. 3, 1882-Aug. 2, 1939; House 1915-33.

JOHNSON, Thomas F. (D Md.) June 26, 1909- —; House 1959-63.

JOHNSON, Tom Loftin (D Ohio) July 18, 1854-April 10, 1911; House 1891-95.

JOHNSON, Waldo Porter (nephew of Joseph Johnson) (D Mo.) Sept. 16, 1817-Aug. 14, 1885; Senate March 17, 1861-Jan. 10, 1862.

JOHNSON, William Cost (W Md.) Jan. 14, 1806-April 14, 1860; House 1833-35, 1837-43.

JOHNSON, William Richard (R Ill.) May 15, 1875-Jan. 2, 1938; House 1925-33.

JOHNSON, William Samuel (— Conn.) Oct. 7, 1727-Nov. 14, 1819; Senate 1789-March 4, 1791; Cont. Cong. 1784-87.

JOHNSON, William Ward (R Calif.) March 9, 1892-June 8, 1963; House 1941-45.

JOHNSTON, Charles (W N.Y.) Feb. 14, 1793-Sept. 1, 1845; House 1839-41.

JOHNSTON, Charles Clement (brother of Joseph Eggleston Johnston, uncle of John Warfield Johnston) (SRD Va.) April 30, 1795-June 17, 1832; House 1831-June 17, 1832.

JOHNSTON, David Emmons (D W.Va.) April 10, 1845-July 7, 1917; House 1899-1901.

JOHNSTON, James Thomas (R Ind.) Jan. 19, 1839-July 19, 1904; House 1885-89.

JOHNSTON, John Bennett Jr. (D La.) June 10, 1932- —; Senate Nov. 14, 1972- —.

JOHNSTON, John Brown (D N.Y.) July 10, 1882-Jan. 11, 1960; House 1919-21.

JOHNSTON, John Warfield (uncle of Henry Bowen, nephew of Charles Clement Johnston and Joseph Eggleston Johnston) (C Va.) Sept. 9, 1818-Feb. 27, 1889; Senate Jan. 26, 1870-March 3, 1871, March 15, 1871-83.

JOHNSTON, Joseph Eggleston (brother of Charles Clement Johnston, uncle of John Warfield Johnston) (D Va.) Feb. 3, 1807-March 21, 1891; House 1879-81.

JOHNSTON, Joseph Forney (D Ala.) March 23, 1843-Aug. 8, 1913; Senate Aug. 6 1907-Aug. 8, 1913; Gov. 1896-1900.

JOHNSTON, Josiah Stoddard (D La.) Nov. 24, 1784-May 19, 1833; House 1821-23; Senate Jan. 15, 1824-May 19, 1833.

JOHNSTON, Olin DeWitt Talmadge (D S.C.) Nov. 18, 1896-April 18, 1965; Senate 1945-April 18, 1965; Gov. 1935-39, 1943-45.

JOHNSTON, Rienzi Melville (cousin of Benjamin Edward Russell) (D Texas) Sept. 9, 1849-Feb. 28, 1926; Senate Jan. 4-Feb. 2, 1913.

JOHNSTON, Rowland Louis (R Mo.) April 23, 1872-Sept. 22, 1939; House 1929-31.

JOHNSTON, Samuel (F N.C.) Dec. 15, 1733-Aug. 18, 1816; Senate Nov. 27, 1789-93; Cont. Cong. 1780-82.

JOHNSTON, Thomas Dillard (D N.C.) April 1, 1840-June 22, 1902; House 1885-89.

JOHNSTON, W. Eugene (R N.C.) March 3, 1936- —; House 1981-83.

JOHNSTON, William (D Ohio) 1819-May 1, 1866; House 1863-65.

JOHNSTONE, George (D S.C.) April 18, 1846-March 8, 1921; House 1891-93.

JOLLEY, John Lawlor (R S.D.) July 14, 1840-Dec. 14, 1926; House Dec. 7, 1891-93.

JONAS, Benjamin Franklin (D La.) July 19, 1834-Dec. 21, 1911; Senate 1879-85.

JONAS, Charles Andrew (father of Charles Raper Jonas) (R N.C.) Aug. 14, 1876-May 25, 1955; House 1929-31.

JONAS, Charles Raper (son of Charles Andrew Jonas) (R N.C.) Dec. 9, 1904- —; House 1953-73.

JONAS, Edgar Allan (R Ill.) Oct. 14, 1885-Nov. 14, 1965; House 1949-55.

JONES, Alexander Hamilton (R N.C.) July 21, 1822-Jan. 29, 1901; House July 6, 1868-71.

JONES, Andrieus Aristieus (D N.M.) May 16, 1862-Dec. 20, 1927; Senate 1917-Dec. 20, 1927.

JONES, Benjamin (D Ohio) April 13, 1787-April 24, 1861; House 1833-37.

JONES, Burr W. (D Wis.) March 9, 1846-Jan. 7, 1935; House 1883-85.

JONES, Charles William (D Fla.) Dec. 24, 1834-Oct. 11, 1897; Senate 1875-87.

JONES, Daniel Terryll (D N.Y.) Aug. 17, 1800-March 29, 1861; House 1851-55.

JONES, Ed (D Tenn.) April 20, 1912- —; House March 25, 1969- —.

JONES, Evan John (R Pa.) Oct. 23, 1872-Jan. 9, 1952; House 1919-23.

JONES, Francis (— Tenn.) ?-?; House 1817-23.

JONES, Frank (D N.H.) Sept. 15, 1832-Oct. 2, 1902; House 1875-79.

JONES, George (— Ga.) Feb. 25, 1766-Nov. 13, 1838; Senate Aug. 27-Nov. 7, 1807.

JONES, George Wallace (— Mich./Wis./Iowa) April 12, 1804-July 22, 1896; House (Terr. Del.) 1835-April 1836 (Mich.), April 1836-Jan. 14, 1839 (Wis.); Senate Dec. 7, 1848-59 (Iowa).

JONES, George Washington (D Tenn.) March 15, 1806-Nov. 14, 1884; House 1843-59.

JONES, George Washington (G Texas) Sept. 5, 1828-July 11, 1903; House 1879-83.

JONES, Hamilton Chamberlain (D N.C.) Sept. 26, 1884-Aug. 10, 1957; House 1947-53.

JONES, Homer Raymond (R Wash.) Sept. 3, 1893-Nov. 26, 1970; House 1947-49.

JONES, Isaac Dashiell (W Md.) Nov. 1, 1806-July 5, 1893; House 1841-43.

JONES, James (R Ga.) ?-Jan. 11, 1801; House 1799-Jan. 11, 1801.

JONES, James (D Va.) Dec. 11, 1772-April 25, 1848; House 1819-23.

JONES, James Chamberlain (W Tenn.) April 20, 1809-Oct. 29, 1859; Senate 1851-57; Gov. 1841-45.

JONES, James Henry (D Texas) Sept. 13, 1830-March 22, 1904; House 1883-87.

JONES, James Kimbrough (D Ark.) Sept. 29, 1839-June 1, 1908; House 1881-Feb. 19, 1885; Senate March 4, 1885-1903; Chrmn. Dem. Nat. Comm. 1896-1904.

JONES, James Robert (D Okla.) May 5, 1939- —; House 1973- —.

JONES, James Taylor (D Ala.) July 20, 1832-Feb. 15, 1895; House 1877-79, Dec. 3, 1883-89.

JONES, Jehu Glancy (D Pa.) Oct. 7, 1811-March 24, 1878; House 1851-53, Feb. 4, 1854-Oct. 30, 1858.

JONES, John James (D Ga.) Nov. 13, 1824-Oct. 19, 1898; House 1859-Jan. 23, 1861.

JONES, John Marvin (D Texas) Feb. 26, 1886-March 4, 1976; House 1917-Nov. 20, 1940.

JONES, John Percival (R Nev.) Jan. 27, 1829-Nov. 27, 1912; Senate 1873-1903.

JONES, John Sills (R Ohio) Feb. 12, 1836-April 11, 1903; House 1877-79.

JONES, John William (W Ga.) April 14, 1806-April 27, 1871; House 1847-49.

JONES, John Winston (D Va.) Nov. 22, 1791-Jan. 29, 1848; House 1835-45; Speaker 1843-45.

JONES, Morgan (D N.Y.) Feb. 26, 1830-July 13, 1894; House 1865-67.

JONES, Nathaniel (D N.Y.) Feb. 17, 1788-July 20, 1866; House 1837-41.

JONES, Owen (D Pa.) Dec. 29, 1819-Dec. 25, 1878; House 1857-59.

JONES, Paul Caruthers (D Mo.) March 12, 1901-Feb. 10, 1981; House Nov. 2, 1948-69.

JONES, Phineas (R N.J.) April 18, 1819-April 19, 1884; House 1881-83.

JONES, Robert Emmett Jr. (D Ala.) June 12, 1912- —; House Jan. 28, 1947-77.

JONES, Robert Franklin (F Ohio) June 25, 1907-June 22, 1968; House 1939-Sept. 2, 1947.

JONES, Roland (D La.) Nov. 18, 1813-Feb. 5, 1869; House 1853-55.

JONES, Seaborn (D Ga.) Feb. 1, 1788-March 18, 1864; House 1833-35; 1845-47.

JONES, Thomas Laurens (D Ky.) Jan. 22, 1819-June 20, 1887; House 1867-71, 1875-77.

JONES, Walter (D Va.) Dec. 18, 1745-Dec. 31, 1815; House 1797-99, 1803-11.

JONES, Walter B. (D N.C.) Aug. 19, 1913- —; House Feb. 5, 1966- —.

JONES, Wesley Livsey (R Wash.) Oct. 9, 1863-Nov. 19, 1932; House 1899-1909; Senate 1909-Nov. 19, 1932.

JONES, William (D Pa.) 1760-Sept. 6, 1831; House 1801-03; Secy. of the Navy 1813-14.

JONES, William Atkinson (D Va.) March 21, 1849-April 17, 1918; House 1891-April 17, 1918.

JONES, William Carey (FSil. R Wash.) April 5, 1855-June 14, 1927; House 1897-99.

JONES, William Theopilus (R Wyo.) Feb. 20, 1842-Oct. 9, 1882; House (Terr. Del.) 1871-73.

JONES, Woodrow Wilson (D N.C.) Jan. 26, 1914- —; House Nov. 7, 1950-57.

JONKMAN, Bartel John (R Mich.) April 28, 1884-June 13, 1955; House Feb. 19, 1940-49.

JORDAN, Barbara Charline (D Texas) Feb. 21, 1936- —; House 1973-79.

JORDAN, Benjamin Everett (D N.C.) Sept. 8, 1896-March 15, 1974; Senate April 19, 1958-73.

JORDAN, Isaac M. (D Ohio) May 5, 1835-Dec. 3, 1890; House 1883-85.

JORDAN, Leonard Beck (R Idaho) May 15, 1899-June 30, 1983; Senate Aug. 6, 1962-73; Gov. 1951-55.

JORDEN, Edwin James (R Pa.) Aug. 30, 1863-Sept. 7, 1903; House Feb. 23-March 4, 1895.

JORGENSEN, Joseph (R Va.) Feb. 11, 1844-Jan. 21, 1888; House 1877-83.

JOSEPH, Antonio (D N.M.) Aug. 25, 1846-April 19, 1910; House (Terr. Del.) 1885-95.

JOST, Henry Lee (D Mo.) Dec. 6, 1873-July 13, 1950; House 1923-25.

JOY, Charles Frederick (R Mo.) Dec. 11, 1849-April 13, 1921; House 1893-April 3, 1894, 1895-1903.

JOYCE, Charles Herbert (R Vt.) Jan. 30, 1830-Nov. 22, 1916; House 1875-83.

JOYCE, James (R Ohio) July 2, 1870-March 25, 1931; House 1909-11.

JUDD, Norman Buel (grandfather of Norman Judd Gould) (R Ill.) Jan. 10, 1815-Nov. 10, 1878; House 1867-71.

JUDD, Walter Henry (R Minn.) Sept. 25, 1898--; House 1943-63.

JUDSON, Andrew Thompson (D Conn.) Nov. 29, 1784-March 17, 1853; House 1835-July 4, 1836.

JULIAN, George Washington (R Ind.) May 5, 1817-July 7, 1899; House 1849-51, 1861-71 (1849-51 Free-Soiler, 1861-71 Republican).

JUNKIN, Benjamin Franklin (R Pa.) Nov. 12, 1822-Oct. 9, 1908; House 1859-61.

JUUL, Niels (R Ill.) April 27, 1859-Dec. 4, 1929; House 1917-21.

K

KADING, Charles August (R Wis.) Jan. 14, 1874-June 19, 1956; House 1927-33.

KAHN, Florence Prag (widow of Julius Kahn) (R Calif.) Nov. 9, 1868-Nov. 16, 1948; House 1925-37.

KAHN, Julius (husband of Florence Prag Kahn) (R Calif.) Feb. 28, 1861-Dec. 18, 1924; House 1899-1903, 1905-Dec. 18, 1924.

KALANIANAOLE, Jonah Kuhio (R Hawaii) March 26, 1871-Jan. 7, 1922; House (Terr. Del.) 1903-Jan. 7, 1922.

KALBFLEISCH, Martin (D N.Y.) Feb. 8, 1804-Feb. 12, 1873; House 1863-65.

KANE, Elias Kent (D Ill.) June 7, 1794-Dec. 12, 1835; Senate 1825-Dec. 12, 1835.

KANE, Nicholas Thomas (D N.Y.) Sept. 12, 1846-Sept. 14, 1887; House March 4-Sept. 14, 1887.

KANJORSKI, Paul E. (D Pa.) April 2, 1937--; House 1985--.

KAPTUR, Marcia Carloyn (D Ohio) June 17, 1946--; House 1983--.

KARCH, Charles Adam (D Ill.) March 17, 1875-Nov. 6, 1932; House 1931-Nov. 6, 1932.

KARST, Raymond Willard (D Mo.) Dec. 31, 1902--; House 1949-51.

KARSTEN, Frank Melvin (D Mo.) Jan. 7, 1913--; House 1947-69.

KARTH, Joseph Edward (D Minn.) Aug. 26, 1922--; House 1959-77.

KASEM, George Albert (D Calif.) April 6, 1919--; House 1959-61.

KASICH, John R. (R Ohio) May 13, 1952--; House 1983--.

KASSEBAUM, Nancy Landon (R Kan.) July 29, 1932--; Senate Dec. 23, 1978--.

KASSON, John Adam (R Iowa) Jan. 11, 1822-May 19, 1910; House 1863-67, 1873-77, 1881-July 13, 1884.

KASTEN, Robert Walter Jr. (R Wis.) June 19, 1942--; House 1975-79; Senate 1981--.

KASTENMEIER, Robert William (D Wis.) Jan. 24, 1924--; House 1959--.

KAUFMAN, David Spangler (D Texas) Dec. 18, 1813-Jan. 31, 1851; House March 30, 1846-Jan. 31, 1851.

KAVANAGH, Edward (D Maine) April 27, 1795-Jan. 20, 1844; House 1831-35; Gov. 1843-44.

KAVANAUGH, William Marmaduke (D Ark.) March 3, 1866-Feb. 21, 1915; Senate Jan. 30-March 3, 1913.

KAYNOR, William Kirk (R Mass.) Nov. 29, 1884-Dec. 20, 1929; House March 4-Dec. 20, 1929.

KAZEN, Abraham Jr. (D Texas) Jan. 17, 1919--; House 1967-85.

KEAN, Hamilton Fish (father of Robert Winthrop Kean, brother of John Kean) (R N.J.) Feb. 27, 1862-Dec. 27, 1941; Senate 1929-35.

KEAN, John (brother of Hamilton Fish Kean, uncle of Robert Winthrop Kean) (R N.J.) Dec. 4, 1852-Nov. 4, 1914; House 1883-85, 1887-89; Senate 1899-1911.

KEAN, Robert Winthrop (son of Hamilton Fish Kean, nephew of John Kean) (R N.J.) Sept. 28, 1893-Sept. 22, 1980; House 1939-59.

KEARNEY, Bernard William (R N.Y.) May 23, 1889-June 3, 1976; House 1943-59.

KEARNS, Carroll Dudley (R Pa.) May 7, 1900-June 11, 1976; House 1947-63.

KEARNS, Charles Cyrus (R Ohio) Feb. 11, 1869-Dec. 17, 1931; House 1915-31.

KEARNS, Thomas (R Utah) April 11, 1862-Oct. 18, 1918; Senate Jan. 23, 1901-05.

KEATING, Edward (D Colo.) July 9, 1875-March 18, 1965; House 1913-19.

KEATING, Kenneth Barnard (R N.Y.) May 18, 1900-May 5, 1975; House 1947-59; Senate 1959-65.

KEATING, William John (R Ohio) March 30, 1927--; House 1971-Jan. 3, 1974.

KEE, James (son of John and Maude Elizabeth Kee) (D W.Va.) April 15, 1917--; House 1965-73.

KEE, John (husband of Maude Elizabeth Kee, father of James Kee) (D W.Va.) Aug. 22, 1874-May 8, 1951; House 1933-May 8, 1951.

KEE, Maude Elizabeth (widow of John Kee, mother of James Kee) (D W.Va.) ?-Feb. 16, 1975; House July 17, 1951-65.

KEEFE, Frank Bateman (R Wis.) Sept. 23, 1887-Feb. 5, 1952; House 1939-51.

KEENEY, Russell Watson (R Ill.) Dec. 29, 1897-Jan. 11, 1958; House 1957-Jan. 11, 1958.

KEESE, Richard (D N.Y.) Nov. 23, 1794-Feb. 7, 1883; House 1827-29.

KEFAUVER, Carey Estes (D Tenn.) July 26, 1903-Aug. 10, 1963; House Sept. 13, 1939-49; Senate 1949-Aug. 10, 1963.

KEHOE, James Nicholas (D Ky.) July 15, 1862-June 16, 1945; House 1901-05.

KEHOE, James Walter (D Fla.) April 25, 1870-Aug. 20, 1938; House 1917-19.

KEHR, Edward Charles (D Mo.) Nov. 5, 1837-April 20, 1918; House 1875-77.

KEIFER, Joseph Warren (R Ohio) Jan. 30, 1836-April 22, 1932; House 1877-85, 1905-11; Speaker 1881-83.

KEIGHTLEY, Edwin William (R Mich.) Aug. 7, 1843-May 4, 1926; House 1877-79.

KEIM, George May (uncle of William High Keim) (D Pa.) March 23, 1805-June 10, 1861; House March 17, 1838-43.

KEIM, William High (nephew of George May Keim) (D Pa.) June 13, 1813-May 18, 1862; House Dec. 7, 1858-59.

KEISTER, Abraham Lincoln (R Pa.) Sept. 10, 1852-May 26, 1917; House 1913-17.

KEITH, Hastings (R Mass.) Nov. 22, 1915--; House 1959-73.

KEITT, Laurence Massillon (D S.C.) Oct. 4, 1824-June 4, 1864; House 1853-July 16, 1856; Aug. 6, 1856-Dec. 1860.

KELIHER, John Austin (D Mass.) Nov. 6, 1866-Sept. 20, 1938; House 1903-11.

KELLER, Kent Ellsworth (D Ill.) June 4, 1867-Sept. 3, 1954; House 1931-41.

KELLER, Oscar Edward (IR Minn.) July 30, 1878-Nov. 21, 1927; House July 1, 1919-27.

KELLEY, Augustine Bernard (D Pa.) July 9, 1883-Nov. 20, 1957; House 1941-Nov. 20, 1957.

KELLEY, Harrison (R Kan.) May 12, 1836-July 24, 1897; House Dec. 2, 1889-91.

KELLEY, John Edward (D/PP S.D.) March 27, 1853-Aug. 5, 1941; House 1897-99.

KELLEY, Patrick Henry (R Mich.) Oct. 7, 1867-Sept. 11, 1925; House 1913-23.

KELLEY, William Darrah (R Pa.) April 12, 1814-Jan. 9, 1890; House 1861-Jan. 9, 1890.

KELLOGG, Charles (— N.Y.) Oct. 3, 1773-May 11, 1842; House 1825-27.

KELLOGG, Francis William (R Mich./Ala.) May 30, 1810-Jan. 13, 1879; House 1859-65 (Mich.); July 22, 1868-69 (Ala.).

KELLOGG, Frank Billings (R Minn.) Dec. 22, 1856-Dec. 21, 1937; Senate 1917-23; Secy. of State 1925-29.

KELLOGG, Orlando (W N.Y.) June 18, 1809-Aug. 24, 1865; House 1847-49; 1863-Aug. 24, 1865.

KELLOGG, Stephen Wright (R Conn.) April 5, 1822-Jan. 27, 1904; House 1869-73.

KELLOGG, William (R Ill.) July 8, 1814-Dec. 20, 1872; House 1857-63.

KELLOGG, William Pitt (R La.) Dec. 8, 1831-Aug. 10, 1918; Senate July 9, 1868-Nov. 1, 1872, 1877-83; House 1883-85; Gov. 1873-77.

KELLY, Edna Flannery (D N.Y.) Aug. 20, 1906-—; House Nov. 8, 1949-69.

KELLY, Edward Austin (D Ill.) April 3, 1892-Aug. 30, 1969; House 1931-43, 1945-47.

KELLY, George Bradshaw (D N.Y.) Dec. 12, 1900-June 26, 1971; House 1937-39.

KELLY, James (— Pa.) July 17, 1760-Feb. 4, 1819; House 1805-09.

KELLY, James Kerr (D Ore.) Feb. 16, 1819-Sept. 15, 1903; Senate 1871-77.

KELLY, John (D N.Y.) April 21, 1821-June 1, 1886; House 1855-Dec. 25, 1858.

KELLY, Melville Clyde (R Pa.) Aug. 4, 1883-April 29, 1935; House 1913-15, 1917-35.

KELLY, Richard (R Fla.) July 31, 1924-—; House 1975-81.

KELLY, William (— Ala.) 1770-1832; Senate Dec. 12, 1822-25.

KELSEY, William Henry (R N.Y.) Oct. 2, 1812-April 20, 1879; House 1855-59, 1867-71 (1855-59 Whig, 1867-71 Republican).

KELSO, John Russell (IRad. Mo.) March 23, 1831-Jan. 26, 1891; House 1865-67.

KEM, James Preston (R Mo.) April 2, 1890-Feb. 24, 1965; Senate 1947-53.

KEM, Omar Madison (P Neb.) Nov. 13, 1855-Feb. 13, 1942; House 1891-97.

KEMBLE, Gouverneur (D N.Y.) Jan. 25, 1786-Sept. 16, 1875; House 1837-41.

KEMP, Bolivar Edwards (D La.) Dec. 28, 1871-June 19, 1933; House 1925-June 19, 1933.

KEMP, Jack French (R N.Y.) July 13, 1935-—; House 1971-—.

KEMPSHALL, Thomas (W N.Y.) about 1796-Jan. 14, 1865; House 1839-41.

KENAN, Thomas (D N.C.) Feb. 26, 1771-Oct. 22, 1843; House 1805-11.

KENDALL, Charles West (D Nev.) April 22, 1828-June 25, 1914; House 1871-75.

KENDALL, Elva Roscoe (R Ky.) Feb. 14, 1893-Jan. 29, 1968; House 1929-31.

KENDALL, John Wilkerson (father of Joseph Morgan Kendall) (D Ky.) June 26, 1834-March 7, 1892; House 1891-March 7, 1892.

KENDALL, Jonas (father of Joseph Gowing Kendall) (F Mass.) Oct. 27, 1757-Oct. 22, 1844; House 1819-21.

KENDALL, Joseph Gowing (son of Jonas Kendall) (— Mass.) Oct. 27, 1788-Oct. 2, 1847; House 1829-33.

KENDALL, Joseph Morgan (son of John Wilkerson Kendall) (D Ky.) May 12, 1863-Nov. 5, 1933; House April 21, 1892-93, 1895-Feb. 18, 1897.

KENDALL, Nathan Edward (R Iowa) March 17, 1868-Nov. 5, 1936; House 1909-13; Gov. 1921-25.

KENDALL, Samuel Austin (R Pa.) Nov. 1, 1859-Jan. 8, 1933; House 1919-Jan. 8, 1933.

KENDRICK, John Benjamin (D Wyo.) Sept. 6, 1857-Nov. 3, 1933; Senate 1917-Nov. 3, 1933; Gov. 1915-17.

KENNA, John Edward (D W.Va.) April 10, 1848-Jan. 11, 1893; House 1877-83; Senate 1883-Jan. 11, 1893.

KENNEDY, Ambrose (R R.I.) Dec. 1, 1875-March 10, 1967; House 1913-23.

KENNEDY, Ambrose Jerome (D Md.) Jan. 6, 1893-Aug. 29, 1950; House Nov. 8, 1932-41.

KENNEDY, Andrew (cousin of Case Broderick) (D Ind.) July 24, 1810-Dec. 31, 1847; House 1841-47.

KENNEDY, Anthony (brother of John Pendleton Kennedy) (U Md.) Dec. 21, 1810-July 31, 1892; Senate 1857-63.

KENNEDY, Charles Augustus (R Iowa) March 24, 1869-Jan. 10, 1951; House 1907-21.

KENNEDY, Edward Moore (brother of John Fitzgerald Kennedy and Robert Francis Kennedy, grandson of John Francis Fitzgerald) (D Mass.) Feb. 22, 1932-—; Senate Nov. 7, 1962-—.

KENNEDY, James (R Ohio) Sept. 3, 1853-Nov. 9, 1928; House 1903-11.

KENNEDY, John Fitzgerald (brother of Edward Moore Kennedy and Robert Francis Kennedy, grandson of John Francis Fitzgerald) (D Mass.) May 29, 1917-Nov. 22, 1963; House 1947-53; Senate 1953-Dec. 22, 1960; President 1961-Nov. 22, 1963.

KENNEDY, John Lauderdale (R Neb.) Oct. 27, 1854-Aug. 30, 1946; House 1905-07.

KENNEDY, John Pendleton (brother of Anthony Kennedy) (W Md.) Oct. 25, 1795-Aug. 18, 1870; House April 25, 1838-39, 1841-45; Secy. of the Navy 1852-53.

KENNEDY, Martin John (D N.Y.) Aug. 29, 1892-Oct. 27, 1955; House March 11, 1930-45.

KENNEDY, Michael Joseph (D N.Y.) Oct. 25, 1897-Nov. 1, 1949; House 1939-43.

KENNEDY, Robert Francis (brother of Edward Moore Kennedy and John Fitzgerald Kennedy, grandson of John Francis Fitzgerald) (D N.Y.) Nov. 20, 1925-June 6, 1968; Senate 1965-June 6, 1968; Atty. Gen. 1961-64.

KENNEDY, Robert Patterson (R Ohio) Jan. 23, 1840-May 6, 1918; House 1887-91.

KENNEDY, William (F N.C.) July 31, 1768-Oct. 11, 1834; House 1803-05, 1809-11, Jan. 30, 1813-15.

KENNEDY, William (D Conn.) Dec. 19, 1854-June 19, 1918; House 1913-15.

KENNELLY, Barbara Bailey (D Conn.) July 10, 1936-—; House Jan. 25, 1982-—.

KENNETT, Luther Martin (AP Mo.) March 15, 1807-April 12, 1873; House 1855-57.

KENNEY, Edward Aloysius (D N.J.) Aug. 11, 1884-Jan. 27, 1938; House 1933-Jan. 27, 1938.

KENNEY, Richard Rolland (D Del.) Sept. 9, 1856-Aug. 14, 1931; Senate Jan. 19, 1897-1901.

KENNON, William Sr. (cousin of William Kennon Jr.) (D Ohio) May 14, 1793-Nov. 2, 1881; House 1829-33, 1835-37.

KENNON, William Jr. (cousin of William Kennon Sr.) (D Ohio) June 12, 1802-Oct. 19, 1867; House 1847-49.

KENT, Everett (D Pa.) Nov. 15, 1888-Oct. 13, 1963; House 1923-25, 1927-29.

KENT, Joseph (NR Md.) Jan. 14, 1779-Nov. 24, 1837; House 1811-15, 1819-Jan. 6, 1826; Senate 1833-Nov. 24, 1837; Gov. 1826-29 (1811-15 Federalist, 1819-26 Democrat, 1833-37 National Republican, 1826-29 Democratic Republican).

KENT, Moss (F N.Y.) April 3, 1766-May 30, 1838; House 1813-17.

KENT, William (I Calif.) March 29, 1864-March 13, 1928; House 1911-17 (1911-13 Progressive Republican, 1913-17 Independent).

KENYON, William Scheuneman (R N.Y.) Dec. 13, 1820-Feb. 10, 1896; House 1859-61.

KENYON, William Squire (R Iowa) June 10, 1869-Sept. 9, 1933; Senate April 12, 1911-Feb. 24, 1922.

KEOGH, Eugene James (D N.Y.) Aug. 30, 1907-—; House 1937-67.

KERN, Frederick John (D Ill.) Sept. 6, 1864-Nov. 9, 1931; House 1901-03.

KERN, John Worth (D Ind.) Dec. 20, 1849-Aug. 17, 1917; Senate 1911-17; Senate majority leader 1913-17.

KERNAN, Francis (D N.Y.) Jan. 14, 1816-Sept. 7, 1892; House 1863-65; Senate 1875-81.

KERR, Daniel (R Iowa) June 18, 1836-Oct. 8, 1916; House 1887-91.

KERR, James (D Pa.) Oct. 2, 1851-Oct. 31, 1908; House 1889-91.

KERR, John (father of John Kerr Jr., cousin of Bartlett Yancey, granduncle of John Hosea Kerr) (D Va.) Aug. 4, 1782-Sept. 29, 1842; House 1813-15, Oct. 30, 1815-17.

KERR, John Jr. (son of John Kerr) (W N.C.) Feb. 10, 1811-Sept. 5, 1879; House 1853-55.

KERR, John Bozman (son of John Leeds Kerr) (W Md.) March 5, 1809-Jan. 27, 1878; House 1849-51.

KERR, John Hosea (grandnephew of John Kerr) (D N.C.) Dec. 31, 1873-June 21, 1958; House Nov. 6, 1923-53.

Biographical Index

KERR, John Leeds (father of John Bozman Kerr) (W Md.) Jan. 15, 1780-Feb. 21, 1844; House 1825-29, 1831-33; Senate Jan. 5, 1841-43.

KERR, Joseph (D Ohio) 1765-Aug. 22, 1837; Senate Dec. 10, 1814-15.

KERR, Josiah Leeds (R Md.) Jan. 10, 1861-Sept. 27, 1920; House Nov. 6, 1900-01.

KERR, Michael Crawford (D Ind.) March 15, 1827-Aug. 19, 1876; House 1865-73, 1875-Aug. 19, 1876; Speaker 1875-76.

KERR, Robert Samuel (D Okla.) Sept. 11, 1896-Jan. 1, 1963; Senate 1949-Jan. 1, 1963; Gov. 1943-47.

KERR, Winfield Scott (R Ohio) June 23, 1852-Sept. 11, 1917; House 1895-1901.

KERRIGAN, James (D N.Y.) Dec. 25, 1828-Nov. 1, 1899; House 1861-63.

KERRY, John Forbes (D Mass.) Dec. 22, 1943- —; Senate 1985- —.

KERSHAW, John (D S.C.) Sept. 12, 1765-Aug. 4, 1829; House 1813-15.

KERSTEN, Charles Joseph (R Wis.) May 26, 1902-Oct. 31, 1972; House 1947-49; 1951-55.

KETCHAM, John Clark (R Mich.) Jan. 1, 1873-Dec. 4, 1941; House 1921-33.

KETCHAM, John Henry (R N.Y.) Dec. 21, 1832-Nov. 4, 1906; House 1865-73, 1877-93, 1897-Nov. 4, 1906.

KETCHUM, William Matthew (R Calif.) Sept. 2, 1921-June 24, 1978; House 1973-June 24, 1978.

KETCHUM, Winthrop Welles (R Pa.) June 29, 1820-Dec. 6, 1879; House 1875-July 19, 1876.

KETTNER, William (D Calif.) Nov. 20, 1864-Nov. 11, 1930; House 1913-21.

KEY, David McKendree (D Tenn.) Jan. 27, 1824-Feb. 3, 1900; Senate Aug. 18, 1875-Jan. 19, 1877; Postmaster Gen. 1877-80.

KEY, John Alexander (D Ohio) Dec. 30, 1871-March 4, 1954; House 1913-19.

KEY, Philip (cousin of Philip Barton Key, great-grandfather of Barnes Compton) (— Md.) 1750-Jan. 4, 1820; House 1791-93.

KEY, Philip Barton (cousin of Philip Key) (F Md.) April 12, 1757-July 28, 1815; House 1807-13.

KEYES, Elias (R Vt.) April 14, 1758-July 9, 1844; House 1821-23.

KEYES, Henry Wilder (R N.H.) May 23, 1863-June 19, 1938; Senate 1919-37; Gov. 1917-19.

KEYS, Martha Elizabeth (wife of Andrew Jacobs Jr., daughter-in-law of Andrew Jacobs Sr.) (D Kan.) Aug. 10, 1930- —; House 1975-79.

KIDDER, David (W Maine) Dec. 8, 1787-Nov. 1, 1860; House 1823-27.

KIDDER, Jefferson Parish (R Dakota) June 4, 1815-Oct. 2, 1883; House (Terr. Del.) 1875-79.

KIDWELL, Zedekiah (D Va.) Jan. 4, 1814-April 27, 1872; House 1853-57.

KIEFER, Andrew Robert (R Minn.) May 25, 1832-May 1, 1904; House 1893-97.

KIEFNER, Charles Edward (R Mo.) Nov. 25, 1869-Dec. 13, 1942; House 1925-27, 1929-31.

KIESS, Edgar Raymond (R Pa.) Aug. 26, 1875-July 20, 1930; House 1913-July 20, 1930.

KILBOURNE, James (D Ohio) Oct. 19, 1770-April 9, 1850; House 1813-17.

KILBURN, Clarence Evans (R N.Y.) April 13, 1893-May 20, 1975; House Feb. 13, 1940-65.

KILDAY, Paul Joseph (D Texas) March 29, 1900-Oct. 12, 1968; House 1939-Sept. 24, 1961.

KILDEE, Dale Edward (D Mich.) Sept. 16, 1929- —; House 1977- —.

KILGORE, Constantine Buckley (D Texas) Feb. 20, 1835-Sept. 23, 1897; House 1887-95.

KILGORE, Daniel (D Ohio) 1793-Dec. 12, 1851; House Dec. 1, 1834-July 4, 1838.

KILGORE, David (R Ind.) April 3, 1804-Jan. 22, 1879; House 1857-61.

KILGORE, Harley Martin (D W.Va.) Jan. 11, 1893-Feb. 28, 1956; Senate 1941-Feb. 28, 1956.

KILGORE, Joe Madison (D Texas) Dec. 10, 1918- —; House 1955-65.

KILLE, Joseph (D N.J.) April 12, 1790-March 1, 1865; House 1839-41.

KILLINGER, John Weinland (R Pa.) Sept. 18, 1824-June 30, 1896; House 1859-63, 1871-75, 1877-81.

KIMBALL, Alanson Mellen (R Wis.) March 12, 1827-May 26, 1913; House 1875-77.

KIMBALL, Henry Mahlon (R Mich.) Aug. 27, 1878-Oct. 19, 1935; House Jan. 3-Oct. 19, 1935.

KIMBALL, William Preston (D Ky.) Nov. 4, 1857-Feb. 24, 1926; House 1907-09.

KIMMEL, William (D Md.) Aug. 15, 1812-Dec. 28, 1886; House 1877-81.

KINCAID, John (D Ky.) Feb. 15, 1791-Feb. 7, 1873; House 1829-31.

KINCHELOE, David Hayes (D Ky.) April 9, 1877-April 16, 1950; House 1915-Oct. 5, 1930.

KINDEL, George John (D Colo.) March 2, 1855-Feb. 28, 1930; House 1913-15.

KINDNESS, Thomas Norman (R Ohio) Aug. 26, 1929- —; House 1975- —.

KINDRED, John Joseph (D N.Y.) July 15, 1864-Oct. 23, 1937; House 1911-13, 1921-29.

KING, Adam (D Pa.) 1790-May 6, 1835; House 1827-33.

KING, Andrew (D Mo.) March 20, 1812-Nov. 18, 1895; House 1871-73.

KING, Austin Augustus (UD Mo.) Sept. 21, 1802-April 22, 1870; House 1863-65; Gov. 1848-53.

KING, Carleton James (R N.Y.) June 15, 1904-Nov. 19, 1977; House 1961-Dec. 31, 1974.

KING, Cecil Rhodes (D Calif.) Jan. 13, 1898-March 17, 1974; House Aug. 25, 1942-69.

KING, Cyrus (half brother of Rufus King) (F Mass.) Sept. 6, 1772-April 25, 1817; House 1813-17.

KING, Daniel Putnam (W Mass.) Jan. 8, 1801-July 25, 1850; House 1843-July 25, 1850.

KING, David Sjodahl (son of William Henry King) (D Utah) June 20, 1917- —; House 1959-63, 1965-67.

KING, Edward John (R Ill.) July 1, 1867-Feb. 17, 1929; House 1915-Feb. 17, 1929.

KING, George Gordon (W R.I.) June 9, 1807-July 17, 1870; House 1849-53.

KING, Henry (brother of Thomas Butler King, uncle of John Floyd King) (D Pa.) July 6, 1790-July 13, 1861; House 1831-35.

KING, James Gore (son of Rufus King, brother of John Alsop King) (W N.J.) May 8, 1791-Oct. 3, 1853; House 1849-51.

KING, John (D N.Y.) 1775-Sept. 1, 1836; House 1831-33.

KING, John Alsop (son of Rufus King, brother of James Gore King) (W N.Y.) Jan. 3, 1788-July 7, 1867; House 1849-51; Gov. 1857-59 (Republican).

KING, John Floyd (son of Thomas Butler King, nephew of Henry King) (D La.) April 20, 1842-May 8, 1915; House 1879-87.

KING, John Pendleton (D Ga.) April 3, 1799-March 19, 1888; Senate Nov. 21, 1833-Nov. 1, 1837.

KING, Karl Clarence (R Pa.) Jan. 26, 1897-April 16, 1974; House Nov. 6, 1951-57.

KING, Perkins (D N.Y.) Jan. 12, 1784-Nov. 29, 1875; House 1829-31.

KING, Preston (R N.Y.) Oct. 14, 1806-Nov. 12, 1865; House 1843-47, 1849-53; Senate 1857-63 (1843-53 Democrat, 1857-63 Republican).

KING, Rufus (half brother of Cyrus King, father of John Alsop King and James Gore King) (F N.Y.) March 24, 1755-April 29, 1827; Senate July 16, 1789-May 23, 1796; 1813-25; Cont. Cong. (Mass.) 1784-87.

KING, Rufus H. (W N.Y.) Jan. 20, 1820-Sept. 13, 1890; House 1855-57.

KING, Samuel Wilder (R Hawaii) Dec. 17, 1886-March 24, 1959; House (Terr. Del.) 1935-43; Gov. (Hawaii Terr.) 1953-57.

KING, Thomas Butler (brother of Henry King, father of John Floyd King) (W Ga.) Aug. 27, 1800-May 10, 1864; House 1839-43, 1845-50.

KING, William Henry (father of David Sjodahl King) (D Utah) June 3, 1863-Nov. 27, 1949; House 1897-99, April 2, 1900-01; Senate 1917-41; Pres. pro tempore 1941.

KING, William Rufus deVane (D N.C./Ala.) April 7, 1786-April 18, 1853; House 1811-Nov. 4, 1816 (N.C.); Senate Dec. 14, 1819-April 15, 1844, July 1, 1848-Dec. 20, 1852 (Ala.); Pres. pro tempore 1835-41, 1849-52; Vice Pres. March 4-April 18, 1853.

KING, William Smith (R Minn.) Dec. 16, 1828-Feb. 24, 1900; House 1875-77.

KINGSBURY, William Wallace (D Minn.) June 4, 1828-April 17, 1892; House (Terr. Del.) 1857-May 11, 1858.

KINKAID, Moses Pierce (R Neb.) Jan. 24, 1856-July 6, 1922; House 1903-July 6, 1922.

KINKEAD, Eugene Francis (D N.J.) March 27, 1876-Sept. 6, 1960; House 1909-Feb. 4, 1915.

KINNARD, George L. (D Ind.) 1803-Nov. 26, 1836; House 1833-Nov. 26, 1836.

KINNEY, John Fitch (D Utah) April 2, 1816-Aug. 16, 1902; House (Terr. Del.) 1863-65.

KINSELLA, Thomas (D N.Y.) Dec. 31, 1832-Feb. 11, 1884; House 1871-73.

KINSEY, Charles (— N.J.) 1773-June 25, 1849; House 1817-19, Feb. 2, 1820-21.

KINSEY, William Medcalf (R Mo.) Oct. 28, 1846-June 20, 1931; House 1889-91.

KINSLEY, Martin (— Mass.) June 2, 1754-June 20, 1835; House 1819-21.

KINZER, John Roland (R Pa.) March 28, 1874-July 25, 1955; House Jan. 28, 1930-47.

KIPP, George Washington (D Pa.) March 28, 1847-July 24, 1911; House 1907-09, March 4-July 24, 1911.

KIRBY, William Fosgate (D Ark.) Nov. 16, 1867-July 26, 1934; Senate Nov. 8, 1916-21.

KIRK, Andrew Jackson (R Ky.) March 19, 1866-May 25, 1933; House Feb. 13, 1926-27.

KIRKLAND, Joseph (— N.Y.) Jan. 18, 1770-Jan. 26, 1844; House 1821-23.

KIRKPATRICK, Littleton (D N.J.) Oct. 19, 1797-Aug. 15, 1859; House 1843-45.

KIRKPATRICK, Sanford (D Iowa) Feb. 11, 1842-Feb. 13, 1932; House 1913-15.

KIRKPATRICK, Snyder Solomon (R Kan.) Feb. 21, 1848-April 5, 1909; House 1895-97.

KIRKPATRICK, William (D N.Y.) Nov. 7, 1769-Sept. 2, 1832; House 1807-09.

KIRKPATRICK, William Huntington (son of William Sebring Kirkpatrick) (R Pa.) Oct. 2, 1885-Nov. 28, 1970; House 1921-23.

KIRKPATRICK, William Sebring (father of William Huntington Kirkpatrick) (R Pa.) April 21, 1844-Nov. 3, 1932; House 1897-99.

KIRKWOOD, Samuel Jordan (R Iowa) Dec. 20, 1813-Sept. 1, 1894; Senate Jan. 13, 1866-67, 1877-March 7, 1881; Gov. 1860-64, 1876-77; Secy. of the Interior 1881-82.

KIRTLAND, Dorrance (— N.Y.) July 28, 1770-May 23, 1840; House 1817-19.

KIRWAN, Michael Joseph (D Ohio) Dec. 2, 1886-July 27, 1970; House 1937-July 27, 1970.

KISSEL, John (R N.Y.) July 31, 1864-Oct. 3, 1938; House 1921-23.

KITCHELL, Aaron (D N.J.) July 10, 1744-June 25, 1820; House 1791-93, Jan. 29, 1795-97, 1799-1801; Senate 1805-March 12, 1809.

KITCHEN, Bethuel Middleton (R W.Va.) March 21, 1812-Dec. 15, 1895; House 1867-69.

KITCHENS, Wade Hampton (D Ark.) Dec. 26, 1878-Aug. 22, 1966; House 1937-41.

KITCHIN, Alvin Paul (nephew of Claude Kitchin and William Walton Kitchin, grandson of William Hodges Kitchin) (D N.C.) Sept. 13, 1908-Oct. 22, 1983; House 1957-63.

KITCHIN, Claude (son of William Hodges Kitchin, brother of William Walton Kitchin, uncle of Alvin Paul Kitchin) (D N.C.) March 24, 1869-May 31, 1923; House 1901-May 31, 1923; House majority leader 1915-19.

KITCHIN, William Hodges (father of Claude Kitchin and William Walton Kitchin, grandfather of Alvin Paul Kitchin) (D N.C.) Dec. 22, 1837-Feb. 2, 1901; House 1879-81.

KITCHIN, William Walton (son of William Hodges Kitchin, brother of Claude Kitchin, uncle of Alvin Paul Kitchin) (D N.C.) Oct. 9, 1866-Nov. 9, 1924; House 1897-Jan. 11, 1909; Gov. 1909-13.

KITTERA, John Wilkes (father of Thomas Kittera) (F Pa.) Nov. 1752-June 6, 1801; House 1791-1801.

KITTERA, Thomas (son of John Wilkes Kittera) (F Pa.) March 21, 1789-June 16, 1839; House Oct. 10, 1826-27.

KITTREDGE, Alfred Beard (R S.D.) March 28, 1861-May 4, 1911; Senate July 11, 1901-09.

KITTREDGE, George Washington (AND N.H.) Jan. 31, 1805-March 6, 1881; House 1853-55.

KLEBERG, Richard Mifflin Sr. (nephew of Rudolph Kleberg, cousin of Robert Christian Eckhardt) (D Texas) Nov. 18, 1887-May 8, 1955; House Nov. 24, 1931-45.

KLEBERG, Rudolph (great-uncle of Robert Christian Eckhardt, uncle of Richard Mifflin Kleberg Sr.) (D Texas) June 26, 1847-Dec. 28, 1924; House April 7, 1896-1903.

KLECZKA, John Casimir (R Wis.) May 6, 1885-April 21, 1959; House 1919-23.

KLECZKA, Gerald (D Wis.) Nov. 26, 1943- —; House Apr. 10, 1984- —.

KLEIN, Arthur George (D N.Y.) Aug. 8, 1904-Feb. 20, 1968; House July 29, 1941-45, Feb. 19, 1946-Dec. 31, 1956.

KLEINER, John Jay (D Ind.) Feb. 8, 1845-April 8, 1911; House 1883-87.

KLEPPE, Thomas S. (R N.D.) July 1, 1919- —; House 1967-71; Secy. of the Interior, July 17, 1975-77.

KLEPPER, Frank B. (R Mo.) June 22, 1864-Aug. 4, 1933; House 1905-07.

KLINE, Ardolph Loges (R N.Y.) Feb. 21, 1858-Oct. 13, 1930; House 1921-23.

KLINE, Isaac Clinton (R Pa.) Aug. 18, 1858-Dec. 2, 1947; House 1921-23.

KLINE, Marcus Charles Lawrence (D Pa.) March 26, 1855-March 10, 1911; House 1903-07.

KLINGENSMITH, John Jr. (D Pa.) 1785-?; House 1835-39.

KLOEB, Frank Le Blond (grandson of Francis Celeste Le Blond) (D Ohio) June 16, 1890-March 11, 1976; House 1933-Aug. 19, 1937.

KLOTZ, Robert (D Pa.) Oct. 27, 1819-May 1, 1895; House 1879-83.

KLUCZYNSKI, John Carl (D Ill.) Feb. 15, 1896-Jan. 26, 1975; House 1951-Jan. 26, 1975.

KLUTTZ, Theodore Franklin (D N.C.) Oct. 4, 1848-Nov. 18, 1918; House 1899-1905.

KNAPP, Anthony Lausett (brother of Robert McCarty Knapp) (D Ill.) June 14, 1828-May 24, 1881; House Dec. 12, 1861-65.

KNAPP, Charles (father of Charles Junius Knapp) (R N.Y.) Oct. 8, 1797-May 14, 1880; House 1869-71.

KNAPP, Charles Junius (son of Charles Knapp) (R N.Y.) June 30, 1845-June 1, 1916; House 1889-91.

KNAPP, Charles Luman (R N.Y.) July 4, 1847-Jan. 3, 1929; House Nov. 5, 1901-11.

KNAPP, Chauncey Langdon (R Mass.) Feb. 26, 1809-May 31, 1898; House 1855-59 (1855-57 American Party, 1857-59 Republican).

KNAPP, Robert McCarty (brother of Anthony Lausett Knapp) (D Ill.) April 21, 1831-June 24, 1889; House 1873-75, 1877-79.

KNICKERBOCKER, Herman (F N.Y.) July 27, 1779-Jan. 30, 1855; House 1809-11.

KNIFFIN, Frank Charles (D Ohio) April 26, 1894-April 30, 1968; House 1931-39.

KNIGHT, Charles Landon (R Ohio) June 18, 1867-Sept. 26, 1933; House 1921-23.

KNIGHT, Jonathan (W Pa.) Nov. 22, 1787-Nov. 22, 1858; House 1855-57.

KNIGHT, Nehemiah (father of Nehemiah Rice Knight) (AF R.I.) March 23, 1746-June 13, 1808; House 1803-June 13, 1808.

KNIGHT, Nehemiah Rice (son of Nehemiah Knight) (D R.I.) Dec. 31, 1780-April 18, 1854; Senate Jan. 9, 1821-41; Gov. 1817-21 (1817-35 Anti-Federalist, 1835-41 Democrat).

KNOPF, Philip (R Ill.) Nov. 18, 1847-Aug. 14, 1920; House 1903-09.

KNOTT, James Proctor (D Ky.) Aug. 29, 1830-June 18, 1911; House 1867-71, 1875-83; Gov. 1883-87.

KNOWLAND, Joseph Russell (father of William Fife Knowland) (R Calif.) Aug. 5, 1873-Feb. 1, 1966; House Nov. 8, 1904-15.

KNOWLAND, William Fife (son of Joseph Russell Knowland) (R Calif.) June 26, 1908-Feb. 23, 1974; Senate Aug. 26, 1945-59; Senate majority leader 1953-55.

KNOWLES, Freeman Tulley (P S.D.) Oct. 10, 1846-June 1, 1910; House 1897-99.

KNOWLTON, Ebenezer (R Maine) Dec. 6, 1815-Sept. 10, 1874; House 1855-57.

KNOX, James (W Ill.) July 4, 1807-Oct. 8, 1876; House 1853-57.

KNOX, Philander Chase (R Pa.) May 6, 1853-Oct. 12, 1921; Senate June 10, 1904-March 4, 1909, 1917-Oct. 12, 1921; Atty. Gen. 1901-04; Secy. of State 1909-13.

KNOX, Samuel (R Mo.) March 21, 1815-March 7, 1905; House June 10, 1864-65.

KNOX, Victor Alfred (R Mich.) Jan. 13, 1899-Dec. 13, 1976; House 1953-65.

KNOX, William Shadrach (R Mass.) Sept. 10, 1843-Sept. 21, 1914; House 1895-1903.

KNUTSON, Coya Gjesdal (DFL Minn.) Aug. 22, 1912- —; House 1955-59.

KNUTSON, Harold (R Minn.) Oct. 20, 1880-Aug. 21, 1953; House 1917-49.

KOCH, Edward Irving (D/L N.Y.) Dec. 12, 1924- —; House 1969-Dec. 31, 1977.

KOCIALKOWSKI, Leo Paul (D Ill.) Aug. 16, 1882-Sept. 27, 1958; House 1933-43.

KOLBE, James Thomas (R Ariz.) June 28, 1942- —; House 1985- —.

KOLTER, Joseph Paul (D Pa.) Sept. 3, 1926- —; House 1983- —.

KOGOVSEK, Raymond Peter (D Colo.) Aug. 19, 1941- —; House 1979-85.

KONIG, George (D Md.) Jan. 26, 1865-May 31, 1913; House 1911-May 31, 1913.

KONOP, Thomas Frank (D Wis.) Aug. 17, 1879-Oct. 17, 1964; House 1911-17.

KOONTZ, William Henry (R Pa.) July 15, 1830-July 4, 1911; House July 18, 1866-69.

KOPP, Arthur William (R Wis.) Feb. 28, 1874-June 2, 1967; House 1909-13.

KOPP, William Frederick (R Iowa) June 20, 1869-Aug. 24, 1938; House 1921-33.

KOPPLEMANN, Herman Paul (D Conn.) May 1, 1880-Aug. 11, 1957; House 1933-39, 1941-43, 1945-47.

KORBLY, Charles Alexander (D Ind.) March 24, 1871-July 26, 1937; House 1909-15.

KORELL, Franklin Frederick (R Ore.) July 23, 1889-June 7, 1965; House Oct. 18, 1927-31.

KORNEGAY, Horace Robinson (D N.C.) March 12, 1924- —; House 1961-69.

KOSTMAYER, Peter Houston (D Pa.) Sept. 27, 1946- —; House 1977-81, 1983- —.

KOWALSKI, Frank (D Conn.) Oct. 18, 1907-Oct. 11, 1974; House 1959-63.

KRAMER, Charles (D Calif.) April 18, 1879-Jan. 20, 1943; House 1933-43.

KRAMER, Kenneth Bentley (R Colo.) Feb. 19, 1942- —; House 1979- —.

KRAUS, Milton (R Ind.) June 26, 1866-Nov. 18, 1942; House 1917-23.

KREBS, Jacob (D Pa.) March 13, 1782-Sept. 26, 1847; House Dec. 4, 1826-March 3, 1827.

KREBS, John Hans (D Calif.) Dec. 17, 1926- —; House 1975-79.

KREBS, Paul J. (D N.J.) May 26, 1912- —; House 1965-67.

KREIDER, Aaron Shenk (R Pa.) June 26, 1863-May 19, 1929; House 1913-23.

KREMER, George (— Pa.) Nov. 21, 1775-Sept. 11, 1854; House 1823-29.

KRIBBS, George Frederic (D Pa.) Nov. 8, 1846-Sept. 8, 1938; House 1891-95.

KRONMILLER, John (R Md.) Dec. 6, 1858-June 19, 1928; House 1909-11.

KRUEGER, Otto (R N.D.) Sept. 7, 1890-June 6, 1963; House 1953-59.

KRUEGER, Robert Charles (D Texas) Sept. 19, 1935- —; House 1975-79.

KRUSE, Edward H. Jr. (D Ind.) Oct. 22, 1918- —; House 1949-51.

KUCHEL, Thomas Henry (R Calif.) Aug. 15, 1910- —; Senate Jan. 2, 1953-69.

KUHNS, Joseph Henry (W Pa.) Sept. 1800-Nov. 16, 1883; House 1851-53.

KULP, Monroe Henry (R Pa.) Oct. 23, 1858-Oct. 19, 1911; House 1895-99.

KUNKEL, Jacob Michael (D Md.) July 13, 1822-April 7, 1870; House 1857-61.

KUNKEL, John Christian (grandfather of John Crain Kunkel) (W Pa.) Sept. 18, 1816-Oct. 14, 1870; House 1855-59.

KUNKEL, John Crain (grandson of John Christian Kunkel, great-grandson of John Sergeant, great-great-grandson of Robert Whitehill) (R Pa.) July 21, 1898-July 27, 1970; House 1939-51, May 16, 1961-Dec. 30, 1966.

KUNZ, Stanley Henry (D Ill.) Sept. 26, 1864-April 23, 1946; House 1921-31, April 5, 1932-33.

KUPFERMAN, Theodore R. (R N.Y.) May 12, 1920- —; House Feb. 8, 1966-69.

KURTZ, Jacob Banks (R Pa.) Oct. 31, 1867-Sept. 18, 1960; House 1923-35.

KURTZ, William Henry (D Pa.) Jan. 31, 1804-June 24, 1868; House 1851-55.

KUSTERMANN, Gustav (R Wis.) May 24, 1850-Dec. 25, 1919; House 1907-11.

KUYKENDALL, Andrew Jackson (R Ill.) March 3, 1815-May 11, 1891; House 1865-67.

KUYKENDALL, Dan H. (R Tenn.) July 9, 1924- —; House 1967-75.

KVALE, Ole Juulson (father of Paul John Kvale (FL Minn.) Feb. 6, 1869-Sept. 11, 1929; House 1923-Sept. 11, 1929 (1923-25 Independent Republican, 1925-29 Farmer Laborite).

KVALE, Paul John (son of Ole Juulson Kvale) (FL Minn.) March 27, 1896-June 14, 1960; House Oct. 16, 1929-39.

KYL, John Henry (R Iowa) May 9, 1919- —; House Dec. 15, 1959-65, 1967-73.

KYLE, James Henderson (I S.D.) Feb. 24, 1854-July 1, 1901; Senate 1891-July 1, 1901.

KYLE, John Curtis (D Miss.) July 17, 1851-July 6, 1913; House 1891-97.

KYLE, Thomas Barton (R Ohio) March 10, 1856-Aug. 13, 1915; House 1901-05.

KYROS, Peter N. (D Maine) July 11, 1925- —; House 1967-75.

L

LA BRANCHE, Alcee Louis (D La.) 1806-Aug. 17, 1861; House 1843-45.

LACEY, Edward Samuel (R Mich.) Nov. 26, 1835-Oct. 2, 1916; House 1881-85.

LACEY, John Fletcher (R Iowa) May 30, 1841-Sept. 29, 1913; House 1889-91, 1893-1907.

LACOCK, Abner (D Pa.) July 9, 1770-April 12, 1837; House 1811-13; Senate 1813-19.

LADD, Edwin Freemont (Nonpart.R N.D.) Dec. 13, 1859-June 22, 1925; Senate 1921-June 22, 1925.

LADD, George Washington (D/G Maine) Sept. 28, 1818-Jan. 30, 1892; House 1879-83.

LA DOW, George Augustus (D Ore.) March 18, 1826-May 1, 1875; House March 4-May 1, 1875.

LAFALCE, John Joseph (D N.Y.) Oct. 6, 1939- —; House 1975- —.

LAFEAN, Daniel Franklin (R Pa.) Feb. 7, 1861-April 18, 1922; House 1903-13, 1915-17.

LAFFERTY, Abraham Walter (PR Ore.) June 10, 1875-Jan. 15, 1964; House 1911-15.

LAFFOON, Polk (D Ky.) Oct. 24, 1844-Oct. 22, 1906; House 1885-89.

LAFLIN, Addison Henry (R N.Y.) Oct. 24, 1823-Sept. 24, 1878; House 1865-71.

LA FOLLETTE, Charles Marion (great-grandson of William Heilman) (R Ind.) Feb. 27, 1898- —; House 1943-47.

LA FOLLETTE, Robert Marion (father of Robert Marion La Follette Jr.) (R Wis.) June 14, 1855-June 18, 1925; House 1885-91; Senate Jan. 2, 1906-June 18, 1925; Gov. 1901-06.

LA FOLLETTE, Robert Marion Jr. (son of Robert Marion La Follette) (Prog. Wis.) Feb. 6, 1895-Feb. 24, 1953; Senate Sept. 30, 1925-35, 1935-47 (1925-35 Republican Progressive, 1935-47 Progressive).

LA FOLLETTE, William Leroy (R Wash.) Nov. 30, 1860-Dec. 20, 1934; House 1911-19.

LAFORE, John Armand Jr. (R Pa.) May 25, 1905- —; House Nov. 5, 1957-61.

LAGAN, Matthew Diamond (D La.) June 20, 1829-April 8, 1901; House 1887-89, 1891-93.

LAGOMARSINO, Robert John (R Calif.) Sept. 4, 1926- —; House March 5, 1974- —.

LA GUARDIA, Fiorello Henry (R Prog. N.Y.) Dec. 11, 1882-Sept. 20, 1947; House 1917-19, 1923-33 (1917-19, 1923-25 Republican, 1925-27 Socialist, 1927-33 Republican Progressive).

LAHM, Samuel (D Ohio) April 22, 1812-June 16, 1876; House 1847-49.

LAIDLAW, William Grant (R N.Y.) Jan. 1, 1840-Aug. 19, 1908; House 1887-91.

LAIRD, James (R Neb.) June 20, 1849-Aug. 17, 1889; House 1883-Aug. 17, 1889.

LAIRD, Melvin Robert (R Wis.) Sept. 1, 1922- —; House 1953-Jan. 21, 1969; Secy. of Defense 1969-73.

LAIRD, William Ramsey III (D W.Va.) June 2, 1916-Jan. 7, 1974; Senate March 13-Nov. 6, 1956.

LAKE, William Augustus (W Miss.) Jan. 6, 1808-Oct. 15, 1861; House 1855-57.

LAMAR, Henry Graybill (D Ga.) July 10, 1798-Sept. 10, 1861; House Dec. 7, 1829-33.

LAMAR, James Robert (D Mo.) March 28, 1866-Aug. 11, 1923; House 1903-05; 1907-09.

LAMAR, John Basil (D Ga.) Nov. 5, 1812-Sept. 15, 1862; House March 4-July 29, 1843.

LAMAR, Lucius Quintus Cincinnatus (uncle of William Bailey Lamar, cousin of Absalom Harris Chappell) (D Miss.) Sept. 17, 1825-Jan. 23, 1893; House 1857-December 1860, 1873-77; Senate 1877-March 6, 1885; Secy. of the Interior 1885-88, Assoc. Justice Supreme Court 1888-93.

LAMAR, William Bailey (nephew of Lucius Quintus Cincinnatus Lamar) (D Fla.) June 12, 1853-Sept. 26, 1928; House 1903-09.

LAMB, Alfred William (D Mo.) March 18, 1824-April 29, 1888; House 1853-55.

LAMB, John (D Va.) June 12, 1840-Nov. 21, 1924; House 1897-1913.

LAMB, John Edward (D Ind.) Dec. 26, 1852-Aug. 23, 1914; House 1883-85.

LAMBERT, John (D N.J.) Feb. 24, 1746-Feb. 4, 1823; House 1805-09; Senate 1809-15.

LAMBERTSON, William Purnell (R Kan.) March 23, 1880-Oct. 26, 1957; House 1929-45.

LAMBETH, John Walter (D N.C.) Jan. 10, 1896-Jan. 12, 1961; House 1931-39.

LAMISON, Charles Nelson (D Ohio) 1826-April 24, 1896; House 1871-75.

LAMNECK, Arthur Philip (D Ohio) March 12, 1880-April 23, 1944; House 1931-39.

LAMPERT, Florian (R Wis.) July 8, 1863-July 18, 1930; House Nov. 5, 1918-July 18, 1930.

LAMPORT, William Henry (R N.Y.) May 27, 1811-July 21, 1891; House 1871-75.

LANCASTER, Columbia (D Wash.) Aug. 26, 1803-Sept. 15, 1893; House (Terr. Del.) April 12, 1854-55.

LANDERS, Franklin (D Ind.) March 22, 1825-Sept. 10, 1901; House 1875-77.

LANDERS, George Marcellus (D Conn.) Feb. 22, 1813-March 27, 1895; House 1875-79.

LANDES, Silas Zephaniah (D Ill.) May 15, 1842-May 23, 1910; House 1885-89.

LANDGREBE, Earl F. (R Ind.) Jan. 21, 1916- —; House 1969-75.

LANDIS, Charles Beary (brother of Frederick Landis) (R Ind.) July 9, 1858-April 24, 1922; House 1897-1909.

LANDIS, Frederick (brother of Charles Beary Landis) (R Ind.) Aug. 18, 1872-Nov. 15, 1934; House 1903-07.

LANDIS, Gerald Wayne (R Ind.) Feb. 23, 1895-Sept. 6, 1971; House 1939-49.

LANDRUM, John Morgan (D La.) July 3, 1815-Oct. 18, 1861; House 1859-61.

LANDRUM, Phillip Mitchell (D Ga.) Sept. 10, 1909- —; House 1953-77.

LANDRY, Joseph Aristide (W La.) July 10, 1817-March 9, 1881; House 1851-53.

LANDY, James (D Pa.) Oct. 13, 1813-July 25, 1875; House 1857-59.

LANE, Amos (father of James Henry Lane) (D Ind.) March 1, 1778-Sept. 2, 1849; House 1833-37.

LANE, Edward (D Ill.) March 27, 1842-Oct. 30, 1912; House 1887-95.

LANE, Harry (grandson of Joseph Lane, nephew of LaFayette Lane) (D Ore.) Aug. 28, 1855-May 23, 1917; Senate 1913-May 23, 1917.

LANE, Henry Smith (R Ind.) Feb. 24, 1811-June 18, 1881; House Aug. 3, 1840-43; Senate 1861-67; Gov. Jan. 14-16, 1861 (1840-43 Whig, 1861-67 Republican).

LANE, James Henry (son of Amos Lane) (D Ind./R Kan.) June 22, 1814-July 11, 1866; House 1853-55; Senate April 4, 1861-July 11, 1866 (1853-55 Democrat Ind., 1861-66 Republican Kan.).

LANE, Joseph (father of LaFayette Lane, grandfather of Harry Lane) (D Ore.) Dec. 14, 1801-April 19, 1881; House (Terr. Del.) 1851-Feb. 14, 1859; Senate Feb. 14, 1859-61; Gov. (Ore. Terr.) 1849-50, May 16-19, 1853.

LANE, Joseph Reed (R Iowa) May 6, 1858-May 1, 1931; House 1899-1901.

LANE, LaFayette (son of Joseph Lane, uncle of Harry Lane) (D Ore.) Nov. 12, 1842-Nov. 23, 1896; House Oct. 25, 1875-77.

LANE, Thomas Joseph (D Mass.) July 6, 1898- —; House Dec. 30, 1941-63.

LANGDON, Chauncey (F Vt.) Nov. 8, 1763-July 23, 1830; House 1815-17.

LANGDON, John (D N.H.) June 25, 1741-Sept. 18, 1819; Senate 1789-1801; Pres. pro tempore 1789, 1792-94; Cont. Cong. 1775-76, 1783; Gov. 1788, 1805-09, 1810-12.

LANGEN, Odin Elsford Stanley (R Minn.) Jan. 5, 1913-July 6, 1976; House 1959-71.

LANGER, William (R N.D.) Sept. 30, 1886-Nov. 8, 1959; Senate 1941-Nov. 8, 1959; Gov. 1933-34, 1937-39.

LANGHAM, Jonathan Nicholas (R Pa.) Aug. 4, 1861-May 21, 1945; House 1909-15.

LANGLEY, John Wesley (husband of Katherine Gudger Langley) (R Ky.) Jan. 14, 1868-Jan. 17, 1932; House 1907-Jan. 11, 1926.

LANGLEY, Katherine Gudger (wife of John Wesley Langley, daughter of James Madison Gudger Jr.) (R Ky.) Feb. 14, 1888-Aug. 15, 1948; House 1927-31.

LANGSTON, John Mercer (R Va.) Dec. 14, 1829-Nov. 15, 1897; House Sept. 23, 1890-91.

LANHAM, Fritz Garland (son of Samuel Willis Tucker Lanham) (D Texas) Jan. 3, 1880-July 31, 1965; House April 19, 1919-47.

LANHAM, Henderson Lovelace (D Ga.) Sept. 14, 1888-Nov. 10, 1957; House 1947-Nov. 10, 1957.

LANHAM, Samuel Willis Tucker (father of Fritz Garland Lanham) (D Texas) July 4, 1846-July 29, 1908; House 1883-93, 1897-Jan. 15, 1903; Gov. 1903-07.

LANING, Jay Ford (R Ohio) May 15, 1853-Sept. 1, 1941; House 1907-09.

LANKFORD, Menalcus (R Va.) March 14, 1883-Dec. 27, 1937; House 1929-33.

LANKFORD, Richard Estep (D Md.) July 22, 1914- —; House 1955-65.

LANKFORD, William Chester (D Ga.) Dec. 7, 1877-Dec. 10, 1964; House 1919-33.

LANMAN, James (D Conn.) June 14, 1767-Aug. 7, 1841; Senate 1819-25.

LANNING, William Mershon (R N.J.) Jan. 1, 1849-Feb. 16, 1912; House 1903-June 6, 1904.

LANSING, Frederick (R N.Y.) Feb. 16, 1838-Jan. 31, 1894; House 1889-91.

LANSING, Gerrit Yates (JD N.Y.) Aug. 4, 1783-Jan. 3, 1862; House 1831-37.

LANSING, William Esselstyne (R N.Y.) Dec. 29, 1821-July 29, 1883; House 1861-63, 1871-75.

LANTAFF, William Courtland (D Fla.) July 31, 1913-Jan. 28, 1970; House 1951-55.

LANTOS, Tom (D Calif.) Feb. 1, 1928- —; House 1981- —.

LANZETTA, James Joseph (D N.Y.) Dec. 21, 1894-Oct. 27, 1956; House 1933-35, 1937-39.

LAPHAM, Elbridge Gerry (R N.Y.) Oct. 18, 1814-Jan. 8, 1890; House 1875-July 29, 1881; Senate Aug. 2, 1881-85.

LAPHAM, Oscar (D R.I.) June 29, 1837-March 29, 1926; House 1891-95.

Biographical Index

LAPORTE, John (− Pa.) Nov. 4, 1798-Aug. 22, 1862; House 1833-37.

LARCADE, Henry Dominique Jr. (D La.) July 12, 1890-March 15, 1966; House 1943-53.

LARNED, Simon (− Mass.) Aug. 3, 1753-Nov. 16, 1817; House Nov. 5, 1804-05.

LARRABEE, Charles Hathaway (D Wis.) Nov. 9, 1820-Jan. 20, 1883; House 1859-61.

LARRABEE, William Henry (D Ind.) Feb. 21, 1870-Nov. 16, 1960; House 1931-43.

LARRAZOLO, Octaviano Ambrosio (R N.M.) Dec. 7, 1859-April 7, 1930; Senate Dec. 7, 1928-29; Gov. 1919-21.

LARRINAGA, Tulio (U P.R.) Jan. 15, 1847-April 28, 1917; House (Res. Comm.) 1905-11.

LARSEN, William Washington (D Ga.) Aug. 12, 1871-Jan. 5, 1938; House 1917-33.

LARSON, Oscar John (R Minn.) May 20, 1871-Aug. 1, 1957; House 1921-25.

LA SERE, Emile (D La.) 1802-Aug. 14, 1882; House Jan. 29, 1846-51.

LASH, Israel George (R N.C.) Aug. 18, 1810-April 1, 1878; House July 20, 1868-71.

LASSITER, Francis Rives (great-nephew of Francis Everod Rives) (D Va.) Feb. 18, 1866-Oct. 31, 1909; House April 19, 1900-03, 1907-Oct. 31, 1909.

LATHAM, George Robert (R W.Va.) March 9, 1832-Dec. 16, 1917; House 1865-67.

LATHAM, Henry Jepson (R N.Y.) Dec. 10, 1908- −; House 1945-Dec. 31, 1958.

LATHAM, Louis Charles (D N.C.) Sept. 11, 1840-Oct. 16, 1895; House 1881-83, 1887-89.

LATHAM, Milton Slocum (D Calif.) May 23, 1827-March 4, 1882; House 1853-55; Senate March 5, 1860-63; Gov. Jan. 9-14, 1860.

LATHROP, Samuel (R Mass.) May 1, 1772-July 11, 1846; House 1819-27.

LATHROP, William (R Ill.) April 17, 1825-Nov. 19, 1907; House 1877-79.

LATIMER, Asbury Churchwell (D S.C.) July 31, 1851-Feb. 20, 1908; House 1893-1903; Senate 1903-Feb. 20, 1908.

LATIMER, Henry (− Del.) April 24, 1752-Dec. 19, 1819; House Feb. 14, 1794-Feb. 7, 1795; Senate Feb. 7, 1795-Feb. 28, 1801.

LATTA, Delbert Leroy (R Ohio) March 5, 1920- −; House 1959- −.

LATTA, James Polk (D Neb.) Oct. 31, 1844-Sept. 11, 1911; House 1909-Sept. 11, 1911.

LATTIMORE, William (− Miss.) Feb. 9, 1774-April 3, 1843; House (Terr. Del.) 1803-07, 1813-17.

LAURANCE, John (− N.Y.) 1750-Nov. 11, 1810; House 1789-93; Senate Nov. 9, 1796-Aug. 1800; Pres. pro tempore 1798-99; Cont. Cong. 1785-87.

LAUSCHE, Frank John (D Ohio) Nov. 14, 1895- −; Senate 1957-69; Gov. 1945-47, 1949-57.

LAUTENBERG, Frank R. (D N.J.) Jan. 23, 1924- −; Senate 1983- −.

LAW, Charles Blakeslee (R N.Y.) Feb. 5, 1872-Sept. 15, 1929; House 1905-11.

LAW, John (son of Lyman Law, grandson of Amasa Learned) (D Ind.) Oct. 28, 1796-Oct. 7, 1873; House 1861-65.

LAW, Lyman (father of John Law) (F Conn.) Aug. 19, 1770-Feb. 3, 1842; House 1811-17.

LAWLER, Frank (D Ill.) June 25, 1842-Jan. 17, 1896; House 1885-91.

LAWLER, Joab (W Ala.) June 12, 1796-May 8, 1838; House 1835-May 8, 1838.

LAWRENCE, Abbott (W Mass.) Dec. 16, 1792-Aug. 18, 1855; House 1835-37, 1839-Sept. 18, 1840.

LAWRENCE, Cornelius Van Wyck (cousin of Effingham Lawrence) (JD N.Y.) Feb. 28, 1791-Feb. 20, 1861; House 1833-May 14, 1834.

LAWRENCE, Effingham (cousin of Cornelius Van Wyck Lawrence) (D La.) March 2, 1820-Dec. 9, 1878; House March 3, 1875.

LAWRENCE, George Pelton (R Mass.) May 19, 1859-Nov. 21, 1917; House Nov. 2, 1897-1913.

LAWRENCE, George Van Eman (son of Joseph Lawrence) (W Pa.) 1786-April 17, 1842; House 1865-69, 1883-85 (1865-69 Whig, 1883-85 Republican).

LAWRENCE, Henry Franklin (R Mo.) Jan. 31, 1868-Jan. 12, 1950; House 1921-23.

LAWRENCE, John Watson (D N.Y.) Aug. 1800-Dec. 20, 1888; House 1845-47.

LAWRENCE, Joseph (father of George Van Eman Lawrence) (W Pa.) 1786-April 17, 1842; House 1825-29, 1841-April 17, 1842.

LAWRENCE, Samuel (brother of William Thomas Lawrence) (− N.Y.) May 23, 1773-Oct. 20, 1837; House 1823-25.

LAWRENCE, Sidney (D N.Y.) Dec. 31, 1801-May 9, 1892; House 1847-49.

LAWRENCE, William (D Ohio) Sept. 2, 1814-Sept. 8, 1895; House 1857-59.

LAWRENCE, William (R Ohio) June 26, 1819-May 8, 1899; House 1865-71, 1873-77.

LAWRENCE, William Thomas (brother of Samuel Lawrence) (− N.Y.) May 7, 1788-Oct. 25, 1859; House 1847-49.

LAWS, Gilbert Lafayette (R Neb.) March 11, 1838-April 25, 1907; House Dec. 2, 1889-91.

LAWSON, John Daniel (R N.Y.) Feb. 18, 1816-Jan. 24, 1896; House 1873-75.

LAWSON, John William (D Va.) Sept. 13, 1837-Feb. 21, 1905; House 1891-93.

LAWSON, Thomas Graves (D Ga.) May 2, 1835-April 16, 1912; House 1891-97.

LAWYER, Thomas (− N.Y.) Oct. 14, 1785-May 21, 1868; House 1817-19.

LAXALT, Paul Dominique (R Nev.) Aug. 2, 1922- −; Senate Dec. 18, 1974- −; Gov. 1967-71.

LAY, Alfred Morrison (D Mo.) May 20, 1836-Dec. 8, 1879; House March 4-Dec. 8, 1879.

LAY, George Washington (W N.Y.) July 26, 1798-Oct. 21, 1860; House 1833-37.

LAYTON, Caleb Rodney (R Del.) Sept. 8, 1851-Nov. 11, 1930; House 1919-23.

LAYTON, Fernando Coello (D Ohio) April 11, 1847-June 22, 1926; House 1891-97.

LAZARO, Ladislas (D La.) June 5, 1872-March 30, 1927; House 1913-March 30, 1927.

LAZEAR, Jesse (D Pa.) Dec. 12, 1804-Sept. 2, 1877; House 1861-65.

LEA, Clarence Frederick (D Calif.) July 11, 1874-June 20, 1964; House 1917-49.

LEA, Luke (brother of Pryor Lea, great-grandfather of the following) (UD Tenn.) Jan. 21, 1783-June 17, 1851; House 1833-37.

LEA, Luke (great-grandson of the preceding) (D Tenn.) April 12, 1879-Nov. 18, 1945; Senate 1911-17.

LEA, Pryor (brother of Luke Lea) (JD Tenn.) Aug. 31, 1794-Sept. 14, 1879; House 1827-31.

LEACH, Anthony Claude (Buddy) Jr. (D La.) March 30, 1934- −; House 1979-81.

LEACH, DeWitt Clinton (R Mich.) Nov. 23, 1822-Dec. 21, 1909; House 1857-61.

LEACH, James A.S. (R Iowa) Oct. 15, 1942- −; House 1977- −.

LEACH, James Madison (C N.C.) Jan. 17, 1815-June 1, 1891; House 1859-61, 1871-75 (1859-61 Whig, 1871-75 Conservative).

LEACH, Robert Milton (R Mass.) April 2, 1879-Feb. 18, 1952; House Nov. 4, 1924-25.

LEADBETTER, Daniel Parkhurst (JD Ohio) Sept. 10, 1797-Feb. 26, 1870; House 1837-41.

LEAHY, Edward Laurence (D R.I.) Feb. 9, 1886-July 22, 1953; Senate Aug. 24, 1949-Dec. 18, 1950.

LEAHY, Patrick Joseph (D Vt.) March 31, 1940- −; Senate 1975- −.

LEAKE, Eugene Walter (D N.J.) July 13, 1877-Aug. 23, 1959; House 1907-09.

LEAKE, Shelton Farrar (D Va.) Nov. 30, 1812-March 4, 1884; House 1845-47, 1859-61.

LEAKE, Walter (D Miss.) May 25, 1762-Nov. 17, 1825; Senate Dec. 10, 1817-May 15, 1820; Gov. 1822-25.

LEARNED, Amasa (grandfather of John Law) (− Conn.) Nov. 15, 1750-May 4, 1825; House 1791-95.

LEARY, Cornelius Lawrence Ludlow (U Md.) Oct. 22, 1813-March 21, 1893; House 1861-63.

LEATH, James Marvin (D Texas) May 6, 1931- —; House 1979- —.

LEATHERWOOD, Elmer O. (R Utah) Sept. 4, 1872-Dec. 24, 1929; House 1921-Dec. 24, 1929.

LEAVENWORTH, Elias Warner (R N.Y.) Dec. 20, 1803-Nov. 25, 1887; House 1875-77.

LEAVITT, Humphrey Howe (JD Ohio) June 18, 1796-March 15, 1873; House Dec. 6, 1830-July 10, 1834.

LEAVITT, Scott (R Mont.) June 16, 1879-Oct. 19, 1966; House 1923-33.

LEAVY, Charles Henry (D Wash.) Feb. 16, 1884-Sept. 25, 1952; House 1937-Aug. 1, 1942.

LE BLOND, Francis Celeste (grandfather of Frank Le Blond Kloeb) (D Ohio) Feb. 14, 1821-Nov. 9, 1902; House 1863-67.

LeBOUTILLIER, John (R N.Y.) May 26, 1953- —; House 1981-83.

LECOMPTE, Joseph (D Ky.) Dec. 15, 1797-April 25, 1851; House 1825-33.

LE COMPTE, Karl Miles (R Iowa) May 25, 1887-Sept. 30, 1972; House 1939-59.

LEDERER, Raymond Francis (D Pa.) May 19, 1938- —; House 1977-May 5, 1981.

LEE, Blair (D Md.) Aug. 9, 1857-Dec. 25, 1944; Senate Jan. 28, 1914-17.

LEE, Frank Hood (D Mo.) March 29, 1873-Nov. 20, 1952; House 1933-35.

LEE, Gary A. (R N.Y.) Aug. 18, 1933- —; House 1979-83.

LEE, Gideon (JD N.Y.) April 27, 1778-Aug. 21, 1841; House Nov. 4, 1835-37.

LEE, Gordon (D Ga.) May 29, 1859-Nov. 7, 1927; House 1905-27.

LEE, Henry (brother of Richard Bland Lee, grandfather of William Henry Fitzhugh Lee) (F Va.) Jan. 29, 1756-March 25, 1818; House 1799-1801; Cont. Cong. 1785-88; Gov. 1791-94.

LEE, John (D Md.) Jan. 30, 1788-May 17, 1871; House 1823-25.

LEE, Joshua (D N.Y.) 1783-Dec. 19, 1842; House 1835-37.

LEE, Joshua Bryan (D Okla.) Jan. 23, 1892-Aug. 10, 1967; House 1935-37; Senate 1937-43.

LEE, Moses Lindley (R N.Y.) May 29, 1805-May 19, 1876; House 1859-61.

LEE, Richard Bland (brother of Henry Lee) (— Va.) Jan. 20, 1761-March 12, 1827; House 1789-95.

LEE, Richard Henry (— Va.) Jan. 20, 1732-June 19, 1794; Senate 1789-Oct. 8, 1792; Pres. pro tempore 1791-92; Cont. Cong. 1774-80, 1784-87.

LEE, Robert Emmett (D Pa.) Oct. 12, 1868-Nov. 19, 1916; House 1911-15.

LEE, Robert Quincy (D Texas) Jan. 12, 1869-April 18, 1930; House 1929-April 18, 1930.

LEE, Silas (F Mass.) July 3, 1760-March 1, 1814; House 1799-Aug. 20, 1801.

LEE, Thomas (D N.J.) Nov. 28, 1780-Nov. 2, 1856; House 1833-37.

LEE, Warren Isbell (R N.Y.) Feb. 5, 1876-Dec. 25, 1955; House 1921-23.

LEE, William Henry Fitzhugh (grandson of Henry Lee) (D Va.) May 31, 1837-Oct. 15, 1891; House 1887-Oct. 15, 1891.

LEECH, James Russell (R Pa.) Nov. 19, 1888-Feb. 5, 1952; House 1927-Jan. 29, 1932.

LEEDOM, John Peter (D Ohio) Dec. 20, 1847-March 18, 1895; House 1881-83.

LEET, Isaac (D Pa.) 1801-June 10, 1844; House 1839-41.

LeFANTE, Joseph Anthony (D N.J.) Sept. 8, 1928- —; House 1977-Dec. 23, 1978.

LE FEVER, Jacob (father of Frank Jacob LeFevre) (R N.Y.) April 20, 1830-Feb. 4, 1905; House 1893-97.

LE FEVER, Joseph (D Pa.) April 3, 1760-Oct. 17, 1826; House 1811-13.

LE FEVRE, Benjamin (D Ohio) Oct. 8, 1838-March 7, 1922; House 1879-87.

LE FEVRE, Frank Jacob (son of Jacob Le Fever) (R N.Y.) Nov. 30, 1874-April 29, 1941; House 1905-07.

LE FEVRE, Jay (R N.Y.) Sept. 6, 1893-April 26, 1970; House 1943-51.

LEFFERTS, John (D N.Y.) Dec. 17, 1785-Sept. 18, 1829; House 1813-15.

LEFFLER, Isaac (brother of Shepherd Leffler) (— Va.) Nov. 7, 1788-March 8, 1866; House 1827-29.

LEFFLER, Shepherd (brother of Isaac Leffler) (D Iowa) April 24, 1811-Sept. 7, 1879; House Dec. 28, 1846-51.

LEFTWICH, Jabez (— Va.) Sept. 22, 1765-June 22, 1855; House 1821-25.

LEFTWICH, John William (D Tenn.) Sept. 7, 1826-March 6, 1870; House July 24, 1866-67.

LEGARDA Y TUASON, Benito (— P.I.) Sept. 27, 1853-Aug. 27, 1915; House (Res. Comm.) Nov. 22, 1907-13.

LEGARE, George Swinton (D S.C.) Nov. 11, 1869-Jan. 31, 1913; House 1903-Jan. 31, 1913.

LEGARE, Hugh Swinton (UD S.C.) Jan. 2, 1797-June 20, 1843; House 1837-39; Atty. Gen. 1841-43; Secy. of State 1843.

LEGGETT, Robert L. (D Calif.) July 26, 1926- —; House 1963-79.

LEHLBACH, Frederick Reimold (nephew of Herman Lehlbach) (R N.J.) Jan. 31, 1876-Aug. 4, 1937; House 1915-37.

LEHLBACH, Herman (uncle of Frederick Reimold Lehlbach) (R N.J.) July 3, 1845-Jan. 11, 1904; House 1885-91.

LEHMAN, Herbert Henry (D N.Y.) March 28, 1878-Dec. 5, 1963; Senate Nov. 9, 1949-57; Gov. 1933-42.

LEHMAN, Richard Henry (D Calif.) July 20, 1948- —; House 1983- —.

LEHMAN, William (D Fla.) Oct. 4, 1913- —; House 1973- —.

LEHMAN, William Eckart (D Pa.) Aug. 21, 1821-July 19, 1895; House 1861-63.

LEHR, John Camillus (D Mich.) Nov. 18, 1878-Feb. 17, 1958; House 1933-35.

LEIB, Michael (D Pa.) Jan. 8, 1760-Dec. 22, 1822; House 1799-Feb. 14, 1806; Senate Jan. 9, 1809-Feb. 14, 1814.

LEIB, Owen D. (D Pa.) ?-June 17, 1848; House 1845-47.

LEIDY, Paul (D Pa.) Nov. 13, 1813-Sept. 11, 1877; House Dec. 7, 1857-59.

LEIGH, Benjamin Watkins (W Va.) June 18, 1781-Feb. 2, 1849; Senate Feb. 26, 1834-July 4, 1836.

LEIGHTY, Jacob D. (R Ind.) Nov. 15, 1839-Oct. 18, 1912; House 1895-97.

LEIPER, George Gray (D Pa.) Feb. 3, 1786-Nov. 18, 1868; House 1829-31.

LEISENRING, John (R Pa.) June 3, 1853-Jan. 19, 1901; House 1895-97.

LEITER, Benjamin Franklin (R Ohio) Oct. 13, 1813-June 17, 1866; House 1855-59.

LELAND, George Thomas (Mickey) (D Texas) Nov. 27, 1944- —; House 1979- —.

LEMKE, William (R N.D.) Aug. 13, 1878-May 30, 1950; House 1933-41, 1943-May 30, 1950 (1933-41 Nonpartisan Republican, 1943-50 Republican).

LE MOYNE, John Valcoulon (D Ill.) Nov. 17, 1828-July 27, 1918; House May 6, 1876-77.

LENAHAN, John Thomas (D Pa.) Nov. 15, 1852-April 28, 1920; House 1907-09.

L'ENGLE, Claude (D Fla.) Oct. 19, 1868-Nov. 6, 1919; House 1913-15.

LENNON, Alton Asa (D N.C.) Aug. 17, 1906- —; Senate July 10, 1953-Nov. 28, 1954; House 1957-73.

LENROOT, Irvine Luther (R Wis.) Jan. 31, 1869-Jan. 26, 1949; House 1909-April 17, 1918; Senate April 18, 1918-27.

LENT, James (JD N.Y.) 1782-Feb. 22, 1833; House 1829-Feb. 22, 1833.

LENT, Norman Frederick (R N.Y.) March 23, 1931- —; House 1971- —.

LENTZ, John Jacob (D Ohio) Jan. 27, 1856-July 27, 1931; House 1897-1901.

LEONARD, Fred Churchill (R Pa.) Feb. 16, 1856-Dec. 5, 1921; House 1895-97.

Biographical Index

LEONARD, George (— Mass.) July 4, 1729-July 26, 1819; House 1789-91, 1795-97.

LEONARD, John Edwards (grandnephew of John Edwards of Pa.) (R La.) Sept. 22, 1845-March 15, 1878; House 1877-March 15, 1878.

LEONARD, Moses Gage (D N.Y.) July 10, 1809-March 20, 1899; House 1843-45.

LEONARD, Stephen Banks (D N.Y.) April 15, 1793-May 8, 1876; House 1835-37, 1839-41.

LESHER, John Vandling (D Pa.) July 27, 1866-May 3, 1932; House 1913-21.

LESINSKI, John (father of John Lesinski Jr.) (D Mich.) Jan. 3, 1885-May 27, 1950; House 1933-May 27, 1950.

LESINSKI, John Jr. (son of John Lesinski) (D Mich.) Dec. 28, 1914-—; House 1951-65.

LESSLER, Montague (R N.Y.) Jan. 1, 1869-Feb. 17, 1938; House Jan. 7, 1902-03.

LESTER, Posey Green (D Va.) March 12, 1850-Feb. 9, 1929; House 1889-93.

LESTER, Rufus Ezekiel (D Ga.) Dec. 12, 1837-June 16, 1906; House 1889-June 16, 1906.

LETCHER, John (D Va.) March 29, 1813-Jan. 26, 1884; House 1851-59; Gov. 1860-64.

LETCHER, Robert Perkins (W Ky.) Feb. 10, 1788-Jan. 24, 1861; House 1823-33, Aug. 6, 1834-35; Gov. 1840-44 (1823-27 Clay Democrat, 1827-44 Whig).

LETTS, Fred Dickinson (cousin of Lester Jesse Dickinson) (R Iowa) April 26, 1875-Jan. 19, 1965; House 1925-31.

LEVER, Asbury Francis (D S.C.) Jan. 5, 1875-April 28, 1940; House Nov. 5, 1901-Aug. 1, 1919.

LEVERING, Robert Woodrow (son-in-law of Usher L. Burdick, brother-in-law of Quentin N. Burdick) (D Ohio) Oct. 3, 1914-—; House 1959-61.

LEVIN, Carl Milton (D Mich.) June 28, 1934-—; Senate 1979-—.

LEVIN, Lewis Charles (AP Pa.) Nov. 10, 1808-March 14, 1860; House 1845-51.

LEVIN, Sander Martin (D Mich.) Sept. 6, 1931-—; House 1983-—.

LEVINE, Mel (D Calif.) June 7, 1943-—; House 1983-—.

LEVITAS, Elliott Harris (D Ga.) Dec. 26, 1930-—; House 1975-85.

LEVY, David (R Fla.) (See YULEE, David Levy.)

LEVY, Jefferson Monroe (D N.Y.) April 16, 1852-March 6, 1924; House 1899-1901, 1911-15.

LEVY, William Mallory (D La.) Oct. 31, 1827-Aug. 14, 1882; House 1875-77.

LEWIS, Abner (W N.Y.) ?-?; House 1845-47.

LEWIS, Barbour (R Tenn.) Jan. 5, 1818-July 15, 1893; House 1873-75.

LEWIS, Burwell Boykin (D Ala.) July 7, 1838-Oct. 11, 1885; House 1875-77, 1879-Oct. 1, 1880.

LEWIS, Charles Swearinger (D Va.) Feb. 26, 1821-Jan. 22, 1878; House Dec. 4, 1854-55.

LEWIS, Clarke (D Miss.) Nov. 8, 1840-March 13, 1896; House 1889-93.

LEWIS, David John (D Md.) May 1, 1869-Aug. 12, 1952; House 1911-17, 1931-39.

LEWIS, Dixon Hall (D Ala.) Aug. 10, 1802-Oct. 25, 1848; House 1829-April 22, 1844; Senate April 22, 1844-Oct. 25, 1848 (1829-44 State Rights Democrat, 1844-48 Democrat).

LEWIS, Earl Ramage (R Ohio) Feb. 22, 1887-Feb. 1, 1956; House 1939-41, 1943-49.

LEWIS, Edward Taylor (D La.) Oct. 26, 1834-April 26, 1927; House 1883-85.

LEWIS, Elijah Banks (D Ga.) March 27, 1854-Dec. 10, 1920; House 1897-1909.

LEWIS, Fred Ewing (R Pa.) Feb. 8, 1865-June 27, 1949; House 1913-15.

LEWIS, James Hamilton (D Wash./Ill.) May 18, 1863-April 9, 1939; House 1897-99 (Wash.); Senate March 26, 1913-19, 1931-April 9, 1939 (Ill.).

LEWIS, Jerry (R Calif.) Oct. 21, 1934-—; House 1979-—.

LEWIS, John Francis (R Va.) March 1, 1818-Sept. 2, 1895; Senate Jan. 26, 1870-75.

LEWIS, John Henry (R Ill.) July 21, 1830-Jan. 6, 1929; House 1881-83.

LEWIS, John William (R Ky.) Oct. 14, 1841-Dec. 20, 1913; House 1895-97.

LEWIS, Joseph Jr. (F Va.) 1772-March 30, 1834; House 1803-17.

LEWIS, Joseph Horace (D Ky.) Oct. 29, 1824-July 6, 1904; House May 10, 1870-73.

LEWIS, Lawrence (D Colo.) June 22, 1879-Dec. 9, 1943; House 1933-Dec. 9, 1943.

LEWIS, Robert Jacob (R Pa.) Dec. 30, 1864-July 24, 1933; House 1901-03.

LEWIS, Thomas (— Va.) ?-?; House 1803-March 5, 1804.

LEWIS, Thomas F. (R Fla.) Oct. 26, 1924-—; House 1983-—.

LEWIS, William (R Ky.) Sept. 22, 1868-Aug. 8, 1959; House April 24, 1948-49.

LEWIS, William J. (D Va.) July 4, 1766-Nov. 1, 1828; House 1817-19.

LIBBEY, Harry (R Va.) Nov. 22, 1843-Sept. 30, 1913; House 1883-87.

LIBONATI, Roland Victor (D Ill.) Dec. 29, 1900-—; House Dec. 31, 1957-65.

LICHTENWALNER, Norton Lewis (D Pa.) June 1, 1889-May 3, 1960; House 1931-33.

LICHTENWALTER, Franklin Herbert (R Pa.) March 28, 1910-March 4, 1973; House Sept. 9, 1947-51.

LIEB, Charles (D Ind.) May 20, 1852-Sept. 1, 1928; House 1913-17.

LIEBEL, Michael Jr. (D Pa.) Dec. 12, 1870-Aug. 8, 1927; House 1915-17.

LIGHTFOOT, Jim Ross (R Iowa) Sept. 27, 1939-—; House 1985-—.

LIGON, Robert Fulwood (D Ala.) Dec. 16, 1823-Oct. 11, 1901; House 1877-79.

LIGON, Thomas Watkins (D Md.) May 10, 1810-Jan. 12, 1881; House 1845-49; Gov. 1854-58.

LILLEY, George Leavens (R Conn.) Aug. 3, 1859-April 21, 1909; House 1903-Jan. 5, 1909; Gov. Jan. 5-April 21, 1909.

LILLEY, Mial Eben (R Pa.) May 30, 1850-Feb. 28, 1915; House 1905-07.

LILLY, Samuel (D N.J.) Oct. 28, 1815-April 3, 1880; House 1853-55.

LILLY, Thomas Jefferson (D W.Va.) June 3, 1878-April 2, 1956; House 1923-25.

LILLY, William (R Pa.) June 3, 1821-Dec. 1, 1893; House March 4-Dec. 1, 1893.

LINCOLN, Abraham (R Ill.) Feb. 12, 1809-April 15, 1865; House 1847-49; President 1861-April 15, 1865 (1847-49 Whig, 1861-65 Republican).

LINCOLN, Enoch (son of Levi Lincoln, brother of Levi Lincoln) (— Mass./Maine) Dec. 28, 1788-Oct. 8, 1829; House Nov. 4, 1818-21 (Mass.), 1821-26 (Maine); Gov. (Maine) 1827-Oct. 8, 1829.

LINCOLN, Levi (father of Enoch Lincoln and Levi Lincoln) (D Mass.) May 15, 1749-April 14, 1820; House Dec. 15, 1800-March 5, 1801; Atty. Gen. 1801-04; Gov. 1808-09.

LINCOLN, Levi (son of the preceding, brother of Enoch Lincoln) (W Mass.) Oct. 25, 1782-May 29, 1868; House Feb. 17, 1834-March 16, 1841; Gov. 1825-34.

LINCOLN, William Slosson (R N.Y.) Aug. 13, 1813-April 21, 1893; House 1867-69.

LIND, James Francis (D Pa.) Oct. 17, 1900-—; House 1949-53.

LIND, John (D Minn.) March 25, 1854-Sept. 18, 1930; House 1887-93, 1903-05; Gov. 1898-1900 (1887-93 Republican, 1898-1900, 1903-05 Democrat).

LINDBERG, Charles Augustus (R Minn.) Jan. 20, 1859-May 24, 1924; House 1907-17.

LINDLEY, James Johnson (W Mo.) Jan. 1, 1822-April 18, 1891; House 1853-57.

LINDQUIST, Francis Oscar (R Mich.) Sept. 27, 1869-Sept. 25, 1924; House 1913-15.

LINDSAY, George Henry (father of George Washington Lindsay) (D N.Y.) Jan. 7, 1837-May 25, 1916; House 1901-13.

LINDSAY, George Washington (son of George Henry Lindsay) (D N.Y.) March 28, 1865-March 15, 1938; House 1923-35.

LINDSAY, John Vliet (R N.Y.) Nov. 24, 1921-—; House 1959-Dec. 31, 1965.

LINDSAY, William (D Ky.) Sept. 4, 1835-Oct. 15, 1909; Senate Feb. 15, 1893-1901.

LINDSEY, Stephen Decatur (R Maine) March 3, 1828-April 26, 1884; House 1877-83.

LINDSLEY, James Girard (R N.Y.) March 19, 1819-Dec. 4, 1898; House 1885-87.

LINDSLEY, William Dell (D Ohio) Dec. 25, 1812-March 11, 1890; House 1853-55.

LINEBERGER, Walter Franklin (R Calif.) July 20, 1883-Oct. 9, 1943; House 1921-27.

LINEHAN, Neil Joseph (D Ill.) Sept. 23, 1895-Aug. 23, 1967; House 1949-51.

LINK, Arthur A. (D N.D.) May 24, 1914- —; House 1971-73; Gov. 1973-81.

LINK, William Walter (D Ill.) Feb. 12, 1884-Sept. 23, 1950; House 1945-47.

LINN, Archibald Ladley (W N.Y.) Oct. 15, 1802-Oct. 10, 1857; House 1841-43.

LINN, James (D N.J.) 1749-Jan. 5, 1821; House 1799-1801.

LINN, John (— N.J.) Dec. 3, 1763-Jan. 5, 1821; House 1817-Jan. 5, 1821.

LINN, Lewis Fields (D Mo.) Nov. 5, 1796-Oct. 3, 1843; Senate Oct. 25, 1833-Oct. 3, 1843.

LINNEY, Romulus Zachariah (R N.C.) Dec. 26, 1841-April 15, 1910; House 1895-1901.

LINTHICUM, John Charles (D Md.) Nov. 26, 1867-Oct. 5, 1932; House 1911-Oct. 5, 1932.

LINTON, William Seelye (R Mich.) Feb. 4, 1856-Nov. 22, 1927; House 1893-97.

LIPINSKI, William Oliver (D Ill.) Dec. 22, 1937- —; House 1983- —.

LIPPITT, Henry Frederick (R R.I.) Oct. 12, 1856-Dec. 28, 1933; Senate 1911-17.

LIPSCOMB, Glenard Paul (R Calif.) Aug. 19, 1915-Feb. 1, 1970; House Nov. 10, 1953-Feb. 1, 1970.

LISLE, Marcus Claiborne (D Ky.) Sept. 23, 1862-July 7, 1894; House 1893-July 7, 1894.

LITCHFIELD, Elisha (D N.Y.) July 12, 1785-Aug. 4, 1859; House 1821-25.

LITTAUER, Lucius Nathan (R N.Y.) Jan. 20, 1859-March 2, 1944; House 1897-1907.

LITTLE, Chauncey Bundy (D Kan.) Feb. 10, 1877-Sept. 29, 1952; House 1925-27.

LITTLE, Edward Campbell (R Kan.) Dec. 14, 1858-June 27, 1924; House 1917-June 27, 1924.

LITTLE, Edward Preble (D Mass.) Nov. 7, 1791-Feb. 6, 1875; House Dec. 13, 1852-53.

LITTLE, John (R Ohio) April 25, 1837-Oct. 18, 1900; House 1885-87.

LITTLE, John Sebastian (D Ark.) March 15, 1853-Oct. 29, 1916; House Dec. 3, 1894-Jan. 14, 1907; Gov. Jan. 8-Feb. 11, 1907.

LITTLE, Joseph James (D N.Y.) June 5, 1841-Feb. 11, 1913; House Nov. 3, 1891-93.

LITTLE, Peter (D Md.) Dec. 11, 1775-Feb. 5, 1830; House 1811-13, Sept. 2, 1816-29.

LITTLEFIELD, Charles Edgar (R Maine) June 21, 1851-May 2, 1915; House June 19, 1899-Sept. 30, 1908.

LITTLEFIELD, Nathaniel Swett (CassD Maine) Sept. 20, 1804-Aug. 15, 1882; House 1841-43, 1849-51 (1841-43 Democrat, 1849-51 Cass Democrat).

LITTLEJOHN, DeWitt Clinton (R N.Y.) Feb. 7, 1818-Oct. 27, 1892; House 1863-65.

LITTLEPAGE, Adam Brown (D W.Va.) April 14, 1859-June 29, 1921; House 1911-13, 1915-19.

LITTLETON, Martin Wiley (D N.Y.) Jan. 12, 1872-Dec. 19, 1934; House 1911-13.

LITTON, Jerry Lon (D Mo.) May 12, 1937-Aug. 3, 1976; House 1973-Aug. 3, 1976.

LIVELY, Robert Maclin (D Texas) Jan. 6, 1855-Jan. 15, 1929; House July 23, 1910-11.

LIVERMORE, Arthur (son of Samuel Livermore, brother of Edward St. Loe Livermore) (D N.H.) July 29, 1766-July 1, 1853; House 1817-21, 1823-25.

LIVERMORE, Edward St. Loe (son of Samuel Livermore, brother of Arthur Livermore) (F Mass.) April 5, 1762-Sept. 15, 1832; House 1807-11.

LIVERMORE, Samuel (father of Arthur Livermore and Edward St. Loe Livermore) (— N.H.) May 14, 1732-May 18, 1803; House 1789-93; Senate 1793-June 12, 1801; Pres. pro tempore 1796, 1800; Cont. Cong. 1780-82, 1785.

LIVERNASH, Edward James (subsequently Edward James de Nivernais) (UL/D Calif.) Feb. 14, 1866-June 1, 1938; House 1903-05.

LIVINGSTON, Edward (D N.Y./La.) May 26, 1764-May 23, 1836; House 1795-1801 (N.Y.), 1823-29 (La.); Senate 1829-May 24, 1831 (La.); Secy. of State 1831-33.

LIVINGSTON, Henry Walter (— N.Y.) 1768-Dec. 22, 1810; House 1803-07.

LIVINGSTON, Leonidas Felix (D Ga.) April 3, 1832-Feb. 11, 1912; House 1891-1911.

LIVINGSTON, Robert LeRoy (F N.Y.) ?-?; House 1809-May 6, 1812.

LIVINGSTON, Robert (Bob) Linligthgow Jr. (R La.) April 30, 1943- —; House Sept. 7, 1977- —.

LLOYD, Edward (D Md.) July 22, 1779-June 2, 1834; House Dec. 3, 1806-09; Senate 1819-Jan. 14, 1826; Gov. 1809-11.

LLOYD, James (D Md.) 1745-1820; Senate Dec. 11, 1797-Dec. 1, 1800.

LLOYD, James (F Mass.) Dec. 1769-April 5, 1831; Senate June 9, 1808-May 1, 1813, June 5, 1822-May 23, 1826.

LLOYD, James Frederick (D Calif.) Sept. 27, 1922- —; House 1975-81.

LLOYD, James Tilghman (D Mo.) Aug. 28, 1857-April 3, 1944; House June 1, 1897-1917.

LLOYD, Marilyn Laird (D Tenn.) Jan. 3, 1929- —; House 1975- —.

LLOYD, Sherman Parkinson (R Utah) Jan. 11, 1914-Dec. 15, 1979; House 1963-65, 1967-73.

LLOYD, Wesley (D Wash.) July 24, 1883-Jan. 10, 1936; House 1933-Jan. 10, 1936.

LOAN, Benjamin Franklin (Rad. Mo.) Oct. 4, 1819-March 30, 1881; House 1863-69 (1863-67 Emancipationist, 1867-69 Radical).

LOBECK, Charles Otto (D Neb.) April 6, 1852-Jan. 30, 1920; House 1911-19.

LOCHER, Cyrus (D Ohio) March 8, 1878-Aug. 17, 1929; Senate April 5-Dec. 14, 1928.

LOCKE, Francis (nephew of Matthew Locke) (D N.C.) Oct. 31, 1776-Jan. 8, 1823; Senate 1814-Dec. 5, 1815.

LOCKE, John (— Mass.) Feb. 14, 1764-March 29, 1855; House 1823-29.

LOCKE, Matthew (uncle of Francis Locke, great-great-great-grandfather of Effiegene (Locke) Wingo) (D N.C.) 1730-Sept. 7, 1801; House 1793-99.

LOCKHART, James (D Ind.) Feb. 13, 1806-Sept. 7, 1857; House 1851-53, March 4-Sept. 7, 1857.

LOCKHART, James Alexander (D N.C.) June 2, 1850-Dec. 24, 1905; House 1895-June 5, 1896.

LOCKWOOD, Daniel Newton (D N.Y.) June 1, 1844-June 1, 1906; House 1877-79, 1891-95.

LODGE, Henry Cabot (grandfather of Henry Cabot Lodge Jr. and John Davis Lodge, great-grandson of George Cabot) (R Mass.) May 12, 1850-Nov. 9, 1924; House 1887-93; Senate 1893-Nov. 9, 1924; Senate majority leader 1919-24.

LODGE, Henry Cabot Jr. (grandson of Henry Cabot Lodge, brother of John Davis Lodge, nephew of Augustus Peabody Gardner) (R Mass.) July 5, 1902- —; Senate 1937-Feb. 3, 1944, 1947-53.

LODGE, John Davis (grandson of Henry Cabot Lodge, brother of Henry Cabot Lodge Jr., nephew of Augustus Peabody Gardner) (R Conn.) Oct. 20, 1903- —; House 1947-51; Gov. 1951-55.

LOEFFLER, Thomas Gilbert (R Texas) Aug. 1, 1946- —; House 1979- —.

LOFLAND, James Ruch (R Del.) Nov. 2, 1823-Feb. 10, 1894; House 1873-75.

LOFT, George William (D N.Y.) Feb. 6, 1865-Nov. 6, 1943; House Nov. 4, 1913-17.

LOFTIN, Scott Marion (D Fla.) Sept. 14, 1878-Sept. 22, 1953; Senate May 26-Nov. 3, 1936.

LOGAN, George (D Pa.) Sept. 9, 1753-April 9, 1821; Senate July 13, 1801-07.

LOGAN, Henry (D Pa.) April 14, 1784-Dec. 26, 1866; House 1835-39.

Biographical Index

LOGAN, John Alexander (R Ill.) Feb. 9, 1826-Dec. 26, 1886; House 1859-April 2, 1862, 1867-71; Senate 1871-77, 1879-Dec. 26, 1886 (1859-62 Democrat, 1867-86 Republican).

LOGAN, Marvel Mills (D Ky.) Jan. 7, 1875-Oct. 3, 1939; Senate 1931-Oct. 3, 1939.

LOGAN, William (D Ky.) Dec. 8, 1776-Aug. 8, 1822; Senate 1819-May 28, 1820.

LOGAN, William Turner (D S.C.) June 21, 1874-Sept. 15, 1941; House 1921-25.

LOGUE, James Washington (D Pa.) Feb. 22, 1863-Aug. 27, 1925; House 1913-15.

LONDON, Meyer (Soc. N.Y.) Dec. 29, 1871-June 6, 1926; House 1915-19, 1921-23.

LONERGAN, Augustine (D Conn.) May 20, 1874-Oct. 18, 1947; House 1913-15, 1917-21, 1931-33; Senate 1933-39.

LONG, Alexander (D Ohio) Dec. 24, 1816-Nov. 28, 1886; House 1863-65.

LONG, Chester Isaiah (R Kan.) Oct. 12, 1860-July 1, 1934; House 1895-97, 1899-March 4, 1903; Senate 1903-09.

LONG, Clarence Dickinson (D Md.) Dec. 11, 1908-—; House 1963-85.

LONG, Edward Henry Carroll (W Md.) Sept. 28, 1808-Oct. 16, 1865; House 1845-47.

LONG, Edward Vaughn (D Mo.) July 18, 1908-Nov. 6, 1972; Senate Sept. 23, 1960-Dec. 27, 1968.

LONG, George Shannon (brother of Huey Pierce Long, brother-in-law of Rose McConnell Long, uncle of Russell Billiu Long, cousin of Gillis William Long) (D La.) Sept. 11, 1883-March 22, 1958; House 1953-March 22, 1958.

LONG, Gillis William (cousin of Huey Pierce Long, Rose McConnell Long, Russell Billiu Long and George Shannon Long) (D La.) May 4, 1923-Jan. 20, 1985; House 1963-65, 1973-Jan. 20, 1985.

LONG, Huey Pierce (husband of Rose McConnell Long, father of Russell Billiu Long, brother of George Shannon Long) (D La.) Aug. 30, 1893-Sept. 10, 1935; Senate Jan. 25, 1932-Sept. 10, 1935; Gov. 1928-32.

LONG, Jefferson Franklin (R Ga.) March 3, 1836-Feb. 5, 1900; House Dec. 22, 1870-71.

LONG, John (W N.C.) Feb. 26, 1785-Aug. 11, 1857; House 1821-29.

LONG, John Benjamin (D Texas) Sept. 8, 1843-April 27, 1924; House 1891-93.

LONG, John Davis (R Mass.) Oct. 27, 1838-Aug. 28, 1915; House 1883-89; Gov. 1880-83; Secy. of the Navy 1897-1902.

LONG, Lewis Marshall (D Ill.) June 22, 1883-Sept. 9, 1957; House 1937-39.

LONG, Oren Ethelbirt (D Hawaii) March 4, 1889-May 6, 1965; Senate Aug. 21, 1959-63; Gov. (Hawaii Terr.) 1951-53.

LONG, Rose McConnell (widow of Huey Pierce Long, mother of Russell Billiu Long, sister-in-law of George Shannon Long) (D La.) April 8, 1892-May 27, 1970; Senate Jan. 31, 1936-37.

LONG, Russell Billiu (son of Huey Pierce Long and Rose McConnell Long, nephew of George Shannon Long) (D La.) Nov. 3, 1918-—; Senate Dec. 31, 1948-—.

LONG, Speedy O. (D La.) June 16, 1928-—; House 1965-73.

LONGFELLOW, Stephen (F Maine) June 23, 1775-Aug. 2, 1849; House 1823-25.

LONGNECKER, Henry Clay (R Pa.) April 17, 1820-Sept. 16, 1871; House 1859-61.

LONGWORTH, Nicholas (nephew of Bellamy Storer) (R Ohio) Nov. 5, 1869-April 9, 1931; House 1903-13, 1915-April 9, 1931; House majority leader 1923-25; Speaker 1925-31.

LONGYEAR, John Wesley (R Mich.) Oct. 22, 1820-March 11, 1875; House 1863-67.

LOOFBOUROW, Frederick Charles (R Utah) Feb. 8, 1874-July 8, 1949; House Nov. 4, 1930-33.

LOOMIS, Andrew Williams (W Ohio) June 27, 1797-Aug. 24, 1873; House March 4-Oct. 20, 1837.

LOOMIS, Arphaxed (D N.Y.) April 9, 1798-Sept. 15, 1885; House 1837-39.

LOOMIS, Dwight (R Conn.) July 27, 1821-Sept. 17, 1903; House 1859-63.

LORD, Bert (R N.Y.) Dec. 4, 1869-May 24, 1939; House 1935-May 24, 1939.

LORD, Frederick William (W N.Y.) Dec. 11, 1800-May 24, 1860; House 1847-49.

LORD, Henry William (R Mich.) March 8, 1821-Jan. 25, 1891; House 1881-83.

LORD, Scott (D N.Y.) Dec. 11, 1820-Sept. 10, 1885; House 1875-77.

LORE, Charles Brown (D Del.) March 16, 1831-March 6, 1911; House 1883-87.

LORIMER, William (R Ill.) April 27, 1861-Sept. 13, 1934; House 1895-1901, 1903-June 17, 1909; Senate June 18, 1909-July 13, 1912.

LORING, George Bailey (R Mass.) Nov. 8, 1817-Sept. 13, 1891; House 1877-81.

LOSER, Joseph Carlton (D Tenn.) Oct. 1, 1892-July 31, 1984; House 1957-63.

LOTT, Chester Trent (R Miss.) Oct. 9, 1941-—; House 1973-—.

LOUD, Eugene Francis (R Calif.) March 12, 1847-Dec. 19, 1908; House 1891-1903.

LOUD, George Alvin (R Mich.) June 18, 1852-Nov. 13, 1925; House 1903-13, 1915-17.

LOUDENSLAGER, Henry Clay (R N.J.) May 22, 1852-Aug. 12, 1911; House 1893-Aug. 12, 1911.

LOUGHRIDGE, William (R Iowa) July 11, 1827-Sept. 26, 1889; House 1867-71, 1873-75.

LOUNSBERY, William (D N.Y.) Dec. 25, 1831-Nov. 8, 1905; House 1879-81.

LOUTTIT, James Alexander (R Calif.) Oct. 16, 1848-July 26, 1906; House 1885-87.

LOVE, Francis Johnson (R W.Va.) Jan. 23, 1901-—; House 1947-49.

LOVE, James (— Ky.) May 12, 1795-June 12, 1874; House 1833-35.

LOVE, John (D Va.) ?-Aug. 17, 1822; House 1807-11.

LOVE, Peter Early (D Ga.) July 7, 1818-Nov. 8, 1866; House 1859-Jan. 23, 1861.

LOVE, Rodney Marvin (D Ohio) July 18, 1908-—; House 1965-67.

LOVE, Thomas Cutting (W N.Y.) Nov. 30, 1789-Sept. 17, 1853; House 1835-37.

LOVE, William Carter (D N.C.) 1784-1835; House 1815-17.

LOVE, William Franklin (D Miss.) March 29, 1850-Oct. 16, 1898; House 1897-Oct. 16, 1898.

LOVEJOY, Owen (cousin of Nathan Allen Farwell) (R Ill.) Jan. 6, 1811-March 25, 1864; House 1857-March 25, 1864.

LOVERING, Henry Bacon (D Mass.) April 8, 1841-April 5, 1911; House 1883-87.

LOVERING, William Croad (R Mass.) Feb. 25, 1835-Feb. 4, 1910; House 1897-Feb. 4, 1910.

LOVETT, John (F N.Y.) Feb. 20, 1761-Aug. 12, 1818; House 1813-17.

LOVETTE, Oscar Byrd (R Tenn.) Dec. 20, 1871-July 6, 1934; House 1931-33.

LOVRE, Harold Orrin (R S.D.) Jan. 30, 1904-Jan. 17, 1972; House 1949-57.

LOW, Frederick Ferdinand (R Calif.) June 30, 1828-July 21, 1894; House June 3, 1862-63; Gov. 1863-67.

LOW, Philip Burrill (R N.Y.) May 6, 1836-Aug. 23, 1912; House 1895-99.

LOWDEN, Frank Orren (R Ill.) Jan. 26, 1861-March 20, 1943; House Nov. 6, 1906-11; Gov. 1917-21.

LOWE, David Perley (R Kan.) Aug. 22, 1823-April 10, 1882; House 1871-75.

LOWE, William Manning (GD Ala.) June 12, 1842-Oct. 12, 1882; House 1879-81, June 3, 1882-Oct. 12, 1882.

LOWELL, Joshua Adams (D Maine) March 20, 1801-March 13, 1874; House 1839-43.

LOWENSTEIN, Allard K. (D-L N.Y.) Jan. 16, 1929-March 14, 1980; House 1969-71.

LOWER, Christian (D Pa.) Jan. 7, 1740-Dec. 19, 1806; House 1805-Dec. 19, 1806.

LOWERY, Bill (R Calif.) May 2, 1947-—; House 1981-—.

LOWNDES, Lloyd Jr. (R Md.) Feb. 21, 1845-Jan. 8, 1905; House 1873-75; Gov. 1896-1900.

LOWNDES, Thomas (brother of William Lowndes) (F S.C.) Jan. 22, 1766-July 8, 1843; House 1801-05.

LOWNDES, William (brother of Thomas Lowndes) (D S.C.) Feb. 11, 1782-Oct. 27, 1822; House 1811-May 8, 1822.

LOWREY, Bill Green (D Miss.) May 25, 1862-Sept. 2, 1947; House 1921-29.

LOWRIE, Walter (D Pa.) Dec. 10, 1784-Dec. 14, 1868; Senate 1819-25.

LOWRY, Michael E. (D Wash.) March 8, 1939- —; House 1979- —.

LOWRY, Robert (D Ind.) April 2, 1824-Jan. 27, 1904; House 1883-87.

LOYALL, George (D Va.) May 29, 1789-Feb. 24, 1868; House March 9, 1830-31, 1833-37.

LOZIER, Ralph Fulton (D Mo.) Jan. 28, 1866-May 28, 1945; House 1923-35.

LUCAS, Edward (brother of William Lucas) (D Va.) Oct. 20, 1780-March 4, 1858; House 1833-37.

LUCAS, John Baptiste Charles (D Pa.) Aug. 14, 1758-Aug. 17, 1842; House 1803-05.

LUCAS, Scott Wike (D Ill.) Feb. 19, 1892-Feb. 22, 1968; House 1935-39; Senate 1939-51; Senate majority leader 1949-51.

LUCAS, William (brother of Edward Lucas) (D Va.) Nov. 30, 1800-Aug. 29, 1877; House 1839-41, 1843-45.

LUCAS, William Vincent (R S.D.) July 3, 1835-Nov. 10, 1921; House 1893-95.

LUCAS, Wingate Hezekiah (D Texas) May 1, 1908- —; House 1947-55.

LUCE, Clare Boothe (stepdaughter of Albert Elmer Austin) (R Conn.) April 10, 1903- —; House 1943-47.

LUCE, Robert (R Mass.) Dec. 2, 1862-April 17, 1946; House 1919-35, 1937-41.

LUCKEY, Henry Carl (D Neb.) Nov. 22, 1868-Dec. 31, 1956; House 1935-39.

LUCKING, Alfred (D Mich.) Dec. 18, 1856-Dec. 1, 1929; House 1903-05.

LUDLOW, Louis Leon (D Ind.) June 24, 1873-Nov. 28, 1950; House 1929-49.

LUECKE, John Frederick (D Mich.) July 4, 1889-March 21, 1952; House 1937-39.

LUFKIN, Willfred Weymouth (R Mass.) March 10, 1879-March 28, 1934; House Nov. 6, 1917-June 30, 1921.

LUGAR, Richard Green (R Ind.) April 4, 1932- —; Senate 1977- —.

LUHRING, Oscar Raymond (R Ind.) Feb. 11, 1879-Aug. 20, 1944; House 1919-23.

LUJAN, Manuel Jr. (R N.M.) May 12, 1928- —; House 1969- —.

LUKEN, Thomas Andrew (D Ohio) July 9, 1925- —; House March 5, 1974-75, 1977- —.

LUKENS, Donald E. (Buz) (R Ohio) Feb. 11, 1931- —; House 1967-71.

LUMPKIN, Alva Moore (D S.C.) Nov. 13, 1886-Aug. 1, 1941; Senate July 22-Aug. 1, 1941.

LUMPKIN, John Henry (nephew of Wilson Lumpkin) (D Ga.) June 13, 1812-July 10, 1860; House 1843-49, 1855-57.

LUMPKIN, Wilson (uncle of John Henry Lumpkin, grandfather of Middleton Pope Barrow) (D Ga.) Jan. 14, 1783-Dec. 28, 1870; House 1815-17, 1827-31; Senate Nov. 22, 1837-41; Gov. 1831-35.

LUNA, Tranquillino (R N.M.) Feb. 25, 1849-Nov. 20, 1892; House (Terr. Del.) 1881-March 5, 1884.

LUNDEEN, Ernest (FL Minn.) Aug. 4, 1878-Aug. 31, 1940; House 1917-19, 1933-37; Senate 1937-Aug. 31, 1940 (1917-19 Republican, 1933-40 Farmer Laborite).

LUNDIN, Frederick (R Ill.) May 18, 1868-Aug. 20, 1947; House 1909-11.

LUNDINE, Stanley N. (D N.Y.) Feb. 4, 1939- —; House March 8, 1976- —.

LUNGREN, Daniel Edward (R Calif.) Sept. 22, 1946- —; House 1979- —.

LUNN, George Richard (D N.Y.) June 23, 1873-Nov. 27, 1948; House 1917-19.

LUSK, Georgia L. (D N.M.) May 12, 1893-Jan. 5, 1971; House 1947-49.

LUSK, Hall Stoner (D Ore.) Sept. 21, 1883-May 15, 1983; Senate March 16-Nov. 8, 1960.

LUTTRELL, John King (D Calif.) June 27, 1831-Oct. 4, 1893; House 1873-79.

LYBRAND, Archibald (R Ohio) May 23, 1840-Feb. 7, 1910; House 1897-1901.

LYLE, Aaron (D Pa.) Nov. 17, 1759-Sept. 24, 1825; House 1809-17.

LYLE, John Emmett Jr. (D Texas) Sept. 4, 1910- —; House 1945-55.

LYMAN, Joseph (R Iowa) Sept. 13, 1840-July 9, 1890; House 1885-89.

LYMAN, Joseph Stebbins (— N.Y.) Feb. 14, 1785-March 21, 1821; House 1819-21.

LYMAN, Samuel (— Mass.) Jan. 25, 1749-June 5, 1802; House 1795-Nov. 6, 1800.

LYMAN, Theodore (I Mass.) Aug. 23, 1833-Sept. 9, 1897; House 1883-85.

LYMAN, William (D Mass.) Dec. 7, 1755-Sept. 2, 1811; House 1793-97.

LYNCH, John (R Maine) Feb. 18, 1825-July 21, 1892; House 1865-73.

LYNCH, John (D Pa.) Nov. 1, 1843-Aug. 17, 1910; House 1887-89.

LYNCH, John Roy (R Miss.) Sept. 10, 1847-Nov. 2, 1939; House 1873-77, April 29, 1882-83.

LYNCH, Thomas (D Wis.) Nov. 21, 1844-May 4, 1898; House 1891-95.

LYNCH, Walter Aloysius (D N.Y.) July 7, 1894-Sept. 10, 1957; House Feb. 20, 1940-51.

LYNDE, William Pitt (D Wis.) Dec. 16, 1817-Dec. 18, 1885; House June 5, 1848-49, 1875-79.

LYON, Asa (F Vt.) Dec. 31, 1763-April 4, 1841; House 1815-17.

LYON, Caleb (I N.Y.) Dec. 7, 1822-Sept. 8, 1875; House 1853-55; Gov. (Idaho Terr.) 1864-66.

LYON, Chittenden (son of Matthew Lyon) (D Ky.) Feb. 22, 1787-Nov. 23, 1842; House 1827-35.

LYON, Francis Strother (W Ala.) Feb. 25, 1800-Dec. 31, 1882; House 1835-39.

LYON, Homer Le Grand (D N.C.) March 1, 1879-May 31, 1956; House 1921-29.

LYON, Lucius (D Mich.) Feb. 26, 1800-Sept. 24, 1851; House (Terr. Del.) 1833-35, (Rep.) 1843-45; Senate Jan. 26, 1837-39.

LYON, Matthew (father of Chittenden Lyon, great-grandfather of William Peters Hepburn) (— Vt./Ky.) July 14, 1746-Aug. 1, 1822; House 1797-1801 (Vt.), 1803-11 (Ky.).

LYTLE, Robert Todd (nephew of John Rowan) (JD Ohio) May 19, 1804-Dec. 22, 1839; House 1833-March 10, 1834, Dec. 27, 1834-35.

M

MAAS, Melvin Joseph (R Minn.) May 14, 1898-April 13, 1964; House 1927-33, 1935-45.

MacCRATE, John (R N.Y.) March 29, 1885-June 9, 1976; House 1919-Dec. 30, 1920.

MacDONALD, John Lewis (D Minn.) Feb. 22, 1838-July 13, 1903; House 1887-89.

MACDONALD, Moses (D Maine) April 8, 1815-Oct. 18, 1869; House 1851-55.

MACDONALD, Torbert Hart (D Mass.) June 6, 1917-May 21, 1976; House 1955-May 21, 1976.

MacDONALD, William Josiah (Prog. Mich.) Nov. 17, 1873-March 29, 1946; House Aug. 26, 1913-15.

MacDOUGALL, Clinton Dugald (R N.Y.) June 14, 1839-May 24, 1914; House 1873-77.

MACE, Daniel (R Ind.) Sept. 5, 1811-July 26, 1867; House 1851-57 (1851-55 Democrat, 1855-57 Republican).

MacGREGOR, Clarence (R N.Y.) Sept. 16, 1872-Feb. 18, 1952; House 1919-Dec. 31, 1928.

MacGREGOR, Clark (R Minn.) July 12, 1922- —; House 1961-71.

MACHEN, Hervey Gilbert (D Md.) Oct. 14, 1916- —; House 1965-69.

MACHEN, Willis Benson (D Ky.) April 10, 1810-Sept. 29, 1893; Senate Sept. 27, 1872-73.

MACHIR, James (— Va.) ?-June 25, 1827; House 1797-99.

MACHROWICZ, Thaddeus Michael (D Mich.) Aug. 21, 1899-Feb. 17, 1970; House 1951-Sept. 18, 1961.

MACIEJEWSKI, Anton Frank (D Ill.) Jan. 3, 1893-Sept. 25, 1949; House 1939-Dec. 8, 1942.

MacINTYRE, Archibald Thompson (D Ga.) Oct. 27, 1822-Jan. 1, 1900; House 1871-73.

Biographical Index

MACIORA, Lucien John (D Conn.) Aug. 17, 1902- —; House 1941-43.

MACK, Connie III (R Fla.) Oct. 29, 1940- —; House 1983- —.

MACK, Peter Francis Jr. (D Ill.) Nov. 1, 1916- —; House 1949-63.

MACK, Russell Vernon (R Wash.) June 13, 1891-March 28, 1960; House June 7, 1947-March 28, 1960.

MACKAY, James Armstrong (D Ga.) June 25, 1919- —; House 1965-67.

MacKAY, Kenneth Hood (D Fla.) March 22, 1933- —; House 1983- —.

MACKEY, Edmund William McGregor (R S.C.) March 8, 1846-Jan. 27, 1884; House 1875-July 19, 1876, May 31, 1882-Jan. 27, 1884 (1875-76 Independent Republican, 1882-84 Republican).

MACKEY, Levi Augustus (D Pa.) Nov. 25, 1819-Feb. 8, 1889; House 1875-79.

MACKIE, John C. (D Mich.) June 1, 1920- —; House 1965-67.

MacKINNON, George Edward (R Minn.) April 22, 1906- —; House 1947-49.

MacLAFFERTY, James Henry (R Calif.) Feb. 27, 1871-June 9, 1937; House Nov. 7, 1922-25.

MACLAY, Samuel (brother of William Maclay, father of William Plunkett Maclay) (— Pa.) June 17, 1741-Oct. 5, 1811; House 1795-97; Senate 1803-Jan. 4, 1809.

MACLAY, William (brother of Samuel Maclay, uncle of William Plunkett Maclay) (D Pa.) July 20, 1737-April 16, 1804; Senate 1789-91.

MACLAY, William (— Pa.) March 22, 1765-Jan. 4, 1825; House 1815-19.

MACLAY, William Brown (D N.Y.) March 20, 1812-Feb. 19, 1882; House 1843-49, 1857-61.

MACLAY, William Plunkett (son of Samuel Maclay, nephew of William Maclay) (D Pa.) Aug. 23, 1774-Sept. 2, 1842; House Oct. 8, 1816-21.

MACON, Nathaniel (uncle of Willis Alston and Micajah Thomas Hawkins, great-grandfather of Charles Henry Martin of North Carolina) (D N.C.) Dec. 17, 1757-June 29, 1837; House 1791-Dec. 13, 1815; Senate Dec. 13, 1815-Nov. 14, 1828; Speaker 1801-07; Pres. pro tempore 1826-27.

MACON, Robert Bruce (D Ark.) July 6, 1859-Oct. 9, 1925; House 1903-13.

MACY, John B. (D Wis.) March 26, 1799-Sept. 24, 1856; House 1853-55.

MACY, William Kingsland (R N.Y.) Nov. 21, 1889-July 15, 1961; House 1947-51.

MADDEN, Martin Barnaby (R Ill.) March 20, 1855-April 27 1928; House 1905-April 27, 1928.

MADDEN, Ray John (D Ind.) Feb. 25, 1892- —; House 1943-77.

MADDOX, John W. (D Ga.) June 3, 1848-Sept. 27, 1922; House 1893-1905.

MADIGAN, Edward Rell (R Ill.) Jan. 13, 1936- —; House 1973- —.

MADISON, Edmond Haggard (R Kan.) Dec. 18, 1865-Sept. 18, 1911; House 1907-Sept. 18, 1911.

MADISON, James (DR Va.) March 16, 1751-June 28, 1836; House 1789-97; Cont. Cong. 1780-83, 1786-88; Secy. of State 1801-09; President 1809-17.

MAFFETT, James Thompson (R Pa.) Feb. 2, 1837-Dec. 19, 1912; House 1887-89.

MAGEE, Clare (D Mo.) March 31, 1899-Aug. 7, 1969; House 1949-53.

MAGEE, James McDevitt (R Pa.) April 5, 1877-April 16, 1949; House 1923-27.

MAGEE, John (D N.Y.) Sept. 3, 1794-April 5, 1868; House 1827-31.

MAGEE, John Alexander (D Pa.) Oct. 14, 1827-Nov. 18, 1903; House 1873-75.

MAGEE, Walter Warren (R N.Y.) May 23, 1861-May 25, 1927; House 1915-May 25, 1927.

MAGINNIS, Martin (D Mont.) Oct. 27, 1841-March 27, 1919; House (Terr. Del.) 1873-85.

MAGNER, Thomas Francis (uncle of John Francis Carew) (D N.Y.) March 8, 1860-Dec. 22, 1945; House 1889-95.

MAGNUSON, Donald Hammer (D Wash.) March 7, 1911-Oct. 5, 1979; House 1953-63.

MAGNUSON, Warren Grant (D Wash.) April 12, 1905- —; House 1937-Dec. 13, 1944; Senate Dec. 14, 1944-81; Pres. pro tempore Jan. 15, 1979-81.

MAGOON, Henry Sterling (R Wis.) Jan. 31, 1832-March 3, 1889; House 1875-77.

MAGRADY, Frederick William (R Pa.) Nov. 24, 1863-Aug. 27, 1954; House 1925-33.

MAGRUDER, Allan Bowie (D La.) 1775-April 15, 1822; Senate Sept. 3, 1812-13.

MAGRUDER, Patrick (— Md.) 1768-Dec. 24, 1819; House 1805-07.

MAGUIRE, Gene Andrew (D N.J.) March 11, 1939- —; House 1975-81.

MAGUIRE, James George (D Calif.) Feb. 22, 1853-June 20, 1920; House 1893-99.

MAGUIRE, John Arthur (D Neb.) Nov. 29, 1870-July 1, 1939; House 1909-15.

MAHAN, Bryan Francis (D Conn.) May 1, 1856-Nov. 16, 1923; House 1913-15.

MAHANY, Rowland Blennerhassett (R N.Y.) Sept. 28, 1864-May 2, 1937; House 1895-99.

MAHER, James Paul (D N.Y.) Nov. 3, 1865-July 31, 1946; House 1911-21.

MAHON, Gabriel Heyward Jr. (D S.C.) Nov. 11, 1889-June 11, 1962; House Nov. 3, 1936-39.

MAHON, George Herman (D Texas) Sept. 22, 1900- —; House 1935-79.

MAHON, Thaddeus Maclay (R Pa.) May 21, 1840-May 31, 1916; House 1893-1907.

MAHONE, William (Read. Va.) Dec. 1, 1826-Oct. 8, 1895; Senate 1881-87.

MAHONEY, Peter Paul (D N.Y.) June 25, 1848-March 27, 1889; House 1885-89.

MAHONEY, William Frank (D Ill.) Feb. 22, 1856-Dec. 27, 1904; House 1901-Dec. 27, 1904.

MAILLIARD, William Somers (R Calif.) June 10, 1917- —; House 1953-March 5, 1974.

MAIN, Verner Wright (R Mich.) Dec. 16, 1885-July 6, 1965; House Dec. 17, 1935-37.

MAISH, Levi (D Pa.) Nov. 22, 1837-Feb. 26, 1899; House 1875-79, 1887-91.

MAJOR, James Earl (D Ill.) Jan. 5, 1887-Jan. 4, 1972; House 1923-25, 1927-29, 1931-Oct. 6, 1933.

MAJOR, Samuel Collier (D Mo.) July 2, 1869-July 28, 1931; House 1919-21, 1923-29, March 4-July 28, 1931.

MAJORS, Thomas Jefferson (R Neb.) June 25, 1841-July 11, 1932; House Nov. 5, 1878-79.

MALBONE, Francis (F R.I.) March 20, 1759-June 4, 1809; House 1793-97; Senate March 4-June 4, 1809.

MALBY, George Roland (R N.Y.) Sept. 16, 1857-July 5, 1912; House 1907-July 5, 1912.

MALLARY, Richard Walker (R Vt.) Feb. 21, 1929- —; House Jan. 7, 1972-75.

MALLARY, Rollin Carolas (— Vt.) May 27, 1784-April 16, 1831; House Jan. 13, 1820-April 16, 1831.

MALLORY, Francis (W Va.) Dec. 12, 1807-March 26, 1860; House 1837-39, Dec. 28, 1840-43.

MALLORY, Meredith (D N.Y.) ?-?; House 1839-41.

MALLORY, Robert (UD Ky.) Nov. 15, 1815-Aug. 11, 1885; House 1859-65.

MALLORY, Rufus (UR Ore.) Jan. 10, 1831-April 30, 1914; House 1867-69.

MALLORY, Stephen Russell (father of the following) (D Fla.) 1812-Nov. 9, 1873; Senate 1851-Jan. 21, 1861.

MALLORY, Stephen Russell (son of the preceding) (D Fla.) Nov. 2, 1848-Dec. 23, 1907; House 1891-95; Senate May 15, 1897-Dec. 23, 1907.

MALONE, George Wilson (R Nev.) Aug. 7, 1890-May 19, 1961; Senate 1947-59.

MALONEY, Francis Thomas (D Conn.) March 31, 1894-Jan. 16, 1945; House 1933-35; Senate 1935-Jan. 16, 1945.

MALONEY, Franklin John (R Pa.) March 29, 1899-Sept. 15, 1958; House 1947-49.

MALONEY, Paul Herbert (D La.) Feb. 14, 1876-March 26, 1967; House 1931-Dec. 15, 1940, 1943-47.

MALONEY, Robert Sarsfield (R Mass.) Feb. 3, 1881-Nov. 8, 1934; House 1921-23.

MANAHAN, James (R Minn.) March 12, 1866-Jan. 8, 1932; House 1913-15.

MANASCO, Carter (D Ala.) Jan. 3, 1902-—; House June 24, 1941-49.

MANDERSON, Charles Frederick (R Neb.) Feb. 9, 1837-Sept. 28, 1911; Senate 1883-95; Pres. pro tempore 1891-93.

MANGUM, Willie Person (W N.C.) May 10, 1792-Sept. 7, 1861; House 1823-March 18, 1826; Senate 1831-Nov. 26, 1836, Nov. 25, 1840-53; Pres. pro tempore 1842-45.

MANKIN, Helen Douglas (D Ga.) Sept. 11, 1896-July 25, 1956; House Feb. 12, 1946-47.

MANLOVE, Joe Jonathan (R Mo.) Oct. 1, 1876-Jan. 31, 1956; House 1923-33.

MANN, Abijah Jr. (D N.Y.) Sept. 24, 1793-Sept. 6, 1868; House 1833-37.

MANN, Edward Coke (D S.C.) Nov. 21, 1880-Nov. 11, 1931; House Oct. 7, 1919-21.

MANN, Horace (FS Mass.) May 4, 1796-Aug. 2, 1859; House April 3, 1848-53 (1848-51 Whig, 1851-53 Free Soiler).

MANN, James (D La.) June 22, 1822-Aug. 26, 1868; House July 18-Aug. 26, 1868.

MANN, James Robert (R Ill.) Oct. 20, 1856-Nov. 30, 1922; House 1897-Nov. 30, 1922.

MANN, James Robert (D S.C.) April 27, 1920-—; House 1969-79.

MANN, Job (D Pa.) March 31, 1795-Oct. 8, 1873; House 1835-37, 1847-51.

MANN, Joel Keith (D Pa.) Aug. 1, 1780-Aug. 28, 1857; House 1831-35.

MANNING, John Jr. (D N.C.) July 30, 1830-Feb. 12, 1899; House Dec. 7, 1870-71.

MANNING, Richard Irvine (D S.C.) May 1, 1789-May 1, 1836; House Dec. 8, 1834-May 1, 1836; Gov. 1824-26.

MANNING, Vannoy Hartrog (D Miss.) July 26, 1839-Nov. 3, 1892; House 1877-83.

MANSFIELD, Joseph Jefferson (D Texas) Feb. 9, 1861-July 12, 1947; House 1917-July 12, 1947.

MANSFIELD, Michael Joseph (Mike) (D Mont.) March 16, 1903-—; House 1943-53; Senate 1953-77; Senate majority leader 1961-77.

MANSON, Mahlon Dickerson (D Ind.) Feb. 20, 1820-Feb. 4, 1895; House 1871-73.

MANSUR, Charles Harley (D Mo.) March 6, 1835-April 16, 1895; House 1887-93.

MANTLE, Lee (R Mont.) Dec. 13, 1851-Nov. 18, 1934; Senate Jan. 16, 1895-99.

MANTON, Thomas J. (D N.Y.) Nov. 3, 1932-—; House 1985-—.

MANZANARES, Francisco Antonio (D N.M.) Jan. 25, 1843-Sept. 17, 1904; House (Terr. Del.) March 5, 1884-85.

MAPES, Carl Edgar (R Mich.) Dec. 26, 1874-Dec. 12, 1939; House 1913-Dec. 12, 1939.

MARABLE, John Hartwell (NR Tenn.) Nov. 18, 1786-April 11, 1844; House 1825-29.

MARAZITI, Joseph James (R N.J.) June 15, 1912-—; House 1973-75.

MARCANTONIO, Vito (AL N.Y.) Dec. 10, 1902-Aug. 9, 1954; House 1935-37, 1939-51 (1935-37 Republican, 1939-51 American Laborite).

MARCHAND, Albert Gallatin (son of David Marchand) (D Pa.) Feb. 27, 1811-Feb. 5, 1848; House 1839-43.

MARCHAND, David (father of Albert Gallatin Marchand) (— Pa.) Dec. 10, 1776-March 11, 1832; House 1817-21.

MARCY, Daniel (D N.H.) Nov. 7, 1809-Nov. 3, 1893; House 1863-65.

MARCY, William Learned (JD N.Y.) Dec. 12, 1786-July 4, 1857; Senate 1831-Jan. 1, 1833; Gov. 1833-39; Secy. of War 1845-49; Secy. of State 1853-57.

MARDIS, Samuel Wright (D Ala.) June 12, 1800-Nov. 14, 1836; House 1831-35.

MARION, Robert (— S.C.) ?-?; House 1805-Dec. 4, 1810.

MARKELL, Henry (son of Jacob Markell) (D N.Y.) Feb. 7, 1792-Aug. 30, 1831; House 1825-29.

MARKELL, Jacob (father of Henry Markell) (F N.Y.) May 8, 1770-Nov. 26, 1852; House 1813-15.

MARKEY, Edward John (D Mass.) July 11, 1946-—; House Nov. 2, 1976-85.

MARKHAM, Henry Harrison (R Calif.) Nov. 16, 1840-Oct. 9, 1923; House 1885-87; Gov. 1891-95.

MARKLEY, Philip Swenk (D Pa.) July 2, 1789-Sept. 12, 1834; House 1823-27.

MARKS, Marc Lincoln (R Pa.) Feb. 12, 1927-—; House 1977-83.

MARKS, William (D Pa.) Oct. 13, 1778-April 10, 1858; Senate 1825-31.

MARLAND, Ernest Whitworth (D Okla.) May 8, 1874-Oct. 4, 1941; House 1933-35; Gov. 1935-39.

MARLENEE, Ronald Charles (R Mont.) Aug. 8, 1935-—; House 1977-—.

MARQUETTE, Turner Mastin (R Neb.) July 19, 1831-Dec. 22, 1894; House March 2-3, 1867.

MARR, Alem (D Pa.) June 18, 1787-March 29, 1843; House 1829-31.

MARR, George Washington Lent (— Tenn.) May 25, 1779-Sept. 5, 1856; House 1817-19.

MARRIOTT, David Daniel (R Utah) Nov. 2, 1939-—; House 1977-85.

MARSALIS, John Henry (D Colo.) May 9, 1904-—; House 1949-51.

MARSH, Benjamin Franklin (R Ill.) 1839-June 2, 1905; House 1877-83, 1893-1901, 1903-June 2, 1905.

MARSH, Charles (father of George Perkins Marsh) (F Vt.) July 10, 1765-Jan. 11, 1849; House 1815-17.

MARSH, George Perkins (son of Charles Marsh) (W Vt.) March 15, 1801-July 24, 1882; House 1843-May 1849.

MARSH, John O. Jr. (D Va.) Aug. 7, 1926-—; House 1963-71.

MARSHALL, Alexander Keith (AP Ky.) Feb. 11, 1808-April 28, 1884; House 1855-57.

MARSHALL, Alfred (D Maine) about 1797-Oct. 2, 1868; House 1841-43.

MARSHALL, Edward Chauncey (D Calif.) June 29, 1821-July 9, 1893; House 1851-53.

MARSHALL, Fred (D Minn.) March 13, 1906-—; House 1949-63.

MARSHALL, George Alexander (D Ohio) Sept. 14, 1851-April 21, 1899; House 1897-99.

MARSHALL, Humphrey (grandfather of the following, father of Thomas Alexander Marshall, cousin of John Marshall) (F Ky.) 1760-July 1, 1841; Senate 1795-1801.

MARSHALL, Humphrey (grandson of the preceding) (AP Ky.) Jan. 13, 1812-March 28, 1872; House 1849-Aug. 4, 1852, 1855-59 (1849-52 Whig, 1855-59 American Party).

MARSHALL, James William (D Va.) March 31, 1844-Nov. 27, 1911; House 1893-95.

MARSHALL, John (uncle of Thomas Francis Marshall, cousin of Humphrey Marshall) (— Va.) Sept. 24, 1755-July 6, 1835; House 1799-June 7, 1800; Secy. of State June 6, 1800-March 4, 1801; Chief Justice Supreme Court Feb. 4, 1801-July 6, 1835.

MARSHALL, Leroy Tate (R Ohio) Nov. 8, 1883-Nov. 22, 1950; House 1933-37.

MARSHALL, Lycurgus Luther (R Ohio) July 9, 1888-Jan. 12, 1958; House 1939-41.

MARSHALL, Samuel Scott (D Ill.) March 12, 1821-July 26, 1890; House 1855-59, 1865-75.

MARSHALL, Thomas Alexander (son of Humphrey Marshall) (W Ky.) Jan. 15, 1794-April 17, 1871; House 1831-35.

MARSHALL, Thomas Francis (nephew of John Marshall) (— Ky.) June 7, 1801-Sept. 22, 1864; House 1841-43.

MARSHALL, Thomas Frank (R N.D.) March 7, 1854-Aug. 20, 1921; House 1901-09.

MARSTON, Gilman (R N.H.) Aug. 20, 1811-July 3, 1890; House 1859-63, 1865-67; Senate March 4-June 18, 1889.

MARTIN, Alexander (— N.C.) 1740-Nov. 10, 1807; Senate 1793-99; Gov. 1782-84, 1789-92.

MARTIN, Augustus Newton (D Ind.) March 23, 1847-July 11, 1901; House 1889-95.

MARTIN, Barclay (uncle of Lewis Tillman) (D Tenn.) Dec. 17, 1802-Nov. 8, 1890; House 1845-47.

MARTIN, Benjamin Franklin (D W.Va.) Oct. 2, 1828-Jan. 20, 1895; House 1877-81.

Biographical Index

MARTIN, Charles (D Ill.) May 20, 1856-Oct. 28, 1917; House March 4-Oct. 28, 1917.

MARTIN, Charles Drake (D Ohio) Aug. 5, 1829-Aug. 27, 1911; House 1859-61.

MARTIN, Charles Henry (great-grandson of Nathaniel Macon) (P N.C.) Aug. 28, 1848-April 19, 1931; House June 5, 1896-99.

MARTIN, Charles Henry (D Ore.) Oct. 1, 1863-Sept. 22, 1946; House 1931-35; Gov. 1935-39.

MARTIN, David O'B. (R N.Y.) April 26, 1944-—; House 1981-—.

MARTIN, David Thomas (R Neb.) July 9, 1907-—; House 1961-Dec. 31, 1974.

MARTIN, Eben Wever (R S.D.) April 12, 1855-May 22, 1932; House 1901-07, Nov. 3, 1908-15.

MARTIN, Edward (R Pa.) Sept. 18, 1879-March 19, 1967; Senate 1947-59; Gov. 1943-47.

MARTIN, Edward Livingston (D Del.) March 29, 1837-Jan. 22, 1897; House 1879-83.

MARTIN, Elbert Sevier (brother of John Preston Martin) (AP Va.) about 1829-Sept. 3, 1876; House 1859-61.

MARTIN, Frederick Stanley (W N.Y.) April 25, 1794-June 28, 1865; House 1851-53.

MARTIN, George Brown (grandson of John Preston Martin) (D Ky.) Aug. 18, 1876-Nov. 12, 1945; Senate Sept. 7, 1918-19.

MARTIN, James D. (R Ala.) Sept. 1, 1918-—; House 1965-67.

MARTIN, James Grubbs (R N.C.) Dec. 11, 1935-—; House 1973-85; Gov. 1985-—.

MARTIN, John (D Kan.) Nov. 12, 1833-Sept. 3, 1913; Senate 1893-95.

MARTIN, John Andrew (D Colo.) April 10, 1868-Dec. 23, 1939; House 1909-13, 1933-Dec. 23, 1939.

MARTIN, John Cunningham (D Ill.) April 29, 1880-Jan. 27, 1952; House 1939-41.

MARTIN, John Mason (son of Joshua Lanier Martin) (D Ala.) Jan. 20, 1837-June 16, 1898; House 1885-87.

MARTIN, John Preston (brother of Elbert Sevier Martin, grandfather of George Brown Martin) (D Ky.) Oct. 11, 1811-Dec. 23, 1862; House 1845-47.

MARTIN, Joseph John (R N.C.) Nov. 21, 1833-Dec. 18, 1900; House 1879-Jan. 29, 1881.

MARTIN, Joseph William Jr. (R Mass.) Nov. 3, 1884-March 6, 1968; House 1925-67; Speaker 1947-49, 1953-55; Chrmn. Rep. Nat. Comm. 1940-42.

MARTIN, Joshua Lanier (father of John Mason Martin) (D Ala.) Dec. 5, 1799-Nov. 2, 1856; House 1835-39; Gov. 1845-47.

MARTIN, Lewis J. (D N.J.) Feb. 22, 1844-May 5, 1913; House March 4-May 5, 1913.

MARTIN, Lynn Morley (R Ill.) Dec. 26, 1939-—; House 1981-—.

MARTIN, Morgan Lewis (cousin of James Duane Doty) (D Wis.) March 31, 1805-Dec. 10, 1887; House (Terr. Del.) 1845-47.

MARTIN, Patrick Minor (R Calif.) Nov. 25, 1924-July 18, 1968; House 1963-65.

MARTIN, Robert Nicols (D Md.) Jan. 14, 1798-July 20, 1870; House 1825-27.

MARTIN, Thomas Ellsworth (R Iowa) Jan. 18, 1893-June 27, 1971; House 1939-55; Senate 1955-61.

MARTIN, Thomas Staples (D Va.) July 29, 1847-Nov. 12, 1919; Senate 1895-Nov. 12, 1919; Senate majority leader 1917-19.

MARTIN, Whitmell Pugh (D La.) Aug. 12, 1867-April 6, 1929; House 1915-April 6, 1929 (1915-19 Progressive, 1919-29 Democrat).

MARTIN, William Dickinson (D S.C.) Oct. 20, 1789-Nov. 17, 1833; House 1827-31.

MARTIN, William Harrison (D Texas) May 23, 1823-Feb. 3, 1898; House Nov. 4, 1887-91.

MARTINDALE, Henry Clinton (W N.Y.) May 6, 1780-April 22, 1860; House 1823-31, 1833-35.

MARTINE, James Edgar (D N.J.) Aug. 25, 1850-Feb. 26, 1925; Senate 1911-17.

MARTINEZ, Matthew G. (D. Calif.) Feb. 14, 1929-—; House July 15, 1982-—.

MARVIN, Dudley (W N.Y.) May 9, 1786-June 25, 1856; House 1823-29, 1847-49 (1823-29 Adams Democrat, 1847-49 Whig).

MARVIN, Francis (R N.Y.) March 8, 1828-Aug. 14, 1905; House 1893-95.

MARVIN, James Madison (U N.Y.) Feb. 27, 1809-April 25, 1901; House 1863-69.

MARVIN, Richard Pratt (W N.Y.) Dec. 23, 1803-Jan. 11, 1892; House 1837-41.

MASON, Armistead Thomson (son of Stevens Thomson Mason) (D Va.) Aug. 4, 1787-Feb. 6, 1819; Senate Jan. 3, 1816-17.

MASON, Harry Howland (D Ill.) Dec. 16, 1873-March 10, 1946; House 1935-37.

MASON, James Brown (F R.I.) Jan. 1775-Aug. 31, 1819; House 1815-19.

MASON, James Murray (JD Va.) Nov. 3, 1798-April 28, 1871; House 1837-39; Senate Jan. 21, 1847-March 28, 1861; Pres. pro tempore 1857.

MASON, Jeremiah (F N.H.) April 27, 1768-Oct. 14, 1848; Senate June 10, 1813-June 16, 1817.

MASON, John Calvin (JD Ky.) Aug. 4, 1802-Aug. 1865; House 1849-53, 1857-59.

MASON, John Thomson (D Md.) May 9, 1815-March 28, 1873; House 1841-43.

MASON, John Young (D Va.) April 18, 1799-Oct. 3, 1859; House 1831-Jan. 11, 1837; Secy. of the Navy 1844-45, 1846-49; Atty. Gen. 1845-46.

MASON, Jonathan (F Mass.) Aug. 30, 1752-Nov. 1, 1831; Senate Nov. 14, 1800-03; House 1817-May 15, 1820.

MASON, Joseph (R N.Y.) March 30, 1828-May 31, 1914; House 1879-83.

MASON, Moses Jr. (D Maine) June 2, 1789-June 25, 1866; House 1833-37.

MASON, Noah Morgan (R Ill.) July 19, 1882-March 29, 1965; House 1937-63.

MASON, Samson (W Ohio) July 24, 1793-Feb. 1, 1869; House 1835-43.

MASON, Stevens Thomson (father of Armistead Thomson Mason) (D Va.) Dec. 29, 1760-May 10, 1803; Senate Nov. 18, 1794-May 10, 1803.

MASON, William (D N.Y.) Sept. 10, 1786-Jan. 13, 1860; House 1835-37.

MASON, William Ernest (father of Winnifred Sprague Mason Huck) (R Ill.) July 7, 1850-June 16, 1921; House 1887-91, 1917-June 16, 1921; Senate 1897-1903.

MASSEY, William Alexander (R Nev.) Oct. 7, 1856-March 5, 1914; Senate July 1, 1912-Jan. 29, 1913.

MASSEY, Zachary David (R Tenn.) Nov. 14, 1864-July 13, 1923; House Nov. 8, 1910-11.

MASSINGALE, Samuel Chapman (D Okla.) Aug. 2, 1870-Jan. 17, 1941; House 1935-Jan. 17, 1941.

MASTERS, Josiah (D N.Y.) Nov. 22, 1763-June 30, 1822; House 1805-09.

MATHEWS, Frank Asbury Jr. (R N.J.) Aug. 3, 1890-Feb. 5, 1964; House Nov. 6, 1945-49.

MATHEWS, George (— Ga.) Aug. 30, 1739-Aug. 30, 1812; House 1789-91; Gov. 1787, 1793-96.

MATHEWS, George Arthur (R Dakota) June 4, 1852-April 19, 1941; House (Terr. Del.) March 4-Nov. 2, 1889.

MATHEWS, James (D Ohio) June 4, 1805-March 30, 1887; House 1841-45.

MATHEWS, Vincent (F N.Y.) June 29, 1766-Aug. 23, 1846; House 1809-11.

MATHEWSON, Elisha (D R.I.) April 18, 1767-Oct. 14, 1853; Senate Oct. 26, 1807-11.

MATHIAS, Charles McC. Jr. (R Md.) July 24, 1922-—; House 1961-69; Senate 1969-—.

MATHIAS, Robert B. (R Calif.) Nov. 17, 1930-—; House 1967-75.

MATHIOT, Joshua (W Ohio) April 4, 1800-July 30, 1849; House 1841-43.

MATHIS, Marvin Dawson (D Ga.) Nov. 30, 1940-—; House 1971-81.

MATLACK, James (— N.J.) Jan. 11, 1775-Jan. 16, 1840; House 1821-25.

MATSON, Aaron (— N.H.) 1770-July 18, 1855; House 1821-25.

MATSON, Courtland Cushing (D Ind.) April 25, 1841-Sept. 4, 1915; House 1881-89.

MATSUI, Robert Takeo (D Calif.) Sept. 17, 1941-—; House 1979-—.

MATSUNAGA, Spark Masayuki (D Hawaii) Oct. 8, 1916-—; House 1963-77; Senate 1977-—.

MATTESON, Orsamus Benajah (W N.Y.) Aug. 28, 1805-Dec. 22, 1889; House 1849-51, 1853-Feb. 27, 1857, March 4, 1857-59.

MATTHEWS, Charles (R Pa.) Oct. 15, 1856-Dec. 12, 1932; House 1911-13.

MATTHEWS, Donald Ray (Billy) (D Fla.) Oct. 3, 1907- —; House 1953-67.

MATTHEWS, Nelson Edwin (R Ohio) April 14, 1852-Oct. 13, 1917; House 1915-17.

MATTHEWS, Stanley (uncle of Henry Watterson) (R Ohio) July 21, 1824-March 22, 1889; Senate March 21, 1877-79; Assoc. Justice Supreme Court 1881-89.

MATTHEWS, William (— Md.) April 26, 1755-?; House 1797-99.

MATTINGLY, Mack (R Ga.) Jan. 7, 1931- —; Senate 1981- —.

MATTOCKS, John (W Vt.) March 4, 1777-Aug. 14, 1847; House 1821-23, 1825-27, 1841-43; Gov. 1843-44.

MATTOON, Ebenezer (F Mass.) Aug. 19, 1755-Sept. 11, 1843; House Feb. 2, 1801-03.

MATTOX, James Albon (D Texas) Aug. 29, 1943- —; House 1977-83.

MAURICE, James (D N.Y.) Nov. 7, 1814-Aug. 4, 1884; House 1853-55.

MAURY, Abram Poindexter (cousin of Fontaine Maury Maverick) (W Tenn.) Dec. 26, 1801-July 22, 1848; House 1835-39.

MAVERICK, Fontaine Maury (cousin of Abram Poindexter Maury, nephew of James Luther Slayden, cousin of John Wood Fishburne) (D Texas) Oct. 23, 1895-June 7, 1954; House 1935-39.

MAVROULES, Nicholas (D Mass.) Nov. 1, 1929- —; House 1979- —.

MAXEY, Samuel Bell (D Texas) March 30, 1825-Aug. 16, 1895; Senate 1875-87.

MAXWELL, Augustus Emmett (grandfather of Emmett Wilson) (D Fla.) Sept. 21, 1820-May 5, 1903; House 1853-57.

MAXWELL, George Clifford (father of John Patterson Bryan Maxwell, uncle of George Maxwell Robeson) (— N.J.) May 31, 1771-March 16, 1816; House 1811-13.

MAXWELL, John Patterson Bryan (son of George Clifford Maxwell, uncle of George Maxwell Robeson) (W N.J.) Sept. 3, 1804-Nov. 14, 1845; House 1837-39, 1841-43.

MAXWELL, Lewis (NR Va.) April 17, 1790-Feb. 13, 1862; House 1827-33.

MAXWELL, Samuel (Fus. Neb.) May 20, 1825-Feb. 11, 1901; House 1897-99.

MAXWELL, Thomas (D N.Y.) Feb. 16, 1792-Nov. 4, 1864; House 1829-31.

MAY, Andrew Jackson (D Ky.) June 24, 1875-Sept. 6, 1959; House 1931-47.

MAY, Catherine Dean (Barnes) (R Wash.) May 18, 1914- —; House 1959-71.

MAY, Edwin Hyland Jr. (R Conn.) May 28, 1924- —; House 1957-59.

MAY, Henry (D Md.) Feb. 13, 1816-Sept. 25, 1866; House 1853-55, 1861-63.

MAY, Mitchell (D N.Y.) July 10, 1870-March 24, 1961; House 1899-1901.

MAY, William L. (D Ill.) about 1793-Sept. 29, 1849; House Dec. 1, 1834-39.

MAYALL, Samuel (D Maine) June 21, 1816-Sept. 17, 1892; House 1853-55.

MAYBANK, Burnet Rhett (D S.C.) March 7, 1899-Sept. 1, 1954; Senate Nov. 5, 1941-Sept. 1, 1954; Gov. 1939-41.

MAYBURY, William Cotter (D Mich.) Nov. 20, 1848-May 6, 1909; House 1883-87.

MAYFIELD, Earle Bradford (D Texas) April 12, 1881-June 23, 1964; Senate 1923-29.

MAYHAM, Stephen Lorenzo (D N.Y.) Oct. 8, 1826-March 3, 1908; House 1869-71, 1877-79.

MAYNARD, Harry Lee (D Va.) June 8, 1861-Oct. 23, 1922; House 1901-11.

MAYNARD, Horace (R Tenn.) Aug. 30, 1814-May 3, 1882; House 1857-63, 1866-75 (1857-63 American Party, 1866-75 Republican); Postmaster Gen. 1880-81.

MAYNARD, John (W N.Y.) ?-March 24, 1850; House 1827-29, 1841-43.

MAYNE, Wiley (R Iowa) Jan. 19, 1917- —; House 1967-75.

MAYO, Robert Murphy (Read. Va.) April 28, 1836-March 29, 1896; House 1883-March 20, 1884.

MAYRANT, William (— S.C.) ?-?; House 1815-Oct. 21, 1816.

MAYS, Dannite Hill (D Fla.) April 28, 1852-May 9, 1930; House 1909-13.

MAYS, James Henry (D Utah) June 29, 1868-April 19, 1926; House 1915-21.

MAZZOLI, Romano Louis (D Ky.) Nov. 2, 1932- —; House 1971- —.

McADOO, William (D N.J.) Oct. 25, 1853-June 7, 1930; House 1883-91.

McADOO, William Gibbs (D Calif.) Oct. 31, 1863-Feb. 1, 1941; Senate 1933-Nov. 8, 1938; Secy. of the Treasury 1913-18.

McALEER, William (D Pa.) Jan. 6, 1838-April 19, 1912; House 1891-95, 1897-1901.

McALLISTER, Archibald (grandson of John Andre Hanna) (D Pa.) Oct. 12, 1813-July 18, 1883; House 1863-65.

McANDREWS, James (D Ill.) Oct. 22, 1862-Aug. 31, 1942; House 1901-05, 1913-21, 1935-41.

McARDLE, Joseph A. (D Pa.) June 29, 1903-Dec. 27, 1967; House 1939-Jan. 5, 1942.

McARTHUR, Clifton Nesmith (grandson of James Willis Nesmith) (R Ore.) June 10, 1879-Dec. 9, 1923; House 1915-23.

McARTHUR, Duncan (D Ohio) June 14, 1772-April 29, 1839; House March 4-April 5, 1813, 1823-25; Gov. 1830-32.

McBRIDE, George Wycliffe (brother of John Rogers McBride) (R Ore.) March 13, 1854-June 18, 1911; Senate 1895-1901.

McBRIDE, John Rogers (brother of George Wycliffe McBride) (R Ore.) Aug. 22, 1832-July 20, 1904; House 1863-65.

McBRYDE, Archibald (D N.C.) Sept. 28, 1766-Feb. 15, 1816; House 1809-13.

McCAIN, John Sidney II (R Ariz.) Aug. 29, 1936- —; House 1983- —.

McCALL, John Ethridge (R Tenn.) Aug. 14, 1859-Aug. 8, 1920; House 1895-97.

McCALL, Samuel Walker (R Mass.) Feb. 28, 1851-Nov. 4, 1923; House 1893-1913; Gov. 1916-19.

McCANDLESS, Alfred A. (R Calif.) July 23, 1927- —; House 1983- —.

McCANDLESS, Lincoln Loy (D Hawaii) Sept. 18, 1859-Oct. 5, 1940; House (Terr. Del.) 1933-35.

McCARRAN, Patrick Anthony (Pat) (D Nev.) Aug. 8, 1876-Sept. 28, 1954; Senate 1933-Sept. 28, 1954.

McCARTHY, Dennis (R N.Y.) March 19, 1814-Feb. 14, 1886; House 1867-71.

McCARTHY, Eugene Joseph (D Minn.) March 29, 1916- —; House 1949-59; Senate 1959-71.

McCARTHY, John Henry (D N.Y.) Nov. 16, 1850-Feb. 5, 1908; House 1889-Jan. 14, 1891.

McCARTHY, John Jay (R Neb.) July 19, 1857-March 30, 1943; House 1903-07.

McCARTHY, Joseph Raymond (R Wis.) Nov. 14, 1908-May 2, 1957; Senate 1947-May 2, 1957.

McCARTHY, Kathryn O'Loughlin (see O'Loughlin, Kathryn Ellen.)

McCARTHY, Richard Dean (D N.Y.) Sept. 24, 1927- —; House 1965-71.

McCARTY, Andrew Zimmerman (W N.Y.) July 14, 1808-April 23, 1879; House 1855-57.

McCARTY, Johnathan (W Ind.) Aug. 3, 1795-March 30, 1852; House 1831-37.

McCARTY, Richard (D N.Y.) Feb. 19, 1780-May 18, 1844; House 1821-23.

McCARTY, William Mason (W Va.) about 1789-Dec. 20, 1863; House Jan. 25, 1840-41; Gov. (Fla. Terr.) 1827.

McCAUSLEN, William Cochran (D Ohio) 1796-March 13, 1863; House 1843-45.

McCLAMMY, Charles Washington (D N.C.) May 29, 1839-Feb. 26, 1896; House 1887-91.

McCLEAN, Moses (D Pa.) June 17, 1804-Sept. 30, 1870; House 1845-47.

McCLEARY, James Thompson (R Minn.) Feb. 5, 1853-Dec. 17, 1924; House 1893-1907.

Biographical Index

McCLEERY, James (R La.) Dec. 2, 1837-Nov. 5, 1871; House March 4-Nov. 5, 1871.

McCLELLAN, Abraham (D Tenn.) Oct. 4, 1789-May 3, 1866; House 1837-43.

McCLELLAN, Charles A. O. (D Ind.) May 25, 1835-Jan. 31, 1898; House 1889-93.

McCLELLAN, George (D N.Y.) Oct. 10, 1856-Feb. 20, 1927; House 1913-15.

McCLELLAN, George Brinton (D N.Y.) Nov. 23, 1865-Nov. 30, 1940; House 1895-Dec. 21, 1903.

McCLELLAN, John Little (D Ark.) Feb. 25, 1896-Nov. 28, 1977; House 1935-39; Senate 1943-Nov. 28, 1977.

McCLELLAN, Robert (D N.Y.) Oct. 2, 1806-June 28, 1860; House 1837-39, 1841-43.

McCLELLAND, Robert (D Mich.) Aug. 1, 1807-Aug. 30, 1880; House 1843-49; Gov. 1851-53; Secy. of the Interior 1853-57.

McCLELLAND, William (D Pa.) March 2, 1842-Feb. 7, 1892; House 1871-73.

McCLENACHAN, Blair (— Pa.) ?-May 8, 1812; House 1797-99.

McCLERNAND, John Alexander (D Ill.) May 30, 1812-Sept. 20, 1900; House 1843-51, Nov. 8, 1859-Oct. 28, 1861.

McCLINTIC, James Vernon (D Okla.) Sept. 8, 1878-April 22, 1948; House 1915-35.

McCLINTOCK, Charles Blaine (R Ohio) May 25, 1886-Feb. 1, 1965; House 1929-33.

McCLORY, Robert (R Ill.) Jan. 31, 1908-—; House 1963-83.

McCLOSKEY, Augustus (D Texas) Sept. 23, 1878-July 21, 1950; House 1929-Feb. 10, 1930.

McCLOSKEY, Francis X. (D Ind.) June 12, 1939-—; House 1983-—.*

McCLOSKEY, Paul N. (Pete) Jr. (R Calif.) Sept. 29, 1927-—; House Dec. 12, 1967-83.

McCLURE, Addison S. (R Ohio) Oct. 10, 1839-April 17, 1903; House 1881-83, 1895-97.

McCLURE, Charles (D Pa.) 1804-Jan. 10, 1846; House 1837-39, Dec. 7, 1840-41.

McCLURE, James A. (R Idaho) Dec. 27, 1924-—; House 1967-73; Senate 1973-—.

McCLURG, Joseph Washington (Rad. Mo.) Feb. 22, 1818-Dec. 2, 1900; House 1863-68; Gov. 1869-71 (1863-65 Emancipationist, 1865-68 Radical, 1869-71 Republican).

McCOID, Moses Ayres (R Iowa) Nov. 5, 1840-May 19, 1904; House 1879-85.

McCOLLISTER, John Yetter (R Neb.) June 10, 1921-—; House 1971-77.

McCOLLUM, Bill (R Fla.) July 12, 1944-—; House 1981-—.

McCOMAS, Louis Emory (grandfather of Katherine Edgar Byron, great-grandfather of Goodloe Edgar Byron) (R Md.) Oct. 28, 1846-Nov. 10, 1907; House 1883-91; Senate 1899-1905.

McCOMAS, William (W Va.) 1795-June 3, 1865; House 1833-37.

McCONNELL, Addison Mitchell Jr. (R Ky.) Feb. 20, 1942-—; Senate 1985-—.

McCONNELL, Felix Grundy (D Ala.) April 1, 1809-Sept. 10, 1846; House 1843-Sept. 10, 1846.

McCONNELL, Samuel Kerns Jr. (R Pa.) April 6, 1901-—; House Jan. 18, 1944-Sept. 1, 1957.

McCONNELL, William John (R Idaho) Sept. 18, 1839-March 30, 1925; Senate Dec. 18, 1890-91; Gov. 1893-97.

McCOOK, Anson George (R N.Y.) Oct. 10, 1835-Dec. 30, 1917; House 1877-83.

McCORD, Andrew (— N.Y.) about 1754-1808; House 1803-05.

McCORD, James Nance (D Tenn.) March 17, 1879-Sept. 2, 1968; House 1943-45; Gov. 1945-49.

McCORD, Myron Hawley (R Wis.) Nov. 26, 1840-April 27, 1908; House 1889-91; Gov. (Ariz. Terr.) 1897-98.

McCORKLE, Joseph Walker (D Calif.) June 24, 1819-March 18, 1884; House 1851-53.

McCORKLE, Paul Grier (D S.C.) Dec. 19, 1863-June 2, 1934; House Feb. 24-March 3, 1917.

McCORMACK, John William (D Mass.) Dec. 21, 1891-Nov. 22, 1980; House Nov. 6, 1928-71; House majority leader 1940-47, 1949-53, 1955-62; Speaker 1962-71.

McCORMACK, Mike (D Wash.) Dec. 14, 1921-—; House 1971-81.

McCORMICK, Henry Clay (R Pa.) June 30, 1844-May 26, 1902; House 1887-91.

McCORMICK, James Robinson (D Mo.) Aug. 1, 1824-May 19, 1897; House Dec. 17, 1867-73.

McCORMICK, John Watts (R Ohio) Dec. 20, 1831-June 25, 1917; House 1883-85.

McCORMICK, (Joseph) Medill (husband of Ruth Hanna McCormick) (R Ill.) May 16, 1877-Feb. 25, 1925; House 1917-19; Senate 1919-Feb. 25, 1925.

McCORMICK, Nelson B. (P Kan.) Nov. 20, 1847-April 10, 1914; House 1897-99.

McCORMICK, Richard Cunningham (U Ariz. & R N.Y.) May 23, 1832-June 2, 1901; House (Terr. Del. Ariz.) 1869-75, (Rep. N.Y.) 1895-97; Gov. (Ariz. Terr.) 1866.

McCORMICK, Ruth Hanna (daughter of Marcus Alonzo Hanna, widow of (Joseph) Medill McCormick and of Albert Gallatin Simms) (R Ill.) March 27, 1880-Dec. 31, 1944; House 1929-31.

McCORMICK, Washington Jay (R Mont.) Jan. 4, 1884-March 7, 1949; House 1921-23.

McCOWEN, Edward Oscar (R Ohio) June 29, 1877-Nov. 4, 1953; House 1943-49.

McCOY, Robert (— Pa.) ?-June 7, 1849; House Nov. 22, 1831-33.

McCOY, Walter Irving (D N.J.) Dec. 8, 1859-July 17, 1933; House 1911-Oct. 3, 1914.

McCOY, William (D Va.) ?-1864; House 1811-33.

McCRACKEN, Robert McDowell (R Idaho) March 15 1874-May 16, 1934; House 1915-17.

McCRARY, George Washington (R Iowa) Aug. 29, 1835-June 23, 1890; House 1869-77; Secy. of War 1877-79.

McCRATE, John Dennis (D Maine) Oct. 1, 1802-Sept. 11, 1879; House 1845-47.

McCREARY, George Deardorff (R Pa.) Sept. 28, 1846-July 26, 1915; House 1903-13.

McCREARY, James Bennett (D Ky.) July 8, 1838-Oct. 8, 1918; House 1885-97; Senate 1903-09; Gov. 1875-79, 1911-15.

McCREARY, John (— S.C.) 1761-Nov. 4, 1833; House 1819-21.

McCREDIE, William Wallace (R Wash.) April 27, 1862-May 10, 1935; House Nov. 2, 1909-11.

McCREERY, Thomas Clay (D Ky.) Dec. 12, 1816-July 10, 1890; Senate Feb. 19, 1868-71, 1873-79.

McCREERY, William (— Md.) 1750-March 8, 1814; House 1803-09.

McCREERY, William (D Pa.) May 17, 1786-Sept. 27, 1841; House 1829-31.

McCULLOCH, George (D Pa.) Feb. 22, 1792-April 6, 1861; House Nov. 20, 1839-41.

McCULLOCH, John (W Pa.) Nov. 15, 1806-May 15, 1879; House 1853-55.

McCULLOCH, Philip Doddridge Jr. (D Ark.) June 23, 1851-Nov. 26, 1928; House 1893-1903.

McCULLOCH, Roscoe Conkling (R Ohio) Nov. 27, 1880-March 17, 1958; House 1915-21; Senate Nov. 5, 1929-Nov. 30, 1930.

McCULLOCH, William Moore (R Ohio) Nov. 24, 1901-Feb. 22, 1980; House Nov. 4, 1947-73.

McCULLOGH, Welty (R Pa.) Oct. 10, 1847-Aug. 31, 1889; House 1887-89.

McCULLOUGH, Hiram (D Md.) Sept. 26, 1813-March 4, 1885; House 1865-69.

McCULLOUGH, Thomas Grubb (— Pa.) April 20, 1785-Sept. 10, 1848; House Oct. 17, 1820-21.

McCUMBER, Porter James (R N.D.) Feb. 3, 1858-May 18, 1933; Senate 1899-1923.

McCURDY, David K. (D Okla.) March 30, 1950-—; House 1981-—.

McDADE, Joseph Michael (R Pa.) Sept. 29, 1931-—; House 1963-—.

McDANIEL, William (D Mo.) ?-about 1854; House Dec. 7, 1846-47.

McDANNOLD, John James (D Ill.) Aug. 29, 1851-Feb. 3, 1904; House 1893-95.

McDEARMON, James Calvin (D Tenn.) June 13, 1844-July 19, 1902; House 1893-97.

McDERMOTT, Allan Langdon (D N.J.) March 30, 1854-Oct. 26, 1908; House Dec. 3, 1900-07.

McDERMOTT, James Thomas (D Ill.) Feb. 13, 1872-Feb. 7, 1938; House 1907-July 21, 1914, 1915-17.

McDILL, Alexander Stuart (R Wis.) March 18, 1822-Nov. 12, 1875; House 1873-75.

McDILL, James Wilson (R Iowa) March 4, 1834-Feb. 28, 1894; House 1873-77; Senate March 8, 1881-83.

McDONALD, Alexander (R Ark.) April 10, 1832-Dec. 13, 1903; Senate June 22, 1868-71.

McDONALD, Edward Francis (D N.J.) Sept. 21, 1844-Nov. 5, 1892; House 1891-Nov. 5, 1892.

McDONALD, Jack H. (R Mich.) June 28, 1932--; House 1967-73.

McDONALD, John (R Md.) May 24, 1837-Jan. 30, 1917; House 1897-99.

McDONALD, Joseph Ewing (D Ind.) Aug. 29, 1819-June 21, 1891; House 1849-51; Senate 1875-81.

McDONALD, Lawrence Patton (D Ga.) April 1, 1935-Sept. 1, 1983; House 1975-Sept. 1, 1983.

McDONOUGH, Gordon Leo (R Calif.) Jan. 2, 1895-June 25, 1968; House 1945-63.

McDOUGALL, James Alexander (D Calif.) Nov. 19, 1817-Sept. 3, 1867; House 1853-55; Senate 1861-67.

McDOWELL, Alexander (R Pa.) March 4, 1845-Sept. 30, 1913; House 1893-95.

McDOWELL, Harris Brown Jr. (D Del.) Feb. 10, 1906--; House 1955-57, 1959-67.

McDOWELL, James (D Va.) Oct. 13, 1796-Aug. 24, 1851; House March 6, 1846-51; Gov. 1843-46.

McDOWELL, James Foster (D Ind.) Dec. 3, 1825-April 18, 1887; House 1863-65.

McDOWELL, John Anderson (D Ohio) Sept. 25, 1853-Oct. 2, 1927; House 1897-1901.

McDOWELL, John Ralph (R Pa.) Nov. 6, 1902-Dec. 11, 1957; House 1939-41, 1947-49.

McDOWELL, Joseph (father of Joseph Jefferson McDowell, cousin of Joseph (P G) McDowell (— N.C.) Feb. 15, 1756-Feb. 5, 1801; House 1797-99.

McDOWELL, Joseph (P G) (cousin of Joseph McDowell) (— N.C.) Feb. 25, 1758-March 7, 1799; House 1793-95.

McDOWELL, Joseph Jefferson (son of Joseph McDowell) (D Ohio) Nov. 13, 1800-Jan. 17, 1877; House 1843-47.

McDUFFIE, George (D S.C.) Aug. 10, 1790-March 11, 1851; House 1821-34; Senate Dec. 23, 1842-Aug. 17, 1846; Gov. 1834-36.

McDUFFIE, John (D Ala.) Sept. 25, 1883-Nov. 1, 1950; House 1919-March 2, 1935.

McDUFFIE, John Van (R Ala.) May 16, 1841-Nov. 18, 1896; House June 4, 1890-91.

McENERY, Samuel Douglas (D La.) May 28, 1837-June 28, 1910; Senate 1897-June 28, 1910; Gov. 1881-88.

McETTRICK, Michael Joseph (D Mass.) June 22, 1848-Dec. 31, 1921; House 1893-95.

McEWAN, Thomas Jr. (R N.J.) Feb. 26, 1854-Sept. 11, 1926; House 1895-99.

McEWEN, Robert Cameron (R N.Y.) Jan. 5, 1920--; House 1965-81.

McEWEN, Robert D. (R Ohio) Jan. 12, 1950--; House 1981--.

McFADDEN, Louis Thomas (R Pa.) July 25, 1876-Oct. 1, 1936; House 1915-35.

McFADDEN, Obadiah Benton (D Wash.) Nov. 18, 1815-June 25, 1875; House (Terr. Del.) 1873-75.

McFALL, John Joseph (D Calif.) Feb. 20, 1918--; House 1957-Dec. 31, 1978.

McFARLAN, Duncan (— N.C.) ?-Sept. 7, 1816; House 1805-07.

McFARLAND, Ernest William (D Ariz.) Oct. 9, 1894-June 8, 1984; Senate 1941-53; Senate majority leader 1951-53; Gov. 1955-59.

McFARLAND, William (D Tenn.) Sept. 15, 1821-April 12, 1900; House 1875-77.

McFARLANE, William Doddridge (D Texas) July 17, 1894-Feb. 18, 1980; House 1933-39.

McGANN, Lawrence Edward (D Ill.) Feb. 2, 1852-July 22, 1928; House 1891-Dec. 2, 1895.

McGARVEY, Robert Neill (R Pa.) Aug. 14, 1888-June 28, 1952; House 1947-49.

McGAUGHEY, Edward Wilson (W Ind.) Jan. 16, 1817-Aug. 6, 1852; House 1845-47, 1849-51.

McGAVIN, Charles (R Ill.) Jan. 10, 1874-Dec. 17, 1940; House 1905-09.

McGEE, Gale William (D Wyo.) March 17, 1915--; Senate 1959-77.

McGEHEE, Daniel Rayford (D Miss.) Sept. 10, 1883-Feb. 9, 1962; House 1935-47.

McGILL, George (D Kan.) Feb. 12, 1879-May 14, 1963; Senate Dec. 1, 1930-39.

McGILLICUDDY, Daniel John (D Maine) Aug. 27, 1859-July 30, 1936; House 1911-17.

McGINLEY, Donald Francis (D Neb.) June 30, 1920--; House 1959-61.

McGLENNON, Cornelius Augustine (D N.J.) Dec. 10, 1878-June 13, 1931; House 1919-21.

McGLINCHEY, Herbert Joseph (D Pa.) Nov. 7, 1904--; House 1945-47.

McGOVERN, George Stanley (D S.D.) July 19, 1922--; House 1957-61; Senate 1963-81.

McGOWAN, Jonas Hartzell (R Mich.) April 2, 1837-July 5, 1909; House 1877-81.

McGRANERY, James Patrick (D Pa.) July 8, 1895-Dec. 23, 1962; House 1937-Nov. 17, 1943; Atty. Gen. 1952-53.

McGRATH, Christopher Columbus (D N.Y.) May 15, 1902--; House 1949-53.

McGRATH, James Howard (D R.I.) Nov. 28, 1903-Sept. 2, 1966; Senate 1947-Aug. 23, 1949; Gov. 1941-45; Chrmn. Dem. Nat. Comm. 1947-49; Atty. Gen. 1949-52.

McGRATH, John Joseph (D Calif.) July 23, 1872-Aug. 25, 1951; House 1933-39.

McGRATH, Raymond J. (R N.Y.) March 27, 1941--; House 1981--.

McGRATH, Thomas C. Jr. (D N.J.) April 22, 1927--; House 1965-67.

McGREGOR, J. Harry (R Ohio) Sept. 30, 1896-Oct. 7, 1958; House Feb. 27, 1940-Oct. 7, 1958.

McGREW, James Clark (R W.Va.) Sept. 14, 1813-Sept. 18, 1910; House 1869-73.

McGROARTY, John Steven (D Calif.) Aug. 20, 1862-Aug. 7, 1944; House 1935-39.

McGUGIN, Harold Clement (R Kan.) Nov. 22, 1893-March 7, 1946; House 1931-35.

McGUIRE, Bird Segle (cousin of William Neville) (R Okla.) Oct. 13, 1865-Nov. 9, 1930; House (Terr. Del.) 1903-07, (Rep.) Nov. 16, 1907-15.

McGUIRE, John Andrew (D Conn.) Feb. 28, 1906-May 28, 1976; House 1949-53.

McHATTON, Robert Lytle (JD Ky.) Nov. 17, 1788-May 20, 1835; House Dec. 7, 1826-29.

McHENRY, Henry Davis (son of John Hardin McHenry) (D Ky.) Feb. 27, 1826-Dec. 17, 1890; House 1871-73.

McHENRY, John Geiser (D Pa.) April 26, 1868-Dec. 27, 1912; House 1907-Dec. 27, 1912.

McHENRY, John Hardin (father of Henry Davis McHenry) (W Ky.) Oct. 13, 1797-Nov. 1, 1871; House 1845-47.

McHUGH, Matthew Francis (D N.Y.) Dec. 6, 1938--; House 1975--.

McILVAINE, Abraham Robinson (W Pa.) Aug. 14, 1804-Aug. 22, 1863; House 1843-49.

McILVAINE, Joseph (D N.J.) Oct. 2, 1769-Aug. 19, 1826; Senate Nov. 12, 1823-Aug. 19, 1826.

McINDOE, Walter Duncan (R Wis.) March 30, 1819-Aug. 22, 1872; House Jan. 26, 1863-67.

McINTIRE, Clifford Guy (R Maine) May 4, 1908-Oct. 1, 1974; House Oct. 22, 1951-65.

McINTIRE, Rufus (JD Maine) Dec. 19, 1784-April 28, 1866; House Sept. 10, 1827-35.

McINTIRE, William Watson (R Md.) June 30, 1850-March 30, 1912; House 1897-99.

McINTOSH, Robert John (R Mich.) Sept. 16, 1922--; House 1957-59.

McINTYRE, John Joseph (D Wyo.) Dec. 17, 1904-Nov. 30, 1974; House 1941-43.

Biographical Index

McINTYRE, Thomas James (D N.H.) Feb. 20, 1915-—; Senate Nov. 7, 1962-79.

McINTYRE, Richard D. (R Ind.) Oct. 5, 1956-—; House 1985-—.*

McJUNKIN, Ebenezer (R Pa.) March 28, 1819-Nov. 10, 1907; House 1871-Jan. 1, 1875.

McKAIG, William McMahone (D Md.) July 29, 1845-June 6, 1907; House 1891-95.

McKAY, James Iver (D N.C.) 1793-Sept. 4, 1853; House 1831-49.

McKAY, Koln Gunn (D Utah) Feb. 23, 1925-—; House 1971-81.

McKEAN, James Bedell (nephew of Samuel McKean) (R N.Y.) Aug. 5, 1821-Jan. 5, 1879; House 1859-63.

McKEAN, Samuel (uncle of James Bedell McKean) (D Pa.) April 7, 1787-Dec. 14, 1841; House 1823-29; Senate 1833-39.

McKEE, George Colin (R Miss.) Oct. 2, 1837-Nov. 17, 1890; House 1869-75.

McKEE, John (— Ala.) 1771-Aug. 12, 1832; House 1823-29.

McKEE, Samuel (D Ky.) Oct. 13, 1774-Oct. 16, 1826; House 1809-17.

McKEE, Samuel (R Ky.) Nov. 5, 1833-Dec. 11, 1898; House 1865-67, June 22, 1868-69.

McKEIGHAN, William Arthur (I Neb.) Jan. 19, 1842-Dec. 15, 1895; House 1891-95 (1891-93 Democrat, 1893-95 Independent).

McKELLAR, Kenneth Douglas (D Tenn.) Jan. 29, 1869-Oct. 25, 1957; House Nov. 9, 1911-17; Senate 1917-53; Pres. pro tempore 1945-47, 1949-53.

McKENNA, Joseph (R Calif.) Aug. 10, 1843-Nov. 21, 1926; House 1885-92; Atty. Gen. 1897-98; Assoc. Justice Supreme Court 1898-1925.

McKENNAN, Thomas McKean Thompson (W Pa.) March 31, 1794-July 9, 1852; House 1831-39, May 30, 1842-43; Secy. of the Interior Aug. 15-Sept. 12, 1850.

McKENNEY, William Robertson (D Va.) Dec. 2, 1851-Jan. 3, 1916; House 1895-May 2, 1896.

McKENTY, Jacob Kerlin (D Pa.) Jan. 19, 1827-Jan. 3, 1866; House Dec. 3, 1860-61.

McKENZIE, Charles Edgar (D La.) Oct. 3, 1896-June 7, 1956; House 1943-47.

McKENZIE, James Andrew (uncle of John McKenzie Moss) (D Ky.) Aug. 1, 1840-June 25, 1904; House 1877-83.

McKENZIE, John Charles (R Ill.) Feb. 18, 1860-Sept. 17, 1941; House 1911-25.

McKENZIE, Lewis (UC Va.) Oct. 7, 1810-June 28, 1895; House Feb. 16-March 3, 1863, Jan. 31, 1870-71 (1863 Unionist, 1870-71 Union Conservative).

McKEON, John (D N.Y.) March 29, 1808-Nov. 22, 1883; House 1835-37, 1841-43.

McKEOUGH, Raymond Stephen (D Ill.) April 29, 1888-Dec. 16, 1979; House 1935-43.

* Contested election. Not seated as of Feb. 25, 1985.

McKEOWN, Thomas Deitz (D Okla.) June 4, 1878-Oct. 22, 1951; House 1917-21, 1923-35.

McKERNAN, John R. Jr. (R Maine) May 20, 1948-—; House 1983-—.

McKEVITT, James Douglas (Mike) (R Colo.) Oct. 26, 1928-—; House 1971-73.

McKIBBIN, Joseph Chambers (D Calif.) May 14, 1824-July 1, 1896; House 1857-59.

McKIM, Alexander (uncle of Isaac McKim) (D Md.) Jan. 10, 1748-Jan. 18, 1832; House 1809-15.

McKIM, Isaac (nephew of Alexander McKim) (D Md.) July 21, 1775-April 1, 1838; House Jan. 4, 1823-25, 1833-April 1, 1838.

McKINIRY, Richard Francis (D N.Y.) March 23, 1878-May 30, 1950; House 1919-21.

McKINLAY, Duncan E. (R Calif.) Oct. 6, 1862-Dec. 30, 1914; House 1905-11.

McKINLEY, John (JD Ala.) May 1, 1780-July 19, 1852; Senate Nov. 27, 1826-31, March 4-April 22, 1837; House 1833-35; Assoc. Justice Supreme Court April 22, 1837-July 19, 1852.

McKINLEY, William (D Va.) ?-?; House Dec. 21, 1810-11.

McKINLEY, William Jr. (R Ohio) Jan. 29, 1843-Sept. 14, 1901; House 1877-May 27, 1884, 1885-91; Gov. 1892-96; President 1897-Sept. 14, 1901.

McKINLEY, William Brown (R Ill.) Sept. 5, 1856-Dec. 7, 1926; House 1905-13, 1915-21; Senate 1921-Dec. 7, 1926.

McKINNEY, James (R Ill.) April 14, 1852-Sept. 29, 1934; House Nov. 7, 1905-13.

McKINNEY, John Franklin (D Ohio) April 12, 1827-June 13, 1903; House 1863-65, 1871-73.

McKINNEY, Luther Franklin (D N.H.) April 25, 1841-July 30, 1922; House 1887-89, 1891-93.

McKINNEY, Stewart Brett (R Conn.) Jan. 30, 1931-—; House 1971-—.

McKINNON, Clinton Dotson (D Calif.) Feb. 5, 1906-—; House 1949-53.

McKISSOCK, Thomas (W N.Y.) April 17, 1790-June 26, 1866; House 1849-51.

McKNEALLY, Martin B. (R N.Y.) Dec. 31, 1914-—; House 1969-71.

McKNIGHT, Robert (R Pa.) Jan. 20, 1820-Oct. 25, 1885; House 1859-63.

McLACHLAN, James (R Calif.) Aug. 1, 1852-Nov. 21, 1940; House 1895-97, 1901-11.

McLAIN, Frank Alexander (D Miss.) Jan. 29, 1852-Oct. 10, 1920; House Dec. 12, 1898-1909.

McLANAHAN, James Xavier (grandson of Andrew Gregg) (D Pa.) 1809-Dec. 16, 1861; House 1849-53.

McLANE, Louis (father of Robert Milligan McLane) (F Del.) May 28, 1786-Oct. 7, 1857; House 1817-27; Senate 1827-April 16, 1829; Secy. of the Treasury 1831-33; Secy. of State 1833-34.

McLANE, Patrick (D Pa.) March 14, 1875-Nov. 13, 1946; House 1919-Feb. 25, 1921.

McLANE, Robert Milligan (son of Louis McLane) (D Md.) June 23, 1815-April 16, 1898; House 1847-51, 1879-83; Gov. 1884-85.

McLAUGHLIN, Charles Francis (D Neb.) June 19, 1887-Feb. 5, 1976; House 1935-43.

McLAUGHLIN, James Campbell (R Mich.) Jan. 26, 1858-Nov. 29, 1932; House 1907-Nov. 29, 1932.

McLAUGHLIN, Joseph (R Pa.) June 9, 1867-Nov. 21, 1926; House 1917-19, 1921-23.

McLAUGHLIN, Melvin Orlando (R Neb.) Aug. 8, 1876-June 18, 1928; House 1919-27.

McLAURIN, Anselm Joseph (D Miss.) March 26, 1848-Dec. 22, 1909; Senate Feb. 7, 1894-95, 1901-Dec. 22, 1909; Gov. 1896-1900.

McLAURIN, John Lowndes (D S.C.) May 9, 1860-July 29, 1934; House Dec. 5, 1892-May 31, 1897; Senate June 1, 1897-1903.

McLEAN, Alney (— Ky.) June 10, 1779-Dec. 30, 1841; House 1815-17, 1819-21.

McLEAN, Donald Holman (R N.J.) March 18, 1884-Aug. 19, 1975; House 1933-45.

McLEAN, Finis Ewing (brother of John McLean, uncle of James David Walker) (W Ky.) Feb. 19, 1806-April 12, 1881; House 1849-51.

McLEAN, George Payne (R Conn.) Oct. 7, 1857-June 6, 1932; Senate 1911-29; Gov. 1901-03.

McLEAN, James Henry (R Mo.) Aug. 13, 1829-Aug. 12, 1886; House Dec. 15, 1882-83.

McLEAN, John (brother of William McLean) (WD Ohio) March 11, 1785-April 4, 1861; House 1813-16; Postmaster Gen. 1823-29; Assoc. Justice Supreme Court 1829-61.

McLEAN, John (brother of Finis Ewing McLean, uncle of James David Walker) (D Ill.) Feb. 4, 1791-Oct. 14, 1830; House Dec. 3, 1818-19; Senate Nov. 23, 1824-25, 1829-Oct. 14, 1830.

McLEAN, Samuel (D Mont.) Aug. 7, 1826-July 16, 1877; House (Terr. Del.) Jan. 6, 1865-67.

McLEAN, William (brother of John McLean) (— Ohio) Aug. 10, 1794-Oct. 12, 1839; House 1823-29.

McLEAN, William Pinkney (D Texas) Aug. 9, 1836-March 13, 1925; House 1873-75.

McLEMORE, Atkins Jefferson (Jeff) (D Texas) March 13, 1857-March 4, 1929; House 1915-19.

McLENE, Jeremiah (D Ohio) 1767-March 19, 1837; House 1833-37.

McLEOD, Clarence John (R Mich.) July 3, 1895-May 15, 1959; House Nov. 2, 1920-21, 1923-37, 1939-41.

McLOSKEY, Robert Thaddeus (R Ill.) June 26, 1907-—; House 1963-65.

McMAHON, Gregory (R N.Y.) March 19, 1915-—; House 1947-49.

McMAHON, James O'Brien (D Conn.) Oct. 6, 1903-July 28, 1952; Senate 1945-July 28, 1952.

McMAHON, John A. (nephew of Clement Laird Vallandigham) (D Ohio) Feb. 19, 1833-March 8, 1923; House 1875-81.

McMANUS, William (− N.Y.) 1780-Jan. 18, 1835; House 1825-27.

McMASTER, William Henry (R S.D.) May 10, 1877-Sept. 14, 1968; Senate 1925-31; Gov. 1921-25.

McMILLAN, Alexander (− N.C.) ?-1817; House 1817.

McMILLAN, Clara Gooding (widow of Thomas Sanders McMillan) (D S.C.) Aug. 17, 1894-Nov. 8, 1976; House Nov. 7, 1939-41.

McMILLAN, J. Alex (R N.C.) May 9, 1932-−; House 1985-−.

McMILLAN, James (R Mich.) May 12, 1838-Aug. 10, 1902; Senate 1889-Aug. 10, 1902.

McMILLAN, John Lanneau (D S.C.) ?-Sept. 3, 1977; House 1939-73.

McMILLAN, Samuel (R N.Y.) Aug. 6, 1850-May 6, 1924; House 1907-09.

McMILLAN, Samuel James Renwick (R Minn.) Feb. 22, 1826-Oct. 3, 1897; Senate 1875-87.

McMILLAN, Thomas Sanders (husband of Clara Gooding McMillan) (D S.C.) Nov. 27, 1888-Sept. 29, 1939; House 1925-Sept. 29, 1939.

McMILLAN, William (− N.W. Terr.) March 2, 1764-May 1804; House (Terr. Del.) Nov. 24, 1800-01.

McMILLEN, Rolla Coral (R Ill.) Oct. 5, 1880-May 6, 1961; House June 13, 1944-51.

McMILLIN, Benton (D Tenn.) Sept. 11, 1845-Jan. 8, 1933; House 1879-Jan. 6, 1899; Gov. 1899-1903.

McMORRAN, Henry Gordon (R Mich.) June 11, 1844-July 19, 1929; House 1903-13.

McMULLEN, Chester Bartow (D Fla.) Dec. 6, 1902-Nov. 3, 1953; House 1951-53.

McMULLEN, Fayette (D Va.) May 18, 1805-Nov. 8, 1880; House 1849-57; Gov. (Wash. Terr.) 1857-61.

McMURRAY, Howard Johnstone (D Wis.) March 3, 1901-Aug. 14, 1961; House 1943-45.

McNAGNY, William Forgy (D Ind.) April 19, 1850-Aug. 24, 1923; House 1893-95.

McNAIR, John (D Pa.) June 8, 1800-Aug. 12, 1861; House 1851-55.

McNAMARA, Patrick Vincent (D Mich.) Oct. 4, 1894-April 30, 1966; Senate 1955-April 30, 1966.

McNARY, Charles Linza (R Ore.) June 12, 1874-Feb. 25, 1944; Senate May 29, 1917-Nov. 5, 1918, Dec. 18, 1918-Feb. 25, 1944.

McNARY, William Sarsfield (D Mass.) March 29, 1863-June 26, 1930; House 1903-07.

McNEELY, Thompson Ware (D Ill.) Oct. 5, 1835-July 23, 1921; House 1869-73.

McNEILL, Archibald (− N.C.) ?-1849; House 1821-23, 1825-27.

McNULTA, John (R Ill.) Nov. 9, 1837-Feb. 22, 1900; House 1873-75.

McNULTY, Frank Joseph (D N.J.) Aug. 10, 1872-May 26, 1926; House 1923-25.

McNULTY, James Francis Jr. (D Ariz.) Oct. 18, 1925-−; House 1983-85.

McPHERSON, Edward (R Pa.) July 31, 1830-Dec. 14, 1895; House 1859-63.

McPHERSON, Isaac Vanbert (R Mo.) March 8, 1868-Oct. 31, 1931; House 1919-23.

McPHERSON, John Rhoderic (D N.J.) May 9, 1833-Oct. 8, 1897; Senate 1877-95.

McPHERSON, Smith (R Iowa) Feb. 14, 1848-Jan. 17, 1915; House 1899-June 6, 1900.

McQUEEN, John (D S.C.) Feb. 9, 1804-Aug. 30, 1867; House Feb. 12, 1849-Dec. 21, 1860.

McRAE, John Jones (SRD Miss.) Jan. 10, 1815-May 31, 1868; Senate Dec. 1, 1851-March 17, 1852; House Dec. 7, 1858-Jan. 12, 1861; Gov. 1854-58 (1851-52, 1854-58 Democrat, 1858-61 State Rights Democrat).

McRAE, Thomas Chipman (cousin of Thomas Banks Cabaniss) (D Ark.) Dec. 21, 1851-June 2, 1929; House Dec. 7, 1885-1903; Gov. 1921-25.

McREYNOLDS, Samuel Davis (D Tenn.) April 16, 1872-July 11, 1939; House 1923-July 11, 1939.

McROBERTS, Samuel (D Ill.) April 12, 1799-March 27, 1843; Senate 1841-March 27, 1843.

McRUER, Donald Campbell (R Calif.) March 10, 1826-Jan. 29, 1898; House 1865-67.

McSHANE, John Albert (D Neb.) Aug. 25, 1850-Nov. 10, 1923; House 1887-89.

McSHERRY, James (− Pa.) July 29, 1776-Feb. 3, 1849; House 1821-23.

McSPADDEN, Clem Rogers (D Okla.) Nov. 9, 1925-−; House 1973-75.

McSWAIN, John Jackson (D S.C.) May 1, 1875-Aug. 6, 1936; House 1921-Aug. 6, 1936.

McSWEEN, Harold Barnett (D La.) July 19, 1926-−; House 1959-63.

McSWEENEY, John (D Ohio) Dec. 19, 1890-Dec. 13, 1969; House 1923-29, 1937-39, 1949-51.

McVEAN, Charles (D N.Y.) 1802-Dec. 22, 1848; House 1833-35.

McVEY, Walter Lewis (R Kan.) Feb. 19, 1922-−; House 1961-63.

McVEY, William Estus (R Ill.) Dec. 13, 1885-Aug. 10, 1958; House 1951-Aug. 10, 1958.

McVICKER, Roy Harrison (D Colo.) Feb. 20, 1924-Sept. 15, 1973; House 1965-67.

McWILLIAMS, John Dacher (R Conn.) July 23, 1891-March 30, 1975; House 1943-45.

McWILLIE, William (D Miss.) Nov. 17, 1795-March 3, 1869; House 1849-51; Gov. 1858-60.

MEACHAM, James (W Vt.) Aug. 16, 1810-Aug. 23, 1856; House Dec. 3, 1849-Aug. 23, 1856.

MEAD, Cowles (− Ga.) Oct. 18, 1776-May 17, 1844; House March 4-Dec. 24, 1805.

MEAD, James Michael (D N.Y.) Dec. 27, 1885-March 15, 1964; House 1919-Dec. 2, 1938; Senate Dec. 3, 1938-47.

MEADE, Edwin Ruthven (D N.Y.) July 6, 1836-Nov. 28, 1889; House 1875-77.

MEADE, Hugh Allen (D Md.) April 4, 1907-July 8, 1949; House 1947-49.

MEADE, Richard Kidder (D Va.) July 29, 1803-April 20, 1862; House Aug. 5, 1847-53.

MEADE, Wendell Howes (R Ky.) Jan. 18, 1912-−; House 1947-49.

MEADER, George (R Mich.) Sept. 13, 1907-−; House 1951-65.

MEANS, Rice William (R Colo.) Nov. 16, 1877-Jan. 30, 1949; Senate Dec. 1, 1924-27.

MEBANE, Alexander (− N.C.) Nov. 26, 1744-July 5, 1795; House 1793-95.

MECHEM, Edwin Leard (R N.M.) July 2, 1912-−; Senate Nov. 30, 1962-Nov. 3, 1964; Gov. 1951-55, 1957-59, 1961-62.

MEDILL, William (D Ohio) 1802-Sept. 2, 1865; House 1839-43; Gov. 1853-56.

MEECH, Ezra (D Vt.) July 26, 1773-Sept. 23, 1856; House 1819-21, 1825-27.

MEEDS, Lloyd (D Wash.) Dec. 11, 1927-−; House 1965-79.

MEEKER, Jacob Edwin (R Mo.) Oct. 7, 1878-Oct. 16, 1918; House 1915-Oct. 16, 1918.

MEEKISON, David (D Ohio) Nov. 14, 1849-Feb. 12, 1915; House 1897-1901.

MEEKS, James Andrew (D Ill.) March 7, 1864-Nov. 10, 1946; House 1933-39.

MEIGS, Henry (D N.Y.) Oct. 28, 1782-May 20, 1861; House 1819-21.

MEIGS, Return Jonathan Jr. (D Ohio) Nov. 16, 1764-March 29, 1825; Senate Dec. 12, 1808-May 1, 1810; Gov. 1810-14; Postmaster Gen. 1814-23.

MEIKLEJOHN, George de Rue (R Neb.) Aug. 26, 1857-April 19, 1929; House 1893-97.

MELCHER, John (D Mont.) Sept. 6, 1924-−; House June 24, 1969-77; Senate 1977-−.

MELLEN, Prentiss (− Mass.) Oct. 11, 1764-Dec. 31, 1840; Senate June 5, 1818-May 15, 1820.

MELLISH, David Batcheller (R N.Y.) Jan. 2, 1831-May 23, 1874; House 1873-May 23, 1874.

MENEFEE, Richard Hickman (W Ky.) Dec. 4, 1809-Feb. 21, 1841; House 1837-39.

MENGES, Franklin (R Pa.) Oct. 26, 1858-May 12, 1956; House 1925-31.

MENZIES, John William (U Ky.) April 12, 1819-Oct. 3, 1897; House 1861-63.

MERCER, Charles Fenton (cousin of Robert Selden Garnett) (D Va.) June 16, 1778-May 4, 1858; House 1817-Dec. 26, 1839.

MERCER, David Henry (R Neb.) July 9, 1857-Jan. 10, 1919; House 1893-1903.

MERCER, John Francis (D Md.) May 17, 1759-Aug. 30, 1821; House Feb. 5, 1792-April 13, 1794; Cont. Cong. (Va.) 1782-85; Gov. (Md.) 1801-03.

MERCUR, Ulysses (R Pa.) Aug. 12, 1818-June 6, 1887; House 1865-Dec. 2, 1872.

MEREDITH, Elisha Edward (D Va.) Dec. 26, 1848-July 29, 1900; House Dec. 9, 1891-97.

MERIWETHER, David (father of James Meriwether) (D Ga.) April 10, 1755-Nov. 16, 1822; House Dec. 6, 1802-07.

MERIWETHER, David (D Ky.) Oct. 30, 1800-April 4, 1893; Senate July 6-Aug. 31, 1852; Gov. (N.M. Terr.) 1853-55.

MERIWETHER, James (son of David Meriwether of Ga., uncle of James A. Meriwether) (— Ga.) 1789-1854; House 1825-27.

MERIWETHER, James A. (nephew of James Meriwether) (W Ga.) Sept. 20, 1806-April 18, 1852; House 1841-43.

MERRIAM, Clinton Levi (R N.Y.) March 25, 1824-Feb. 18, 1900; House 1871-75.

MERRICK, William Duhurst (father of William Matthew Merrick) (W Md.) Oct. 25, 1793-Feb. 5, 1857; Senate Jan. 4, 1838-45.

MERRICK, William Matthew (son of William Duhurst Merrick) (D Md.) Sept. 1, 1818-Feb. 4, 1889; House 1871-73.

MERRILL, D. Bailey (R Ind.) Nov. 22, 1912-—; House 1953-55.

MERRILL, Orsamus Cook (D Vt.) June 18, 1775-April 12, 1865; House 1817-Jan. 12, 1820.

MERRIMAN, Truman Adams (D N.Y.) Sept. 5, 1839-April 16, 1892; House 1885-89.

MERRIMON, Augustus Summerfield (D N.C.) Sept. 15, 1830-Nov. 14, 1892; Senate 1873-79.

MERRITT, Edwin Albert (R N.Y.) July 25, 1860-Dec. 4, 1914; House Nov. 5, 1912-Dec. 4, 1914.

MERRITT, Matthew Joseph (D N.Y.) April 2, 1895-Sept. 29, 1946; House 1935-45.

MERRITT, Samuel Augustus (D Idaho) Aug. 15, 1827-Sept. 8, 1910; House (Terr. Del.) 1871-73.

MERRITT, Schuyler (R Conn.) Dec. 16, 1853-April 1, 1953; House Nov. 6, 1917-31, 1933-37.

MERROW, Chester Earl (R N.H.) Nov. 15, 1906-Feb. 10, 1974; House 1943-63.

MERWIN, Orange (— Conn.) April 7, 1777-Sept. 4, 1853; House 1825-29.

MESICK, William Smith (R Mich.) Aug. 26, 1856-Dec. 1, 1942; House 1897-1901.

MESKILL, Thomas J. (R Conn.) Jan. 30, 1928-—; House 1967-71; Gov. 1971-75.

METCALF, Arunah (D N.Y.) Aug. 15, 1771-Aug. 15, 1848; House 1811-13.

METCALF, Jesse Houghton (R R.I.) Nov. 16, 1860-Oct. 9, 1942; Senate Nov. 5, 1924-37.

METCALF, Lee Warren (D Mont.) Jan. 28, 1911-Jan. 12, 1978; House 1953-61; Senate 1961-Jan. 12, 1978.

METCALF, Victor Howard (R Calif.) Oct. 10, 1853-Feb. 20, 1936; House 1899-July 1, 1904; Secy. of Commerce and Labor 1904-06; Secy of the Navy 1906-08.

METCALFE, Henry Bleecker (D N.Y.) Jan. 20, 1805-Feb. 7, 1881; House 1875-77.

METCALFE, Lyne Shackelford (R Mo.) April 21, 1822-Jan. 31, 1906; House 1877-79.

METCALFE, Ralph Harold (D Ill.) May 29, 1910-Oct. 10, 1978; House 1971-Oct. 10, 1978.

METCALFE, Thomas (D Ky.) March 20, 1780-Aug. 18, 1855; House 1819-June 1, 1828; Senate June 23, 1848-49; Gov. 1828-32.

METZ, Herman August (D N.Y.) Oct. 19, 1867-May 17, 1934; House 1913-15.

METZENBAUM, Howard Morton (D Ohio) June 4, 1917-—; Senate Jan. 4-Dec. 23, 1974, Dec. 29, 1976-—.

MEYER, Adolph (D La.) Oct. 19, 1842-March 8, 1908; House 1891-March 8, 1908.

MEYER, Herbert Alton (R Kan.) Aug. 30, 1886-Oct. 2, 1950; House 1947-Oct. 2, 1950.

MEYER, John Ambrose (D Md.) May 15, 1899-Oct. 2, 1969; House 1941-43.

MEYER, William Henry (D Vt.) Dec. 29, 1914-Dec. 16, 1983; House 1959-61.

MEYERS, Benjamin Franklin (D Pa.) July 6, 1833-Aug. 11, 1918; House 1871-73.

MEYERS, Jan (R Kan.) July 20, 1928-—; House 1985-—.

MEYNER, Helen Stevenson (D N.J.) March 5, 1929-—; House 1975-79.

MEZVINSKY, Edward Maurice (D Iowa) Jan. 17, 1937-—; House 1973-77.

MICA, Daniel Andrew (D Fla.) Feb. 4, 1944-—; House 1979-—.

MICHAELSON, Magne Alfred (R Ill.) Sept. 7, 1878-Oct. 26, 1949; House 1921-31.

MICHALEK, Anthony (R Ill.) Jan. 16, 1878-Dec. 21, 1916; House 1905-07.

MICHEL, Robert Henry (R Ill.) March 2, 1923-—; House 1957-—.

MICHENER, Earl Cory (R Mich.) Nov. 30, 1876-July 4, 1957; House 1919-33, 1935-51.

MICKEY, J. Ross (D Ill.) Jan. 5, 1856-March 20, 1928; House 1901-03.

MIDDLESWARTH, Ner (W Pa.) Dec. 12, 1783-June 2, 1865; House 1853-55.

MIDDLETON, George (D N.J.) Oct. 14, 1800-Dec. 31, 1888; House 1863-65.

MIDDLETON, Henry (D S.C.) Sept. 28, 1770-June 14, 1846; House 1815-19; Gov. 1810-12.

MIERS, Robert Walter (D Ind.) Jan. 27, 1848-Feb. 20, 1930; House 1897-1905.

MIKULSKI, Barbara Ann (D Md.) July 20, 1936-—; House 1977-—.

MIKVA, Abner J. (D Ill.) Jan. 21, 1926-—; House 1969-73; 1975-Sept. 26, 1979.

MILES, Frederick (R Conn.) Dec. 19, 1815-Nov. 20, 1896; House 1879-83, 1889-91.

MILES, John Esten (D N.M.) July 28, 1884-Oct. 7, 1971; House 1949-51; Gov. 1939-43.

MILES, Joshua Weldon (D Md.) Dec. 9, 1858-March 4, 1929; House 1895-97.

MILES, William Porcher (D S.C.) July 4, 1822-May 11, 1899; House 1857-Dec. 1860.

MILFORD, Dale (D Texas) Feb. 18, 1926-—; House 1973-79.

MILLARD, Charles Dunsmore (R N.Y.) Dec. 1, 1873-Dec. 11, 1944; House 1931-Sept. 29, 1937.

MILLARD, Joseph Hopkins (R Neb.) April 20, 1836-Jan. 13, 1922; Senate March 28, 1901-07.

MILLARD, Stephen Columbus (R N.Y.) Jan. 14, 1841-June 21, 1914; House 1883-87.

MILLEDGE, John (— Ga.) 1757-Feb. 9, 1818; House Nov. 22, 1792-93, 1795-99, 1801-May 1802; Senate June 19, 1806-Nov. 14, 1809; Pres. pro tempore 1809; Gov. 1802-06.

MILLEN, John (D Ga.) 1804-Oct. 15, 1843; House March 4-Oct. 15, 1843.

MILLER, Arthur Lewis (R Neb.) May 24, 1892-March 16, 1967; House 1943-59.

MILLER, Bert Henry (D Idaho) Dec. 15, 1879-Oct. 8, 1949; Senate Jan. 3-Oct. 8, 1949.

MILLER, Clarence Benjamin (R Minn.) March 13, 1872-Jan. 10, 1922; House 1909-19.

MILLER, Clarence E. (R Ohio) Nov. 1, 1917-—; House 1967-—.

MILLER, Clement Woodnutt (nephew of Thomas Woodnutt Miller) (D Calif.) Oct. 28, 1916-Oct. 7, 1962; House 1959-Oct. 7, 1962.

MILLER, Daniel Fry (W Iowa) Oct. 4, 1814-Dec. 9, 1895; House Dec. 20, 1850-51.

MILLER, Daniel H. (JD Pa.) ?-1846; House 1823-31.

MILLER, Edward Edwin (R Ill.) July 22, 1880-Aug. 1, 1946; House 1923-25.

MILLER, Edward Tylor (R Md.) Feb. 1, 1895-Jan. 20, 1968; House 1947-59.

MILLER, George (D Calif.) May 17, 1945- —; House 1975- —.

MILLER, George Funston (R Pa.) Sept. 5, 1809-Oct. 21, 1885; House 1865-69.

MILLER, George Paul (D Calif.) Jan. 15, 1891-Dec. 29, 1982; House 1945-73.

MILLER, Homer Virgil Milton (D Ga.) April 29, 1814-May 31, 1896; Senate Feb. 24-March 3, 1871.

MILLER, Howard Shultz (D Kan.) Feb. 27, 1879-Jan. 2, 1970; House 1953-55.

MILLER, Jack Richard (R Iowa) June 6, 1916- —; Senate 1961-73.

MILLER, Jacob Welsh (W N.J.) Aug. 29, 1800-Sept. 30, 1862; Senate 1841-53.

MILLER, James Francis (D Texas) Aug. 1, 1830-July 3, 1902; House 1883-87.

MILLER, James Monroe (R Kan.) May 6, 1852-Jan. 20, 1926; House 1899-1911.

MILLER, Jesse (father of William Henry Miller) (D Pa.) 1800-Aug. 20, 1850; House 1833-Oct. 30, 1836.

MILLER, John (— N.Y.) Nov. 10, 1774-March 31, 1862; House 1825-27.

MILLER, John (VBD Mo.) Nov. 25, 1781-March 18, 1846; House 1837-43; Gov. 1826-32.

MILLER, John (R Wash.) May 23, 1938- —; House 1985- —.

MILLER, John Elvis (D Ark.) May 15, 1888-Jan. 30, 1981; House 1931-Nov. 14, 1937; Senate Nov. 15, 1937-March 31, 1941.

MILLER, John Franklin (R Calif.) (uncle of the following) Nov. 21, 1831-March 8, 1886; Senate 1881-March 8, 1886.

MILLER, John Franklin (nephew of the preceding) (R Wash.) June 9, 1862-May 28, 1936; House 1917-31.

MILLER, John Gaines (W Mo.) Nov. 29, 1812-May 11, 1856; House 1851-May 11, 1856.

MILLER, John Krepps (D Ohio) May 25, 1819-Aug. 11, 1863; House 1847-51.

MILLER, Joseph (D Ohio) Sept. 9, 1819-May 27, 1862; House 1857-59.

MILLER, Killian (W N.Y.) July 30, 1785-Jan. 9, 1859; House 1855-57.

MILLER, Louis Ebenezer (R Mo.) April 30, 1899-Nov. 1, 1952; House 1943-45.

MILLER, Lucas Miltiades (D Wis.) Sept. 15, 1824-Dec. 4, 1902; House 1891-93.

MILLER, Morris Smith (father of Rutger Bleecker Miller) (F N.Y.) July 31, 1779-Nov. 16, 1824; House 1813-15.

MILLER, Orrin Larrabee (R Kan.) Jan. 11, 1856-Sept. 11, 1926; House 1895-97.

MILLER, Pleasant Moorman (— Tenn.) ?-1849; House 1809-11.

MILLER, Rutger Bleecker (son of Morris Smith Miller) (D N.Y.) July 28, 1805-Nov. 12, 1877; House Nov. 9, 1836-37.

MILLER, Samuel Franklin (R N.Y.) May 27, 1827-March 16, 1892; House 1863-65, 1875-77.

MILLER, Samuel Henry (R Pa.) April 19, 1840-Sept. 4, 1918; House 1881-85, 1915-17.

MILLER, Smith (D Ind.) May 30, 1804-March 21, 1872; House 1853-57.

MILLER, Stephen Decatur (N S.C.) May 8, 1787-March 8, 1838; House Jan. 2, 1817-19; Senate 1831-March 2, 1833; Gov. 1828-30 (1817-19, 1828-30 Democrat, 1831-33 Nullifier).

MILLER, Thomas Byron (R Pa.) Aug. 11, 1896-March 20, 1976; House May 9, 1942-45.

MILLER, Thomas Ezekiel (R S.C.) June 17, 1849-April 8, 1938; House Sept. 24, 1890-91.

MILLER, Thomas Woodnutt (uncle of Clement Woodnutt Miller) (R Del.) June 26, 1886-May 5, 1973; House 1915-17.

MILLER, Ward MacLaughlin (R Ohio) Nov. 29, 1902- —; House Nov. 8, 1960-61.

MILLER, Warner (R N.Y.) Aug. 12, 1838-March 21, 1918; House 1879-July 26, 1881; Senate July 27, 1881-87.

MILLER, Warren (R W.Va.) April 2, 1847-Dec. 29, 1920; House 1895-99.

MILLER, William Edward (R N.Y.) March 22, 1914-June 24, 1983; House 1951-65; Chrmn. Rep. Nat. Comm. 1961-64.

MILLER, William Henry (son of Jesse Miller) (D Pa.) Feb. 28, 1829-Sept. 12, 1870; House 1863-65.

MILLER, William Jennings (R Conn.) March 12, 1899-Nov. 22, 1950; House 1939-41, 1943-45, 1947-49.

MILLER, William Starr (— N.Y.) Aug. 22, 1793-Nov. 9, 1854; House 1845-47.

MILLIGAN, Jacob Le Roy (D Mo.) March 9, 1889-March 9, 1951; House Feb. 14, 1920-21, 1923-35.

MILLIGAN, John Jones (W Del.) Dec. 10, 1795-April 20, 1875; House 1831-39.

MILLIKEN, Charles William (D Ky.) Aug. 15, 1827-Oct. 16, 1915; House 1873-77.

MILLIKEN, Seth Llewellyn (R Maine) Dec. 12, 1831-April 18, 1897; House 1883-April 18, 1897.

MILLIKEN, William H. Jr. (R Pa.) Aug. 19, 1897-July 4, 1969; House 1959-65.

MILLIKIN, Eugene Donald (R Colo.) Feb. 12, 1891-July 26, 1958; Senate Dec. 20, 1941-57.

MILLINGTON, Charles Stephen (R N.Y.) March 13, 1855-Oct. 25, 1913; House 1909-11.

MILLS, Daniel Webster (R Ill.) Feb. 25, 1838-Dec. 16, 1904; House 1897-99.

MILLS, Elijah Hunt (F Mass.) Dec. 1, 1776-May 5, 1829; House 1815-19; Senate June 12, 1820-27.

MILLS, Newt Virgus (D La.) Sept. 27, 1899- —; House 1937-43.

MILLS, Ogden Livingston (R N.Y.) Aug. 23, 1884-Oct. 11, 1937; House 1921-27; Secy. of the Treasury 1932-33.

MILLS, Roger Quarles (D Texas) March 30, 1832-Sept. 2, 1911; House 1873-March 28, 1892; Senate March 29, 1892-99.

MILLS, Wilbur Daigh (D Ark.) May 24, 1909- —; House 1939-77.

MILLS, William Oswald (R Md.) Aug. 12, 1924-May 24, 1973; House May 27, 1971-May 24, 1973.

MILLSON, John Singleton (D Va.) Oct. 1, 1808-March 1, 1874; House 1849-61.

MILLSPAUGH, Frank Crenshaw (R Mo.) Jan. 14, 1872-July 8, 1947; House 1921-Dec. 5, 1922.

MILLWARD, William (W Pa.) June 30, 1822-Nov. 28, 1871; House 1855-57, 1859-61.

MILNES, Alfred (R Mich.) May 28, 1844-Jan. 15, 1916; House Dec. 2, 1895-97.

MILNES, William Jr. (C Va.) Dec. 8, 1827-Aug. 14, 1889; House Jan. 27, 1870-71.

MILNOR, James (F Pa.) June 20, 1773-April 8, 1844; House 1811-13.

MILNOR, William (F Pa.) June 26, 1769-Dec. 13, 1848; House 1807-11, 1815-17, 1821-May 8, 1822.

MILTON, John Gerald (D N.J.) Jan. 21, 1881-April 14, 1977; Senate Jan. 18-Nov. 8, 1938.

MILTON, William Hall (D Fla.) March 2, 1864-Jan. 4, 1942; Senate March 27, 1908-09.

MINAHAN, Daniel Francis (D N.J.) Aug. 8, 1877-April 29, 1947; House 1919-21, 1923-25.

MINER, Ahiman Louis (W Vt.) Sept. 23, 1804-July 19, 1886; House 1851-53.

MINER, Charles (F Pa.) Feb. 1, 1780-Oct. 26, 1865; House 1825-29.

MINER, Henry Clay (D N.Y.) March 23, 1842-Feb. 22, 1900; House 1895-97.

MINER, Phineas (W Conn.) Nov. 27, 1777-Sept. 15, 1839; House Dec. 1, 1834-35.

MINETA, Norman Yoshio (D Calif.) Nov. 12, 1931- —; House 1975- —.

MINISH, Joseph George (D N.J.) Sept. 1, 1916- —; House 1963-85.

MINK, Patsy Takemoto (D Hawaii) Dec. 6, 1927- —; House 1965-77.

MINOR, Edward Sloman (R Wis.) Dec. 13, 1840-July 26, 1924; House 1895-1907.

MINSHALL, William Edwin Jr. (R Ohio) Oct. 24, 1911- —; House 1955-75.

MINTON, Sherman (D Ind.) Oct. 20, 1890-April 9, 1965; Senate 1935-41; Assoc. Justice Supreme Court 1949-56.

MITCHEL, Charles Burton (D Ark.) Sept. 19, 1815-Sept. 20, 1864; Senate March 4-July 11, 1861.

MOODY, Gideon Curtis (R S.D.) Oct. 16, 1832-March 17, 1904; Senate Nov. 2, 1889-91.

MOODY, James Montraville (R N.C.) Feb. 12, 1858-Feb. 5, 1903; House 1901-Feb. 5, 1903.

MOODY, Jim (D Wis.) Sept. 2, 1935- —; House 1983- —.

MOODY, Malcolm Adelbert (R Ore.) Nov. 30, 1854-March 19, 1925; House 1899-1903.

MOODY, William Henry (R Mass.) Dec. 23, 1853-July 2, 1917; House Nov. 5, 1895-May 1, 1902; Secy. of the Navy 1902-04; Atty. Gen. 1904-06; Assoc. Justice Supreme Court 1906-10.

MOON, John Austin (D Tenn.) April 22, 1855-June 26, 1921; House 1897-1921.

MOON, John Wesley (R Mich.) Jan. 18, 1836-April 5, 1898; House 1893-95.

MOON, Reuben Osborne (R Pa.) July 22, 1847-Oct. 25, 1919; House Nov. 2, 1903-13.

MOONEY, Charles Anthony (D Ohio) Jan. 5, 1879-May 29, 1931; House 1919-21, 1923-May 29, 1931.

MOONEY, William Crittenden (R Ohio) June 15, 1855-July 24, 1918; House 1915-17.

MOOR, Wyman Bradbury Seavy (D Maine) Nov. 11, 1811-March 10, 1869; Senate Jan. 5-June 7, 1848.

MOORE, Allen Francis (R Ill.) Sept. 30, 1869-Aug. 18, 1945; House 1921-25.

MOORE, Andrew (father of Samuel McDowell Moore) (— Va.) 1752-April 14, 1821; House 1789-97, March 5-Aug. 11, 1804; Senate Aug. 11, 1804-09.

MOORE, Arch Alfred Jr. (R W.Va.) April 16, 1923- —; House 1957-69; Gov. 1969-77, 1985- —.

MOORE, Arthur Harry (D N.J.) July 3, 1879-Nov. 18, 1952; Senate 1935-Jan. 17, 1938; Gov. 1926-29, 1932-35, 1938-41.

MOORE, Charles Ellis (R Ohio) Jan. 3, 1884-April 2, 1941; House 1919-33.

MOORE, Edward Hall (R Okla.) Nov. 19, 1871-Sept. 2, 1950; Senate 1943-49.

MOORE, Eliakim Hastings (R Ohio) June 19, 1812-April 4, 1900; House 1869-71.

MOORE, Ely (D N.Y.) July 4, 1798-Jan. 27, 1861; House 1835-39.

MOORE, Gabriel (— Ala.) 1785-June 9, 1845; House 1821-29; Senate 1831-37; Gov. 1829-31.

MOORE, Heman Allen (D Ohio) Aug. 27, 1809-April 3, 1844; House 1843-April 3, 1844.

MOORE, Henry Dunning (W Pa.) April 13, 1817-Aug. 11, 1887; House 1849-53.

MOORE, Horace Ladd (D Kan.) Feb. 25, 1837-May 1, 1914; House Aug. 2, 1894-95.

MOORE, Jesse Hale (R Ill.) April 22, 1817-July 11, 1883; House 1869-73.

MOORE, John (W La.) 1788-June 17, 1867; House Dec. 17, 1840-43, 1851-53.

MOORE, John Matthew (D Texas) Nov. 18, 1862-Feb. 3, 1940; House June 6, 1905-13.

MOORE, John William (D Ky.) June 9, 1877-Dec. 11, 1941; House Nov. 3, 1925-29, June 1, 1929-33.

MOORE, Joseph Hampton (R Pa.) March 8, 1864-May 2, 1950; House Nov. 6, 1906-Jan. 4, 1920.

MOORE, Laban Theodore (Nat.A. Ky.) Jan. 13, 1829-Nov. 9, 1892; House 1859-61.

MOORE, Littleton Wilde (D Texas) March 25, 1835-Oct. 29, 1911; House 1887-93.

MOORE, Nicholas Ruxton (D Md.) July 21, 1756-Oct. 7, 1816; House 1803-11, 1813-15.

MOORE, Orren Cheney (R N.H.) Aug. 10, 1839-May 12, 1893; House 1889-91.

MOORE, Oscar Fitzallen (R Ohio) Jan. 27, 1817-June 24, 1885; House 1855-57.

MOORE, Paul John (D N.J.) Aug. 5, 1868-Jan. 10, 1938; House 1927-29.

MOORE, Robert (grandfather of Michael Daniel Harter) (— Pa.) March 30, 1778-Jan. 14, 1831; House 1817-21.

MOORE, Robert Lee (D Ga.) Nov. 27, 1867-Jan. 14, 1940; House 1923-25.

MOORE, Robert Walton (D Va.) Feb. 6, 1859-Feb. 8, 1941; House May 27, 1919-31.

MOORE, Samuel (D Pa.) Feb. 8, 1774-Feb. 18, 1861; House Oct. 13, 1818-May 20, 1822.

MOORE, Samuel McDowell (son of Andrew Moore) (W Va.) Feb. 9, 1796-Sept. 17, 1875; House 1833-35.

MOORE, Sydenham (D Ala.) May 25, 1817-May 31, 1862; House 1857-Jan. 21, 1861.

MOORE, Thomas (— S.C.) 1759-July 11, 1822; House 1801-13, 1815-17.

MOORE, Thomas Love (— Va.) ?-1862; House Nov. 13, 1820-23.

MOORE, Thomas Patrick (D Ky.) 1797-July 21, 1853; House 1823-29.

MOORE, William (R N.J.) Dec. 25, 1810-April 26, 1878; House 1867-71.

MOORE, William Henson (R La.) Oct. 4, 1939- —; House Jan. 7, 1975- —.

MOORE, William Robert (R Tenn.) March 28, 1830-June 12, 1909; House 1881-83.

MOORE, William Sutton (R Pa.) Nov. 18, 1822-Dec. 30, 1877; House 1873-75.

MOOREHEAD, Tom Van Horn (R Ohio) April 12, 1898- —; House 1961-63.

MOORES, Merrill (R Ind.) April 21, 1856-Oct. 21, 1929; House 1915-25.

MOORHEAD, Carlos John (R Calif.) May 6, 1922- —; House 1973- —.

MOORHEAD, James Kennedy (R Pa.) Sept. 7, 1806-March 6, 1884; House 1859-69.

MOORHEAD, William Singer (D Pa.) April 8, 1923- —; House 1959-81.

MOORMAN, Henry DeHaven (D Ky.) June 9, 1880-Feb. 3, 1939; House 1927-29.

MORAN, Edward Carleton Jr. (D Maine) Dec. 29, 1894-July 12, 1967; House 1933-37.

MORANO, Albert Paul (R Conn.) Jan. 18, 1908- —; House 1951-59.

MOREHEAD, Charles Slaughter (W Ky.) July 7, 1802-Dec. 21, 1868; House 1847-51; Gov. 1855-59 (American Party).

MOREHEAD, James Turner (W Ky.) May 24, 1797-Dec. 28, 1854; Senate 1841-47; Gov. 1834-36.

MOREHEAD, James Turner (W N.C.) Jan. 11, 1799-May 5, 1875; House 1851-53.

MOREHEAD, John Henry (D Neb.) Dec. 3, 1861-May 31, 1942; House 1923-35; Gov. 1913-17.

MOREHEAD, John Motley (R N.C.) July 20, 1866-Dec. 13, 1923; House 1909-11.

MOREY, Frank (R La.) July 11, 1840-Sept. 22, 1889; House 1869-June 8, 1876.

MOREY, Henry Lee (R Ohio) April 8, 1841-Dec. 29, 1902; House 1881-June 20, 1884, 1889-91.

MORGAN, Charles Henry (R Mo.) July 5, 1842-Jan. 4, 1912; House 1875-79, 1883-85, 1893-95, 1909-11 (1875-95 Democrat, 1909-11 Republican).

MORGAN, Christopher (brother of Edwin Barbour Morgan, nephew of Noyes Barber) (W N.Y.) June 4, 1808-April 3, 1877; House 1839-43.

MORGAN, Daniel (F Va.) 1736-July 6, 1802; House 1797-99.

MORGAN, Dick Thompson (R Okla.) Dec. 6, 1853-July 4, 1920; House 1909-July 4, 1920.

MORGAN, Edwin Barbour (brother of Christopher Morgan, nephew of Noyes Barber) (R N.Y.) May 2, 1806-Oct. 13, 1881; House 1853-59.

MORGAN, Edwin Dennison (cousin of Morgan Gardner Bulkeley) (UR N.Y.) Feb. 8, 1811-Feb. 14, 1883; Senate 1863-69; Chrmn. Rep. Nat. Comm. 1856-64, 1872-76; Gov. 1859-63.

MORGAN, George Washington (D Ohio) Sept. 20, 1820-July 26, 1893; House 1867-June 3, 1868, 1869-73.

MORGAN, James (F N.J.) Dec. 29, 1756-Nov. 11, 1822; House 1811-13.

MORGAN, James Bright (D Miss.) March 14, 1833-June 18, 1892; House 1885-91.

MORGAN, John Jordan (father-in-law of John Adams Dix) (D N.Y.) 1770-July 29, 1849; House 1821-25, Dec. 1, 1834-35.

MORGAN, John Tyler (D Ala.) June 20, 1824-June 11, 1907; Senate 1877-June 11, 1907.

MORGAN, Lewis Lovering (D La.) March 2, 1876-June 10, 1950; House Nov. 5, 1912-17.

MORGAN, Robert Burren (D N.C.) Oct. 5, 1925- —; Senate 1975-81.

MORGAN, Stephen (R Ohio) Jan. 25, 1854-Feb. 9, 1928; House 1899-1905.

MORGAN, Thomas Ellsworth (D Pa.) Oct. 13, 1906-—; House 1945-77.

MORGAN, William Mitchell (R Ohio) Aug. 1, 1870-Sept. 17, 1935; House 1921-31.

MORGAN, William Stephen (D Va.) Sept. 7, 1801-Sept. 3, 1878; House 1835-39.

MORIN, John Mary (R Pa.) April 18, 1868-March 3, 1942; House 1913-29.

MORITZ, Theodore Leo (D Pa.) Feb. 10, 1892- —; House 1935-37.

MORPHIS, Joseph Lewis (R Miss.) April 17, 1831-July 29, 1913; House Feb. 23, 1870-73.

MORRELL, Daniel Johnson (R Pa.) Aug. 8, 1821-Aug. 20, 1885; House 1867-71.

MORRELL, Edward de Veaux (R Pa.) Aug. 7, 1863-Sept. 1, 1917; House Nov. 6, 1900-07.

MORRIL, David Lawrence (Ad.D N.H.) June 10, 1772-Jan. 28, 1849; Senate 1817-23; Gov. 1824-27.

MORRILL, Anson Peaslee (brother of Lot Myrick Morrill) (R Maine) June 10, 1803-July 4, 1887; House 1861-63; Gov. 1855-56.

MORRILL, Edmund Needham (R Kan.) Feb. 12, 1834-March 14, 1909; House 1883-91; Gov. 1895-97.

MORRILL, Justin Smith (UR Vt.) April 14, 1810-Dec. 28, 1898; House 1855-67; Senate 1867-Dec. 28, 1898 (1855-67 Whig, 1867-98 Union Republican).

MORRILL, Lot Myrick (brother of Anson Peaslee Morrill) (R Maine) May 3, 1813-Jan. 10, 1883; Senate Jan. 17, 1861-69, Oct. 30, 1869-July 7, 1876; Gov. 1858-61; Secy. of the Treasury 1876-77.

MORRILL, Samuel Plummer (R Maine) Feb. 11, 1816-Aug. 4, 1892; House 1869-71.

MORRIS, Calvary (W Ohio) Jan. 15, 1798-Oct. 13, 1871; House 1837-43.

MORRIS, Daniel (R N.Y.) Jan. 4, 1812-April 22, 1889; House 1863-67.

MORRIS, Edward Joy (W Pa.) July 16, 1815-Dec. 31, 1881; House 1843-45; 1857-June 8, 1861.

MORRIS, Gouverneur (uncle of Lewis Robert Morris) (F N.Y.) Jan. 31, 1752-Nov. 6, 1816; Senate April 3, 1800-03; Cont. Cong. 1777-78.

MORRIS, Isaac Newton (son of Thomas Morris of Ohio, brother of Jonathan David Morris) (D Ill.) Jan. 22, 1812-Oct. 29, 1879; House 1857-61.

MORRIS, James Remley (son of Joseph Morris) (D Ohio) Jan. 10, 1819-Dec. 24, 1899; House 1861-65.

MORRIS, Jonathan David (son of Thomas Morris of Ohio, brother of Isaac Newton Morris) (D Ohio) Oct. 8, 1804-May 16, 1875; House 1847-51.

MORRIS, Joseph (father of James Remley Morris) (D Ohio) Oct. 16, 1795-Oct. 23, 1854; House 1843-47.

MORRIS, Joseph Watkins (D Ky.) Feb. 26, 1879-Dec. 21, 1937; House Nov. 30, 1923-25.

MORRIS, Lewis Robert (nephew of Gouverneur Morris) (F Vt.) Nov. 2, 1760-Dec. 29, 1825; House 1797-1803.

MORRIS, Mathias (W Pa.) Sept. 12, 1787-Nov. 9, 1839; House 1835-39.

MORRIS, Robert (father of Thomas Morris of N.Y.) (— Pa.) Jan. 20, 1734-May 8, 1806; Senate 1789-95; Cont. Cong. 1776-78.

MORRIS, Robert Page Walter (R Minn.) June 30, 1853-Dec. 16, 1924; House 1897-1903.

MORRIS, Samuel Wells (D Pa.) Sept. 1, 1786-May 25, 1847; House 1837-41.

MORRIS, Thomas (son of Robert Morris) (— N.Y.) Feb. 26, 1771-March 12, 1849; House 1801-03.

MORRIS, Thomas (father of Isaac Newton Morris and Jonathan David Morris) (D Ohio) Jan. 3, 1776-Dec. 7, 1844; Senate 1833-39.

MORRIS, Thomas Gayle (D N.M.) Aug. 20, 1919-—; House 1959-69.

MORRIS, Toby (D Okla.) Feb. 28, 1899-Sept. 1, 1973; House 1947-53, 1957-61.

MORRISON, Bruce A. (D Conn.) Oct. 8, 1944-—; House 1983-—.

MORRISON, Cameron A. (D N.C.) Oct. 5, 1869-Aug. 20, 1953; Senate Dec. 13, 1930-Dec. 4, 1932; House 1943-45; Gov. 1921-25.

MORRISON, George Washington (D N.H.) Oct. 16, 1809-Dec. 21, 1888; House Oct. 8, 1850-51, 1853-55.

MORRISON, James Hobson (D La.) Dec. 8, 1908-—; House 1943-67.

MORRISON, James Lowery Donaldson (D Ill.) April 12, 1816-Aug. 14, 1888; House Nov. 4, 1856-57.

MORRISON, John Alexander (D Pa.) Jan. 31, 1814-July 25, 1904; House 1851-53.

MORRISON, Martin Andrew (D Ind.) April 15, 1862-July 9, 1944; House 1909-17.

MORRISON, Sid (R Wash.) May 13, 1933-—; House 1981-—.

MORRISON, William Ralls (D Ill.) Sept. 14, 1825-Sept. 29, 1909; House 1863-65, 1873-87.

MORRISSEY, John (D N.Y.) Feb. 12, 1831-May 1, 1878; House 1867-71.

MORROW, Dwight Whitney (R N.J.) Jan. 11, 1873-Oct. 5, 1931; Senate Dec. 3, 1930-Oct. 5, 1931.

MORROW, Jeremiah (W Ohio) Oct. 6, 1771-March 22, 1852; House Oct. 17, 1803-13, Oct. 13, 1840-43; Senate 1813-19 (1803-13, 1813-19 Democrat, 1840-43 Whig); Gov. 1822-26.

MORROW, John (— Va.) ?-?; House 1805-09.

MORROW, John (D N.M.) April 19, 1865-Feb. 25, 1935; House 1923-29.

MORROW, William W. (R Calif.) July 15, 1843-July 24, 1929; House 1885-91.

MORSE, Elijah Adams (R Mass.) May 25, 1841-June 5, 1898; House 1889-97.

MORSE, Elmer Addison (R Wis.) May 11, 1870-Oct. 4, 1945; House 1907-13.

MORSE, F. Bradford (R Mass.) Aug. 7, 1921-—; House 1961-May 1, 1972.

MORSE, Freeman Harlow (R Maine) Feb. 19, 1807-Feb. 5, 1891; House 1843-45, 1857-61 (1843-45 Whig, 1857-61 Republican).

MORSE, Isaac Edward (D La.) May 22, 1809-Feb. 11, 1866; House Dec. 2, 1844-51.

MORSE, Leopold (D Mass.) Aug. 15, 1831-Dec. 15, 1892; House 1877-85, 1887-89.

MORSE, Oliver Andrew (R N.Y.) March 26, 1815-April 20, 1870; House 1857-59.

MORSE, Wayne Lyman (D Ore.) Oct. 20, 1900-July 22, 1974; Senate 1945-69 (1945-Oct. 24, 1952 Republican, Oct. 24, 1952-Feb. 17, 1955 Independent, Feb. 17, 1955-69 Democrat).

MORTON, Jackson (brother of Jeremiah Morton) (W Fla.) Aug. 10, 1794-Nov. 20, 1874; Senate 1849-55.

MORTON, Jeremiah (brother of Jackson Morton) (W Va.) Sept. 3, 1799-Nov. 28, 1878; House 1849-51.

MORTON, Levi Parson (R N.Y.) May 16, 1824-May 16, 1920; House 1879-March 21, 1881; Vice Pres. 1889-93; Gov. 1895-97.

MORTON, Marcus (D Mass.) Dec. 19, 1784-Feb. 6, 1864; House 1817-21; Gov. 1840-41, 1843-44.

MORTON, Oliver Hazard Perry Throck (UR Ind.) Aug. 4, 1823-Nov. 1, 1877; Senate 1867-Nov. 1, 1877; Gov. 1861-67.

MORTON, Rogers Clark Ballard (brother of Thruston Ballard Morton) (R Md.) Sept. 19, 1914-April 19, 1979; House 1963-Jan. 29, 1971; Chrmn. Rep. Nat. Comm. 1969-71; Secy. of the Interior 1971-75; Secy. of Commerce 1975-76.

MORTON, Thruston Ballard (brother of Rogers Clark Ballard Morton) (R Ky.) Aug. 19, 1907-August 14, 1982; House 1947-53; Senate 1957-Dec. 16, 1968; Chrmn. Rep. Nat. Comm. 1959-61.

MOSELEY, Jonathan Ogden (R Conn.) April 9, 1762-Sept. 9, 1838; House 1805-21.

MOSELEY, William Abbott (W N.Y.) Oct. 20, 1798-Nov. 19, 1873; House 1843-47.

MOSER, Guy Louis (D Pa.) Jan. 23, 1866-May 9, 1961; House 1937-43.

MOSES, Charles Leavell (D Ga.) May 2, 1856-Oct. 10, 1910; House 1891-97.

MOSES, George Higgins (R N.H.) Feb. 9, 1869-Dec. 20, 1944; Senate Nov. 6, 1918-33; Pres. pro tempore 1925-33.

MOSES, John (D N.D.) June 12, 1885-March 3, 1945; Senate Jan. 3-March 3, 1945; Gov. 1939-45.

MOSGROVE, James (D/G Pa.) June 14, 1821-Nov. 27, 1900; House 1881-83.

MOSHER, Charles Adams (R Ohio) May 7, 1906-Nov. 16, 1984; House 1961-77.

MOSIER, Harold Gerard (D Ohio) July 24, 1889-Aug. 7, 1971; House 1937-39.

MOSS, Frank Edward (D Utah) Sept. 23, 1911- —; Senate 1959-77.

MOSS, Hunter Holmes Jr. (R W.Va.) May 26, 1874-July 15, 1916; House 1913-July 15, 1916.

MOSS, John Emerson Jr. (D Calif.) April 13, 1913- —; House 1953-Dec. 31, 1978.

MOSS, John McKenzie (nephew of James Andrew McKenzie) (R Ky.) Jan. 3, 1868-June 11, 1929; House March 25, 1902-03.

MOSS, Ralph Wilbur (D Ind.) April 21, 1862-April 26, 1919; House 1909-17.

MOTT, Gordon Newell (R Nev.) Oct. 21, 1812-April 27, 1887; House (Terr. Del.) 1863-Oct. 31, 1864.

MOTT, James (D N.J.) Jan. 18, 1739-Oct. 18, 1823; House 1801-05.

MOTT, James Wheaton (R Ore.) Nov. 12, 1883-Nov. 12, 1945; House 1933-Nov. 12, 1945.

MOTT, Luther Wright (R N.Y.) Nov. 30, 1874-July 10, 1923; House 1911-July 10, 1923.

MOTT, Richard (R Ohio) July 21, 1804-Jan. 22, 1888; House 1855-59.

MOTTL, Ronald Milton (D Ohio) Feb. 6, 1934- —; House 1975-83.

MOULDER, Morgan Moore (D Mo.) Aug. 31, 1904-Nov. 12, 1976; House 1949-63.

MOULTON, Mace (D N.H.) May 2, 1796-May 5, 1867; House 1845-47.

MOULTON, Samuel Wheeler (D Ill.) Jan. 20, 1821-June 3, 1905; House 1865-67, 1881-85.

MOUSER, Grant Earl (father of Grant Earl Mouser Jr.) (R Ohio) Sept. 11, 1868-May 6, 1949; House 1905-09.

MOUSER, Grant Earl Jr. (son of Grant Earl Mouser) (R Ohio) Feb. 20, 1895-Dec. 21, 1943; House 1929-33.

MOUTON, Alexander (D La.) Nov. 19, 1804-Feb. 12, 1885; Senate Jan. 12, 1837-March 1, 1842; Gov. 1842-46.

MOUTON, Robert Louis (D La.) Oct. 20, 1892-Nov. 26, 1956; House 1937-41.

MOXLEY, William James (R Ill.) May 22, 1851-Aug. 4, 1938; House Nov. 23, 1909-11.

MOYNIHAN, Daniel Patrick (D N.Y.) March 16, 1927- —; Senate 1977- —.

MOYNIHAN, Patrick Henry (R Ill.) Sept. 25, 1869-May 20, 1946; House 1933-35.

MOZLEY, Norman Adolphus (R Mo.) Dec. 11, 1865-May 9, 1922; House 1895-97.

MRAZEK, Robert J. (D N.Y.) Nov. 5, 1945- —; House 1983- —.

MRUK, Joseph (R N.Y.) Nov. 6, 1903- —; House 1943-45.

MUDD, Sydney Emanuel (father of the following) (R Md.) Feb. 12, 1858-Oct. 21, 1911; House March 20, 1890-91, 1897-1911.

MUDD, Sydney Emanuel (son of the preceding) (R Md.) June 20, 1885-Oct. 11, 1924; House 1915-Oct. 11, 1924.

MUHLENBERG, Francis Swaine (son of John Peter Gabriel Muhlenberg, nephew of Frederick Augustus Conrad Muhlenberg) (NR Ohio) April 22, 1795-Dec. 17, 1831; House Dec. 19, 1828-29.

MUHLENBERG, Frederick Augustus (great-great-grandson of Frederick Augustus Conrad Muhlenberg, great-great-grandnephew of John Peter Gabriel Muhlenberg) (R Pa.) Sept. 25, 1887-Jan 19, 1980; House 1947-49.

MUHLENBERG, Frederick Augustus Conrad (brother of John Peter Gabriel Muhlenberg, uncle of Francis Swaine Muhlenberg and Henry Augustus Philip Muhlenberg, great-great-grandfather of Frederick Augustus Muhlenberg) (— Pa.) Jan. 1, 1750-June 5, 1801; House 1789-97; Speaker 1789-91, 1793-95; Cont. Cong. 1779-80.

MUHLENBERG, Henry Augustus (son of Henry Augustus Philip Muhlenberg, grandson of Joseph Hiester) (D Pa.) July 21, 1823-Jan. 9, 1854; House 1853-Jan. 9, 1854.

MUHLENBERG, Henry Augustus Philip (father of Henry Augustus Muhlenberg, nephew of John Peter Gabriel Muhlenberg and Frederick Augustus Conrad Muhlenberg) (JD Pa.) May 13, 1782-Aug. 11, 1844; House 1829-Feb. 9, 1838.

MUHLENBERG, John Peter Gabriel (father of Francis Swaine Muhlenberg, brother of Frederick Augustus Conrad Muhlenberg, uncle of Henry Augustus Philip Muhlenberg, great-great-granduncle of Frederick Augustus Muhlenberg) (D Pa.) Oct. 1, 1746-Oct. 1, 1807; House 1789-91, 1793-95, 1799-1801; Senate March 4-June 30, 1801.

MULDOWNEY, Michael Joseph (R Pa.) Aug. 10, 1889-March 30, 1947; House 1933-35.

MULDROW, Henry Lowndes (D Miss.) Feb. 8, 1837-March 1, 1905; House 1877-85.

MULKEY, Frederick William (nephew of Joseph Norton Dolph) (R Ore.) Jan. 6, 1874-May 5, 1924; Senate Jan. 23-March 3, 1907, Nov. 6-Dec. 17, 1918.

MULKEY, William Oscar (D Ala.) July 27, 1871-June 30, 1943; House June 29, 1914-15.

MULLER, Nicholas (D N.Y.) Nov. 15, 1836-Dec. 12, 1917; House 1877-81, 1883-87, 1899-Dec. 1, 1902.

MULLIN, Joseph (R N.Y.) Aug. 6, 1811-May 17, 1882; House 1847-49.

MULLINS, James (R Tenn.) Sept. 15, 1807-June 26, 1873; House 1867-69.

MULTER, Abraham Jacob (D N.Y.) Dec. 24, 1900- —; House Nov. 4, 1947-Dec. 31, 1967.

MUMFORD, George (D N.C.) ?-Dec. 31, 1818; House 1817-Dec. 31, 1818.

MUMFORD, Gurdon Saltonstall (F N.Y.) Jan. 29, 1764-April 30, 1831; House 1805-11.

MUMMA, Walter Mann (R Pa.) Nov. 20, 1890-Feb. 25, 1961; House 1951-Feb. 25, 1961.

MUNDT, Karl Earl (R S.D.) June 3, 1900-Aug. 16, 1974; House 1939-Dec. 30, 1948; Senate Dec. 31, 1948-73.

MUNGEN, William (D Ohio) May 12, 1821-Sept. 9, 1887; House 1867-71.

MURCH, Thompson Henry (G Lab. Ref. Maine) March 29, 1838-Dec. 15, 1886; House 1879-83.

MURDOCK, John Robert (D Ariz.) April 20, 1885-Feb. 14, 1972; House 1937-53.

MURDOCK, Orrice Abram Jr. (Abe) (D Utah) July 18, 1893-Sept. 15, 1979; House 1933-41; Senate 1941-47.

MURDOCK, Victor (R Kan.) March 18, 1871-July 8, 1945; House May 26, 1903-15; Chrmn. Prog. Party Nat. Comm. 1915-16.

MURFREE, William Hardy (uncle of David W. Dickinson) (D N.C.) Oct. 2, 1781-Jan. 19, 1827; House 1813-17.

MURKOWSKI, Frank H. (R Alaska) March 28, 1933- —; Senate 1981- —.

MURPHEY, Charles (D Ga.) May 9, 1799-Jan. 16, 1861; House 1851-53.

MURPHY, Arthur Phillips (R Mo.) Dec. 10, 1870-Feb. 1, 1914; House 1905-07, 1909-11.

MURPHY, Austin J. (D Pa.) June 17, 1927- —; House 1977- —.

MURPHY, Benjamin Franklin (R Ohio) Dec. 24, 1867-March 6, 1938; House 1919-33.

MURPHY, Edward Jr. (D N.Y.) Dec. 15, 1836-Aug. 3, 1911; Senate 1893-99.

MURPHY, Everett Jerome (R Ill.) July 24, 1852-April 10, 1922; House 1895-97.

MURPHY, George Lloyd (R Calif.) July 4, 1902- —; Senate Jan. 1, 1965-Jan. 2, 1971.

MURPHY, Henry Cruse (D N.Y.) July 5, 1810-Dec. 1, 1882; House 1843-45, 1847-49.

MURPHY, James Joseph (D N.Y.) Nov. 3, 1898-Oct. 19, 1962; House 1949-53.

MURPHY, James William (D Wis.) April 17, 1858-July 11, 1927; House 1907-09.

MURPHY, Jeremiah Henry (D Iowa) Feb. 19, 1835-Dec. 11, 1893; House 1883-87.

MURPHY, John (D Ala.) 1786-Sept. 21, 1841; House 1833-35; Gov. 1825-29.

MURPHY, John Michael (D N.Y.) Aug. 3, 1926- —; House 1963-81.

MURPHY, John William (D Pa.) April 26, 1902-March 28, 1962; House 1943-July 17, 1946.

MURPHY, Maurice J. Jr. (R N.H.) Oct. 3, 1927- —; Senate Dec. 7, 1961-Nov. 6, 1962.

MURPHY, Morgan Francis (D Ill.) April 16, 1933- —; House 1971-81.

MURPHY, Nathan Oakes (R Ariz.) Oct. 14, 1849-Aug. 22, 1908; House (Terr. Del.) 1895-97; Gov. (Ariz. Terr.) 1892-94, 1898-1902.

MURPHY, Richard Louis (D Iowa) Nov. 6, 1875-July 16, 1936; Senate 1933-July 16, 1936.

MURPHY, William Thomas (D Ill.) Aug. 7, 1899-Jan. 29, 1978; House 1959-71.

MURRAY, Ambrose Spencer (brother of William Murray) (R N.Y.) Nov. 27, 1807-Nov. 8, 1885; House 1855-59.

MURRAY, George Washington (R S.C.) Sept. 22, 1853-April 21, 1926; House 1893-95, June 4, 1896-97.

MURRAY, James Cunningham (D Ill.) May 16, 1917- —; House 1955-57.

MURRAY, James Edward (D Mont.) May 3, 1876-March 23, 1961; Senate Nov. 7, 1934-61.

MURRAY, John (cousin of Thomas Murray Jr.) (— Pa.) 1768-March 7, 1834; House Oct. 14, 1817-21.

MURRAY, John L. (D Ky.) Jan. 25, 1806-Jan. 31, 1842; House 1837-39.

MURRAY, Reid Fred (R Wis.) Oct. 16, 1887-April 29, 1952; House 1939-April 29, 1952.

MURRAY, Robert Maynard (D Ohio) Nov. 28, 1841-Aug. 2, 1913; House 1883-85.

MURRAY, Thomas Jr. (cousin of John Murray) (D Pa.) 1770-Aug. 26, 1823; House Oct. 9, 1821-23.

MURRAY, Thomas Jefferson (D Tenn.) Aug. 1, 1894-Nov. 28, 1971; House 1943-67.

MURRAY, William (brother of Ambrose Spencer Murray) (D N.Y.) Oct. 1, 1803-Aug. 25, 1875; House 1851-55.

MURRAY, William Francis (D Mass.) Sept. 7, 1881-Sept. 21, 1918; House 1911-Sept. 28, 1914.

MURRAY, William Henry (D Okla.) Nov. 21, 1869-Oct. 15, 1956; House 1913-17; Gov. 1931-35.

MURRAY, William Vans (F Md.) Feb. 9, 1760-Dec. 11, 1803; House 1791-97.

MURTHA, John Patrick Jr. (D Pa.) Jan. 17, 1932- —; House Feb. 5, 1974- —.

MUSKIE, Edmund Sixtus (D Maine) March 28, 1914- —; Senate 1959-May 7, 1980; Gov. 1955-59; Secy. of State May 8, 1980-81.

MUSSELWHITE, Harry Webster (D Mich.) May 23, 1868-Dec. 14, 1955; House 1933-35.

MUSTO, Raphael (D Pa.) March 30, 1929- —; House April 15, 1980-81.

MUTCHLER, Howard (son of William Mutchler) (D Pa.) Feb. 12, 1859-Jan. 4, 1916; House Aug. 7, 1893-95, 1901-03.

MUTCHLER, William (father of Howard Mutchler) (D Pa.) Dec. 21, 1831-June 23, 1893; House 1875-77, 1881-85, 1889-June 23, 1893.

MYERS, Amos (R Pa.) April 23, 1824-Oct. 18, 1893; House 1863-65.

MYERS, Francis John (D Pa.) Dec. 18, 1901-July 5, 1956; House 1939-45; Senate 1945-51.

MYERS, Gary Arthur (R Pa.) Aug. 16, 1937- —; House 1975-79.

MYERS, Henry Lee (D Mont.) Oct. 9, 1862-Nov. 11, 1943; Senate 1911-23.

MYERS, John Thomas (R Ind.) Feb. 8, 1927- —; House 1967- —.

MYERS, Leonard (R Pa.) Nov. 13, 1827-Feb. 11, 1905; House 1863-69, April 9, 1869-75.

MYERS, Michael J. (Ozzie) (D Pa.) May 4, 1943- —; House Nov. 2, 1976-Oct. 2, 1980.

MYERS, William Ralph (D Ind.) June 12, 1836-April 18, 1907; House 1879-81.

N

NABERS, Benjamin Duke (U Miss.) Nov. 7, 1812-Sept. 6, 1878; House 1851-53.

NAPHEN, Henry Francis (D Mass.) Aug. 14, 1852-June 8, 1905; House 1899-1903.

NAPIER, John L. (R S.C.) May 16, 1947- —; House 1981-83.

NAREY, Harry Elsworth (R Iowa) May 15, 1885-Aug. 18, 1962; House Nov. 3, 1942-43.

NASH, Charles Edmund (R La.) May 23, 1844-June 21, 1913; House 1875-77.

NATCHER, William Huston (D Ky.) Sept. 11, 1909- —; House Aug. 1, 1953- —.

NAUDAIN, Arnold (NR Del.) Jan. 6, 1790-Jan. 4, 1872; Senate Jan. 13, 1830-June 16, 1836.

NAYLOR, Charles (W Pa.) Oct. 6, 1806-Dec. 24, 1872; House June 29, 1837-41.

NEAL, Henry Safford (R Ohio) Aug. 25, 1828-July 13, 1906; House 1877-83.

NEAL, John Randolph (D Tenn.) Nov. 26, 1836-March 26, 1889; House 1885-89.

NEAL, Lawrence Talbot (D Ohio) Sept. 22, 1844-Nov. 2, 1905; House 1873-77.

NEAL, Stephen Lybrook (D N.C.) Nov. 7, 1934- —; House 1975- —.

NEAL, William Elmer (R W.Va.) Oct. 14, 1875-Nov. 12, 1959; House 1953-55, 1957-59.

NEALE, Raphael (— Md.) ?-Oct. 19, 1833; House 1819-25.

NEDZI, Lucien Norbert (D Mich.) May 28, 1925- —; House Nov. 7, 1961-81.

NEECE, William Henry (D Ill.) Feb. 26, 1831-Jan. 3, 1909; House 1883-87.

NEEDHAM, James Carson (R Calif.) Sept. 17, 1864-July 11, 1942; House 1899-1913.

NEELEY, George Arthur (D Kan.) Aug. 1, 1879-Jan. 1, 1919; House Nov. 11, 1912-15.

NEELY, Matthew Mansfield (D W.Va.) Nov. 9, 1874-Jan. 18, 1958; House Oct. 14, 1913-21, 1945-47; Senate 1923-29, 1931-Jan. 12, 1941, 1949-Jan. 18, 1958; Gov. 1941-45.

NEGLEY, James Scott (R Pa.) Dec. 22, 1826-Aug. 7, 1901; House 1869-75, 1885-87.

NEILL, Robert (D Ark.) Nov. 12, 1838-Feb. 16, 1907; House 1893-97.

NELLIGAN, James L. (R Pa.) Feb. 14, 1929- —; House 1981-83.

NELSEN, Ancher (R Minn.) Oct. 11, 1904- —; House 1959- 75.

NELSON, Adolphus Peter (R Wis.) March 28, 1872-Aug. 21, 1927; House Nov. 5, 1918-23.

NELSON, Arthur Emanuel (R Minn.) May 10, 1892-April 11, 1955; Senate Nov. 18, 1942-43.

NELSON, Charles Pembroke (son of John Edward Nelson) (R Maine) July 2, 1907-June 8, 1962; House 1949-57.

NELSON, Clarence William (Bill) (D Fla.) Sept. 29, 1942- —; House 1979- —.

NELSON, Gaylord (D Wis.) June 4, 1916- —; Senate 1963-81; Gov. 1959-63.

NELSON, Homer Augustus (D N.Y.) Aug. 31, 1829-April 25, 1891; House 1863-65.

NELSON, Hugh (D Va.) Sept. 30, 1768-March 18, 1836; House 1811-Jan. 14, 1823.

NELSON, Jeremiah (F Mass.) Sept. 14, 1769-Oct. 2, 1838; House 1805-07, 1815-25, 1831-33.

NELSON, John (son of Roger Nelson) (D Md.) June 1, 1794-Jan. 18, 1860; House 1821-23; Atty. Gen. 1843-45.

NELSON, John Edward (father of Charles Pembroke Nelson) (R Maine) July 12, 1874-April 11, 1955; House March 27, 1922-33.

NELSON, John Mandt (R Wis.) Oct. 10, 1870-Jan. 29, 1955; House Sept. 4, 1906-19, 1921-33.

NELSON, Knute (R Minn.) Feb. 2, 1843-April 28, 1923; House 1883-89; Senate 1895-April 28, 1923; Gov. 1893-95.

NELSON, Roger (father of John Nelson) (D Md.) 1759-June 7, 1815; House Nov. 6, 1804-May 14, 1810.

NELSON, Thomas Amos Rogers (U Tenn.) March 19, 1812-Aug. 24, 1873; House 1859-61.

NELSON, Thomas Maduit (D Va.) Sept. 27, 1782-Nov. 10, 1853; House Dec. 4, 1816-19.

NELSON, William (W N.Y.) June 29, 1784-Oct. 3, 1869; House 1847-51.

NELSON, William Lester (D Mo.) Aug. 4, 1875-Dec. 31, 1946; House 1919-21, 1925-33, 1935-43.

NES, Henry (I Pa.) May 20, 1799-Sept. 10, 1850; House 1843-45, 1847-Sept. 10, 1850.

NESBIT, Walter (D Ill.) May 1, 1878-Dec. 6, 1938; House 1933-35.

NESBITT, Wilson (D S.C.) ?-May 13, 1861; House 1817-19.

NESMITH, James Willis (cousin of Joseph Gardner Wilson, grandfather of Clifton Nesmith McArthur) (D Ore.) July 23, 1820-June 17, 1885; Senate 1861-67; House Dec. 1, 1873-75.

NEUBERGER, Maurine Brown (widow of Richard Lewis Neuberger) (D Ore.) Jan. 9, 1907- —; Senate Nov. 9, 1960-67.

NEUBERGER, Richard Lewis (husband of Maurine Brown Neuberger) (D Ore.) Dec. 26, 1912-March 9, 1960; Senate 1955-March 9, 1960.

NEVILLE, Joseph (— Va.) 1730-March 4, 1819; House 1793-95.

NEVILLE, William (cousin of Bird Segle McGuire) (P Neb.) Dec. 29, 1843-April 5, 1909; House Dec. 4, 1899-1903.

NEVIN, Robert Murphy (R Ohio) May 5, 1850-Dec. 17, 1912; House 1901-07.

NEW, Anthony (D Va./Ky.) 1747-March 2, 1833; House 1793-1805 (Va.), 1811-13, 1817-19, 1821-23 (Ky.).

NEW, Harry Stewart (R Ind.) Dec. 31, 1858-May 9, 1937; Senate 1917-23; Chrmn. Rep. Nat. Comm. 1907-08; Postmaster Gen. 1923-29.

NEW, Jeptha Dudley (D Ind.) Nov. 28, 1830-July 9, 1892; House 1875-77, 1879-81.

NEWBERRY, John Stoughton (father of Truman Handy Newberry) (R Mich.) Nov. 18, 1826-Jan. 2, 1887; House 1879-81.

NEWBERRY, Truman Handy (son of John Stoughton Newberry) (R Mich.) Nov. 5, 1864-Oct. 3, 1945; Senate 1919-Nov. 18, 1922; Secy. of the Navy 1908-09.

NEWBERRY, Walter Cass (D Ill.) Dec. 23, 1835-July 20, 1912; House 1891-93.

NEWBOLD, Thomas (D N.J.) Aug. 2, 1760-Dec. 18, 1823; House 1807-13.

NEWCOMB, Carman Adam (R Mo.) July 1, 1830-April 6, 1902; House 1867-69.

NEWELL, William Augustus (R N.J.) Sept. 5, 1817-Aug. 8, 1901; House 1847-51, 1865-67 (1845-51 Whig, 1865-67 Republican); Gov. 1857-60 (N.J.), 1880-84 (Wash. Terr.).

NEWHALL, Judson Lincoln (R Ky.) March 26, 1870-July 23, 1952; House 1929-31.

NEWHARD, Peter (D Pa.) July 26, 1783-Feb. 19, 1860; House 1839-43.

NEWLANDS, Francis Griffith (D Nev.) Aug. 28, 1848-Dec. 24, 1917; House 1893-1903; Senate 1903-Dec. 24, 1917.

NEWMAN, Alexander (D Va.) Oct. 5, 1804-Sept. 8, 1849; House March 4-Sept. 8, 1849.

NEWNAN, Daniel (SRD Ga.) about 1780-Jan. 16, 1851; House 1831-33.

NEWSHAM, Joseph Parkinson (R La.) May 24, 1837-Oct. 22, 1919; House July 18, 1868-69, May 23, 1870-71.

NEWSOME, John Parks (D Ala.) Feb. 13, 1893-Nov. 10, 1961; House 1943-45.

NEWTON, Cherubusco (D La.) May 15, 1848-May 26, 1910; House 1887-89.

NEWTON, Cleveland Alexander (R Mo.) Sept. 3, 1873-Sept. 17, 1945; House 1919-27.

NEWTON, Eben (W Ohio) Oct. 16, 1795-Nov. 6, 1885; House 1851-53.

NEWTON, Thomas Jr. (D Va.) Nov. 21, 1768-Aug. 5, 1847; House 1801-March 3, 1829, March 4, 1829-March 9, 1830, 1831-33.

NEWTON, Thomas Willoughby (W Ark.) Jan. 18, 1804-Sept. 22, 1853; House Feb. 6-March 3, 1847.

NEWTON, Walter Hughes (R Minn.) Oct. 10, 1880-Aug. 10, 1941; House 1919-June 30, 1929.

NEWTON, Willoughby (W Va.) Dec. 2, 1802-May 23, 1874; House 1843-45.

NIBLACK, Silas Leslie (cousin of William Ellis Niblack) (D Fla.) March 17, 1825-Feb. 13, 1883; House Jan. 29-March 3, 1873.

NIBLACK, William Ellis (cousin of Silas Leslie Niblack) (D Ind.) May 19, 1822-May 7, 1893; House Dec. 7, 1857-61, 1865-75.

NICHOLAS, John (brother of Wilson Cary Nicholas, uncle of Robert Carter Nicholas) (D Va.) about 1757-Dec. 31, 1819; House 1793-1801.

NICHOLAS, Robert Carter (nephew of John Nicholas and Wilson Cary Nicholas) (D La.) 1793-Dec. 24, 1857; Senate Jan. 13, 1836-41.

NICHOLAS, Wilson Cary (brother of John Nicholas, uncle of Robert Carter Nicholas) (D Va.) Jan. 31, 1761-Oct. 10, 1820; Senate Dec. 5, 1799-May 22, 1804; House 1807-Nov. 27, 1809; Gov. 1814-16.

NICHOLLS, John Calhoun (D Ga.) April 25, 1834-Dec. 25, 1893; House 1879-81, 1883-85.

NICHOLLS, Samuel Jones (D S.C.) May 7, 1885-Nov. 23, 1937; House Sept. 14, 1915-21.

NICHOLLS, Thomas David (D Pa.) Sept. 16, 1870-Jan. 19, 1931; House 1907-11.

NICHOLS, Charles Archibald (R Mich.) Aug. 25, 1876-April 25, 1920; House 1915-April 25, 1920.

NICHOLS, John (I N.C.) Nov. 14, 1834-Sept. 22, 1917; House 1887-89.

NICHOLS, John Conover (Jack) (D Okla.) Aug. 31, 1896-Nov. 7, 1945; House 1935-July 3, 1943.

NICHOLS, Matthias H. (R Ohio) Oct. 3, 1824-Sept. 15, 1862; House 1853-59 (1853-55 Whig, 1855-59 Republican).

NICHOLS, William (D Ala.) Oct. 16, 1918- —; House 1967- —.

NICHOLSON, Alfred Osborn Pope (D Tenn.) Aug. 31, 1808-March 23, 1876; Senate Dec. 25, 1840-Feb. 7, 1842, 1859-61.

NICHOLSON, Donald William (R Mass.) Aug. 11, 1888-Feb. 16, 1968; House Nov. 18, 1947-59.

NICHOLSON, John (D N.Y.) 1765-Jan. 20, 1820; House 1809-11.

NICHOLSON, John Anthony (D Del.) Nov. 17, 1827-Nov. 4, 1906; House 1865-69.

NICHOLSON, Joseph Hopper (D Md.) May 15, 1770-March 4, 1817; House 1799-March 1, 1806.

NICHOLSON, Samuel Danford (R Colo.) Feb. 22, 1859-March 24, 1923; Senate 1921-March 24, 1923.

NICKLES, Donald L. (R Okla.) Dec. 6, 1948- —; Senate 1981- —.

NICOLL, Henry (D N.Y.) Oct. 23, 1812-Nov. 28, 1879; House 1847-49.

NIEDRINGHAUS, Frederick Gottlieb (uncle of Henry Frederick Niedringhaus) (R Mo.) Oct. 21, 1837-Nov. 25, 1922; House 1889-91.

NIEDRINGHAUS, Henry Frederick (nephew of Frederick Gottlieb Niedringhaus) (R Mo.) Dec. 15, 1864-Aug. 3, 1941; House 1927-33.

NIELSON, Howard Curtis (R Utah) Sept. 12, 1924- —; House 1983- —.

NILES, Jason (R Miss.) Dec. 19, 1814-July 7, 1894; House 1873-75.

NILES, John Milton (D Conn.) Aug. 20, 1787-May 31, 1856; Senate Dec. 21, 1835-39, 1843-49; Postmaster Gen. 1840-41.

NILES, Nathaniel (— Vt.) April 3, 1741-Oct. 31, 1828; House Oct. 17, 1791-95.

NIMTZ, F. Jay (R Ind.) Dec. 1, 1915- —; House 1957-59.

NISBET, Eugenius Aristides (cousin of Mark Anthony Cooper) (W Ga.) Dec. 7, 1803-March 18, 1871; House 1839-Oct. 12, 1841.

NIVEN, Archibald Campbell (D N.Y.) Dec. 8, 1803-Feb. 21, 1882; House 1845-47.

NIX, Robert Nelson Cornelius Sr. (D Pa.) Aug. 9, 1905- —; House May 20, 1958-79.

NIXON, George Stuart (R Nev.) April 2, 1860-June 5, 1912; Senate 1905-June 5, 1912.

NIXON, John Thompson (R N.J.) Aug. 31, 1820-Sept. 28, 1889; House 1859-63.

NIXON, Richard Milhous (R Calif.) Jan. 9, 1913- —; House 1947-Nov. 30, 1950; Senate Dec. 1, 1950-Jan. 1, 1953; Vice Pres. 1953-61; President 1969-Aug. 9, 1974.

NOBLE, David Addison (D Mich.) Nov. 9, 1802-Oct. 13, 1876; House 1853-55.

NOBLE, James (DR Ind.) Dec. 16, 1785-Feb. 26, 1831; Senate Dec. 11, 1816-Feb. 26, 1831.

NOBLE, Warren Perry (D Ohio) June 14, 1820-July 9, 1903; House 1861-65.

NOBLE, William Henry (D N.Y.) Sept. 22, 1788-Feb. 5, 1850; House 1837-39.

NODAR, Robert Joseph Jr. (R N.Y.) March 23, 1916- — ; House 1947-49.

NOELL, John William (father of Thomas Estes Noell) (D Mo.) Feb. 22, 1816-March 14, 1863; House 1859-March 14, 1863.

NOELL, Thomas Estes (son of John William Noell) (Rad. Mo.) April 3, 1839-Oct. 3, 1867; House 1865-Oct. 3, 1867.

NOLAN, John Ignatius (husband of Mae Ella Nolan) (R Calif.) Jan. 14, 1874-Nov. 18, 1922; House 1913-Nov. 18, 1922.

NOLAN, Mae Ella (widow of John Ignatius Nolan) (R Calif.) Sept. 20, 1886-July 9, 1973; House Jan. 23, 1923-25.

NOLAN, Michael Nicholas (D N.Y.) May 4, 1833-May 31, 1905; House 1881-83.

NOLAN, Richard Michael (D Minn.) Dec. 17, 1943- — ; House 1975-81.

NOLAN, William Ignatius (R Minn.) May 14, 1874-Aug. 3, 1943; House June 17, 1929-33.

NOLAND, James E. (D Ind.) April 22, 1920- — ; House 1949-51.

NOONAN, Edward Thomas (D Ill.) Oct. 23, 1861-Dec. 19, 1923; House 1899-1901.

NOONAN, George Henry (R Texas) Aug. 20, 1828-Aug. 17, 1907; House 1895-97.

NORBECK, Peter (R S.D.) Aug. 27, 1870-Dec. 20, 1936; Senate 1921-Dec. 20, 1936; Gov. 1917-21.

NORBLAD, Albin Walter Jr. (R Ore.) Sept. 12, 1908-Sept. 20, 1964; House Jan. 11, 1946-Sept. 20, 1964.

NORCROSS, Amasa (R Mass.) Jan. 26, 1824-April 2, 1898; House 1877-83.

NORMAN, Fred Barthold (R Wash.) March 21, 1882-April 18, 1947; House 1943-45, Jan. 3-April 18, 1947.

NORRELL, Catherine Dorris (widow of William Frank Norrell) (D Ark.) March 30, 1901-Aug. 26, 1981; House April 18, 1961-63.

NORRELL, William Frank (husband of Catherine Dorris Norrell) (D Ark.) Aug. 29, 1896-Feb. 15, 1961; House 1939-Feb. 15, 1961.

NORRIS, Benjamin White (R Ala.) Jan. 22, 1819-Jan. 26, 1873; House July 21, 1868-69.

NORRIS, George William (IR Neb.) July 11, 1861-Sept. 2, 1944; House 1903-13; Senate 1913-43 (1913-37 Republican, 1937-43 Independent Republican).

NORRIS, Moses Jr. (D N.H.) Nov. 8, 1799-Jan. 11, 1855; House 1843-47; Senate 1849-Jan. 11, 1855.

NORTH, Solomon Taylor (R Pa.) May 24, 1853-Oct. 19, 1917; House 1915-17.

NORTH, William (F N.Y.) 1755-Jan. 3, 1836; Senate May 5-Aug. 17, 1798.

NORTHWAY, Stephen Asa (R Ohio) June 19, 1833-Sept. 8, 1898; House 1893-Sept. 8, 1898.

NORTON, Daniel Sheldon (UC Minn.) April 12, 1829-July 13, 1870; Senate 1865-July 13, 1870.

NORTON, Ebenezer Foote (D N.Y.) Nov. 7, 1774-May 11, 1851; House 1829-31.

NORTON, Elijah Hise (D Mo.) Nov. 24, 1821-Aug. 5, 1914; House 1861-63.

NORTON, James (D S.C.) Oct. 8, 1843-Oct. 14, 1920; House Dec. 6, 1897-1901.

NORTON, James Albert (D Ohio) Nov. 11, 1843-July 24, 1912; House 1897-1903.

NORTON, Jesse Olds (R Ill.) Dec. 25, 1812-Aug. 3, 1875; House 1853-57, 1863-65.

NORTON, John Nathaniel (D Neb.) May 12, 1878-Oct. 5, 1960; House 1927-29, 1931-33.

NORTON, Mary Teresa (D N.J.) March 7, 1875-Aug. 2, 1959; House 1925-51.

NORTON, Miner Gibbs (R Ohio) May 11, 1857-Sept. 7, 1926; House 1921-23.

NORTON, Nelson Ira (R N.Y.) March 30, 1820-Oct. 28, 1887; House Dec. 6, 1875-77.

NORTON, Patrick Daniel (R N.D.) May 17, 1876-Oct. 14, 1953; House 1913-19.

NORTON, Richard Henry (D Mo.) Nov. 6, 1849-March 15, 1918; House 1889-93.

NORVELL, John (D Mich.) Dec. 21, 1789-April 24, 1850; Senate Jan. 26, 1837-41.

NORWOOD, Thomas Manson (D Ga.) April 26, 1830-June 19, 1913; Senate Nov. 14, 1871-77; House 1885-89.

NOTT, Abraham (F S.C.) Feb. 5, 1768-June 19, 1830; House 1799-1801.

NOURSE, Amos (— Maine) Dec. 17, 1794-April 7, 1877; Senate Jan. 16-March 3, 1857.

NOWAK, Henry James (D N.Y.) Feb. 21, 1935- — ; House 1975- — .

NOYES, John (F Vt.) April 2, 1764-Oct. 26, 1841; House 1815-17.

NOYES, Joseph Cobham (W Maine) Sept. 22, 1798-July 28, 1868; House 1837-39.

NUCKOLLS, Stephen Friel (D Wyo.) Aug. 16, 1825-Feb. 14, 1879; House (Terr. Del.) Dec. 6, 1869-71.

NUCKOLLS, William Thompson (— S.C.) Feb. 23, 1801-Sept. 27, 1855; House 1827-33.

NUGEN, Robert Hunter (D Ohio) July 16, 1809-Feb. 28, 1872; House 1861-63.

NUGENT, John Frost (D Idaho) June 28, 1868-Sept. 18, 1931; Senate Jan. 22, 1918-Jan. 14, 1921.

NUNN, David Alexander (R Tenn.) July 26, 1833-Sept. 11, 1918; House 1867-69, 1873-75.

NUNN, Samuel Augustus (D Ga.) Sept. 8, 1938- — ; Senate Nov. 8, 1972- — .

NUTE, Alonzo (R N.H.) Feb. 12, 1826-Dec. 24, 1892; House 1889-91.

NUTTING, Newton Wright (R N.Y.) Oct. 22, 1840-Oct. 15, 1889; House 1883-85, 1887-Oct. 15, 1889.

NYE, Frank Mellen (R Minn.) March 7, 1852-Nov. 29, 1935; House 1907-13.

NYE, Gerald Prentice (R N.D.) Dec. 19, 1892-July 17, 1971; Senate Nov. 14, 1925-45.

NYE, James Warren (R Nev.) June 10, 1815-Dec. 25, 1876; Senate Dec. 16, 1864-73; Gov. (Nev. Terr.) 1861-64.

NYGAARD, Hjalmar (R N.D.) March 24, 1906-July 18, 1963; House 1961-July 18, 1963.

O

OAKAR, Mary Rose (D Ohio) March 5, 1940- — ; House 1977- — .

OAKEY, Peter Davis (R Conn.) Feb. 25, 1861-Nov. 18, 1920; House 1915-17.

OAKLEY, Thomas Jackson (Clinton D. N.Y.) Nov. 10, 1783-May 11, 1857; House 1813-15, 1827-May 9, 1828 (1813-15 Federalist, 1827-28 Clinton Democrat).

OAKMAN, Charles Gibb (R Mich.) Sept. 4, 1903-Oct. 28, 1973; House 1953-55.

OATES, William Calvin (D Ala.) Nov. 30, 1835-Sept. 9, 1910; House 1881-Nov. 5, 1894; Gov. 1894-96.

OBERSTAR, James Louis (D Minn.) Sept. 10, 1934- — ; House 1975-85.

OBEY, David Ross (D Wis.) Oct. 3, 1938- — ; House April 1, 1969- — .

O'BRIEN, Charles Francis Xavier (D N.J.) March 7, 1879-Nov. 14, 1940; House 1921-25.

O'BRIEN, George Donoghue (D Mich.) Jan. 1, 1900-Oct. 25, 1957; House 1937-39, 1941-47, 1949-55.

O'BRIEN, George Miller (R Ill.) June 17, 1917- — ; House 1973- — .

O'BRIEN, James (ATD N.Y.) March 13, 1841-March 5, 1907; House 1879-81.

O'BRIEN, James Henry (D N.Y.) July 15, 1860-Sept. 2, 1924; House 1913-15.

O'BRIEN, Jeremiah (D Maine) Jan. 21, 1778-May 30, 1858; House 1823-29.

O'BRIEN, Joseph John (R N.Y.) Oct. 9, 1897-Jan. 23, 1953; House 1939-45.

O'BRIEN, Leo William (D N.Y.) Sept. 21, 1900-May 4, 1982; House April 1, 1952-67.

O'BRIEN, Thomas Joseph (D Ill.) April 30, 1878-April 14, 1964; House 1933-39, 1943-April 14, 1964.

O'BRIEN, William James (D Md.) May 28, 1836-Nov. 13, 1905; House 1873-77.

O'BRIEN, William Smith (D W.Va.) Jan. 8, 1862-Aug. 10, 1948; House 1927-29.

OCAMPO, Pablo (— P.I.) Jan. 25, 1853-Feb. 5, 1925; House (Res. Comm.) Nov. 22, 1907-Nov. 22, 1909.

OCHILTREE, Thomas Peck (I Texas) Oct. 26, 1837-Nov. 25, 1902; House 1883-85.

O'CONNELL, David Joseph (D N.Y.) Dec. 25, 1868-Dec. 29, 1930; House 1919-21, 1923-Dec. 29, 1930.

O'CONNELL, Jeremiah Edward (D R.I.) July 8, 1883-Sept. 18, 1964; House 1923-27, 1929-May 9, 1930.

O'CONNELL, Jerry Joseph (D Mont.) June 14, 1909-Jan. 16, 1956; House 1937-39.

O'CONNELL, John Matthew (D R.I.) Aug. 10, 1872-Dec. 6, 1941; House 1933-39.

O'CONNELL, Joseph Francis (D Mass.) Dec. 7, 1872-Dec. 10, 1942; House 1907-11.

O'CONNOR, Charles (R Okla.) Oct. 26, 1878-Nov. 15, 1940; House 1929-31.

O'CONNOR, James (D La.) April 4, 1870-Jan. 7, 1941; House June 5, 1919-31.

O'CONNOR, James Francis (D Mont.) May 7, 1878-Jan. 15, 1945; House 1937-Jan. 15, 1945.

O'CONNOR, John Joseph (D N.Y.) Nov. 23, 1885-Jan. 26, 1960; House Nov. 6, 1923-39.

O'CONNOR, Michael Patrick (D S.C.) Sept. 29, 1831-April 26, 1881; House 1879-April 26, 1881.

O'CONOR, Herbert Romulus (D Md.) Nov. 17, 1896-March 4, 1960; Senate 1947-53; Gov. 1939-47.

O'DANIEL, Wilbert Lee (D Texas) March 11, 1890-May 11, 1969; Senate Aug. 4, 1941-49; Gov. 1939-41.

O'DAY, Caroline Love Goodwin (D N.Y.) June 22, 1875-Jan. 4, 1943; House 1935-43.

ODDIE, Tasker Lowndes (R Nev.) Oct. 24, 1870-Feb. 17, 1950; Senate 1921-33; Gov. 1911-15.

ODELL, Benjamin Baker Jr. (R N.Y.) Jan. 14, 1854-May 9, 1926; House 1895-99; Gov. 1901-05.

ODELL, Moses Fowler (D N.Y.) Feb. 24, 1818-June 13, 1866; House 1861-65.

ODELL, Nathaniel (D N.Y.) Oct. 10, 1828-Oct. 30, 1904; House 1875-77.

O'DONNELL, James (R Mich.) March 25, 1840-March 17, 1915; House 1885-93.

O'FERRALL, Charles Triplett (D Va.) Oct. 21, 1840-Sept. 22, 1905; House May 5, 1884-Dec. 28, 1893; Gov. 1894-98.

OGDEN, Aaron (F N.J.) Dec. 3, 1756-April 19, 1839; Senate Feb. 28, 1801-03; Gov. 1812-13.

OGDEN, Charles Franklin (R Ky.) ?-April 10, 1933; House 1919-23.

OGDEN, David A. (F N.Y.) Jan. 10, 1770-June 9, 1829; House 1817-19.

OGDEN, Henry Warren (D La.) Oct. 21, 1842-July 23, 1905; House May 12, 1894-99.

OGLE, Alexander (father of Charles Ogle, grandfather of Andrew Jackson Ogle) (D Pa.) Aug. 10, 1766-Oct. 14, 1832; House 1817-19.

OGLE, Andrew Jackson (grandson of Alexander Ogle) (W Pa.) March 25, 1822-Oct. 14, 1852; House 1849-51.

OGLE, Charles (son of Alexander Ogle) (W Pa.) 1798-May 10, 1841; House 1837-May 10, 1841.

OGLESBY, Richard James (cousin of Woodson Ratcliffe Oglesby) (R Ill.) July 25, 1824-April 24, 1899; Senate 1873-79; Gov. 1865-69, Jan. 13-23, 1873, 1885-89.

OGLESBY, Woodson Ratcliffe (cousin of Richard James Oglesby) (D N.Y.) Feb. 9, 1867-April 30, 1955; House 1913-17.

O'GORMAN, James Aloysius (D N.Y.) May 5, 1860-May 17, 1943; Senate 1911-17.

O'GRADY, James Mary Early (R N.Y.) March 31, 1863-Nov. 3, 1928; House 1899-1901.

O'HAIR, Frank Trimble (D Ill.) March 12, 1870-Aug. 3, 1932; House 1913-15.

O'HARA, Barratt (D Ill.) April 28, 1882-Aug. 11, 1969; House 1949-51, 1953-69.

O'HARA, James Edward (R N.C.) Feb. 26, 1844-Sept. 15, 1905; House 1883-87.

O'HARA, James Grant (D Mich.) Nov. 8, 1925--; House 1959-77.

O'HARA, Joseph Patrick (R Minn.) Jan. 23, 1895-March 4, 1975; House 1941-59.

OHLIGER, Lewis Phillip (D Ohio) Jan. 3, 1843-Jan. 9, 1923; House Dec. 5, 1892-93.

O'KONSKI, Alvin Edward (R Wis.) May 26, 1904--; House 1943-73.

OLCOTT, Jacob Van Vechten (R N.Y.) May 17, 1856-June 1, 1940; House 1905-11.

OLCOTT, Simeon (F N.H.) Oct. 1, 1735-Feb. 22, 1815; Senate June 17, 1801-05.

OLDFIELD, Pearl Peden (widow of William Allan Oldfield) (D Ark.) Dec. 2, 1876-April 12, 1962; House Jan. 9, 1929-31.

OLDFIELD, William Allan (husband of Pearl Peden Oldfield) (D Ark.) Feb. 4, 1874-Nov. 19, 1928; House 1909-Nov. 19, 1928.

OLDS, Edson Baldwin (D Ohio) June 3, 1802-Jan. 24, 1869; House 1849-55.

O'LEARY, Denis (D N.Y.) Jan. 22, 1863-Sept. 27, 1943; House 1913-Dec. 31, 1914.

O'LEARY, James Aloysius (D N.Y.) April 23, 1889-March 16, 1944; House 1935-March 16, 1944.

OLIN, Abram Baldwin (son of Gideon Olin) (R N.Y.) Sept. 21, 1808-July 7, 1879; House 1857-63.

OLIN, Gideon (father of Abram Baldwin Olin, uncle of Henry Olin) (D Vt.) Nov. 2, 1743-Jan. 21, 1823; House 1803-07.

OLIN, Henry (nephew of Gideon Olin) (Jeff.D Vt.) May 7, 1768-Aug. 16, 1837; House Dec. 13, 1824-25.

OLIN, James R. (D Va.) Feb. 28, 1920--; House 1983--.

OLIVER, Andrew (D N.Y.) Jan. 16, 1815-March 6, 1889; House 1853-57.

OLIVER, Daniel Charles (D N.Y.) Oct. 6, 1865-March 26, 1924; House 1917-19.

OLIVER, Frank (D N.Y.) Oct. 2, 1883-Jan. 1, 1968; House 1923-June 18, 1934.

OLIVER, George Tener (R Pa.) Jan. 26, 1848-Jan. 22, 1919; Senate March 17, 1909-17.

OLIVER, James Churchill (D Maine) Aug. 6, 1895--; House 1937-43; 1959-61 (1937-43 Republican, 1959-61 Democrat).

OLIVER, Mordecai (W Mo.) Oct. 22, 1819-April 25, 1898; House 1853-57.

OLIVER, Samuel Addison (R Iowa) July 21, 1833-July 7, 1912; House 1875-79.

OLIVER, William Bacon (cousin of Sydney Parham Epes) (D Ala.) May 23, 1867-May 27, 1948; House 1915-37.

OLIVER, William Morrison (D N.Y.) Oct. 15, 1792-July 21, 1863; House 1841-43.

OLMSTED, Marlin Edgar (R Pa.) May 21, 1847-July 19, 1913; House 1897-1913.

OLNEY, Richard (D Mass.) Jan. 5, 1871-Jan. 15, 1939; House 1915-21.

O'LOUGHLIN, Kathryn Ellen (later married and served as Kathryn O'Loughlin McCarthy) (D Kan.) April 24, 1894-Jan. 16, 1952; House 1933-35.

OLPP, Archibald Ernest (R N.J.) May 12, 1882-July 26, 1949; House 1921-23.

OLSEN, Arnold (D Mont.) Dec. 17, 1916--; House 1961-71.

OLSON, Alec G. (D Minn.) Sept. 11, 1930--; House 1963-67.

O'MAHONEY, Joseph Christopher (D Wyo.) Nov. 5, 1884-Dec. 1, 1962; Senate Jan. 1, 1934-53; Nov. 29, 1954-61.

O'MALLEY, Matthew Vincent (D N.Y.) June 26, 1878-May 26, 1931; House March 4-May 26, 1931.

O'MALLEY, Thomas David Patrick (D Wis.) March 24, 1903--; House 1933-39.

O'NEAL, Emmet (D Ky.) April 14, 1887-July 18, 1967; House 1935-47.

O'NEAL, Maston Emmett Jr. (D Ga.) July 19, 1907--; House 1965-71.

O'NEALL, John Henry (D Ind.) Oct. 30, 1838-July 15, 1907; House 1887-91.

O'NEIL, Joseph Henry (D Mass.) March 23, 1853-Feb. 19, 1935; House 1889-95.

Biographical Index

O'NEILL, Charles (R Pa.) March 21, 1821-Nov. 25, 1893; House 1863-71; 1873-Nov. 25, 1893.

O'NEILL, Edward Leo (D N.J.) July 10, 1903-Dec. 12, 1948; House 1937-39.

O'NEILL, Harry Patrick (D Pa.) Feb. 10, 1889-June 24, 1953; House 1949-53.

O'NEILL, John (D Ohio) Dec. 17, 1822-May 25, 1905; House 1863-65.

O'NEILL, John Joseph (D Mo.) June 25, 1846-Feb. 19, 1898; House 1883-89, 1891-93, April 3, 1894-95.

O'NEILL, Thomas Phillip Jr. (D Mass.) Dec. 9, 1912-—; House 1953-—; House majority leader 1973-77; Speaker 1977-—.

O'REILLY, Daniel (D N.Y.) June 3, 1838-Sept. 23, 1911; House 1879-81.

ORMSBY, Stephen (D Ky.) 1759-1844; House 1811-13, April 20, 1813-17.

ORR, Alexander Dalrymple (nephew of William Grayson, cousin of William John Grayson (— Ky.) Nov. 6, 1761-June 21, 1835; House Nov. 8, 1792-97.

ORR, Benjamin (F Mass.) Dec. 1, 1772-Sept. 3, 1828; House 1817-19.

ORR, Jackson (R Iowa) Sept. 21, 1832-March 15, 1926; House 1871-75.

ORR, James Lawrence (D S.C.) May 12, 1822-May 5, 1873; House 1849-59; Speaker 1857-59; Gov. 1865-68 (Republican).

ORR, Robert Jr. (D Pa.) March 5, 1786-May 22, 1876; House Oct. 11, 1825-29.

ORTH, Godlove Stein (R Ind.) April 22, 1817-Dec. 16, 1882; House 1863-71, 1873-75, 1879-Dec. 16, 1882.

ORTIZ, Solomon Porfirio (D Texas) June 3, 1937-—; House 1983-—.

OSBORN, Thomas Ward (R Fla.) March 9, 1836-Dec. 18, 1898; Senate June 25, 1868-73.

OSBORNE, Edwin Sylvanus (R Pa.) Aug. 7, 1839-Jan. 1, 1900; House 1885-91.

OSBORNE, Henry Zenas (R Calif.) Oct. 4, 1848-Feb. 8, 1923; House 1917-Feb. 8, 1923.

OSBORNE, John Eugene (D Wyo.) June 19, 1858-April 24, 1943; House 1897-99; Gov. 1893-95.

OSBORNE, Thomas Burr (W Conn.) July 8, 1798-Sept. 2, 1869; House 1839-43.

OSGOOD, Gayton Pickman (D Mass.) July 4, 1797-June 26, 1861; House 1833-35.

O'SHAUNESSY, George Francis (D R.I.) May 1, 1868-Nov. 28, 1934; House 1911-19.

OSIAS, Camilo (Nat. P.I.) March 23, 1889-—; House (Res. Comm.) 1929-35.

OSMER, James H. (R Pa.) Jan. 23, 1832-Oct. 3, 1912; House 1879-81.

OSMERS, Frank Charles Jr. (R N.J.) Dec. 30, 1907-May 21, 1977; House 1939-43, Nov. 6, 1951-65.

OSTERTAG, Harold Charles (R N.Y.) June 22, 1896-—; House 1951-65.

O'SULLIVAN, Eugene Daniel (D Neb.) May 31, 1883-Feb. 7, 1968; House 1949-51.

O'SULLIVAN, Patrick Brett (D Conn.) Aug. 11, 1887-Nov. 10, 1978; House 1923-25.

OTERO, Mariano Sabino (nephew of Miguel Antonio Otero) (R N.M.) Aug. 29, 1844-Feb. 1, 1904; House (Terr. Del.) 1879-81.

OTERO, Miguel Antonio (uncle of Mariano Sabino Otero) (D N.M.) June 21, 1829-May 30, 1882; House (Terr. Del.) July 23, 1856-61.

OTEY, Peter Johnston (D Va.) Dec. 22, 1840-May 4, 1902; House 1895-May 4, 1902.

OTIS, Harrison Gray (F Mass.) Oct. 8, 1765-Oct. 28, 1848; House 1797-1801; Senate 1817-May 30, 1822.

OTIS, John (W Maine) Aug. 3, 1801-Oct. 17, 1856; House 1849-51.

OTIS, John Grant (PP Kan.) Feb. 10, 1838-Feb. 22, 1916; House 1891-93.

OTIS, Norton Prentiss (R N.Y.) March 18, 1840-Feb. 20, 1905; House 1903-Feb. 20, 1905.

OTJEN, Theobald (R Wis.) Oct. 27, 1851-April 11, 1924; House 1895-1907.

O'TOOLE, Donald Lawrence (D N.Y.) Aug. 1, 1902-Sept. 12, 1964; House 1937-53.

OTTINGER, Richard Lawrence (D N.Y.) Jan. 27, 1929-—; House 1965-71, 1975-85.

OURY, Granville Henderson (D Ariz.) March 12, 1825-Jan. 11, 1891; House (Terr. Del.) 1881-85.

OUTHWAITE, Joseph Hodson (D Ohio) Dec. 5, 1841-Dec. 9, 1907; House 1885-95.

OUTLAND, George Elmer (D Calif.) Oct. 8, 1906-—; House 1943-47.

OUTLAW, David (cousin of George Outlaw) (W N.C.) Sept. 14, 1806-Oct. 22, 1868; House 1847-53.

OUTLAW, George (cousin of David Outlaw) (JD N.C.) ?-Aug. 15, 1825; House Jan. 19-March 3, 1825.

OVERMAN, Lee Slater (D N.C.) Jan. 3, 1854-Dec. 12, 1930; Senate 1903-Dec. 12, 1930.

OVERMYER, Arthur Warren (D Ohio) May 31, 1879-March 8, 1952; House 1915-19.

OVERSTREET, James (— S.C.) Feb. 11, 1773-May 24, 1822; House 1819-May 24, 1822.

OVERSTREET, James Whetstone (D Ga.) Aug. 28, 1866-Dec. 4, 1938; House Oct. 3, 1906-07, 1917-23.

OVERSTREET, Jesse (R Ind.) Dec. 14, 1859-May 27, 1910; House 1895-1909.

OVERTON, Edward Jr. (R Pa.) Feb. 4, 1836-Sept. 18, 1903; House 1877-81.

OVERTON, John Holmes (uncle of Overton Brooks) (D La.) Sept. 17, 1875-May 14, 1948; House May 12, 1931-33; Senate 1933-May 14, 1948.

OVERTON, Walter Hampden (D La.) 1788-Dec. 24, 1845; House 1829-31.

OWEN, Allen Ferdinand (W Ga.) Oct. 9, 1816-April 7, 1865; House 1849-51.

OWEN, Emmett Marshall (D Ga.) Oct. 19, 1877-June 21, 1939; House 1933-June 21, 1939.

OWEN, George Washington (— Ala.) Oct. 20, 1796-Aug. 18, 1837; House 1823-29.

OWEN, James (D N.C.) Dec. 7, 1784-Sept. 4, 1865; House 1817-19.

OWEN, Robert Dale (D Ind.) Nov. 9, 1800-June 24, 1877; House 1843-47.

OWEN, Robert Latham (D Okla.) Feb. 3, 1856-July 19, 1947; Senate Dec. 11, 1907-25.

OWEN, Ruth Bryan (later Mrs. Borge Rohde, daughter of William Jennings Bryan) (D Fla.) Oct. 2, 1885-July 26, 1954; House 1929-33.

OWEN, William Dale (R Ind.) Sept. 6, 1846-1906; House 1885-91.

OWENS, Douglas Wayne (D Utah) May 2, 1937-—; House 1973-75.

OWENS, George Welshman (U Ga.) Aug. 29, 1786-March 2, 1856; House 1835-39.

OWENS, James W. (D Ohio) Oct. 24, 1837-March 30, 1900; House 1889-93.

OWENS, Major Robert Odell (D N.Y.) June 28, 1936-—; House 1983-—.

OWENS, Thomas Leonard (R Ill.) Dec. 21, 1897-June 7, 1948; House 1947-June 7, 1948.

OWENS, William Claiborne (D Ky.) Oct. 17, 1849-Nov. 18, 1925; House 1895-97.

OWSLEY, Bryan Young (W Ky.) Aug. 19, 1798-Oct. 27, 1849; House 1841-43.

OXLEY, Michael Garver (R Ohio) Feb. 11, 1944-—; House July 21, 1981-—.

P

PACE, Stephen (D Ga.) March 9, 1891-April 5, 1970; House 1937-51.

PACHECO, Romualdo (R Calif.) Oct. 31, 1831-Jan. 23, 1899; House 1877-Feb. 7, 1878, 1879-83; Gov. Feb. 27-Dec. 9, 1875.

PACKARD, Jasper (R Ind.) Feb. 1, 1832-Dec. 13, 1899; House 1869-75.

PACKARD, Ron (R Calif.) Jan. 19, 1931-—; House 1983-—.

PACKER, Asa (D Pa.) Dec. 29, 1805-May 17, 1879; House 1853-57.

PACKER, Horace Billings (R Pa.) Oct. 11, 1851-April 13, 1940; House 1897-1901.

PACKER, John Black (R Pa.) March 21, 1824-July 7, 1891; House 1869-77.

PACKWOOD, Robert William (R Ore.) Sept. 11, 1932-—; Senate 1969-—.

PADDOCK, Algernon Sidney (R Neb.) Nov. 9, 1830-Oct. 17, 1897; Senate 1875-81, 1887-93.

PADDOCK, George Arthur (R Ill.) March 24, 1885-Dec. 29, 1964; House 1941-43.

PADGETT, Lemuel Phillips (D Tenn.) Nov. 28, 1855-Aug. 2, 1922; House 1901-Aug. 2, 1922.

PAGAN, Bolivar (Coal. P.R.) May 16, 1897-Feb. 9, 1961; House (Res. Comm.) Dec. 26, 1939-45.

PAGE, Carroll Smalley (R Vt.) Jan. 10, 1843-Dec. 3, 1925; Senate Oct. 21, 1908-23; Gov. 1890-92.

PAGE, Charles Harrison (D R.I.) July 19, 1843-July 21, 1912; House Feb. 21-March 3, 1887, 1891-93, April 5, 1893-95.

PAGE, Henry (D Md.) June 28, 1841-Jan. 7, 1913; House 1891-Sept. 3, 1892.

PAGE, Horace Francis (R Calif.) Oct. 20, 1833-Aug. 23, 1890; House 1873-83.

PAGE, John (D Va.) April 17, 1744-Oct. 11, 1808; House 1789-97; Gov. 1802-05.

PAGE, John (D N.H.) May 21, 1787-Sept. 8, 1865; Senate June 8, 1836-37; Gov. 1839-42.

PAGE, Robert (F Va.) Feb. 4, 1765-Dec. 8, 1840; House 1799-1801.

PAGE, Robert Newton (D N.C.) Oct. 26, 1859-Oct. 3, 1933; House 1903-17.

PAGE, Sherman (JD N.Y.) May 9, 1779-Sept. 27, 1853; House 1833-37.

PAIGE, Calvin DeWitt (R Mass.) May 20, 1848-April 24, 1930; House Nov. 26, 1913-25.

PAIGE, David Raymond (D Ohio) April 8, 1844-June 30, 1901; House 1883-85.

PAINE, Elijah (F Vt.) Jan. 21, 1757-April 28, 1842; Senate 1795-Sept. 1, 1801.

PAINE, Halbert Eleazer (R Wis.) Feb. 4, 1826-April 14, 1905; House 1865-71.

PAINE, Robert Treat (AP N.C.) Feb. 18, 1812-Feb. 8, 1872; House 1855-57.

PAINE, William Wiseham (D Ga.) Oct. 10, 1817-Aug. 5, 1882; House Dec. 22, 1870-71.

PALEN, Rufus (W N.Y.) Feb. 25, 1807-April 26, 1844; House 1839-41.

PALFREY, John Gorham (W Mass.) May 2, 1796-April 26, 1881; House 1847-49.

PALMER, Alexander Mitchell (D Pa.) May 4, 1872-May 11, 1936; House 1909-15; Atty. Gen. 1919-21.

PALMER, Beriah (— N.Y.) 1740-May 20, 1812; House 1803-05.

PALMER, Cyrus Maffet (R Pa.) Feb. 12, 1887-Aug. 16, 1959; House 1927-29.

PALMER, Francis Wayland (Frank) (R Iowa) Oct. 11, 1827-Dec. 3, 1907; House 1869-73.

PALMER, George William (nephew of John Palmer, cousin of William Elisha Haynes) (R N.Y.) Jan. 13, 1818-March 2, 1916; House 1857-61.

PALMER, Henry Wilber (R Pa.) July 10, 1839-Feb. 15, 1913; House 1901-07, 1909-11.

PALMER, John (uncle of George William Palmer) (D N.Y.) Jan. 29, 1785-Dec. 8, 1840; House 1817-19, 1837-39.

PALMER, John McAuley (D Ill.) Sept. 13, 1817-Sept. 25, 1900; Senate 1891-97; Gov. 1869-73 (Republican).

PALMER, John William (R Mo.) Aug. 20, 1866-Nov. 3, 1958; House 1929-31.

PALMER, Thomas Witherell (R Mich.) Jan. 25, 1830-June 1, 1913; Senate 1883-89.

PALMER, William Adams (D Vt.) Sept. 12, 1781-Dec. 3, 1860; Senate Oct. 20, 1818-25; Gov. 1831-35.

PALMISANO, Vincent Luke (D Md.) Aug. 5, 1882-Jan. 12, 1953; House 1927-39.

PANETTA, Leon Edward (D Calif.) June 28, 1938- ; House 1977- .

PANTIN, Santiago Iglesias (See IGLESIAS, Santiago).

PAREDES, Quintin (Nat. P.I.) Sept. 9, 1884- ; House (Res. Comm.) Feb. 14, 1936-Sept. 29, 1938.

PARK, Frank (D Ga.) March 3, 1864-Nov. 20, 1925; House Nov. 5, 1913-25.

PARKE, Benjamin (D Ind.) Sept. 22, 1777-July 12, 1835; House (Terr. Del.) Dec. 12, 1805-March 1, 1808.

PARKER, Abraham X. (R N.Y.) Nov. 14, 1831-Aug. 9, 1909; House 1881-89.

PARKER, Amasa Junius (D N.Y.) June 2, 1807-May 13, 1890; House 1837-39.

PARKER, Andrew (D Pa.) May 21, 1805-Jan. 15, 1864; House 1851-53.

PARKER, Homer Cling (D Ga.) Sept. 25, 1885-June 22, 1946; House Sept. 10, 1931-35.

PARKER, Hosea Washington (D N.H.) May 30, 1833-Aug. 21, 1922; House 1871-75.

PARKER, Isaac (— Mass.) June 17, 1768-July 26, 1830; House 1797-99.

PARKER, Isaac Charles (R Mo.) Oct. 15, 1838-Nov. 17, 1896; House 1871-75.

PARKER, James (D Mass.) 1768-Nov. 9, 1837; House 1813-15, 1819-21.

PARKER, James (grandfather of Richard Wayne Parker) (D N.J.) March 3, 1776-April 1, 1868; House 1833-37.

PARKER, James Southworth (R N.Y.) June 3, 1867-Dec. 19, 1933; House 1913-Dec. 19, 1933.

PARKER, John Mason (W N.Y.) June 14, 1805-Dec. 16, 1873; House 1855-59.

PARKER, Josiah (— Va.) May 11, 1751-March 18, 1810; House 1789-1801.

PARKER, Nahum (— N.H.) March 4, 1760-Nov. 12, 1839; Senate 1807-June 1, 1810.

PARKER, Richard (D Va.) Dec. 22, 1810-Nov. 10, 1893; House 1849-51.

PARKER, Richard Elliott (D Va.) Dec. 27, 1783-Sept. 6, 1840; Senate Dec. 12, 1836-March 13, 1837.

PARKER, Richard Wayne (grandson of James Parker) (R N.J.) Aug. 6, 1848-Nov. 28, 1923; House 1895-1911, Dec. 1, 1914-19, 1921-23.

PARKER, Samuel Wilson (W Ind.) Sept. 9, 1805-Feb. 1, 1859; House 1851-55.

PARKER, Severn Eyre (— Va.) July 19, 1787-Oct. 21, 1836; House 1819-21.

PARKER, William Henry (— S.D.) May 5, 1847-June 26, 1908; House 1907-June 26, 1908.

PARKS, Gorham (D Maine) May 27, 1794-Nov. 23, 1877; House 1833-37.

PARKS, Tilman Bacon (D Ark.) May 14, 1872-Feb. 12, 1950; House 1921-37.

PARMENTER, William (D Mass.) March 30, 1789-Feb. 25, 1866; House 1837-45.

PARRAN, Thomas (R Md.) Feb. 12, 1860-March 29, 1955; House 1911-13.

PARRETT, William Fletcher (D Ind.) Aug. 10, 1825-June 30, 1895; House 1889-93.

PARRIS, Albion Keith (cousin of Virgil Delphini Parris) (D Mass./Maine) Jan. 19, 1788-Feb. 22, 1857; House (Mass.) 1815-Feb. 3, 1818; Senate (Maine) 1827-Aug. 26, 1828; Gov. (Maine) 1822-27.

PARRIS, Stanford E. (R Va.) Sept. 9, 1929- ; House 1973-75; Senate 1981- .

PARRIS, Virgil Delphini (cousin of Albion Keith Parris) (SRD Maine) Feb. 18, 1807-June 13, 1874; House May 29, 1838-41.

PARRISH, Isaac (D Ohio) March 1804-Aug. 9, 1860; House 1839-41, 1845-47.

PARRISH, Lucian Walton (D Texas) Jan. 10, 1878-March 27, 1922; House 1919-March 27, 1922.

PARROTT, John Fabyan (D N.H.) Aug. 8, 1767-July 9, 1836; House 1817-19; Senate 1819-25.

PARROTT, Marcus Junius (R Kan.) Oct. 27, 1828-Oct. 4, 1879; House (Terr. Del.) 1857-Jan. 29, 1861.

PARSONS, Claude VanCleve (D Ill.) Oct. 7, 1895-May 23, 1941; House Nov. 4, 1930-41.

PARSONS, Edward Young (D Ky.) Dec. 12, 1841-July 8, 1876; House 1875-July 8, 1876.

PARSONS, Herbert (R N.Y.) Oct. 28, 1869-Sept. 16, 1925; House 1905-11.

PARSONS, Richard Chappel (R Ohio) Oct. 10, 1826-Jan. 9, 1899; House 1873-75.

PARTRIDGE, Donald Barrows (R Maine) June 7, 1891-June 5, 1946; House 1931-33.

PARTRIDGE, Frank Charles (R Vt.) May 7, 1861-March 2, 1943; Senate Dec. 23, 1930-March 31, 1931.

PARTRIDGE, George (— Mass.) Feb. 8, 1740-July 7, 1828; House 1789-Aug. 14, 1790; Cont. Cong. 1779-82, 1783-85.

PARTRIDGE, Samuel (D N.Y.) Nov. 29, 1790-March 30, 1883; House 1841-43.

PASCHAL, Thomas Moore (D Texas) Dec. 15, 1845-Jan. 28, 1919; House 1893-95.

PASCO, Samuel (D Fla.) June 28, 1834-March 13, 1917; Senate May 19, 1887-April 19, 1899.

PASHAYAN, Charles Sahag (Chip) Jr. (R Calif.) March 27, 1941-—; House 1979-—.

PASSMAN, Otto Ernest (D La.) June 27, 1900-—; House 1947-77.

PASTORE, John Orlando (D R.I.) March 17, 1907-—; Senate Dec. 19, 1950-Dec. 28, 1976; Gov. 1945-50.

PATERSON, John (— N.Y.) 1744-July 19, 1808; House 1803-05.

PATERSON, William (F N.J.) Dec. 24, 1745-Sept. 9, 1806; Senate 1789-Nov. 13, 1790; Cont. Cong. 1780-81, 1787; Gov. 1790-92; Assoc. Justice Supreme Court 1793-1806.

PATMAN, William N. (D Texas) March 26, 1927-—; House 1981-85.

PATMAN, Wright (D Texas) Aug. 6, 1893-March 7, 1976; House 1929-March 7, 1976.

PATRICK, Luther (D Ala.) Jan. 23, 1894-May 26, 1957; House 1937-43, 1945-47.

PATTEN, Edward James (D N.J.) Aug. 22, 1905-—; House 1963-81.

PATTEN, Harold Ambrose (D Ariz.) Oct. 6, 1907-Sept. 6, 1969; House 1949-55.

PATTEN, John (— Del.) April 26, 1746-Dec. 26, 1800; House 1793-Feb. 14, 1794, 1795-97; Cont. Cong. 1785-86.

PATTEN, Thomas Gedney (D N.Y.) Sept. 12, 1861-Feb. 23, 1939; House 1911-17.

PATTERSON, David Trotter (D Tenn.) Feb. 28, 1818-Nov. 3, 1891; Senate July 24, 1866-69.

PATTERSON, Edward White (D Kan.) Oct. 4, 1895-March 6, 1940; House 1935-39.

PATTERSON, Ellis Ellwood (D Calif.) Nov. 28, 1897-—; House 1945-47.

PATTERSON, Francis Ford Jr. (R N.J.) July 30, 1867-Nov. 30, 1935; House Nov. 2, 1920-27.

PATTERSON, George Robert (R Pa.) Nov. 9, 1863-March 21, 1906; House 1901-March 21, 1906.

PATTERSON, George Washington (brother of William Patterson) (R N.Y.) Nov. 11, 1799-Oct. 15, 1879; House 1877-79.

PATTERSON, Gilbert Brown (D N.C.) May 29, 1863-Jan. 26, 1922; House 1903-07.

PATTERSON, James O'Hanlon (D S.C.) June 25, 1857-Oct. 25, 1911; House 1905-11.

PATTERSON, James Thomas (R Conn.) Oct. 20, 1908-—; House 1947-59.

PATTERSON, James Willis (R N.H.) July 2, 1823-May 4, 1893; House 1863-67; Senate 1867-73.

PATTERSON, Jerry Mumford (D Calif.) Oct. 25, 1934-—; House 1975-85.

PATTERSON, John (half brother of Thomas Patterson) (D Ohio) Feb. 10, 1771-Feb. 7, 1848; House 1823-25.

PATTERSON, John James (R S.C.) Aug. 8, 1830-Sept. 28, 1912; Senate 1873-79.

PATTERSON, Josiah (father of Malcolm Rice Patterson) (D Tenn.) April 14, 1837-Feb. 10, 1904; House 1891-97.

PATTERSON, Lafayette Lee (D Ala.) Aug. 23, 1888-—; House Nov. 6, 1928-33.

PATTERSON, Malcolm Rice (son of Josiah Patterson) (D Tenn.) June 7, 1861-March 8, 1935; House 1901-Nov. 5, 1906; Gov. 1907-11.

PATTERSON, Roscoe Conkling (R Mo.) Sept. 15, 1876-Oct. 22, 1954; House 1921-23; Senate 1929-35.

PATTERSON, Thomas (half brother of John Patterson) (D Pa.) Oct. 1, 1764-Nov. 16, 1841; House 1817-25.

PATTERSON, Thomas J. (W N.Y.) about 1808-?; House 1843-45.

PATTERSON, Thomas MacDonald (D Colo.) Nov. 4, 1839-July 23, 1916; House (Terr. Del.) 1875-Aug. 1, 1876; (Rep.) Dec. 13, 1877-79; Senate 1901-07.

PATTERSON, Walter (— N.Y.) ?-?; House 1821-23.

PATTERSON, William (brother of George Washington Patterson, uncle of Augustus Frank) (W N.Y.) June 4, 1789-Aug. 14, 1838; House 1837-Aug. 14, 1838.

PATTERSON, William (D Ohio) 1790-Aug. 17, 1868; House 1833-37.

PATTISON, Edward Worthington (D N.Y.) April 29, 1932-—; House 1975-79.

PATTISON, John M. (D Ohio) June 13, 1847-June 18, 1906; House 1891-93; Gov. Jan. 8-June 18, 1906.

PATTON, Charles Emory (son of John Patton, brother of John Patton Jr.) (— Pa.) July 5, 1859-Dec. 15, 1937; House 1911-15.

PATTON, David Henry (D Ind.) Nov. 26, 1837-Jan. 17, 1914; House 1891-93.

PATTON, John (father of Charles Emory Patton and John Patton Jr., uncle of William Irvin Swoope) (R Pa.) Jan. 6, 1823-Dec. 23, 1897; House 1861-63, 1887-89.

PATTON, John Jr. (son of John Patton, brother of Charles Emory Patton) (R Mich.) Oct. 30, 1850-May 24, 1907; Senate May 5, 1894-Jan. 14, 1895.

PATTON, John Denniston (D Pa.) Nov. 28, 1829-Feb. 22, 1904; House 1883-85.

PATTON, John Mercer (D Va.) Aug. 10, 1797-Oct. 29, 1858; House Nov. 25, 1830-April 7, 1838.

PATTON, Nat (D Texas) Feb. 26, 1884-July 27, 1957; House 1935-45.

PAUL, John (father of the following) (Read. Va.) June 30, 1839-Nov. 1, 1901; House 1881-Sept. 5, 1883.

PAUL, John (son of the preceding) (R Va.) Dec. 9, 1883-Feb. 13, 1964; House Dec. 15, 1922-23.

PAUL, Ronald Ernest (R Texas) Aug. 20, 1935-—; House April 3, 1976-77, 1979-85.

PAULDING, William Jr. (D N.Y.) March 7, 1770-Feb. 11, 1854; House 1811-13.

PAWLING, Levi (D Pa.) July 25, 1773-Sept. 7, 1845; House 1817-19.

PAYNE, Frederick George (R Maine) July 24, 1904-June 15, 1978; Senate 1953-59; Gov. 1949-53.

PAYNE, Henry B. (grandfather of Frances Payne Bolton) (D Ohio) Nov. 30, 1810-Sept. 9, 1896; House 1875-77; Senate 1885-91.

PAYNE, Sereno Elisha (R N.Y.) June 26, 1843-Dec. 10, 1914; House 1883-87, 1889-Dec. 10, 1914; House majority leader 1899-1911.

PAYNE, William Winter (D Ala.) Jan. 2, 1807-Sept. 2, 1874; House 1841-47.

PAYNTER, Lemuel (D Pa.) 1788-Aug. 1, 1863; House 1837-41.

PAYNTER, Thomas Hanson (D Ky.) Dec. 9, 1851-March 8, 1921; House 1889-Jan. 5, 1895; Senate 1907-13.

PAYSON, Lewis Edwin (R Ill.) Sept. 17, 1840-Oct. 4, 1909; House 1881-91.

PEACE, Roger Craft (D S.C.) May 19, 1899-Aug. 20, 1968; Senate Aug. 5-Nov. 4, 1941.

PEARCE, Charles Edward (R Mo.) May 29, 1842-Jan. 30, 1902; House 1897-1901.

PEARCE, Dutee Jerauld (D R.I.) April 3, 1789-May 9, 1849; House 1825-37.

PEARCE, James Alfred (D Md.) Dec. 8, 1804-Dec. 20, 1862; House 1835-39, 1841-43; Senate 1843-Dec. 20, 1862 (1835-39, 1841-43, 1843-62 Whig, March 4 1862-Dec. 20, 1862 Democrat).

PEARCE, John Jamison (W Pa.) Feb. 28, 1826-May 26, 1912; House 1855-57.

PEARRE, George Alexander (R Md.) July 16, 1860-Sept. 19, 1923; House 1899-1911.

PEARSON, Albert Jackson (D Ohio) May 20, 1846-May 15, 1905; House 1891-95.

PEARSON, Herron Carney (D Tenn.) July 31, 1890-April 24, 1953; House 1935-43.

PEARSON, James Blackwood (R Kan.) May 7, 1920-—; Senate Jan. 31, 1962-Dec. 23, 1978.

PEARSON, John James (W Pa.) Oct. 25, 1800-May 30, 1888; House Dec. 5, 1836-37.

PEARSON, Joseph (F N.C.) 1776-Oct. 27, 1834; House 1809-15.

PEARSON, Richmond (R N.C.) Jan. 26, 1852-Sept. 12, 1923; House 1895-99, May 10, 1900-01.

PEASE, Donald James (D Ohio) Sept. 26, 1931- —; House 1977- —.

PEASE, Henry Roberts (R Miss.) Feb. 19, 1835-Jan. 2, 1907; Senate Feb. 3, 1874-75.

PEASLEE, Charles Hazen (D N.H.) Feb. 6, 1804-Sept. 18, 1866; House 1847-53.

PEAVEY, Hubert Haskell (R Wis.) Jan. 12, 1881-Nov. 21, 1937; House 1923-35.

PECK, Erasmus Darwin (R Ohio) Sept. 16, 1808-Dec. 25, 1876; House April 23, 1870-73.

PECK, George Washington (D Mich.) June 4, 1818-June 30, 1905; House 1855-57.

PECK, Jared Valentine (D N.Y.) Sept. 21, 1816-Dec. 25, 1891; House 1853-55.

PECK, Lucius Benedict (D Vt.) Nov. 17, 1802-Dec. 28, 1866; House 1847-51.

PECK, Luther Christopher (W N.Y.) Jan. 1800-Feb. 5, 1876; House 1837-41.

PECKHAM, Rufus Wheeler (D N.Y.) Dec. 20, 1809-Nov. 22, 1873; House 1853-55.

PEDDIE, Thomas Baldwin (R N.J.) Feb. 11, 1808-Feb. 16, 1889; House 1877-79.

PEDEN, Preston Elmer (D Okla.) June 28, 1914- —; House 1947-49.

PEEK, Harmanus (— N.Y.) June 24, 1782, Sept. 27, 1838; House 1819-21.

PEEL, Samuel West (D Ark.) Sept. 13, 1831-Dec. 18, 1924; House 1883-93.

PEELLE, Stanton Judkins (R Ind.) Feb. 11, 1843-Sept. 4, 1928; House 1881-May 22, 1884.

PEERY, George Campbell (D Va.) Oct. 28, 1873-Oct. 14, 1952; House 1923-29; Gov. 1934-38.

PEFFER, William Alfred (P Kan.) Sept. 10, 1831-Oct. 7, 1912; Senate 1891-97.

PEGRAM, John (— Va.) Nov. 16, 1773-April 8, 1831; House April 21, 1818-19.

PEIRCE, Joseph (— N.H.) June 25, 1748-Sept. 12, 1812; House 1801-02.

PEIRCE, Robert Bruce Fraser (R Ind.) Feb. 17, 1843-Dec. 5, 1898; House 1881-83.

PELHAM, Charles (R Ala.) March 12, 1835-Jan. 18, 1908; House 1873-75.

PELL, Claiborne de Borda (son of Herbert Claiborne Pell Jr.) (D R.I.) Nov. 22, 1918- —; Senate 1961- —.

PELL, Herbert Claiborne Jr. (great-grandson of John Francis Hamtramck Claiborne, great-great-grandnephew of William Charles Cole Claiborne and Nathaniel Herbert Claiborne, father of Claiborne de Borda Pell) (D N.Y.) Feb. 16, 1884-July 17, 1961; House 1919-21.

PELLY, Thomas Minor (R Wash.) Aug. 22, 1902-Nov. 21, 1973; House 1953-73.

PELTON, Guy Ray (W N.Y.) Aug. 3, 1824-July 24, 1890; House 1855-57.

PENCE, Lafayette (P/Sil.D Colo.) Dec. 23, 1857-Oct. 22, 1923; House 1893-95.

PENDLETON, Edmund Henry (W N.Y.) 1788-Feb. 25, 1862; House 1831-33.

PENDLETON, George Cassety (D Texas) April 23, 1845-Jan. 19, 1913; House 1893-97.

PENDLETON, George Hunt (son of Nathanael Greene Pendleton) (D Ohio) July 19, 1825-Nov. 24, 1889; House 1857-65; Senate 1879-85.

PENDLETON, James Monroe (R R.I.) Jan. 10, 1822-Feb. 16, 1889; House 1871-75.

PENDLETON, John Overton (D W.Va.) July 4, 1851-Dec. 24, 1916; House 1889-Feb. 26, 1890, 1891-95.

PENDLETON, John Strother (W Va.) March 1, 1802-Nov. 19, 1868; House 1845-49.

PENDLETON, Nathanael Green (father of George Hunt Pendleton) (W Ohio) Aug. 25, 1793-June 16, 1861; House 1841-43.

PENINGTON, John Brown (D Del.) Dec. 20, 1825-June 1, 1902; House 1887-91.

PENN, Alexander Gordon (D La.) May 10, 1799-May 7, 1866; House Dec. 30, 1850-53.

PENNIMAN, Ebenezer Jenckes (W/FS Mich.) Jan. 11, 1804-April 12, 1890; House 1851-53.

PENNINGTON, Alexander Cumming McWhorter (cousin of William Pennington) (W N.J.) July 2, 1810-Jan. 25, 1867; House 1853-57.

PENNINGTON, William (cousin of Alexander Cumming McWhorter Pennington) (W N.J.) May 4, 1796-Feb. 16, 1862; House 1859-61; Speaker 1859-61; Gov. 1837-43.

PENNY, Timothy J. (D Minn.) Nov. 19, 1951- —; House 1983- —.

PENNYBACKER, Isaac Samuels (cousin of Green Berry Samuels) (D Va.) Sept. 3, 1805-Jan. 12, 1847; House 1837-39; Senate Dec. 3, 1845-Jan. 12, 1847.

PENROSE, Boies (R Pa.) Nov. 1, 1860-Dec. 31, 1921; Senate 1897-Dec. 31, 1921.

PEPPER, Claude Denson (D Fla.) Sept. 8, 1900- —; Senate Nov. 4, 1936-51; House 1963- —.

PEPPER, George Wharton (R Pa.) March 16, 1867-May 24, 1961; Senate Jan. 9, 1922-27.

PEPPER, Irvin St. Clair (D Iowa) June 10, 1876-Dec. 22, 1913; House 1911-Dec. 22, 1913.

PERCE, Legrand Winfield (R Miss.) June 19, 1836-March 16, 1911; House Feb. 23, 1870-73.

PERCY, Charles Harting (R Ill.) Sept. 27, 1919- —; Senate 1967-85.

PERCY, Le Roy (D Miss.) Nov. 9, 1860-Dec. 24, 1929; Senate Feb. 23, 1910-13.

PEREA, Francisco (cousin of Pedro Perea) (R N.M.) Jan. 9, 1830-May 21, 1913; House (Terr. Del.) 1863-65.

PEREA, Pedro (cousin of Francisco Perea) (R N.M.) April 22, 1852-Jan. 11, 1906; House (Terr. Del.) 1899-1901.

PERHAM, Sidney (R Maine) March 27, 1819-April 10, 1907; House 1863-69; Gov. 1871-74.

PERKINS, Bishop (D N.Y.) Sept. 5, 1787-Nov. 20, 1866; House 1853-55.

PERKINS, Bishop Walden (R Kan.) Oct. 18, 1841-June 20, 1894; House 1883-91; Senate Jan. 1, 1892-93.

PERKINS, Carl Dewey (D Ky.) Oct. 15, 1912-Aug. 3, 1984; House 1949-Aug. 3, 1984.

PERKINS, Carl C. "Chris" (son of Carl Dewey Perkins) (D Ky.) Aug. 6, 1954- —; House 1985- —.

PERKINS, Elias (F Conn.) April 5, 1767-Sept. 27, 1845; House 1801-03.

PERKINS, George Clement (R Calif.) Aug. 23, 1839-Feb. 26, 1923; Senate July 26, 1893-1915; Gov. 1880-83.

PERKINS, George Douglas (R Iowa) Feb. 29, 1840-Feb. 3, 1914; House 1891-99.

PERKINS, James Breck (R N.Y.) Nov. 4, 1847-March 11, 1910; House 1901-March 11, 1910.

PERKINS, Jared (W N.H.) Jan. 5, 1793-Oct. 15, 1854; House 1851-53.

PERKINS, John Jr. (D La.) July 1, 1819-Nov. 28, 1885; House 1853-55.

PERKINS, Randolph (R N.J.) Nov. 30, 1871-May 25, 1936; House 1921-May 25, 1936.

PERKY, Kirtland Irving (D Idaho) Feb. 8, 1867-Jan. 9, 1939; Senate Nov. 18, 1912-Feb. 5, 1913.

PERLMAN, Nathan David (R N.Y.) Aug. 2, 1887-June 29, 1952; House Nov. 2, 1920-27.

PERRILL, Augustus Leonard (D Ohio) Jan. 20, 1807-June 2, 1882; House 1845-47.

PERRY, Aaron Fyfe (R Ohio) Jan. 1, 1815-March 11, 1893; House 1871-72.

PERRY, Eli (D N.Y.) Dec. 25, 1799-May 17, 1881; House 1871-75.

PERRY, John Jasiel (R Maine) Aug. 2, 1811-May 2, 1897; House 1855-57, 1859-61.

PERRY, Nehemiah (Const.U N.J.) March 30, 1816-Nov. 1, 1881; House 1861-65.

PERRY, Thomas Johns (D Md.) Feb. 17, 1807-June 27, 1871; House 1845-47.

PERRY, William Hayne (D S.C.) June 9, 1839-July 7, 1902; House 1885-91.

PERSON, Seymour Howe (R Mich.) Feb. 2, 1879-April 7, 1957; House 1931-33.

PERSONS, Henry (D Ga.) Jan. 30, 1834-June 17, 1910; House 1879-81.

PESQUERA, Jose Lorenzo (Nonpart. P.R.) Aug. 10, 1882-July 25, 1950; House (Res. Comm.) April 15, 1932-33.

PETER, George (D Md.) Sept. 28, 1779-June 22, 1861; House Oct. 7, 1816-19, 1825-27.

Biographical Index

PETERS, Andrew James (D Mass.) April 3, 1872-June 26, 1938; House 1907-Aug. 15, 1914.

PETERS, John Andrew (uncle of the following) (R Maine) Oct. 9, 1822-April 2, 1904; House 1867-73.

PETERS, John Andrew (nephew of the preceding) (R Maine) Aug. 13, 1864-Aug. 22, 1953; House Sept. 8, 1913-Jan. 2, 1922.

PETERS, Mason Summers (D/P Kan.) Sept. 3, 1844-Feb. 14, 1914; House 1897-99.

PETERS, Samuel Ritter (R Kan.) Aug. 16, 1842-April 21, 1910; House 1883-91.

PETERSEN, Andrew Nicholas (R N.Y.) March 10, 1870-Sept. 28, 1952; House 1921-23.

PETERSON, Hugh (D Ga.) Aug. 21, 1898-Oct. 3, 1961; House 1935-47.

PETERSON, James Hardin (D Fla.) Feb. 11, 1894-March 28, 1978; House 1933-51.

PETERSON, John Barney (cousin of Horatio Clifford Claypool and Harold Kile Claypool) (D Ind.) July 4, 1850-July 16, 1944; House 1913-15.

PETERSON, Morris Blaine (D Utah) March 26, 1906--; House 1961-63.

PETRI, Thomas E. (R Wis.) May 28, 1940--; House April 9, 1979--.

PETRIE, George (R N.Y.) Sept. 8, 1793-May 8, 1879; House 1847-49.

PETRIKIN, David (D Pa.) Dec. 1, 1788-March 1, 1847; House 1837-41.

PETTENGILL, Samuel Barrett (nephew of William Horace Clagett) (D Ind.) Jan. 19, 1886-March 20, 1974; House 1931-39.

PETTIBONE, Augustus Herman (R Tenn.) Jan. 21, 1835-Nov. 26, 1918; House 1881-87.

PETTIGREW, Ebenezer (W N.C.) March 10, 1783-July 8, 1848; House 1835-37.

PETTIGREW, Richard Franklin (R S.D.) July 23, 1848-Oct. 5, 1926; House (Terr. Del.) 1881-83; Senate Nov. 2, 1889-1901.

PETTIS, Jerry Lyle (husband of Shirley Neal Pettis) (R Calif.) July 18, 1916-Feb. 14, 1975; House 1967-Feb. 14, 1975.

PETTIS, Shirley Neal (widow of Jerry Lyle Pettis) (R Calif.) July 12, 1924--; House April 29, 1975-79.

PETTIS, Solomon Newton (R Pa.) Oct. 10, 1827-Sept. 18, 1900; House Dec. 7, 1868-69.

PETTIS, Spencer Darwin (D Mo.) 1802-Aug. 28, 1831; House 1829-Aug. 28, 1831.

PETTIT, John (D Ind.) June 24, 1807-Jan. 17, 1877; House 1843-49; Senate Jan. 11, 1853-55.

PETTIT, John Upfold (R Ind.) Sept. 11, 1820-March 21, 1881; House 1855-61.

PETTUS, Edmund Winston (D Ala.) July 6, 1821-July 27, 1907; Senate 1897-July 27, 1907.

PEYSER, Peter A. (D N.Y.) Sept. 7, 1921--; House 1971-77, 1979-83.

PEYSER, Theodore Albert (D N.Y.) Feb. 18, 1873-Aug. 8, 1937; House 1933-Aug. 8, 1937.

PEYTON, Balie (brother of Joseph Hopkins Peyton) (W Tenn.) Nov. 26, 1803-Aug. 18, 1878; House 1833-37.

PEYTON, Joseph Hopkins (brother of Balie Peyton) (W Tenn.) May 20, 1808-Nov. 11, 1845; House 1843-Nov. 11, 1845.

PEYTON, Samuel Oldham (D Ky.) Jan. 8, 1804-Jan. 4, 1870; House 1847-49, 1857-61.

PFEIFER, Joseph Lawrence (D N.Y.) Feb. 6, 1892-April 19, 1974; House 1935-51.

PFEIFFER, William Louis (R N.Y.) May 29, 1907--; House 1949-51.

PFOST, Gracie Bowers (D Idaho) March 12, 1906-Aug. 11, 1965; House 1953-63.

PHEIFFER, William Townsend (R N.Y.) July 15, 1898--; House 1941-43.

PHELAN, James (D Tenn.) Dec. 7, 1856-Jan. 30, 1891; House 1887-Jan. 30, 1891.

PHELAN, James Duval (D Calif.) April 20, 1861-Aug. 7, 1930; Senate 1915-21.

PHELAN, Michael Francis (D Mass.) Oct. 22, 1875-Oct. 12, 1941; House 1913-21.

PHELPS, Charles Edward (UC Md.) May 1, 1833-Dec. 27, 1908; House 1865-69 (1865-67 Union War Party, 1867-69 Union Conservative).

PHELPS, Darwin (R Pa.) April 17, 1807-Dec. 14, 1879; House 1869-71.

PHELPS, Elisha (father of John Smith Phelps) (D Conn.) Nov. 16, 1779-April 6, 1847; House 1819-21, 1825-29.

PHELPS, James (son of Lancelot Phelps) (D Conn.) Jan. 12, 1822-Jan. 15, 1900; House 1875-83.

PHELPS, John Smith (son of Elisha Phelps) (D Mo.) Dec. 22, 1814-Nov. 20, 1886; House 1845-63; Gov. 1877-81.

PHELPS, Lancelot (father of James Phelps) (D Conn.) Nov. 9, 1784-Sept. 1, 1866; House 1835-39.

PHELPS, Oliver (D N.Y.) Oct. 21, 1749-Feb. 21, 1809; House 1803-05.

PHELPS, Samuel Shethar (W Vt.) May 13, 1793-March 25, 1855; Senate 1839-51; Jan. 17, 1853-March 16, 1854.

PHELPS, Timothy Guy (R Calif.) Dec. 20, 1824-June 11, 1899; House 1861-63.

PHELPS, William Wallace (D Minn.) June 1, 1826-Aug. 3, 1873; House May 11, 1858-59.

PHELPS, William Walter (R N.J.) Aug. 24, 1839-June 17, 1894; House 1873-75, 1883-89.

PHILBIN, Philip Joseph (D Mass.) May 29, 1898-June 14, 1972; House 1943-71.

PHILIPS, John Finis (D Mo.) Dec. 31, 1834-March 13, 1919; House 1875-77; Jan. 10, 1880-81.

PHILLIPS, Alfred Noroton (D Conn.) April 23, 1894-Jan. 18, 1970; House 1937-39.

PHILLIPS, Dayton Edward (R Tenn.) March 29, 1910-Oct. 23, 1980; House 1947-51.

PHILLIPS, Fremont Orestes (R Ohio) March 16, 1856-Feb. 21, 1936; House 1899-1901.

PHILLIPS, Henry Myer (D Pa.) June 30, 1811-Aug. 28, 1884; House 1857-59.

PHILLIPS, John (F Pa.) ?-?; House 1821-23.

PHILLIPS, John (R Calif.) Sept. 11, 1887-Dec. 18, 1983; House 1943-57.

PHILLIPS, Philip (D Ala.) Dec. 13, 1807-Jan. 14, 1884; House 1853-55.

PHILLIPS, Stephen Clarendon (W Mass.) Nov. 4, 1801-June 26, 1857; House Dec. 1, 1834-Sept. 28, 1838.

PHILLIPS, Thomas Wharton (father of Thomas Wharton Phillips Jr.) (R Pa.) Feb. 23, 1835-July 21, 1912; House 1893-97.

PHILLIPS, Thomas Wharton Jr. (son of Thomas Wharton Phillips) (R Pa.) Nov. 21, 1874-Jan. 2, 1956; House 1923-27.

PHILLIPS, William Addison (R Kan.) Jan. 14, 1824-Nov. 30, 1893; House 1873-79.

PHILSON, Robert (— Pa.) 1759-July 25, 1831; House 1819-21.

PHIPPS, Lawrence Cowle (R Colo.) Aug. 30, 1862-March 1, 1958; Senate 1919-31.

PHISTER, Elijah Conner (D Ky.) Oct. 8, 1822-May 16, 1887; House 1879-83.

PHOENIX, Jonas Phillips (W N.Y.) Jan. 14, 1788-May 4, 1859; House 1843-45, 1849-51.

PICKENS, Andrew (grandfather of Francis Wilkinson Pickens) (D S.C.) Sept. 13, 1739-Aug. 11, 1817; House 1793-95.

PICKENS, Francis Wilkinson (grandson of Andrew Pickens) (ND S.C.) April 7, 1805-Jan. 25, 1869; House Dec. 8, 1834-43; Gov. 1860-62.

PICKENS, Israel (D N.C./Ala.) Jan. 30, 1780-April 24, 1827; House (N.C.) 1811-17; Senate (Ala.) Feb. 17, 1826-Nov. 27, 1826; Gov. (Ala.) 1821-25.

PICKERING, Timothy (F Mass.) July 17, 1745-Jan. 29, 1829; Senate 1803-11; House 1813-17; Postmaster Gen. 1791-95; Secy. of War 1795; Secy. of State 1795-1800.

PICKETT, Charles Edgar (R Iowa) Jan. 14, 1866-July 20, 1930; House 1909-13.

PICKETT, Thomas Augustus (Tom) (D Texas) Aug. 14, 1906-June 7, 1980; House 1945-June 30, 1952.

PICKLE, J. J. (Jake) (D Texas) Oct. 11, 1913--; House Dec. 21, 1963--.

PICKLER, John Alfred (R S.D.) Jan. 24, 1844-June 13, 1910; House Nov. 2, 1889-97.

PICKMAN, Benjamin Jr. (— Mass.) Sept. 30, 1763-Aug. 16, 1843; House 1809-11.

PIDCOCK, James Nelson (cousin of Alvah Augustus Clark) (D N.J.) Feb. 8, 1836-Dec. 17, 1899; House 1885-89.

PIERCE, Charles Wilson (D Ala.) Oct. 7, 1823-Feb. 18, 1907; House July 21, 1868-69.

PIERCE, Franklin (D N.H.) Nov. 23, 1804-Oct. 8, 1869; House 1833-37; Senate 1837-Feb. 28, 1842; President 1853-57.

PIERCE, Gilbert Ashville (R N.D.) Jan. 11, 1839-Feb. 15, 1901; Senate Nov. 21, 1889-91; Gov. (N.D. Terr.) 1884-86.

PIERCE, Henry Lillie (R Mass.) Aug. 23, 1825-Dec. 17, 1896; House Dec. 1, 1873-77.

PIERCE, Ray Vaughn (R N.Y.) Aug. 6, 1840-Feb. 4, 1914; House 1879-Sept. 18, 1880.

PIERCE, Rice Alexander (D Tenn.) July 3, 1848-July 12, 1936; House 1883-85, 1889-93, 1897-1905.

PIERCE, Wallace Edgar (R N.Y.) Dec. 9, 1881-Jan. 3, 1940; House 1939-Jan. 3, 1940.

PIERCE, Walter Marcus (D Ore.) May 30, 1861-March 27, 1954; House 1933-43; Gov. 1923-27.

PIERSON, Isaac (W N.J.) Aug. 15, 1770-Sept. 22, 1833; House 1827-31.

PIERSON, Jeremiah Halsey (F N.Y.) Sept. 13, 1766-Dec. 12, 1855; House 1821-23.

PIERSON, Job (D N.Y.) Sept. 23, 1791-April 9, 1860; House 1831-35.

PIGOTT, James Protus (D Conn.) Sept. 11, 1852-July 1, 1919; House 1893-95.

PIKE, Austin Franklin (R N.H.) Oct. 16, 1819-Oct. 8, 1886; House 1873-75; Senate 1883-Oct. 8, 1886.

PIKE, Frederick Augustus (R Maine) Dec. 9, 1816-Dec. 2, 1886; House 1861-69.

PIKE, James (AP N.H.) Nov. 10, 1818-July 26, 1895; House 1855-59.

PIKE, Otis G. (D N.Y.) Aug. 31, 1921-—; House 1961-79.

PILCHER, John Leonard (D Ga.) Aug. 27, 1898-Aug. 20, 1981; House Feb. 4, 1953-65.

PILE, William Anderson (R Mo.) Feb. 11, 1829-July 7, 1889; House 1867-69; Gov. (N.M.) 1869-70.

PILES, Samuel Henry (R Wash.) Dec. 28, 1858-March 11, 1940; Senate 1905-11.

PILLION, John Raymond (R N.Y.) Aug. 10, 1904-Dec. 31, 1978; House 1953-65.

PILSBURY, Timothy (Cal.D Texas) April 12, 1789-Nov. 23, 1858; House March 30, 1846-49.

PINCKNEY, Charles (father of Henry Laurens Pinckney) (D S.C.) Oct. 26, 1757-Oct. 29, 1824; Senate Dec. 6, 1798-1801; House 1819-21; Cont. Cong. 1784-87; Gov. 1789-92, 1796-98, 1806-08.

PINCKNEY, Henry Laurens (son of Charles Pinckney) (D S.C.) Sept. 24, 1794-Feb. 3, 1863; House 1833-37.

PINCKNEY, John McPherson (D Texas) May 4, 1845-April 24, 1905; House Nov. 17, 1903-April 24, 1905.

PINCKNEY, Thomas (F S.C.) Oct. 23, 1750-Nov. 2, 1828; House Nov. 23, 1797-1801; Gov. 1787-89.

PINDALL, James (F Va.) about 1783-Nov. 22, 1825; House 1817-July 26, 1820.

PINDAR, John Sigsbee (D N.Y.) Nov. 18, 1835-June 30, 1907; House 1885-87; Nov. 4, 1890-91.

PINE, William Bliss (R Okla.) Dec. 30, 1877-Aug. 25, 1942; Senate 1925-31.

PINERO, Jesus T. (PD P.R.) April 16, 1897-Nov. 19, 1952; House (Res. Comm.) 1945-Sept. 2, 1946; Gov. 1946-48.

PINKNEY, William (— Md.) March 17, 1764-Feb. 25, 1822; House March 4-Nov. 1791, 1815-April 18, 1816; Senate Dec. 21, 1819-Feb. 25, 1822; Atty. Gen. 1811-14.

PIPER, William (— Pa.) Jan. 1, 1774-1852; House 1811-17.

PIPER, William Adam (D Calif.) May 21, 1826-Aug. 5, 1899; House 1875-77.

PIRCE, William Almy (R R.I.) Feb. 29, 1824-March 5, 1891; House 1885-Jan. 25, 1887.

PIRNIE, Alexander (R N.Y.) April 16, 1903-June 12, 1982; House 1959-73.

PITCHER, Nathaniel (D N.Y.) 1777-May 25, 1836; House 1819-23, 1831-33.

PITKIN, Timothy (F Conn.) Jan. 21, 1766-Dec. 18, 1847; House Sept. 16, 1805-19.

PITMAN, Charles Wesley (W Pa.) ?-June 8, 1871; House 1849-51.

PITNEY, Mahlon (R N.J.) Feb. 5, 1858-Dec. 9, 1924; House 1895-Jan. 10, 1899; Assoc. Justice Supreme Court 1912-22.

PITTENGER, William Alvin (R Minn.) Dec. 29, 1885-Nov. 26, 1951; House 1929-33, 1935-37, 1939-47.

PITTMAN, Key (D Nev.) Sept. 19, 1872-Nov. 10, 1940; Senate Jan. 29, 1913-Nov. 10, 1940; Pres. pro tempore March 9, 1933-Nov. 10, 1940.

PLAISTED, Harris Merrill (R Maine) Nov. 2, 1828-Jan. 31, 1898; House Sept. 13, 1875-77; Gov. 1881-83.

PLANT, David (NR Conn.) March 29, 1783-Oct. 18, 1851; House 1827-29.

PLANTS, Tobias Avery (R Ohio) March 17, 1811-June 19, 1887; House 1865-69.

PLATER, Thomas (— Md.) May 9, 1769-May 1, 1830; House 1801-05.

PLATT, Edmund (R N.Y.) Feb. 2, 1865-Aug. 7, 1939; House 1913-June 7, 1920.

PLATT, James Henry Jr. (R Va.) July 13, 1837-Aug. 13, 1894; House Jan. 26, 1870-75.

PLATT, Jonas (F N.Y.) June 30, 1769-Feb. 22, 1834; House 1799-1801.

PLATT, Orville Hitchcock (R Conn.) July 19, 1827-April 21, 1905; Senate 1879-April 21, 1905.

PLATT, Thomas Collier (R N.Y.) July 15, 1833-March 6, 1910; House 1873-77; Senate March 4-May 16, 1881, 1897-1909.

PLAUCHE, Vance Gabriel (D La.) Aug. 25, 1897-April 2, 1976; House 1941-43.

PLEASANTS, James (D Va.) Oct. 24, 1769-Nov. 9, 1836; House 1811-Dec. 14, 1819; Senate Dec. 14, 1819-Dec. 15, 1822; Gov. 1822-25.

PLOESER, Walter Christian (R Mo.) Jan. 7, 1907-—; House 1941-49.

PLOWMAN, Thomas Scales (D Ala.) June 8, 1843-July 26, 1919; House 1897-Feb. 9, 1898.

PLUMB, Preston B. (R Kan.) Oct. 12, 1837-Dec. 20, 1891; Senate 1877-Dec. 20, 1891.

PLUMB, Ralph (R Ill.) March 29, 1816-April 8, 1903; House 1885-89.

PLUMER, Arnold (D Pa.) June 6, 1801-April 28, 1869; House 1837-39, 1841-43.

PLUMER, George (D Pa.) Dec. 5, 1762-June 8, 1843; House 1821-27.

PLUMER, William (father of William Plumer Jr.) (F N.H.) June 25, 1759-Dec. 22, 1850; Senate June 17, 1802-07; Gov. 1812-13, 1816-19 (1812-19 Democrat).

PLUMER, William Jr. (son of William Plumer) (D N.H.) Feb. 9, 1789-Sept. 18, 1854; House 1819-25.

PLUMLEY, Charles Albert (son of Frank Plumley) (R Vt.) April 14, 1875-Oct. 31, 1964; House Jan. 16, 1934-51.

PLUMLEY, Frank (father of Charles Albert Plumley) (R Vt.) Dec. 17, 1844-April 30, 1924; House 1909-15.

PLUMMER, Franklin E. (— Miss.) ?-Sept. 24, 1847; House 1831-35.

POAGE, William Robert (D Texas) Dec. 28, 1899-—; House 1937-Dec. 31, 1978.

PODELL, Bertram L. (D N.Y.) Dec. 27, 1925-—; House Feb. 20, 1968-75.

POEHLER, Henry (D Minn.) Aug. 22, 1833-July 18, 1912; House 1879-81.

POFF, Richard Harding (R Va.) Oct. 19, 1923-—; House 1953-Aug. 29, 1972.

POINDEXTER, George (— Miss.) 1779-Sept. 5, 1855; House (Terr. Del.) 1807-13; (Rep.) Dec. 10, 1817-19; Senate Oct. 15, 1830-35; Pres. pro tempore 1834; Gov. 1820-22.

POINDEXTER, Miles (R Wash.) April 22, 1868-Sept. 21, 1946; House 1909-11; Senate 1911-23.

POINSETT, Joel Roberts (D S.C.) March 2, 1779-Dec. 12, 1851; House 1821-March 7, 1825; Secy. of War 1837-41.

POLANCO-ABREU, Santiago (PD P.R.) Oct. 30, 1920- —; House 1965-69.

POLAND, Luke Potter (R Vt.) Nov. 1, 1815-July 2, 1887; Senate Nov. 21, 1865-67; House 1867-75, 1883-85.

POLK, Albert Fawcett (D Del.) Oct. 11, 1869-Feb. 14, 1955; House 1917-19.

POLK, James Gould (D Ohio) Oct. 6, 1896-April 28, 1959; House 1931-41, 1949-April 28, 1959.

POLK, James Knox (brother of William Hawkins Polk) (D Tenn.) Nov. 2, 1795-June 15, 1849; House 1825-39; Speaker 1835-39; Gov. 1839-41; President 1845-49.

POLK, Rufus King (D Pa.) Aug. 23, 1866-March 5, 1902; House 1899-March 5, 1902.

POLK, Trusten (D Mo.) May 29, 1811-April 16, 1876; Senate 1857-Jan. 10, 1862; Gov. 1857.

POLK, William Hawkins (brother of James Knox Polk) (D Tenn.) May 24, 1815-Dec. 16, 1862; House 1851-53.

POLLARD, Ernest Mark (R Neb.) April 15, 1869-Sept. 24, 1939; House July 18, 1905-09.

POLLARD, Henry Moses (R Mo.) June 14, 1836-Feb. 23, 1904; House 1877-79.

POLLOCK, Howard W. (R Alaska) April 11, 1920- —; House 1967-71.

POLLOCK, James (W Pa.) Sept. 11, 1810-April 19, 1890; House April 5, 1844-49; Gov. 1855-58.

POLLOCK, William Pegues (D S.C.) Dec. 9, 1870-June 2, 1922; Senate Nov. 6, 1918-19.

POLSLEY, Daniel Haymond (R W.Va.) Nov. 28, 1803-Oct. 14, 1877; House 1867-69.

POMERENE, Atlee (D Ohio) Dec. 6, 1863-Nov. 12, 1937; Senate 1911-23.

POMEROY, Charles (R Iowa) Sept. 3, 1825-Feb. 11, 1891; House 1869-71.

POMEROY, Samuel Clarks (R Kan.) Jan. 3, 1816-Aug. 27, 1891; Senate April 4, 1861-73.

POMEROY, Theodore Medad (R N.Y.) Dec. 31, 1824-March 23, 1905; House 1861-69; Speaker, Dec. 7, 1868-March 3, 1869.

POND, Benjamin (D N.Y.) 1768-Oct. 6, 1814; House 1811-13.

POOL, Joe Richard (D Texas) Feb. 18, 1911-July 14, 1968; House 1963-July 14, 1968.

POOL, John (uncle of Walter Freshwater Pool) (W N.C.) June 16, 1826-Aug. 16, 1884; Senate July 4, 1868-73.

POOL, Walter Freshwater (nephew of John Pool) (R N.C.) Oct. 10, 1850-Aug. 25, 1883; House March 4-Aug. 25, 1883.

POOLE, Theodore Lewis (R N.Y.) April 10, 1840-Dec. 23, 1900; House 1895-97.

POPE, James Pinckney (D Idaho) March 31, 1884-Jan. 23, 1966; Senate 1933-39.

POPE, John (D Ky.) 1770-July 12, 1845; Senate 1807-13; House 1837-43; Pres. pro tempore 1811; Gov. (Ark. Terr.) 1829-35.

POPE, Nathaniel (— Ill.) Jan. 5, 1784-Jan. 22, 1850; House (Terr. Del.) Sept. 5, 1816-Sept. 5, 1818.

POPE, Patrick Hamilton (D Ky.) March 17, 1806-May 4, 1841; House 1833-35.

POPPLETON, Earley Franklin (D Ohio) Sept. 29, 1834-May 6, 1899; House 1875-77.

PORTER, Albert Gallatin (R Ind.) April 20, 1824-May 3, 1897; House 1859-63; Gov. 1881-85.

PORTER, Alexander (W La.) 1786-Jan. 13, 1844; Senate Dec. 19, 1833-Jan. 5, 1837.

PORTER, Augustus Seymour (nephew of Peter Buell Porter) (W Mich.) Jan. 18, 1798-Sept. 18, 1872; Senate Jan. 20, 1840-45.

PORTER, Charles Howell (R Va.) June 21, 1833-July 9, 1897; House Jan. 26, 1870-73.

PORTER, Charles Orlando (D Ore.) April 4, 1919- —; House 1957-61.

PORTER, Gilchrist (W Mo.) Nov. 1, 1817-Nov. 1, 1894; House 1851-53, 1855-57.

PORTER, Henry Kirke (— Pa.) Nov. 24, 1840-April 10, 1921; House 1903-05.

PORTER, James (D N.Y.) April 18, 1787-Feb. 7, 1839; House 1817-19.

PORTER, John (— Pa.) ?-?; House Dec. 8, 1806-11.

PORTER, John Edward (R Ill.) June 1, 1935- —; House Jan. 24, 1980- —.

PORTER, Peter Augustus (grandson of Peter Buell Porter) (IR/D N.Y.) Oct. 10, 1853-Dec. 15, 1925; House 1907-09.

PORTER, Peter Buell (grandfather of Peter Augustus Porter, uncle of Augustus Seymour Porter) (D N.Y.) Aug. 4, 1773-March 20, 1844; House 1809-13, 1815-Jan. 23, 1816; Secy. of War 1828-29.

PORTER, Stephen Geyer (R Pa.) May 18, 1869-June 27, 1930; House 1911-June 27, 1930.

PORTER, Timothy H. (— N.Y.) ?-about 1840; House 1825-27.

POSEY, Francis Blackburn (R Ind.) April 28, 1848-Oct. 31, 1915; House Jan. 29-March 3, 1889.

POSEY, Thomas (— La.) July 9, 1750-March 19, 1818; Senate Oct. 8, 1812-Feb. 4, 1813; Gov. (Ind. Terr.) 1813-16.

POST, George Adams (D Pa.) Sept. 1, 1854-Oct. 31, 1925; House 1883-85.

POST, James Douglas (D Ohio) Nov. 25, 1863-April 1, 1921; House 1911-15.

POST, Jotham Jr. (F N.Y.) April 4, 1771-May 15, 1817; House 1813-15.

POST, Morton Everel (D Wyo.) Dec. 25, 1840-March 19, 1933; House (Terr. Del.) 1881-85.

POST, Philip Sidney (R Ill.) March 19, 1833-Jan. 6, 1895; House 1887-Jan. 6, 1895.

POSTON, Charles Debrille (R Ariz.) April 20, 1825-June 24, 1902; House (Terr. Del.) Dec. 5, 1864-65.

POTTER, Allen (I Mich.) Oct. 2, 1818-May 8, 1885; House 1875-77.

POTTER, Charles Edward (R Mich.) Oct. 30, 1916-Nov. 23, 1979; House Aug. 26, 1947-Nov. 4, 1952; Senate Nov. 5, 1952-59.

POTTER, Clarkson Nott (D N.Y.) April 25, 1825-Jan. 23, 1882; House 1869-75, 1877-79.

POTTER, Elisha Reynolds (father of the following) (F R.I.) Nov. 5, 1764-Sept. 26, 1835; House Nov. 15, 1796-97, 1809-15.

POTTER, Elisha Reynolds (son of the preceding) (W R.I.) June 20, 1811-April 10, 1882; House 1843-45.

POTTER, Emery Davis (D Ohio) Oct. 7, 1804-Feb. 12, 1896; House 1843-45, 1849-51.

POTTER, John Fox (R Wis.) May 11, 1817-May 18, 1899; House 1857-63.

POTTER, Orlando Brunson (UD N.Y.) March 10, 1823-Jan. 2, 1894; House 1883-85.

POTTER, Robert (JD N.C.) about 1800-March 2, 1841; House 1829-Nov. 1831.

POTTER, Samuel John (— R.I.) June 29, 1753-Oct. 14, 1804; Senate 1803-Oct. 14, 1804.

POTTER, William Wilson (D Pa.) Dec. 18, 1792-Oct. 28, 1839; House 1837-Oct. 28, 1839.

POTTLE, Emory Bemsley (R N.Y.) July 4, 1815-April 18, 1891; House 1857-61.

POTTS, David Jr. (W Pa.) Nov. 27, 1794-June 1, 1863; House 1831-39.

POTTS, David Matthew (R N.Y.) March 12, 1906-Sept. 11, 1976; House 1947-49.

POTTS, Richard (F Md.) July 19, 1753-Nov. 26, 1808; Senate Jan. 10, 1793-Oct. 24, 1796; Cont. Cong. 1781-82.

POU, Edward William (cousin of James Paul Buchanan) (D N.C.) Sept. 9, 1863-April 1, 1934; House 1901-April 1, 1934.

POULSON, C. Norris (R Calif.) July 23, 1895-Sept. 25, 1982; House 1943-45, 1947-June 11, 1953.

POUND, Thaddeus Coleman (R Wis.) Dec. 6, 1833-Nov. 21, 1914; House 1877-83.

POWELL, Adam Clayton Jr. (D N.Y.) Nov. 29, 1908-April 4, 1972; House 1945-67, 1969-71.

POWELL, Alfred H. (— Va.) March 6, 1781-1831; House 1825-27.

POWELL, Cuthbert (son of Levin Powell) (W Va.) March 4, 1775-May 8, 1849; House 1841-43.

POWELL, Joseph (D Pa.) June 23, 1828-April 24, 1904; House 1875-77.

POWELL, Lazarus Whitehead (D Ky.) Oct. 6, 1812-July 3, 1867; Senate 1859-65; Gov. 1851-55.

POWELL, Levin (father of Cuthbert Powell) (F Va.) 1737-Aug. 23, 1810; House 1799-1801.

POWELL, Paulus (D Va.) 1809-June 10, 1874; House 1849-59.

POWELL, Samuel (– Tenn.) July 10, 1776-Aug. 2, 1841; House 1815-17.

POWELL, Walter E. (R Ohio) April 25, 1931-–; House 1971-75.

POWER, Thomas Charles (R Mont.) May 22, 1839-Feb. 16, 1923; Senate Jan. 2, 1890-95.

POWERS, Caleb (R Ky.) Feb. 1, 1869-July 25, 1932; House 1911-19.

POWERS, David Lane (R N.J.) July 29, 1896-March 28, 1968; House 1933-Aug. 30, 1945.

POWERS, Gershom (JD N.Y.) July 11, 1789-June 25, 1831; House 1829-31.

POWERS, Horace Henry (R Vt.) May 29, 1835-Dec. 8, 1913; House 1891-1901.

POWERS, Llewellyn (R Maine) Oct. 14, 1836-July 28, 1908; House 1877-79; April 8, 1901-July 28, 1908; Gov. 1897-1901.

POWERS, Samuel Leland (R Mass.) Oct. 26, 1848-Nov. 30, 1929; House 1901-05.

POYDRAS, Julien de Lallande (– Orleans) April 3, 1740-June 14, 1824; House (Terr. Del.) 1809-11.

PRACHT, Charles Frederick (R Pa.) Oct. 20, 1880-Dec. 22, 1950; House 1943-45.

PRALL, Anning Smith (D N.Y.) Sept. 17, 1870-July 23, 1937; House Nov. 6, 1923-35.

PRATT, Charles Clarence (R Pa.) April 23, 1854-Jan. 27, 1916; House 1909-11.

PRATT, Daniel Darwin (R Ind.) Oct. 26, 1813-June 17, 1877; Senate 1869-75.

PRATT, Eliza Jane (D N.C.) March 5, 1902-May 13, 1981; House May 25, 1946-47.

PRATT, Harcourt Joseph (R N.Y.) Oct. 23, 1866-May 21, 1934; House 1925-33.

PRATT, Harry Hayt (R N.Y.) Nov. 11, 1864-Nov. 13, 1932; House 1915-19.

PRATT, Henry Otis (R Iowa) Feb. 11, 1838-May 22, 1931; House 1873-77.

PRATT, James Timothy (D Conn.) Dec. 14, 1802-April 11, 1887; House 1853-55.

PRATT, Joseph Marmaduke (R Pa.) Sept. 4, 1891-July 19, 1946; House Jan. 18, 1944-45.

PRATT, Le Gage (D N.J.) Dec. 14, 1852-March 9, 1911; House 1907-09.

PRATT, Ruth Sears Baker (R N.Y.) Aug. 24, 1877-Aug. 23, 1965; House 1929-33.

PRATT, Thomas George (W Md.) Feb. 18, 1804-Nov. 9, 1869; Senate Jan. 12, 1850-57; Gov. 1845-48.

PRATT, Zadock (D N.Y.) Oct. 30, 1790-April 6, 1871; House 1837-39, 1843-45.

PRAY, Charles Nelson (R Mont.) April 6, 1868-Sept. 12, 1963; House 1907-13.

PRENTISS, John Holmes (brother of Samuel Prentiss) (D N.Y.) April 17, 1784-June 26, 1861; House 1837-41.

PRENTISS, Samuel (brother of John Holmes Prentiss) (W Vt.) March 31, 1782-Jan. 15, 1857; Senate 1831-April 11, 1842.

PRENTISS, Sergeant Smith (– Miss.) Sept. 30, 1808-July 1, 1850; House May 30, 1838-39.

PRESCOTT, Cyrus Dan (R N.Y.) Aug. 15, 1836-Oct. 23, 1902; House 1879-83.

PRESSLER, Larry Lee (R S.D.) March 29, 1942-–; House 1975-79; Senate 1979-–.

PRESTON, Francis (father of William Campbell Preston, uncle of William Ballard Preston and William Preston) (– Va.) Aug. 2, 1765-May 26, 1836; House 1793-97.

PRESTON, Jacob Alexander (W Md.) March 12, 1796-Aug. 2, 1868; House 1843-45.

PRESTON, Prince Hulon Jr. (D Ga.) July 5, 1908-Feb. 8, 1961; House 1947-61.

PRESTON, William (nephew of Francis Preston) (W Ky.) Oct. 16, 1816-Sept. 21, 1887; House Dec. 6, 1852-55.

PRESTON, William Ballard (nephew of Francis Preston) (W Va.) Nov. 25, 1805-Nov. 16, 1862; House 1847-49; Secy. of the Navy 1849-50.

PRESTON, William Campbell (son of Francis Preston) (Cal.N S.C.) Dec. 27, 1794-May 22, 1860; House Nov. 26, 1833-Nov. 29, 1842.

PREYER, Lunsford Richardson (D N.C.) Jan. 11, 1919-–; House 1969-81.

PRICE, Andrew (D La.) April 2, 1854-Feb. 5, 1909; House Dec. 2, 1889-97.

PRICE, Charles Melvin (D Ill.) Jan. 1, 1905-–; House 1945-–.

PRICE, Emory Hilliard (D Fla.) Dec. 3, 1899-Feb. 11, 1976; House 1943-49.

PRICE, Hiram (R Iowa) Jan. 10, 1814-May 30, 1901; House 1863-69, 1877-81.

PRICE, Hugh Hiram (son of William Thompson Price) (R Wis.) Dec. 2, 1859-Dec. 25, 1904; House Jan. 18-March 3, 1887.

PRICE, Jesse Dashiell (D Md.) Aug. 15, 1863-May 14, 1939; House Nov. 3, 1914-19.

PRICE, Robert Dale (Bob) (R Texas) Sept. 7, 1927-–; House 1967-75.

PRICE, Rodman McCamley (D N.J.) May 5, 1816-June 7, 1894; House 1851-53; Gov. 1854-57.

PRICE, Samuel (– W.Va.) July 28, 1805-Feb. 25, 1884; Senate Aug. 26, 1876-Jan. 26, 1877.

PRICE, Sterling (D Mo.) Sept. 20, 1809-Sept. 29, 1867; House 1845-Aug. 12, 1846; Gov. 1853-57.

PRICE, Thomas Lawson (D Mo.) Jan. 19, 1809-July 15, 1870; House Jan. 21, 1862-63.

PRICE, William Pierce (D Ga.) Jan. 29, 1835-Nov. 4, 1908; House Dec. 22, 1870-73.

PRICE, William Thompson (father of Hugh Hiram Price) (R Wis.) June 17, 1824-Dec. 6, 1886; House 1883-Dec. 6, 1886.

PRIDEMORE, Auburn Lorenzo (D Va.) June 27, 1837-May 17, 1900; House 1877-79.

PRIEST, James Percy (D Tenn.) April 1, 1900-Oct. 12, 1956; House 1941-Oct. 12, 1956.

PRINCE, Charles Henry (R Ga.) May 9, 1837-April 3, 1912; House July 25, 1868-69.

PRINCE, George Washington (R Ill.) March 4, 1854-Sept. 26, 1939; House Dec. 2, 1895-1913.

PRINCE, Oliver Hillhouse (– Ga.) 1787-Oct. 9, 1837; Senate Nov. 7, 1828-29.

PRINCE, William (– Ind.) 1772-Sept. 8, 1824; House 1823-Sept. 8, 1824.

PRINDLE, Elizur H. (R N.Y.) May 6, 1829-Oct. 7, 1890; House 1871-73.

PRINGEY, Joseph Colburn (R Okla.) May 22, 1858-Feb. 11, 1935; House 1921-23.

PRINGLE, Benjamin (W N.Y.) Nov. 9, 1807-June 7, 1887; House 1853-57.

PRITCHARD, George Moore (son of Jeter Connelly Pritchard) (R N.C.) Jan. 4, 1886-April 24, 1955; House 1929-31.

PRITCHARD, Jeter Connelly (father of George Moore Pritchard) (R N.C.) July 12, 1857-April 10, 1921; Senate Jan. 23, 1895-1903.

PRITCHARD, Joel McFee (R Wash.) May 5, 1925-–; House 1973-85.

PROCTOR, Redfield (R Vt.) June 1, 1831-March 4, 1908; Senate Nov. 2, 1891-March 4, 1908; Gov. 1878-80; Secy. of War 1889-91.

PROFFIT, George H. (W Ind.) Sept. 7, 1807-Sept. 7, 1847; House 1839-43.

PROKOP, Stanley A. (D Pa.) ?-Nov. 11, 1977; House 1959-61.

PROSSER, William Farrand (R Tenn.) March 16, 1834-Sept. 23, 1911; House 1869-71.

PROUTY, Solomon Francis (R Iowa) Jan. 17, 1854-July 16, 1927; House 1911-15.

PROUTY, Winston Lewis (R Vt.) Sept. 1, 1906-Sept. 10, 1971; House 1951-59; Senate 1959-Sept. 10, 1971.

PROXMIRE, William (D Wis.) Nov. 11, 1915-–; Senate Aug. 28, 1957-–.

PRUYN, John Van Schaick Lansing (D N.Y.) June 22, 1811-Nov. 21, 1877; House Dec. 7, 1863-65, 1867-69.

PRYOR, David Hampton (D Ark.) Aug. 29, 1934-–; House Nov. 8, 1966-73; Senate 1979-–; Gov. 1975-79.

PRYOR, Luke (D Ala.) July 5, 1820-Aug. 5, 1900; Senate Jan. 7-Nov. 23, 1880; House 1883-85.

PRYOR, Roger Atkinson (D Va.) July 19, 1828-March 14, 1919; House Dec. 7, 1859-61.

PUCINSKI, Roman Conrad (D Ill.) May 13, 1919-–; House 1959-73.

PUGH, George Ellis (D Ohio) Nov. 28, 1822-July 19, 1876; Senate 1855-61.

PUGH, James Lawrence (D Ala.) Dec. 12, 1820-March 9, 1907; House 1859-Jan. 21, 1861; Senate Nov. 24, 1880-97.

PUGH, John (D Pa.) June 2, 1761-July 13, 1842; House 1805-09.

PUGH, John Howard (R N.J.) June 23, 1827-April 30, 1905; House 1877-79.

PUGH, Samuel Johnson (R Ky.) Jan. 28, 1850-April 17, 1922; House 1895-1901.

PUGSLEY, Cornelius Amory (D N.Y.) July 17, 1850-Sept. 10, 1936; House 1901-03.

PUGSLEY, Jacob Joseph (R Ohio) Jan. 25, 1838-Feb. 5, 1920; House 1887-91.

PUJO, Arsène Paulin (D La.) Dec. 16, 1861-Dec. 31, 1939; House 1903-13.

PULITZER, Joseph (D N.Y.) April 10, 1847-Oct. 29, 1911; House 1885-April 10, 1886.

PURCELL, Graham Boynton Jr. (D Texas) May 5, 1919- —; House Jan. 27, 1962-73.

PURCELL, William Edward (D N.D.) Aug. 3, 1856-Nov. 23, 1928; Senate Feb. 1, 1910-Feb. 1, 1911.

PURDY, Smith Meade (D N.Y.) July 31, 1796-March 30, 1870; House 1843-45.

PURMAN, William James (R Fla.) April 11, 1840-Aug. 14, 1928; House 1873-Jan. 25, 1875, March 4, 1875-77.

PURNELL, Fred Sampson (R Ind.) Oct. 25, 1882-Oct. 21, 1939; House 1917-33.

PURSELL, Carl Duane (R Mich.) Dec. 19, 1932- —; House 1977- —.

PURTELL, William Arthur (R Conn.) May 6, 1897-May 31, 1978; Senate Aug. 29-Nov. 4, 1952, 1953-59.

PURVIANCE, Samuel Anderson (W Pa.) Jan. 10, 1809-Feb. 14, 1882; House 1855-59.

PURVIANCE, Samuel Dinsmore (F N.C.) Jan. 7, 1774-about 1806; House 1803-05.

PURYEAR, Richard Clauselle (W N.C.) Feb. 9, 1801-July 30, 1867; House 1853-57.

PUSEY, William Henry Mills (D Iowa) July 29, 1826-Nov. 15, 1900; House 1883-85.

PUTNAM, Harvey (W N.Y.) Jan. 5, 1793-Sept. 20, 1855; House Nov. 7, 1838-39, 1847-51.

PYLE, Gladys (R S.D.) Oct. 4, 1890- —; Senate Nov. 9, 1938-39.

Q

QUACKENBUSH, John Adam (R N.Y.) Oct. 15, 1828-May 11, 1908; House 1889-93.

QUARLES, James Minor (W Tenn.) Feb. 8, 1823-March 3, 1901; House 1859-61.

QUARLES, Joseph Very (R Wis.) Dec. 16, 1843-Oct. 7, 1911; Senate 1899-1905.

QUARLES, Julian Minor (D Va.) Sept. 25, 1848-Nov. 18, 1929; House 1899-1901.

QUARLES, Tunstall (D Ky.) about 1770-Jan. 7, 1855; House 1817-June 15, 1820.

QUAY, Matthew Stanley (R Pa.) Sept. 30, 1833-May 28, 1904; Senate 1887-99, Jan. 16, 1901-May 28, 1904; Chrmn. Rep. Nat. Comm. 1888-91.

QUAYLE, James Danforth (R Ind.) Feb. 4, 1947- —; House 1977-81; Senate 1981- —.

QUAYLE, John Francis (D N.Y.) Dec. 1, 1868-Nov. 27, 1930; House 1923-Nov. 27, 1930.

QUEZON, Manuel Luis (Nat. P.I.) Aug. 19, 1878-Aug. 1, 1944; House (Res. Comm.) Nov. 23, 1909-Oct. 15, 1916; Pres. (P.I.) 1935-44.

QUIE, Albert Harold (R Minn.) Sept. 18, 1923- —; House Feb. 18, 1958-79; Gov. 1979-83.

QUIGG, Lemuel Ely (R N.Y.) Feb. 12, 1863-July 1, 1919; House Jan. 30, 1894-99.

QUIGLEY, James Michael (D Pa.) March 30, 1918- —; House 1955-57, 1959-61.

QUILLEN, James H. (Jimmy) (R Tenn.) Jan. 11, 1916- —; House 1963- —.

QUIN, Percy Edwards (D Miss.) Oct. 30, 1872-Feb. 4, 1932; House 1913-Feb. 4, 1932.

QUINCY, Josiah (F Mass.) Feb. 4, 1772-July 1, 1864; House 1805-13.

QUINN, James Leland (D Pa.) Sept. 8, 1875-Nov. 12, 1960; House 1935-39.

QUINN, John (D N.Y.) Aug. 9, 1839-Feb. 23, 1903; House 1889-91.

QUINN, Peter Anthony (D N.Y.) May 10, 1904-Dec. 23, 1974; House 1945-47.

QUINN, Terence John (D N.Y.) Oct. 16, 1836-June 18, 1878; House 1877-June 18, 1878.

QUINN, Thomas Vincent (D N.Y.) March 16, 1903- —; House 1949-Dec. 30, 1951.

QUITMAN, John Anthony (D Miss.) Sept. 1, 1799-July 17, 1858; House 1855-July 17, 1858; Gov. 1850-51.

R

RABAUT, Louis Charles (D Mich.) Dec. 5, 1886-Nov. 12, 1961; House 1935-47, 1949-Nov. 12, 1961.

RABIN, Benjamin J. (D N.Y.) June 3, 1896-Feb. 22, 1969; House 1945-Dec. 31, 1947.

RACE, John Abner (D Wis.) May 12, 1914-Nov. 10, 1983; House 1965-67.

RADCLIFFE, Amos Henry (R N.J.) Jan. 16, 1870-Dec. 29, 1950; House 1919-23.

RADCLIFFE, George Lovick (D Md.) Aug. 22, 1877-July 29, 1974; Senate 1935-47.

RADFORD, William (D N.Y.) June 24, 1814-Jan. 18, 1870; House 1863-67.

RADWAN, Edmund Patrick (R N.Y.) Sept. 22, 1911-Sept. 7, 1959; House 1951-59.

RAGON, Heartsill (D Ark.) March 20, 1885-Sept. 15, 1940; House 1923-June 16, 1933.

RAGSDALE, James Willard (D S.C.) Dec. 14, 1872-July 23, 1919; House 1913-July 23, 1919.

RAHALL, Nick Joe II (D W.Va.) May 20, 1949- —; House 1977- —.

RAILSBACK, Thomas F. (R Ill.) Jan. 22, 1932- —; House 1967-83.

RAINES, John (R N.Y.) May 6, 1840-Dec. 16, 1909; House 1889-93.

RAINEY, Henry Thomas (D Ill.) Aug. 20, 1860-Aug. 19, 1934; House 1903-21, 1923-Aug. 19, 1934; House majority leader 1931-33; Speaker 1933-34.

RAINEY, John William (D Ill.) Dec. 21, 1880-May 4, 1923; House April 2, 1918-May 4, 1923.

RAINEY, Joseph Hayne (R S.C.) June 21, 1832-Aug. 2, 1887; House Dec. 12, 1870-79.

RAINEY, Lilius Bratton (D Ala.) July 27, 1876-Sept. 27, 1959; House Sept. 30, 1919-23.

RAINS, Albert M. (D Ala.) March 11, 1902- —; House 1945-65.

RAKER, John Edward (D Calif.) Feb. 22, 1863-Jan. 22, 1926; House 1911-Jan. 22, 1926.

RALSTON, Samuel Moffett (D Ind.) Dec. 1, 1857-Oct. 14, 1925; Senate 1923-Oct. 14, 1925; Gov. 1913-17.

RAMEY, Frank Marion (R Ill.) Sept. 23, 1881-March 27, 1942; House 1929-31.

RAMEY, Homer Alonzo (R Ohio) March 2, 1891-April 13, 1960; House 1943-49.

RAMSAY, Robert Lincoln (D W.Va.) March 24, 1877-Nov. 14, 1956; House 1933-39, 1941-43, 1949-53.

RAMSEY, Alexander (W Pa./R Minn.) Sept. 8, 1815-April 22, 1903; House (W Pa.) 1843-47; Senate (R Minn.) 1863-75; Gov. 1849-53 (Minn. Terr.), 1860-63 (Minn. State); Secy. of War 1879-81.

RAMSEY, John Rathbone (R N.J.) April 25, 1862-April 10, 1933; House 1917-21.

RAMSEY, Robert (W Pa.) Feb. 15, 1780-Dec. 12, 1849; House 1833-35, 1841-43.

RAMSEY, William (D Pa.) Sept. 7, 1779-Sept. 29, 1831; House 1827-Sept. 29, 1831.

RAMSEY, William Sterrett (D Pa.) June 12, 1810-Oct. 17, 1840; House 1839-Oct. 17, 1840.

RAMSEYER, Christian William (R Iowa) March 13, 1875-Nov. 1, 1943; House 1915-33.

RAMSPECK, Robert C. Word (D Ga.) Sept. 5, 1890-Sept. 10, 1972; House Oct. 2, 1929-Dec. 31, 1945.

RANDALL, Alexander (W Md.) Jan. 3, 1803-Nov. 21, 1881; House 1841-43.

RANDALL, Benjamin (W Maine) Nov. 14, 1789-Oct. 11, 1859; House 1839-43.

RANDALL, Charles Hiram (Prohib./D/R/Prog. Calif.) July 23, 1865-Feb. 18, 1951; House 1915-21.

RANDALL, Charles Sturtevant (R Mass.) Feb. 20, 1824-Aug. 17, 1904; House 1889-95.

RANDALL, Clifford Ellsworth (R Wis.) Dec. 25, 1876-Oct. 16, 1934; House 1919-21.

RANDALL, Samuel Jackson (D Pa.) Oct. 10, 1828-April 13, 1890; House 1863-April 13, 1890; Speaker 1876-81.

RANDALL, William Harrison (R Ky.) July 15, 1812-Aug. 1, 1881; House 1863-67.

RANDALL, William Joseph (D Mo.) July 16, 1909- —; House March 3, 1959-77.

RANDELL, Choice Boswell (nephew of Lucius Jeremiah Gartrell) (D Texas) Jan. 1, 1857-Oct. 19, 1945; House 1901-13.

RANDOLPH, James Fitz (father of Theodore Fitz Randolph) (— N.J.) June 26, 1791-Jan. 25, 1872; House Dec. 1, 1827-33.

RANDOLPH, James Henry (R Tenn.) Oct. 18, 1825-Aug. 22, 1900; House 1877-79.

RANDOLPH, Jennings (D W.Va.) March 8, 1902- —; House 1933-47; Senate Nov. 5, 1958-85.

RANDOLPH, John (SRD Va.) June 2, 1773-May 24, 1833; House 1799-1813, 1815-17, 1819-Dec. 26, 1825, 1827-29, March 4-May 24, 1833; Senate Dec. 26, 1825-27.

RANDOLPH, Joseph Fitz (W N.J.) March 14, 1803-March 20, 1873; House 1837-43.

RANDOLPH, Theodore Fitz (son of James Fitz Randolph) (D N.J.) June 24, 1826-Nov. 7, 1883; Senate 1875-81; Gov. 1869-72.

RANDOLPH, Thomas Mann (D Va.) Oct. 1, 1768-June 20, 1828; House 1803-07; Gov. 1819-22.

RANEY, John Henry (R Mo.) Sept. 28, 1849-Jan. 23, 1928; House 1895-97.

RANGEL, Charles Bernard (D N.Y.) June 1, 1930- —; House 1971- —.

RANKIN, Christopher (D Miss.) 1788-March 14, 1826; House 1819-March 14, 1826.

RANKIN, Jeannette (R Mont.) June 11, 1880-May 18, 1973; House 1917-19, 1941-43.

RANKIN, John Elliott (D Miss.) March 29, 1882-Nov. 26, 1960; House 1921-53.

RANKIN, Joseph (D Wis.) Sept. 25, 1833-Jan. 24, 1886; House 1883-Jan. 24, 1886.

RANNEY, Ambrose Arnold (R Mass.) April 17, 1821-March 5, 1899; House 1881-87.

RANSDELL, Joseph Eugene (D La.) Oct. 7, 1858-July 27, 1954; House Aug. 29, 1899-1913; Senate 1913-31.

RANSIER, Alonzo Jacob (R S.C.) Jan. 3, 1834-Aug. 17, 1882; House 1873-75.

RANSLEY, Harry Clay (R Pa.) Feb. 5, 1863-Nov. 7, 1941; House Nov. 2, 1920-37.

RANSOM, Matt Whitaker (cousin of Wharton Jackson Green) (D N.C.) Oct. 8, 1826-Oct. 8, 1904; Senate Jan. 30, 1872-95; Pres. pro tempore 1895.

RANTOUL, Robert Jr. (D Mass.) Aug. 13, 1805-Aug. 7, 1852; Senate Feb. 1-March 3, 1851; House March 4, 1851-Aug. 7, 1852.

RAPIER, James Thomas (R Ala.) Nov. 13, 1837-May 31, 1883; House 1873-75.

RARICK, John Richard (D La.) Jan. 29, 1924- —; House 1967-75.

RARIDEN, James (W Ind.) Feb. 14, 1795-Oct. 20, 1856; House 1837-41.

RATCHFORD, William Richard (D Conn.) May 24, 1934- —; House 1979-85.

RATHBONE, Henry Riggs (grandson of Ira Harris) (R Ill.) Feb. 12, 1870-July 15, 1928; House 1923-July 15, 1928.

RATHBUN, George Oscar (D N.Y.) 1803-Jan. 5, 1870; House 1843-47.

RAUCH, George Washington (D Ind.) Feb. 22, 1876-Nov. 4, 1940; House 1907-17.

RAUM, Green Berry (R Ill.) Dec. 3, 1829-Dec. 18, 1909; House 1867-69.

RAWLINS, Joseph Lafayette (D Utah) March 28, 1850-May 24, 1926; House (Terr. Del.) 1893-95; Senate 1897-1903.

RAWLS, Morgan (D Ga.) June 29, 1829-Oct. 18, 1906; House 1873-March 24, 1874.

RAWSON, Charles Augustus (R Iowa) May 29, 1867-Sept. 2, 1936; Senate Feb. 24-Dec. 1, 1922.

RAY, George Washington (R N.Y.) Feb. 3, 1844-Jan. 10, 1925; House 1883-85, 1891-Sept. 11, 1902.

RAY, John Henry (R N.Y.) Sept. 27, 1886-May 21, 1975; House 1953-63.

RAY, Joseph Warren (R Pa.) May 25, 1849-Sept. 15, 1928; House 1889-91.

RAY, Ossian (R N.H.) Dec. 13, 1835-Jan. 28, 1892; House Jan. 8, 1881-85.

RAY, Richard Belmont (D Ga.) Feb. 2, 1927- —; House 1983- —.

RAY, William Henry (R Ill.) Dec. 14, 1812-Jan. 25, 1881; House 1873-75.

RAYBURN, Sam (D Texas) Jan. 6 1882-Nov. 16, 1961; House 1913-Nov. 16, 1961; House majority leader 1937-1940; Speaker 1940-47, 1949-53, 1955-61.

RAYFIEL, Leo Frederick (D N.Y.) March 22, 1888-Nov. 18, 1978; House 1945-Sept. 13, 1947.

RAYMOND, Henry Jarvis (R N.Y.) Jan. 24, 1820-June 18, 1869; House 1865-67; Chrmn. Rep. Nat. Comm. 1864-66.

RAYMOND, John Baldwin (R Dakota) Dec. 5, 1844-Jan. 3, 1886; House (Terr. Del.) 1883-85.

RAYNER, Isidor (D Md.) April 11, 1850-Nov. 25, 1912; House 1887-89, 1891-95; Senate 1905-Nov. 25, 1912.

RAYNER, Kenneth (W N.C.) June 20, 1808-March 4, 1884; House 1839-45.

REA, David (D Mo.) Jan. 19, 1831-June 13, 1901; House 1875-79.

REA, John (D Pa.) Jan. 27, 1755-Feb. 26, 1829; House 1803-11, May 11, 1813-15.

READ, Almon Heath (D Pa.) June 12, 1790-June 3, 1844; House March 18, 1842-June 3, 1844.

READ, George (— Del.) Sept. 18, 1733-Sept. 21, 1798; Senate 1789-Sept. 18, 1793; Cont. Cong. 1774-77.

READ, Jacob (F S.C.) 1751-July 17, 1816; Senate 1795-1801; Pres. pro tempore 1798; Cont. Cong. 1783-85.

READ, Nathan (F Mass.) July 2, 1759-Jan. 20, 1849; House Nov. 25, 1800-03.

READ, William Brown (D Ky.) Dec. 14, 1817-Aug. 5, 1880; House 1871-75.

READE, Edwin Godwin (AP N.C.) Nov. 13, 1812-Oct. 18, 1894; House 1855-57.

READING, John Roberts (D Pa.) Nov. 1, 1826-Feb. 14, 1886; House 1869-April 13, 1870.

READY, Charles (uncle of William T. Haskell) (W Tenn.) Dec. 22, 1802-June 4, 1878; House 1853-59.

REAGAN, John Henninger (D Texas) Oct. 8, 1818-March 6, 1905; House 1857-61, 1875-March 4, 1887; Senate March 4, 1887-June 10, 1891.

REAMES, Alfred Evan (D Ore.) Feb. 5, 1870-March 4, 1943; Senate Feb. 1-Nov. 8, 1938.

REAMS, Henry Frazier (I Ohio) Jan. 15, 1897-Sept. 15, 1971; House 1951-55.

REAVIS, Charles Frank (R Neb.) Sept. 5, 1870-May 26, 1932; House 1915-June 3, 1922.

REBER, John (R Pa.) Feb. 1, 1858-Sept. 26, 1931; House 1919-23.

REDDEN, Monroe Minor (D N.C.) Sept. 24, 1901- —; House 1947-53.

REDFIELD, William Cox (D N.Y.) June 18, 1858-June 13, 1932; House 1911-13; Secy. of Commerce 1913-19.

REDING, John Randall (D N.H.) Oct. 18, 1805-Oct. 8, 1892; House 1841-45.

REDLIN, Rolland W. (D N.D.) Feb. 29, 1920- —; House 1965-67.

REECE, Brazilla Carroll (husband of Louise Goff Reece) (R Tenn.) Dec. 22, 1889-March 19, 1961; House 1921-31, 1933-47, 1951-March 19, 1961; Chrmn. Rep. Nat. Comm. 1946-48.

REECE, Louise Goff (widow of Brazilla Carroll Reece, daughter of Guy Despard Goff, granddaughter of Nathan Goff) (R Tenn.) Nov. 6, 1898-May 14, 1970; House May 16, 1961-63.

REED, Charles Manning (W Pa.) April 3, 1803-Dec. 16, 1871; House 1843-45.

REED, Chauncey William (R Ill.) June 2, 1890-Feb. 9, 1956; House 1935-Feb. 9, 1956.

REED, Clyde Martin (R Kan.) Oct. 19, 1871-Nov. 8, 1949; Senate 1939-Nov. 8, 1949; Gov. 1929-31.

REED, Daniel Alden (R N.Y.) Sept. 15, 1875-Feb. 19, 1959; House 1919-Feb. 19, 1959.

REED, David Aiken (R Pa.) Dec. 21, 1880-Feb. 10, 1953; Senate Aug. 8, 1922-35.

REED, Edward Cambridge (D N.Y.) March 8, 1793-May 1, 1883; House 1831-33.

REED, Eugene Elliott (D N.H.) April 23, 1866-Dec. 15, 1940; House 1913-15.

REED, Isaac (W Maine) Aug. 22, 1809-Sept. 19, 1887; House June 25, 1852-53.

REED, James Alexander (D Mo.) Nov. 9, 1861-Sept. 8, 1944; Senate 1911-29.

REED, James Byron (D Ark.) Jan. 2, 1881-April 27, 1935; House Oct. 20, 1923-29.

REED, John (father of the following) (F Mass.) Nov. 11, 1751-Feb. 17, 1831; House 1795-1801.

REED, John (son of the preceding) (W Mass.) Sept. 2, 1781-Nov. 25, 1860; House 1813-17, 1821-41 (1813-17 Federalist, 1821-41 Whig).

REED, Joseph Rea (R Iowa) March 12, 1835-April 2, 1925; House 1889-91.

REED, Philip (— Md.) 1760-Nov. 2, 1829; Senate Nov. 25, 1806-13; House 1817-19, March 19, 1822-23.

REED, Robert Rentoul (W Pa.) March 12, 1807-Dec. 14, 1864; House 1849-51.

REED, Stuart Felix (R W.Va.) Jan. 8, 1866-July 4, 1935; House 1917-25.

REED, Thomas Brackett (R Maine) Oct. 18, 1839-Dec. 7, 1902; House 1877-Sept. 4, 1899; Speaker 1889-91, 1895-99.

REED, Thomas Buck (D Miss.) May 7, 1787-Nov. 26, 1829; Senate Jan. 28, 1826-27, March 4-Nov. 26, 1829.

REED, William (F Mass.) June 6, 1776-Feb. 18, 1837; House 1811-15.

REEDER, William Augustus (R Kan.) Aug. 28, 1849-Nov. 7, 1929; House 1899-1911.

REES, Edward Herbert (R Kan.) June 3, 1886-Oct. 25, 1969; House 1937-61.

REES, Rollin Raymond (R Kan.) Jan. 10, 1865-May 30, 1935; House 1911-13.

REES, Thomas M. (D Calif.) March 26, 1925- —; House Dec. 15, 1965-77.

REESE, David Addison (W Ga.) March 3, 1794-Dec. 16, 1871; House 1853-55.

REESE, Seaborn (D Ga.) Nov. 28, 1846-March 1, 1907; House Dec. 4, 1882-87.

REEVES, Albert Lee Jr. (R Mo.) May 31, 1906- —; House 1947-49.

REEVES, Henry Augustus (D N.Y.) Dec. 7, 1832-March 4, 1916; House 1869-71.

REEVES, Walter (R Ill.) Sept. 25, 1848-April 9, 1909; House 1895-1903.

REGAN, Kenneth Mills (D Texas) March 6, 1893-Aug. 15, 1959; House Aug. 23, 1947-55.

REGULA, Ralph Strauss (R Ohio) Dec. 3, 1924- —; House 1973- —.

REID, Charles Chester (D Ark.) June 15, 1868-May 20, 1922; House 1901-11.

REID, Charlotte Thompson (R Ill.) Sept. 27, 1913- —; House 1963-Oct. 7, 1971.

REID, David Settle (nephew of Thomas Settle) (D N.C.) April 19, 1813-June 19, 1891; House 1843-47; Senate Dec. 6, 1854-59; Gov. 1851-54.

REID, Frank R. (R Ill.) April 18, 1879-Jan. 25, 1945; House 1923-35.

REID, Harry (D Nev.) Dec. 2, 1939- —; House 1983- —.

REID, James Wesley (D N.C.) June 11, 1849-Jan. 1, 1902; House Jan. 28, 1885-Dec. 31, 1886.

REID, John William (D Mo.) June 14, 1821-Nov. 22, 1881; House March 4-Aug. 3, 1861.

REID, Ogden Rogers (D N.Y.) June 24, 1925- —; House 1963-75 (1963-March 22, 1972 Republican, March 22, 1972-75 Democrat).

REID, Robert Raymond (D Ga.) Sept. 8, 1789-July 1, 1841; House Feb. 18, 1819-23; Gov. (Fla. Terr.) 1839-41.

REIFEL, Benjamin (R S.D.) Sept. 19, 1906- —; House 1961-71.

REILLY, James Bernard (D Pa.) Aug. 12, 1845-May 14, 1924; House 1875-79, 1889-95.

REILLY, John (D Pa.) Feb. 22, 1836-April 19, 1904; House 1875-77.

REILLY, Michael Kieran (D Wis.) July 15, 1869-Oct. 14, 1944; House 1913-17, Nov. 4, 1930-39.

REILLY, Thomas Lawrence (D Conn.) Sept. 20, 1859-July 6, 1924; House 1911-15.

REILLY, Wilson (D Pa.) Aug. 8, 1811-Aug. 26, 1885; House 1857-59.

REILY, Luther (D Pa.) Oct. 17, 1794-Feb. 20, 1854; House 1837-39.

REINECKE, Edwin (R Calif.) Jan. 7, 1924- —; House 1965-Jan. 21, 1969.

RELFE, James Hugh (D Mo.) Oct. 17, 1791-Sept. 14, 1863; House 1843-47.

REMANN, Frederick (R Ill.) May 10, 1847-July 14, 1895; House March 4-July 14, 1895.

RENCHER, Abraham (D N.C.) Aug. 12, 1798-July 6, 1883; House 1829-39, 1841-43; Gov. (N.M.) 1857-61.

RESA, Alexander John (D Ill.) Aug. 4, 1887-July 4, 1964; House 1945-47.

RESNICK, Joseph Yale (D N.Y.) July 13, 1924-Oct. 6, 1969; House 1965-69.

REUSS, Henry Schoellkopf (D Wis.) Feb. 22, 1912- —; House 1955-83.

REVELS, Hiram Rhodes (R Miss.) Sept. 27, 1827-Jan. 16, 1901; Senate Feb. 23, 1870-71.

REVERCOMB, William Chapman (R W.Va.) July 20, 1895-Oct. 6, 1979; Senate 1943-49, Nov. 7, 1956-59.

REYBURN, John Edgar (father of William Stuart Reyburn) (R Pa.) Feb. 7, 1845-Jan. 4, 1914; House Feb. 18, 1890-97, Nov. 6, 1906-March 31, 1907.

REYBURN, William Stuart (son of John Edgar Reyburn) (R Pa.) Dec. 17, 1882-July 25, 1946; House May 23, 1911-13.

REYNOLDS, Edwin Ruthvin (R N.Y.) Feb. 16, 1816-July 4, 1908; House Dec. 5, 1860-61.

REYNOLDS, Gideon (W N.Y.) Aug. 9, 1813-July 13, 1896; House 1847-51.

REYNOLDS, John (D Ill.) Feb. 26, 1789-May 8, 1865; House Dec. 1, 1834-37, 1839-43; Gov. 1830-34.

REYNOLDS, John Hazard (R N.Y.) June 21, 1819-Sept. 24, 1875; House 1859-61.

REYNOLDS, John Merriman (R Pa.) March 5, 1848-Sept. 14, 1933; House 1905-Jan. 17, 1911.

REYNOLDS, Joseph (D N.Y.) Sept. 14, 1785-Sept. 24, 1864; House 1835-37.

REYNOLDS, Robert Rice (D N.C.) June 18, 1884-Feb. 13, 1963; Senate Dec. 5, 1932-45.

REYNOLDS, Samuel Williams (R Neb.) Aug. 11, 1890- —; Senate July 3-Nov. 7, 1954.

RHEA, John (D Tenn.) 1753-May 27, 1832; House 1803-15, 1817-23.

RHEA, John Stockdale (D/P Ky.) March 9, 1855-July 29, 1924; House 1897-March 25, 1902, 1903-05.

RHEA, William Francis (D Va.) April 20, 1858-March 23, 1931; House 1899-1903.

RHETT, Robert Barnwell (formerly Robert Barnwell Smith) (D S.C.) Dec. 24, 1800-Sept. 14, 1876; House 1837-49; Senate Dec. 18, 1850-May 7, 1852.

RHINOCK, Joseph Lafayette (D Ky.) Jan. 4, 1863-Sept. 20, 1926; House 1905-11.

RHODES, George Milton (D Pa.) Feb. 24, 1898-Oct. 23, 1978; House 1949-69.

RHODES, John Jacob (R Ariz.) Sept. 18, 1916- —; House 1953-83.

RHODES, Marion Edwards (R Mo.) Jan. 4, 1868-Dec. 25, 1928; House 1905-07, 1919-23.

RIBICOFF, Abraham Alexander (D Conn.) April 9, 1910- —; House 1949-53; Senate 1963-81; Gov. 1955-61; Secy. of HEW 1961-62.

RICAUD, James Barroll (AP Md.) Feb. 11, 1808-Jan. 24, 1866; House 1855-59.

RICE, Alexander Hamilton (R Mass.) Aug. 30, 1818-July 22, 1895; House 1859-67; Gov. 1876-79.

RICE, Americus Vespucius (D Ohio) Nov. 18, 1835-April 4, 1904; House 1875-79.

RICE, Benjamin Franklin (R Ark.) May 26, 1828-Jan. 19, 1905; Senate June 23, 1868-73.

RICE, Edmund (brother of Henry Mower Rice) (D Minn.) Feb. 14, 1819-July 11, 1889; House 1887-89.

RICE, Edward Young (D Ill.) Feb. 8, 1820-April 16, 1883; House 1871-73.

RICE, Henry Mower (brother of Edmund Rice) (D Minn.) Nov. 29, 1817-Jan. 15, 1894; House (Terr. Del.) 1853-57; Senate May 11, 1858-63.

RICE, John Birchard (R Ohio) June 23, 1832-Jan. 14, 1893; House 1881-83.

RICE, John Blake (R Ill.) May 28, 1809-Dec. 17, 1874; House 1873-Dec. 17, 1874.

RICE, John Hovey (R Maine) Feb. 5, 1816-March 14, 1911; House 1861-67.

RICE, John McConnell (D Ky.) Feb. 19, 1831-Sept. 18, 1895; House 1869-73.

RICE, Theron Moses (Nat.G Mo.) Sept. 21, 1829-Nov. 7, 1895; House 1881-83.

RICE, Thomas (— Mass.) March 30, 1768-Aug. 25, 1854; House 1815-19.

RICE, William Whitney (R Mass.) March 7, 1826-March 1, 1896; House 1877-87.

RICH, Carl West (R Ohio) Sept. 12, 1898-June 26, 1972; House 1963-65.

RICH, Charles (D Vt.) Sept. 13, 1771-Oct. 15, 1824; House 1813-15.

RICH, John Tyler (R Mich.) April 23, 1841-March 28, 1926; House April 5, 1881-83; Gov. 1893-97.

RICH, Robert Fleming (R Pa.) June 23, 1883-April 28, 1968; House Nov. 4, 1930-43, 1945-51.

RICHARD, Gabriel (— Mich.) Oct. 15, 1767-Sept. 13, 1832; House (Terr. Del.) 1823-25.

RICHARDS, Charles Lenmore (D Nev.) Oct. 3, 1877-Dec. 22, 1953; House 1923-25.

RICHARDS, Jacob (D Pa.) 1773-July 20, 1816; House 1803-09.

RICHARDS, James Alexander Dudley (D Ohio) March 22, 1845-Dec. 4, 1911; House 1893-95.

RICHARDS, James Prioleau (D S.C.) Aug. 31, 1894-Feb. 21, 1979; House 1933-57.

RICHARDS, John (brother of Matthias Richards) (— Pa.) April 18, 1753-Nov. 13, 1822; House 1795-97.

RICHARDS, John (— N.Y.) April 13, 1765-April 18, 1850; House 1823-25.

RICHARDS, Mark (D Vt.) July 15, 1760-Aug. 10, 1844; House 1817-21.

RICHARDS, Matthias (brother of John Richards) (— Pa.) Feb. 26, 1758-Aug. 4, 1830; House 1807-11.

RICHARDSON, David Plunket (R N.Y.) May 28, 1833-June 21, 1904; House 1879-83.

RICHARDSON, George Frederick (D Mich.) July 1, 1850-March 1, 1923; House 1893-95.

RICHARDSON, Harry Alden (R Del.) Jan. 1, 1853-June 16, 1928; Senate 1907-13.

RICHARDSON, James Daniel (D Tenn.) March 10, 1843-July 24, 1914; House 1885-1905.

RICHARDSON, James Montgomery (D Ky.) July 1, 1858-Feb. 9, 1925; House 1905-07.

RICHARDSON, John Peter (SRD S.C.) April 14, 1801-Jan. 24, 1864; House Dec. 19, 1836-39; Gov. 1840-42.

RICHARDSON, John Smythe (D S.C.) Feb. 29, 1828-Feb. 24, 1894; House 1879-83.

RICHARDSON, Joseph (— Mass.) Feb. 1, 1778-Sept. 25, 1871; House 1827-31.

RICHARDSON, William (D Ala.) May 8, 1839-March 31, 1914; House Aug. 6, 1900-March 31, 1914.

RICHARDSON, William Alexander (D Ill.) Jan. 16, 1811-Dec. 27, 1875; House Dec. 6, 1847-Aug. 25, 1856, 1861-Jan. 29, 1863; Senate Jan. 30, 1863-65.

RICHARDSON, William Blaine (D N.M.) Nov. 15, 1947-—; House 1983-—.

RICHARDSON, William Emanuel (D Pa.) Sept. 3, 1886-Nov. 3, 1948; House 1933-37.

RICHARDSON, William Merchant (F Mass.) Jan. 4, 1774-March 15, 1838; House Nov. 4, 1811-April 18, 1814.

RICHMOND, Frederick William (D N.Y.) Nov. 15, 1923-—; House 1975-August 25, 1982.

RICHMOND, Hiram Lawton (R Pa.) May 17, 1810-Feb. 19, 1885; House 1873-75.

RICHMOND, James Buchanan (D Va.) Feb. 27, 1842-April 30, 1910; House 1879-81.

RICHMOND, Jonathan (— N.Y.) July 31, 1774-July 28, 1853; House 1819-21.

RICKETTS, Edwin Darlington (R Ohio) Aug. 3, 1867-July 3, 1937; House 1915-17, 1919-23.

RIDDICK, Carl Wood (R Mont.) Feb. 25, 1872-July 9, 1960; House 1919-23.

RIDDLE, Albert Gallatin (R Ohio) May 28, 1816-May 16, 1902; House 1861-63.

RIDDLE, George Read (D Del.) 1817-March 29, 1867; House 1851-55; Senate Feb. 2, 1864-March 29, 1867.

RIDDLE, Haywood Yancey (D Tenn.) June 20, 1834-March 28, 1879; House Dec. 14, 1875-79.

RIDDLEBERGER, Harrison Holt (Read. Va.) Oct. 4, 1844-Jan. 24, 1890; Senate 1883-89.

RIDER, Ira Edgar (D N.Y.) Nov. 17, 1868-May 29, 1906; House 1903-05.

RIDGE, Thomas Joseph (R Pa.) Aug. 26, 1945-—; House 1983-—.

RIDGELY, Edwin Reed (PP/D Kan.) May 9, 1844-April 23, 1927; House 1897-1901.

RIDGELY, Henry Moore (F Del.) Aug. 6, 1779-Aug. 6, 1847; House 1811-15; Senate Jan. 12, 1827-29.

RIDGWAY, Joseph (W Ohio) May 6, 1783-Feb. 1, 1861; House 1837-43.

RIDGWAY, Robert (C Va.) April 21, 1823-Oct. 16, 1870; House Jan. 27-Oct. 16, 1870.

RIEGLE, Donald Wayne Jr. (D Mich.) Feb. 4, 1938-—; House 1967-Dec. 30, 1976; Senate Dec. 30, 1976-— (1967-Feb. 27, 1973 Republican, Feb. 27, 1973-— Democrat).

RIEHLMAN, Roy Walter (R N.Y.) Aug. 26, 1899-July 16, 1978; House 1947-65.

RIFE, John Winebrenner (R Pa.) Aug. 14, 1846-April 17, 1908; House 1889-93.

RIGGS, James Milton (D Ill.) April 17, 1839-Nov. 18, 1933; House 1883-87.

RIGGS, Jetur Rose (D N.J.) June 20, 1809-Nov. 5, 1869; House 1859-61.

RIGGS, Lewis (D N.Y.) Jan. 16, 1789-Nov. 6, 1870; House 1841-43.

RIGNEY, Hugh McPheeters (D Ill.) July 31, 1873-Oct. 12, 1950; House 1937-39.

RIKER, Samuel (— N.Y.) April 8, 1743-May 19, 1823; House Nov. 5, 1804-05, 1807-09.

RILEY, Corinne Boyd (widow of John Jacob Riley) (D S.C.) July 4, 1893-April 12, 1979; House April 10, 1962-63.

RILEY, John Jacob (husband of Corinne Boyd Riley) (D S.C.) Feb. 1, 1895-Jan. 1, 1962; House 1945-49, 1951-Jan. 1, 1962.

RINAKER, John Irving (R Ill.) Nov. 1, 1830-Jan. 15, 1915; House June 5, 1896-97.

RINALDO, Matthew John (R N.J.) Sept. 1, 1931-—; House 1973-—.

RINGGOLD, Samuel (D Md.) Jan. 15, 1770-Oct. 18, 1829; House Oct. 15, 1810-15, 1817-21.

RIORDAN, Daniel Joseph (D N.Y.) July 7, 1870-April 28, 1923; House 1899-1901, Nov. 6, 1906-April 28, 1923.

RIPLEY, Eleazar Wheelock (brother of James Wheelock Ripley) (D La.) April 15, 1782-March 2, 1839; House 1835-March 2, 1839.

RIPLEY, James Wheelock (brother of Eleazar Wheelock Ripley) (D Maine) March 12, 1786-June 17, 1835; House Sept. 11, 1826-March 12, 1830.

RIPLEY, Thomas C. (— N.Y.) ?-?; House Dec. 7, 1846-47.

RISENHOOVER, Theodore Marshall (D Okla.) Nov. 3, 1934-—; House 1975-79.

RISK, Charles Francis (R R.I.) Aug. 19, 1897-Dec. 26, 1943; House Aug. 6, 1935-37, 1939-41.

RISLEY, Elijah (W N.Y.) May 7, 1787-Jan. 9, 1870; House 1849-51.

RITCHEY, Thomas (D Ohio) Jan. 19, 1801-March 9, 1863; House 1847-49, 1853-55.

Biographical Index

RITCHIE, Byron Foster (son of James Monroe Ritchie) (D Ohio) Jan. 29, 1853-Aug. 22, 1928; House 1893-95.

RITCHIE, David (R Pa.) Aug. 19, 1812-Jan. 24, 1867; House 1853-59.

RITCHIE, James Monroe (father of Byron Foster Ritchie) (R Ohio) July 28, 1829-Aug. 17, 1918; House 1881-83.

RITCHIE, John (D Md.) Aug. 12, 1831-Oct. 27, 1887; House 1871-73.

RITTER, Burwell Clark (uncle of Walter Evans) (C Ky.) Jan. 6, 1810-Oct. 1, 1880; House 1865-67.

RITTER, Donald Lawrence (R Pa.) Oct. 21, 1940- —; House 1979- —.

RITTER, John (D Pa.) Feb. 6, 1779-Nov. 24, 1851; House 1843-47.

RIVERA, Luis Munoz (U P.R.) July 17, 1859-Nov. 15, 1916; House (Res. Comm.) 1911-Nov. 15, 1916.

RIVERS, Lucius Mendel (D S.C.) Sept. 28, 1905-Dec. 28, 1970; House 1941-Dec. 28, 1970.

RIVERS, Ralph Julian (D Alaska) May 23, 1903-Aug. 14, 1976; House 1959-67.

RIVERS, Thomas (AP Tenn.) Sept. 18, 1819-March 18, 1863; House 1855-57.

RIVES, Francis Everod (great-uncle of Francis Rives Lassiter) (D Va.) Jan. 14, 1792-Dec. 26, 1861; House 1837-41.

RIVES, William Cabell (W Va.) May 4, 1792-April 25, 1868; House 1823-29; Senate Dec. 10, 1832-Feb. 22, 1834, 1836-39, Jan. 18, 1841-45 (1823-29, 1832-34, 1836-39 Democrat, 1841-45 Whig).

RIVES, Zeno John (R Ill.) Feb. 22, 1874-Sept. 2, 1939; House 1905-07.

RIXEY, John Franklin (D Va.) Aug. 1, 1854-Feb. 8, 1907; House 1897-Feb. 8, 1907.

RIZLEY, Ross (R Okla.) July 5, 1892-March 4, 1969; House 1941-49.

ROACH, Sidney Crain (R Mo.) July 25, 1876-June 29, 1934; House 1921-25.

ROACH, William Nathaniel (D N.D.) Sept. 25, 1840-Sept. 7, 1902; Senate 1893-99.

ROANE, John (father of John Jones Roane) (D Va.) Feb. 9, 1766-Nov. 15, 1838; House 1809-15, 1827-31, 1835-37.

ROANE, John Jones (son of John Roane) (D Va.) Oct. 31, 1794-Dec. 18, 1869; House 1831-33.

ROANE, William Henry (D Va.) Sept. 17, 1787-May 11, 1845; House 1815-17; Senate March 14, 1837-41.

ROARK, Charles Wickliffe (R Ky.) Jan. 22, 1887-April 5, 1929; House March 4-April 5, 1929.

ROBB, Edward (D Mo.) March 19, 1857-March 13, 1934; House 1897-1905.

ROBBINS, Asher (W R.I.) Oct. 26, 1757-Feb. 25, 1845; Senate Oct. 31, 1825-39.

ROBBINS, Edward Everett (R Pa.) Sept. 27, 1860-Jan. 25, 1919; House 1897-99, 1917-Jan. 25, 1919.

ROBBINS, Gaston Ahi (D Ala.) Sept. 26, 1858-Feb. 22, 1902; House 1893-March 13, 1896, 1899-March 8, 1900.

ROBBINS, George Robbins (W N.J.) Sept. 24, 1808-Feb. 22, 1875; House 1855-59.

ROBBINS, John (D Pa.) 1808-April 27, 1880; House 1849-55, 1875-77.

ROBBINS, William McKendree (D N.C.) Oct. 26, 1828-May 5, 1905; House 1873-79.

ROBERTS, Anthony Ellmaker (grandfather of Robert Grey Bushong) (W Pa.) Oct. 29, 1803-Jan. 25, 1885; House 1855-59.

ROBERTS, Brigham Henry (D Utah) March 13, 1857-Sept. 27, 1933; House 1899-Jan. 25, 1900.

ROBERTS, Charles Boyle (D Md.) April 19, 1842-Sept. 10, 1899; House 1875-79.

ROBERTS, Clint (R S.D.) Jan. 30, 1935- —; House 1981-83.

ROBERTS, Edwin Ewing (R Nev.) Dec. 12, 1870-Dec. 11, 1933; House 1911-19.

ROBERTS, Ellis Henry (R N.Y.) Sept. 30, 1827-Jan. 8, 1918; House 1871-75.

ROBERTS, Ernest William (R Mass.) Nov. 22, 1858-Feb. 27, 1924; House 1899-1917.

ROBERTS, Herbert Ray (D Texas) March 28, 1913- —; House Jan. 30, 1962-81.

ROBERTS, Jonathan (DR Pa.) Aug. 16, 1771-July 24, 1854; House 1811-Feb. 24, 1814; Senate Feb. 24, 1814-21.

ROBERTS, Kenneth Allison (D Ala.) Nov. 1, 1912- —; House 1951-65.

ROBERTS, Pat (R Kan.) April 20, 1936- —; House 1981- —.

ROBERTS, Robert Whyte (D Miss.) Nov. 28, 1784-Jan. 4, 1865; House 1843-47.

ROBERTS, William Randall (D N.Y.) Feb. 6, 1830-Aug. 9, 1897; House 1871-75.

ROBERTSON, Alice Mary (R Okla.) Jan. 2, 1854-July 1, 1931; House 1921-23.

ROBERTSON, A. Willis (D Va.) May 27, 1887-Nov. 1, 1971; House 1933-Nov. 5, 1946; Senate Nov. 6, 1946-67.

ROBERTSON, Charles Raymond (R N.D.) Sept. 5, 1889-Feb. 18, 1951; House 1941-43, 1945-49.

ROBERTSON, Edward Vivian (R Wyo.) May 27, 1881-April 15, 1963; Senate 1943-49.

ROBERTSON, Edward White (father of Samuel Matthews Robertson) (D La.) June 13, 1823-Aug. 2, 1887; House 1877-83, March 4-Aug. 2, 1887.

ROBERTSON, George (— Ky.) Nov. 18, 1790-May 16, 1874; House 1817-21.

ROBERTSON, John (brother of Thomas Bolling Robertson) (W Va.) April 13, 1787-July 5, 1873; House Dec. 8, 1834-39.

ROBERTSON, Samuel Matthews (son of Edward White Robertson) (D La.) Jan. 1, 1852-Dec. 24, 1911; House Dec. 5, 1887-1907.

ROBERTSON, Thomas Austin (D Ky.) Sept. 9, 1848-July 18, 1892; House 1883-87.

ROBERTSON, Thomas Bolling (brother of John Robertson) (D La.) Feb. 27, 1779-Oct. 5, 1828; House April 30, 1812-April 20, 1818; Gov. 1820-24.

ROBERTSON, Thomas James (R S.C.) Aug. 3, 1823-Oct. 13, 1897; Senate July 15, 1868-77.

ROBERTSON, William Henry (R N.Y.) Oct. 10, 1823-Dec. 7, 1898; House 1867-69.

ROBESON, Edward John Jr. (D Va.) Aug. 9, 1890-March 10, 1966; House May 2, 1950-59.

ROBESON, George Maxwell (nephew of George Clifford Maxwell) (R N.J.) March 16, 1829-Sept. 27, 1897; House 1879-83; Secy. of the Navy 1869-77.

ROBIE, Reuben (D N.Y.) July 15, 1799-Jan. 21, 1872; House 1851-53.

ROBINSON, Arthur Raymond (R Ind.) March 12, 1881-March 17, 1961; Senate Oct. 20, 1925-35.

ROBINSON, Christopher (AP R.I.) May 15, 1806-Oct. 3, 1889; House 1859-61.

ROBINSON, Edward (W Maine) Nov. 25, 1796-Feb. 19, 1857; House April 28, 1838-39.

ROBINSON, George Dexter (R Mass.) Jan. 20, 1834-Feb. 22, 1896; House 1877-Jan. 7, 1884; Gov. 1884-87.

ROBINSON, James Carroll (D Ill.) Aug. 19, 1823-Nov. 3, 1886; House 1859-65, 1871-75.

ROBINSON, James Kenneth (R Va.) May 14, 1916- —; House 1971-85.

ROBINSON, James McClellan (D Ind.) May 31, 1861-Jan. 16, 1942; House 1897-1905.

ROBINSON, James Sidney (R Ohio) Oct. 14, 1827-Jan. 14, 1892; House 1881-Jan. 12, 1885.

ROBINSON, James Wallace (R Ohio) Nov. 26, 1826-June 28, 1898; House 1873-75.

ROBINSON, James William (D Utah) Jan. 19, 1878-Dec. 2, 1964; House 1933-47.

ROBINSON, John Buchanan (R Pa.) May 23, 1846-Jan. 28, 1933; House 1891-97.

ROBINSON, John Larne (D Ind.) May 3, 1813-March 21, 1860; House 1847-53.

ROBINSON, John McCracken (D Ill.) April 10, 1794-April 25, 1843; Senate Dec. 11, 1830-41.

ROBINSON, John Seaton (D Neb.) May 4, 1856-May 25, 1903; House 1899-1903.

ROBINSON, Jonathan (brother of Moses Robinson) (— Vt.) Aug. 11, 1756-Nov. 3, 1819; Senate Oct. 10, 1807-15.

ROBINSON, Joseph Taylor (D Ark.) Aug. 26, 1872-July 14, 1937; House 1903-Jan. 14, 1913; Senate 1913-July 14, 1937; Senate majority leader 1933-1937; Gov. Jan. 16-March 8, 1913.

ROBINSON, Leonidas Dunlap (D N.C.) April 22, 1867-Nov. 7, 1941; House 1917-21.

ROBINSON, Milton Stapp (R Ind.) April 20, 1832-July 28, 1892; House 1875-79.

ROBINSON, Moses (brother of Jonathan Robinson) (D Vt.) March 20, 1741-May 26, 1813; Senate Oct. 17, 1791-Oct. 15, 1796; Gov. 1789-90.

ROBINSON, Orville (D N.Y.) Oct. 28, 1801-Dec. 1, 1882; House 1843-45.

ROBINSON, Thomas Jr. (D Del.) 1800-Oct. 28, 1843; House 1839-41.

ROBINSON, Thomas John Bright (R Iowa) Aug. 12, 1868-Jan. 27, 1958; House 1923-33.

ROBINSON, Tommy (D Ark.) March 7, 1942-—; House 1985-—.

ROBINSON, William Erigena (D N.Y.) May 6, 1814-Jan. 23, 1892; House 1867-69, 1881-85.

ROBISON, David Fullerton (nephew of David Fullerton) (W Pa.) May 28, 1816-June 24, 1859; House 1855-57.

ROBISON, Howard Winfield (R N.Y.) Oct. 30, 1915-—; House Jan. 14, 1958-75.

ROBSION, John Marshall (father of John Marshall Robsion Jr.) (R Ky.) Jan. 2, 1873-Feb. 17, 1948; House 1919-Jan. 10, 1930, 1935-Feb. 17, 1948; Senate Jan. 11-Nov. 30, 1930.

ROBSION, John Marshall Jr. (son of John Marshall Robsion) (R Ky.) Aug. 28, 1904-—; House 1953-59.

ROCHESTER, William Beatty (D N.Y.) Jan. 29, 1789-June 14, 1838; House 1821-April 1823.

ROCKEFELLER, John Davison "Jay" IV (D W.Va.) June 18, 1937-—; Senate 1985-—; Gov. 1977-85.

ROCKEFELLER, Lewis Kirby (R N.Y.) Nov. 25, 1875-Sept. 18, 1948; House Nov. 2, 1937-43.

ROCKHILL, William (D Ind.) Feb. 10, 1793-Jan. 15, 1865; House 1847-49.

ROCKWELL, Francis Williams (son of Julius Rockwell) (R Mass.) May 26, 1844-June 26, 1929; House Jan. 17, 1884-91.

ROCKWELL, Hosea Hunt (D N.Y.) May 31, 1840-Dec. 18, 1918; House 1891-93.

ROCKWELL, John Arnold (W Conn.) Aug. 27, 1803-Feb. 10, 1861; House 1845-49.

ROCKWELL, Julius (father of Francis Williams Rockwell) (W Mass.) April 26, 1805-May 19, 1888; House 1843-51; Senate June 3, 1854-Jan. 31, 1855.

ROCKWELL, Robert Fay (R Colo.) Feb. 11, 1886-Sept. 29, 1950; House Dec. 9, 1941-49.

RODDENBERY, Seaborn Anderson (D Ga.) Jan. 12, 1870-Sept. 25, 1913; House Feb. 16, 1910-Sept. 25, 1913.

RODENBERG, William August (R Ill.) Oct. 30, 1865-Sept. 10, 1937; House 1899-1901, 1903-13, 1915-23.

RODEY, Bernard Shandon (R N.M.) March 1, 1856-March 10, 1927; House (Terr. Del.) 1901-05.

RODGERS, Harold (Hal) (R Ky.) Dec. 31, 1937-—; House 1981-—.

RODGERS, Robert Lewis (R Pa.) June 2, 1875-May 9, 1960; House 1939-47.

RODINO, Peter Wallace Jr. (D N.J.) June 7, 1909-—; House 1949-—.

RODMAN, William (D Pa.) Oct. 7, 1757-July 27, 1824; House 1811-13.

RODNEY, Caesar Augustus (cousin of George Brydges Rodney) (D Del.) Jan. 4, 1772-June 10, 1824; House 1803-05, 1821-Jan. 24, 1822; Senate Jan. 24, 1822-Jan. 29, 1823; Atty. Gen. 1807-11.

RODNEY, Daniel (F Del.) Sept. 10, 1764-Sept. 2, 1846; House Oct. 1, 1822-23; Senate Nov. 8, 1826-Jan. 12, 1827; Gov. 1814-17.

RODNEY, George Brydges (cousin of Caesar Augustus Rodney) (W Del.) April 2, 1803-June 18, 1883; House 1841-45.

ROE, Dudley George (D Md.) March 23, 1881-Jan. 4, 1970; House 1945-47.

ROE, James A. (D N.Y.) July 9, 1896-April 22, 1967; House 1945-47.

ROE, Robert A. (D N.J.) Feb. 28, 1924-—; House Nov. 4, 1969-—.

ROEMER, Buddy (D La.) Oct. 4, 1943-—; House 1981-—.

ROGERS, Andrew Jackson (D N.J.) July 1, 1828-May 22, 1900; House 1863-67.

ROGERS, Anthony Astley Cooper (D Ark.) Feb. 14, 1821-July 27, 1899; House 1869-71.

ROGERS, Byron Giles (D Colo.) Aug. 1, 1900-Dec. 31, 1983; House 1951-71.

ROGERS, Charles (W N.Y.) April 30, 1800-Jan. 13, 1874; House 1843-45.

ROGERS, Dwight Laing (father of Paul Grant Rogers) (D Fla.) Aug. 17, 1886-Dec. 1, 1954; House 1945-Dec. 1, 1954.

ROGERS, Edith Nourse (widow of John Jacob Rogers) (R Mass.) 1881-Sept. 10, 1960; House June 30, 1925-Sept. 10, 1960.

ROGERS, Edward (D N.Y.) May 30, 1787-May 29, 1857; House 1839-41.

ROGERS, George Frederick (D N.Y.) March 19, 1887-Nov. 20, 1948; House 1945-47.

ROGERS, Harold (R Ky.) Dec. 31, 1937-—; House 1981-—.

ROGERS, James (D S.C.) Oct. 24, 1795-Dec. 21, 1873; House 1835-37, 1839-43.

ROGERS, John (D N.Y.) May 9, 1813-May 11, 1879; House 1871-73.

ROGERS, John Henry (D Ark.) Oct. 9, 1845-April 16, 1911; House 1883-91.

ROGERS, John Jacob (husband of Edith Nourse Rogers) (R Mass.) Aug. 18, 1881-March 28, 1925; House 1913-March 28, 1925.

ROGERS, Paul Grant (son of Dwight Laing Rogers) (D Fla.) June 4, 1921-—; House Jan. 11, 1955-79.

ROGERS, Sion Hart (D N.C.) Sept. 30, 1825-Aug. 14, 1874; House 1853-55, 1871-73 (1853-55 Whig, 1871-73 Democrat).

ROGERS, Thomas Jones (father of William Findlay Rogers) (D Pa.) 1781-Dec. 7, 1832; House March 3, 1818-April 20, 1824.

ROGERS, Walter Edward (D Texas) July 19, 1908-—; House 1951-67.

ROGERS, Will (D Okla.) Dec. 12, 1898-Aug. 3, 1983; House 1933-43.

ROGERS, Will Jr. (D Calif.) Oct. 20, 1911-—; House 1943-May 23, 1944.

ROGERS, William Findlay (son of Thomas Jones Rogers) (D N.Y.) March 1, 1820-Dec. 16, 1899; House 1883-85.

ROGERS, William Nathaniel (D N.H.) Jan. 10, 1892-Sept. 25, 1945; House 1923-25, Jan. 5, 1932-37.

ROHRBOUGH, Edward Gay (R W.Va.) 1874-Dec. 12, 1956; House 1943-45, 1947-49.

ROLLINS, Edward Henry (R N.H.) Oct. 3, 1824-July 31, 1889; House 1861-67; Senate 1877-83.

ROLLINS, James Sidney (C Mo.) April 19, 1812-Jan. 9, 1888; House 1861-65.

ROLPH, Thomas (R Calif.) Jan. 17, 1885-May 10, 1956; House 1941-45.

ROMAN, James Dixon (W Md.) Aug. 11, 1809-Jan. 19, 1867; House 1847-49.

ROMEIS, Jacob (R Ohio) Dec. 1, 1835-March 8, 1904; House 1885-89.

ROMERO, Trinidad (R N.M.) June 15, 1835-Aug. 28, 1918; House (Terr. Del.) 1877-79.

ROMJUE, Milton Andrew (D Mo.) Dec. 5, 1874-Jan. 23, 1968; House 1917-21, 1923-43.

ROMULO, Carlos Pena (— P.I.) Jan. 14, 1901-—; House (Res. Comm.) Aug. 10, 1944-July 4, 1946.

RONAN, Daniel J. (D Ill.) July 13, 1914-Aug. 13, 1969; House 1965-Aug. 13, 1969.

RONCALIO, Teno (D Wyo.) March 23, 1916-—; House 1965-67, 1971-Dec. 30, 1978.

RONCALLO, Angelo Dominick (R N.Y.) May 28, 1927-—; House 1973-75.

ROONEY, Fred B. (D Pa.) Nov. 6, 1925-—; House July 30, 1963-79.

ROONEY, John James (D N.Y.) Nov. 29, 1903-Oct. 26, 1975; House June 6, 1944-Dec. 31, 1974.

ROOSEVELT, Franklin Delano Jr. (son of Franklin Delano Roosevelt, brother of James Roosevelt) (D N.Y.) Aug. 17, 1914-—; House May 17, 1949-55 (1949-51 Liberal/Four Freedoms, 1951-55 Democrat).

ROOSEVELT, James (son of Franklin Delano Roosevelt, brother of Franklin Delano Roosevelt Jr.) (D Calif.) Dec. 23, 1907-—; House 1955-Sept. 30, 1965.

ROOSEVELT, James I. (uncle of Robert Barnwell Roosevelt) (D N.Y.) Dec. 14, 1795-April 5, 1875; House 1841-43.

ROOSEVELT, Robert Barnwell (nephew of James I. Roosevelt, uncle of Theodore Roosevelt) (D N.Y.) Aug. 7, 1829-June 14, 1906; House 1871-73.

ROOT, Elihu (R N.Y.) Feb. 15, 1845-Feb. 7, 1937; Senate 1909-15; Secy. of War 1899-1904; Secy. of State 1905-09.

ROOT, Erastus (D N.Y.) March 16, 1773-Dec. 24, 1846; House 1803-05, 1809-11, Dec. 26, 1815-17, 1831-33.

ROOT, Joseph Mosley (W Ohio) Oct. 7, 1807-April 7, 1879; House 1845-51.

ROOTS, Logan Holt (R Ark.) March 26, 1841-May 30, 1893; House June 22, 1868-71.

ROSE, Charles Gradison III (D N.C.) Aug. 10, 1939-—; House 1973-—.

ROSE, John Marshall (R Pa.) May 18, 1856-April 22, 1923; House 1917-23.

ROSE, Robert Lawson (son of Robert Selden Rose, son-in-law of Nathaniel Allen) (W N.Y.) Oct. 12, 1804-March 14, 1877; House 1847-51.

ROSE, Robert Selden (father of Robert Lawson Rose) (— N.Y.) Feb. 24, 1774-Nov. 24, 1835; House 1823-27, 1829-31.

ROSECRANS, William Starke (D Calif.) Sept. 6, 1819-March 11, 1898; House 1881-85.

ROSENBLOOM, Benjamin Louis (R W.Va.) June 3, 1880-March 22, 1965; House 1921-25.

ROSENTHAL, Benjamin S. (D/L N.Y.) June 8, 1923-Jan. 4, 1983; House Feb. 20, 1962-Jan. 4, 1983.

ROSIER, Joseph (D W.Va.) Jan. 24, 1870-Oct. 7, 1951; Senate Jan. 13, 1941-Nov. 17, 1942.

ROSS, Edmund Gibson (R Kan.) Dec. 7, 1826-May 8, 1907; Senate July 19, 1866-71; Gov. (N.M. Terr.) 1885-89 (Democrat).

ROSS, Henry Howard (W N.Y.) May 9, 1790-Sept. 14, 1862; House 1825-27.

ROSS, James (F Pa.) July 12, 1762-Nov. 27, 1847; Senate April 24, 1794-1803; Pres. pro tempore 1798-99.

ROSS, John (father of Thomas Ross) (— Pa.) Feb. 24, 1770-Jan. 31, 1834; House 1809-11, 1815-Feb. 24, 1818.

ROSS, Jonathan (R Vt.) April 30, 1826-Feb. 23, 1905; Senate Jan. 11, 1899-Oct. 18, 1900.

ROSS, Lewis Winans (D Ill.) Dec. 8, 1812-Oct. 20, 1895; House 1863-69.

ROSS, Miles (D N.J.) April 30, 1827-Feb. 22, 1903; House 1875-83.

ROSS, Robert Tripp (R N.Y.) June 4, 1903-October 1, 1981; House 1947-49, Feb. 19, 1952-53.

ROSS, Sobieski (R Pa.) May 16, 1828-Oct. 24, 1877; House 1873-77.

ROSS, Thomas (son of John Ross) (D Pa.) Dec. 1, 1806-July 7, 1865; House 1849-53.

ROSS, Thomas Randolph (D Ohio) Oct. 26, 1788-June 28, 1869; House 1819-25.

ROSSDALE, Albert Berger (R N.Y.) Oct. 23, 1878-April 17, 1968; House 1921-23.

ROSTENKOWSKI, Daniel David (Dan) (D Ill.) Jan. 2, 1928-—; House 1959-—.

ROTH, Tobias A. (R Wis.) Oct. 10, 1938-—; House 1979-—.

ROTH, William V. Jr. (R Del.) July 22, 1921-—; House 1967-Dec. 31, 1970; Senate Jan. 1, 1971-—.

ROTHERMEL, John Hoover (D Pa.) March 7, 1856-Aug. 1922; House 1907-15.

ROTHWELL, Gideon Frank (D Mo.) April 24, 1836-Jan. 18, 1894; House 1879-81.

ROUDEBUSH, Richard Lowell (R Ind.) Jan. 18, 1918-—; House 1961-71.

ROUKEMA, Marge (R N.J.) Sept. 19, 1929-—; House 1981-—.

ROUSE, Arthur Blythe (D Ky.) June 20, 1874-Jan. 25, 1956; House 1911-27.

ROUSH, John Edward (D Ind.) Sept. 12, 1920-—; House 1959-69, 1971-77.

ROUSSEAU, Lovell Harrison (R Ky.) Aug. 4, 1818-Jan. 7, 1869; House 1865-July 21, 1866, Dec. 3, 1866-67.

ROUSSELOT, John Harbin (R Calif.) Nov. 1, 1927-—; House 1961-63, June 30, 1970-83.

ROUTZOHN, Harry Nelson (R Ohio) Nov. 4, 1881-April 14, 1953; House 1939-41.

ROWAN, John (uncle of Robert Todd Lytle) (D Ky.) July 12, 1773-July 13, 1843; House 1807-09; Senate 1825-31.

ROWAN, Joseph (D N.Y.) Sept. 8, 1870-Aug. 3, 1930; House 1919-21.

ROWAN, William A. (D Ill.) Nov. 24, 1882-May 31, 1961; House 1943-47.

ROWBOTTOM, Harry Emerson (R Ind.) Nov. 3, 1884-March 22, 1934; House 1925-31.

ROWE, Edmund (Ed) (R Ohio) Dec. 21, 1892-—; House 1943-45.

ROWE, Frederick William (R N.Y.) March 19, 1863-June 20, 1946; House 1915-21.

ROWE, Peter (D N.Y.) March 10, 1807-April 17, 1876; House 1853-55.

ROWELL, Jonathan Harvey (R Ill.) Feb. 10, 1833-May 15, 1908; House 1883-91.

ROWLAND, Alfred (D N.C.) Feb. 9, 1844-Aug. 2, 1898; House 1887-91.

ROWLAND, Charles Hedding (R Pa.) Dec. 20, 1860-Nov. 24, 1921; House 1915-19.

ROWLAND, James Roy Jr. (D Ga.) Feb. 3, 1926-—; House 1983-—.

ROWLAND, John G. (R Conn.) May 24, 1957-—; House 1985-—.

ROY, Alphonse (D N.H.) Oct. 26, 1897-Oct. 5, 1967; House June 9, 1938-39.

ROY, William Robert (D Kan.) Feb. 23, 1926-—; House 1971-75.

ROYBAL, Edward R. (D Calif.) Feb. 10, 1916-—; House 1963-—.

ROYCE, Homer Elihu (R Vt.) June 14, 1819-April 24, 1891; House 1857-61.

ROYER, William H. (R Calif.) April 11, 1920-—; House April 9, 1979-81.

ROYSE, Lemuel Willard (R Ind.) Jan. 19, 1847-Dec. 18, 1946; House 1895-99.

RUBEY, Thomas Lewis (D Mo.) Sept. 27, 1862-Nov. 2, 1928; House 1911-21, 1923-Nov. 2, 1928.

RUCKER, Atterson Walden (D Colo.) April 3, 1847-July 19, 1924; House 1909-13.

RUCKER, Tinsley White (D Ga.) March 24, 1848-Nov. 18, 1926; House Jan. 11-March 3, 1917.

RUCKER, William Waller (D Mo.) Feb. 1, 1855-May 30, 1936; House 1899-1923.

RUDD, Eldon Dean (R Ariz.) July 15, 1920-—; House 1977-—.

RUDD, Stephen Andrew (D N.Y.) Dec. 11, 1874-March 31, 1936; House 1931-March 31, 1936.

RUDMAN, Warren (R N.H.) May 13, 1930-—; Senate Dec. 29, 1980-—.

RUFFIN, James Edward (D Mo.) July 24, 1893-April 9, 1977; House 1933-35.

RUFFIN, Thomas (D N.C.) Sept. 9, 1820-Oct. 13, 1863; House 1853-61.

RUGGLES, Benjamin (D Ohio) Feb. 21, 1783-Sept. 2, 1857; Senate 1815-33.

RUGGLES, Charles Herman (— N.Y.) Feb. 10, 1789-June 16, 1865; House 1821-23.

RUGGLES, John (D Maine) Oct. 8, 1789-June 20, 1874; Senate Jan. 20, 1835-41.

RUGGLES, Nathaniel (F Mass.) Nov. 11, 1761-Dec. 19, 1819; House 1813-19.

RUMPLE, John Nicholas William (R Iowa) March 4, 1841-Jan. 31, 1903; House 1901-Jan. 31, 1903.

RUMSEY, David (W N.Y.) Dec. 25, 1810-March 12, 1883; House 1847-51.

RUMSEY, Edward (W Ky.) Nov. 5, 1796-April 6, 1868; House 1837-39.

RUMSFELD, Donald (R Ill.) July 9, 1932-—; House 1963-May 25, 1969; Secy. of Defense 1975-77.

RUNK, John (W N.J.) July 3, 1791-Sept. 22, 1872; House 1845-47.

RUNNELS, Harold Lowell (D N.M.) March 17, 1924-Aug. 5, 1980; House 1971-Aug. 5, 1980.

RUPLEY, Arthur Ringwalt (PR Pa.) Nov. 13, 1868-Nov. 11, 1920; House 1913-15.

RUPPE, Philip E. (R Mich.) Sept. 29, 1926-—; House 1967-79.

RUPPERT, Jacob Jr. (D N.Y.) Aug. 5, 1867-Jan. 13, 1939; House 1899-1907.

RUSK, Harry Welles (D Md.) Oct. 17, 1852-Jan. 28, 1926; House Nov. 2, 1886-97.

RUSK, Jeremiah McLain (R Wis.) June 17, 1830-Nov. 21, 1893; House 1871-77; Gov. 1882-89; Secy. of Agric. 1889-93.

RUSK, Thomas Jefferson (D Texas) Dec. 5, 1803-July 29, 1857; Senate Feb. 21, 1846-July 29, 1857; Pres. pro tempore 1857.

RUSS, John (D Conn.) Oct. 29, 1767-June 22, 1833; House 1819-23.

RUSSELL, Benjamin Edward (cousin of Rienzi Melville Johnston) (D Ga.) Oct. 5, 1845-Dec. 4, 1909; House 1893-97.

RUSSELL, Charles Addison (R Conn.) March 2, 1852-Oct. 23, 1902; House 1887-Oct. 23, 1902.

RUSSELL, Charles Hinton (R Nev.) Dec. 27, 1903-—; House 1947-49; Gov. 1951-59.

RUSSELL, Daniel Lindsay (R N.C.) Aug. 7, 1845-May 14, 1908; House 1879-81; Gov. 1897-1901.

RUSSELL, David Abel (W N.Y.) 1780-Nov. 24, 1861; House 1835-41.

RUSSELL, Donald Stuart (D S.C.) Feb. 22, 1906-—; Senate April 22, 1965-67; Gov. 1963-65.

RUSSELL, Gordon James (D Texas) Dec. 22, 1859-Sept. 14, 1919; House Nov. 4, 1902-June 14, 1910.

RUSSELL, James McPherson (father of Samuel Lyon Russell) (W Pa.) Nov. 10, 1786-Nov. 14, 1870; House Dec. 21, 1841-43.

RUSSELL, Jeremiah (D N.Y.) Jan. 26, 1786-Sept. 30, 1867; House 1843-45.

RUSSELL, John (— N.Y.) Sept. 7, 1772-Aug. 2, 1842; House 1805-09.

RUSSELL, John Edwards (D Mass.) Jan. 20, 1834-Oct. 28, 1903; House 1887-89.

RUSSELL, Jonathan (D Mass.) Feb. 27, 1771-Feb. 16, 1832; House 1821-23.

RUSSELL, Joseph (D N.Y.) ?-?; House 1845-57, 1851-53.

RUSSELL, Joseph James (D Mo.) Aug. 23, 1854-Oct. 22, 1922; House 1907-09, 1911-19.

RUSSELL, Joshua Edward (R Ohio) Aug. 9, 1867-June 21, 1953; House 1915-17.

RUSSELL, Leslie W. (— N.Y.) April 15, 1840-Feb. 3, 1903; House March 4-Sept. 11, 1891.

RUSSELL, Richard Brevard (D Ga.) Nov. 2, 1897-Jan. 21, 1971; Senate Jan. 12, 1933-Jan. 21, 1971; Pres. pro tempore 1969-71; Gov. 1931-33.

RUSSELL, Richard Manning (D Mass.) March 3, 1891-Feb. 27, 1977; House 1935-37.

RUSSELL, Sam Morris (D Texas) Aug. 9, 1889-Oct. 19, 1971; House 1941-47.

RUSSELL, Samuel Lyon (son of James McPherson Russell) (W Pa.) July 30, 1816-Sept. 27, 1891; House 1853-55.

RUSSELL, William (W Ohio) 1782-Sept. 28, 1845; House 1827-33, 1841-43 (1827-33 Jackson Democrat, 1841-43 Whig).

RUSSELL, William Augustus (R Mass.) April 22, 1831-Jan. 10, 1899; House 1879-85.

RUSSELL, William Fiero (D N.Y.) Jan. 14, 1812-April 29, 1896; House 1857-59.

RUSSO, Martin Anthony (D Ill.) Jan. 23, 1944-—; House 1975-—.

RUST, Albert (D Ark.) ?-April 3, 1870; House 1855-57; 1859-61.

RUTH, Earl B. (R N.C.) Feb. 7, 1916-—; House 1969-75.

RUTHERFORD, Albert Greig (R Pa.) Jan. 3, 1879-Aug. 10, 1941; House 1937-Aug. 10, 1941.

RUTHERFORD, J. T. (D Texas) May 30, 1921-—; House 1955-63.

RUTHERFORD, Robert (— Va.) Oct. 20, 1728-Oct. 1803; House 1793-97.

RUTHERFORD, Samuel (D Ga.) March 15, 1870-Feb. 4, 1932; House 1925-Feb. 4, 1932.

RUTHERFURD, John (F N.J.) Sept. 20, 1760-Feb. 23, 1840; Senate 1791-Dec. 5, 1799.

RUTLEDGE, John Jr. (F S.C.) 1766-Sept. 1, 1819; House 1797-1803.

RYALL, Daniel Bailey (D N.J.) Jan. 30, 1798-Dec. 17, 1864; House 1839-41.

RYAN, Elmer James (D Minn.) May 26, 1907-Feb. 1, 1958; House 1935-41.

RYAN, Harold M. (D Mich.) Feb. 6, 1911-—; House Feb. 13, 1962-65.

RYAN, James Wilfrid (D Pa.) Oct. 16, 1858-Feb. 26, 1907; House 1899-1901.

RYAN, Leo Joseph (D Calif.) May 5, 1925-Nov. 18, 1978; House 1973-Nov. 18, 1978.

RYAN, Thomas (R Kan.) Nov. 25, 1837-April 5, 1914; House 1877-April 4, 1889.

RYAN, Thomas Jefferson (R N.Y.) June 17, 1890-Nov. 10, 1968; House 1921-23.

RYAN, William (D N.Y.) March 8, 1840-Feb. 18, 1925; House 1893-95.

RYAN, William Fitts (D/L N.Y.) June 28, 1922-Sept. 17, 1972; House 1961-Sept. 17, 1972.

RYAN, William Henry (D N.Y.) May 10, 1860-Nov. 18, 1939; House 1899-1909.

RYON, John Walker (D Pa.) March 4, 1825-March 12, 1901; House 1879-81.

RYTER, John Francis (D Conn.) Feb. 4, 1914-Feb. 5, 1978; House 1945-47.

S

SABATH, Adolph Joachim (D Ill.) April 4, 1866-Nov. 6, 1952; House 1907-Nov. 6, 1952.

SABIN, Alvah (W Vt.) Oct. 23, 1793-Jan. 22, 1885; House 1853-57.

SABIN, Dwight May (R Minn.) April 25, 1843-Dec. 22, 1902; Senate 1883-39; Chrmn. Rep. Nat. Comm. 1883-84.

SABINE, Lorenzo (W Mass.) Feb. 28, 1803-April 14, 1877; House Dec. 13, 1852-53.

SABO, Martin Olav (D Minn.) Feb. 28, 1938-—; House 1979-—.

SACKETT, Frederick Mosley (R Ky.) Dec. 17, 1868-May 18, 1941; Senate 1925-Jan. 9, 1930.

SACKETT, William Augustus (W N.Y.) Nov. 18, 1811-Sept. 6, 1895; House 1849-53.

SACKS, Leon (D Pa.) Oct. 7, 1902-March 11, 1972; House 1937-43.

SADLAK, Antoni Nicholas (R Conn.) June 13, 1908-Oct. 18, 1969; House 1947-59.

SADLER, Thomas William (D Ala.) April 17, 1831-Oct. 29, 1896; House 1885-87.

SADOWSKI, George Gregory (D Mich.) March 12, 1903-Oct. 9, 1961; House 1933-39, 1943-51.

SAGE, Ebenezer (D N.Y.) Aug. 16, 1755-Jan. 20, 1834; House 1809-15.

SAGE, Russell (W N.Y.) Aug. 4, 1816-July 22, 1906; House 1853-57.

SAILLY, Peter (D N.Y.) April 20, 1754-March 16, 1826; House 1805-07.

ST. GEORGE, Katharine Price Collier (R N.Y.) July 12, 1896-May 2, 1983; House 1947-65.

ST GERMAIN, Fernand Joseph (D R.I.) Jan. 9, 1928-—; House 1961-—.

ST. JOHN, Charles (R N.Y.) Oct. 8, 1818-July 6, 1891; House 1871-75.

ST. JOHN, Daniel Bennett (W N.Y.) Oct. 8, 1808-Feb. 18, 1890; House 1847-49.

ST. JOHN, Henry (D Ohio) July 16, 1783-May 1869; House 1843-47.

ST. MARTIN, Louis (D La.) May 17, 1820-Feb. 9, 1893; House 1851-53; 1885-87.

ST. ONGE, William Leon (D Conn.) Oct. 9, 1914-May 1, 1970; House 1963-May 1, 1970.

SALINGER, Pierre Emil George (D Calif.) June 14, 1925-—; Senate Aug. 4-Dec. 31, 1964.

SALMON, Joshua S. (D N.J.) Feb. 2, 1846-May 6, 1902; House 1899-May 6, 1902.

SALMON, William Charles (D Tenn.) April 3, 1868-May 13, 1925; House 1923-25.

Biographical Index

SALTONSTALL, Leverett (great-grandfather of the following) (W Mass.) June 13, 1783-May 8, 1845; House Dec. 5, 1838-43.

SALTONSTALL, Leverett (great-grandson of the preceding) (R Mass.) Sept. 1, 1892-June 17, 1979; Senate Jan. 4, 1945-67; Gov. 1939-45.

SAMFORD, William James (D Ala.) Sept. 16, 1844-June 11, 1901; House 1879-81; Gov. 1900-01.

SAMMONS, Thomas (grandfather of John Henry Starin) (D N.Y.) Oct. 1, 1762-Nov. 20, 1838; House 1803-07, 1809-13.

SAMPLE, Samuel Caldwell (D Ind.) Aug. 15, 1796-Dec. 2, 1855; House 1843-45.

SAMPSON, Ezekiel Silas (R Iowa) Dec. 6, 1831-Oct. 7, 1892; House 1875-79.

SAMPSON, Zabdiel (D Mass.) Aug. 22, 1781-July 19, 1828; House 1817-July 26, 1820.

SAMUEL, Edmund William (R Pa.) Nov. 27, 1857-March 7, 1930; House 1905-07.

SAMUELS, Green Berry (cousin of Isaac Samuels Pennybacker) (D Va.) Feb. 1, 1806-Jan. 5, 1859; House 1839-41.

SANBORN, John Carfield (R Idaho) Sept. 28, 1885-May 16, 1968; House 1947-51.

SANDAGER, Harry (R R.I.) April 12, 1887-Dec. 24, 1955; House 1939-41.

SANDERS, Archie Dovell (R N.Y.) June 17, 1857-July 15, 1941; House 1917-33.

SANDERS, Everett (R Ind.) March 8, 1882-May 12, 1950; House 1917-25; Chrmn. Rep. Nat. Comm. 1932-34.

SANDERS, Jared Young (father of Jared Young Sanders Jr.) (D La.) Jan. 29, 1869-March 23, 1944; House 1917-21; Gov. 1908-12.

SANDERS, Jared Young Jr. (son of Jared Young Sanders) (D La.) April 20, 1892-Nov. 29, 1960; House May 1, 1934-37, 1941-43.

SANDERS, Morgan Gurley (D Texas) July 14, 1878-Jan. 7, 1956; House 1921-39.

SANDERS, Newell (R Tenn.) July 12, 1850-Jan. 26, 1939; Senate April 11, 1912-Jan. 24, 1913.

SANDERS, Wilbur Fiske (R Mont.) May 2, 1834-July 7, 1905; Senate Jan. 1, 1890-93.

SANDFORD, James T. (— Tenn.) ?-?; House 1823-25.

SANDFORD, Thomas (D Ky.) 1762-Dec. 10, 1808; House 1803-07.

SANDIDGE, John Milton (D La.) Jan. 7, 1817-March 30, 1890; House 1855-59.

SANDLIN, John Nicholas (D La.) Feb. 24, 1872-Dec. 25, 1957; House 1921-37.

SANDMAN, Charles William Jr. (R N.J.) Oct. 23, 1921- —; House 1967-75.

SANDS, Joshua (— N.Y.) Oct. 12, 1757-Sept. 13, 1835; House 1803-05, 1825-27.

SANFORD, John (father of Stephen Sanford, grandfather of the following) (D N.Y.) June 3, 1803-Oct. 4, 1857; House 1841-43.

SANFORD, John (son of Stephen Sanford, grandson of the preceding) (R N.Y.) Jan. 18, 1851-Sept. 26, 1939; House 1889-93.

SANFORD, John W.A. (UD Ga.) Aug. 28, 1798-Sept. 12, 1870; House March 4-July 25, 1835.

SANFORD, Jonah (great-grandfather of Rollin Brewster Sanford) (JD N.Y.) Nov. 30, 1790-Dec. 25, 1867; House Nov. 3, 1830-31.

SANFORD, Nathan (D N.Y.) Nov. 4, 1777-Oct. 17, 1838; Senate 1815-21, Jan. 14, 1826-31.

SANFORD, Rollin Brewster (great-grandson of Jonah Sanford) (R N.Y.) May 18, 1874-May 16, 1957; House 1915-21.

SANFORD, Stephen (son of John Sanford born in 1803, father of John Sanford born in 1851) (R N.Y.) May 26, 1826-Feb. 13, 1913; House 1869-71.

SANTANGELO, Alfred Edward (D N.Y.) June 4, 1912-March 30, 1978; House 1957-63.

SANTINI, James David (D Nev.) Aug. 13, 1937- —; House 1975-83.

SAPP, William Fletcher (nephew of William Robinson Sapp) (R Iowa) Nov. 20, 1824-Nov. 22, 1890; House 1877-81.

SAPP, William Robinson (uncle of William Fletcher Sapp) (W Ohio) March 4, 1804-Jan. 3, 1875; House 1853-57.

SARASIN, Ronald Arthur (R Conn.) Dec. 31, 1934- —; House 1973-79.

SARBACHER, George William Jr. (R Pa.) Sept. 30, 1919-March 4, 1973; House 1947-49.

SARBANES, Paul Spyros (D Md.) Feb. 3, 1933- —; House 1971-77; Senate 1977- —.

SARGENT, Aaron Augustus (R Calif.) Sept. 28, 1827-Aug. 14, 1887; House 1861-63, 1869-73; Senate 1873-79.

SASSCER, Lansdale Ghiselin (D Md.) Sept. 30, 1893-Nov. 5, 1964; House Feb. 3, 1939-53.

SASSER, James Ralph (D Tenn.) Sept. 30, 1931- —; Senate 1977- —.

SATTERFIELD, Dave Edward Jr. (father of David Edward Satterfield III) (D Va.) Sept. 11, 1894-Dec. 27, 1946; House Nov. 2, 1937-Feb. 15, 1945.

SATTERFIELD, Dave Edward III (son of Dave Edward Satterfield Jr.) (D Va.) Dec. 2, 1920- —; House 1965-81.

SAUERHERING, Edward (R Wis.) June 24, 1864-March 1, 1924; House 1895-99.

SAULSBURY, Eli (brother of Willard Saulsbury born in 1820, uncle of Willard Saulsbury born in 1861) (D Del.) Dec. 29, 1817-March 22, 1893; Senate 1871-89.

SAULSBURY, Willard (brother of Eli Saulsbury, father of the following) (D Del.) June 2, 1820-April 6, 1892; Senate 1859-71.

SAULSBURY, Willard (son of the preceding, nephew of Eli Saulsbury) (D Del.) April 17, 1861-Feb. 20, 1927; Senate 1913-19; Pres. pro tempore 1916-19.

SAUND, Daliph Singh (D Calif.) Sept. 20, 1899-April 22, 1973; House 1957-63.

SAUNDERS, Alvin (grandfather of William Henry Harrison of Wyoming) (R Neb.) July 12, 1817-Nov. 1, 1899; Senate March 5, 1877-83; Gov. (Neb. Terr.) 1861-67.

SAUNDERS, Edward Watts (D Va.) Oct. 20, 1860-Dec. 16, 1921; House Nov. 6, 1906-Feb. 29, 1920.

SAUNDERS, Romulus Mitchell (D N.C.) March 3, 1791-April 21, 1867; House 1821-27, 1841-45.

SAUTHOFF, Harry (Prog. Wis.) June 3, 1879-June 16, 1966; House 1935-39, 1941-45.

SAVAGE, Charles Raymon (D Wash.) April 12, 1906-Jan. 14, 1976; House 1945-47.

SAVAGE, Gus (D Ill.) Oct. 30, 1925- —; House 1981- —.

SAVAGE, John (D N.Y.) Feb. 22, 1779-Oct. 19, 1863; House 1815-19.

SAVAGE, John Houston (— Tenn.) Oct. 9, 1815-April 5, 1904; House 1849-53, 1855-59.

SAVAGE, John Simpson (D Ohio) Oct. 30, 1841-Nov. 24, 1884; House 1875-77.

SAWTELLE, Cullen (D Maine) Sept. 25, 1805-Nov. 10, 1887; House 1845-47; 1849-51.

SAWYER, Frederick Adolphus (R S.C.) Dec. 12, 1822-July 31, 1891; Senate July 16, 1868-73.

SAWYER, Harold S. (R Mich.) March 21, 1920- —; House 1977-85.

SAWYER, John Gilbert (R N.Y.) June 5, 1825-Sept. 5, 1898; House 1885-91.

SAWYER, Lemuel (D N.C.) 1777-Jan. 9, 1852; House 1807-13, 1817-23, 1825-29.

SAWYER, Lewis Ernest (D Ark.) June 24, 1867-May 5, 1923; House March 4-May 5, 1923.

SAWYER, Philetus (R Wis.) Sept. 22, 1816-March 29, 1900; House 1865-75; Senate 1881-93.

SAWYER, Samuel Locke (D Mo.) Nov. 27, 1813-March 29, 1890; House 1879-81.

SAWYER, Samuel Tredwell (D N.C.) 1800-Nov. 29, 1865; House 1837-39.

SAWYER, William (D Ohio) Aug. 5, 1803-Sept. 18, 1877; House 1845-49.

SAXBE, William B. (R Ohio) June 24, 1916- —; Senate 1969-Jan. 3, 1974; Atty. Gen. 1974-75.

SAXTON, H. James (R N.J.) Jan. 22, 1943- —; House 1985- —.

SAY, Benjamin (— Pa.) 1756-April 23, 1813; House Nov. 16, 1808-June 1809.

SAYERS, Joseph Draper (D Texas) Sept. 23, 1841-May 15, 1929; House 1885-Jan. 16, 1899; Gov. 1899-1903.

SAYLER, Henry Benton (cousin of Milton Sayler) (R Ind.) March 31, 1836-June 18, 1900; House 1873-75.

SAYLER, Milton (cousin of Henry Benton Sayler) (D Ohio) Nov. 4, 1831-Nov. 17, 1892; House 1873-79; Speaker pro tempore 1876.

SAYLOR, John Phillips (R Pa.) July 23, 1908-Oct. 28, 1973; House Sept. 13, 1949-Oct. 28, 1973.

SCALES, Alfred Moore (D N.C.) Nov. 26, 1827-Feb. 9, 1892; House 1857-59, 1875-Dec. 30, 1884; Gov. 1885-89.

SCAMMAN, John Fairfield (D Maine) Oct. 24, 1786-May 22, 1858; House 1845-47.

SCANLON, Thomas Edward (D Pa.) Sept. 18, 1896-Aug. 9, 1955; House 1941-45.

SCARBOROUGH, Robert Bethea (D S.C.) Oct. 29 1861-Nov. 23, 1927; House 1901-05.

SCHADEBERG, Henry C. (R Wis.) Oct. 12, 1913- —; House 1961-65, 1967-71.

SCHAEFER, Daniel L. (R Colo.) Jan. 25, 1936- —; House April 7, 1983- —.

SCHAEFER, Edwin Martin (D Ill.) May 14, 1887-Nov. 8, 1950; House 1933-43.

SCHAFER, John Charles (R Wis.) May 7, 1893-June 9, 1962; House 1923-33; 1939-41.

SCHALL, Thomas David (R Minn.) June 4, 1878-Dec. 22, 1935; House 1915-25; Senate 1925-Dec. 22, 1935.

SCHELL, Richard (D N.Y.) May 15, 1810-Nov. 10, 1879; House Dec. 7, 1874-75.

SCHENCK, Abraham Henry (uncle of Isaac Teller) (D N.Y.) Jan. 22, 1775-June 1, 1831; House 1815-17.

SCHENCK, Ferdinand Schureman (JD N.J.) Feb. 11, 1790-May 16, 1860; House 1833-37.

SCHENCK, Paul Fornshell (R Ohio) April 19, 1899-Nov. 30, 1968; House Nov. 6, 1951-65.

SCHENCK, Robert Cumming (R Ohio) Oct. 4, 1809-March 23, 1890; House 1843-51, 1863-Jan. 5, 1871 (1843-51 Whig, 1863-71 Republican).

SCHERER, Gordon Harry (R Ohio) Dec. 26, 1906- —; House 1953-63.

SCHERLE, William Joseph (R Iowa) March 14, 1923- —; House 1967-75.

SCHERMERHORN, Abraham Maus (W N.Y.) Dec. 11, 1791-Aug. 22, 1855; House 1849-53.

SCHERMERHORN, Simon Jacob (D N.Y.) Sept. 25, 1827-July 21, 1901; House 1893-95.

SCHEUER, James Haas (D N.Y.) Feb. 6, 1920- —; House 1965-73, 1975- —.

SCHIFFLER, Andrew Charles (R W.Va.) Aug. 10, 1889-March 27, 1970; House 1939-41, 1943-45.

SCHIRM, Charles Reginald (R Md.) Aug. 12, 1864-Nov. 2, 1918; House 1901-03.

SCHISLER, Darwin Gale (D Ill.) March 2, 1933- —; House 1965-67.

SCHLEICHER, Gustave (D Texas) Nov. 19, 1823-Jan. 10, 1879; House 1875-Jan. 10, 1879.

SCHLEY, William (D Ga.) Dec. 15, 1786-Nov. 20, 1858; House 1833-July 1, 1835; Gov. 1835-37.

SCHMIDHAUSER, John Richard (D Iowa) Jan. 3, 1922- —; House 1965-67.

SCHMITT, Harrison Hagan (R N.M.) July 3, 1935- —; Senate 1977-83.

SCHMITZ, John George (R Calif.) Aug. 12, 1930- —; House June 30, 1970-73.

SCHNEEBELI, Gustav Adolphus (R Pa.) May 23, 1853-Feb. 6, 1923; House 1905-07.

SCHNEEBELI, Herman T. (R Pa.) July 7, 1907-May 6, 1982; House April 26, 1960-77.

SCHNEIDER, Claudine (R R.I.) March 25, 1947- —; House 1981- —.

SCHNEIDER, George John (Prog. Wis.) Oct. 30, 1877-March 12, 1939; House 1923-33, 1935-39 (1923-33 Republican, 1935-39 Progressive).

SCHOEPPEL, Andrew Frank (R Kan.) Nov. 23, 1894-Jan. 21, 1962; Senate 1949-Jan. 21, 1962; Gov. 1943-47.

SCHOOLCRAFT, John Lawrence (W N.Y.) 1804-July 7, 1860; House 1849-53.

SCHOONMAKER, Cornelius Corneliusen (grandfather of Marius Schoonmaker) (— N.Y.) June 1745-96; House 1791-93.

SCHOONMAKER, Marius (grandson of Cornelius Corneliusen Schoonmaker) (W N.Y.) April 24, 1811-Jan. 5, 1894; House 1851-53.

SCHROEDER, Patricia Scott (D Colo.) July 30, 1940- —; House 1973- —.

SCHUETTE, William Duncan (R Mich.) Oct. 13, 1953- —; House 1985- —.

SCHUETZ, Leonard William (D Ill.) Nov. 16, 1887-Feb. 13, 1944; House 1931-Feb. 13, 1944.

SCHULTE, William Theodore (D Ind.) Aug. 19, 1890-Dec. 7, 1966; House 1933-43.

SCHULZE, Richard Taylor (R Pa.) Aug. 7, 1929- —; House 1975- —.

SCHUMAKER, John Godfrey (D N.Y.) June 27, 1826-Nov. 23, 1905; House 1869-71, 1873-77.

SCHUMER, Charles E. (D N.Y.) Nov. 23, 1951- —; House 1981- —.

SCHUNEMAN, Martin Gerretsen (D N.Y.) Feb. 10, 1764-Feb. 21, 1827; House 1805-07.

SCHUREMAN, James (F N.J.) Feb. 12, 1756-Jan. 22, 1824; House 1789-91, 1797-99, 1813-15; Senate 1799-Feb. 16, 1801; Cont. Cong. 1786-87.

SCHURZ, Carl (R Mo.) March 2, 1829-May 14, 1906; Senate 1869-75; Secy. of the Interior 1877-81.

SCHUYLER, Karl Cortlandt (R Colo.) April 3, 1877-July 31, 1933; Senate Dec. 7, 1932-33.

SCHUYLER, Philip Jeremiah (son of Philip John Schuyler) (— N.Y.) Jan. 21, 1768-Feb. 21, 1835; House 1817-19.

SCHUYLER, Philip John (father of Philip Jeremiah Schuyler) (F N.Y.) Nov. 20, 1733-Nov. 18, 1804; Senate 1789-91, 1797-Jan. 3, 1798; Cont. Cong. 1775-81.

SCHWABE, George Blaine (brother of Max Schwabe) (R Okla.) July 26, 1886-April 2, 1952; House 1945-49, 1951-April 2, 1952.

SCHWABE, Max (brother of George Blaine Schwabe) (R Mo.) Dec. 6, 1905- —; House 1943-49.

SCHWARTZ, Henry Herman (Harry) (D Wyo.) May 18, 1869-April 24, 1955; Senate 1937-43.

SCHWARTZ, John (D Pa.) Oct. 27, 1793-June 20, 1860; House 1859-June 20, 1860.

SCHWEIKER, Richard Schultz (R Pa.) June 1, 1926- —; House 1961-69; Senate 1969-81. Secy. of Health and Human Services 1981-83.

SCHWELLENBACH, Lewis Baxter (D Wash.) Sept. 20, 1894-June 10, 1948; Senate 1935-Dec. 16, 1940; Secy. of Labor 1945-48.

SCHWENGEL, Frederick Delbert (R Iowa) May 28, 1907- —; House 1955-65, 1967-73.

SCHWERT, Pius Louis (D N.Y.) Nov. 22, 1892-March 11, 1941; House 1939-March 11, 1941.

SCOBLICK, James Paul (R Pa.) May 10, 1909- —; House Nov. 5, 1946-49.

SCOFIELD, Glenni William (R Pa.) March 11, 1817-Aug. 30, 1891; House 1863-75.

SCOTT, Byron Nicholson (D Calif.) March 21, 1903- —; House 1935-39.

SCOTT, Charles Frederick (R Kan.) Sept. 7, 1860-Sept. 18, 1938; House 1901-11.

SCOTT, Charles Lewis (D Calif.) Jan. 23, 1827-April 30, 1899; House 1857-61.

SCOTT, David (— Pa.) ?-?; House 1817.

SCOTT, Frank Douglas (R Mich.) Aug. 25, 1878-Feb. 12, 1951; House 1915-27.

SCOTT, George Cromwell (R Iowa) Aug. 8, 1864-Oct. 6, 1948; House Nov. 5, 1912-15, 1917-19.

SCOTT, Hardie (son of John Roger Kirkpatrick Scott) (R Pa.) June 7, 1907- —; House 1947-53.

SCOTT, Harvey David (R Ind.) Oct. 18, 1818-July 11, 1891; House 1855-57.

SCOTT, Hugh Doggett Jr. (R Pa.) Nov. 11, 1900- —; House 1941-45, 1947-59; Senate 1959-77; Chrmn. Rep. Nat. Comm. 1948-49.

SCOTT, John (— Mo.) May 18, 1785-Oct. 1, 1861; House (Terr. Del.) Aug. 6, 1816-Jan. 13, 1817, Aug. 5, 1817-March 3, 1821, (Rep.) Aug. 10, 1821-27.

SCOTT, John (father of the following) (— Pa.) Dec. 25, 1784-Sept. 22, 1850; House 1829-31.

SCOTT, John (son of the preceding) (R Pa.) July 24, 1824-Nov. 29, 1896; Senate 1869-75.

SCOTT, John Guier (D Mo.) Dec. 26, 1819-May 16, 1892; House Dec. 7, 1863-65.

Biographical Index

SCOTT, John Roger Kirkpatrick (father of Hardie Scott) (R Pa.) July 6, 1873-Dec. 9, 1945; House 1915-Jan. 5, 1919.

SCOTT, Lon Allen (R Tenn.) Sept. 25, 1888-Feb. 11, 1931; House 1921-23.

SCOTT, Nathan Bay (R W.Va.) Dec. 18, 1842-Jan. 2, 1924; Senate 1899-1911.

SCOTT, Owen (D Ill.) July 6, 1848-Dec. 21, 1928; House 1891-93.

SCOTT, Ralph James (D N.C.) Oct. 15, 1905-Aug. 5, 1983; House 1957-67.

SCOTT, Thomas (— Pa.) 1739-March 2, 1796; House 1789-91, 1793-95.

SCOTT, William Kerr (D N.C.) April 17, 1896-April 16, 1958; Senate Nov. 29, 1954-April 16, 1958; Gov. 1949-53.

SCOTT, William Lawrence (D Pa.) July 2, 1828-Sept. 19, 1891; House 1885-89.

SCOTT, William Lloyd (R Va.) July 1, 1915-—; House 1967-73; Senate 1973-Jan. 1, 1979.

SCOVILLE, Jonathan (D N.Y.) July 14, 1830-March 4, 1891; House Nov. 12, 1880-83.

SCRANTON, George Whitfield (second cousin of Joseph Augustine Scranton) (R Pa.) May 11, 1811-March 24, 1861; House 1859-March 24, 1861.

SCRANTON, Joseph Augustine (second cousin of George Whitfield Scranton) (R Pa.) July 26, 1838-Oct. 12, 1908; House 1881-83, 1885-87, 1889-91, 1893-97.

SCRANTON, William Warren (R Pa.) July 19, 1917-—; House 1961-63; Gov. 1963-67.

SCRIVNER, Errett Power (R Kan.) March 20, 1898-May 5, 1978; House Sept. 14, 1943-59.

SCROGGY, Thomas Edmund (R Ohio) March 18, 1843-March 6, 1915; House 1905-07.

SCRUGHAM, James Graves (D Nev.) Jan. 19, 1880-June 23, 1945; House 1933-Dec. 7, 1942; Senate Dec. 7, 1942-June 23, 1945; Gov. 1923-27.

SCUDDER, Henry Joel (uncle of Townsend Scudder) (R N.Y.) Sept. 18, 1825-Feb. 10, 1886; House 1873-75.

SCUDDER, Hubert Baxter (R Calif.) Nov. 5, 1888-July 4, 1968; House 1949-59.

SCUDDER, Isaac Williamson (R N.J.) 1816-Sept. 10, 1881; House 1873-75.

SCUDDER, John Anderson (D N.J.) March 22, 1759-Nov. 6, 1836; House Oct. 31, 1810-11.

SCUDDER, Townsend (nephew of Henry Joel Scudder) (D N.Y.) July 26, 1865-Feb. 22, 1960; House 1899-1901, 1903-05.

SCUDDER, Tredwell (— N.Y.) Jan. 1, 1778-Oct. 31, 1834; House 1817-19.

SCUDDER, Zeno (W Mass.) Aug. 18, 1807-June 26, 1857; House 1851-March 4, 1854.

SCULL, Edward (R Pa.) Feb. 5, 1818-July 10, 1900; House 1887-93.

SCULLY, Thomas Joseph (D N.J.) Sept. 19, 1868-Dec. 14, 1921; House 1911-21.

SCURRY, Richardson (D Texas) Nov. 11, 1811-April 9, 1862; House 1851-53.

SEAMAN, Henry John (AP N.Y.) April 16, 1805-May 3, 1861; House 1845-47.

SEARING, John Alexander (D N.Y.) May 14, 1805-May 6, 1876; House 1857-59.

SEARS, William Joseph (D Fla.) Dec. 4, 1874-March 30, 1944; House 1915-29, 1933-37.

SEARS, Willis Gratz (R Neb.) Aug. 16, 1860-June 1, 1949; House 1923-31.

SEATON, Frederick Andrew (R Neb.) Dec. 11, 1909-Jan. 16, 1974; Senate Dec. 10, 1951-Nov. 4, 1952; Secy. of the Interior 1956-61.

SEAVER, Ebenezer (D Mass.) July 5, 1763-March 1, 1844; House 1803-13.

SEBASTIAN, William King (D Ark.) 1812-May 20, 1865; Senate May 12, 1848-July 11, 1861.

SEBELIUS, Keith George (R Kan.) Sept. 10, 1916-Aug. 5, 1982; House 1969-81.

SECCOMBE, James (R Ohio) Feb. 12, 1893-Aug. 23, 1970; House 1939-41.

SECREST, Robert Thompson (D Ohio) Jan. 22, 1904-—; House 1933-Aug. 3, 1942, 1949-Sept. 26, 1954, 1963-Jan. 3, 1967.

SEDDON, James Alexander (D Va.) July 13, 1815-Aug. 19, 1880; House 1845-47, 1849-51.

SEDGWICK, Charles Baldwin (R N.Y.) March 15, 1815-Feb. 3, 1883; House 1859-63.

SEDGWICK, Theodore (F Mass.) May 9, 1746-Jan. 24, 1813; House 1789-June 1796, 1799-1801; Senate June 11, 1796-99; Speaker 1799-1801; Pres. pro tempore 1798; Cont. Cong. 1785-88.

SEELEY, John Edward (R N.Y.) Aug. 1, 1810-March 30, 1875; House 1871-73.

SEELY-BROWN, Horace Jr. (R Conn.) May 12, 1908-April 9, 1982; House 1947-49, 1951-59, 1961-63.

SEELYE, Julius Hawley (I Mass.) Sept. 14, 1824-May 12, 1895; House 1875-77.

SEERLEY, John Joseph (D Iowa) March 13, 1852-Feb. 23, 1931; House 1891-93.

SEGAR, Joseph Eggleston (U Va.) June 1, 1804-April 30, 1880; House March 15, 1862-63.

SEGER, George Nicholas (R N.J.) Jan. 4, 1866-Aug. 26, 1940; House 1923-Aug. 26, 1940.

SEIBERLING, Francis (R Ohio) Sept. 20, 1870-Feb. 1, 1945; House 1929-33.

SEIBERLING, John Frederick (D Ohio) Sept. 8, 1918-—; House 1971-—.

SELBY, Thomas Jefferson (D Ill.) Dec. 4, 1840-March 10, 1917; House 1901-03.

SELDEN, Armistead Inge Jr. (D Ala.) Feb. 20, 1921-—; House 1953-69.

SELDEN, Dudley (D N.Y.) ?-Nov. 7, 1855; House 1833-July 1, 1834.

SELDOMRIDGE, Harry Hunter (D Colo.) Oct. 1, 1864-Nov. 2, 1927; House 1913-15.

SELLS, Sam Riley (R Tenn.) Aug. 2, 1871-Nov. 2, 1935; House 1911-21.

SELVIG, Conrad George (R Minn.) Oct. 11, 1877-Aug. 2, 1953; House 1927-33.

SELYE, Lewis (I N.Y.) July 11, 1803-Jan. 27, 1883; House 1867-69.

SEMMES, Benedict Joseph (D Md.) Nov. 1, 1789-Feb. 10, 1863; House 1829-33.

SEMPLE, James (D Ill.) Jan. 5, 1798-Dec. 20, 1866; Senate Dec. 4, 1843-47.

SENER, James Beverley (R Va.) May 18, 1837-Nov. 18, 1903; House 1873-75.

SENEY, George Ebbert (D Ohio) May 29, 1832-June 11, 1905; House 1883-91.

SENEY, Joshua (— Md.) March 4, 1756-Oct. 20, 1798; House 1789-May 1, 1792; Cont. Cong. 1787-88.

SENNER, George Frederick Jr. (D Ariz.) Nov. 24, 1921-—; House 1963-67.

SENSENBRENNER, Frank James Jr. (R Wis.) June 14, 1943-—; House 1979-—.

SENTER, William Tandy (W Tenn.) May 12, 1801-Aug. 28, 1848; House 1843-45.

SERGEANT, John (grandfather of John Sergeant Wise and Richard Alsop Wise, great-grandfather of John Crain Kunkel) (F Pa.) Dec. 5, 1779-Nov. 23, 1852; House Oct. 10, 1815-23, 1827-29, 1837-Sept. 15, 1841.

SESSINGHAUS, Gustavus (R Mo.) Nov. 8, 1838-Nov. 16, 1887; House March 2-3, 1883.

SESSIONS, Walter Loomis (R N.Y.) Oct. 4, 1820-May 27, 1896; House 1871-75, 1885-87.

SETTLE, Evan Evans (D Ky.) Dec. 1, 1848-Nov. 16, 1899; House 1897-Nov. 16, 1899.

SETTLE, Thomas (uncle of David Settle Reid, grandfather of the following) (D N.C.) March 9, 1789-Aug. 5, 1857; House 1817-21.

SETTLE, Thomas (grandson of the preceding) (R N.C.) March 10, 1865-Jan. 20, 1919; House 1893-97.

SEVERANCE, Luther (W Maine) Oct. 26, 1797-Jan. 25, 1855; House 1843-47.

SEVIER, Ambrose Hundley (cousin of Henry Wharton Conway) (D Ark.) Nov. 10, 1801-Dec. 31, 1848; House (Terr. Del.) Feb. 13, 1828-June 15, 1836; Senate Sept. 18, 1836-March 15, 1848 (1828-36 Whig, 1836-48 Democrat).

SEVIER, John (D N.C./Tenn.) Sept. 23, 1745-Sept. 24, 1815; House 1789-91 (N.C.) 1811-Sept. 24, 1815 (Tenn.); Gov. (Tenn.) 1796-1801, 1803-09.

SEWALL, Charles S. (— Md.) 1779-Nov. 3, 1848; House Oct. 1, 1832-33, Jan. 2-March 3, 1843.

SEWALL, Samuel (— Mass.) Dec. 11, 1757-June 8, 1814; House Dec. 7, 1796-Jan. 10, 1800.

SEWARD, James Lindsay (D Ga.) Oct. 30, 1813-Nov. 21, 1886; House 1853-59.

SEWARD, William Henry (R N.Y.) May 16, 1801-Oct. 16, 1872; Senate 1849-61 (1849-55 Whig, 1855-61 Republican); Secy. of State 1861-69; Gov. 1839-43.

SEWELL, William Joyce (R N.J.) Dec. 6, 1835-Dec. 27, 1901; Senate 1881-87, 1895-Dec. 27, 1901.

SEXTON, Leonidas (R Ind.) May 19, 1827-July 4, 1880; House 1877-79.

SEYBERT, Adam (D Pa.) May 16, 1773-May 2, 1825; House Oct. 10, 1809-15, 1817-19.

SEYMOUR, David Lowrey (D N.Y.) Dec. 2, 1803-Oct. 11, 1867; House 1843-45, 1851-53.

SEYMOUR, Edward Woodruff (son of Origen Storrs Seymour) (D Conn.) Aug. 30, 1832-Oct. 16, 1892; House 1883-87.

SEYMOUR, Henry William (R Mich.) July 21, 1834-April 7, 1906; House Feb. 14, 1888-89.

SEYMOUR, Horatio (uncle of Origen Storrs Seymour) (CD Vt.) May 31, 1778-Nov. 21, 1857; Senate 1821-33.

SEYMOUR, Origen Storrs (father of Edward Woodruff Seymour, nephew of Horatio Seymour) (D Conn.) Feb. 9, 1804-Aug. 12, 1881; House 1851-55.

SEYMOUR, Thomas Hart (D Conn.) Sept. 29, 1807-Sept. 3, 1868; House 1843-45; Gov. 1850-53.

SEYMOUR, William (D N.Y.) about 1780-Dec. 28, 1848; House 1835-37.

SHACKELFORD, John Williams (D N.C.) Nov. 16, 1844-Jan. 18, 1883; House 1881-Jan. 18, 1883.

SHACKLEFORD, Dorsey William (D Mo.) Aug. 27, 1853-July 15, 1936; House Aug. 29, 1899-1919.

SHAFER, Jacob K. (D Idaho) Dec. 26, 1823-Nov. 22, 1876; House (Terr. Del.) 1869-71.

SHAFER, Paul Werntz (R Mich.) April 27, 1893-Aug. 17, 1954; House 1937-Aug. 17, 1954.

SHAFFER, Joseph Crockett (R Va.) Jan. 19, 1880-Oct. 19, 1958; House 1929-31.

SHAFROTH, John Franklin (D Colo.) June 9, 1854-Feb. 20, 1922; House 1895-Feb. 15, 1904; Senate 1913-19; Gov. 1909-13 (1895-97 Republican, 1897-1903 Silver Republican/Democrat, 1903-19 Democrat).

SHALLENBERGER, Ashton Cokayne (D Neb.) Dec. 23, 1862-Feb. 22, 1938; House 1901-03, 1915-19, 1923-29, 1931-35; Gov. 1909-11.

SHALLENBERGER, William Shadrack (R Pa.) Nov. 24, 1839-April 15, 1914; House 1877-83.

SHAMANSKY, Robert N. (D Ohio) April 18, 1927-—; House 1981-83.

SHANKLIN, George Sea (D Ky.) Dec. 23, 1807-April 1, 1883; House 1865-67.

SHANKS, John Peter Cleaver (R Ind.) June 17, 1826-Jan. 23, 1901; House 1861-63, 1867-75.

SHANLEY, James Andrew (D Conn.) April 1, 1896-April 5, 1965; House 1935-43.

SHANNON, James Michael (D Mass.) April 4, 1952-—; House 1979-85.

SHANNON, Joseph Bernard (D Mo.) March 17, 1867-March 28, 1943; House 1931-43.

SHANNON, Richard Cutts (R N.Y.) Feb. 12, 1839-Oct. 5, 1920; House 1895-99.

SHANNON, Thomas (brother of Wilson Shannon) (D Ohio) Nov. 15, 1786-March 16, 1843; House Dec. 4, 1826-27.

SHANNON, Thomas Bowles (R Calif.) Sept. 21, 1827-Feb. 21, 1897; House 1863-65.

SHANNON, Wilson (brother of Thomas Shannon) (D Ohio) Feb. 24, 1802-Aug. 31, 1877; House 1853-55; Gov. 1838-40, 1842-44 (Ohio), 1855-56 (Kansas Terr.).

SHARON, William (R Neb.) Jan. 9, 1821-Nov. 13, 1885; Senate 1875-81.

SHARP, Edgar Allan (R N.Y.) June 3, 1876-Nov. 27, 1948; House 1945-47.

SHARP, Philip Riley (D Ind.) July 15, 1942-—; House 1975-—.

SHARP, Solomon P. (D Ky.) 1780-Nov. 7, 1825; House 1813-17.

SHARP, William Graves (D Ohio) March 14, 1859-Nov. 17, 1922; House 1909-July 23, 1914.

SHARPE, Peter (— N.Y.) ?-?; House 1823-25.

SHARTEL, Cassius McLean (R Mo.) April 27, 1860-Sept. 27, 1943; House 1905-07.

SHATTUC, William Bunn (R Ohio) June 11, 1841-July 13, 1911; House 1897-1903.

SHAW, Aaron (D Ill.) Dec. 19, 1811-Jan. 7, 1887; House 1857-59, 1883-85.

SHAW, Albert Duane (R N.Y.) Dec. 21, 1841-Feb. 10, 1901; House Nov. 6, 1900-Feb. 10, 1901.

SHAW, E. Clay (R Fla.) April 19, 1939-—; House 1981-—.

SHAW, Frank Thomas (D Md.) Oct. 7, 1841-Feb. 24, 1923; House 1885-89.

SHAW, George Bullen (R Wis.) March 12, 1854-Aug. 27, 1894; House 1893-Aug. 27, 1894.

SHAW, Guy Loren (R Ill.) May 16, 1881-May 19, 1950; House 1921-23.

SHAW, Henry (son of Samuel Shaw) (F Mass.) 1788-Oct. 17, 1857; House 1817-21.

SHAW, Henry Marchmore (D N.C.) Nov. 20, 1819-Nov. 1, 1864; House 1853-55, 1857-59.

SHAW, John Gilbert (D N.C.) Jan. 16, 1859-July 21, 1932; House 1895-97.

SHAW, Samuel (father of Henry Shaw) (D Vt.) Dec. 1768-Oct. 23, 1827; House Sept. 6, 1808-13.

SHAW, Tristram (— N.H.) May 23, 1786-March 14, 1843; House 1839-43.

SHEAFE, James (F N.H.) Nov. 16, 1755-Dec. 5, 1829; House 1799-1801; Senate 1801-June 14, 1802.

SHEAKLEY, James (D Pa.) April 24, 1829-Dec. 10, 1917; House 1875-77; Gov. (Alaska Terr.) 1893-97.

SHEATS, Charles Christopher (R Ala.) April 10, 1839-May 27, 1904; House 1873-75.

SHEEHAN, Timothy Patrick (R Ill.) Feb. 21, 1909-—; House 1951-59.

SHEFFER, Daniel (D Pa.) May 24, 1783-Feb. 16, 1880; House 1837-39.

SHEFFEY, Daniel (F Va.) 1770-Dec. 3, 1830; House 1809-17.

SHEFFIELD, William Paine (father of the following) (R R.I.) Aug. 30, 1820-June 2, 1907; House 1861-63; Senate Nov. 19, 1884-Jan. 20, 1885.

SHEFFIELD, William Paine (son of the preceding) (R R.I.) June 1, 1857-Oct. 19, 1919; House 1909-11.

SHELBY, Richard Craig (D Ala.) May 6, 1934-—; House 1979-—.

SHELDEN, Carlos Douglas (R Mich.) June 10, 1840-June 24, 1904; House 1897-1903.

SHELDON, Lionel Allen (R La.) Aug. 30, 1828-Jan. 17, 1917; House 1869-75; Gov. (N.M. Terr.) 1881-85.

SHELDON, Porter (R N.Y.) Sept. 29, 1831-Aug. 15, 1908; House 1869-71.

SHELL, George Washington (D S.C.) Nov. 13, 1831-Dec. 15, 1899; House 1891-95.

SHELLABARGER, Samuel (R Ohio) Dec. 10, 1817-Aug. 7, 1896; House 1861-63, 1865-69, 1871-73.

SHELLEY, Charles Miller (D Ala.) Dec. 28, 1833-Jan. 20, 1907; House 1877-81, Nov. 7, 1882-Jan. 9, 1885.

SHELLEY, John Francis (D Calif.) Sept. 3, 1905-Sept. 1, 1974; House Nov. 8, 1949-Jan. 7, 1964.

SHELTON, Samuel Azariah (R Mo.) Sept. 3, 1858-Sept. 13, 1948; House 1921-23.

SHEPARD, Charles Biddle (D N.C.) Dec. 5, 1807-Oct. 31, 1843; House 1837-41.

SHEPARD, William (— Mass.) Dec. 1, 1737-Nov. 16, 1817; House 1797-1803.

SHEPARD, William Biddle (NR N.C.) May 14, 1799-June 20, 1852; House 1829-37.

SHEPLER, Matthias (D Ohio) Nov. 11, 1790-April 7, 1863; House 1837-39.

SHEPLEY, Ether (D Maine) Nov. 2, 1789-Jan. 15, 1877; Senate 1833-March 3, 1836.

SHEPPARD, Harry Richard (D Calif.) Jan. 10, 1885-April 28, 1969; House 1937-65.

SHEPPARD, John Levi (father of Morris Sheppard) (D Texas) April 13, 1852-Oct. 11, 1902; House 1899-Oct. 11, 1902.

Biographical Index

SHEPPARD, Morris (son of John Levi Sheppard) (D Texas) May 28, 1875-April 9, 1941; House Nov. 15, 1902-Feb. 3, 1913; Senate Feb. 3, 1913-April 9, 1941.

SHEPPERD, Augustine Henry (W N.C.) Feb. 24, 1792-July 11, 1864; House 1827-39, 1841-43, 1847-51.

SHERBURNE, John Samuel (— N.H.) 1757-Aug. 2, 1830; House 1793-97.

SHEREDINE, Upton (D Md.) 1740-Jan. 14, 1800; House 1791-93.

SHERIDAN, George Augustus (L La.) Feb. 22, 1840-Oct. 7, 1896; House 1873-75.

SHERIDAN, John Edward (D Pa.) Sept. 15, 1902- —; House Nov. 7, 1939-47.

SHERLEY, Joseph Swagar (D Ky.) Nov. 28, 1871-Feb. 13, 1941; House 1903-19.

SHERMAN, James Schoolcraft (R N.Y.) Oct. 24, 1855-Oct. 30, 1912; House 1887-91, 1893-1909; Vice Pres. 1909-Oct. 30, 1912.

SHERMAN, John (R Ohio) May 10, 1823-Oct. 22, 1900; House 1855-March 21, 1861; Senate March 21, 1861-March 8, 1877, 1881-March 4, 1897; Pres. pro tempore 1886; Secy. of the Treasury 1877-81; Secy. of State 1897-98.

SHERMAN, Judson W. (R N.Y.) 1808-Nov. 12, 1881; House 1857-59.

SHERMAN, Lawrence Yates (R Ill.) Nov. 8, 1858-Sept. 15, 1939; Senate March 26, 1913-21.

SHERMAN, Roger (grandfather of William Maxwell Evarts) (— Conn.) April 19, 1721-July 23, 1793; House 1789-91; Senate June 13, 1791-July 23, 1793; Cont. Cong. 1774-81, 1783-84.

SHERMAN, Socrates Norton (R N.Y.) July 22, 1801-Feb. 1, 1873; House 1861-63.

SHERRILL, Eliakim (W N.Y.) Feb. 16, 1813-July 4, 1863; House 1847-49.

SHERROD, William Crawford (D Ala.) Aug. 17, 1835-March 24, 1919; House 1869-71.

SHERWIN, John Crocker (R Ill.) Feb. 8, 1838-Jan. 1, 1904; House 1879-83.

SHERWOOD, Henry (D Pa.) Oct. 9, 1813-Nov. 10, 1896; House 1871-73.

SHERWOOD, Isaac R. (D Ohio) Aug. 13, 1835-Oct. 15, 1925; House 1873-75, 1907-21, 1923-25 (1873-75 Republican, 1907-21, 1923-25 Democrat).

SHERWOOD, Samuel (F N.Y.) April 24, 1779-Oct. 31, 1862; House 1813-15.

SHERWOOD, Samuel Burr (F Conn.) Nov. 26, 1767-April 27, 1833; House 1817-19.

SHIEL, George Knox (D Ore.) 1825-Dec. 12, 1893; House July 30, 1861-63.

SHIELDS, Benjamin Glover (W Ala.) 1808-?; House 1841-43.

SHIELDS, Ebenezer J. (W Tenn.) Dec. 22, 1778-April 21, 1846; House 1835-39.

SHIELDS, James (uncle of the following) (JD Ohio) April 13, 1762-Aug. 13, 1831; House 1829-31.

SHIELDS, James (nephew of the preceding) (D Ill./Minn./Mo.) May 10, 1810-June 1, 1879; Senate March 6-15, 1849, Oct. 27, 1849-55 (Ill.), May 11, 1858-59 (Minn.), Jan. 27-March 3, 1879 (Mo.).

SHIELDS, John Knight (D Tenn.) Aug. 15, 1858-Sept. 30, 1934; Senate 1913-25.

SHINN, William Norton (JD N.J.) Oct. 24, 1782-Aug. 18, 1871; House 1833-37.

SHIPHERD, Zebulon Rudd (F N.Y.) Nov. 15, 1768-Nov. 1, 1841; House 1813-15.

SHIPLEY, George Edward (D Ill.) April 21, 1927- —; House 1959-79.

SHIPSTEAD, Henrik (R Minn.) Jan. 8, 1881-June 26, 1960; Senate 1923-47 (1923-41 Farmer Laborite, 1941-47 Republican).

SHIRAS, George 3d (IR Pa.) Jan. 1, 1859-March 24, 1942; House 1903-05.

SHIVELY, Benjamin Franklin (D Ind.) March 20, 1857-March 14, 1916; House Dec. 1, 1884-85, 1887-93; Senate 1909-March 14, 1916 (1884-85 National Anti-Monopolist, 1887-1916 Democrat).

SHOBER, Francis Edwin (father of Francis Emanuel Shober) (D N.C.) March 12, 1831-May 29, 1896; House 1869-73.

SHOBER, Francis Emanuel (son of Francis Edwin Shober) (D N.Y.) Oct. 24, 1860-Oct. 7, 1919; House 1903-05.

SHOEMAKER, Francis Henry (FL Minn.) April 25, 1889-July 24, 1958; House 1933-35.

SHOEMAKER, Lazarus Denison (R Pa.) Nov. 5, 1819-Sept. 9, 1893; House 1871-75.

SHONK, George Washington (R Pa.) April 26, 1850-Aug. 14, 1900; House 1891-93.

SHORT, Dewey Jackson (R Mo.) April 7, 1898-Nov. 19, 1979; House 1929-31, 1935-57.

SHORT, Don Levingston (R N.D.) June 22, 1903-May 10, 1982; House 1959-65.

SHORTER, Eli Sims (D Ala.) March 15, 1823-April 29, 1879; House 1855-59.

SHORTRIDGE, Samuel Morgan (R Calif.) Aug. 3, 1861-Jan. 15, 1952; Senate 1921-33.

SHOTT, Hugh Ike (R W Va.) Sept. 3, 1866-Oct. 12, 1953; House 1929-33; Senate Nov. 18, 1942-43.

SHOUP, George Laird (grandfather of Richard Garner Shoup) (R Idaho) June 15, 1836-Dec. 21, 1904; Senate Dec. 18, 1890-1901; Gov. 1889-90 (Idaho Terr.), Oct. 1-Dec. 1890 (Idaho).

SHOUP, Richard Garner (grandson of George Laird Shoup) (R Mont.) Nov. 29, 1923- —; House 1971-75.

SHOUSE, Jouett (D Kan.) Dec. 10, 1879-June 2, 1968; House 1915-19.

SHOWALTER, Joseph Baltzell (R Pa.) Feb. 11, 1851-Dec. 3, 1932; House April 20, 1897-1903.

SHOWER, Jacob (I Md.) Feb. 22, 1803-May 25, 1879; House 1853-55.

SHREVE, Milton William (R Pa.) May 3, 1858-Dec. 23, 1939; House 1913-15, 1919-33.

SHRIVER, Garner E. (R Kan.) July 6, 1912- —; House 1961-77.

SHUFORD, Alonzo Craig (P N.C.) March 1, 1858-Feb. 8, 1933; House 1895-99.

SHUFORD, George Adams (D N.C.) Sept. 5, 1895-Dec. 8, 1962; House 1953-59.

SHULL, Joseph Horace (D Pa.) Aug. 17, 1848-Aug. 9, 1944; House 1903-05.

SHULTZ, Emanuel (R Ohio) July 25, 1819-Nov. 5, 1912; House 1881-83.

SHUMWAY, Norman David (R Calif.) July 28, 1934- —; House 1979- —.

SHUSTER, E. G. (Bud) (R Pa.) Jan. 23, 1932- —; House 1973- —.

SIBAL, Abner Woodruff (R Conn.) April 11, 1921- —; House 1961-65.

SIBLEY, Henry Hastings (son of Solomon Sibley) (— Wis./Minn.) Feb. 20, 1811-Feb. 18, 1891; House (Terr. Del.) Oct. 30, 1848-49 (Wis.), July 7, 1849-53 (Minn.); Gov. (Minn.) 1858-60.

SIBLEY, Jonas (D Mass.) March 7, 1762-Feb. 5, 1834; House 1823-25.

SIBLEY, Joseph Crocker (R Pa.) Feb. 18, 1850-May 19, 1926; House 1893-95, 1899-1907 (1893-95 Democrat/People's Party/Prohibitionist, 1899-1901 Democrat, 1901-07 Republican).

SIBLEY, Mark Hopkins (W N.Y.) 1796-Sept. 8, 1852; House 1837-79.

SIBLEY, Solomon (father of Henry Hastings Sibley) (— Mich.) Oct. 7, 1769-April 4, 1846; House (Terr. Del.) Nov. 20, 1820-23.

SICKLES, Carlton R. (D Md.) June 15, 1921- —; House 1963-67.

SICKLES, Daniel Edgar (D N.Y.) Oct. 10, 1825-May 3, 1914; House 1857-61, 1893-95.

SICKLES, Nicholas (D N.Y.) Sept. 11, 1801-May 13, 1845; House 1835-37.

SIEGEL, Isaac (R N.Y.) April 12, 1880-June 29, 1947; House 1915-23.

SIEMINSKI, Alfred Dennis (D N.J.) Aug. 23, 1911- —; House 1951-59.

SIKES, Robert Louis Fulton (D Fla.) June 3, 1906- —; House 1941-Oct. 19, 1944, 1945-79.

SIKORSKI, Gerry (D Minn.) April 26, 1948- —; House 1983- —.

SILER, Eugene (R Ky.) June 26, 1900- —; House 1955-65.

SILJANDER, Mark Deli (R Mich.) June 11, 1951- —; House April 28, 1981- —.

SILL, Thomas Hale (NR Pa.) Oct. 11, 1783-Feb. 7, 1856; House March 14, 1826-27, 1829-31.

SILSBEE, Nathaniel (D Mass.) Jan. 14, 1773-July 14, 1850; House 1817-21; Senate May 31, 1826-35.

SILVESTER, Peter (grandfather of Peter Henry Silvester) (— N.Y.) 1734-Oct. 15, 1808; House 1789-93.

SILVESTER, Peter Henry (grandson of Peter Silvester) (W N.Y.) Feb. 17, 1807-Nov. 29, 1882; House 1847-51.

SIMKINS, Eldred (D S.C.) Aug. 30, 1779-Nov. 17, 1831; House Jan. 24, 1818-21.

SIMMONS, Furnifold McLendel (D N.C.) Jan. 20, 1854-April 30, 1940; House 1887-89; Senate 1901-31.

SIMMONS, George Abel (W N.Y.) Sept. 8, 1791-Oct. 27, 1857; House 1853-57.

SIMMONS, James Fowler (W R.I.) Sept. 10, 1795-July 10, 1864; Senate 1841-47, 1857-Aug. 15, 1862.

SIMMONS, James Samuel (nephew of Milton George Urner) (R N.Y.) Nov. 25, 1861-Nov. 28, 1935; House 1909-13.

SIMMONS, Robert Glenmore (R Neb.) Dec. 25, 1891-Dec. 27, 1969; House 1923-33.

SIMMS, Albert Gallatin (husband of Ruther Hanna McCormick) (R N.M.) Oct. 8, 1882-Dec. 29, 1964; House 1929-31.

SIMMS, William Emmett (D Ky.) Jan. 2, 1822-June 25, 1898; House 1859-61.

SIMON, Joseph (R Ore.) Feb. 7, 1851-Feb. 14, 1935; Senate Oct. 8, 1898-1903.

SIMON, Paul Martin (D Ill.) Nov. 29, 1928-—; House 1975-85; Senate 1985-—.

SIMONDS, William Edgar (R Conn.) Nov. 24, 1842-March 14, 1903; House 1889-91.

SIMONS, Samuel (D Conn.) 1792-Jan. 13, 1847; House 1843-45.

SIMONTON, Charles Bryson (D Tenn.) Sept. 8, 1838-June 10, 1911; House 1879-83.

SIMONTON, William (W Pa.) Feb. 12, 1788-May 17, 1846; House 1839-43.

SIMPKINS, John (R Mass.) June 27, 1862-March 27, 1898; House 1895-March 27, 1898.

SIMPSON, Alan Kooi (R Wyo.) Sept. 2, 1931-—; Senate Jan. 1, 1979-—.

SIMPSON, Edna Oakes (widow of Sidney Elmer Simpson) (R Ill.) Oct. 28, 1891-—; House 1959-61.

SIMPSON, James Jr. (R Ill.) Jan. 7, 1905-Feb. 29, 1960; House 1933-35.

SIMPSON, Jeremiah (Jerry) (P Kan.) March 31, 1842-Oct. 23, 1905; House 1891-95, 1897-99.

SIMPSON, Kenneth Farrand (R N.Y.) May 4, 1895-Jan. 25, 1941; House Jan. 3-Jan. 25, 1941.

SIMPSON, Milward Lee (R Wyo.) Nov. 12, 1897-—; Senate Nov. 7, 1962-67; Gov. 1955-59.

SIMPSON, Richard Franklin (D S.C.) March 24, 1798-Oct. 28, 1882; House 1843-49.

SIMPSON, Richard Murray (R Pa.) Aug. 30, 1900-Jan. 7, 1960; House May 11, 1937-Jan. 7, 1960.

SIMPSON, Sidney Elmer (Sid) (husband of Edna Oakes Simpson) (R Ill.) Sept. 20, 1894-Oct. 26, 1958; House 1943-Oct. 26, 1958.

SIMS, Alexander Dromgoole (nephew of George Coke Dromgoole) (D S.C.) June 12, 1803-Nov. 22, 1848; House 1845-Nov. 22, 1848.

SIMS, Hugo Sheridan Jr. (D S.C.) Oct. 14, 1921-—; House 1949-51.

SIMS, Leonard Henly (D Mo.) Feb. 6, 1807-Feb. 28, 1886; House 1845-47.

SIMS, Thetus Willrette (D Tenn.) April 25, 1852-Dec. 17, 1939; House 1897-1921.

SINCLAIR, James Herbert (R N.D.) Oct. 9, 1871-Sept. 5, 1943; House 1919-35.

SINGISER, Theodore Frelinghuysen (R Idaho) March 15, 1845-Jan. 23, 1907; House (Terr. Del.) 1883-85.

SINGLETON, James Washington (D Ill.) Nov. 23, 1811-April 4, 1892; House 1879-83.

SINGLETON, Otho Robards (D Miss.) Oct. 14, 1814-Jan. 11, 1889; House 1853-55, 1857-Jan. 12, 1861, 1875-87.

SINGLETON, Thomas Day (N S.C.) ?-Nov. 25, 1833; House March 3-Nov. 25, 1833.

SINNICKSON, Clement Hall (grandnephew of Thomas Sinnickson) (R N.J.) Sept. 16, 1834-July 24, 1919; House 1875-79.

SINNICKSON, Thomas (granduncle of Clement Hall Sinnickson, uncle of the following) (— N.J.) Dec. 21, 1744-May 15, 1817; House 1789-91, 1797-99.

SINNICKSON, Thomas (nephew of the preceding) (— N.J.) Dec. 13, 1786-Feb. 17, 1873; House Dec. 1, 1828-29.

SINNOTT, Nicholas John (R Ore.) Dec. 6, 1870-July 20, 1929; House 1913-May 31, 1928.

SIPE, William Allen (D Pa.) July 1, 1844-Sept. 10, 1935; House Dec. 5, 1892-95.

SIROVICH, William Irving (D N.Y.) March 18, 1882-Dec. 17, 1939; House 1927-Dec. 17, 1939.

SISISKY, Norman (D Va.) June 9, 1927-—; House 1983-—.

SISK, Bernice Frederic (D Calif.) Dec. 14, 1910-—; House 1955-79.

SISSON, Frederick James (D N.Y.) March 31, 1879-Oct. 20, 1949; House 1933-37.

SISSON, Thomas Upton (D Miss.) Sept. 22, 1869-Sept. 26, 1923; House 1909-23.

SITES, Frank Crawford (D Pa.) Dec. 24, 1864-May 23, 1935; House 1923-25.

SITGREAVES, Charles (D N.J.) April 22, 1803-March 17, 1878; House 1865-69.

SITGREAVES, Samuel (F Pa.) March 16, 1764-April 4, 1827; House 1795-98.

SITTLER, Edward Lewis Jr. (R Pa.) April 21, 1908-Dec. 26, 1978; House 1951-53.

SKEEN, Joseph R. (R N.M.) June 30, 1927-—; House 1981-—.

SKELTON, Charles (D N.J.) April 19, 1806-May 20, 1879; House 1851-55.

SKELTON, Ike N. (D Mo.) Dec. 20, 1931-—; House 1977-—.

SKILES, William Woodburn (R Ohio) Dec. 11, 1849-Jan. 9, 1904; House 1901-Jan. 9, 1904.

SKINNER, Charles Rufus (R N.Y.) Aug. 4, 1844-June 30, 1928; House Nov. 8, 1881-85.

SKINNER, Harry (brother of Thomas Gregory Skinner) (P N.C.) May 25, 1855-May 19, 1929; House 1895-99.

SKINNER, Richard (D Vt.) May 30, 1778-May 23, 1833; House 1813-15; Gov. 1820-23.

SKINNER, Thomas Gregory (brother of Harry Skinner) (D N.C.) Jan. 22, 1842-Dec. 22, 1907; House Nov. 20, 1883-87, 1889-91.

SKINNER, Thomas Joseph (D Mass.) May 24, 1752-Jan. 20, 1809; House Jan. 27, 1797-99, 1803-Aug. 10, 1804.

SKUBITZ, Joe (R Kan.) May 6, 1906-—; House 1963-Dec. 31, 1978.

SLACK, John Mark Jr. (D W.Va.) March 18, 1915-March 17, 1980; House 1959-March 17, 1980.

SLADE, Charles (D Ill.) ?-July 26, 1834; House 1833-July 26, 1834.

SLADE, William (W Vt.) May 9, 1786-Jan. 18, 1859; House Nov. 1, 1831-43; Gov. 1844-46.

SLATER, James Harvey (D Ore.) Dec. 28, 1826-Jan. 28, 1899; House 1871-73; Senate 1879-85.

SLATTERY, James Charles (D Kan.) Aug. 4, 1948-—; House 1983-—.

SLATTERY, James Michael (D Ill.) July 29, 1878-Aug. 28, 1948; Senate April 14, 1939-Nov. 21, 1940.

SLAUGHTER, Daniel French Jr. (R Va.) May 20, 1925-—; House 1985-—.

SLAUGHTER, Roger Caldwell (D Mo.) July 17, 1905-June 2, 1974; House 1943-47.

SLAYDEN, James Luther (uncle of Fontaine Maury Maverick) (D Texas) June 1, 1853-Feb. 24, 1924; House 1897-1919.

SLAYMAKER, Amos (— Pa.) March 11, 1755-June 12, 1837; House Oct. 11, 1814-15.

SLEMONS, William Ferguson (D Ark.) March 15, 1830-Dec. 10, 1918; House 1875-81.

SLEMP, Campbell (father of Campbell Bascom Slemp) (R Va.) Dec. 2, 1839-Oct. 13, 1907; House 1903-Oct. 13, 1907.

Biographical Index

SLEMP, Campbell Bascom (son of Campbell Slemp) (R Va.) Sept. 4, 1870-Aug. 7, 1943; House Dec. 17, 1907-23.

SLIDELL, John (SRD La.) 1793-July 26, 1871; House 1843-Nov. 10, 1845; Senate Dec. 5, 1853-Feb. 4, 1861.

SLINGERLAND, John I. (R N.Y.) March 1, 1804-Oct. 26, 1861; House 1847-49.

SLOAN, Andrew (R Ga.) June 10, 1845-Sept. 22, 1883; House March 24, 1874-75.

SLOAN, Andrew Scott (brother of Ithamar Conkey Sloan) (R Wis.) June 12, 1820-April 8, 1895; House 1861-63.

SLOAN, Charles Henry (R Neb.) May 2, 1863-June 2, 1946; House 1911-19, 1929-31.

SLOAN, Ithamar Conkey (brother of Andrew Scott Sloan) (R Wis.) May 9, 1822-Dec. 24, 1898; House 1863-67.

SLOAN, James (— N.J.) ?-Nov. 1811; House 1803-09.

SLOANE, John (W Ohio) 1779-May 15, 1856; House 1819-29.

SLOANE, Jonathan (W Ohio) Nov. 1785-April 25, 1854; House 1833-37.

SLOCUM, Henry Warner (D N.Y.) Sept. 24, 1827-April 14, 1894; House 1869-73, 1883-85.

SLOCUMB, Jesse (F N.C.) 1780-Dec. 20, 1820; House 1817-Dec. 20, 1820.

SLOSS, Joseph Humphrey (Con.D Ala.) Oct. 12, 1826-Jan. 27, 1911; House 1871-75.

SMALL, Frank Jr. (R Md.) July 15, 1896-Oct. 24, 1973; House 1953-55.

SMALL, John Humphrey (D N.C.) Aug. 29, 1858-July 13, 1946; House 1899-1921.

SMALL, William Bradbury (R N.H.) May 17, 1817-April 7, 1878; House 1873-75.

SMALLS, Robert (R S.C.) April 5, 1839-Feb. 22, 1915; House 1875-79, July 19, 1882-83, March 18, 1884-87.

SMART, Ephraim Knight (D Maine) Sept. 3, 1813-Sept. 29, 1872; House 1847-49, 1851-53.

SMART, James Stevenson (R N.Y.) June 14, 1842-Sept. 17, 1903; House 1873-75.

SMATHERS, George Armistead (nephew of William Howell Smathers) (D Fla.) Nov. 14, 1913- —; House 1947-51; Senate 1951-69.

SMATHERS, William Howell (uncle of George Armistead Smathers) (D N.J.) Jan. 7, 1891-Sept. 24, 1955; Senate April 15, 1937-43.

SMELT, Dennis (— Ga.) about 1750-?; House Sept. 1, 1806-11.

SMILIE, John (D Pa.) 1741-Dec. 30, 1812; House 1793-95, 1799-Dec. 30, 1812.

SMITH, Abraham Herr (R Pa.) March 7, 1815-Feb. 16, 1894; House 1873-85.

SMITH, Addison Taylor (R Idaho) Sept. 5, 1862-July 5, 1956; House 1913-33.

SMITH, Albert (D Maine) Jan. 3, 1793-May 29, 1867; House 1839-41.

SMITH, Albert (R N.Y.) June 22, 1805-Aug. 27, 1870; House 1843-47.

SMITH, Albert Lee (R Ala.) Aug. 31, 1931- —; House 1981-83.

SMITH, Arthur (— Va.) Nov. 15, 1785-March 30, 1853; House 1821-25.

SMITH, Ballard (— Va.) ?-?; House 1815-21.

SMITH, Benjamin A. II (D Mass.) March 26, 1916- —; Senate Dec. 27, 1960-Nov. 7, 1962.

SMITH, Bernard (— N.Y.) July 5, 1776-July 16, 1835; House 1819-21.

SMITH, Caleb Blood (W Ind.) April 16, 1808-Jan. 7, 1864; House 1843-49; Secy. of the Interior 1861-63.

SMITH, Charles Bennett (D N.Y.) Sept. 14, 1870-May 21, 1939; House 1911-19.

SMITH, Charles Brooks (R W.Va.) Feb. 24, 1844-Dec. 7, 1899; House Feb. 3, 1890-91.

SMITH, Christopher H. (R N.J.) March 4, 1953- —; House 1981- —.

SMITH, Clyde Harold (husband of Margaret Chase Smith) (R Maine) June 9, 1876-April 8, 1940; House 1937-April 8, 1940.

SMITH, Daniel (— Tenn.) Oct. 28, 1748-June 6, 1818; Senate Oct. 6, 1798-99, 1805-March 31, 1809.

SMITH, David Highbaugh (D Ky.) Dec. 19, 1854-Dec. 17, 1928; House 1897-1907.

SMITH, Delazon (D Ore.) Oct. 5, 1816-Nov. 19, 1860; Senate Feb. 14-March 3, 1859.

SMITH, Denny (R Ore.) Jan. 19, 1938- —; House 1981- —.

SMITH, Dietrich Conrad (R Ill.) April 4, 1840-April 18, 1914; House 1881-83.

SMITH, Edward Henry (D N.Y.) May 5, 1809-Aug. 7, 1885; House 1861-63.

SMITH, Ellison DuRant (D S.C.) Aug. 1, 1866-Nov. 17, 1944; Senate 1909-Nov. 17, 1944.

SMITH, Frances Ormand Jonathan (D Maine) Nov. 23, 1806-Oct. 14, 1876; House 1833-39.

SMITH, Francis Raphael (D Pa.) Sept. 25, 1911- —; House 1941-43.

SMITH, Frank Ellis (D Miss.) Feb. 21, 1918- —; House 1951-Nov. 14, 1962.

SMITH, Frank Leslie (R Ill.) Nov. 24, 1867-Aug. 30, 1950; House 1919-21; Senate (elected 1926 but never served).

SMITH, Frank Owens (D Md.) Aug. 27, 1859-Jan. 29, 1924; House 1913-15.

SMITH, Frederick Cleveland (R Ohio) July 29, 1844-July 16, 1956; House 1939-51.

SMITH, George (— Pa.) ?-?; House 1809-13.

SMITH, George Joseph (R N.Y.) Nov. 7, 1859-Dec. 24, 1913; House 1903-05.

SMITH, George Luke (R La.) Dec. 11, 1837-July 9, 1884; House Nov. 24, 1873-75.

SMITH, George Ross (R Minn.) May 28, 1864-Nov. 7, 1952; House 1913-17.

SMITH, George Washington (R Ill.) Aug. 18, 1846-Nov. 30, 1907; House 1889-Nov. 30, 1907.

SMITH, Gerrit (UA N.Y.) March 6, 1797-Dec. 28, 1874; House 1853-Aug. 7, 1854.

SMITH, Gomer Griffith (D Okla.) July 11, 1896-May 26, 1953; House Dec. 10, 1937-39.

SMITH, Green Clay (son of John Speed Smith) (U Ky.) July 4, 1826-June 29, 1895; House 1863-July 13, 1866; Gov. (Mont. Terr.) 1866-69.

SMITH, H. Allen (R Calif.) Oct. 8, 1909- —; House 1957-73.

SMITH, Henry (PP Wis.) July 22, 1838-Sept. 16, 1916; House 1887-89.

SMITH, Henry Cassorte (R Mich.) June 2, 1856-Dec. 7, 1911; House 1899-1903.

SMITH, Henry P. III (R N.Y.) Sept. 29, 1911- —; House 1965-75.

SMITH, Hezekiah Bradley (D/G N.J.) July 24, 1816-Nov. 3, 1887; House 1879-81.

SMITH, Hiram Ypsilanti (R Iowa) March 22, 1843-Nov. 4, 1894; House Dec. 2, 1884-85.

SMITH, Hoke (D Ga.) Sept. 2, 1855-Nov. 27, 1931; Senate Nov. 16, 1911-21; Secy. of the Interior 1893-96; Gov. 1907-09, 1911.

SMITH, Horace Boardman (R N.Y.) Aug. 18, 1826-Dec. 26, 1888; House 1871-75.

SMITH, Howard Alexander (uncle of Peter H. Dominick) (R N.J.) Jan. 30, 1880-Oct. 27, 1966; Senate Dec. 7, 1944-59.

SMITH, Howard Worth (D Va.) Feb. 2, 1883-Oct. 3, 1976; House 1931-67.

SMITH, Isaac (F N.J.) 1740-Aug. 29, 1807; House 1795-97.

SMITH, Isaac (D Pa.) Jan. 4, 1761-April 4, 1834; House 1813-15.

SMITH, Israel (D Vt.) April 4, 1759-Dec. 2, 1810; House Oct. 17, 1791-97, 1801-03; Senate 1803-Oct. 1, 1807; Gov. 1807-08.

SMITH, James Jr. (D N.J.) June 12, 1851-April 1, 1927; Senate 1893-99.

SMITH, James Strudwick (D N.C.) Oct. 15, 1790-Aug. 1859; House 1817-21.

SMITH, James Vernon (R Okla.) July 23, 1926-June 23, 1973; House 1967-69.

SMITH, Jedediah Kilburn (— N.H.) Nov. 7, 1770-Dec. 17, 1828; House 1807-09.

SMITH, Jeremiah (brother of Samuel Smith of N.H., uncle of Robert Smith) (F N.H.) Nov. 29, 1759-Sept. 21, 1842; House 1791-July 26, 1797; Gov. 1809-10.

SMITH, John (D Ohio) 1735-June 10, 1816; Senate April 1, 1803-April 25, 1808.

SMITH, John (D Va.) May 7, 1750-March 5, 1836; House 1801-15.

SMITH, John (D N.Y.) Feb. 12, 1752-Aug. 12, 1816; House Feb. 6, 1800-Feb. 23, 1804; Senate Feb. 23, 1804-13.

SMITH, John (father of Worthington Curtis Smith) (D Vt.) Aug. 12, 1789-Nov. 26, 1858; House 1839-41.

SMITH, John Ambler (R Va.) Sept. 23, 1847-Jan. 6, 1892; House 1873-75.

SMITH, John Armstrong (R Ohio) Sept. 23, 1814-March 7, 1892; House 1869-73.

SMITH, John Cotton (F Conn.) Feb. 12, 1765-Dec. 7, 1845; House Nov. 17, 1800-Aug. 1806; Gov. 1812-17.

SMITH, John Hyatt (IR/D N.Y.) April 10, 1824-Dec. 7, 1886; House 1881-83.

SMITH, John Joseph (D Conn.) Jan. 25, 1904-Feb. 16, 1980; House 1935-Nov. 4, 1941.

SMITH, John M. C. (R Mich.) Feb. 6, 1853-March 30, 1923; House 1911-21, June 28, 1921-March 30, 1923.

SMITH, John Quincy (R Ohio) Nov. 5, 1824-Dec. 30, 1901; House 1873-75.

SMITH, John Speed (father of Green Clay Smith) (D Ky.) July 1, 1792-June 6, 1854; House Aug. 6, 1821-23.

SMITH, John T. (D Pa.) ?-?; House 1843-45.

SMITH, John Walter (D Md.) Feb. 5, 1845-April 19, 1925; House 1899-Jan. 12, 1900; Senate March 25, 1908-21; Gov. 1900-04.

SMITH, Joseph F. (D Pa.) Jan. 24, 1920-—; House July 28, 1981-—.

SMITH, Joseph Luther (D W.Va.) May 22, 1880-Aug. 23, 1962; House 1929-45.

SMITH, Joseph Showalter (D Ore.) June 20, 1824-July 13, 1884; House 1869-71.

SMITH, Josiah (— Mass.) Feb. 26, 1738-April 4, 1803; House 1801-03.

SMITH, Lawrence Henry (R Wis.) Sept. 15, 1892-Jan. 22, 1958; House Aug. 29, 1941-Jan. 22, 1958.

SMITH, Lawrence Jack (D Fla.) April 25, 1941-—; House 1983-—.

SMITH, Madison Roswell (D Mo.) July 9, 1850-June 18, 1919; House 1907-09.

SMITH, Marcus Aurelius (D Ariz.) Jan. 24, 1851-April 7, 1924; House (Terr. Del.) 1887-95, 1897-99, 1901-03, 1905-09; Senate March 27, 1912-21.

SMITH, Margaret Chase (widow of Clyde Harold Smith) (R Maine) Dec. 14, 1897-—; House June 3, 1940-49; Senate 1949-73.

SMITH, Martin Fernand (D Wash.) May 28, 1891-Oct. 25, 1954; House 1933-43.

SMITH, Nathan (brother of Nathaniel Smith, uncle of Truman Smith) (W Conn.) Jan. 8, 1770-Dec. 6, 1835; Senate 1833-Dec. 6, 1835.

SMITH, Nathaniel (brother of Nathan Smith, uncle of Truman Smith) (F Conn.) Jan. 6, 1762-March 9, 1822; House 1795-99.

SMITH, Neal Edward (D Iowa) March 23, 1920-—; House 1959-—.

SMITH, O'Brien (— S.C.) about 1756-April 27, 1811; House 1805-07.

SMITH, Oliver Hampton (W Ind.) Oct. 23, 1794-March 19, 1859; House 1827-29, Senate 1837-43 (1827-29 Jackson Democrat, 1837-43 Whig).

SMITH, Perry (D Conn.) May 12, 1783-June 8, 1852; Senate 1837-43.

SMITH, Ralph Tyler (R Ill.) Oct. 6, 1915-Aug. 13, 1972; Senate Sept. 17, 1969-Nov. 3, 1970.

SMITH, Robert (nephew of Jeremiah Smith and Samuel Smith of N.H.) (D Ill.) June 12, 1802-Dec. 21, 1867; House 1843-49, 1857-59.

SMITH, Robert Barnwell (*See* RHETT, Robert Barnwell).

SMITH, Robert Clinton (R N.H.) March 30, 1941-—; House 1985-—.

SMITH, Robert Freeman (R Ore.) June 16, 1931-—; House 1983-—.

SMITH, Samuel (D Md.) July 27, 1752-April 22, 1839; House 1793-1803, Jan. 31, 1816-Dec. 17, 1822; Senate 1803-15, Dec. 17, 1822-23; Pres. pro tempore 1805-08.

SMITH, Samuel (— Pa.) ?-?; House Nov. 7, 1805-11.

SMITH, Samuel (brother of Jeremiah Smith, uncle of Robert Smith) (F N.H.) Nov. 11, 1765-April 25, 1842; House 1813-15.

SMITH, Samuel A. (ID Pa.) 1795-May 15, 1861; House Oct. 13, 1829-33.

SMITH, Samuel Axley (D Tenn.) June 26, 1822-Nov. 25, 1863; House 1853-59.

SMITH, Samuel William (R Mich.) Aug. 23, 1852-June 19, 1931; House 1897-1915.

SMITH, Sylvester Clark (R Calif.) Aug. 26, 1858-Jan. 26, 1913; House 1905-Jan. 26, 1913.

SMITH, Thomas (F Pa.) ?-Jan. 29, 1846; House 1815-17.

SMITH, Thomas (D Ind.) May 1, 1799-April 12, 1876; House 1839-41, 1843-47.

SMITH, Thomas Alexander (D Md.) Sept. 3, 1850-May 1, 1932; House 1905-07.

SMITH, Thomas Francis (D N.Y.) July 24, 1865-April 11, 1923; House April 12, 1917-21.

SMITH, Thomas Vernor (D Ill.) April 26, 1890-May 24, 1964; House 1939-41.

SMITH, Truman (nephew of Nathan Smith and Nathaniel Smith) (W Conn.) Nov. 27, 1791-May 3, 1884; House 1839-43, 1845-49; Senate 1849-May 24, 1854.

SMITH, Virginia Dodd (R Neb.) June 30, 1911-—; House 1975-—.

SMITH, Walter Inglewood (R Iowa) July 10, 1862-Jan. 27, 1922; House Dec. 3, 1900-March 15, 1911.

SMITH, William (F Md.) April 12, 1728-March 27, 1814; House 1789-91; Cont. Cong. 1777-78.

SMITH, William (D S.C.) 1762-June 26, 1840; Senate Dec. 4, 1816-23, Nov. 29, 1826-31.

SMITH, William (— S.C.) Sept. 20, 1751-June 22, 1837; House 1797-99.

SMITH, William (— Va.) ?-?; House 1821-27.

SMITH, William (D Va.) Sept. 6, 1797-May 18, 1887; House 1841-43, 1853-61; Gov. 1846-49, 1864-65.

SMITH, William Alden (R Mich.) May 12, 1859-Oct. 11, 1932; House 1895-Feb. 9, 1907; Senate Feb. 9, 1907-19.

SMITH, William Alexander (R N.C.) Jan. 9, 1828-May 16, 1888; House 1873-75.

SMITH, William Ephraim (D Ga.) March 14, 1829-March 11, 1890; House 1875-81.

SMITH, William Jay (R Tenn.) Sept. 24, 1823-Nov. 29, 1913; House 1869-71.

SMITH, William Loughton (F S.C.) 1758-Dec. 19, 1812; House 1789-July 10, 1797.

SMITH, William Nathan Harrell (D N.C.) Sept. 24, 1812-Nov. 14, 1889; House 1859-61.

SMITH, William Orlando (R Pa.) June 13, 1859-May 12, 1932; House 1903-07.

SMITH, William Robert (D Texas) Aug. 18, 1863-Aug. 16, 1924; House 1903-17.

SMITH, William Russell (AP Ala.) March 27, 1815-Feb. 26, 1896; House 1851-57 (1851-55 Union Whig, 1855-57 American Party).

SMITH, William Stephens (F N.Y.) Nov. 8, 1755-June 10, 1816; House 1813-15.

SMITH, Willis (D N.C.) Dec. 19, 1887-June 26, 1953; Senate Nov. 27, 1950-June 26, 1953.

SMITH, Wint (R Kan.) Oct. 7, 1892-April 27, 1976; House 1947-61.

SMITH, Worthington Curtis (son of John Smith of Vt.) (R Vt.) April 23, 1823-Jan. 2, 1894; House 1867-73.

SMITHERS, Nathaniel Barratt (R Del.) Oct. 8, 1818-Jan. 16, 1896; House Dec. 7, 1863-65.

SMITHWICK, John Harris (D Fla.) July 17, 1872-Dec. 2, 1948; House 1919-27.

SMOOT, Reed (R Utah) Jan. 10, 1862-Feb. 9, 1941; Senate 1903-33.

SMYSER, Martin Luther (R Ohio) April 3, 1851-May 6, 1908; House 1889-91, 1905-07.

SMYTH, Alexander (— Va.) 1765-April 17, 1830; House 1817-25, 1827-April 17, 1830.

SMYTH, George Washington (D Texas) May 16, 1803-Feb. 21, 1866; House 1853-55.

SMYTH, William (R Iowa) Jan. 3, 1824-Sept. 30, 1870; House 1869-Sept. 30, 1870.

Biographical Index

SNAPP, Henry (father of Howard Malcolm Snapp) (R Ill.) June 30, 1822-Nov. 26, 1895; House Dec. 4, 1871-73.

SNAPP, Howard Malcolm (son of Henry Snapp) (R Ill.) Sept. 27, 1855-Aug. 14, 1938; House 1903-11.

SNEED, William Henry (AP Tenn.) Aug. 27, 1812-Sept. 18, 1869; House 1855-57.

SNELL, Bertrand Hollis (R N.Y.) Dec. 9, 1870-Feb. 2, 1958; House Nov. 2, 1915-39.

SNIDER, Samuel Prather (R Minn.) Oct. 9, 1845-Sept. 24, 1928; House 1889-91.

SNODGRASS, Charles Edward (nephew of Henry Clay Snodgrass) (D Tenn.) Dec. 28, 1866-Aug. 3, 1936; House 1899-1903.

SNODGRASS, Henry Clay (uncle of Charles Edward Snodgrass) (D Tenn.) March 29, 1848-April 22, 1931; House 1891-95.

SNODGRASS, John Fryall (D Va.) March 2, 1804-June 5, 1854; House 1853-June 5, 1854.

SNOOK, John Stout (D Ohio) Dec. 18, 1862-Sept. 19, 1952; House 1901-05, 1917-19.

SNOVER, Horace Greeley (R Mich.) Sept. 21, 1847-July 21, 1924; House 1895-99.

SNOW, Donald Francis (R Maine) Sept. 6, 1877-Feb. 12, 1958; House 1929-33.

SNOW, Herman Wilber (D Ill.) July 3, 1836-Aug. 25, 1914; House 1891-93.

SNOW, William W. (D N.Y.) April 27, 1812-Sept. 3, 1886; House 1851-53.

SNOWE, Olympia Jean Bouchles (R Maine) Feb. 21, 1947- ; House 1979- .

SNYDER, Adam Wilson (VBD Ill.) Oct. 6, 1799-May 14, 1842; House 1837-39.

SNYDER, Charles Philip (D W.Va.) June 9, 1847-Aug. 21, 1915; House May 15, 1883-89.

SNYDER, Homer Peter (R N.Y.) Dec. 6, 1863-Dec. 30, 1937; House 1915-25.

SNYDER, John (— Pa.) Jan. 29, 1793-Aug. 15, 1850; House 1841-43.

SNYDER, John Buell (D Pa.) July 30, 1877-Feb. 24, 1946; House 1933-Feb. 24, 1946.

SNYDER, Marion Gene (R Ky.) Jan. 26, 1928- ; House 1963-65, 1967- .

SNYDER, Melvin Claude (R W.Va.) Oct. 29, 1898- ; House 1947-49.

SNYDER, Oliver P. (R Ark.) Nov. 13, 1833-Nov. 22, 1882; House 1871-75.

SOLARZ, Stephen Joshua (D N.Y.) Sept. 12, 1940- ; House 1975- .

SOLLERS, Augustus Rhodes (W Md.) May 1, 1814-Nov. 26, 1862; House 1841-43, 1853-55.

SOLOMON, Gerald B. (R N.Y.) Aug. 14, 1930- ; House 1979- .

SOMERS, Andrew Lawrence (D N.Y.) March 21, 1895-April 6, 1949; House 1925-April 6, 1949.

SOMERS, Peter J. (D Wis.) April 12, 1850-Feb. 15, 1924; House Aug. 27, 1893-95.

SOMES, Daniel Eton (R Maine) May 20, 1815-Feb. 13, 1888; House 1859-61.

SORG, Paul John (D Ohio) Sept. 23, 1840-May 28, 1902; House May 21, 1894-97.

SOSNOWSKI, John Bartholomew (R Mich.) Dec. 8, 1883-July 16, 1968; House 1925-27.

SOULE, Nathan (— N.Y.) ?-?; House 1831-33.

SOULE, Pierre (SRD La.) Aug. 28, 1801-March 26, 1870; Senate Jan. 21-March 3, 1847, 1849-April 11, 1853.

SOUTH, Charles Lacy (D Texas) July 22, 1892-Dec. 20, 1965; House 1935-43.

SOUTHALL, Robert Goode (D Va.) Dec. 26, 1852-May 25, 1924; House 1903-07.

SOUTHARD, Henry (father of Isaac Southard and Samuel Lewis Southard) (D N.J.) Oct. 7, 1747-May 22, 1842; House 1801-11, 1815-21.

SOUTHARD, Isaac (son of Henry Southard, brother of Samuel Lewis Southard) (CD N.J.) Aug. 30, 1783-Sept. 18, 1850; House 1831-33.

SOUTHARD, James Harding (R Ohio) Jan. 20, 1851-Feb. 20, 1919; House 1895-1907.

SOUTHARD, Milton Isaiah (D Ohio) Oct. 20, 1836-May 4, 1905; House 1873-79.

SOUTHARD, Samuel Lewis (son of Henry Southard, brother of Isaac Southard) (W N.J.) June 9, 1787-June 26, 1842; Senate Jan. 26, 1821-23, 1833-June 26, 1842; Pres. pro tempore 1841-42 (1821-23 Democrat, 1833-42 Whig); Secy. of the Navy 1823-29; Gov. 1832-33.

SOUTHGATE, William Wright (W Ky.) Nov. 27, 1800-Dec. 26, 1849; House 1837-39.

SOUTHWICK, George Newell (R N.Y.) March 7, 1863-Oct. 17, 1912; House 1895-99, 1901-11.

SOWDEN, William Henry (D Pa.) June 6, 1840-March 3, 1907; House 1885-89.

SPAIGHT, Richard Dobbs (grandfather of Richard Spaight Donnell, father of Richard Dobbs Spaight Jr.) (D N.C.) March 25, 1758-Sept. 6, 1802; House Dec. 10, 1798-1801; Cont. Cong. 1782-85; Gov. 1792-95.

SPAIGHT, Richard Dobbs Jr. (son of Richard Dobbs Spaight) (D N.C.) 1796-May 2, 1850; House 1823-25; Gov. 1835-36.

SPALDING, Burleigh Folsom (R N.D.) Dec. 3, 1853-March 17, 1934; House 1899-1901; 1903-05.

SPALDING, George (R Mich.) Nov. 12, 1836-Sept. 13, 1915; House 1895-99.

SPALDING, Rufus Paine (WD Ohio) May 3, 1798-Aug. 29, 1886; House 1863-69.

SPALDING, Thomas (— Ga.) March 26, 1774-Jan. 5, 1851; House Dec. 24, 1805-06.

SPANGLER, David (W Ohio) Dec. 2, 1796-Oct. 18, 1856; House 1833-37.

SPANGLER, Jacob (F Pa.) Nov. 28, 1767-June 17, 1843; House 1817-April 20, 1818.

SPARKMAN, John Jackson (D Ala.) Dec. 20, 1899- ; House 1937-Nov. 5, 1946; Senate Nov. 6, 1946-79.

SPARKMAN, Stephen Milancthon (D Fla.) July 29, 1849-Sept. 26, 1929; House 1895-1917.

SPARKS, Charles Isaac (R Kan.) Dec. 20, 1872-April 30, 1937; House 1929-33.

SPARKS, William Andrew Jackson (D Ill.) Nov. 19, 1828-May 7, 1904; House 1875-83.

SPAULDING, Elbridge Gerry (U N.Y.) Feb. 24, 1809-May 5, 1897; House 1849-51, 1859-63 (1849-51 Whig, 1859-63 Unionist).

SPAULDING, Oliver Lyman (R Mich.) Aug. 2, 1833-July 30, 1922; House 1881-83.

SPEAKS, John Charles (R Ohio) Feb. 11, 1859-Nov. 6, 1945; House 1921-31.

SPEARING, James Zacharie (D La.) April 23, 1864-Nov. 2, 1942; House April 22, 1924-31.

SPECTER, Arlen (R Pa.) Feb. 12, 1930- ; Senate 1981- .

SPEED, Thomas (— Ky.) Oct. 25, 1768-Feb. 20, 1842; House 1817-19.

SPEER, Emory (I Ga.) Sept. 3, 1848-Dec. 13, 1918; House 1879-83 (1879-81 Democrat, 1881-83 Independent).

SPEER, Peter Moore (R Pa.) Dec. 29, 1862-Aug. 3, 1933; House 1911-13.

SPEER, Robert Milton (D Pa.) Sept. 8, 1838-Jan. 17, 1890; House 1871-75.

SPEER, Thomas Jefferson (R Ga.) Aug. 31, 1837-Aug. 18, 1872; House 1871-Aug. 18, 1872.

SPEIGHT, Jesse (D N.C./Miss.) Sept. 22, 1795-May 1, 1847; House 1829-37 (N.C.); Senate 1845-May 1, 1847 (Miss.).

SPELLMAN, Gladys Noon (D Md.) March 1, 1918- ; House 1975-Feb. 24, 1981.

SPENCE, Brent (D Ky.) Dec. 24, 1874-Sept. 18, 1967; House 1931-63.

SPENCE, Floyd Davidson (R S.C.) April 9, 1928- ; House 1971- .

SPENCE, John Selby (uncle of Thomas Ara Spence) (D Md.) Feb. 29, 1788-Oct. 24, 1840; House 1823-25, 1831-33; Senate Dec. 31, 1836-Oct. 24, 1840.

SPENCE, Thomas Ara (nephew of John Selby Spence) (W Md.) Feb. 20, 1810-Nov. 10, 1877; House 1843-45.

SPENCER, Ambrose (father of John Canfield Spencer) (D N.Y.) Dec. 13, 1765-March 13, 1848; House 1829-31.

SPENCER, Elijah (D N.Y.) 1775-Dec. 15, 1852; House 1821-23.

SPENCER, George Eliphaz (R Ala.) Nov. 1, 1836-Feb. 19, 1893; Senate July 13, 1868-79.

SPENCER, George Lloyd (D Ark.) March 27, 1893-Jan. 14, 1981; Senate April 1, 1941-43.

SPENCER, James Bradley (D N.Y.) April 26, 1781-March 26, 1848; House 1837-39.

SPENCER, James Grafton (D Miss.) Sept. 13, 1844-Feb. 22, 1926; House 1895-97.

SPENCER, John Canfield (son of Ambrose Spencer) (D N.Y.) Jan. 8, 1788-May 18, 1855; House 1817-19; Secy. of War 1841-43; Secy. of the Treasury 1843-44.

SPENCER, Richard (D Md.) Oct. 29, 1796-Sept. 3, 1868; House 1829-31.

SPENCER, Selden Palmer (R Mo.) Sept. 16, 1862-May 16, 1925; Senate Nov. 6, 1918-May 16, 1925.

SPENCER, William Brainerd (D La.) Feb. 5, 1835-Feb. 12, 1882; House June 8, 1876-Jan. 8, 1877.

SPERRY, Lewis (D Conn.) Jan. 23, 1848-June 22, 1922; House 1891-95.

SPERRY, Nehemiah Day (R Conn.) July 10, 1827-Nov. 13, 1911; House 1895-1911.

SPIGHT, Thomas (D Miss.) Oct. 25, 1841-Jan. 5, 1924; House July 5, 1898-1911.

SPINK, Cyrus (R Ohio) March 24, 1793-May 31, 1859; House March 4-May 31, 1859.

SPINK, Solomon Lewis (R Dakota) March 20, 1831-Sept. 22, 1881; House (Terr. Del.) 1869-71.

SPINNER, Francis Elias (D N.Y.) Jan. 21, 1802-Dec. 31, 1890; House 1855-61.

SPINOLA, Francis Barretto (D N.Y.) March 19, 1821-April 14, 1891; House 1887-April 14, 1891.

SPONG, William Belser Jr. (D Va.) Sept. 29, 1920-—; Senate Dec. 31, 1966-73.

SPOONER, Henry Joshua (R R.I.) Aug. 6, 1839-Feb. 9, 1918; House Dec. 5, 1881-91.

SPOONER, John Coit (R Wis.) Jan. 6, 1843-June 11, 1919; Senate 1885-91, 1897-April 30, 1907.

SPRAGUE, Charles Franklin (grandson of Peleg Sprague) (R Mass.) June 10, 1857-Jan. 30, 1902; House 1897-1901.

SPRAGUE, Peleg (— N.H.) Dec. 10, 1756-April 20, 1800; House Dec. 15, 1797-99.

SPRAGUE, Peleg (grandfather of Charles Franklin Sprague) (NR Maine) April 27, 1793-Oct. 13, 1880; House 1825-29; Senate 1829-Jan. 1, 1835.

SPRAGUE, William (W Mich.) Feb. 23, 1809-Sept. 19, 1868; House 1849-51.

SPRAGUE, William (uncle of the following) (W R.I.) Nov. 3, 1799-Oct. 19, 1856; House 1835-37; Senate Feb. 18, 1842-Jan. 17, 1844; Gov. 1838-39.

SPRAGUE, William (nephew of the preceding) (R R.I.) Sept. 12, 1830-Sept. 11, 1915; Senate 1863-75; Gov. 1860-63 (Unionist).

SPRAGUE, William Peter (R Ohio) May 21, 1827-March 3, 1899; House 1871-75.

SPRATT, John M. Jr. (D S.C.) Nov. 1, 1942-—; House 1983-—.

SPRIGG, James Cresap (brother of Michael Cresap Sprigg) (— Ky.) 1802-Oct. 3, 1852; House 1841-43.

SPRIGG, Michael Cresap (brother of James Cresap Sprigg) (D Md.) July 1, 1791-Dec. 18, 1845; House 1827-31.

SPRIGG, Richard Jr. (nephew of Thomas Sprigg) (— Md.) ?-?; House May 5, 1796-99, 1801-Feb. 11, 1802.

SPRIGG, Thomas (uncle of Richard Sprigg Jr.) (— Md.) 1747-Dec. 13, 1809; House 1793-97.

SPRIGGS, John Thomas (D N.Y.) April 5, 1825-Dec. 23, 1888; House 1883-87.

SPRINGER, Raymond Smiley (R Ind.) April 26, 1882-Aug. 28, 1947; House 1939-Aug. 28, 1947.

SPRINGER, William Lee (R Ill.) April 12, 1909-—; House 1951-73.

SPRINGER, William McKendree (D Ill.) May 30, 1836-Dec. 4, 1903; House 1875-95.

SPROUL, Elliott Wilford (R Ill.) Dec. 28, 1856-June 22, 1935; House 1921-31.

SPROUL, William Henry (R Kan.) Oct. 14, 1867-Dec. 27, 1932; House 1923-31.

SPRUANCE, Presley (W Del.) Sept. 11, 1785-Feb. 13, 1863; Senate 1847-53.

SQUIRE, Watson Carvosso (R Wash.) May 18, 1838-June 7, 1926; Senate Nov. 20, 1889-97; Gov. (Wash. Terr.) 1884-87.

STACK, Edmund John (D Ill.) Jan. 31, 1874-April 12, 1957; House 1911-13.

STACK, Edward John (D Fla.) April 29, 1910-—; House 1979-81.

STACK, Michael Joseph (D Pa.) Sept. 29, 1888-Dec. 14, 1960; House 1935-39.

STACKHOUSE, Eli Thomas (D S.C.) March 27, 1824-June 14, 1892; House 1891-June 14, 1892.

STAEBLER, Neil (D Mich.) July 11, 1905-—; House 1963-65.

STAFFORD, Robert Theodore (R Vt.) Aug. 8, 1913-—; House 1961-Sept. 16, 1971; Senate Sept. 16, 1971-—; Gov. 1959-61.

STAFFORD, William Henry (R Wis.) Oct. 12, 1869-April 22, 1957; House 1903-11, 1913-19, 1921-23, 1929-33.

STAGGERS, Harley Orrin (father of Harley Orrin Staggers Jr.) (D W.Va.) Aug. 3, 1907-—; House 1949-81.

STAGGERS, Harley Orrin Jr. (son of Harley Orrin Staggers) (D W. Va.) Feb. 22, 1951-—; House 1983-—.

STAHLE, James Alonzo (R Pa.) Jan. 11, 1829-Dec. 21, 1912; House 1895-97.

STAHLNECKER, William Griggs (D N.Y.) June 20, 1849-March 26, 1902; House 1885-93.

STALBAUM, Lynn Ellsworth (D Wis.) May 15, 1920-—; House 1965-67.

STALKER, Gale Hamilton (R N.Y.) Nov. 7, 1889-—; House 1923-35.

STALLINGS, Jesse Francis (D Ala.) April 4, 1856-March 18, 1928; House 1893-1901.

STALLINGS, Richard (D Idaho) Oct. 10, 1940-—; House 1985-—.

STALLWORTH, James Adams (D Ala.) April 7, 1822-Aug. 31, 1861; House 1857-Jan. 21, 1861.

STANARD, Edwin Obed (R Mo.) Jan. 5, 1832-March 12, 1914; House 1873-75.

STANBERY, William (JD Ohio) Aug. 10, 1788-Jan. 23, 1873; House Oct. 9, 1827-33.

STANDIFER, James (W Tenn.) ?-Aug. 20, 1837; House 1823-25, 1829-Aug. 20, 1837.

STANDIFORD, Elisha David (D Ky.) Dec. 28, 1831-July 26, 1887; House 1873-75.

STANFIELD, Robert Nelson (R Ore.) July 9, 1877-April 13 1945; Senate 1921-27.

STANFIL, William Abner (R Ky.) Jan. 16, 1892-June 12, 1971; Senate Nov. 19, 1945-Nov. 5, 1946.

STANFORD, Leland (R Calif.) March 9, 1824-June 21, 1893; Senate 1885-June 21, 1893; Gov. 1862-63.

STANFORD, Richard (grandfather of William Robert Webb) (D N.C.) March 2, 1767-April 9, 1816; House 1797-April 9, 1816.

STANGELAND, Arlan Ingehart (R Minn.) Feb. 8, 1930-—; House March 1, 1977-—.

STANLEY, Augustus Owsley (D Ky.) May 21, 1867-Aug. 13, 1958; House 1903-15; Senate May 19, 1919-25; Gov. 1915-19.

STANLEY, Thomas Bahnson (D Va.) July 16, 1890-July 10, 1970; House Nov. 5, 1946-Feb. 3, 1953; Gov. 1954-58.

STANLEY, Winifred Claire (R N.Y.) Aug. 14, 1909-—; House 1943-45.

STANLY, Edward (son of John Stanly) (W N.C.) July 13, 1810-July 12, 1872; House 1837-43, 1849-53.

STANLY, John (father of Edward Stanly) (— N.C.) April 9, 1774-Aug. 2, 1834; House 1801-03; 1809-11.

STANTON, Benjamin (W Ohio) June 4, 1809-June 2, 1872; House 1851-53, 1855-61.

STANTON, Frederick Perry (D Tenn.) Dec. 22, 1814-June 4, 1894; House 1845-55; Gov. (Kan. Terr.) 1858-61.

STANTON, James Vincent (D Ohio) Feb. 27, 1932-—; House 1971-77.

STANTON, John William (R Ohio) Feb. 20, 1924-—; House 1965-83.

STANTON, Joseph Jr. (D R.I.) July 19, 1739-1807; Senate June 7, 1790-93; House 1801-07.

Biographical Index

STANTON, Richard Henry (D Ky.) Sept. 9, 1812-March 20, 1891; House 1849-55.

STANTON, William Henry (D Pa.) July 28, 1843-March 28, 1900; House Nov. 7, 1876-77.

STARIN, John Henry (grandson of Thomas Sammons) (R N.Y.) Aug. 27, 1825-March 21, 1909; House 1877-81.

STARK, Benjamin (D Ore.) June 26, 1820-Oct. 10, 1898; Senate Oct. 29, 1861-Sept. 12, 1862.

STARK, Fortney Hillman (D Calif.) Nov. 11, 1931-—; House 1973-—.

STARK, William Ledyard (D Neb.) July 29, 1853-Nov. 11, 1922; House 1897-1903.

STARKEY, Frank Thomas (D Minn.) Feb. 18, 1892-May 14, 1968; House 1945-47.

STARKWEATHER, David Austin (D Ohio) Jan. 21, 1802-July 12, 1876; House 1839-41, 1845-47.

STARKWEATHER, George Anson (D N.Y.) May 19, 1794-Oct. 15, 1879; House 1847-49.

STARKWEATHER, Henry Howard (R Conn.) April 29, 1826-Jan. 28, 1876; House 1867-Jan. 28, 1876.

STARNES, Joe (D Ala.) March 31, 1895-Jan. 9, 1962; House 1935-45.

STARR, John Farson (R N.J.) March 25, 1818-Aug. 9, 1904; House 1863-67.

STATON, David Mick (R W. Va.) Feb. 11, 1940-—; House 1981-83.

STAUFFER, Simon Walter (R Pa.) Aug. 13, 1888-Sept. 26, 1975; House 1953-55, 1957-59.

STEAGALL, Henry Bascom (D Ala.) May 19, 1873-Nov. 22, 1943; House 1915-Nov. 22, 1943.

STEARNS, Asahel (F Mass.) June 17, 1774-Feb. 5, 1839; House 1815-17.

STEARNS, Foster Waterman (R N.H.) July 29, 1881-June 4, 1956; House 1939-45.

STEARNS, Ozora Pierson (R Minn.) Jan. 15, 1831-June 2, 1896; Senate Jan. 23-March 3, 1871.

STEBBINS, Henry George (WD N.Y.) Sept. 15, 1811-Dec. 9, 1881; House 1863-Oct. 24, 1864.

STECK, Daniel Frederick (D Iowa) Dec. 16, 1881-Dec. 31, 1950; Senate April 12, 1926-31.

STEDMAN, Charles Manly (D N.C.) Jan. 29, 1841-Sept. 23, 1930; House 1911-Sept. 23, 1930.

STEDMAN, William (F Mass.) Jan. 21, 1765-Aug. 31, 1831; House 1803-July 16, 1810.

STEED, Thomas Jefferson (D Okla.) March 2, 1904-June 7, 1983; House 1949-81.

STEELE, George Washington (R Ind.) Dec. 13, 1839-July 12, 1922; House 1881-89, 1895-1903; Gov. (Okla. Terr.) 1890-91.

STEELE, Henry Joseph (D Pa.) May 10, 1860-March 19, 1933; House 1915-21.

STEELE, John (F N.C.) Nov. 1, 1764-Aug. 14, 1815; House 1789-93.

STEELE, John Benedict (D N.Y.) March 28, 1814-Sept. 24, 1866; House 1861-65.

STEELE, John Nevett (W Md.) Feb. 22, 1796-Aug. 13, 1853; House May 29, 1834-37.

STEELE, Leslie Jasper (D Ga.) Nov. 21, 1868-July 24, 1929; House 1927-July 24, 1929.

STEELE, Robert Hampton (R Conn.) Nov. 3, 1938-—; House Nov. 3, 1970-75.

STEELE, Thomas Jefferson (D Iowa) March 19, 1853-March 20, 1920; House 1915-17.

STEELE, Walter Leak (D N.C.) April 18, 1823-Oct. 16, 1891; House 1877-81.

STEELE, William Gaston (D N.J.) Dec. 17, 1820-April 22, 1892; House 1861-65.

STEELE, William Randolph (D Wyo) July 24, 1842-Nov. 30, 1901; House (Terr. Del.) 1873-77.

STEELMAN, Alan Watson (R Texas) March 15, 1942-—; House 1973-77.

STEENERSON, Halvor (R Minn.) June 30, 1852-Nov. 22, 1926; House 1903-23.

STEENROD, Lewis (D Va.) May 27, 1810-Oct. 3, 1862; House 1839-45.

STEERS, Newton Ivan Jr. (R Md.) Jan 13, 1917-—; House 1977-79.

STEFAN, Karl (R Neb.) March 1, 1884-Oct. 2, 1951; House 1935-Oct. 2, 1951.

STEIGER, Sam (R Ariz.) March 10, 1929-—; House 1967-77.

STEIGER, William Albert (R Wis.) May 15, 1938-Dec. 4, 1978; House 1967-Dec. 4, 1978.

STEIWER, Frederick (R Ore.) Oct. 13, 1883-Feb. 3, 1939; Senate 1927-Jan. 31, 1938.

STENGER, William Shearer (D Pa.) Feb. 13, 1840-March 29, 1918; House 1875-79.

STENGLE, Charles Irwin (D N.Y.) Dec. 5, 1869-Nov. 23, 1953; House 1923-25.

STENHOLM, Charles Walter (D Texas) Oct. 26, 1938-—; House 1979-—.

STENNIS, John Cornelius (D Miss.) Aug. 3, 1901-—; Senate Nov. 5, 1947-—.

STEPHENS, Abraham P. (D N.Y.) Feb. 18, 1796-Nov. 25, 1859; House 1851-53.

STEPHENS, Alexander Hamilton (great-great-uncle of Robert Grier Stephens Jr.) (D Ga.) Feb. 11, 1812-March 4, 1883; House Oct. 2, 1843-59, Dec. 1, 1873-Nov. 4, 1882; Gov. 1882-83.

STEPHENS, Ambrose Everett Burnside (R Ohio) June 3, 1862-Feb. 12, 1927; House 1919-Feb. 12, 1927.

STEPHENS, Dan Voorhees (D Neb.) Nov. 4, 1868-Jan. 13, 1939; House Nov. 7, 1911-19.

STEPHENS, Hubert Durrett (D Miss.) July 2, 1875-March 14, 1946; House 1911-21; Senate 1923-35.

STEPHENS, John Hall (D Texas) Nov. 22, 1847-Nov. 18, 1924; House 1897-1917.

STEPHENS, Philander (JD Pa.) 1788-July 8, 1842; House 1829-33.

STEPHENS, Robert Grier Jr. (great-great-nephew of Alexander Hamilton Stephens) (D Ga.) Aug. 14, 1913-—; House 1961-77.

STEPHENS, William Dennison (R Calif.) Dec. 26, 1859-April 25, 1944; House 1911-July 22, 1916; Gov. 1917-23.

STEPHENSON, Benjamin (D Ill.) ?-Oct. 10, 1822; House (Terr. Del.) Sept. 3, 1814-16.

STEPHENSON, Isaac (brother of Samuel Merritt Stephenson) (R Wis.) June 18, 1829-March 15, 1918; House 1883-89; Senate May 17, 1907-15.

STEPHENSON, James (F Va.) March 20, 1764-Aug. 7, 1833; House 1803-05, 1809-11, Oct. 28, 1822-25.

STEPHENSON, Samuel Merritt (brother of Isaac Stephenson) (R Mich.) Dec. 23, 1831-July 31, 1907; House 1889-97.

STERETT, Samuel (AF Md.) 1758-July 12, 1833; House 1791-93.

STERIGERE, John Benton (D Pa.) July 31, 1793-Oct. 13, 1852; House 1827-31.

STERLING, Ansel (brother of Micah Sterling) (— Conn.) Feb. 3, 1782-Nov. 6, 1853; House 1821-25.

STERLING, Bruce Foster (D Pa.) Sept. 28, 1870-April 26, 1945; House 1917-19.

STERLING, John Allen (brother of Thomas Sterling) (R Ill.) Feb. 1, 1857-Oct. 17, 1918; House 1903-13, 1915-Oct. 17, 1918.

STERLING, Micah (brother of Ansel Sterling) (F N.Y.) Nov. 5, 1784-April 11, 1844; House 1821-23.

STERLING, Thomas (brother of John Allen Sterling) (R S.D.) Feb. 21, 1851-Aug. 26, 1930; Senate 1913-25.

STETSON, Charles (D Maine) Nov. 2, 1801-March 27, 1863; House 1849-51.

STETSON, Lemuel (D N.Y.) March 13, 1804-May 17, 1868; House 1843-45.

STEVENS, Aaron Fletcher (R N.H.) Aug. 9, 1819-May 10, 1887; House 1867-71.

STEVENS, Bradford Newcomb (D Ill.) Jan. 3, 1813-Nov. 10, 1885; House 1871-73.

STEVENS, Charles Abbot (brother of Moses Tyler Stevens, cousin of Isaac Ingalls Stevens) (R Mass.) Aug. 9, 1816-April 7, 1892; House Jan. 27-March 3, 1875.

STEVENS, Frederick Clement (R Minn.) Jan. 1, 1861-July 1, 1923; House 1897-1915.

STEVENS, Hestor Lockhart (D Mich.) Oct. 1, 1803-May 7, 1864; House 1853-55.

STEVENS, Hiram Sanford (D Ariz.) March 20, 1832-March 22, 1893; House (Terr. Del.) 1875-79.

STEVENS, Isaac Ingalls (cousin of Charles Abbot Stevens and Moses Tyler Stevens) (D Wash.) March 25, 1818-Sept. 1, 1862; House (Terr. Del.) 1857-61; Gov. (Wash. Terr.) 1853-57.

STEVENS, James (D Conn.) July 4, 1768-April 4, 1835; House 1819-21.

STEVENS, Moses Tyler (brother of Charles Abbot Stevens, cousin of Isaac Ingalls Stevens) (D Mass.) Oct. 10, 1825-March 25, 1907; House 1891-95.

STEVENS, Raymond Bartlett (D N.H.) June 18, 1874-May 18, 1942; House 1913-15.

STEVENS, Robert Smith (D N.Y.) March 27, 1824-Feb. 23, 1893; House 1883-85.

STEVENS, Thaddeus (R Pa.) April 4, 1792-Aug. 11, 1868; House 1849-53, 1859-Aug. 11, 1868 (1849-53 Whig, 1859-68 Republican).

STEVENS, Theodore F. (Ted) (R Alaska) Nov. 18, 1923-−; Senate Dec. 24, 1968-−.

STEVENSON, Adlai Ewing (great-grandfather of Adlai Ewing Stevenson III) (D Ill.) Oct. 23, 1835-June 14, 1914; House 1875-77, 1879-81; Vice Pres. 1893-97.

STEVENSON, Adlai Ewing III (great-grandson of Adlai Ewing Stevenson) (D Ill.) Oct. 10, 1930-−; Senate Nov. 17, 1970-81.

STEVENSON, Andrew (father of John White Stevenson) (D Va.) Jan. 21, 1784-Jan. 25, 1857; House 1821-June 2, 1834; Speaker 1827-34.

STEVENSON, James S. (− Pa.) 1780-Oct. 16, 1831; House 1825-29.

STEVENSON, Job Evans (R Ohio) Feb. 10, 1832-July 24, 1922; House 1869-73.

STEVENSON, John White (son of Andrew Stevenson) (D Ky.) May 4, 1812-Aug. 10, 1886; House 1857-61; Senate 1871-77; Gov. 1867-71.

STEVENSON, William Francis (D S.C.) Nov. 23, 1861-Feb. 12, 1942; House 1917-33.

STEVENSON, William Henry (R Wis.) Sept. 23, 1891-March 19, 1978; House 1941-49.

STEWARD, Lewis (D Ill.) Nov. 21, 1824-Aug. 27, 1896; House 1891-93.

STEWART, Alexander (R Wis.) Sept. 12, 1829-May 24, 1912; House 1895-1901.

STEWART, Andrew (father of the following) (W Pa.) June 11, 1791-July 16, 1872; House 1821-29, 1831-35, 1843-49 (1821-29, 1831-35 Democrat, 1843-49 Whig).

STEWART, Andrew (son of the preceding) (R Pa.) April 6, 1836-Nov. 9, 1903; House 1891-Feb. 26, 1892.

STEWART, Arthur Thomas (Tom) (D Tenn.) Jan. 11, 1892-Oct. 10, 1972; Senate Jan. 16, 1939-49.

STEWART, Bennett McVey (D Ill.) Aug. 6, 1915-−; House 1979-81.

STEWART, Charles (D Texas) May 30, 1836-Sept. 21, 1895; House 1883-93.

STEWART, David (W Md.) Sept. 13, 1800-Jan. 5, 1858; Senate Dec. 6, 1849-Jan. 12, 1850.

STEWART, David Wallace (R Iowa) Jan. 22, 1887-Feb. 10, 1974; Senate Aug. 7, 1926-27.

STEWART, Donald Wilbur (D Ala.) Feb. 8, 1940-−; Senate Nov. 8, 1978-81.

STEWART, Jacob Henry (R Minn.) Jan. 15, 1829-Aug. 25, 1884; House 1877-79.

STEWART, James (− N.C.) Nov. 11, 1775-Dec. 29, 1821; House Jan. 5, 1818-19.

STEWART, James Augustus (D Md.) Nov. 24, 1808-April 3, 1879; House 1855-61.

STEWART, James Fleming (R N.J.) June 15, 1851-Jan. 21, 1904; House 1895-1903.

STEWART, John (D Pa.) ?-1820; House Jan. 15, 1801-05.

STEWART, John (D Conn.) Feb. 10, 1795-Sept. 16, 1860; House 1843-45.

STEWART, John David (D Ga.) Aug. 2, 1833-Jan. 28, 1894; House 1887-91.

STEWART, John George (R Del.) June 2, 1890-May 24, 1970; House 1935-37.

STEWART, John Knox (R N.Y.) Oct. 20, 1853-June 27, 1919; House 1899-1903.

STEWART, John Wolcott (R Vt.) Nov. 24, 1825-Oct. 29, 1915; House 1883-91; Senate March 24-Oct. 21, 1908; Gov. 1870-72.

STEWART, Paul (D Okla.) Feb. 27, 1892-Nov. 13, 1950; House 1943-47.

STEWART, Percy Hamilton (D N.J.) Jan. 10, 1867-June 30, 1951; House Dec. 1, 1931-33.

STEWART, Thomas Elliott (CR N.Y.) Sept. 22, 1824-Jan. 9, 1904; House 1867-69.

STEWART, William (R Pa.) Sept. 10, 1810-Oct. 17, 1876; House 1857-61.

STEWART, William Morris (R Nev.) Aug. 9, 1827-April 23, 1909; Senate Dec. 15, 1864-75, 1887-1905.

STIGLER, William Grady (D Okla.) July 7, 1891-Aug. 21, 1952; House March 28, 1944-Aug. 21, 1952.

STILES, John Dodson (D Pa.) Jan. 15, 1822-Oct. 29, 1896; House June 3, 1862-65, 1869-71.

STILES, William Henry (D Ga.) Jan. 1, 1808-Dec. 20, 1865; House 1843-45.

STILLWELL, Thomas Neel (R Ind.) Aug. 29, 1830-Jan. 14, 1874; House 1865-67.

STINESS, Walter Russell (R R.I.) March 13, 1854-March 17, 1924; House 1915-23.

STINSON, K. William (Bill) (R Wash.) April 20, 1930-−; House 1963-65.

STIVERS, Moses Dunning (R N.Y.) Dec. 30, 1828-Feb. 2, 1895; House 1889-91.

STOBBS, George Russell (R Mass.) Feb. 7, 1877-Dec. 23, 1966; House 1925-31.

STOCKBRIDGE, Francis Brown (R Mich.) April 9, 1826-April 30, 1894; Senate 1887-April 30, 1894.

STOCKBRIDGE, Henry Jr. (R Md.) Sept. 18, 1856-March 22, 1924; House 1889-91.

STOCKDALE, Thomas Ringland (D Miss.) March 28, 1828-Jan. 8, 1899; House 1887-95.

STOCKMAN, David Alan (R Mich.) Nov. 10, 1946-−; House 1977-81; Director, Office of Management and Budget 1981-−.

STOCKMAN, Lowell (R Ore.) April 12, 1901-Aug. 10, 1962; House 1943-53.

STOCKSLAGER, Strother Madison (D Ind.) May 7, 1842-June 1, 1930; House 1881-85.

STOCKTON, John Potter (son of Robert Field Stockton, grandson of Richard Stockton) (D N.J.) Aug. 2, 1826-Jan. 22, 1900; Senate March 15, 1865-March 27, 1866, 1869-75.

STOCKTON, Richard (father of Robert Field Stockton, grandfather of John Potter Stockton) (F N.J.) April 17, 1764-March 7, 1828; Senate Nov. 12, 1796-99; House 1813-15.

STOCKTON, Robert Field (son of Richard Stockton, father of John Potter Stockton) (D N.J.) Aug. 20, 1795-Oct. 7, 1866; Senate 1851-Jan. 10, 1853.

STODDARD, Ebenezer (− Conn.) May 6, 1785-Aug. 19, 1847; House 1821-25.

STODDERT, John Truman (JD Md.) Oct. 1, 1790-July 19, 1870; House 1833-35.

STOKELY, Samuel (W Ohio) Jan. 25, 1796-May 23, 1861; House 1841-43.

STOKES, Edward Lowber (R Pa.) Sept. 29, 1880-Nov. 8, 1964; House Nov. 3, 1931-35.

STOKES, James William (D S.C.) Dec. 12, 1853-July 6, 1901; House 1895-June 1, 1896; Nov. 3, 1896-July 6, 1901.

STOKES, Louis (D Ohio) Feb. 23, 1925-−; House 1969-−.

STOKES, Montfort (D N.C.) March 12, 1762-Nov. 4, 1842; Senate Dec. 4, 1816-23; Gov. 1830-32.

STOKES, William Brickly (R Tenn.) Sept. 9, 1814-March 14, 1897; House 1859-61, July 24, 1866-71 (1859-61 Whig, 1866-71 Republican).

STOLL, Philip Henry (D S.C.) Nov. 5, 1874-Oct. 29, 1958; House Oct. 7, 1919-23.

STONE, Alfred Parish (D Ohio) June 28, 1813-Aug. 2, 1865; House Oct. 8, 1844-45.

STONE, Charles Warren (R Pa.) June 29, 1843-Aug. 15, 1912; House Nov. 4, 1890-99.

STONE, Claudius Ulysses (D Ill.) May 11, 1879-Nov. 13, 1957; House 1911-17.

STONE, David (D N.C.) Feb. 17, 1770-Oct. 7, 1818; House 1799-1801; Senate 1801-Feb. 17, 1807, 1813-Dec. 24, 1814; Gov. 1808-10.

STONE, Eben Francis (R Mass.) Aug. 3, 1822-Jan. 22, 1895; House 1881-87.

Biographical Index

STONE, Frederick (grandson of Michael Jenifer Stone) (D Md.) Feb. 7, 1820-Oct. 17, 1899; House 1867-71.

STONE, James W. (D Ky.) 1813-Oct. 13, 1854; House 1843-45, 1851-53.

STONE, John Wesley (R Mich.) July 18, 1838-March 24, 1922; House 1877-81.

STONE, Joseph Champlin (R Iowa) July 30, 1829-Dec. 3, 1902; House 1877-79.

STONE, Michael Jenifer (grandfather of Frederick Stone) (— Md.) 1747-1812; House 1789-91.

STONE, Richard Bernard (D Fla.) Sept. 22, 1928- —; Senate Jan. 1, 1975-Dec. 31, 1980.

STONE, Ulysses Stevens (R Okla.) Dec. 17, 1878-Dec. 8, 1962; House 1929-31.

STONE, William (W Tenn.) Jan. 26, 1791-Feb. 18, 1853; House Sept. 14, 1837-39.

STONE, William Alexis (R Pa.) April 18, 1846-March 1, 1920; House 1891-Nov. 9, 1898; Gov. 1899-1903.

STONE, William Henry (D Mo.) Nov. 7, 1828-July 9, 1901; House 1873-77.

STONE, William Joel (D Mo.) May 7, 1848-April 14, 1918; House 1885-91; Senate 1903-April 14, 1918; Gov. 1893-97.

STONE, William Johnson (D Ky.) June 26, 1841-March 12, 1923; House 1885-95.

STORER, Bellamy (father of the following) (W Ohio) March 26, 1796-June 1, 1875; House 1835-37.

STORER, Bellamy (son of the preceding, uncle of Nicholas Longworth) (R Ohio) Aug. 28, 1847-Nov. 12, 1922; House 1891-95.

STORER, Clement (— N.H.) Sept. 20, 1760-Nov. 21, 1830; House 1807-09; Senate June 27, 1817-19.

STORKE, Thomas More (D Calif.) Nov. 23, 1876-Oct. 12, 1971; Senate Nov. 9, 1938-39.

STORM, Frederic (R N.Y.) July 2, 1844-June 9, 1935; House 1901-03.

STORM, John Brutzman (D Pa.) Sept. 19, 1838-Aug. 13, 1901; House 1871-75, 1883-87.

STORRS, Henry Randolph (brother of William Lucius Storrs) (F N.Y.) Sept. 3, 1787-July 29, 1837; House 1817-21, 1823-31.

STORRS, William Lucius (brother of Henry Randolph Storrs) (W Conn.) March 25, 1795-June 25, 1861; House 1829-33, 1839-June 1840.

STORY, Joseph (D Mass.) Sept. 18, 1779-Sept. 10, 1845; House May 23, 1808-09; Assoc. Justice Supreme Court 1811-Sept. 10, 1845.

STOUGHTON, William Lewis (R Mich.) March 20, 1827-June 6, 1888; House 1869-73.

STOUT, Byron Gray (D Mich.) Jan. 12, 1829-June 19, 1896; House 1891-93.

STOUT, Lansing (D Ore.) March 27, 1828-March 4, 1871; House 1859-61.

STOUT, Tom (D Mont.) May 20, 1879-Dec. 26, 1965; House 1913-17.

STOVER, John Hubler (R Mo.) April 24, 1833-Oct. 27, 1889; House Dec. 7, 1868-69.

STOW, Silas (F N.Y.) Dec. 21, 1773-Jan. 19, 1827; House 1811-13.

STOWELL, William Henry Harrison (R Va.) July 26, 1840-April 27, 1922; House 1871-77.

STOWER, John G. (JD N.Y.) ?-?; House 1827-29.

STRADER, Peter Wilson (D Ohio) Nov. 6, 1818-Feb. 25, 1881; House 1869-71.

STRAIT, Horace Burton (R Minn.) Jan. 26, 1835-Feb. 25, 1894; House 1873-79, 1881-87.

STRAIT, Thomas Jefferson (Alliance D S.C.) Dec. 25, 1846-April 18, 1924; House 1893-99.

STRANAHAN, James Samuel Thomas (W N.Y.) April 25, 1808-Sept. 3, 1898; House 1855-57.

STRANG, Michael Lathrop (R Col.) June 17, 1929- —; House 1985- —.

STRANGE, Robert (D N.C.) Sept. 20, 1796-Feb. 19, 1854; Senate Dec. 5, 1836-Nov. 16, 1840.

STRATTON, Charles Creighton (uncle of Benjamin Franklin Howey) (W N.J.) March 6, 1796-March 30, 1859; House 1837-39, 1841-43; Gov. 1845-48.

STRATTON, John (— Va.) Aug. 19, 1769-May 10, 1804; House 1801-03.

STRATTON, John Leake Newbold (R N.J.) Nov. 27, 1817-May 17, 1899; House 1859-63.

STRATTON, Nathan Taylor (D N.J.) March 17, 1813-March 9, 1887; House 1851-55.

STRATTON, Samuel Studdiford (D N.Y.) Sept. 27, 1916- —; House 1959- —.

STRATTON, William Grant (R Ill.) Feb. 26, 1914- —; House 1941-43, 1947-49; Gov. 1953-61.

STRAUB, Christian Markle (D Pa.) 1804-?; House 1853-55.

STRAUS, Isidor (D N.Y.) Feb. 6, 1845-April 15, 1912; House Jan. 30, 1894-95.

STRAWBRIDGE, James Dale (R Pa.) April 7, 1824-July 19, 1890; House 1873-75.

STREET, Randall S. (D N.Y.) 1780-Nov. 21, 1841; House 1819-21.

STRICKLAND, Randolph (R Mich.) Feb. 4, 1823-May 5, 1880; House 1869-71.

STRINGER, Lawrence Beaumont (D Ill.) Feb. 24, 1866-Dec. 5, 1942; House 1913-15.

STRINGFELLOW, Douglas (R Utah) Sept. 24, 1922-Oct. 19, 1966; House 1953-55.

STRODE, Jesse Burr (R Neb.) Feb. 18, 1845-Nov. 10, 1924; House 1895-99.

STROHM, John (W Pa.) Oct. 16, 1793-Sept. 12, 1884; House 1845-49.

STRONG, Caleb (F Mass.) Jan. 9, 1745-Nov. 7, 1819; Senate 1789-June 1, 1796; Gov. 1800-07, 1812-16.

STRONG, James (F N.Y.) 1783-Aug. 8, 1847; House 1819-21, 1823-31.

STRONG, James George (R Kan.) April 23, 1870-Jan. 11, 1938; House 1919-33.

STRONG, Julius Levi (R Conn.) Nov. 8, 1828-Sept. 7, 1872; House 1869-Sept. 7, 1872.

STRONG, Luther Martin (R Ohio) June 23, 1838-April 26, 1903; House 1893-97.

STRONG, Nathan Leroy (R Pa.) Nov. 12, 1859-Dec. 14, 1939; House 1917-35.

STRONG, Selah Brewster (D N.Y.) May 1, 1792-Nov. 29, 1872; House 1843-45.

STRONG, Solomon (F Mass.) March 2, 1780-Sept. 16, 1850; House 1815-19.

STRONG, Stephen (D N.Y.) Oct. 11, 1791-April 15, 1866; House 1845-47.

STRONG, Sterling Price (D Texas) Aug. 17, 1852-March 28, 1936; House 1933-35.

STRONG, Theron Rudd (cousin of William Strong of Pa.) (D N.Y.) Nov. 7, 1802-May 14, 1873; House 1839-41.

STRONG, William (D Vt.) 1763-Jan. 28, 1840; House 1811-15, 1819-21.

STRONG, William (cousin of Theron Rudd Strong) (D Pa.) May 6, 1808-Aug. 19, 1895; House 1847-51; Assoc. Justice Supreme Court 1870-80.

STROTHER, George French (father of James French Strother of Va., great-grandfather of James French Strother of W.Va.) (D Va.) 1783-Nov. 28, 1840; House 1817-Feb. 10, 1820.

STROTHER, James French (son of George French Strother, grandfather of the following) (W Va.) Sept. 4, 1811-Sept. 20, 1860; House 1851-53.

STROTHER, James French (grandson of the preceding, great-grandson of George French Strother) (R W.Va.) June 29, 1868-April 10, 1930; House 1925-29.

STROUSE, Myer (D Pa.) Dec. 16, 1825-Feb. 11, 1878; House 1863-67.

STROWD, William Franklin (P N.C.) Dec. 7, 1832-Dec. 12, 1911; House 1895-99.

STRUBLE, Isaac S. (R Iowa) Nov. 3, 1843-Feb. 17, 1913; House 1883-91.

STRUDWICK, William Francis (F N.C.) ?-1812; House Nov. 28, 1796-97.

STUART, Alexander Hugh Holmes (cousin of Archibald Stuart) (W Va.) April 2, 1807-Feb. 13, 1891; House 1841-43; Secy. of the Interior 1850-53.

STUART, Andrew (D Ohio) Aug. 3, 1823-April 30, 1872; House 1853-55.

STUART, Archibald (cousin of Alexander Hugh Holmes Stuart) (W Va.) Dec. 2, 1795-Sept. 20, 1855; House 1837-39.

STUART, Charles Edward (D Mich.) Nov. 25, 1810-May 19, 1887; House Dec. 6, 1847-49, 1851-53; Senate 1853-59.

STUART, David (D Mich.) March 12, 1816-Sept. 12, 1868; House 1853-55.

STUART, John Todd (D Ill.) Nov. 10, 1807-Nov. 23, 1885; House 1839-43, 1863-65 (1839-43 Whig, 1863-65 Democrat).

STUART, Philip (F Md.) 1760-Aug. 14, 1830; House 1811-19.

STUBBLEFIELD, Frank Albert (D Ky.) April 5, 1907-Oct. 14, 1977; House 1959-Dec. 31, 1974.

STUBBS, Henry Elbert (D Calif.) March 4, 1881-Feb. 28, 1937; House 1933-Feb. 28, 1937.

STUCKEY, Williamson Sylvester Jr. (D Ga.) May 25, 1935- —; House 1967-77.

STUDDS, Gerry Eastman (D Mass.) May 12, 1937- —; House 1973- —.

STUDLEY, Elmer Ebenezer (R N.Y.) Sept. 24, 1869-Sept. 6, 1942; House 1933-35.

STULL, Howard William (R Pa.) April 11, 1876-April 22, 1949; House April 26, 1932-33.

STUMP, Herman (D Md.) Aug. 8, 1837-Jan. 9, 1917; House 1889-93.

STUMP, Robert (R Ariz.) April 4, 1927- —; House 1977- — (1977-83 Democrat, 1983- — Republican).

STURGEON, Daniel (D Pa.) Oct. 27, 1789-July 3, 1878; Senate Jan. 14, 1840-51.

STURGES, Jonathan (father of Lewis Burr Sturges) (— Conn.) Aug. 23, 1740-Oct. 4, 1819; House 1789-93; Cont. Cong. 1774-87.

STURGES, Lewis Burr (son of Jonathan Sturges) (F Conn.) March 15, 1763-March 30, 1844; House Sept. 16, 1805-17.

STURGISS, George Cookman (R W.Va.) Aug. 16, 1842-Feb. 26, 1925; House 1907-11.

STURTEVANT, John Cirby (R Pa.) Feb. 20, 1835-Dec. 20, 1912; House 1897-99.

SULLIVAN, Christopher Daniel (D N.Y.) July 14, 1870-Aug. 3, 1942; House 1917-41.

SULLIVAN, George (— N.H.) Aug. 29, 1771-April 14, 1838; House 1811-13.

SULLIVAN, John Andrew (D Mass.) May 10, 1868-May 31, 1927; House 1903-07.

SULLIVAN, John Berchmans (husband of Leonor Kretzer Sullivan) (D Mo.) Oct. 10, 1897-Jan. 29, 1951; House 1941-43, 1945-47, 1949-Jan. 29, 1951.

SULLIVAN, Leonor Kretzer (widow of John Berchmans Sullivan) (D Mo.) Aug. 21, 1903- —; House 1953-77.

SULLIVAN, Maurice Joseph (D Nev.) Dec. 7, 1884-Aug. 9, 1953; House 1943-45.

SULLIVAN, Patrick Joseph (R Wyo.) March 17, 1865-April 8, 1935; Senate Dec. 5, 1929-Nov. 20, 1930.

SULLIVAN, Patrick Joseph (R Pa.) Oct. 12, 1877-Dec. 31, 1946; House 1929-33.

SULLIVAN, Timothy Daniel (D N.Y.) July 23, 1862-Aug. 31, 1913; House 1903-July 27, 1906, March 4-Aug. 31, 1913.

SULLIVAN, William Van Amberg (D Miss.) Dec. 18, 1857-March 21, 1918; House 1897-May 31, 1898; Senate May 31, 1898-1901.

SULLOWAY, Cyrus Adams (R N.H.) June 8, 1839-March 11, 1917; House 1895-1913, 1915-March 11, 1917.

SULZER, Charles August (brother of William Sulzer) (D Alaska) Feb. 24, 1879-April 28, 1919; House (Terr Del) 1917-Jan. 7, 1919, March 4-April 28, 1919.

SULZER, William (brother of Charles August Sulzer) (D N.Y.) March 18, 1863-Nov. 6, 1941; House 1895-Dec. 31, 1912; Gov. 1913.

SUMMERS, George William (W Va.) March 4, 1804-Sept. 19, 1868; House 1841-45.

SUMMERS, John William (R Wash.) April 29, 1870-Sept. 25, 1937; House 1919-33.

SUMNER, Charles (R Mass.) Jan. 6, 1811-March 11, 1874; Senate April 24, 1851-March 11, 1874 (1851-57 Democrat/Free-Soiler, 1857-74 Republican).

SUMNER, Charles Allen (D Calif.) Aug. 2, 1835-Jan. 31, 1903; House 1883-85.

SUMNER, Daniel Hadley (D Wis.) Sept. 15, 1837-May 29, 1903; House 1883-85.

SUMNER, Jessie (R Ill.) July 17, 1898- —; House 1939-47.

SUMNERS, Hatton William (D Texas) May 30, 1875-April 19, 1962; House 1913-47.

SUMTER, Thomas (grandfather of Thomas De Lage Sumter) (D S.C.) Aug. 14, 1734-June 1, 1832; House 1789-93, 1797-Dec. 15, 1801; Senate Dec. 15, 1801-Dec. 16, 1810.

SUMTER, Thomas De Lage (grandson of Thomas Sumter) (D S.C.) Nov. 14, 1809-July 2, 1874; House 1839-43.

SUNDQUIST, Donald Kenneth (R Tenn.) March 15, 1936- —; House 1983- —.

SUNDSTROM, Frank Leander (R N.J.) Jan. 5, 1901-May 23, 1980; House 1943-49.

SUNIA, Fofo I.F. (D American Samoa) March 13, 1937- —; House 1981- —.

SUTHERLAND, Daniel Alexander (R Alaska) April 17, 1869-March 24, 1955; House (Terr. Del.) 1921-31.

SUTHERLAND, George (R Utah) March 25, 1862-July 18, 1942; House 1901-03; Senate 1905-17; Assoc. Justice Supreme Court 1922-38.

SUTHERLAND, Howard (R W.Va.) Sept. 8, 1865-March 12, 1950; House 1913-17; Senate 1917-23.

SUTHERLAND, Jabez Gridley (D Mich.) Oct. 6, 1825-Nov. 20, 1902; House 1871-73.

SUTHERLAND, Joel Barlow (JD Pa.) Feb. 26, 1792-Nov. 15, 1861; House 1827-37.

SUTHERLAND, Josiah (D N.Y.) June 12, 1804-May 25, 1887; House 1851-53.

SUTHERLAND, Roderick Dhu (P Neb.) April 27, 1862-Oct. 18, 1915; House 1897-1901.

SUTPHIN, William Halstead (D N.J.) Aug. 30, 1887-Oct. 14, 1972; House 1931-43.

SUTTON, James Patrick (Pat) (D Tenn.) Oct. 31, 1915- —; House 1949-55.

SWAN, Samuel (— N.J.) 1771-Aug. 24, 1844; House 1821-31.

SWANK, Fletcher B. (D Okla.) April 24, 1875-March 16, 1950; House 1921-29, 1931-35.

SWANN, Edward (D N.Y.) March 10, 1862-Sept. 19, 1945; House Nov. 4, 1902-03.

SWANN, Thomas (D Md.) Feb. 3, 1809-July 24, 1883; House 1869-79; Gov. 1866-69 (Unionist).

SWANSON, Charles Edward (R Iowa) Jan. 3, 1879-Aug. 22, 1970; House 1929-33.

SWANSON, Claude Augustus (D Va.) March 31, 1862-July 7, 1939; House 1893-Jan. 30, 1906; Senate Aug. 1, 1910-33; Gov. 1906-10; Secy. of the Navy 1933-39.

SWANWICK, John (D Pa.) 1740-Aug. 1, 1798; House 1795-Aug. 1, 1798.

SWART, Peter (— N.Y.) July 5, 1752-Nov. 3, 1829; House 1807-09.

SWARTZ, Joshua William (R Pa.) June 9, 1867-May 27, 1959; House 1925-27.

SWASEY, John Philip (R Maine) Sept. 4, 1839-May 27, 1928; House Nov. 3, 1908-11.

SWEARINGEN, Henry (D Ohio) about 1792-?; House Dec. 3, 1838-41.

SWEAT, Lorenzo De Medici (D Maine) May 26, 1818-July 26, 1898; House 1863-65.

SWEENEY, Mac (R Texas) Sept. 15, 1955- —; House 1985- —.

SWEENEY, Martin Leonard (father of Robert E. Sweeney) (D Ohio) April 15, 1885-May 1, 1960; House Nov. 3, 1931-43.

SWEENEY, Robert E. (son of Martin Leonard Sweeney) (D Ohio) Nov. 4, 1924- —; House 1965-67.

SWEENEY, William Northcut (D Ky.) May 5, 1832-April 21, 1895; House 1869-71.

SWEENY, George (— Ohio) Feb. 22, 1796-Oct. 10, 1877; House 1839-43.

SWEET, Burton Erwin (R Iowa) Dec. 10, 1867-Jan. 3, 1957; House 1915-23.

SWEET, Edwin Forrest (D Mich.) Nov. 21, 1847-April 2, 1935; House 1911-13.

SWEET, John Hyde (R Neb.) Sept. 1, 1880-April 4, 1964; House April 9, 1940-41.

SWEET, Thaddeus C. (R N.Y.) Nov. 16, 1872-May 1, 1928; House Nov. 6, 1923-May 1, 1928.

SWEET, Willis (R Idaho) Jan. 1, 1856-July 9, 1925; House Oct. 1, 1890-95.

SWEETSER, Charles (D Ohio) Jan. 22, 1808-April 14, 1864; House 1849-53.

Biographical Index

SWENEY, Joseph Henry (R Iowa) Oct. 2, 1845-Nov. 11, 1918; House 1889-91.

SWICK, Jesse Howard (R Pa.) Aug. 6, 1879-Nov. 17, 1952; House 1927-35.

SWIFT, Allen (D Wash.) Sept. 12, 1935- —; House 1979- —.

SWIFT, Benjamin (F Vt.) April 3, 1781-Nov. 11, 1847; House 1827-31; Senate 1833-39.

SWIFT, George Robinson (D Ala.) Dec. 19, 1887-Sept. 10, 1972; Senate June 15-Nov. 5, 1946.

SWIFT, Oscar William (R N.Y.) April 11, 1869-June 30, 1940; House 1915-19.

SWIFT, Zephaniah (F Conn.) Feb. 27, 1759-Sept. 27, 1823; House 1793-97.

SWIGERT, John Leonard (R Col.) Aug. 30, 1931-Dec. 27, 1982; elected to House 1982, but did not serve.

SWINBURNE, John (R N.Y.) May 30, 1820-March 28, 1889; House 1885-87.

SWINDALL, Charles (R Okla.) Feb. 13, 1876-June 19, 1939; House Nov. 2, 1920-21.

SWINDALL, Patrick Lynn (R Ga.) Oct. 18, 1950- —; House 1985- —.

SWING, Philip David (R Calif.) Nov. 30, 1884-Aug. 8, 1963; House 1921-33.

SWITZER, Robert Mauck (R Ohio) March 6, 1863-Oct. 28, 1952; House 1911-19.

SWOOPE, Jacob (F Va.) ?-1832; House 1809-11.

SWOOPE, William Irvin (nephew of John Patton) (R Pa.) Oct. 3, 1862-Oct. 9, 1930; House 1923-27.

SWOPE, Guy Jacob (D Pa.) Dec. 26, 1892-July 25, 1969; House 1937-39; Gov. (Puerto Rico) 1941.

SWOPE, John Augustus (D Pa.) Dec. 25, 1827-Dec. 6, 1910; House Dec. 23, 1884-March 3, 1885, Nov. 3, 1885-87.

SWOPE, King (R Ky.) Aug. 10, 1893-April 23, 1961; House Aug. 2, 1919-21.

SWOPE, Samuel Franklin (R Ky.) March 1, 1809-April 19, 1865; House 1855-57 (1855-56 American Party, 1856-57 Republican).

SYKES, George (D N.J.) Sept. 20, 1802-Feb. 25, 1880; House 1843-45, Nov. 4, 1845-47.

SYMES, George Gifford (R Colo.) April 28, 1840-Nov. 3, 1893; House 1885-89.

SYMINGTON, James Wadsworth (son of William Stuart Symington) (D Mo.) Sept. 28, 1927- —; House 1969-77.

SYMINGTON, William Stuart (father of James Wadsworth Symington) (D Mo.) June 26, 1901- —; Senate 1953-Dec. 27, 1976.

SYMMS, Steven Douglas (R Idaho) April 23, 1938- —; House 1973-81; Senate 1981- —.

SYNAR, Michael Lynn (D Okla.) Oct. 17, 1950- —; House 1979- —.

SYPHER, Jacob Hale (R La.) June 22, 1837-May 9, 1905; House July 18, 1868-69, Nov. 7, 1870-75.

T

TABER, John (R N.Y.) May 5, 1880-Nov. 22, 1965; House 1923-63.

TABER, Stephen (son of Thomas Taber 2d) (D N.Y.) March 7, 1821-April 23, 1886; House 1865-69.

TABER, Thomas 2d (father of Stephen Taber) (D N.Y.) May 19, 1785-March 21, 1862; House Nov. 5, 1828-29.

TABOR, Horace Austin Warner (R Colo.) Nov. 26, 1830-April 10, 1899; Senate Jan. 27-March 3, 1883.

TACKETT, Boyd (D Ark.) May 9, 1911- —; House 1949-53.

TAFFE, John (R Neb.) Jan. 30, 1827-March 14, 1884; House 1867-73.

TAFT, Charles Phelps (brother of President William Howard Taft, uncle of Robert Alphonso Taft) (R Ohio) Dec. 21, 1843-Dec. 31, 1929; House 1895-97.

TAFT, Kingsley Arter (R Ohio) July 19, 1903-March 28, 1970; Senate Nov. 5, 1946-47.

TAFT, Robert Alphonso (son of President William Howard Taft, father of Robert Taft Jr., nephew of Charles Phelps Taft) (R Ohio) Sept. 8, 1889-July 31, 1953; Senate 1939-July 31, 1953; Senate majority leader 1953.

TAFT, Robert Jr. (son of Robert Alphonso Taft, grandson of President William Howard Taft, grandnephew of Charles Phelps Taft) (R Ohio) Feb. 26, 1917- —; House 1963-65, 1967-71; Senate 1971-Dec. 28, 1976.

TAGGART, Joseph (D Kan.) June 15, 1867-Dec. 3, 1938; House Nov. 7, 1911-17.

TAGGART, Samuel (F Mass.) March 24, 1754-April 25, 1825; House 1803-17.

TAGGART, Thomas (D Ind.) Nov. 17, 1856-March 6, 1929; Senate March 20-Nov. 7, 1916; Chrmn. Dem. Nat. Comm. 1904-08.

TAGUE, Peter Francis (D Mass.) June 4, 1871-Sept. 17, 1941; House 1915-19, Oct. 23, 1919-25.

TAIT, Charles (D Ga.) Feb. 1, 1768-Oct. 7, 1835; Senate Nov. 27, 1809-19.

TALBERT, William Jasper (D S.C.) Oct. 6, 1846-Feb. 5, 1931; House 1893-1903.

TALBOT, Isham (— Ky.) 1773-Sept. 25, 1837; Senate Jan. 3, 1815-19, Oct. 19, 1820-25.

TALBOT, Joseph Edward (R Conn.) March 18, 1901-April 30, 1966; House Jan. 20, 1942-47.

TALBOT, Silas (F N.Y.) Jan. 11, 1751-June 30, 1813; House 1793-95.

TALBOTT, Albert Gallatin (uncle of William Clayton Anderson) (D Ky.) April 4, 1808-Sept. 9, 1887; House 1855-59.

TALBOTT, Joshua Frederick Cockey (D Md.) July 29, 1843-Oct. 5, 1918; House 1879-85, 1893-95, 1903-Oct. 5, 1918.

TALCOTT, Burt L. (R Calif.) Feb. 22, 1920- —; House 1963-77.

TALCOTT, Charles Andrew (D N.Y.) June 10, 1857-Feb. 27, 1920; House 1911-15.

TALIAFERRO, Benjamin (— Ga.) 1750-Sept. 3, 1821; House 1799-1802.

TALIAFERRO, James Piper (D Fla.) Sept. 30, 1847-Oct. 6, 1934; Senate April 20, 1899-1911.

TALIAFERRO, John (W Va.) 1768-Aug. 12, 1852; House 1801-03, Nov. 29, 1811-13, March 24, 1824-31, 1835-43 (1801-03, 1811-13, 1824-31 Democrat, 1835-43 Whig).

TALLE, Henry Oscar (R Iowa) Jan. 12, 1892-March 14, 1969; House 1939-59.

TALLMADGE, Benjamin (father of Frederick Augustus Tallmadge) (F Conn.) Feb. 25, 1754-March 7, 1835; House 1801-17.

TALLMADGE, Frederick Augustus (son of Benjamin Tallmadge) (W N.Y.) Aug. 29, 1792-Sept. 17, 1869; House 1847-49.

TALLMADGE, James Jr. (D N.Y.) Jan. 20, 1778-Sept. 29, 1853; House June 6, 1817-19.

TALLMADGE, Nathaniel Pitcher (D N.Y.) Feb. 8, 1795-Nov. 2, 1864; Senate 1833-June 17, 1844; Gov. (Wis. Terr.) 1844-45.

TALLMAN, Peleg (D Mass.) July 24, 1764-March 12, 1840; House 1811-13.

TALLON, Robert M. (D S.C.) Aug. 8, 1946- —; House 1983- —.

TALMADGE, Herman Eugene (D Ga.) Aug. 9, 1913- —; Senate 1957-81; Gov. 1947, 1948-55.

TANNEHILL, Adamson (D Pa.) May 23, 1750-Dec. 23, 1820; House 1813-15.

TANNER, Adolphus Hitchcock (R N.Y.) May 23, 1833-Jan. 14, 1882; House 1869-71.

TAPPAN, Benjamin (D Ohio) May 25, 1773-April 12, 1857; Senate 1839-45.

TAPPAN, Mason Weare (R N.H.) Oct. 20, 1817-Oct. 25, 1886; House 1855-61.

TARBOX, John Kemble (D Mass.) May 6, 1838-May 28, 1887; House 1875-77.

TARR, Christian (— Pa.) May 25, 1765-Feb. 24, 1833; House 1817-21.

TARSNEY, John Charles (D Mo.) Nov. 7, 1845-Sept. 4, 1920; House 1889-Feb. 17, 1896.

TARSNEY, Timothy Edward (D Mich.) Feb. 4, 1849-June 8, 1909; House 1885-89.

TARVER, Malcolm Connor (D Ga.) Sept. 25, 1885-March 5, 1960; House 1927-47.

TATE, Farish Carter (D Ga.) Nov. 20, 1856-Feb. 7, 1922; House 1893-1905.

TATE, Magnus (F Va.) 1760-March 30, 1823; House 1815-17.

TATGENHORST, Charles Jr. (R Ohio) Aug. 19, 1883-Jan. 13, 1961; House Nov. 8, 1927-29.

TATOM, Absalom (R N.C.) 1742-Dec. 20, 1802; House 1795-June 1, 1796.

TATNALL, Josiah (— Ga.) 1764-June 6, 1803; Senate Feb. 20, 1796-99; Gov. 1801-02.

TATTNALL, Edward Fenwick (— Ga.) 1788-Nov. 21, 1832; House 1821-27.

TAUKE, Thomas Joseph (R Iowa) Oct. 11, 1950- —; House 1979- —.

TAUL, Micah (grandfather of Taul Bradford) (D Ky.) May 14, 1785-May 27, 1850; House 1815-17.

TAULBEE, William Preston (D Ky.) Oct. 22, 1851-March 11, 1890; House 1885-89.

TAURIELLO, Anthony Francis (D N.Y.) Aug. 14, 1899-Dec. 21, 1983; House 1949-51.

TAUZIN, W.J. (Billy) (D La.) June 14, 1943- —; House May 22, 1980- —.

TAVENNER, Clyde Howard (D Ill.) Feb. 4, 1882-Feb. 6, 1942; House 1913-17.

TAWNEY, James Albertus (R Minn.) Jan. 3, 1855-June 12, 1919; House 1893-1911.

TAYLER, Robert Walker (R Ohio) Nov. 26, 1852-Nov. 25, 1910; House 1895-1903.

TAYLOR, Abner (R Ill.) 1829-April 13, 1903; House 1889-93.

TAYLOR, Alexander Wilson (R Pa.) March 22, 1815-May 7, 1893; House 1873-75.

TAYLOR, Alfred Alexander (son of Nathaniel Green Taylor, brother of Robert Love Taylor) (R Tenn.) Aug. 6, 1848-Nov. 25, 1931; House 1889-95; Gov. 1921-23.

TAYLOR, Arthur Herbert (D Ind.) Feb. 29, 1852-Feb. 20, 1922; House 1893-95.

TAYLOR, Benjamin Irving (D N.Y.) Dec. 21, 1877-Sept. 5, 1946; House 1913-15.

TAYLOR, Caleb Newbold (R Pa.) July 27, 1813-Nov. 15, 1887; House 1867-69, April 13, 1870-71.

TAYLOR, Chester William (son of Samuel Mitchell Taylor) (D Ark.) July 16, 1883-July 17, 1931; House Oct. 31, 1921-23.

TAYLOR, Dean Park (R N.Y.) Jan. 1, 1902-Oct. 16, 1977; House 1943-61.

TAYLOR, Edward Livingston Jr. (R Ohio) Aug. 10, 1869-March 10, 1938; House 1905-13.

TAYLOR, Edward Thomas (D Colo.) June 19, 1858-Sept. 3, 1941; House 1909-Sept. 3, 1941.

TAYLOR, Ezra Booth (R Ohio) July 9, 1823-Jan. 29, 1912; House Dec. 13, 1880-93.

TAYLOR, Gene (R Mo.) Feb. 10, 1928- —; House 1973- —.

TAYLOR, George (D N.Y.) Oct. 19, 1820-Jan. 18, 1894; House 1857-59.

TAYLOR, George Washington (D Ala.) Jan. 16, 1849-Dec. 21, 1932; House 1897-1915.

TAYLOR, Glen Hearst (D Idaho) April 12, 1904-April 28, 1984; Senate 1945-51.

TAYLOR, Herbert Worthington (R N.J.) Feb. 19, 1869-Oct. 15, 1931; House 1921-23, 1925-27.

TAYLOR, Isaac Hamilton (R Ohio) April 18, 1840-Dec. 18, 1936; House 1885-87.

TAYLOR, James Alfred (D W.Va.) Sept. 25, 1878-June 9, 1956; House 1923-27.

TAYLOR, James Willis (R Tenn.) Aug. 28, 1880-Nov. 14, 1939; House 1919-Nov. 14, 1939.

TAYLOR, John (D Va.) May 17, 1754-Aug. 20, 1824; Senate Oct. 18, 1792-May 11, 1794, June 4-Dec. 7, 1803, Dec. 18, 1822-Aug. 20, 1824.

TAYLOR, John (D S.C.) May 4, 1770-April 16, 1832; House 1807-Dec. 30, 1810; Senate Dec. 31, 1810-Nov. 1816; Gov. 1826-28.

TAYLOR, John (— S.C.) ?-?; House 1815-17.

TAYLOR, John Clarence (D S.C.) March 2, 1890-March 25, 1983; House 1933-39.

TAYLOR, John James (D N.Y.) April 27, 1808-July 1, 1892; House 1853-55.

TAYLOR, John Lampkin (W Ohio) March 7, 1805-Sept. 6, 1870; House 1847-55.

TAYLOR, John May (D Tenn.) May 18, 1838-Feb. 17, 1911; House 1883-87.

TAYLOR, John W. (D N.Y.) March 26, 1784-Sept. 8, 1854; House 1813-33; Speaker 1820-21, 1825-27.

TAYLOR, Jonathan (D Ohio) 1796-April 1848; House 1839-41.

TAYLOR, Joseph Danner (R Ohio) Nov. 7, 1830-Sept. 19, 1899; House Jan. 2, 1883-85, 1887-93.

TAYLOR, Miles (D La.) July 16, 1805-Sept. 23, 1873; House 1855-Feb. 5, 1861.

TAYLOR, Nathaniel Green (father of Alfred Alexander Taylor and Robert Love Taylor) (W Tenn.) Dec. 29, 1819-April 1, 1887; House March 30, 1854-55, July 24, 1866-67.

TAYLOR, Nelson (D N.Y.) June 8, 1821-Jan. 16, 1894; House 1865-67.

TAYLOR, Robert (— Va.) April 29, 1763-July 3, 1845; House 1825-27.

TAYLOR, Robert Love (son of Nathaniel Green Taylor, brother of Alfred Alexander Taylor (D Tenn.) July 31, 1850-March 31, 1912; House 1879-81; Senate 1907-March 31, 1912; Gov. 1887-91, 1897-99.

TAYLOR, Roy Arthur (D N.C.) Jan. 31, 1910- —; House June 25, 1960-77.

TAYLOR, Samuel Mitchell (father of Chester William Taylor) (D Ark.) May 25, 1852-Sept. 13, 1921; House Jan. 15, 1913-Sept. 13, 1921.

TAYLOR, Vincent Albert (R Ohio) Dec. 6, 1845-Dec. 2, 1922; House 1891-93.

TAYLOR, Waller (D Ind.) before 1786-Aug. 26, 1826; Senate Dec. 11, 1816-25.

TAYLOR, William (D N.Y.) Oct. 12, 1791-Sept. 16, 1865; House 1833-39.

TAYLOR, William (D Va.) April 5, 1788-Jan. 17, 1846; House 1843-Jan. 17, 1846.

TAYLOR, William Penn (W Va.) ?-?; House 1833-35.

TAYLOR, Zachary (R Tenn.) May 9, 1849-Feb. 19, 1921; House 1885-87.

TAZEWELL, Henry (father of Littleton Waller Tazewell) (— Va.) Nov. 15, 1753-Jan. 24, 1799; Senate Dec. 29, 1794-Jan. 24, 1799; Pres. pro tempore 1794-96.

TAZEWELL, Littleton Waller (son of Henry Tazewell) (D Va.) Dec. 17, 1774-May 6, 1860; House Nov. 26, 1800-01; Senate Dec. 7, 1824-July 16, 1832; Pres. pro tempore 1832; Gov. 1834-36.

TEAGUE, Charles McKevett (R Calif.) Sept. 18, 1909-Jan. 1, 1974; House 1955-Jan. 1, 1974.

TEAGUE, Olin Earl (D Texas) April 6, 1910-Jan. 23, 1981; House Aug. 24, 1946-Dec. 31, 1978.

TEESE, Frederick Halstead (D N.J.) Oct. 21, 1823-Jan. 7, 1894; House 1875-77.

TEIGAN, Henry George (FL Minn.) Aug. 7, 1881-March 12, 1941; House 1937-39.

TELFAIR, Thomas (D Ga.) March 2, 1780-Feb. 18, 1818; House 1813-17.

TELLER, Henry Moore (D Colo.) May 23, 1830-Feb. 23, 1914; Senate Nov. 15, 1876-April 17, 1882, 1885-1909 (1876-82, 1885-97 Republican, 1897-1903 Independent Silver Republican, 1903-09 Democrat); Secy. of the Interior 1882-85.

TELLER, Isaac (nephew of Abraham Henry Schenck) (D N.Y.) Feb. 7, 1799-April 30, 1868; House Nov. 7, 1854-55.

TELLER, Ludwig (D N.Y.) June 22, 1911-Oct. 4, 1965; House 1957-61.

TEMPLE, Henry Wilson (R Pa.) March 31, 1864-Jan. 11, 1955; House 1913-15, Nov. 2, 1915-33 (1913-15 Progressive Republican, 1915-33 Republican).

TEMPLE, William (D Del.) Feb. 28, 1814-May 28, 1863; House March 4-May 28, 1863.

TEMPLETON, Thomas Weir (R Pa.) Nov. 8, 1867-Sept. 5, 1935; House 1917-19.

TENER, John Kinley (R Pa.) July 25, 1863-May 19, 1946; House 1909-Jan. 16, 1911; Gov. 1911-15.

TENEROWICZ, Rudolph Gabriel (D Mich.) June 14, 1890-Aug. 31, 1963; House 1939-43.

TEN EYCK, Egbert (— N.Y.) April 18, 1779-April 11, 1844; House 1823-Dec. 15, 1825.

TEN EYCK, John Conover (R N.J.) March 12, 1814-Aug. 24, 1879; Senate 1859-65.

TEN EYCK, Peter Gansevoort (D N.Y.) Nov. 7, 1873-Sept. 2, 1944; House 1913-15, 1921-23.

TENNEY, Samuel (— N.H.) Nov. 27, 1748-Feb. 6, 1816; House Dec. 8, 1800-07.

TENZER, Herbert (D N.Y.) Nov. 1, 1905- —; House 1965-69.

TERRELL, George Butler (D Texas) Dec. 5, 1862-April 18, 1947; House 1933-35.

Biographical Index

TERRELL, James C. (UD Ga.) Nov. 7, 1806-Dec. 1, 1835; House March 4-July 8, 1835.

TERRELL, Joseph Meriwether (D Ga.) June 6, 1861-Nov. 17, 1912; Senate Nov. 17, 1910-July 14, 1911; Gov. 1902-07.

TERRELL, William (D Ga.) 1778-July 4, 1855; House 1817-21.

TERRY, David Dickson (son of William Leake Terry) (D Ark.) Jan. 31, 1881-Oct. 7, 1963; House Dec. 19, 1933-43.

TERRY, John H. (R N.Y.) Nov. 14, 1924- —; House 1971-73.

TERRY, Nathaniel (— Conn.) Jan. 30, 1768-June 14, 1844; House 1817-19.

TERRY, William (C Va.) Aug. 14, 1824-Sept. 5, 1888; House 1871-73, 1875-77.

TERRY, William Leake (father of David Dickson Terry) (D Ark.) Sept. 27, 1850-Nov. 4, 1917; House 1891-1901.

TEST, John (W Ind.) Nov. 12, 1771-Oct. 9, 1849; House 1823-27, 1829-31 (1823-27 Clay Democrat, 1829-31 Whig).

TEWES, Donald Edgar (R Wis.) Aug. 4, 1916- —; House 1957-59.

THACHER, George (F Mass.) April 12, 1754-April 6, 1824; House 1789-1801; Cont. Cong. 1787.

THACHER, Thomas Chandler (D Mass.) July 20, 1858-April 11, 1945; House 1913-15.

THATCHER, Maurice Hudson (R Ky.) Aug. 15, 1870-Jan. 6, 1973; House 1923-33.

THATCHER, Samuel (D Mass.) July 1, 1776-July 18, 1872; House Dec. 6, 1802-05.

THAYER, Andrew Jackson (D Ore.) Nov. 27, 1818-April 28, 1873; House March 4-July 30, 1861.

THAYER, Eli (father of John Alden Thayer) (R Mass.) June 11, 1819-April 15, 1899; House 1857-61.

THAYER, Harry Irving (R Mass.) Sept. 10, 1869-March 10, 1926; House 1925-March 10, 1926.

THAYER, John Alden (son of Eli Thayer) (D Mass.) Dec. 22, 1857-July 31, 1917; House 1911-13.

THAYER, John Milton (uncle of Arthur Laban Bates) (R Neb.) Jan. 24, 1820-March 19, 1906; Senate March 1, 1867-71; Gov. 1875-79 (Wyo. Terr.), 1887-91 (Neb.).

THAYER, John Randolph (D Mass.) March 9, 1845-Dec. 19, 1916; House 1899-1905.

THAYER, Martin Russell (R Pa.) Jan. 27, 1819-Oct. 14, 1906; House 1863-67.

THEAKER, Thomas Clarke (R Ohio) Feb. 1, 1812-July 16, 1883; House 1859-61.

THIBODEAUX, Bannon Goforth (— La.) Dec. 22, 1812-March 5, 1866; House 1845-49.

THILL, Lewis Dominic (R Wis.) Oct. 18, 1903- —; House 1939-43.

THISTLEWOOD, Napoleon Bonaparte (R Ill.) March 30, 1837-Sept. 15, 1915; House Feb. 15, 1908-13.

THOM, William Richard (D Ohio) July 7, 1885-Aug. 28, 1960; House 1933-39, 1941-43, 1945-47.

THOMAS, Albert (husband of Lera M. Thomas) (D Texas) April 12, 1898-Feb. 15, 1966; House 1937-Feb. 15, 1966.

THOMAS, Benjamin Franklin (CU Mass.) Feb. 12, 1813-Sept. 27, 1878; House June 11, 1861-63.

THOMAS, Charles Randolph (father of the following) (R N.C.) Feb. 7, 1827-Feb. 18, 1891; House 1871-75.

THOMAS, Charles Randolph (son of the preceding) (D N.C.) Aug. 21, 1861-March 8, 1931; House 1899-1911.

THOMAS, Charles Spalding (D Colo.) Dec. 6, 1849-June 24, 1934; Senate Jan. 15, 1913-21; Gov. 1899-1901.

THOMAS, Christopher Yancy (R Va.) March 24, 1818-Feb. 11, 1879; House March 5, 1874-75.

THOMAS, David (D N.Y.) June 11, 1762-Nov. 11, 1831; House 1801-May 1, 1808.

THOMAS, Elbert Duncan (D Utah) June 17, 1883-Feb. 11, 1953; Senate 1933-51.

THOMAS, Francis (UR Md.) Feb. 3, 1799-Jan. 22, 1876; House 1831-41, 1861-69); Gov. 1842-45 (1831-45 Democrat, 1861-69 Union Republican).

THOMAS, George Morgan (R Ky.) Nov. 23, 1828-Jan. 7, 1914; House 1887-89.

THOMAS, Henry Franklin (R Mich.) Dec. 17, 1843-April 16, 1912; House 1893-97.

THOMAS, Isaac (D Tenn.) Nov. 4, 1784-Feb. 2, 1859; House 1815-17.

THOMAS, James Houston (D Tenn.) Sept. 22, 1808-Aug. 4, 1876; House 1847-51, 1859-61.

THOMAS, Jesse Burgess (W Ind./Ill.) 1777-May 4, 1853; House (Terr. Del.) Oct. 22, 1808-09 (Ind.); Senate Dec. 3, 1818-29 (Ill.).

THOMAS, John (R Idaho) Jan. 4, 1874-Nov. 10, 1945; Senate June 30, 1928-33, Jan. 27, 1940-Nov. 10, 1945.

THOMAS, John Chew (F Md.) Oct. 15, 1764-May 10, 1836; House 1799-1801.

THOMAS, John Lewis Jr. (R Md.) May 20, 1835-Oct. 15, 1893; House Dec. 4, 1865-67.

THOMAS, John Parnell (R N.J.) Jan. 16, 1895-Nov. 19, 1970; House 1937-Jan. 2, 1950.

THOMAS, John Robert (R Ill.) Oct. 11, 1846-Jan. 19, 1914; House 1879-89.

THOMAS, John William Elmer (D Okla.) Sept. 8, 1876-Sept. 19, 1965; House 1923-27; Senate 1927-51.

THOMAS, Lera M. (widow of Albert Thomas) (D Texas) Aug. 3, 1900- —; House March 30, 1966-67.

THOMAS, Lot (R Iowa) Oct. 17, 1843-March 17, 1905; House 1899-1905.

THOMAS, Ormsby Brunson (R Wis.) Aug. 21, 1832-Oct. 24, 1904; House 1885-91.

THOMAS, Philemon (D La.) Feb. 9, 1763-Nov. 18, 1847; House 1831-35.

THOMAS, Phillip Francis (D Md.) Sept. 12, 1810-Oct. 2, 1890; House 1839-41, 1875-77; Gov. 1848-51; Secy. of the Treasury 1860-61.

THOMAS, Richard (F Pa.) Dec. 30, 1744-Jan. 19, 1832; House 1795-1801.

THOMAS, Robert Lindsay (D Ga.) Nov. 20, 1943- —; House 1983- —.

THOMAS, Robert Young Jr. (D Ky.) July 13, 1855-Sept. 3, 1925; House 1909-Sept. 3, 1925.

THOMAS, William Aubrey (R Ohio) June 7, 1866-Sept. 8, 1951; House Nov. 8, 1904-11.

THOMAS, William David (R N.Y.) March 22, 1880-May 17, 1936; House Jan. 30, 1934-May 17, 1936.

THOMAS, William Marshall (R Calif.) Dec. 6, 1941- —; House 1979- —.

THOMASON, Robert Ewing (D Texas) May 30, 1879-Nov. 8, 1973; House 1931-July 31, 1947.

THOMASSON, William Poindexter (W Ky.) Oct. 8, 1797-Dec. 29, 1882; House 1843-47.

THOMPSON, Albert Clifton (R Ohio) Jan. 23, 1842-Jan. 26, 1910; House 1885-91.

THOMPSON, Benjamin (W Mass.) Aug. 5, 1798-Sept. 24, 1852; House 1845-47, 1851-Sept. 24, 1852.

THOMPSON, Charles James (R Ohio) Jan. 24, 1862-March 27, 1932; House 1919-31.

THOMPSON, Charles Perkins (D Mass.) July 30, 1827-Jan. 19, 1894; House 1875-77.

THOMPSON, Charles Winston (D Ala.) Dec. 30, 1860-March 20, 1904; House 1901-March 20, 1904.

THOMPSON, Chester Charles (D Ill.) Sept. 19, 1893-Jan. 30, 1971; House 1933-39.

THOMPSON, Clark Wallace (D Texas) Aug. 6, 1896-Dec. 16, 1981; House June 24, 1933-35, Aug. 23, 1947-Dec. 30, 1966.

THOMPSON, Fountain Land (D N.D.) Nov. 18, 1854-Feb. 4, 1942; Senate Nov. 10, 1909-Jan. 31, 1910.

THOMPSON, Frank Jr. (D N.J.) July 26, 1918- —; House 1955-81.

THOMPSON, George Western (D Va.) May 14, 1806-Feb. 24, 1888; House 1851-July 30, 1852.

THOMPSON, Hedge (— N.J.) Jan. 28, 1780-July 23, 1828; House 1827-July 23, 1828.

THOMPSON, Jacob (D Miss.) May 15, 1810-March 24, 1885; House 1839-51; Secy. of the Interior 1857-61.

THOMPSON, James (D Pa.) Oct. 1, 1806-Jan. 28, 1874; House 1845-51.

THOMPSON, Joel (F N.Y.) Oct. 3, 1760-Feb. 8, 1843; House 1813-15.

THOMPSON, John (D N.Y.) March 20, 1749-1823; House 1799-1801, 1807-11.

THOMPSON, John (R N.Y.) July 4, 1809-June 1, 1890; House 1857-59.

THOMPSON, John Burton (W Ky.) Dec. 14, 1810-Jan. 7, 1874; House Dec. 7, 1840-43, 1847-51; Senate 1853-59.

THOMPSON, John McCandless (brother of William George Thompson) (R Pa.) Jan. 4, 1829-Sept. 3, 1903; House Dec. 22, 1874-75, 1877-79.

THOMPSON, Joseph Bryan (D Okla.) April 29, 1871-Sept. 18, 1919; House 1913-Sept. 18, 1919.

THOMPSON, Philip (— Ky.) Aug. 20, 1789-Nov. 25, 1836; House 1823-25.

THOMPSON, Philip Burton Jr. (D Ky.) Oct. 15, 1845-Dec. 15, 1909; House 1879-85.

THOMPSON, Philip Rootes (D Va.) March 26, 1766-July 27, 1837; House 1801-07.

THOMPSON, Richard Wigginton (W Ind.) June 9, 1809-Feb. 9, 1900; House 1841-43, 1847-49; Secy. of the Navy 1877-80.

THOMPSON, Robert Augustine (father of Thomas Larkin Thompson) (D Va.) Feb. 14, 1805-Aug. 31, 1876; House 1847-49.

THOMPSON, Ruth (R Mich.) Sept. 15, 1887-April 5, 1970; House 1951-57.

THOMPSON, Standish Fletcher (R Ga.) Feb. 5, 1925-—; House 1967-73.

THOMPSON, Theo Ashton (D La.) March 31, 1916-July 1, 1965; House 1953-July 1, 1965.

THOMPSON, Thomas Larkin (son of Robert Augustine Thompson) (D Calif.) May 31, 1838-Feb. 1, 1898; House 1887-89.

THOMPSON, Thomas Weston (— N.H.) March 15, 1766-Oct. 1, 1821; House 1805-07; Senate June 24, 1814-17.

THOMPSON, Waddy Jr. (W S.C.) Jan. 8, 1798-Nov. 23, 1868; House Sept. 10, 1835-41.

THOMPSON, Wiley (D Ga.) Sept. 23, 1781-Dec. 28, 1835; House 1821-33.

THOMPSON, William (D Iowa) Nov. 10, 1813-Oct. 6, 1897; House 1847-June 29, 1850.

THOMPSON, William George (brother of John McCandless Thompson) (R Iowa) Jan. 17, 1830-April 2, 1911; House Oct. 14, 1879-83.

THOMPSON, William Henry (D Neb.) Dec. 14, 1853-June 6, 1937; Senate May 24, 1933-Nov. 6, 1934.

THOMPSON, William Howard (D Kan.) Oct. 14, 1871-Feb. 9, 1928; Senate 1913-19.

THOMSON, Alexander (— Pa.) Jan. 12, 1788-Aug. 2, 1848; House Dec. 6, 1824-May 1, 1826.

THOMSON, Charles Marsh (PR Ill.) Feb. 13, 1877-Dec. 30, 1943; House 1913-15.

THOMSON, Edwin Keith (R Wyo) Feb. 8, 1919-Dec. 9, 1960; House 1955-Dec. 9, 1960.

THOMSON, John (D Ohio) Nov. 20, 1780-Dec. 2, 1852; House 1825-27, 1829-37.

THOMSON, John Renshaw (D N.J.) Sept. 25, 1800-Sept. 12, 1862; Senate 1853-Sept. 12, 1862.

THOMSON, Mark (F N.J.) 1739-Dec. 14, 1803; House 1795-99.

THOMSON, Vernon Wallace (R Wis.) Nov. 5, 1905-—; House 1961-Dec. 31, 1974; Gov. 1957-59.

THONE, Charles (R Neb.) Jan. 4, 1924-—; House 1971-79.

THORINGTON, James (W Iowa) May 7, 1816-June 13, 1887; House 1855-57.

THORKELSON, Jacob (R Mont.) Sept. 24, 1876-Nov. 20, 1945; House 1939-41.

THORNBERRY, William Homer (D Texas) Jan. 9, 1909-—; House 1949-Dec. 20, 1963.

THORNBURGH, Jacob Montgomery (R Tenn.) July 3, 1837-Sept. 19, 1890; House 1873-79.

THORNTON, Anthony (D Ill.) Nov. 9, 1814-Sept. 10, 1904; House 1865-67.

THORNTON, John Randolph (D La.) Aug. 25, 1846-Dec. 28, 1917; Senate Dec. 7, 1910-15.

THORNTON, Raymond Hoyt Jr. (D Ark.) July 16, 1928-—; House 1973-79.

THORP, Robert Taylor (R Va.) March 12, 1850-Nov. 26, 1938; House May 2, 1896-97, March 23, 1898-99.

THORPE, Roy Henry (R Neb.) Dec. 13, 1874-Sept. 19, 1951; House Nov. 7, 1922-23.

THROCKMORTON, James Webb (D Texas) Feb. 1, 1825-April 21, 1894; House 1875-79, 1883-87; Gov. 1866-67.

THROOP, Enos Thompson (D N.Y.) Aug. 21, 1784-Nov. 1, 1874; House 1815-June 4, 1816; Gov. 1829-33.

THROPP, Joseph Earlston (R Pa.) Oct. 4, 1847-July 27, 1927; House 1899-1901.

THRUSTON, Buckner (D Ky.) Feb. 8, 1764-Aug. 30, 1845; Senate 1805-Dec. 18, 1809.

THURMAN, Allen Granberry (D Ohio) Nov. 13, 1813-Dec. 12, 1895; House 1845-47; Senate 1869-81; Pres. pro tempore 1879-81.

THURMAN, John Richardson (W N.Y.) Oct. 6, 1814-July 24, 1854; House 1849-51.

THURMOND, James Strom (R S.C.) Dec. 5, 1902-—; Senate Dec. 24, 1954-April 4, 1956, Nov. 7, 1956-—; Pres. pro tempore 1981-—. Gov. 1947-51 (1947-51, 1954-56, 1956-Sept. 16, 1964 Democrat, Sept. 16, 1964-— Republican).

THURSTON, Benjamin Babcock (D R.I.) June 29, 1804-May 17, 1886; House 1847-49, 1851-57.

THURSTON, John Mellen (R Neb.) Aug. 21, 1847-Aug. 9, 1916; Senate 1895-1901.

THURSTON, Lloyd (R Iowa) March 27, 1880-May 7, 1970; House 1925-39.

THURSTON, Samuel Royal (D Ore.) April 15, 1816-April 9, 1851; House (Terr. Del.) 1849-51.

THYE, Edward John (R Minn.) April 26, 1896-Aug. 28, 1969; Senate 1947-59; Gov. 1943-47.

TIBBATTS, John Wooleston (D Ky.) June 12, 1802-July 5, 1852; House 1843-47.

TIBBITS, George (F N.Y.) Jan. 14, 1763-July 19, 1849; House 1803-05.

TIBBOTT, Harve (R Pa.) May 27, 1885-Dec. 31, 1969; House 1939-49.

TICHENOR, Isaac (F Vt.) Feb. 8, 1754-Dec. 11, 1838; Senate Oct. 18, 1796-Oct. 17, 1797, 1815-21; Gov. 1797-1807, 1808-09.

TIERNAN, Robert Owens (D R.I.) Feb. 24, 1929-—; House March 28, 1967-75.

TIERNEY, William Laurence (D Conn.) Aug. 6, 1876-April 13, 1958; House 1931-33.

TIFFIN, Edward (D Ohio) June 19, 1766-Aug. 9, 1829; Senate 1807-09; Gov. 1803-07.

TIFT, Nelson (D Ga.) July 23, 1810-Nov. 21, 1891; House July 25, 1868-69.

TILDEN, Daniel Rose (W Ohio) Nov. 5, 1804-March 4, 1890; House 1843-47.

TILLINGHAST, Joseph Leonard (cousin of Thomas Tillinghast) (W R.I.) 1791-Dec. 30, 1844; House 1837-43.

TILLINGHAST, Thomas (cousin of Joseph Leonard Tillinghast) (— R.I.) Aug. 21, 1742-Aug. 26, 1821; House Nov. 13, 1797-99, 1801-03.

TILLMAN, Benjamin Ryan (brother of George Dionysius Tillman) (D S.C.) Aug. 11, 1847-July 3, 1918; Senate 1895-July 3, 1918; Gov. 1890-94.

TILLMAN, George Dionysius (brother of Benjamin Ryan Tillman) (D S.C.) Aug. 21, 1826-Feb. 2, 1902; House 1879-June 19, 1882, 1883-93.

TILLMAN, John Newton (D Ark.) Dec. 13, 1859-March 9, 1929; House 1915-29.

TILLMAN, Lewis (nephew of Barclay Martin) (R Tenn.) Aug. 18, 1816-May 3, 1886; House 1869-71.

TILLOTSON, Thomas (— N.Y.) 1750-May 5, 1832; House March 4-Aug. 10, 1801.

TILSON, John Quillin (R Conn.) April 5, 1866-Aug. 14, 1958; House 1909-13, 1915-Dec. 3, 1932; House majority leader 1925-31.

TIMBERLAKE, Charles Bateman (R Colo.) Sept. 25, 1854-May 31, 1941; House 1915-33.

TINCHER, Jasper Napoleon (R Kan.) Nov. 2, 1878-Nov. 6, 1951; House 1919-27.

TINKHAM, George Holden (R Mass.) Oct. 29, 1870-Aug. 28, 1956; House 1915-43.

TIPTON, John (D Ind.) Aug. 14, 1786-April 5, 1839; Senate Jan. 3, 1832-39.

TIPTON, Thomas Foster (R Ill.) Aug. 29, 1833-Feb. 7, 1904; House 1877-79.

TIPTON, Thomas Weston (R Neb.) Aug. 5, 1817-Nov. 26, 1899; Senate March 1, 1867-75.

TIRRELL, Charles Quincy (R Mass.) Dec. 10, 1844-July 31, 1910; House 1901-July 31, 1910.

TITUS, Obadiah (D N.Y.) Jan. 20, 1789-Sept. 2, 1854; House 1837-39.

TOBEY, Charles William (R N.H.) July 22, 1880-July 24, 1953; House 1933-39; Senate 1939-July 24, 1953; Gov. 1929-31.

TOD, John (D Pa.) 1779-March 1830; House 1821-24.

TODD, Albert May (Fus. Mich.) June 3, 1850-Oct. 6, 1931; House 1897-99.

TODD, John Blair Smith (D Dakota) April 4, 1814-Jan. 5, 1872; House (Terr. Del.) Dec. 9, 1861-63, June 17, 1864-65.

TODD, Lemuel (R Pa.) July 29, 1817-May 12, 1891; House 1855-57, 1873-75.

TODD, Paul Harold Jr. (D Mich.) Sept. 22, 1921- —; House 1965-67.

TOLAN, John Harvey (D Calif.) Jan. 15, 1877-June 30, 1947; House 1937-47.

TOLAND, George Washington (W Pa.) Feb. 8, 1796-Jan. 30, 1869; House 1837-43.

TOLL, Herman (D Pa.) March 15, 1907-July 26, 1967; House 1959-67.

TOLLEFSON, Thor Carl (R Wash.) May 2, 1901-Dec. 30, 1982; House 1947-65.

TOLLEY, Harold Sumner (R N.Y.) Jan. 16, 1894-May 20, 1956; House 1925-27.

TOMLINSON, Gideon (D Conn.) Dec. 31, 1780-Oct. 8, 1854; House 1819-27; Senate 1831-37; Gov. 1827-31.

TOMLINSON, Thomas Ash (W N.Y.) March 1802-June 18, 1872; House 1841-43.

TOMPKINS, Arthur Sidney (R N.Y.) Aug. 26, 1865-Jan. 20, 1938; House 1899-1903.

TOMPKINS, Caleb (— N.Y.) Dec. 22, 1759-Jan. 1, 1846; House 1817-21.

TOMPKINS, Christopher (— Ky.) March 24, 1780-Aug. 9, 1858; House 1831-35.

TOMPKINS, Cydnor Bailey (father of Emmett Tompkins) (R Ohio) Nov. 8, 1810-July 23, 1862; House 1857-61.

TOMPKINS, Emmett (son of Cydnor Bailey Tompkins) (R Ohio) Sept. 1, 1853-Dec. 18, 1917; House 1901-03.

TOMPKINS, Patrick Watson (W Miss.) 1804-May 8, 1953; House 1847-49.

TONGUE, Thomas H. (R Ore.) June 23, 1844-Jan. 11, 1903; House 1897-Jan. 11, 1903.

TONRY, Richard Alvin (D La.) June 25, 1935- —; House 1977- —.

TONRY, Richard Joseph (D N.Y.) Sept. 30, 1893-Jan. 17, 1971; House 1935-37.

TOOLE, Joseph Kemp (D Mont.) May 12, 1851-March 11, 1929; House (Terr. Del.) 1885-89; Gov. 1889-93, 1901-08.

TOOMBS, Robert (SRD Ga.) July 2, 1810-Dec. 15, 1885; House 1845-53; Senate 1853-Feb. 4, 1861.

TORRICELLI, Robert G. (D N.J.) Aug. 26, 1951- —; House 1983- —.

TORRENS, James H. (D N.Y.) Sept. 12, 1874-April 5, 1952; House Feb. 29, 1944-47.

TORRES, Estaban Edward (D Calif.) Jan. 27, 1930- —; House 1983- —.

TOUCEY, Isaac (D Conn.) Nov. 5, 1796-July 30, 1869; House 1835-39; Senate May 12, 1852-57; Gov. 1846-47; Atty. Gen. 1848-49; Secy. of the Navy 1857-61.

TOU VELLE, William Ellsworth (D Ohio) Nov. 23, 1862-Aug. 14, 1951; House 1907-11.

TOWE, Harry Lancaster (R N.J.) Nov. 3, 1898- —; House 1943-Sept. 7, 1951.

TOWELL, David Gilmer (R Nev.) June 9, 1937- —; House 1973-75.

TOWER, John Goodwin (R Texas) Sept. 29, 1925- —; Senate June 15, 1961-85.

TOWEY, Frank William Jr. (D N.J.) Nov. 5, 1895-Sept. 4, 1979; House 1937-39.

TOWNE, Charles Arnette (D Minn./N.Y.) Nov. 21, 1858-Oct. 22, 1928; House 1895-97 (Minn.), 1905-07 (N.Y.); Senate Dec. 5, 1900-Jan. 28, 1901 (Minn.) (1895-97 Republican, 1900-07 Democrat).

TOWNER, Horace Mann (R Iowa) Oct. 23, 1855-Nov. 23, 1937; House 1911-April 1, 1923; Gov. (Puerto Rico) 1923-29.

TOWNS, Edolphus (D N.Y.) July 21, 1934- —; House 1983- —.

TOWNS, George Washington Bonaparte (D Ga.) May 4, 1801-July 15, 1854; House 1835-Sept. 1, 1836, 1837-39, Jan. 5, 1846-47; Gov. 1847-51 (1835-39 Union Democrat, 1846-51 Democrat).

TOWNSEND, Amos (R Ohio) 1821-March 17, 1895; House 1877-83.

TOWNSEND, Charles Champlain (R Pa.) Nov. 24, 1841-July 10, 1910; House 1889-91.

TOWNSEND, Charles Elroy (R Mich.) Aug. 15, 1856-Aug. 3, 1924; House 1903-11; Senate 1911-23.

TOWNSEND, Dwight (D N.Y.) Sept. 26, 1826-Oct. 29, 1899; House Dec. 5, 1864-65, 1871-73.

TOWNSEND, Edward Waterman (D N.J.) Feb. 10, 1855-March 15, 1942; House 1911-15.

TOWNSEND, George (D N.Y.) 1769-Aug. 17, 1844; House 1815-19.

TOWNSEND, Hosea (R Colo.) June 16, 1840-March 4, 1909; House 1889-93.

TOWNSEND, John Gillis Jr. (R Del.) May 31, 1871-April 10, 1964; Senate 1929-41; Gov. 1917-21.

TOWNSEND, Martin Ingham (R N.Y.) Feb. 6, 1810-March 8, 1903; House 1875-79.

TOWNSEND, Washington (R Pa.) Jan. 20, 1813-March 18, 1894; House 1869-77.

TOWNSHEND, Norton Strange (D Ohio) Dec. 25, 1815-July 13, 1895; House 1851-53.

TOWNSHEND, Richard Wellington (D Ill.) April 30, 1840-March 9, 1889; House 1877-March 9, 1889.

TRACEWELL, Robert John (R Ind.) May 7, 1852-July 28, 1922; House 1895-97.

TRACEY, Charles (D N.Y.) May 27, 1847-March 24, 1905; House Nov. 8, 1887-95.

TRACEY, John Plank (R Mo.) Sept. 18, 1836-July 24, 1910; House 1895-97.

TRACY, Albert Haller (brother of Phineas Lyman Tracy) (D N.Y.) June 17, 1793-Sept. 19, 1859; House 1819-25.

TRACY, Andrew (W Vt.) Dec. 15, 1797-Oct. 28, 1868; House 1853-55.

TRACY, Henry Wells (IR Pa.) Sept. 24, 1807-April 11, 1886; House 1863-65.

TRACY, Phineas Lyman (brother of Albert Haller Tracy) (W N.Y.) Dec. 25, 1786-Dec. 22, 1876; House Nov. 5, 1827-33.

TRACY, Uri (D N.Y.) Feb. 8, 1764-July 21, 1838; House 1805-07, 1809-13.

TRACY, Uriah (F Conn.) Feb. 2, 1755-July 19, 1807; House 1793-Oct. 13, 1796; Senate Oct. 13, 1796-July 19, 1807; Pres. pro tempore 1800.

TRAEGER, William Isham (R Calif.) Feb. 26, 1880-Jan. 20, 1935; House 1933-35.

TRAFICANT, James A. Jr. (D Ohio) May 8, 1941- —; House 1985- —.

TRAFTON, Mark (AP Mass.) Aug. 1, 1810-March 8, 1901; House 1855-57.

TRAIN, Charles Russell (R Mass.) Oct. 18, 1817-July 28, 1885; House 1859-63.

TRAMMELL, Park (D Fla.) April 9, 1876-May 8, 1936; Senate 1917-May 8, 1936; Gov. 1913-17.

TRANSUE, Andrew Jackson (D Mich.) Jan. 12, 1903- —; House 1937-39.

TRAXLER, Jerome Bob (D Mich.) July 21, 1931- —; House April 16, 1974- —.

TRAYNOR, Philip Andrew (D Del.) May 31, 1874-Dec. 5, 1962; House 1941-43, 1945-47.

TREADWAY, Allen Towner (R Mass.) Sept. 16, 1867-Feb. 16, 1947; House 1913-45.

TREADWAY, William Marshall (D Va.) Aug. 24, 1807-May 1, 1891; House 1845-47.

TREDWELL, Thomas (grandfather of Thomas Treadwell Davis) (— N.Y.) Feb. 6, 1743-Dec. 30, 1831; House May 1791-95.

TREEN, David Conner (R La.) July 16, 1928- —; House 1973- —.

TRELOAR, William Mitchellson (R Mo.) Sept. 21, 1850-July 3, 1935; House 1895-97.

TREMAIN, Lyman (R N.Y.) June 14, 1819-Nov. 30, 1878; House 1873-75.

TREZVANT, James (— Va.) ?-Sept. 2, 1841; House 1825-31.

TRIBBLE, Samuel Joelah (D Ga.) Nov. 15, 1869-Dec. 8, 1916; House 1911-Dec. 8, 1916.

TRIBLE, Paul Seward Jr. (R Va.) Dec. 29, 1946- —; House 1977-83; Senate 1983- —.

TRIGG, Abram (brother of John Johns Trigg) (— Va.) 1750-?; House 1797-1809.

TRIGG, Connally Findlay (D Va.) Sept. 18, 1847-April 23, 1907; House 1885-87.

TRIGG, John Johns (brother of Abram Trigg) (— Va.) 1748-May 17, 1804; House 1797-May 17, 1804.

TRIMBLE, Carey Allen (R Ohio) Sept. 13, 1813-May 4, 1887; House 1859-63.

TRIMBLE, David (D Ky.) June 1782-Oct. 20, 1842; House 1817-27.

TRIMBLE, James William (D Ark.) Feb. 3, 1894-March 10, 1972; House 1945-67.

TRIMBLE, John (R Tenn.) Feb. 7, 1812-Feb. 23, 1884; House 1867-69.

TRIMBLE, Lawrence Strother (D Ky.) Aug. 26, 1825-Aug. 9, 1904; House 1865-71.

TRIMBLE, South (D Ky.) April 13, 1864-Nov. 23, 1946; House 1901-07.

TRIMBLE, William Allen (— Ohio) April 4, 1786-Dec. 13, 1821; Senate 1819-Dec. 13, 1821.

TRIPLETT, Philip (W Ky.) Dec. 24, 1799-March 30, 1852; House 1839-43.

TRIPPE, Robert Pleasant (W Ga.) Dec. 21, 1819-July 22, 1900; House 1855-59.

TROTTER, James Fisher (D Miss.) Nov. 5, 1802-March 9, 1866; Senate Jan. 22-July 10, 1838.

TROTTI, Samuel Wilds (— S.C.) July 18, 1810-June 24, 1856; House Dec. 17, 1842-43.

TROUP, George Michael (SRD Ga.) Sept. 8, 1780-April 26, 1856; House 1807-15; Senate Nov. 13, 1816-Sept. 23, 1818, 1829-Nov. 8, 1833 (1807-15 Democrat, 1816-18, 1829-33 State Rights Democrat); Gov. 1823-27.

TROUT, Michael Carver (D Pa.) Sept. 30, 1810-June 25, 1873; House 1853-55.

TROUTMAN, William Irvin (R Pa.) Jan. 13, 1905-Jan. 27, 1971; House 1943-Jan. 2, 1945.

TROWBRIDGE, Rowland Ebenezer (R Mich.) June 18, 1821-April 20, 1881; House 1861-63, 1865-69.

TRUAX, Charles Vilas (D Ohio) Feb. 1, 1887-Aug. 9, 1935; House 1933-Aug. 9, 1935.

TRUMAN, Harry S (D Mo.) May 8, 1884-Dec. 26, 1972; Senate 1935-Jan. 17, 1945; Vice Pres. Jan. 20-April 12, 1945; President April 12, 1945-53.

TRUMBO, Andrew (W Ky.) Sept. 15, 1797-Aug. 21, 1871; House 1845-47.

TRUMBULL, Jonathan (F Conn.) March 26, 1740-Aug. 7, 1809; House 1789-95; Senate 1795-June 10, 1796; Speaker 1791-93; Gov. 1797-1809.

TRUMBULL, Joseph (W Conn.) Dec. 7, 1782-Aug. 4, 1861; House Dec. 1, 1834-35, 1839-43; Gov. 1849-50.

TRUMBULL, Lyman (R Ill.) Oct. 12, 1813-June 25, 1896; Senate 1855-73.

TSONGAS, Paul Efthemios (D Mass.) Feb. 14, 1941- —; House 1975-79; Senate 1979-85.

TUCK, Amos (I N.H.) Aug. 2, 1810-Dec. 11, 1879; House 1847-53.

TUCK, William Munford (D Va.) Sept. 28, 1896-June 9, 1983; House April 14, 1953-69; Gov. 1946-50.

TUCKER, Ebenezer (— N.J.) Nov. 15, 1758-Sept. 5, 1845; House 1825-29.

TUCKER, George (cousin of Henry St. George Tucker) (D Va.) Aug. 20, 1775-April 10, 1861; House 1819-25.

TUCKER, Henry St. George (father of John Randolph Tucker, grandfather of the following, cousin of George Tucker, nephew of Thomas Tudor Tucker) (— Va.) Dec. 29, 1780-Aug. 28, 1848; House 1815-19.

TUCKER, Henry St. George (son of John Randolph Tucker, grandson of the preceding) (D Va.) April 5, 1853-July 23, 1932; House 1889-97, March 21, 1922-July 23, 1932.

TUCKER, James Guy (D Ark.) June 13, 1943- —; House 1977-79.

TUCKER, John Randolph (son of Henry St. George Tucker, father of Henry St. George Tucker) (D Va.) Dec. 24, 1823-Feb. 13, 1897; House 1875-87.

TUCKER, Starling (— S.C.) 1770-Jan. 3, 1834; House 1817-31.

TUCKER, Thomas Tudor (uncle of Henry St. George Tucker) (F S.C.) June 25, 1745-May 2, 1828; House 1789-93; Cont. Cong. 1787-88.

TUCKER, Tilghman Mayfield (D Miss.) Feb. 5, 1802-April 3, 1859; House 1843-45; Gov. 1842-44.

TUFTS, John Quincy (R Iowa) July 12, 1840-Aug. 10, 1908; House 1875-77.

TULLY, Pleasant Britton (D Calif.) March 21, 1829-March 24, 1897; House 1883-85.

TUMULTY, Thomas James (D N.J.) March 2, 1913-Nov. 23, 1981; House 1955-57.

TUNNELL, James Miller (D Del.) Aug. 2, 1879-Nov. 14, 1957; Senate 1941-47.

TUNNEY, John Varick (D Calif.) June 26, 1934- —; House 1965-Jan. 2, 1971; Senate Jan. 2, 1971-Jan. 1, 1977.

TUPPER, Stanley Roger (R Maine) Jan. 25, 1921- —; House 1961-67.

TURLEY, Thomas Battle (D Tenn.) April 5, 1845-July 1, 1910; Senate July 20, 1897-1901.

TURNBULL, Robert (D Va.) Jan. 11, 1850-Jan. 22, 1920; House March 8, 1910-13.

TURNER, Benjamin Sterling (R Ala.) March 17, 1825-March 21, 1894; House 1871-73.

TURNER, Charles Jr. (WD Mass.) June 20, 1760-May 16, 1839; House June 28, 1809-13.

TURNER, Charles Henry (D N.Y.) May 26, 1861-Aug. 31, 1913; House Dec. 9, 1889-91.

TURNER, Clarence Wyly (D Tenn.) Oct. 22, 1866-March 23, 1939; House Nov. 7, 1922-23, 1933-March 23, 1939.

TURNER, Daniel (son of James Turner) (D N.C.) Sept. 21, 1796-July 21, 1860, House 1827-29.

TURNER, Erastus Johnson (R Kan.) Dec. 26, 1846-Feb. 10, 1933; House 1887-91.

TURNER, George (Fus. Wash.) Feb. 25, 1850-Jan. 26, 1932; Senate 1897-1903.

TURNER, Henry Gray (D Ga.) March 20, 1839-June 9, 1904; House 1881-97.

TURNER, James (father of Daniel Turner) (D N.C.) Dec. 20, 1766-Jan. 15, 1824; Senate 1805-Nov. 21, 1816; Gov. 1802-05.

TURNER, James (D Md.) Nov. 7, 1783-March 28, 1861; House 1833-37.

TURNER, Oscar (father of the following) (ID Ky.) Feb. 3, 1825-Jan. 22, 1896; House 1879-85.

TURNER, Oscar (son of the preceding) (D Ky.) Oct. 19, 1867-July 17, 1902; House 1899-1901.

TURNER, Smith Spangler (D Va.) Nov. 21, 1842-April 8, 1898; House Jan. 30, 1894-97.

TURNER, Thomas (D Ky.) Sept. 10, 1821-Sept. 11, 1900; House 1877-81.

TURNER, Thomas Johnston (D Ill.) April 5, 1815-April 4, 1874; House 1847-49.

TURNEY, Hopkins Lacy (D Tenn.) Oct. 3, 1797-Aug. 1 1857; House 1837-43; Senate 1845-51.

TURNEY, Jacob (D Pa.) Feb. 18, 1825-Oct. 4, 1891; House 1875-79.

TURPIE, David (D Ind.) July 8, 1828-April 21, 1909; Senate Jan. 14-March 3 1863, 1887-99.

TURPIN, Charles Murray (R Pa.) March 4, 1878-June 4, 1946; House June 4, 1929-37.

TURPIN, Louis Washington (D Ala.) Feb. 22, 1849-Feb. 3, 1903; House 1889-June 4, 1890, 1891-95.

TURRILL, Joel (JD N.Y.) Feb. 22, 1794-Dec. 28, 1859; House 1833-37.

TUTEN, James Russell (D Ga.) July 23, 1911-Aug. 16, 1968; House 1963-67.

TUTHILL, Joseph Hasbrouck (nephew of Selah Tuthill) (D N.Y.) Feb. 25, 1811-July 27, 1877; House 1871-73.

TUTHILL, Selah (uncle of Joseph Hasbrouck Tuthill) (— N.Y.) Oct. 26, 1771- Sept. 7, 1821; House March 4-Sept. 7, 1821.

TUTTLE, William Edgar Jr. (D N.J.) Dec. 10, 1870-Feb. 11, 1923; House 1911-15.

TWEED, William Marcy (D N.Y.) April 3, 1823-April 12, 1878; House 1853-55.

TWEEDY, John Hubbard (W Wis.) Nov. 9, 1814-Nov. 12, 1891; House (Terr. Del.) 1847-May 29, 1848.

TWEEDY, Samuel (W Conn.) March 8, 1776-July 1, 1868; House 1833-35.

TWICHELL, Ginery (R Mass.) Aug. 26, 1811-July 23, 1883; House 1867-73.

TWYMAN, Robert Joseph (R Ill.) June 18, 1897-June 28, 1976; House 1947-49.

TYDINGS, Joseph Davies (son of Millard Evelyn Tydings) (D Md.) May 4, 1928--; Senate 1965-71.

TYDINGS, Millard Evelyn (father of Joseph Davies Tydings) (D Md.) April 6, 1890-Feb. 9, 1961; House 1923-27; Senate 1927-51.

TYLER, Asher (W N.Y.) May 10, 1798-Aug. 1, 1875; House 1843-45.

TYLER, David Gardiner (son of John Tyler) (D Va.) July 12, 1846-Sept. 5, 1927; House 1893-97.

TYLER, James Manning (R Vt.) April 27, 1835-Oct. 13, 1926; House 1879-83.

TYLER, John (father of David Gardiner Tyler) (DR Va.) March 29, 1790-Jan. 18, 1862; House Dec. 16, 1817-21; Senate 1827-Feb. 29, 1836; Pres. pro tempore 1834-35; Gov. 1825-27; Vice Pres. March 4-April 4, 1841; President April 6, 1841-45.

TYNDALL, William Thomas (R Mo.) Jan. 16, 1862-Nov. 26, 1928; House 1905-07.

TYNER, James Noble (R Ind.) Jan. 17, 1826-Dec. 5, 1904; House 1869-75; Postmaster Gen. 1876-77.

TYSON, Jacob (— N.Y.) Oct. 8, 1773-July 16, 1848; House 1823-25.

TYSON, Joe Roberts (W Pa.) Feb. 8, 1803-June 27, 1858; House 1855-57.

TYSON, John Russell (D Ala.) Nov. 28, 1856-March 27, 1923; House 1921-March 27, 1923.

TYSON, Lawrence Davis (D Tenn.) July 4, 1861-Aug. 24, 1929; Senate 1925-Aug. 24, 1929.

U

UDALL, Morris King (brother of Stewart Lee Udall) (D Ariz.) June 15, 1922--; House May 2, 1961--.

UDALL, Stewart Lee (brother of Morris King Udall) (D Ariz.) Jan. 31, 1920--; House 1955-Jan. 18, 1961; Secy. of the Interior 1961-69.

UDREE, Daniel (D Pa.) Aug. 5, 1751-July 15, 1828; House Oct. 12, 1813-15, Dec. 26, 1820-21, Dec. 10, 1822-25.

ULLMAN, Albert Conrad (D Ore.) March 9, 1914--; House 1957-81.

UMSTEAD, William Bradley (D N.C.) May 13, 1895-Nov. 7, 1954; House 1933-39; Senate Dec. 18, 1946-Dec. 30, 1948; Gov. 1953-54.

UNDERHILL, Charles Lee (R Mass.) July 20, 1867-Jan. 28, 1946; House 1921-33.

UNDERHILL, Edwin Stewart (D N.Y.) Oct. 7, 1861-Feb. 7, 1929; House 1911-15.

UNDERHILL, John Quincy (D N.Y.) Feb. 19, 1848-May 21, 1907; House 1899-1901.

UNDERHILL, Walter (W N.Y.) Sept. 12, 1795-Aug. 17, 1866; House 1849-51.

UNDERWOOD, John William Henderson (D Ga.) Nov. 20, 1816-July 18, 1888; House 1859-Jan. 23, 1861.

UNDERWOOD, Joseph Rogers (brother of Warner Lewis Underwood, grandfather of Oscar Wilder Underwood) (W Ky.) Oct. 24, 1791-Aug. 23, 1876; House 1835-43; Senate 1847-53.

UNDERWOOD, Mell Gilbert (D Ohio) Jan. 30, 1892-March 8, 1972; House 1923-April 10, 1936.

UNDERWOOD, Oscar Wilder (grandson of Joseph Rogers Lewis Underwood) (D Ala.) May 6, 1862-Jan. 25, 1929; House 1895-June 9, 1896, 1897-1915; House majority leader 1911-15; Senate 1915-27.

UNDERWOOD, Thomas Rust (D Ky.) March 3, 1898-June 29, 1956; House 1949-March 17, 1951; Senate March 19, 1951-Nov. 4, 1952.

UNDERWOOD, Warner Lewis (brother of Joseph Rogers Underwood) (AP Ky.) Aug. 7, 1808-March 12, 1872; House 1855-59.

UPDEGRAFF, Jonathan Taylor (R Ohio) May 13, 1822-Nov. 30, 1882; House 1879-Nov. 30, 1882.

UPDEGRAFF, Thomas (R Iowa) April 3, 1834-Oct. 4, 1910; House 1879-83, 1893-99.

UPDIKE, Ralph Eugene (R Ind.) May 27, 1894-Sept. 16, 1953; House 1925-29.

UPHAM, Charles Wentworth (cousin of George Baxter Upham and Jabez Upham) (W Mass.) May 4, 1802-June 15, 1875; House 1853-55.

UPHAM, George Baxter (brother of Jabez Upham, cousin of Charles Wentworth Upham) (— N.H.) Dec. 27 1768-Feb. 10, 1848; House 1801-03.

UPHAM, Jabez (brother of George Baxter Upham, cousin of Charles Wentworth Upham) (— Mass.) Aug. 23, 1764-Nov. 8, 1811; House 1807-10.

UPHAM, Nathaniel (D N.H.) June 9, 1774-July 10, 1829; House 1817-23.

UPHAM, William (W Vt.) Aug. 5, 1792-Jan. 14, 1853; Senate 1843-Jan. 14, 1853.

UPSHAW, William David (D Ga.) Oct. 15, 1866-Nov. 21, 1952; House 1919-27.

UPSON, Charles (R Mich.) March 19, 1821-Sept. 5, 1885; House 1863-69.

UPSON, Christopher Columbus (D Texas) Oct. 17, 1829-Feb. 8, 1902; House April 15, 1879-83.

UPSON, William Hanford (R Ohio) Jan. 11, 1823-April 13, 1910; House 1869-73.

UPTON, Charles Horace (R Va.) Aug. 23, 1812-June 17, 1877; House May 23, 1861-Feb. 27, 1862.

UPTON, Robert William (R N.H.) Feb. 3, 1884-April 28, 1972; Senate Aug. 14, 1953-Nov. 7, 1954.

URNER, Milton George (uncle of James Samuel Simmons) (R Md.) July 29, 1839-Feb. 9, 1926; House 1879-83.

UTT, James Boyd (R Calif.) March 11, 1899-March 1, 1970; House 1953-March 1, 1970.

UTTER, George Herbert (R R.I.) July 24, 1854-Nov. 3, 1912; House 1911-Nov. 3, 1912; Gov. 1905-07.

UTTERBACK, Hubert (cousin of John Gregg Utterback) (D Iowa) June 28, 1880-May 12, 1942; House 1935-37.

UTTERBACK, John Gregg (cousin of Hubert Utterback) (D Maine) July 12, 1872-July 11, 1955; House 1933-35.

V

VAIL, George (D N.J.) July 21, 1809-May 23, 1875; House 1853-57.

VAIL, Henry (D N.Y.) 1782-June 25, 1853; House 1837-39.

VAIL, Richard Bernard (R Ill.) Aug. 31, 1895-July 29, 1955; House 1947-49, 1951-53.

VAILE, William Newell (R Colo.) June 22, 1876-July 2, 1927; House 1919-July 2, 1927.

VALENTINE, Edward Kimble (R Neb.) June 1, 1843-April 11, 1916; House 1879-85.

VALENTINE, Tim (D N.C.) March 15, 1926--; House 1983--.

VALK, William Weightman (AP N.Y.) Oct. 12, 1806-Sept. 20, 1879; House 1855-57.

VALLANDIGHAM, Clement Laird (uncle of John A. McMahon) (D Ohio) July 29, 1820-June 17, 1871; House May 25, 1858-63.

VAN AERNAM, Henry (R N.Y.) March 11, 1819-June 1, 1894; House 1865-69, 1879-83.

VAN ALEN, James Isaac (half brother of Martin Van Buren) (F N.Y.) 1776-Dec. 23, 1870; House 1807-09.

VAN ALEN, John Evert (— N.Y.) 1749-March 1807; House 1793-99.

VAN ALSTYNE, Thomas Jefferson (D N.Y.) July 25, 1827-Oct. 26, 1903; House 1883-85.

VAN AUKEN, Daniel Myers (D Pa.) Jan. 15, 1826-Nov. 7, 1908; House 1867-71.

VAN BUREN, John (D N.Y.) May 13, 1799-Jan. 16, 1855; House 1841-43.

VAN BUREN, Martin (half brother of James Isaac Van Alen) (D N.Y.) Dec. 5, 1782-July 24, 1862; Senate 1821-Dec. 20, 1828; Gov. 1829; Secy. of State 1829-31; Vice Pres. 1833-37; President 1837-41.

VANCE, John Luther (D Ohio) July 19, 1839-June 10, 1921; House 1875-77.

VANCE, Joseph (W Ohio) March 21, 1786-Aug. 24, 1852; House 1821-35, 1843-47 (1821-35 Democrat, 1843-47 Whig); Gov. 1836-38.

VANCE, Robert Brank (uncle of Zebulon Baird Vance and the following) (D N.C.) 1793-1827; House 1823-25.

VANCE, Robert Brank (nephew of the preceding, brother of Zebulon Baird Vance (D N.C.) April 24, 1828-Nov. 28, 1899; House 1873-85.

VANCE, Robert Johnstone (D Conn.) March 15, 1854-June 15, 1902; House 1887-89.

VANCE, Zebulon Baird (brother of Robert Brank Vance, nephew of Robert Brank Vance) (D N.C.) May 13, 1830-April 14, 1894; House Dec. 7, 1858-61; Senate 1879-April 14, 1894; Gov. 1862-65, 1877-79.

VAN CORTLANDT, Philip (brother of Pierre Van Cortlandt Jr.) (D N.Y.) Aug. 21, 1749-Nov. 1, 1831; House 1793-1809.

VAN CORTLANDT, Pierre Jr. (brother of Philip Van Cortlandt) (D N.Y.) Aug. 29, 1762-July 13, 1848; House 1811-13.

VAN DEERLIN, Lionel (D Calif.) July 25, 1914--; House 1963-81.

VANDENBERG, Arthur Hendrick (R Mich.) March 22, 1884-April 18, 1951; Senate March 31, 1928-April 18, 1951; Pres. pro tempore 1947-49.

VANDERGRIFF, Tom (D Texas) Jan. 29, 1926--; House 1983-85.

VANDER JAGT, Guy Adrian (R Mich.) Aug. 26, 1931--; House Nov. 8, 1966--.

VANDERPOEL, Aaron (D N.Y.) Feb. 5, 1799-July 18, 1870; House 1833-37, 1839-41.

VANDER VEEN, Richard Franklin (D Mich.) Nov. 26, 1922--; House Feb. 18, 1974-77.

VANDERVEER, Abraham (D N.Y.) 1781-July 21, 1839; House 1837-39.

VANDEVER, William (R Iowa/Calif.) March 31, 1817-July 23, 1893; House 1859-Sept. 24, 1861 (Iowa), 1887-91 (Calif.).

VANDIVER, Willard Duncan (D Mo.) March 30, 1854-May 30, 1932; House 1897-1905.

VAN DUZER, Clarence Dunn (D Nev.) May 4, 1866-Sept. 28, 1947; House 1903-07.

VAN DYKE, Carl Chester (D Minn.) Feb. 18, 1881-May 20, 1919; House 1915-May 20, 1919.

VAN DYKE, John (W N.J.) April 3, 1807-Dec. 24, 1878; House 1847-51.

VAN DYKE, Nicholas (F Del.) Dec. 20, 1769-May 21, 1826; House Oct. 6, 1807-11; Senate 1817-May 21, 1826.

VAN EATON, Henry Smith (D Miss.) Sept. 14, 1826-May 30, 1898; House 1883-87.

VAN GAASBECK, Peter (AF N.Y.) Sept. 27, 1754-1797; House 1793-95.

VAN HORN, Burt (R N.Y.) Oct. 28, 1823-April 1, 1896; House 1861-63 1865-69.

VAN HORN, George (D N.Y.) Feb. 5, 1850-May 3, 1904; House 1891-93.

VAN HORN, Robert Thompson (R Mo.) May 19, 1824-Jan. 3, 1916; House 1865-71, 1881-83, Feb. 27, 1896-97.

VAN HORNE, Archibald (— Md.) ?-1817; House 1807-11.

VAN HORNE, Espy (D Pa.) 1795-Aug. 25, 1829; House 1825-29.

VAN HORNE, Isaac (D Pa.) Jan. 13, 1754-Feb. 2, 1834; House 1801-05.

VAN HOUTEN, Isaac B. (D N.Y.) June 4, 1776-Aug. 16, 1850; House 1833-35.

VANIK, Charles Albert (D Ohio) April 7, 1913--; House 1955-81.

VANMETER, John Inskeep (W Ohio) Feb. 1798-Aug. 3, 1875; House 1843-45.

VAN NESS, John Peter (D N.Y.) 1770-March 7, 1846; House Oct. 6, 1801-Jan. 17, 1803.

VAN NUYS, Frederick (D Ind.) April 16, 1874-Jan. 25, 1944; Senate 1933-Jan. 25, 1944.

VAN PELT, William Kaiser (R Wis.) March 10, 1905--; House 1951-65.

VAN RENSSELAER, Henry Bell (son of Stephen Van Rensselaer) (W N.Y.) May 14, 1810-March 23, 1864; House 1841-43.

VAN RENSSELAER, Jeremiah (father of Solomon Van Vechten Van Rensselaer, cousin of Killian Killian Van Rensselaer) (— N.Y.) Aug. 27, 1738-Feb. 19, 1810; House 1789-91.

VAN RENSSELAER, Killian Killian (cousin of Jeremiah Van Rensselaer, uncle of Solomon Van Vechten Van Renssealer) (D N.Y.) June 9, 1763-June 18, 1845; House 1801-11.

VAN RENSSELAER, Solomon Van Vechten (son of Jeremiah Van Rensselaer, nephew of Killian Killian Van Rensselaer) (F N.Y.) Aug. 6, 1774-April 23, 1852; House 1819-Jan. 14, 1822.

VAN RENSSELAER, Stephen (father of Henry Bell Van Rensselaer) (— N.Y.) Nov. 1, 1764-Jan. 26, 1839; House Feb. 27, 1822-29.

VAN SANT, Joshua (D Md.) Dec. 31, 1803-April 8, 1884; House 1853-55.

VAN SCHAICK, Isaac Whitbeck (uncle of Aaron Van Schaick Cochrane) (R Wis.) Dec. 7, 1817-Aug. 22, 1901; House 1885-87, 1889-91.

VAN SWEARINGEN, Thomas (— Va.) May 5, 1784-Aug. 19, 1822; House 1819-Aug. 19, 1822.

VAN TRUMP, Philadelph (D Ohio) Nov. 15, 1810-July 31, 1874; House 1867-73.

VAN VALKENBURGH, Robert Bruce (R N.Y.) Sept. 4, 1821-Aug. 1, 1888; House 1861-65.

VAN VOORHIS, Henry Clay (R Ohio) May 11, 1852-Dec. 12, 1927; House 1893-1905.

VAN VOORHIS, John (R N.Y.) Oct. 22, 1826-Oct. 20, 1905; House 1879-83, 1893-95.

VAN VORHES, Nelson Holmes (R Ohio) Jan. 23, 1822-Dec. 4, 1882; House 1875-79.

VAN WINKLE, Marshall (grandnephew of Peter Godwin Van Winkle) (R N.J.) Sept. 28, 1869-May 10, 1957; House 1905-07.

VAN WINKLE, Peter Godwin (granduncle of Marshall Van Winkle) (U W.Va.) Sept. 7, 1808-April 15, 1872; Senate Aug. 4, 1863-69.

VAN WYCK, Charles Henry (R N.Y./Neb.) May 10, 1824-Oct. 24, 1895; House 1859-63, 1867-69, Feb. 17, 1870-71 (N.Y.); Senate 1881-87 (Neb.).

VAN WYCK, William William (D N.Y.) Aug. 9, 1777-Aug. 27, 1840; House 1821-25.

VAN ZANDT, James Edward (R Pa.) Dec. 18, 1898--; House 1939-Sept. 24, 1943, 1947-63.

VARDAMAN, James Kimble (D Miss.) July 26, 1861-June 25, 1930; Senate 1913-19; Gov. 1904-08.

VARE, William Scott (R Pa.) Dec. 24, 1867-Aug. 7, 1934; House April 24, 1912-Jan. 2, 1923, March 4, 1923-27, Senate (elected 1926 but never served).

VARNUM, John (F Mass.) June 25, 1778-July 23, 1836; House 1825-31.

VARNUM, Joseph Bradley (— Mass.) Jan. 29, 1750-Sept. 21, 1821; House 1795-June 29, 1811; Senate June 29, 1811-17; Speaker 1807-11; Pres. pro tempore 1813-14.

VAUGHAN, Horace Worth (D Texas) Dec. 2, 1867-Nov. 10, 1922; House 1913-15.

VAUGHAN, William Wirt (D Tenn.) July 2, 1831-Aug. 19, 1878; House 1871-73.

VAUGHN, Albert Clinton Sr. (R Pa.) Oct. 9, 1894-Sept. 1, 1951; House Jan. 3-Sept. 1, 1951.

VAUX, Richard (D Pa.) Dec. 19, 1816-March 22, 1895; House May 20, 1890-91.

VEEDER, William Davis (D N.Y.) May 19, 1835-Dec. 2, 1910; House 1877-79.

VEHSLAGE, John Herman George (D N.Y.) Dec. 20, 1842-July 21, 1904; House 1897-99.

VELDE, Harold Himmel (R Ill.) April 1, 1910--; House 1949-57.

VENABLE, Abraham Bedford (uncle of Abraham Watkins Venable) (— Va.) Nov. 20, 1758-Dec. 26, 1811; House 1791-99; Senate Dec. 7, 1803-June 7, 1804.

VENABLE, Abraham Watkins (nephew of Abraham Bedford Venable) (D N.C.) Oct. 17, 1799-Feb. 24, 1876; House 1847-53.

VENABLE, Edward Carrington (D Va.) Jan. 31, 1853-Dec. 8, 1908; House 1889-Sept. 23, 1890.

VENABLE, William Webb (D Miss.) Sept. 25, 1880-Aug. 2, 1948; House Jan. 4, 1916-21.

VENTO, Bruce Frank (D Minn.) Oct. 7, 1940--; House 1977--.

Biographical Index

VERPLANCK, Daniel Crommelin (father of Gulian Crommelin Verplanck) (F N.Y.) March 19, 1762-March 29, 1834; House Oct. 17, 1803-09.

VERPLANCK, Gulian Crommelin (son of Daniel Crommelin Verplanck) (D N.Y.) Aug. 6, 1786-March 18, 1870; House 1825-33.

VERREE, John Paul (R Pa.) March 9, 1817-June 27, 1889; House 1859-63.

VEST, George Graham (D Mo.) Dec. 6, 1830-Aug. 9, 1904; Senate 1879-1903.

VESTAL, Albert Henry (R Ind.) Jan. 18, 1875-April 1, 1932; House 1917-April 1, 1932.

VEYSEY, Victor V. (R Calif.) April 14, 1915- — ; House 1971-75.

VIBBARD, Chauncey (D N.Y.) Nov. 11, 1811-June 5, 1891; House 1861-63.

VICKERS, George (D Md.) Nov. 19, 1801-Oct. 8, 1879; Senate March 7, 1868-73.

VIDAL, Michel (R La.) Oct. 1, 1824-?; House July 18, 1868-69.

VIELE, Egbert Ludoricus (D N.Y.) June 17, 1825-April 22, 1902; House 1885-87.

VIGORITO, Joseph Phillip (D Pa.) Nov. 10, 1918- — ; House 1965-77.

VILAS, William Freeman (D Wis.) July 9, 1840-Aug. 28, 1908; Senate 1891-97; Postmaster Gen. 1885-88; Secy. of the Interior 1888-89.

VINCENT, Beverly Mills (D Ky.) March 28, 1890- — ; House 1937-45.

VINCENT, Bird J. (R Mich.) March 6, 1880-July 18, 1931; House 1923-July 18, 1931.

VINCENT, Earl W. (R Iowa) March 27, 1886-May 22, 1953; House June 4, 1928-29.

VINCENT, William Davis (P Kan.) Oct. 11, 1852-Feb. 28, 1922; House 1897-99.

VINING, John (— Del.) Dec. 23, 1758-Feb. 1802; House 1789-93; Senate 1793-Jan. 19, 1798; Cont. Cong. 1784-86.

VINSON, Carl (D Ga.) Nov. 18, 1883-June 1, 1981; House Nov. 3, 1914-65.

VINSON, Frederick Moore (Fred) (D Ky.) Jan. 22, 1890-Sept. 8, 1953; House Jan. 12, 1924-29, 1931-May 12, 1938; Secy. of the Treasury 1945-46; Chief Justice Supreme Court 1946-53.

VINTON, Samuel Finley (W Ohio) Sept. 25, 1792-May 11, 1862; House 1823-37, 1843-51.

VISCLOSKY, Peter John (D Ind.) Aug. 13, 1949- — ; House 1985- — .

VIVIAN, Weston Edward (D Mich.) Oct. 25, 1924- — ; House 1965-67.

VOIGT, Edward (R Wis.) Dec. 1, 1873-Aug. 26, 1934; House 1917-27.

VOLK, Lester David (R N.Y.) Sept. 17, 1884-April 30, 1962; House Nov. 2, 1920-23.

VOLKMER, Harold Lee (D Mo.) April 4, 1931- — ; House 1977- — .

VOLLMER, Henry (D Iowa) July 28, 1867-Aug. 25, 1930; House Feb. 10, 1914-15.

VOLSTEAD, Andrew John (R Minn.) Oct. 31, 1860-Jan. 20, 1947; House 1903-23.

VOORHEES, Charles Stewart (son of Daniel Wolsey Voorhees) (D Wash.) June 4, 1853-Dec. 26, 1909; House (Terr. Del.) 1885-89.

VOORHEES, Daniel Wolsey (father of Charles Stewart Voorhees) (D Ind.) Sept. 26, 1827-April 9, 1897; House 1861-Feb. 23, 1866, 1869-73; Senate Nov. 6, 1877-97.

VOORHIS, Charles Henry (R N.J.) March 13, 1833-April 15, 1896; House 1879-81.

VOORHIS, Horace Jerry (D Calif.) April 6, 1901-Sept. 11, 1984; House 1937-47.

VORYS, John Martin (R Ohio) June 16, 1896-Aug. 25, 1968; House 1939-59.

VOSE, Roger (F N.H.) Feb. 24, 1763-Oct. 26, 1841; House 1813-17.

VREELAND, Albert Lincoln (R N.J.) July 2, 1901-May 3, 1975; House 1939-43.

VREELAND, Edward Butterfield (R N.Y.) Dec. 7, 1856-May 8, 1936; House Nov. 7, 1899-1913.

VROOM, Peter Dumont (D N.J.) Dec. 12, 1791-Nov. 18, 1873; House 1839-41; Gov. 1829-32, 1833-36.

VUCANOVICH, Barbara Farrell (R Nev.) June 22, 1921- — ; House 1983- — .

VURSELL, Charles Wesley (R Ill.) Feb. 8, 1881-Sept. 21, 1974; House 1943-59.

W

WACHTER, Frank Charles (R Md.) Sept. 16, 1861-July 1, 1910; House 1899-1907.

WADDELL, Alfred Moore (D N.C.) Sept. 16, 1834-March 17, 1912; House 1871-79.

WADDILL, Edmund Jr. (R Va.) May 22, 1855-April 9, 1931; House April 12, 1890-91.

WADDILL, James Richard (D Mo.) Nov. 22, 1842-June 14, 1917; House 1879-81.

WADE, Benjamin Franklin (brother of Edward Wade) (R Ohio) Oct. 27, 1800-March 2, 1878; Senate March 15, 1851-69; Pres. pro tempore 1867-69 (1851-57 Whig, 1857-69 Republican).

WADE, Edward (brother of Benjamin Franklin Wade) (R Ohio) Nov. 22, 1802-Aug. 13, 1866; House 1853-61 (1853-55 Free-Soiler, 1855-61 Republican).

WADE, Martin Joseph (D Iowa) Oct. 20, 1861-April 16, 1931; House 1903-05.

WADE, William Henry (R Mo.) Nov. 3, 1835-Jan. 13, 1911; House 1885-91.

WADLEIGH, Bainbridge (R N.H.) Jan. 4, 1831-Jan. 24, 1891; Senate 1873-79.

WADSWORTH, James Wolcott (father of James Wolcott Wadsworth Jr.) (R N.Y.) Oct. 12, 1846-Dec. 24, 1926; House Nov. 8, 1881-85, 1891-1907.

WADSWORTH, James Wolcott Jr. (son of James Wolcott Wadsworth) (R N.Y.) Aug. 12, 1877-June 21, 1952; Senate 1915-27; House 1933-51.

WADSWORTH, Jeremiah (F Conn.) July 12, 1743-April 30, 1804; House 1789-95; Cont. Cong. 1787-88.

WADSWORTH, Peleg (— Mass.) May 6, 1748-Nov. 12, 1829; House 1793-1807.

WADSWORTH, William Henry (R Ky.) July 4, 1821-April 2, 1893; House 1861-65, 1885-87 (1861-65 Unionist, 1885-87 Republican).

WAGENER, David Douglas (D Pa.) Oct. 11, 1792-Oct. 1, 1860; House 1833-41.

WAGGAMAN, George Augustus (NR La.) 1790-March 22, 1843; Senate Nov. 15, 1831-35.

WAGGONNER, Joseph David Jr. (D La.) Sept. 7, 1918- — ; House Dec. 19, 1961-79.

WAGNER, Earl Thomas (D Ohio) April 27, 1908- — ; House 1949-51.

WAGNER, Peter Joseph (W N.Y.) Aug. 14, 1795-Sept. 13, 1884; House 1839-41.

WAGNER, Robert Ferdinand (D N.Y.) June 8, 1877-May 4, 1953; Senate 1927-June 28, 1949.

WAGONER, George Chester Robinson (R Mo.) Sept. 3, 1863-April 27, 1946; House Feb. 26-March 3, 1903.

WAINWRIGHT, Jonathan Mayhew (R N.Y.) Dec. 10, 1864-June 3, 1945; House 1923-31.

WAINWRIGHT, Stuyvesant II (R N.Y.) March 16, 1921- — ; House 1953-61.

WAIT, John Turner (R Conn.) Aug. 27, 1811-April 21, 1899; House April 12, 1876-87.

WAKEFIELD, James Beach (R Minn.) March 21, 1825-Aug. 25, 1910; House 1883-87.

WAKEMAN, Abram (W N.Y.) May 31, 1824-June 29, 1889; House 1855-57.

WAKEMAN, Seth (R N.Y.) Jan. 15, 1811-Jan. 4, 1880; House 1871-73.

WALBRIDGE, David Safford (R Mich.) July 30, 1802-June 15, 1868; House 1855-59.

WALBRIDGE, Henry Sanford (cousin of Hiram Walbridge) (W N.Y.) April 8, 1801-Jan. 27, 1869; House 1851-53.

WALBRIDGE, Hiram (cousin of Henry Sanford Walbridge) (D N.Y.) Feb. 2, 1821-Dec. 6, 1870; House 1853-55.

WALCOTT, Frederic Collin (R Conn.) Feb. 19, 1869-April 27, 1949; Senate 1929-35.

WALDEN, Hiram (D N.Y.) Aug. 21, 1800-July 21, 1880; House 1849-51.

WALDEN, Madison Miner (R Iowa) Oct. 6, 1836-July 24, 1891; House 1871-73.

WALDIE, Jerome Russell (D Calif.) Feb. 15, 1925- — ; House June 7, 1966-75.

WALDO, George Ernest (R N.Y.) Jan. 11, 1851-June 16, 1942; House 1905-09.

WALDO, Loren Pinckney (D Conn.) Feb. 2, 1802-Sept. 8, 1881; House 1849-51.

WALDOW, William Frederick (R N.Y.) Aug. 26, 1882-April 16, 1930; House 1917-19.

WALDRON, Alfred Marpole (R Pa.) Sept. 21, 1865-June 28, 1952; House 1933-35.

WALDRON, Henry (R Mich.) Oct. 11, 1819-Sept. 13, 1880; House 1855-61, 1871-77.

WALES, George Edward (— Vt.) May 13, 1792-Jan. 8, 1860; House 1825-29.

WALES, John (— Del.) July 31, 1783-Dec. 3, 1863; Senate Feb. 3, 1849-51.

WALGREN, Douglas (D Pa.) Dec. 28, 1940-—; House 1977-—.

WALKER, Amasa (R Mass.) May 4, 1799-Oct. 29, 1875; House Dec. 1, 1862-63.

WALKER, Benjamin (D N.Y.) 1753-Jan. 13, 1818; House 1801-03.

WALKER, Charles Christopher Brainerd (D N.Y.) June 27, 1824-Jan. 26, 1888; House 1875-77.

WALKER, David (brother of George Walker, grandfather of James David Walker) (— Ky.) ?-March 1, 1820; House 1817-March 1, 1820.

WALKER, E. S. Johnny (D N.M.) June 18, 1911-—; House 1965-69.

WALKER, Felix (D N.C.) July 19, 1753-1828; House 1817-23.

WALKER, Francis (brother of John Walker) (— Va.) June 22, 1764-March 1806; House 1793-95.

WALKER, Freeman (D Ga.) Oct. 25, 1780-Sept. 23, 1827; Senate Nov. 6, 1819-Aug. 6, 1821.

WALKER, George (brother of David Walker) (— Ky.) 1763-1819; Senate Aug. 30-Dec. 16, 1814.

WALKER, Gilbert Carlton (D Va.) Aug. 1, 1833-May 11, 1885; House 1875-79 (1875-77 Conservative, 1877-79 Democrat); Gov. 1869-74.

WALKER, Isaac Pigeon (D Wis.) Nov. 2, 1815-March 29, 1872; Senate June 8, 1848-55.

WALKER, James Alexander (R Va.) Aug. 27, 1832-Oct. 21, 1901; House 1895-99.

WALKER, James David (grandson of David Walker, nephew of Finis Ewing McLean and John McLean of Ill., cousin of Wilkinson Call) (D Ark.) Dec. 13, 1830-Oct. 17, 1906; Senate 1879-85.

WALKER, James Peter (D Mo.) March 14, 1851-July 19, 1890; House 1887-July 19, 1890.

WALKER, John (brother of Francis Walker) (— Va.) Feb. 13, 1744-Dec. 2, 1809; Senate March 31-Nov. 9, 1790; Cont. Cong. 1780.

WALKER, John Randall (D Ga.) Feb. 23, 1874-?; House 1913-19.

WALKER, John Williams (father of Percy Walker) (D Ala.) Aug. 12, 1783-April 23, 1823; Senate Dec. 14, 1819-Dec. 12, 1822.

WALKER, Joseph Henry (R Mass.) Dec. 21, 1829-April 3, 1907; House 1889-99.

WALKER, Lewis Leavell (R Ky.) Feb. 15, 1873-June 30, 1944; House 1929-31.

WALKER, Percy (son of John Williams Walker) (AP Ala.) Dec. 1812-Dec. 31, 1880; House 1855-57.

WALKER, Prentiss Lafayette (R Miss.) Aug. 23, 1917-—; House 1965-67.

WALKER, Robert James (D Miss.) July 23, 1801-Nov. 11, 1869; Senate 1835-March 5, 1845; Secy. of the Treasury 1845-49; Gov. (Kan. Terr.) 1857.

WALKER, Robert Jarvis Cochran (R Pa.) Oct. 20, 1838-Dec. 19, 1903; House 1881-83.

WALKER, Robert Smith (R Pa.) Dec. 23, 1942-—; House 1977-—.

WALKER, Walter (D Colo.) April 3, 1883-Oct. 8, 1956; Senate Sept. 26-Dec. 6, 1932.

WALKER, William Adams (D N.Y.) June 5, 1805-Dec. 18, 1861; House 1853-55.

WALL, Garret Dorset (father of James Walter Wall) (D N.J.) March 10, 1783-Nov. 22, 1850; Senate 1835-41.

WALL, James Walter (son of Garret Dorset Wall) (D N.J.) May 26, 1820-June 9, 1872; Senate Jan. 14-March 3, 1863.

WALL, William (R N.Y.) March 20, 1800-April 20, 1872; House 1861-63.

WALLACE, Alexander Stuart (R S.C.) Dec. 30, 1810-June 27, 1893; House May 27, 1870-77.

WALLACE, Daniel (W S.C.) May 9, 1801-May 13, 1859; House June 12, 1848-53.

WALLACE, David (W Ind.) April 4, 1799-Sept. 4, 1859; House 1841-43; Gov. 1837-40.

WALLACE, James M. (— Pa.) 1750-Dec. 17, 1823; House Oct. 10, 1815-21.

WALLACE, John Winfield (R Pa.) Dec. 20, 1818-June 24, 1889; House 1861-63, 1875-77.

WALLACE, Jonathan Hasson (D Ohio) Oct. 31, 1824-Oct. 28, 1892; House May 27, 1884-85.

WALLACE, Nathaniel Dick (D La.) Oct. 27, 1845-July 16, 1894; House Dec. 9, 1886-87.

WALLACE, Robert Minor (D Ark.) Aug. 6, 1856-Nov. 9, 1942; House 1903-11.

WALLACE, Rodney (R Mass.) Dec. 21, 1823-Feb. 27, 1903; House 1889-91.

WALLACE, William Andrew (D Pa.) Nov. 28, 1827-May 22, 1896; Senate 1875-81.

WALLACE, William Copeland (R N.Y.) May 21, 1856-Sept. 4, 1901; House 1889-91.

WALLACE, William Henson (R Wash./Idaho) July 19, 1811-Feb. 7, 1879; House (Terr. Del.) 1861-63 (Wash.), Feb. 1, 1864-65 (Idaho); Gov. (Idaho Terr.) 1863.

WALLEY, Samuel Hurd (W Mass.) Aug. 31, 1805-Aug. 27, 1877; House 1853-55.

WALLGREN, Monrad Charles (D Wash.) April 17, 1891-Sept. 18, 1961; House 1933-Dec. 19, 1940; Senate Dec. 19, 1940-Jan. 9, 1945; Gov. 1945-49.

WALLHAUSER, George Marvin (R N.J.) Feb. 10, 1900-—; House 1959-65.

WALLIN, Samuel (R N.Y.) July 31, 1856-Dec. 1, 1917; House 1913-15.

WALLING, Ansel Tracy (D Ohio) Jan. 10, 1824-June 22, 1896; House 1875-77.

WALLOP, Malcolm (R Wyo.) Feb. 27, 1933-—; Senate 1977-—.

WALLS, Josiah Thomas (R Fla.) Dec. 30, 1842-May 5, 1905; House 1871-Jan. 29, 1873, March 4, 1873-April 19, 1876.

WALN, Robert (F Pa.) Feb. 22, 1765-Jan. 24, 1836; House Dec. 3, 1798-1801.

WALSH, Allan Bartholomew (D N.J.) Aug. 29, 1874-Aug. 5, 1953; House 1913-15.

WALSH, Arthur (D N.J.) Feb. 26, 1896-Dec. 13, 1947; Senate Nov. 26, 1943-Dec. 7, 1944.

WALSH, David Ignatius (D Mass.) Nov. 11, 1872-June 11, 1947; Senate 1919-25, Dec. 6, 1926-47; Gov. 1914-16.

WALSH, James Joseph (D N.Y.) May 22, 1858-May 8, 1909; House 1895-June 2, 1896.

WALSH, John Richard (D Ind.) May 22, 1913-—; House 1949-51.

WALSH, Joseph (R Mass.) Dec. 16, 1875-Jan. 13, 1946; House 1915-Aug. 2, 1922.

WALSH, Michael (D N.Y.) March 8, 1810-March 18, 1859; House 1853-55.

WALSH, Patrick (D Ga.) Jan. 1, 1840-March 19, 1899; Senate April 2, 1894-95.

WALSH, Thomas James (D Mont.) June 12, 1859-March 2, 1933; Senate 1913-March 2, 1933.

WALSH, Thomas Yates (W Md.) 1809-Jan. 20, 1865; House 1851-53.

WALSH, William (D Md.) May 11, 1828-May 17, 1892; House 1875-79.

WALSH, William Francis (R N.Y.) July 11, 1912-—; House 1973-79.

WALTER, Francis Eugene (D Pa.) May 26, 1894-May 31, 1963; House 1933-May 31, 1963.

WALTERS, Anderson Howell (R Pa.) May 18, 1862-Dec. 7, 1927; House 1913-15, 1919-23, 1925-27.

WALTERS, Herbert Sanford (D Tenn.) Nov. 17, 1891-Aug. 17, 1973; Senate Aug. 20, 1963-Nov. 3, 1964.

WALTHALL, Edward Cary (D Miss.) April 4, 1831-April 21, 1898; Senate March 9, 1885-Jan. 24, 1894, 1895-April 21, 1898.

WALTON, Charles Wesley (R Maine) Dec. 9, 1819-Jan. 24, 1900; House 1861-May 26, 1862.

WALTON, Eliakim Persons (R Vt.) Feb. 17, 1812-Dec. 19, 1890; House 1857-63.

Biographical Index

WALTON, George (cousin of Matthew Walton) (— Ga.) 1750-Feb. 2, 1804; Senate Nov. 16, 1795-Feb. 20, 1796; Cont. Cong. 1776-78, 1780-81, 1787-88; Gov. 1779, 1789.

WALTON, Matthew (cousin of George Walton) (D Ky.) ?-Jan. 18, 1819; House 1803-07.

WALTON, William Bell (D N.M.) Jan. 23, 1871-April 14, 1939; House 1917-19.

WALWORTH, Reuben Hyde (D N.Y.) Oct. 26, 1788-Nov. 27, 1867; House 1821-23.

WAMPLER, Fred (D Ind.) Oct. 15, 1909- —; House 1959-61.

WAMPLER, William Creed (R Va.) April 21, 1926- —; House 1953-55, 1967-83.

WANGER, Irving Price (R Pa.) March 5, 1852-Jan. 14, 1940; House 1893-1911.

WARBURTON, Herbert Birchby (R Del.) Sept. 21, 1916-July 30, 1983; House 1953-55.

WARBURTON, Stanton (R Wash.) April 13, 1865-Dec. 24, 1926; House 1911-13.

WARD, Aaron (uncle of Elijah Ward) (D N.Y.) July 5, 1790-March 2, 1867; House 1825-29, 1831-37, 1841-43.

WARD, Andrew Harrison (D Ky.) Jan. 3, 1815-April 16, 1904; House Dec. 3, 1866-67.

WARD, Artemas (father of Artemas Ward Jr.) (F Mass.) Nov. 26, 1727-Oct. 28, 1800; House 1791-95; Cont. Cong. 1780-82.

WARD, Artemas Jr. (son of Artemas Ward) (F Mass.) Jan. 9, 1762-Oct. 7, 1847; House 1813-17.

WARD, Charles Bonnell (R N.Y.) April 27, 1879-May 27, 1946; House 1915-25.

WARD, David Jenkins (D Md.) Sept. 17, 1871-Feb. 18, 1961; House June 6, 1939-45.

WARD, Elijah (nephew of Aaron Ward) (D N.Y.) Sept. 16, 1816-Feb. 7, 1882; House 1857-59, 1861-65, 1875-77.

WARD, Hallett Sydney (D N.C.) Aug. 31, 1870-March 31, 1956; House 1921-25.

WARD, Hamilton (R N.Y.) July 3, 1829-Dec. 28, 1898; House 1865-71.

WARD, James Hugh (D Ill.) Nov. 30, 1853-Aug. 15, 1916; House 1885-87.

WARD, Jasper Delos (R Ill.) Feb. 1, 1829-Aug. 6, 1902; House 1873-75.

WARD, Jonathan (D N.Y.) Sept. 21, 1768-Sept. 28, 1842; House 1815-17.

WARD, Marcus Lawrence (R N.J.) Nov. 9, 1812-April 25, 1884; House 1873-75; Gov. 1866-69; Chrmn. Rep. Nat. Comm. 1866-68.

WARD, Matthias (D Texas) Oct. 13, 1805-Oct. 5, 1861; Senate Sept. 27, 1858-Dec. 5, 1859.

WARD, Thomas (D N.J.) about 1759-March 4, 1842; House 1813-17.

WARD, Thomas Bayless (D Ind.) April 27, 1835-Jan. 1, 1892; House 1883-87.

WARD, William (R Pa.) Jan. 1, 1837-Feb. 27, 1895; House 1877-83.

WARD, Wiliam Lukens (R N.Y.) Sept. 2, 1856-July 16, 1933; House 1897-99.

WARD, William Thomas (W Ky.) Aug. 9, 1808-Oct. 12, 1878; House 1851-53.

WARDWELL, Daniel (R N.Y.) May 28, 1791-March 27, 1878; House 1831-37.

WARE, John Haines III (R Pa.) Aug. 29, 1908- —; House Nov. 3, 1970-1975.

WARE, Nicholas (— Ga.) 1769-Sept. 7, 1824; Senate Nov. 10, 1821-Sept. 7, 1824.

WARE, Orie Solomon (D Ky.) May 11, 1882-Dec. 16, 1974; House 1927-29.

WARFIELD, Henry Ridgely (F Md.) Sept. 14, 1774-March 18, 1839; House 1819-25.

WARNER, Adoniram Judson (D Ohio) Jan. 13, 1834-Aug. 12, 1910; House 1879-81; 1883-87.

WARNER, Hiram (D Ga.) Oct. 29, 1802-June 30, 1881; House 1855-57.

WARNER, John De Witt (D N.Y.) Oct. 30, 1851-May 27, 1925; House 1891-95.

WARNER, John William (R Va.) Feb. 18, 1927- —; Senate Jan. 2, 1979- —.

WARNER, Levi (brother of Samuel Larkin Warner) (D Conn.) Oct. 10, 1831-April 12, 1911; House Dec. 4, 1876-79.

WARNER, Richard (D Tenn.) Sept. 19, 1835-March 4, 1915; House 1881-85.

WARNER, Samuel Larkin (brother of Levi Warner) (R Conn.) June 14, 1828-Feb. 6, 1893; House 1865-67.

WARNER, Vespasian (R Ill.) April 23, 1842-March 31, 1925; House 1895-1905.

WARNER, Willard (R Ala.) Sept. 4, 1826-Nov. 23, 1906; Senate July 13, 1868-71.

WARNER, William (R Mo.) June 11, 1840-Oct. 4, 1916; House 1885-89; Senate March 18, 1905-11.

WARNOCK, William Robert (R Ohio) Aug. 29, 1838-July 30, 1918; House 1901-05.

WARREN, Cornelius (W N.Y.) March 15, 1790-July 28, 1849; House 1847-49.

WARREN, Edward Allen (D Ark.) May 2, 1818-July 2, 1875; House 1853-55, 1857-59.

WARREN, Francis Emroy (R Wyo.) June 20, 1844-Nov. 24, 1929; Senate Nov. 18, 1890-93; 1895-Nov. 24, 1929; Gov. 1885-86, 1889-90 (Wyo. Terr.), Sept. 11-Nov. 24, 1890 (Wyo.).

WARREN, Joseph Mabbett (D N.Y.) Jan. 28, 1813-Sept. 9, 1896; House 1871-73.

WARREN, Lindsay Carter (D N.C.) Dec. 16, 1889-Dec. 28, 1976; House 1925-Oct. 31, 1940.

WARREN, Lott (W Ga.) Oct. 30, 1797-June 17, 1861; House 1839-43.

WARREN, William Wirt (D Mass.) Feb. 27, 1834-May 2, 1880; House 1875-77.

WARWICK, John George (D Ohio) Dec. 23, 1830-Aug. 14, 1892; House 1891-Aug. 14, 1892.

WASHBURN, Cadwallader Colden (brother of Israel Washburn Jr., Elihu Benjamin Washburne and William Drew Washburn) (R Wis.) April 22, 1818-May 15, 1882; House 1855-61, 1867-71; Gov. 1872-74.

WASHBURN, Charles Grenfill (R Mass.) Jan. 28, 1857-May 25, 1928; House Dec. 18, 1906-11.

WASHBURN, Henry Dana (R Ind.) March 28, 1832-Jan. 26, 1871; House Feb. 23, 1866-69.

WASHBURN, Israel Jr. (brother of Elihu Benjamin Washburne, Cadwallader Colden Washburn and William Drew Washburn) (R Maine) June 6, 1813-May 12, 1883; House 1851-Jan. 1, 1861 (1851-55 Whig, 1855-61 Republican); Gov. 1861-63.

WASHBURN, William Barrett (R Mass.) Jan. 31, 1820-Oct. 5, 1887; House 1863-Dec. 5, 1871; Senate April 17, 1874-75; Gov. 1872-74.

WASHBURN, William Drew (brother of Israel Washburn Jr., Elihu Benjamin Washburne and Cadwallader Colden Washburn) (R Minn.) Jan. 14, 1831-July 29, 1912; House 1879-85; Senate 1889-95.

WASHBURNE, Elihu Benjamin (brother of Israel Washburn Jr., Cadwallader Colden Washburn and William Drew Washburn) (W Ill.) Sept. 23, 1816-Oct. 22, 1887; House 1853-March 6, 1869; Secy. of State 1869.

WASHINGTON, George Corbin (grandnephew of President George Washington) (— Md.) Aug. 20, 1789-July 17, 1854; House 1827-33, 1835-37.

WASHINGTON, Harold (D Ill.) April 15, 1922- —; House 1981-April 30, 1983.

WASHINGTON, Joseph Edwin (D Tenn.) Nov. 10, 1851-Aug. 28, 1915; House 1887-97.

WASHINGTON, William Henry (W N.C.) Feb. 7, 1813-Aug. 12, 1860; House 1841-43.

WASIELEWSKI, Thaddeus Francis Boleslaw (D Wis.) Dec. 2, 1904-April 25, 1976; House 1941-47.

WASKEY, Frank Hinman (D Alaska) April 20, 1875-Jan. 18, 1964; House (Terr. Del.) Aug. 14, 1906-07.

WASON, Edward Hills (R N.H.) Sept. 2, 1865-Feb. 6, 1941; House 1915-33.

WATERMAN, Charles Winfield (R Colo.) Nov. 2, 1861-Aug. 27, 1932; Senate 1927-Aug. 27, 1932.

WATERS, Russell Judson (R Calif.) June 6, 1843-Sept. 25, 1911; House 1899-1901.

WATKINS, Albert Galiton (D Tenn.) May 5, 1818-Nov. 9, 1895; House 1849-53, 1855-59 (1849-53 Whig, 1855-59 Democrat).

WATKINS, Arthur Vivian (R Utah) Dec. 18, 1886-Sept. 1, 1973; Senate 1947-59.

WATKINS, Elton (D Ore.) July 6, 1881-June 24, 1956; House 1923-25.

WATKINS, George Robert (R Pa.) May 21, 1902-Aug. 7, 1970; House 1965-Aug. 7, 1970.

WATKINS, John Thomas (D La.) Jan. 15, 1854-April 25, 1925; House 1905-21.

WATKINS, Wesley Wade (D Okla.) Dec. 15, 1938-—; House 1977-—.

WATMOUGH, John Goddard (— Pa.) Dec. 6, 1793-Nov. 27, 1861; House 1831-35.

WATRES, Laurence Hawley (R Pa.) July 18, 1882-Feb. 6, 1964; House 1923-31.

WATSON, Albert William (R S.C.) Aug. 30, 1922-—; House 1963-Feb. 1, 1965, June 15, 1965-71 (1963-65 Democrat, 1965-71 Republican).

WATSON, Clarence Wayland (D W.Va.) May 8, 1864-May 24, 1940; Senate Feb. 1, 1911-13.

WATSON, Cooper Kinderdine (FS Ohio) June 18, 1810-May 20, 1880; House 1855-57.

WATSON, David Kemper (R Ohio) June 8, 1849-Sept. 28, 1918; House 1895-97.

WATSON, Henry Winfield (R Pa.) June 24, 1856-Aug. 27, 1933; House 1915-Aug. 27, 1933.

WATSON, James (D N.Y.) April 6, 1750-May 15, 1806; Senate Aug. 17, 1798-March 19, 1800.

WATSON, James Eli (R Ind.) Nov. 2, 1863-July 29, 1948; House 1895-97, 1899-1909; Senate Nov. 8, 1916-33; Senate majority leader 1929-33.

WATSON, Lewis Findlay (R Pa.) April 14, 1819-Aug. 25, 1890; House 1877-79, 1881-83, 1889-Aug. 25, 1890.

WATSON, Thomas Edward (D Ga.) Sept. 5, 1856-Sept. 26, 1922; House 1891-93; Senate 1921-Sept. 26, 1922 (1891-93 Populist, 1921-22 Democrat).

WATSON, Walter Allen (D Va.) Nov. 25, 1867-Dec. 24, 1919; House 1913-Dec. 24, 1919.

WATTERSON, Harvey Magee (father of Henry Watterson) (D Tenn.) Nov. 23, 1811-Oct. 11, 1891; House 1839-43.

WATTERSON, Henry (son of Harvey Magee Watterson, nephew of Stanley Matthews) (D Ky.) Feb. 16, 1840-Dec. 22, 1921; House Aug. 12, 1876-77.

WATTS, John (— N.Y.) Aug. 27, 1749-Sept. 3, 1836; House 1793-95.

WATTS, John Clarence (D Ky.) July 9, 1902-Sept. 24, 1971; House April 14, 1951-Sept. 24, 1971.

WATTS, John Sebrie (R N.M.) Jan. 19, 1816-June 11, 1876; House (Terr. Del.) 1861-63.

WAUGH, Daniel Webster (R Ind.) March 7, 1842-March 14, 1921; House 1891-95.

WAXMAN, Henry Arnold (D Calif.) Sept. 12, 1939-—; House 1975-—.

WAYNE, Anthony (father of Isaac Wayne) (— Ga.) Jan. 1, 1745-Dec. 15, 1796; House 1791-March 21, 1792.

WAYNE, Isaac (son of Anthony Wayne) (F Pa.) 1772-Oct. 25, 1852; House 1823-25.

WAYNE, James Moore (JD Ga.) 1790-July 5, 1867; House 1829-Jan. 13, 1835; Assoc. Justice Supreme Court 1835-67.

WEADOCK, Thomas Addis Emmet (D Mich.) Jan. 1, 1850-Nov. 18, 1938; House 1891-95.

WEAKLEY, Robert (N Tenn.) July 20, 1764-Feb. 4, 1845; House 1809-11.

WEARIN, Otha Donner (D Iowa) Jan. 10, 1903-—; House 1933-39.

WEATHERFORD, Zadoc Lorenzo (D Ala.) Feb. 4, 1888-—; House Nov. 5, 1940-41.

WEAVER, Archibald Jerard (grandfather of Phillip Hart Weaver) (R Neb.) April 15, 1844-April 18, 1887; House 1883-87.

WEAVER, Claude (D Okla.) March 19, 1867-May 19, 1954; House 1913-15.

WEAVER, James Baird (D/G-Lab. Iowa) June 12, 1833-Feb. 6, 1912; House 1879-81, 1885-89 (1879-81, 1885-87 Greenbacker, 1887-89 Democrat/Greenback Laborite).

WEAVER, James Dorman (R Pa.) Sept. 27, 1920-—; House 1963-65.

WEAVER, James Howard (D Ore.) Aug. 8, 1927-—; House 1975-—.

WEAVER, Phillip Hart (grandson of Archibald Jerard Weaver) (R Neb.) April 9, 1919-—; House 1955-63.

WEAVER, Walter Lowrie (R Ohio) April 1, 1851-May 26, 1909; House 1897-1901.

WEAVER, Zebulon (D. N.C.) May 12, 1872-Oct. 29, 1948; House 1917-March 1, 1919, March 4, 1919-29, 1931-47.

WEBB, Edwin Yates (D N.C.) May 23, 1872-Feb. 7, 1955; House 1903-Nov. 10, 1919.

WEBB, William Robert (grandson of Richard Stanford) (D Tenn.) Nov. 11, 1842-Dec. 19, 1926; Senate Jan. 24-March 3, 1913.

WEBBER, Amos Richard (R Ohio) Jan. 21, 1852-Feb. 25, 1948; House Nov. 8, 1904-07.

WEBBER, George Washington (R Mich.) Nov. 25, 1825-Jan. 15, 1900; House 1881-83.

WEBER, Ed (R Ohio) July 26, 1931-—; House 1981-—.

WEBER, John Baptiste (R N.Y.) Sept. 21, 1842-Dec. 18, 1926; House 1885-89.

WEBER, Vin (R Minn.) July 24, 1952-—; House 1981-83.

WEBSTER, Daniel (W N.H./Mass.) Jan. 18, 1782-Oct. 24, 1852; House 1813-17 (N.H.), 1823-May 30, 1827 (Mass.) Senate (Mass.) May 30, 1827-Feb. 22, 1841, 1845-July 22, 1850 (1813-17, 1823-41 Federalist, 1845-50 Whig); Secy. of State 1841-43, 1850-52.

WEBSTER, Edwin Hanson (R Md.) March 31, 1829-April 24, 1893; House 1859-July 1865.

WEBSTER, John Stanley (R Wash.) Feb. 22, 1877-Dec. 24, 1962; House 1919-May 8, 1923.

WEBSTER, Taylor (JD Ohio) Oct. 1, 1800-April 27, 1876; House 1833-39.

WEDEMEYER, William Walter (R Mich.) March 22, 1873-Jan. 2, 1913; House 1911-Jan. 2, 1913.

WEEKS, Edgar (cousin of John Wingate Weeks of Mass.) (R Mich.) Aug. 3, 1839-Dec. 17, 1904; House 1899-1903.

WEEKS, John Eliakim (R Vt.) June 14, 1853-Sept. 10, 1949; House 1931-33; Gov. 1927-31.

WEEKS, John Wingate (great-uncle of the following) (— N.H.) March 31, 1781-April 3, 1853; House 1829-33.

WEEKS, John Wingate (father of Sinclair Weeks, cousin of Edgar Weeks) (R Mass.) April 11, 1860-July 12, 1926; House 1905-March 4, 1913; Senate March 4, 1913-19; Secy. of War 1921-25.

WEEKS, Joseph (grandfather of Joseph Weeks Babcock) (D N.H.) Feb. 13, 1773-Aug. 4, 1845; House 1835-39.

WEEKS, Sinclair (son of John Wingate Weeks of Mass.) (R Mass.) June 15, 1893-Feb. 7, 1972; Senate Feb. 8-Dec. 19, 1944; Secy. of Commerce 1953-58.

WEEMS, Capell Lane (R Ohio) July 7, 1860-Jan. 5, 1913; House Nov. 3, 1903-09.

WEEMS, John Crompton (D Md.) 1778-Jan. 20, 1862; House Feb. 1, 1826-29.

WEFALD, Knud (FL Minn.) Nov. 3, 1869-Oct. 25, 1936; House 1923-27.

WEICHEL, Alvin F. (R Ohio) Sept. 11, 1891-Nov. 27, 1956; House 1943-55.

WEICKER, Lowell Palmer Jr. (R Conn.) May 16, 1931-—; House 1969-71; Senate 1971-—.

WEIDEMAN, Carl May (D Mich.) March 5, 1898-March 5, 1972; House 1933-35.

WEIGHTMAN, Richard Hanson (D N.M.) Dec. 28, 1816-Aug. 10, 1861; House (Terr. Del.) 1851-53.

WEIS, Jessica McCullough (R N.Y.) July 8, 1901-May 1, 1963; House 1959-63.

WEISS, Samuel Arthur (D Pa.) April 15, 1902-Feb. 1, 1977; House 1941-Jan. 7, 1946.

WEISS, Theodore S. (D N.Y.) Sept. 17, 1927-—; House 1977-—.

WEISSE, Charles Herman (D Wis.) Oct. 24, 1866-Oct. 8, 1919; House 1903-11.

WELBORN, John (R Mo.) Nov. 20, 1857-Oct. 27, 1907; House 1905-07.

WELCH, Adonijah Strong (R Fla.) April 12, 1821-March 14, 1889; Senate June 25, 1868-69.

WELCH, Frank (R Neb.) Feb. 10, 1835-Sept. 4, 1878; House 1877-Sept. 4, 1878.

WELCH, John (W Ohio) Oct. 28, 1805-Aug. 5, 1891; House 1851-53.

WELCH, Philip James (D Mo.) April 4, 1895-April 26, 1963; House 1949-53.

Biographical Index

WELCH, Richard Joseph (R Calif.) Feb. 13, 1869-Sept. 10, 1949, House Aug. 31, 1926-Sept. 10, 1949.

WELCH, William Wickham (AP Conn.) Dec. 10, 1818-July 30, 1892; House 1855-57.

WELKER, Herman (R Idaho) Dec. 11, 1906-Oct. 30, 1957; Senate 1951-57.

WELKER, Martin (R Ohio) April 25, 1819-March 15, 1902; House 1865-71.

WELLBORN, Marshall Johnson (D Ga.) May 29, 1808-Oct. 16, 1874; House 1849-51.

WELLBORN, Olin (D Texas) June 18, 1843-Dec. 6, 1921; House 1879-87.

WELLER, John B. (UD Ohio/Calif.) Feb. 22, 1812-Aug. 17, 1875; House 1839-45 (Ohio); Senate Jan. 30, 1852-57 (Calif.); (1839-45 Democrat, 1852-57 Union Democrat); Gov. (Calif.) 1858-60.

WELLER, Luman Hamlin (Nat.G/D Iowa) Aug. 24, 1833-March 2, 1914; House 1883-85.

WELLER, Ovington Eugene (R Md.) Jan. 23, 1862-Jan. 5, 1947; Senate 1921-27.

WELLER, Royal Hurlburt (D N.Y.) July 2, 1881-March 1, 1929; House 1923-March 1, 1929.

WELLING, Milton Holmes (D Utah) Jan. 25, 1876-May 28, 1947; House 1917-21.

WELLINGTON, George Louis (R Md.) Jan. 28, 1852-March 20, 1927; House 1895-97; Senate 1897-1903.

WELLS, Alfred (R N.Y.) May 27, 1814-July 18, 1867; House 1859-61.

WELLS, Daniel Jr. (D Wis.) July 16, 1808-March 18, 1902; House 1853-57.

WELLS, Erastus (D Mo.) Dec. 2, 1823-Oct. 2, 1893; House 1869-77; 1879-81.

WELLS, Guilford Wiley (R Miss.) Feb. 14, 1840-March 21, 1909; House 1875-77.

WELLS, John (W N.Y.) July 1, 1817-May 30, 1877; House 1851-53.

WELLS, John Sullivan (— N.H.) Oct. 18, 1803-Aug. 1, 1860; Senate Jan. 16-March 3, 1855.

WELLS, Owen Augustine (D Wis.) Feb. 4, 1844-Jan. 29, 1935; House 1893-95.

WELLS, William Hill (— Del.) Jan. 7, 1769-March 11, 1829; Senate Jan. 17, 1799-Nov. 6, 1804, May 28, 1813-17.

WELSH, George Austin (R Pa.) Aug. 9, 1878-Oct. 22, 1970; House 1923-May 31, 1932.

WELTNER, Charles Longstreet (D Ga.) Dec. 17, 1927-—; House 1963-67.

WELTY, Benjamin Franklin (D Ohio) Aug. 9, 1870-Oct. 23, 1962; House 1917-21.

WEMPLE, Edward (D N.Y.) Oct. 23, 1843-Dec. 18, 1920; House 1883-85.

WENDOVER, Peter Hercules (D N.Y.) Aug. 1, 1768-Sept. 24, 1834; House 1815-21.

WENE, Elmer H. (D N.J.) May 1, 1892-Jan. 25, 1957; House 1937-39, 1941-45.

WENTWORTH, John (R Ill.) March 5, 1815-Oct. 16, 1888; House 1843-51, 1853-55, 1865-67 (1843-51, 1853-55 Democrat, 1865-67 Republican).

WENTWORTH, Tappan (W Mass.) Feb. 24, 1802-June 12, 1875; House 1853-55.

WERDEL, Thomas Harold (R Calif.) Sept. 13, 1905-Sept. 30, 1966; House 1949-53.

WERNER, Theodore B. (D S.D.) June 2, 1892-—; House 1933-37.

WERTZ, George M. (R Pa.) July 19, 1856-Nov. 19, 1928; House 1923-25.

WEST, Charles Franklin (D Ohio) Jan. 12, 1895-Dec. 27, 1955; House 1931-35.

WEST, George (R N.Y.) Feb. 17, 1823-Sept. 20, 1901; House 1881-83, 1885-89.

WEST, Joseph Rodman (R La.) Sept. 19, 1822-Oct. 31, 1898; Senate 1871-77.

WEST, Milton Horace (D Texas) June 30, 1888-Oct. 28, 1948; House April 22, 1933-Oct. 28, 1948.

WEST, William Stanley (D Ga.) Aug. 23, 1849-Dec. 22, 1914; Senate March 2-Nov. 3, 1914.

WESTBROOK, John (D Pa.) Jan. 9, 1789-Oct. 8, 1852; House 1841-43.

WESTBROOK, Theodoric Romeyn (D N.Y.) Nov. 20, 1821-Oct. 6, 1885; House 1853-55.

WESTCOTT, James Diament Jr. (D Fla.) May 10, 1802-Jan. 19, 1880; Senate July 1, 1845-49.

WESTERLO, Rensselaer (F N.Y.) April 29, 1776-April 18, 1851; House 1817-19.

WESTLAND, Aldred John (Jack) (R Wash.) Dec. 14, 1904-Nov. 3, 1982; House 1953-65.

WETHERED, John (D Md.) May 8, 1809-Feb. 15, 1888; House 1843-45.

WETMORE, George Peabody (R R.I.) Aug. 2, 1846-Sept. 11, 1921; Senate 1895-1907, Jan. 22, 1908-13; Gov. 1885-87.

WEVER, John Madison (R N.Y.) Feb. 24, 1847-Sept. 27, 1914; House 1891-95.

WEYMOUTH, George Warren (R Mass.) Aug. 25, 1850-Sept. 7, 1910; House 1897-1901.

WHALEN, Charles William Jr. (R Ohio) July 31, 1920-—; House 1967-79.

WHALEY, Kellian Van Rensalear (R Va./W.Va.) May 6, 1821-May 20, 1876; House 1861-63 (Va.), Dec. 7, 1863-67 (W.Va.).

WHALEY, Richard Smith (D S.C.) July 15, 1874-Nov. 8, 1951; House April 29, 1913-21.

WHALLEY, John Irving (R Pa.) Sept. 14, 1902-March 8, 1980; House Nov. 8, 1960-73.

WHALLON, Reuben (JD N.Y.) Dec. 7, 1776-April 15, 1843; House 1833-35.

WHARTON, Charles Stuart (R Ill.) April 22, 1875-Sept. 4, 1939; House 1905-07.

WHARTON, James Ernest (R N.Y.) Oct. 4, 1899-—; House 1951-65.

WHARTON, Jesse (grandfather of Wharton Jackson Green) (— Tenn.) July 29, 1782-July 22, 1833; House 1807-09; Senate March 17, 1814-Oct. 10, 1815.

WHEAT, Alan D. (D Mo.) Oct. 16, 1951-—; House 1983-—.

WHEAT, William Howard (R Ill.) Feb. 19, 1879-Jan. 16, 1944; House 1939-Jan. 16, 1944.

WHEATON, Horace (D N.Y.) Feb. 24, 1803-June 23, 1882; House 1843-47.

WHEATON, Laban (F Mass.) March 13, 1754-March 23, 1846; House 1809-17.

WHEELER, Burton Kendall (D Mont.) Feb. 27, 1882-Jan. 6, 1975; Senate 1923-47.

WHEELER, Charles Kennedy (D Ky.) April 18, 1863-June 15, 1933; House 1897-1903.

WHEELER, Ezra (D Wis.) Dec. 23, 1820-Sept. 19, 1871; House 1863-65.

WHEELER, Frank Willis (R Mich.) March 2, 1853-Aug. 9, 1921; House 1889-91.

WHEELER, Grattan Henry (— N.Y.) Aug. 25, 1783-March 11, 1852; House 1831-33.

WHEELER, Hamilton Kinkaid (R Ill.) Aug. 5, 1848-July 19, 1918; House 1893-95.

WHEELER, Harrison H. (D Mich.) March 22, 1839-July 28, 1896; House 1891-93.

WHEELER, John (D N.Y.) Feb. 11, 1823-April 1, 1906; House 1853-57.

WHEELER, Joseph (D Ala.) Sept. 10, 1836-Jan. 25, 1906; House 1881-June 3, 1882; Jan. 15-March 3, 1883; 1885-April 20, 1900.

WHEELER, Loren Edgar (R Ill.) Oct. 7, 1862-Jan. 8, 1932; House 1915-23, 1925-27.

WHEELER, Nelson Platt (R Pa.) Nov. 4, 1841-March 3, 1920; House 1907-11.

WHEELER, William Almon (R N.Y.) June 19, 1819-June 4, 1887; House 1861-63, 1869-77; Vice Pres. 1877-81.

WHEELER, William McDonald (D Ga.) July 11, 1915-—; House 1947-55.

WHELCHEL, Benjamin Frank (D Ga.) Dec. 16, 1895-May 11, 1954; House 1935-45.

WHERRY, Kenneth Spicer (R Neb.) Feb. 28, 1892-Nov. 29, 1951; Senate 1943-Nov. 29, 1951.

WHIPPLE, Thomas Jr. (— N.H.) 1787-Jan. 23, 1835; House 1821-29.

WHITACRE, John Jefferson (D Ohio) Dec. 28, 1860-Dec. 2, 1938; House 1911-15.

WHITAKER, John Albert (grandson of Addison Davis James) (D Ky.) Oct. 31, 1901-Dec. 15, 1951; House April 17, 1948-Dec. 15, 1951.

WHITCOMB, James (D Ind.) Dec. 1, 1795-Oct. 4, 1852; Senate 1849-Oct. 4, 1852; Gov. 1843-49.

WHITE, Addison (cousin of John White) (W Ky.) May 1, 1824-Feb. 4, 1909; House 1851-53.

WHITE, Albert Smith (R Ind.) Oct. 24, 1803-Sept. 24, 1864; House 1837-39, 1861-63; Senate 1839-45 (1837-45 Whig, 1861-63 Republican).

WHITE, Alexander (F Va.) 1738-Sept. 19, 1804; House 1789-93.

WHITE, Alexander (R Ala.) Oct. 16, 1816-Dec. 13, 1893; House 1851-53, 1873-75 (1851-53 Union Whig, 1873-75 Republican).

WHITE, Alexander Colwell (R Pa.) Dec. 12, 1833-June 11, 1906; House 1885-87.

WHITE, Allison (D Pa.) Dec. 21, 1816-April 5, 1886; House 1857-59.

WHITE, Bartow (— N.Y.) Nov. 7, 1776-Dec. 12, 1862; House 1825-27.

WHITE, Benjamin (D Maine) May 13, 1790-June 7, 1860; House 1843-45.

WHITE, Campbell Patrick (JD N.Y.) Nov. 30, 1787-Feb. 12, 1859; House 1829-35.

WHITE, Cecil Fielding (D Calif.) Dec. 12, 1900- —; House 1949-51.

WHITE, Chilton Allen (D Ohio) Feb. 6, 1826-Dec. 7, 1900; House 1861-65.

WHITE, Compton Ignatius (father of Compton Ignatius White Jr.) (D Idaho) July 31, 1877-March 31, 1956; House 1933-47, 1949-51.

WHITE, Compton Ignatius Jr. (son of Compton Ignatius White) (D Idaho) Dec. 19, 1920- —; House 1963-67.

WHITE, David (— Ky.) 1785-Oct. 19, 1834; House 1823-25.

WHITE, Dudley Allen (R Ohio) Jan. 3, 1901-Oct. 14, 1957; House 1937-41.

WHITE, Edward Douglass (son of James White, father of the following) (W La.) March 1795-April 18, 1847; House 1829-Nov. 15, 1834, 1839-43; Gov. 1834-38.

WHITE, Edward Douglass (grandson of James White, son of the preceding) (D La.) Nov. 3, 1845-May 19, 1921; Senate 1891-March 12, 1894; Assoc. Justice Supreme Court 1894-1910; Chief Justice Supreme Court 1910-21.

WHITE, Francis (— Va.) ?-Nov. 1826; House 1813-15.

WHITE, Francis Shelley (Frank) (D Ala.) March 13, 1847-Aug. 1, 1922; Senate May 11, 1914-15.

WHITE, Frederick Edward (D Iowa) Jan. 19, 1844-Jan. 14, 1920; House 1891-93.

WHITE, George (D Ohio) Aug. 21, 1872-Dec. 15, 1953; House 1911-15, 1917-19; Chrmn. Dem. Nat. Comm. 1920-21; Gov. 1931-35.

WHITE, George Elon (R Ill.) March 7, 1848-May 17, 1935; House 1895-99.

WHITE, George Henry (R N.C.) Dec. 18, 1852-Dec. 28, 1918; House 1897-1901.

WHITE, Harry (R Pa.) Jan. 12, 1834-June 23, 1920; House 1877-81.

WHITE, Hays Baxter (R Kan.) Sept. 21, 1855-Sept. 29, 1930; House 1919-29.

WHITE, Hugh (R N.Y.) Dec. 25, 1798-Oct. 6, 1870; House 1845-51.

WHITE, Hugh Lawson (— Tenn.) Oct. 30, 1773-April 10, 1840; Senate Oct. 28, 1825-Jan. 13, 1840; Pres. pro tempore 1832-33.

WHITE, James (father of Edward Douglass White born in 1845, grandfather of Edward Douglass White born in 1795) (— Tenn.) June 16, 1749-Oct. 1809; House (Terr. Del.) Sept. 3, 1794-June 1, 1796; Cont. Cong. (N.C.) 1786-88.

WHITE, James Bain (R Ind.) June 26, 1835-Oct. 9, 1897; House 1887-89.

WHITE, James Bamford (D Ky.) June 6, 1842-March 25, 1931; House 1901-03.

WHITE, John (cousin of Addison White, uncle of John Daugherty White) (W Ky.) Feb. 14, 1802-Sept. 22, 1845; House 1835-45; Speaker 1841-43.

WHITE, John Daugherty (nephew of John White) (R Ky.) Jan. 16, 1849-Jan. 5, 1920; House 1875-77, 1881-85.

WHITE, Joseph Livingston (W Ind.) ?-Jan. 12, 1861; House 1841-43.

WHITE, Joseph M. (D Fla.) May 10, 1781-Oct. 19, 1839; House (Terr. Del.) 1825-37.

WHITE, Joseph Worthington (D Ohio) Oct. 2, 1822-Aug. 6, 1892; House 1863-65.

WHITE, Leonard (D Mass.) May 3, 1767-Oct. 10, 1849; House 1811-13.

WHITE, Michael Doherty (R Ind.) Sept. 8, 1827-Feb. 6, 1917; House 1877-79.

WHITE, Milo (R Minn.) Aug. 17, 1830-May 18, 1913; House 1883-87.

WHITE, Phineas (D Vt.) Oct. 30, 1770-July 6, 1847; House 1821-23.

WHITE, Richard Crawford (D Texas) April 29, 1923- —; House 1965-83.

WHITE, Samuel (F Del.) 1770-Nov. 4, 1809; Senate Feb. 28, 1801-Nov. 4, 1809.

WHITE, Sebastian Harrison (D Colo.) Dec. 24, 1864-Dec. 21, 1945; House Nov. 15, 1927-29.

WHITE, Stephen Mallory (D Calif.) Jan. 19, 1853-Feb. 21, 1901; Senate 1893-99.

WHITE, Stephen Van Culen (R N.Y.) Aug. 1, 1831-Jan. 18, 1913; House 1887-89.

WHITE, Wallace Humphrey Jr. (grandson of William Pierce Frye) (R Maine) Aug. 6, 1877-March 31, 1952; House 1917-31; Senate 1931-49; Senate majority leader 1947-49.

WHITE, Wilbur McKee (R Ohio) Feb. 22, 1890-Dec. 31, 1973; House 1931-33.

WHITE, William John (R Ohio) Oct. 7, 1850-Feb. 16, 1923; House 1893-95.

WHITEAKER, John (D Ore.) May 4, 1820-Oct. 2, 1902; House 1879-81; Gov. 1859-62.

WHITEHEAD, Joseph (D Va.) Oct. 31, 1867-July 8, 1938; House 1925-31.

WHITEHEAD, Thomas (C Va.) Dec. 27, 1825-July 1, 1901; House 1873-75.

WHITEHILL, James (son of John Whitehill, nephew of Robert Whitehill) (— Pa.) Jan. 31, 1762-Feb. 26, 1822; House 1813-Sept. 1, 1814.

WHITEHILL, John (father of James Whitehill, brother of Robert Whitehill) (— Pa.) Dec. 11, 1729-Sept. 16, 1815; House 1803-07.

WHITEHILL, Robert (brother of John Whitehill, uncle of James Whitehill, great-great-grand-father of John Crain Kunkel) (— Pa.) July 21, 1738-April 8, 1813; House Nov. 7, 1805-April 8, 1813.

WHITEHOUSE, John Osborne (LD N.Y.) July 19, 1817-Aug. 24, 1881; House 1873-77.

WHITEHURST, George William (R Va.) March 12, 1925- —; House 1969- —.

WHITELAW, Robert Henry (D Mo.) Jan. 30, 1854-July 27, 1937; House Nov. 4, 1890-91.

WHITELEY, Richard Henry (R Ga.) Dec. 22, 1830-Sept. 26, 1890; House Dec. 22, 1870-75.

WHITELEY, William Gustavus (D Del.) Aug. 7, 1819-April 23, 1886; House 1857-61.

WHITENER, Basil Lee (D N.C.) May 14, 1915- —; House 1957-69.

WHITESIDE, Jenkin (— Tenn.) 1772-Sept. 25, 1822; Senate April 11, 1809-Oct. 8, 1811.

WHITESIDE, John (D Pa.) 1773-July 28, 1830; House 1815-19.

WHITFIELD, John Wilkins (D Kan.) March 11, 1818-Oct. 27, 1879; House (Terr. Del.) Dec. 20, 1854-Aug. 1, 1856; Dec. 9, 1856-57.

WHITING, Justin Rice (D/G Mich.) Feb. 18, 1847-Jan. 31, 1903; House 1887-95.

WHITING, Richard Henry (uncle of Ira Clifton Copley) (R Ill.) Jan. 17, 1826-May 24, 1888; House 1875-77.

WHITING, William (R Mass.) March 3, 1813-June 29, 1873; House March 4-June 29, 1873.

WHITING, William (R Mass.) May 24, 1841-Jan. 9, 1911; House 1883-89.

WHITLEY, Charles Orville (D N.C.) Jan. 3, 1927- —; House 1977- —.

WHITLEY, James Lucius (R N.Y.) May 24, 1872-May 17, 1959; House 1929-35.

WHITMAN, Ezekiel (F Mass./Maine) March 9, 1776-Aug. 1, 1866; House 1809-11, 1817-21 (Mass.), 1821-June 1, 1822 (Maine).

WHITMAN, Lemuel (D Conn.) June 8, 1780-Nov. 13, 1841; House 1823-25.

WHITMORE, Elias (D N.Y.) March 2, 1772-Dec. 26, 1853; House 1825-27.

WHITMORE, George Washington (R Texas) Aug. 26, 1824-Oct. 14, 1876; House March 30, 1870-71.

WHITNEY, Thomas Richard (AP N.Y.) May 2, 1807-April 12, 1858; House 1855-57.

Biographical Index

WHITTAKER, Robert (R Kan.) Sept. 18, 1939-—; House 1979-—.

WHITTEMORE, Benjamin Franklin (R S.C.) May 18, 1824-Jan. 25, 1894; House July 18, 1868-Feb. 24, 1870.

WHITTEN, Jamie Lloyd (D Miss.) April 18, 1910-—; House Nov. 4, 1941-—.

WHITTHORNE, Washington Curran (D Tenn.) April 19, 1825-Sept. 21, 1891; House 1871-83, 1887-91; Senate April 16, 1886-87.

WHITTINGTON, William Madison (D Miss.) May 4, 1878-Aug. 20, 1962; House 1925-51.

WHITTLESEY, Elisha (uncle of William Augustus Whittlesey, cousin of Frederick Whittlesey and Thomas Tucker Whittlesey) (— Ohio) Oct. 19, 1783-Jan. 7, 1863; House 1823-July 9, 1838.

WHITTLESEY, Frederick (cousin of Elisha Whittlesey and Thomas Tucker Whittlesey) (W N.Y.) June 12, 1799-Sept. 19, 1851; House 1831-35.

WHITTLESEY, Thomas Tucker (cousin of Elisha Whittlesey and Frederick Whittlesey) (VBD Conn.) Dec. 8, 1798-Aug. 20, 1868; House April 29, 1836-39.

WHITTLESEY, William Augustus (nephew of Elisha Whittlesey) (D Ohio) July 14, 1796-Nov. 6, 1866; House 1849-51.

WHYTE, William Pinkney (D Md.) Aug. 9, 1824-March 17, 1908; Senate July 13, 1868-69, 1875-81, June 8, 1906-March 17, 1908; Gov. 1872-74.

WICK, William Watson (D Ind.) Feb. 23, 1796-May 19, 1868; House 1839-41, 1845-49.

WICKERSHAM, James (R Alaska) Aug. 24, 1857-Oct. 24, 1939; House (Terr. Del.) 1909-17, Jan. 7-March 3, 1919, March 1-3, 1921, 1931-33.

WICKERSHAM, Victor Eugene (D Okla.) Feb. 9, 1906-—; House April 1, 1941-47, 1949-57, 1961-65.

WICKES, Eliphalet (— N.Y.) April 1, 1769-June 7, 1850; House 1805-07.

WICKHAM, Charles Preston (R Ohio) Sept. 15, 1836-March 18, 1925; House 1887-91.

WICKLIFFE, Charles Anderson (grandfather of Robert Charles Wickliffe and John Crepps Wickliffe Beckham) (UW Ky.) June 8, 1788-Oct. 31, 1869; House 1823-33, 1861-63 (1823-33 Democrat, 1861-63 Union Whig); Gov. 1839-40; Postmaster Gen. 1841-45.

WICKLIFFE, Robert Charles (grandson of Charles Anderson Wickliffe, cousin of John Crepps Wickliffe Beckham) (D La.) May 1, 1874-June 11, 1912; House 1909-June 11, 1912.

WIDGERY, William (D Mass.) about 1753-July 31, 1822; House 1811-13.

WIDNALL, William Beck (R N.J.) March 17, 1906-Dec. 28, 1983; House Feb. 6, 1950-Dec. 31, 1974.

WIER, Roy William (D Minn.) Feb. 25, 1888-June 27, 1963; House 1949-61.

WIGFALL, Louis Tresvant (D Texas) April 21, 1816-Feb. 18, 1874; Senate Dec. 5, 1859-March 23, 1861.

WIGGINS, Charles Edward (R Calif.) Dec. 3, 1927-—; House 1967-79.

WIGGINTON, Peter Dinwiddie (D Calif.) Sept. 6, 1839-July 7, 1890; House 1875-77, Feb. 7, 1878-79.

WIGGLESWORTH, Richard Bowditch (R Mass.) April 25, 1891-Oct. 22, 1960; House Nov. 6, 1928-Nov. 13, 1958.

WIKE, Scott (D Ill.) April 6, 1834-Jan. 15, 1901; House 1875-77, 1889-93.

WILBER, David (father of David Forrest Wilber) (R N.Y.) Oct. 5, 1820-April 1, 1890; House 1873-75, 1879-81, 1887-April 1, 1890.

WILBER, David Forrest (son of David Wilber) (R N.Y.) Dec. 7, 1859-Aug. 14, 1928; House 1895-99.

WILBOUR, Isaac (F R.I.) April 25, 1763-Oct. 4, 1837; House 1807-09.

WILCOX, James Mark (D Fla.) May 21, 1890-Feb. 3, 1956; House 1933-39.

WILCOX, Jeduthun (father of Leonard Wilcox) (F N.H.) Nov. 18, 1768-July 18, 1838; House 1813-17.

WILCOX, John A. (UW Miss.) April 18, 1819-Feb. 7, 1864; House 1851-53.

WILCOX, Leonard (son of Jeduthun Wilcox) (D N.H.) Jan. 29, 1799-June 18, 1850; Senate March 1, 1842-43.

WILCOX, Robert William (— Hawaii) Feb. 15, 1855-Oct. 23, 1903; House (Terr. Del.) Nov. 6, 1900-03.

WILDE, Richard Henry (D Ga.) Sept. 24, 1789-Sept. 10, 1847; House 1815-17, Feb. 7-March 3, 1825, Nov. 17, 1827-35.

WILDER, Abel Carter (R Kan.) March 18, 1828-Dec. 22, 1875; House 1863-65.

WILDER, William Henry (R Mass.) May 14, 1855-Sept. 11, 1913; House 1911-Sept. 11, 1913.

WILDMAN, Zalmon (D Conn.) Feb. 16, 1775-Dec. 10, 1835; House March 4-Dec. 10, 1835.

WILDRICK, Isaac (D N.J.) March 3, 1803-March 22, 1892; House 1849-53.

WILEY, Alexander (R Wis.) May 26, 1884-May 26, 1967; Senate 1939-63.

WILEY, Ariosto Appling (brother of Oliver Cicero Wiley) (D Ala.) Nov. 6, 1848-June 17, 1908; House 1901-June 17, 1908.

WILEY, James Sullivan (D Maine) Jan. 22, 1808-Dec. 21, 1891; House 1847-49.

WILEY, John McClure (D N.Y.) Aug. 11, 1846-Aug. 13, 1912; House 1889-91.

WILEY, Oliver Cicero (brother of Ariosto Appling Wiley) (D Ala.) Jan. 30, 1851-Oct. 18, 1917; House Nov. 3, 1908-09.

WILEY, William Halsted (R N.J.) July 10, 1842-May 2, 1925; House 1903-07, 1909-11.

WILFLEY, Xenophon Pierce (D Mo.) March 18, 1871-May 4, 1931; Senate April 30-Nov. 5, 1918.

WILKIN, James Whitney (father of Samuel Jones Wilkin) (D N.Y.) 1762-Feb. 23, 1845; House June 7, 1815-19.

WILKIN, Samuel Jones (son of James Whitney Wilkin) (D N.Y.) Dec. 17, 1793-March 11, 1866; House 1831-33.

WILKINS, Beriah (D Ohio) July 10, 1846-June 7, 1905; House 1883-89.

WILKINS, William (D Pa.) Dec. 20, 1779-June 23, 1865; Senate 1831-June 30, 1834; House 1843-Feb. 14, 1844; (1831-34 Democrat/Anti Mason, 1843-44 Democrat); Secy. of War 1844-45.

WILKINSON, Morton Smith (R Minn.) Jan. 22, 1819-Feb. 4, 1894; Senate 1859-65; House 1869-71.

WILKINSON, Theodore Stark (D La.) Dec. 18, 1847-Feb. 1, 1921; House 1887-91.

WILLARD, Charles Wesley (R Vt.) June 18, 1827-June 8, 1880; House 1869-75.

WILLARD, George (R Mich.) March 20, 1824-March 26, 1901; House 1873-77.

WILLCOX, Washington Frederick (D Conn.) Aug. 22, 1834-March 8, 1909; House 1889-93.

WILLETT, William Forte Jr. (D N.Y.) Nov. 27, 1869-Feb. 12, 1938; House 1907-11.

WILLEY, Calvin (D Conn.) Sept. 15, 1776-Aug. 23, 1858; Senate May 4, 1825-31.

WILLEY, Earle Dukes (R Del.) July 21, 1889-March 17, 1950; House 1943-45.

WILLEY, Waitman Thomas (— Va./R W.Va.) Oct. 18, 1811-May 2, 1900; Senate July 9, 1861-63 (Va.); Aug. 4, 1863-71 (W.Va.).

WILLFORD, Albert Clinton (D Iowa) Sept. 21, 1877-March 10, 1937; House 1933-35.

WILLIAMS, Abram Pease (R Calif.) Feb. 3, 1832-Oct. 17, 1911; Senate Aug. 4, 1886-87.

WILLIAMS, Alpheus Starkey (D Mich.) Sept. 20, 1810-Dec. 20, 1878; House 1875-Dec. 20, 1878.

WILLIAMS, Andrew (R N.Y.) Aug. 27, 1828-Oct. 6, 1907; House 1875-79.

WILLIAMS, Archibald Hunter Arrington (nephew of Archibald Hunter Arrington) (D N.C.) Oct. 22, 1842-Sept. 5, 1895; House 1891-93.

WILLIAMS, Arthur Bruce (R Mich.) Jan. 27, 1872-May 1, 1925; House June 19, 1923-May 1, 1925.

WILLIAMS, Benjamin (— N.C.) Jan. 1, 1751-July 20, 1814; House 1793-95; Gov. 1799-1802, 1807-08.

WILLIAMS, Charles Grandison (R Wis.) Oct. 18, 1829-March 30, 1892; House 1873-83.

WILLIAMS, Christopher Harris (grandfather of John Sharp Williams) (W Tenn.) Dec. 18, 1798-Nov. 27, 1857; House 1837-43, 1849-53.

WILLIAMS, Clyde (D Mo.) Oct. 13, 1873-Nov. 12, 1954; House 1927-29; 1931-43.

WILLIAMS, David Rogerson (D S.C.) March 8, 1776-Nov. 17, 1830; House 1805-09, 1811-13; Gov. 1814-16.

WILLIAMS, Elihu Stephen (R Ohio) Jan. 24, 1835-Dec. 1, 1903; House 1887-91.

WILLIAMS, George Fred (D Mass.) July 10, 1852-July 11, 1932; House 1891-93.

WILLIAMS, George Henry (UR Ore.) March 23, 1823-April 4, 1910; Senate 1865-71; Atty. Gen. 1872-75.

WILLIAMS, George Howard (R Mo.) Dec. 1, 1871-Nov. 25, 1963; Senate May 25, 1925-Dec. 5, 1926.

WILLIAMS, George Short (R Del.) Oct. 21, 1877-Nov. 22, 1961; House 1939-41.

WILLIAMS, Guinn (D Texas) April 22, 1871-Jan. 9, 1948; House May 13, 1922-33.

WILLIAMS, Harrison Arlington Jr. (D N.J.) Dec. 10, 1919- —; House Nov. 3, 1953-57; Senate 1959-March 11, 1982.

WILLIAMS, Henry (D Mass.) Nov. 30, 1805-May 8, 1887; House 1839-41, 1843-45.

WILLIAMS, Hezekiah (D Maine) July 28, 1798-Oct. 23, 1856; House 1845-49.

WILLIAMS, Isaac Jr. (D N.Y.) April 5, 1777-Nov. 9, 1860; House Dec. 20, 1813-15, 1817-19, 1823-25.

WILLIAMS, James (D Del.) Aug. 4, 1825-April 12, 1899; House 1875-79.

WILLIAMS, James Douglas (D Ind.) Jan. 16, 1808-Nov. 20, 1880; House 1875-Dec. 1, 1876; Gov. 1877-80.

WILLIAMS, James Robert (D Ill.) Dec. 27, 1850-Nov. 8, 1923; House Dec. 2, 1889-95, 1899-1905.

WILLIAMS, James Wray (D Md.) Oct. 8, 1792-Dec. 2, 1842; House 1841-Dec. 2, 1842.

WILLIAMS, Jared (JD Va.) March 4, 1766-Jan. 2, 1831; House 1819-25.

WILLIAMS, Jared Warner (D N.H.) Dec. 22, 1796-Sept. 29, 1864; House 1837-41; Senate Nov. 29, 1853-July 15, 1854; Gov. 1847-49.

WILLIAMS, Jeremiah Norman (D Ala.) May 29, 1829-May 8, 1915; House 1875-79.

WILLIAMS, John (— N.Y.) Sept. 1752-July 22, 1806; House 1795-99.

WILLIAMS, John (brother of Lewis Williams and Robert Williams, father of Joseph Lanier Williams, cousin of Marmaduke Williams) (— Tenn.) Jan. 29, 1778-Aug. 10, 1837; Senate Oct. 10, 1815-23.

WILLIAMS, John (D N.Y.) Jan. 7, 1807-March 26, 1875; House 1855-57.

WILLIAMS, John Bell (D Miss.) Dec. 4, 1918-March 25, 1983; House 1947-Jan. 16, 1968; Gov. 1968-72.

WILLIAMS, John James (R Del.) May 17, 1904- —; Senate 1947-Dec. 31, 1970.

WILLIAMS, John McKeown Snow (R Mass.) Aug. 13, 1818-March 19, 1886; House 1873-75.

WILLIAMS, John Sharp (grandson of Christopher Harris Williams) (D Miss.) July 30, 1854-Sept. 27, 1932; House 1893-1909; Senate 1911-23.

WILLIAMS, John Stuart (D Ky.) July 10, 1818-July 17, 1898; Senate 1879-85.

WILLIAMS, Jonathan (— Pa.) May 20, 1750-May 16, 1815; House March 4-May 16, 1815.

WILLIAMS, Joseph Lanier (son of John Williams of Tenn.) (W Tenn.) Oct. 23, 1810-Dec. 14, 1865; House 1837-43.

WILLIAMS, Lawrence Gordon (R Pa.) Sept. 15, 1913-July 13, 1975; House 1967-75.

WILLIAMS, Lemuel (— Mass.) June 18, 1747-Nov. 8, 1828; House 1799-1805.

WILLIAMS, Lewis (brother of John Williams of Tenn. and Robert Williams, cousin of Marmaduke Williams) (— N.C.) Feb. 1, 1782-Feb. 23, 1842; House 1815-Feb. 23, 1842.

WILLIAMS, Lyle (R Ohio) Aug. 23, 1942-—; House 1979-85.

WILLIAMS, Marmaduke (cousin of John Williams of Tenn., Lewis Williams and Robert Williams) (D N.C.) April 6, 1774-Oct. 29, 1850; House 1803-09.

WILLIAMS, Morgan B. (R Pa.) Sept. 17, 1831-Oct. 13, 1903; House 1897-99.

WILLIAMS, Nathan (D N.Y.) Dec. 19, 1773-Sept. 25, 1835; House 1805-07

WILLIAMS, Pat (D Mont.) Oct. 30, 1937-—; House 1979-—.

WILLIAMS, Reuel (D Maine) June 2, 1783-July 25, 1862; Senate 1837-Feb. 15, 1843.

WILLIAMS, Richard (R Ore.) Nov. 15, 1836-June 19, 1914; House 1877-79.

WILLIAMS, Robert (brother of John Williams of Tenn. and Lewis Williams, cousin of Marmaduke Williams) (— N.C.) July 12, 1773-Jan. 25, 1836; House 1797-1803; Gov. (Miss. Terr.) 1805-09.

WILLIAMS, Seward Henry (R Ohio) Nov. 7, 1870-Sept. 2, 1922; House 1915-17.

WILLIAMS, Sherrod (W Ky.) 1804-?; House 1835-41.

WILLIAMS, Thomas (R Pa.) Aug. 28, 1806-June 16, 1872; House 1863-69.

WILLIAMS, Thomas (D Ala.) Aug. 11, 1825-April 13, 1903; House 1879-85.

WILLIAMS, Thomas Hickman (D Miss.) Jan. 20, 1801-May 3, 1851; Senate Nov. 12, 1838-39.

WILLIAMS, Thomas Hill (D Miss.) 1780-1840; Senate Dec. 10, 1817-29.

WILLIAMS, Thomas Scott (— Conn.) June 26, 1777-Dec. 22, 1861; House 1817-19.

WILLIAMS, Thomas Sutler (R Ill.) Feb. 14, 1872-April 5, 1940; House 1915-Nov. 11, 1929.

WILLIAMS, Thomas Wheeler (W Conn.) Sept. 28, 1789-Dec. 31, 1874; House 1839-43.

WILLIAMS, William (D N.Y.) Sept. 6, 1815-Sept. 10, 1876; House 1871-73.

WILLIAMS, William (R Ind.) May 11, 1821-April 22, 1896; House 1867-75.

WILLIAMS, William Brewster (R Mich.) July 28, 1826-March 4, 1905; House Dec. 1, 1873-77.

WILLIAMS, William Elza (D Ill.) May 5, 1857-Sept. 13, 1921; House 1899-1901, 1913-17.

WILLIAMS, William Robert (R N.Y.) Aug. 11, 1884-May 9, 1972; House 1951-59.

WILLIAMSON, Ben Mitchell (D Ky.) Oct. 16, 1864-June 23, 1941; Senate Dec. 1, 1930-31.

WILLIAMSON, Hugh (F N.C.) Dec. 5, 1735-May 22, 1819; House 1789-93; Cont. Cong. 1782-85, 1787-88.

WILLIAMSON, John Newton (R Ore.) Nov. 8, 1855-Aug. 29, 1943; House 1903-07.

WILLIAMSON, William (R S.D.) Oct. 7, 1875-July 15, 1972; House 1921-33.

WILLIAMSON, William Durkee (D Maine) July 31, 1779-May 27, 1846; House 1821-23; Gov. 1821.

WILLIE, Asa Hoxie (D Texas) Oct. 11, 1829-March 16, 1899; House 1873-75.

WILLIS, Albert Shelby (D Ky.) Jan. 22, 1843-Jan. 6, 1897; House 1877-87.

WILLIS, Benjamin Albertson (D N.Y.) March 24, 1840-Oct. 14, 1886; House 1875-79.

WILLIS, Edwin Edward (D La.) Oct. 2, 1904-Oct. 24, 1972; House 1949-69.

WILLIS, Francis (— Ga.) Jan. 5, 1745-Jan. 25, 1829; House 1791-93.

WILLIS, Frank Bartlett (R Ohio) Dec. 28, 1871-March 30, 1928; House 1911-Jan. 9, 1915; Senate Jan. 14, 1921-March 30, 1928; Gov. 1915-17.

WILLIS, Jonathan Spencer (R Del.) April 5, 1830-Nov. 24, 1903; House 1895-97.

WILLIS, Raymond Eugene (R Ind.) Aug. 11, 1875-March 21, 1956; Senate 1941-47.

WILLITS, Edwin (R Mich.) April 24, 1830-Oct. 22, 1896; House 1877-83.

WILLOUGHBY, Westel Jr. (D N.Y.) Nov. 20, 1769-Oct. 3, 1844; House Dec. 13, 1815-17.

WILMOT, David (R Pa.) Jan. 20, 1814-March 16, 1868; House 1845-51; Senate March 14, 1861-63 (1845-51 Democrat, 1861-63 Republican).

WILSHIRE, William Wallace (C Ark.) Sept. 8, 1830-Aug. 19, 1888; House 1873-June 16, 1874, 1875-77 (1873-74 Republican, 1875-77 Conservative).

Biographical Index

WILSON, Alexander (— Va.) ?-?; House Dec. 4, 1804-09.

WILSON, Benjamin (D W.Va.) April 30, 1825-April 26, 1901; House 1875-83.

WILSON, Charles (D Texas) June 1, 1933-—; House 1973-—.

WILSON, Charles Herbert (D Calif.) Feb. 15, 1917-July 21, 1984; House 1963-81.

WILSON, Earl (R Ind.) April 18, 1906-—; House 1941-59, 1961-65.

WILSON, Edgar (Sil.R/D Idaho) Feb. 25, 1861-Jan. 3, 1915; House 1895-97, 1899-1901 (1895-97 Republican, 1899-1901 Silver Republican/Democrat).

WILSON, Edgar Campbell (son of Thomas Wilson of Va., father of Eugene McLanahan Wilson) (W Va.) Oct. 18, 1800-April 24, 1860; House 1833-35.

WILSON, Emmett (grandson of Augustus Emmett Maxwell) (D Fla.) Sept. 17, 1882-May 29, 1918; House 1913-17.

WILSON, Ephraim King (father of the following) (D Md.) Sept. 15, 1771-Jan. 2, 1834; House 1827-31.

WILSON, Ephraim King (son of the preceding) (D Md.) Dec. 22, 1821-Feb. 24, 1891; House 1873-75; Senate 1885-Feb. 24, 1891.

WILSON, Eugene McLanahan (son of Edgar Campbell Wilson, grandson of Thomas Wilson of Va., great-grandson of Isaac Griffin) (D Minn.) Dec. 25, 1833-April 10, 1890; House 1869-71.

WILSON, Francis Henry (R N.Y.) Feb. 11, 1844-Sept. 25, 1910; House 1895-Sept. 30, 1897.

WILSON, Frank Eugene (D N.Y.) Dec. 22, 1857-July 12, 1935; House 1899-1905, 1911-15.

WILSON, George Allison (R Iowa) April 1, 1884-Sept. 8, 1953; Senate Jan. 14, 1943-49; Gov. 1939-43.

WILSON, George Howard (D Okla.) Aug. 21, 1905-—; House 1949-51.

WILSON, George Washington (R Ohio) Feb. 22, 1840-Nov. 27, 1909; House 1893-97.

WILSON, Henry (D Pa.) 1778-Aug. 14, 1826; House 1823-Aug. 14, 1826.

WILSON, Henry (FS/AP/D Mass.) Feb. 16, 1812-Nov. 22, 1875; Senate Jan. 31, 1855-73; Vice Pres. 1873-75 (Republican).

WILSON, Isaac (— N.Y.) June 25, 1780-Oct. 25, 1848; House 1823-Jan. 7, 1824.

WILSON, James (father of the following) (F N.H.) Aug. 16, 1766-Jan. 4, 1839; House 1809-11.

WILSON, James (son of the preceding) (W N.H.) March 18, 1797-May 29, 1881; House 1847-Sept. 9, 1850.

WILSON, James (D Pa.) April 28, 1779-July 19, 1868; House 1823-39.

WILSON, James (father of John Lockwood Wilson) (R Ind.) April 9, 1825-Aug. 8, 1867; House 1857-61.

WILSON, James (R Iowa) Aug. 16, 1835-Aug. 26, 1920; House 1873-77, 1883-85; Secy. of Agriculture 1897-1913.

WILSON, James Clifton (D Texas) June 21, 1874-Aug. 3, 1951; House 1917-19.

WILSON, James Falconer (R Iowa) Oct. 19, 1828-April 22, 1895; House Oct. 8, 1861-69; Senate 1883-95.

WILSON, James Jefferson (D N.J.) 1775-July 28, 1834; Senate 1815-Jan. 8, 1821.

WILSON, Jeremiah Morrow (R Ind.) Nov. 25, 1828-Sept. 24, 1901; House 1871-75.

WILSON, John (— S.C.) Aug. 11, 1773-Aug. 13, 1828; House 1821-27.

WILSON, John (F Mass.) Jan. 10, 1777-Aug. 9, 1848; House 1813-15, 1817-19.

WILSON, John Frank (D Ariz.) May 7, 1846-April 7, 1911; House (Terr. Del.) 1899-1901, 1903-05.

WILSON, John Haden (D Pa.) Aug. 20, 1867-Jan. 28, 1946; House 1919-21.

WILSON, John Henry (R Ky.) Jan. 30, 1846-Jan. 14, 1923; House 1889-93.

WILSON, John Lockwood (son of James Wilson of Ind.) (R Wash.) Aug. 7, 1850-Nov. 6, 1912; House Nov. 20, 1889-Feb. 18, 1895; Senate Feb. 19, 1895-99.

WILSON, John Thomas (R Ohio) April 16, 1811-Oct. 6, 1891; House 1867-73.

WILSON, Joseph Franklin (D Texas) March 18, 1901-Oct. 13, 1968; House 1947-55.

WILSON, Joseph Gardner (cousin of James Willis Nesmith) (R Ore.) Dec. 13, 1826-July 2, 1873; House March 4-July 2, 1873.

WILSON, Nathan (D N.Y.) Dec. 23, 1758-July 25, 1834; House June 3, 1808-09.

WILSON, Pete (R Calif.) Aug. 23, 1933-—; Senate 1983-—.

WILSON, Riley Joseph (D La.) Nov. 12, 1871-Feb. 23, 1946; House 1915-37.

WILSON, Robert (U Mo.) Nov. 1803-May 10, 1870; Senate Jan. 17, 1862-Nov. 13, 1863

WILSON, Robert Carlton (Bob) (R Calif.) April 5, 1916-—; House 1953-81.

WILSON, Robert Patterson Clark (D Mo.) Aug. 8, 1834-Dec. 21, 1916; House Dec. 2, 1889-93.

WILSON, Stanyarne (D S.C.) Jan. 10, 1860-Feb. 14, 1928; House 1895-1901.

WILSON, Stephen Fowler (R Pa.) Sept. 4, 1821-March 30, 1897; House 1865-69.

WILSON, Thomas (father of Edgar Campbell Wilson, grandfather of Eugene McLanahan Wilson) (F Va.) Sept. 11, 1765-Jan. 24, 1826; House 1811-13.

WILSON, Thomas (D Pa.) 1772-Oct. 4, 1824; House May 4, 1813-17.

WILSON, Thomas (D Minn.) May 16, 1827-April 3, 1910; House 1887-89.

WILSON, Thomas Webber (D Miss.) Jan. 24, 1893-Jan. 31, 1948; House 1923-29.

WILSON, William (— Pa.) ?-?; House 1815-19.

WILSON, William (— Ohio) March 19, 1773-June 6, 1827; House 1823-June 6, 1827.

WILSON, William Bauchop (D Pa.) April 2, 1862-May 25, 1934; House 1907-13; Secy. of Labor 1913-21.

WILSON, William Edward (D Ind.) March 9, 1870-Sept. 29, 1948; House 1923-25.

WILSON, William Henry (R Pa.) Dec. 6, 1877-Aug. 11, 1937; House 1935-37.

WILSON, William Lyne (D W.Va.) May 3, 1843-Oct. 17, 1900; House 1883-95; Postmaster Gen. 1895-97.

WILSON, William Warfield (R Ill.) March 2, 1868-July 22, 1942; House 1903-13, 1915-21.

WINNANS, Edwin Baruch (D Mich.) May 16, 1826-July 4, 1894; House 1883-87; Gov. 1891-93.

WINANS, James January (R Ohio) June 7, 1818-April 28, 1879; House 1869-71.

WINANS, John (ID Wis.) Sept. 27, 1831-Jan. 17, 1907; House 1883-85.

WINCHESTER, Boyd (D Ky.) Sept. 23, 1836-May 18, 1923; House 1869-73.

WINDOM, William (R Minn.) May 10, 1827-Jan. 29, 1891; House 1859-69; Senate July 15, 1870-Jan. 22, 1871; March 4, 1871-March 7, 1881; Nov. 15, 1881-83; Secy. of the Treasury 1881, 1889-91.

WINFIELD, Charles Henry (D N.Y.) April 22, 1822-June 10, 1888; House 1863-67.

WING, Austin Eli (W Mich.) Feb. 3, 1792-Aug. 27, 1849; House (Terr. Del.) 1825-29, 1831-33.

WINGATE, Joseph Ferdinand (D Maine) June 29, 1786-?; House 1827-31.

WINGATE, Paine (F N.H.) May 14, 1739-March 7, 1838; Senate 1789-93; House 1793-95; Cont. Cong. 1787-88.

WINGO, Effiegene (Locke) (widow of Otis Theodore Wingo, great-great-great-granddaughter of Matthew Locke) (D Ark.) April 13, 1883-Sept. 19, 1962; House Nov. 4, 1930-33.

WINGO, Otis Theodore (husband of Effiegene Wingo) (D Ark.) June 18, 1877-Oct. 21, 1930; House 1913-Oct. 21, 1930.

WINN, Larry Jr. (R Kan.) Aug. 22, 1919-—; House 1967-85.

WINN, Richard (D S.C.) 1750-Dec. 19, 1818; House 1793-97, Jan. 24, 1803-13.

WINN, Thomas Elisha (Alliance D Ga.) May 2, 1839-June 5, 1925; House 1891-93.

WINSLOW, Samuel Ellsworth (R Mass.) April 11, 1862-July 11, 1940; House 1913-25.

WINSLOW, Warren (D N.C.) Jan. 1, 1810- Aug. 16, 1862; House 1855-61.

WINSTEAD, William Arthur (D Mass.) Jan. 6, 1904- —; House 1943-65.

WINSTON, Joseph (D N.C.) June 17, 1746-April 21, 1815; House 1793-95, 1803-07.

WINTER, Charles Edwin (R Wyo.) Sept. 13, 1870-April 22, 1948; House 1923-29.

WINTER, Elisha I. (F N.Y.) July 15, 1781-June 30, 1849; House 1813-15.

WINTER, Thomas Daniel (R Kan.) July 7, 1896-Nov. 7, 1951; House 1939-47.

WINTHROP, Robert Charles (W Mass.) May 12, 1809-Nov. 16, 1894; House Nov. 9, 1840-May 25, 1842, Nov. 29, 1842-July 30, 1850; Senate July 30, 1850-Feb. 1, 1851; Speaker, 1847-49.

WIRTH, Timothy Endicott (D Colo.) Sept. 22, 1939- —; House 1975- —.

WISE, George Douglas (cousin of John Sergeant Wise and Richard Alsop Wise, nephew of Henry Alexander Wise) (D Va.) June 4, 1831-Feb. 4, 1898; House 1881-April 10, 1890, 1891-95.

WISE, Henry Alexander (father of John Sergeant Wise and Richard Alsop Wise, uncle of George Douglas Wise) (Tyler D Va.) Dec. 3, 1806-Sept. 12, 1876; House 1833-Feb. 12, 1844 (1833-37 Jackson Democrat, 1837-43 Whig, 1843-44 Tyler Democrat); Gov. 1856-60.

WISE, James Walter (D Ga.) March 3, 1868-Sept. 8, 1925; House 1915-25.

WISE, John Sergeant (son of Henry Alexander Wise, grandson of John Sergeant, brother of Richard Alsop Wise, cousin of George Douglas Wise) (Read. Va.) Dec. 27, 1846-May 12, 1913; House 1883-85.

WISE, Morgan Ringland (D Pa.) June 7, 1825-April 13, 1903; House 1879-83.

WISE, Richard Alsop (son of Henry Alexander Wise, grandson of John Sergeant, brother of John Sergeant Wise, cousin of George Douglas Wise) (R Va.) Sept. 2, 1843-Dec. 21, 1900; House April 26, 1898-99, March 12-Dec. 21, 1900.

WISE, Robert Ellsworth Jr. (D W.Va.) Jan. 6, 1948- —; House 1983- —.

WITCHER, John Seashoal (R W.Va.) July 15, 1839-July 8, 1906; House 1869-71.

WITHERELL, James (D Vt.) June 16, 1759-Jan. 9, 1838; House 1807-May 1, 1808.

WITHERS, Garrett Lee (D Ky.) June 21, 1884-April 30, 1953; Senate Jan. 20, 1949-Nov. 26, 1950; House Aug. 2, 1952-April 30, 1953.

WITHERS, Robert Enoch (cousin of Thomas Withers Chinn) (C Va.) Sept. 18, 1821-Sept. 21, 1907; Senate 1875-81.

WITHERSPOON, Robert (great-great-grandfather of Robert Witherspoon Hemphill) (D S.C.) Jan. 29, 1767-Oct. 11, 1837; House 1809-11.

WITHERSPOON, Samuel Andrew (D Miss.) May 4, 1855-Nov. 24, 1915; House 1911-Nov. 24, 1915.

WITHROW, Gardner Robert (R Wis.) Oct. 5, 1892-Sept. 23, 1964; House 1931-39, 1949-61 (1931-35 Republican, 1935-39 Progressive, 1949-61 Republican).

WITTE, William Henry (D Pa.) Oct. 4, 1817-Nov. 24, 1876; House 1853-55.

WOFFORD, Thomas Albert (D S.C.) Sept. 27, 1908-Feb. 25, 1978; Senate April 5-Nov. 6, 1956.

WOLCOTT, Edward Oliver (R Colo.) March 26, 1848-March 1, 1905; Senate 1889-1901.

WOLCOTT, Jesse Paine (R Mich.) March 3, 1893-Jan. 28, 1969; House 1931-57.

WOLCOTT, Josiah Oliver (D Del.) Oct. 31, 1877-Nov. 11, 1938; Senate 1917-July 2, 1921.

WOLD, John Schiller (R Wyo.) Aug. 31, 1916- —; House 1969-71.

WOLF, Frank R. (R Va.) Jan. 30, 1939- —; House 1981- —.

WOLF, George (D Pa.) Aug. 12, 1777-March 11, 1840; House Dec. 9, 1824-29; Gov. 1829-35.

WOLF, Harry Benjamin (D Md.) June 16, 1880-Feb. 17, 1944; House 1907-09.

WOLF, Leonard George (D Iowa) Oct. 29, 1925-March 28, 1970; House 1959-61.

WOLF, William Penn (R Iowa) Dec. 1, 1833-Sept. 19, 1896; House Dec. 6, 1870-71.

WOLFE, Simeon Kalfius (D Ind.) Feb. 14, 1824-Nov. 18, 1888; House 1873-75.

WOLFENDEN, James (R Pa.) July 25, 1889-April 8, 1949; House Nov. 6, 1928-47.

WOLFF, Joseph Scott (D Mo.) June 14, 1878-Feb. 27, 1958; House 1923-25.

WOLFF, Lester Lionel (D N.Y.) Jan. 4, 1919- —; House 1965-81.

WOLFORD, Frank Lane (D Ky.) Sept. 2, 1817-Aug. 2, 1895; House 1883-87.

WOLPE, Howard Eliot (D Mich.) Nov. 2, 1939- —; House 1979- —.

WOLVERTON, Charles Anderson (R N.J.) Oct. 24, 1880-May 16, 1969; House 1927-59.

WOLVERTON, John Marshall (R W.Va.) Jan. 31, 1872-Aug. 19, 1944; House 1925-27, 1929-31.

WOLVERTON, Simon Peter (D Pa.) Jan. 28, 1837-Oct. 25, 1910; House 1891-95.

WON PAT, Antonio Borja (D Guam) Dec. 10, 1908- —; House 1973-85.

WOOD, Abiel (F Mass.) July 22, 1772-Oct. 26, 1834; House 1813-15.

WOOD, Alan Jr. (nephew of John Wood) (R Pa.) July 6, 1834-Oct. 31, 1902; House 1875-77.

WOOD, Amos Eastman (D Ohio) Jan. 2, 1810-Nov. 19, 1850; House Dec. 3, 1849-Nov. 19, 1850.

WOOD, Benjamin (brother of Fernando Wood) (D N.Y.) Oct. 13, 1820-Feb. 21, 1900; House 1861-65; 1881-83.

WOOD, Benson (R Ill.) March 31, 1839-Aug. 27, 1915; House 1895-97.

WOOD, Bradford Ripley (D N.Y.) Sept. 3, 1800-Sept. 26, 1889; House 1845-47.

WOOD, Ernest Edward (D Mo.) Aug. 24, 1875-Jan. 10, 1952; House 1905-June 23, 1906.

WOOD, Fernando (brother of Benjamin Wood) (D N.Y.) June 14, 1812-Feb. 13, 1881; House 1841-43, 1863-65, 1867-Feb. 13, 1881 (1841-43 Tammany Democrat, 1863-65, 1867-81 Democrat).

WOOD, Ira Wells (R N.J.) June 19, 1856-Oct. 5, 1931; House Nov. 8, 1904-13.

WOOD, John (uncle of Alan Wood Jr.) (R Pa.) Sept. 6, 1816-May 28, 1898; House 1859-61.

WOOD, John Jacob (JD N.Y.) Feb. 16, 1784-May 20, 1874; House 1827-29.

WOOD, John M. (R Maine) Nov. 17, 1813-Dec. 24, 1864; House 1855-59.

WOOD, John Stephens (D Ga.) Feb. 8, 1885-Sept. 12, 1968; House 1931-35, 1945-53.

WOOD, John Travers (R Idaho) Nov. 25, 1878-Nov. 2, 1954; House 1951-53.

WOOD, Reuben Terrell (D Mo.) Aug. 7, 1884-July 16, 1955; House 1933-41.

WOOD, Silas (D N.Y.) Sept. 14, 1769-March 2, 1847; House 1819-29.

WOOD, Thomas Jefferson (D Ind.) Sept. 30, 1844-Oct. 13, 1908; House 1883-85.

WOOD, Walter Abbott (R N.Y.) Oct. 23, 1815-Jan. 15, 1892; House 1879-83.

WOOD, William Robert (R Ind.) Jan. 5, 1861-March 7, 1933; House 1915-33.

WOODARD, Frederick Augustus (D N.C.) Feb. 12, 1854-May 8, 1915; House 1893-97.

WOODBRIDGE, Frederick Enoch (R Vt.) Aug. 29, 1818-April 25, 1888; House 1863-69.

WOODBRIDGE, William W. (W/D Mich.) Aug. 20, 1780-Oct. 20, 1861; House (Terr. Del.) 1819-Aug. 9, 1820; Senate 1841-47; Gov. 1840-41.

WOODBURN, William (R Nev.) April 14, 1838-Jan. 15, 1915; House 1875-77, 1885-89.

WOODBURY, Levi (D N.H.) Dec. 22, 1789-Sept. 4, 1851; Senate March 16, 1825-31, 1841-Nov. 20, 1845; Gov. 1823-24; Secy. of the Navy 1831-34; Secy. of the Treasury 1834-41; Assoc. Justice Supreme Court 1845-51.

WOODCOCK, David (D N.Y.) 1785-Sept. 18, 1835; House 1821-23, 1827-29.

WOODFORD, Stewart Lyndon (R N.Y.) Sept. 3, 1835-Feb. 14, 1913; House 1873-July 1, 1874.

WOODHOUSE, Chase Going (D Conn.) 1890-Dec. 12, 1984; House 1945-47, 1949-51.

WOODMAN, Charles Walhart (R Ill.) March 11, 1844-March 18, 1898; House 1895-97.

WOODRUFF, George Catlin (D Conn.) Dec. 1, 1805-Nov. 21, 1885; House 1861-63.

WOODRUFF, John (AP Conn.) Feb. 12, 1826-May 20, 1868; House 1855-57; 1859-61.

WOODRUFF, Roy Orchard (R Mich.) March 14, 1876-Feb. 12, 1953; House 1913-15, 1921-53 (1913-15 Progressive Republican, 1921-53 Republican).

WOODRUFF, Thomas M. (D N.Y.) May 3, 1804-March 28, 1855; House 1845-47.

WOODRUM, Clifton Alexander (D Va.) April 27, 1887-Oct. 6, 1950; House 1923-Dec. 31, 1945.

WOODS, Frank Plowman (R Iowa) Dec. 11, 1868-April 25, 1944; House 1909-19.

WOODS, Henry (brother of John Woods of Pa.) (— Pa.) 1764-1826; House 1799-1803.

WOODS, James Pleasant (D Va.) Feb. 4, 1868-July 7, 1948; House Feb. 25, 1919-23.

WOODS, John (brother of Henry Woods) (F Pa.) 1761-Dec. 16, 1816; House (elected 1814 but never served).

WOODS, John (W Ohio) Oct. 18, 1794-July 30, 1855; House 1825-29.

WOODS, Samuel Davis (R Calif.) Sept. 19, 1845-Dec. 24, 1915; House Dec. 3, 1900-03.

WOODS, William (D N.Y.) 1790-Aug. 7, 1837; House Nov. 3, 1823-25.

WOODSON, Samuel Hughes (father of the following) (— Ky.) Sept. 15, 1777-July 28, 1827; House 1821-23.

WOODSON, Samuel Hughes (son of the preceding) (AP Mo.) Oct. 24, 1815-June 23, 1881; House 1857-61.

WOODWARD, George Washington (D Pa.) March 26, 1809-May 10, 1875; House Nov. 21, 1867-71.

WOODWARD, Gilbert Motier (D Wis.) Dec. 25, 1835-March 13, 1913; House 1883-85.

WOODWARD, Joseph Addison (D S.C.) April 11, 1806-Aug. 3, 1885; House 1843-53.

WOODWARD, William (— S.C.) ?-?; House 1815-17.

WOODWORTH, James Hutchinson (R Ill.) Dec. 4, 1804-March 26, 1869; House 1855-57.

WOODWORTH, Laurin Dewey (R Ohio) Sept. 10, 1837-March 13, 1897; House 1873-77.

WOODWORTH, William W. (D N.Y.) March 16, 1807-Feb. 13, 1873; House 1845-47.

WOODYARD, Harry Chapman (R W.Va.) Nov. 13, 1867-June 21, 1929; House 1903-11, Nov. 7, 1916-23, 1925-27.

WOOMER, Ephraim Milton (R Pa.) Jan. 14, 1844-Nov. 29, 1897; House 1893-97.

WOOTEN, Dudley Goodall (D Texas) June 19, 1860-Feb. 7, 1929; House July 13, 1901-03.

WORCESTER, Samuel Thomas (R Ohio) Aug. 30, 1804-Dec. 6, 1882; House July 4, 1861-63.

WORD, Thomas Jefferson (W Miss.) ?-?; House May 30, 1838-39.

WORKS, John Downey (R Calif.) March 29, 1847-June 6, 1928; Senate 1911-17.

WORLEY, Francis Eugene (D Texas) Oct. 10, 1908-Dec. 17, 1974; House 1941-April 3, 1950.

WORMAN, Ludwig (F Pa.) 1761-Oct. 17, 1822; House 1821-Oct. 17, 1822.

WORTENDYKE, Jacob Reynier (D N.J.) Nov. 27, 1818-Nov. 7, 1868; House 1857-59.

WORTHINGTON, Henry Gaither (R Nev.) Feb. 9, 1828-July 29, 1909; House Oct. 31, 1864-65.

WORTHINGTON, John Tolley Hood (D Md.) Nov. 1, 1788-April 27, 1849; House 1831-33, 1837-41.

WORTHINGTON, Nicholas Ellsworth (D Ill.) March 30, 1836-March 4, 1916; House 1883-87.

WORTHINGTON, Thomas (D Ohio) July 16, 1773-June 20, 1827; Senate April 1, 1803-07, Dec. 15, 1810-Dec. 1, 1814; Gov. 1814-18.

WORTHINGTON, Thomas Contee (nephew of Benjamin Contee) (D Md.) Nov. 25, 1782-April 12, 1847; House 1825-27.

WORTLEY, George (R N.Y.) Dec. 8, 1928-—; House 1981-—.

WREN, Thomas (R Nev.) Jan. 2, 1826-Feb. 5, 1904; House 1877-79.

WRIGHT, Ashley Bascom (R Mass.) May 25, 1841-Aug. 14, 1897; House 1893-Aug. 14, 1897.

WRIGHT, Augustus Romaldus (D Ga.) June 16, 1813-March 31, 1891; House 1857-59.

WRIGHT, Charles Frederick (brother of Myron Benjamin Wright) (R Pa.) May 3, 1856-Nov. 10, 1925; House 1899-1905.

WRIGHT, Daniel Boone (D Miss.) Feb. 17, 1812-Dec. 27, 1887; House 1853-57.

WRIGHT, Edwin Ruthvin Vincent (D N.J.) Jan. 2, 1812-Jan. 21, 1871; House 1865-67.

WRIGHT, George Grover (brother of Joseph Albert Wright) (R Iowa) March 24, 1820-Jan. 11, 1896; Senate 1871-77.

WRIGHT, George Washington (I Calif.) June 4, 1816-April 7, 1885; House Sept. 11, 1850-51.

WRIGHT, Hendrick Bradley (D Pa.) April 24, 1808-Sept. 2, 1881; House 1853-55; July 4, 1861-63, 1877-81.

WRIGHT, James Assion (D Pa.) Aug. 11, 1902-Nov. 7, 1963; House 1941-45.

WRIGHT, James Claude Jr. (D Texas) Dec. 22, 1922-—; House 1955-—; House majority leader 1977-—.

WRIGHT, John Crafts (Ad.D Ohio) Aug. 17, 1783-Feb. 13, 1861; House 1823-29.

WRIGHT, John Vines (D Tenn.) June 28, 1828-June 11, 1908; House 1855-61.

WRIGHT, Joseph Albert (brother of George Grover Wright) (D Ind.) April 17, 1810-May 11, 1867; House 1843-45; Senate Feb. 24, 1862-Jan. 14, 1863; Gov. 1849-57.

WRIGHT, Myron Benjamin (brother of Charles Frederick Wright) (R Pa.) June 12, 1847-Nov. 13, 1894; House 1889-Nov. 13, 1894.

WRIGHT, Robert (D Md.) Nov. 20, 1752-Sept. 7, 1826; Senate Nov. 19, 1801-Nov. 12, 1806; House Nov. 29, 1810-17, 1821-23; Gov. 1806-09.

WRIGHT, Samuel Gardiner (W N.J.) Nov. 18, 1781-July 30, 1845; House March 4-July 30, 1845.

WRIGHT, Silas Jr. (D N.Y.) May 24, 1795-Aug. 27, 1847; House 1827-Feb. 16, 1829, Senate Jan. 4, 1833-Nov. 26, 1844; Gov. 1845-47.

WRIGHT, William (D N.J.) Nov. 13, 1790-Nov. 1, 1866; House 1843-47; Senate 1853-59, 1863-Nov. 1, 1866 (1843-47 Clay Whig, 1853-66 Democrat).

WRIGHT, William Carter (D Ga.) Jan. 6, 1866-June 11, 1933; House Jan. 24, 1918-33.

WURTS, John (NR Pa.) Aug. 13, 1792-April 23, 1861; House 1825-27.

WURZBACH, Harry McLeary (uncle of Robert Christian Eckhardt) (R Texas) May 19, 1874-Nov. 6, 1931; House 1921-29, Feb. 10, 1930-Nov. 6, 1931.

WYANT, Adam Martin (R Pa.) Sept. 15, 1869-Jan. 5, 1935; House 1921-33.

WYATT, Joseph Peyton Jr. (D Texas) Oct. 12, 1941-—; House 1979-81.

WYATT, Wendell (R Ore.) June 15, 1917-—; House Nov. 3, 1964-75.

WYDEN, Ron (D Ore.) May 3, 1949-—; House 1981-—.

WYDLER, John Waldemar (R N.Y.) June 9, 1924-—; House 1963-81.

WYLIE, Chalmers Pangburn (R Ohio) Nov. 23, 1920-—; House 1967-—.

WYMAN, Louis Crosby (R N.H.) March 16, 1917-—; House 1963-65, 1967-Dec. 31, 1974; Senate Dec. 31, 1974-Jan. 3, 1975.

WYNKOOP, Henry (— Pa.) March 2, 1737-March 25, 1816; House 1789-91; Cont. Cong. 1779-83.

WYNN, William Joseph (UL/D Calif.) June 12, 1860-Jan. 4, 1935; House 1903-05.

WYNNS, Thomas (F N.C.) 1764-June 3, 1825; House Dec. 7, 1802-07.

Y

YANCEY, Bartlett (cousin of John Kerr) (— N.C.) Feb. 19, 1785-Aug. 30, 1828; House 1813-17.

YANCEY, Joel (D Ky.) Oct. 21, 1773-April 1838; House 1827-31.

YANCEY, William Lowndes (uncle of Joseph Haynsworth Earle) (D Ala.) Aug. 10, 1814-July 28, 1863; House Dec. 2, 1844-Sept. 1, 1846.

YANGCO, Teodoro Rafael (Nat. P.I.) Nov. 9, 1861-April 20, 1939; House (Res. Comm.) 1917-20.

YAPLE, George Lewis (U Mich.) Feb. 20, 1851-Dec. 16, 1939; House 1883-85.

YARBOROUGH, Ralph Webster (D Texas) June 8, 1903- —; Senate April 29, 1957-71.

YARDLEY, Robert Morris (R Pa.) Oct. 9, 1850-Dec. 8, 1902; House 1887-91.

YATES, John Barentse (D N.Y.) Feb. 1, 1784-July 10, 1836; House 1815-17.

YATES, Richard (father of the following) (UR Ill.) Jan. 18, 1818-Nov. 27, 1873; House 1851-55; Senate 1865-71; Gov. 1861-65 (1851-55 Whig, 1865-71 Union Republican).

YATES, Richard (son of the preceding) (R Ill.) Dec. 12, 1860-April 11, 1936; House 1919-33; Gov. 1901-05.

YATES, Sidney Richard (D Ill.) Aug. 27, 1909- —; House 1949-63, 1965- —.

YATRON, Gus (D Pa.) Oct. 16, 1927- —; House 1969- —.

YEAMAN, George Helm (U Ky.) Nov. 1, 1829-Feb. 23, 1908; House Dec. 1, 1862-65.

YEATES, Jesse Johnson (D N.C.) May 29, 1829-Sept. 5, 1892; House 1875-79; Jan. 29-March 3, 1881.

YELL, Archibald (VBD Ark.) 1797-Feb. 22, 1847; House Aug. 1, 1836-39; 1845-July 1, 1846; Gov. 1840-44.

YOAKUM, Charles Henderson (D Texas) July 10, 1849-Jan. 1, 1909; House 1895-97.

YOCUM, Seth Hartman (R Pa.) Aug. 2, 1834-April 19, 1895; House 1879-81.

YODER, Samuel S. (D Ohio) Aug. 16, 1841-May 11, 1921; House 1887-91.

YON, Thomas Alva (D Fla.) March 14, 1882-Feb. 16, 1971; House 1927-33.

YORK, Tyre (LD N.C.) May 4, 1836-Jan. 28, 1916; House 1883-85.

YORKE, Thomas Jones (W N.J.) March 25, 1801-April 4, 1882; House 1837-39, 1841-43.

YORTY, Samuel William (D Calif.) Oct. 1, 1909- —; House 1951-55.

YOST, Jacob (R Va.) April 1, 1853-Jan. 25, 1933; House 1887-89, 1897-99.

YOST, Jacob Senewell (D Pa.) July 29, 1801-March 7, 1872; House 1843-47.

YOUMANS, Henry Melville (D Mich.) May 15, 1832-July 8, 1920; House 1891-93.

YOUNG, Andrew Jackson (D Ga.) March 12, 1932- —; House 1973-77.

YOUNG, Augustus (W Vt.) March 20, 1784-June 17, 1857; House 1841-43.

YOUNG, Bryan Rust (brother of William Singleton Young, uncle of John Young Brown born in 1835) (D Ky.) Jan. 14, 1800-May 14, 1882; House 1845-47.

YOUNG, Charles William (Bill) (R Fla.) Dec. 16, 1930- —; House 1971- —.

YOUNG, Clarence Clifton (R Nev.) Nov. 7, 1922- —; House 1953-57.

YOUNG, Donald Edwin (R Alaska) June 9, 1933- —; House March 6, 1973- —.

YOUNG, Ebenezer (F Conn.) Dec. 25, 1783-Aug. 18, 1851; House 1829-35.

YOUNG, Edward Lunn (R S.C.) Sept. 7, 1920- —; House 1973-75.

YOUNG, George Morley (R N.D.) Dec. 11, 1870-May 27, 1932; House 1913-Sept. 2, 1924.

YOUNG, Hiram Casey (D Tenn.) Dec. 14, 1828-Aug. 17, 1899; House 1875-81, 1883-85.

YOUNG, Horace Olin (R Mich.) Aug. 4, 1850-Aug. 5, 1917; House March 4, 1903-May 16, 1913.

YOUNG, Isaac Daniel (R Kan.) March 29, 1849-Dec. 10, 1927; House 1911-13.

YOUNG, James (D Texas) July 18, 1866-April 29, 1942; House 1911-21.

YOUNG, James Rankin (R Pa.) March 10, 1847-Dec. 18, 1924; House 1897-1903.

YOUNG, John (W N.Y.) June 12, 1802-April 23, 1852; House Nov. 9, 1836-37, 1841-43; Gov. 1847-49.

YOUNG, John Andrew (D Texas) Nov. 10, 1916- —; House 1957-79.

YOUNG, John Duncan (D Ky.) Sept. 22, 1823-Dec. 26, 1910; House 1873-75.

YOUNG, John Smith (D La.) Nov. 4, 1834-Oct. 11, 1916; House Nov. 5, 1878-79.

YOUNG, Lafayette (R Iowa) May 10, 1848-Nov. 15, 1926; Senate Nov. 12, 1910-April 11, 1911.

YOUNG, Milton Ruben (R N.D.) Dec. 6, 1897-May 31, 1983; Senate March 12, 1945-81.

YOUNG, Pierce Manning Butler (D Ga.) Nov. 15, 1836-July 6, 1896; House July 25, 1868-69, Dec. 22, 1870-75.

YOUNG, Richard (R N.Y.) Aug. 6, 1846-June 9, 1935; House 1909-11.

YOUNG, Richard Montgomery (D Ill.) Feb. 20, 1798-Nov. 28, 1861; Senate 1837-43.

YOUNG, Robert A. (D Mo.) Nov. 27, 1923- —; House 1977- —.

YOUNG, Samuel Hollingsworth (R Ill.) Dec. 26, 1922- —; House 1973-75.

YOUNG, Stephen Marvin (D Ohio) May 4, 1889-Dec. 1, 1984; House 1933-37, 1941-43, 1949-51; Senate 1959-71.

YOUNG, Thomas Lowry (R Ohio) Dec. 14, 1832-July 20, 1888; House 1879-83.

YOUNG, Timothy Roberts (D Ill.) Nov. 19, 1811-May 12, 1898; House 1849-51.

YOUNG, William Albin (D Va.) May 17, 1860-March 12, 1928; House 1897-April 26, 1898, 1899-March 12, 1900.

YOUNG, William Singleton (brother of Bryan Rust Young, uncle of John Young Brown born in 1835) (D Ky.) April 10, 1790-Sept. 20, 1827; House 1825-Sept. 20, 1827.

YOUNGBLOOD, Harold Francis (R Mich.) Aug. 7, 1907- —; House 1947-49.

YOUNGDAHL, Oscar Ferdinand (R Minn.) Oct. 13, 1893-Feb. 3, 1946; House 1939-43.

YOUNGER, Jesse Arthur (R Calif.) April 11, 1893-June 20, 1967; House 1953-June 20, 1967.

YULEE, David Levy (formerly David Levy) (WD Fla.) June 12, 1810-Oct. 10, 1886; House (Terr. Del.) 1841-45; Senate July 1, 1845-51, 1855-Jan. 21, 1861.

Z

ZABLOCKI, Clement John (D Wis.) Nov. 18, 1912-Dec. 3, 1983; House 1949-Dec. 3, 1983.

ZEFERETTI, Leo C. (D N.Y.) July 15, 1927- —; House 1975-83.

ZELENKO, Herbert (D N.Y.) March 16, 1906-Feb. 23, 1979; House 1955-63.

ZENOR, William Tayor (D Ind.) April 30, 1846-June 2, 1916; House 1897-1907.

ZIEGLER, Edward Danner (D Pa.) March 3, 1844-Dec. 21, 1931; House 1899-1901.

ZIHLMAN, Frederick Nicholas (R Md.) Oct. 2, 1879-April 22, 1935; House 1917-31.

ZIMMERMAN, Orville (D Mo.) Dec. 31, 1880-April 7, 1948; House 1935-April 7, 1948.

ZION, Roger Herschel (R Ind.) Sept. 17, 1921- —; House 1967-75.

ZIONCHECK, Marion Anthony (D Wash.) Dec. 5, 1901-Aug. 7, 1936; House 1933-Aug. 7, 1936.

ZOLLICOFFER, Felix Kirk (SRW Tenn.) May 19, 1812-Jan. 19, 1862; House 1853-59.

ZORINSKY, Edward (D Neb.) Nov. 11, 1928- —; Senate Dec. 28, 1976- —.

ZSCHAU, Ed (R Calif.) Jan. 6, 1940- —; House 1983- —.

ZWACH, John Matthew (R Minn.) Feb. 8, 1907- —; House 1967-75.

Members of Congress Congressional Statistics

Sessions of the U.S. Congress, 1789-1985

Source: Official Congressional Directory

Congress	Session	Date of beginning[1]	Date of adjournment[2]	Length in days	President pro tempore of the Senate[3]	Speaker of the House of Representatives
1st	1	Mar. 4, 1789	Sept. 29, 1789	210	John Langdon of New Hampshire	Frederick A. C. Muhlenberg of Pennsylvania
	2	Jan. 4, 1790	Aug. 12, 1790	221		
	3	Dec. 6, 1790	Mar. 3, 1791	88		
2nd	1	Oct. 24, 1791	May 8, 1792	197	Richard Henry Lee of Virginia	Jonathan Trumbull of Connecticut
	2	Nov. 5, 1792	Mar. 2, 1793	119	John Langdon of New Hampshire	
3rd	1	Dec. 2, 1793	June 9, 1794	190	Langdon Ralph Izard of South Carolina	Frederick A. C. Muhlenberg of Pennsylvania
	2	Nov. 3, 1794	Mar. 3, 1795	121	Henry Tazewell of Virginia	
4th	1	Dec. 7, 1795	June 1, 1796	177	Tazewell Samuel Livermore of New Hampshire	Jonathan Dayton of New Jersey
	2	Dec. 5, 1796	Mar. 3, 1797	89	William Bingham of Pennsylvania	
5th	1	May 15, 1797	July 10, 1797	57	William Bradford of Rhode Island	Dayton
	2	Nov. 13, 1797	July 16, 1798	246	Jacob Read of South Carolina Theodore Sedgwick of Massachusetts	George Dent of Maryland[5]
	3	Dec. 3, 1798	Mar. 3, 1799	91	John Laurence of New York James Ross of Pennsylvania	
6th	1	Dec. 2, 1799	May 14, 1800	164	Samuel Livermore of New Hampshire Uriah Tracy of Connecticut	Theodore Sedgwick of Massachusetts
	2	Nov. 17, 1800	Mar. 3, 1801	107	John E. Howard of Maryland James Hillhouse of Connecticut	
7th	1	Dec. 7, 1801	May 3, 1802	148	Abraham Baldwin of Georgia	Nathaniel Macon of North Carolina
	2	Dec. 6, 1802	Mar. 3, 1803	88	Stephen R. Bradley of Vermont	
8th	1	Oct. 17, 1803	Mar. 27, 1804	163	John Brown of Kentucky Jesse Franklin of North Carolina	Macon
	2	Nov. 5, 1804	Mar. 3, 1805	119	Joseph Anderson of Tennessee	
9th	1	Dec. 2, 1805	Apr. 21, 1806	141	Samuel Smith of Maryland	Macon
	2	Dec. 1, 1806	Mar. 3, 1807	93		
10th	1	Oct. 26, 1807	Apr. 25, 1808	182	Smith	Joseph B. Varnum of Massachusetts

(Footnotes, p. 179)

Congress	Session	Date of beginning[1]	Date of adjournment[2]	Length in days	President pro tempore of the Senate[3]	Speaker of the House of Representatives
	2	Nov. 7, 1808	Mar. 3, 1809	117	Stephen R. Bradley of Vermont	
					John Milledge of Georgia	
11th	1	May 22, 1809	June 28, 1809	38	Andrew Gregg of Pennsylvania	Varnum
	2	Nov. 27, 1809	May 1, 1810	156	John Gaillard of South Carolina	
	3	Dec. 3, 1810	Mar. 3, 1811	91	John Pope of Kentucky	
12th	1	Nov. 4, 1811	July 6, 1812	245	William H. Crawford of Georgia	Henry Clay of Kentucky
	2	Nov. 2, 1812	Mar. 3, 1813	122	Crawford	
13th	1	May 24, 1813	Aug. 2, 1813	71		Clay
	2	Dec. 6, 1813	Apr. 18, 1814	134	Joseph B. Varnum of Massachusetts	
	3	Sept. 19, 1814	Mar. 3, 1815	166	John Gaillard of South Carolina	Langdon Cheves of South Carolina[6]
14th	1	Dec. 4, 1815	Apr. 30, 1816	148	Gaillard	Henry Clay of Kentucky
	2	Dec. 2, 1816	Mar. 3, 1817	92	Gaillard	
15th	1	Dec. 1, 1817	Apr. 20, 1818	141	Gaillard	Clay
	2	Nov. 16, 1818	Mar. 3, 1819	108	James Barbour of Virginia	
16th	1	Dec. 6, 1819	May 15, 1820	162	John Gaillard of South Carolina	Clay
	2	Nov. 13, 1820	Mar. 3, 1821	111	Gaillard	John W. Taylor of New York[7]
17th	1	Dec. 3, 1821	May 8, 1822	157	Gaillard	Philip P. Barbour of Virginia
	2	Dec. 2, 1822	Mar. 3, 1823	92	Gaillard	
18th	1	Dec. 1, 1823	May 27, 1824	178	Gaillard	Henry Clay of Kentucky
	2	Dec. 6, 1824	Mar. 3, 1825	88	Gaillard	
19th	1	Dec. 5, 1825	May 22, 1826	169	Nathaniel Macon of North Carolina	John W. Taylor of New York
	2	Dec. 4, 1826	Mar. 3, 1827	90	Macon	
20th	1	Dec. 3, 1827	May 26, 1828	175	Samuel Smith of Maryland	Andrew Stevenson of Virginia
	2	Dec. 1, 1828	Mar. 3, 1829	93	Smith	
21st	1	Dec. 7, 1829	May 31, 1830	176	Smith	Stevenson
	2	Dec. 6, 1830	Mar. 3, 1831	88	Littleton Waller Tazewell of Virginia	
22nd	1	Dec. 5, 1831	July 16, 1832	225	Tazewell	Stevenson
	2	Dec. 3, 1832	Mar. 2, 1833	91	Hugh Lawson White of Tennessee	
23rd	1	Dec. 2, 1833	June 30, 1834	211	George Poindexter of Mississippi	Stevenson
	2	Dec. 1, 1834	Mar. 3, 1835	93	John Tyler of Virginia	John Bell of Tennessee[8]
24th	1	Dec. 7, 1835	July 4, 1836	211	William R. King of Alabama	James K. Polk of Tennessee
	2	Dec. 5, 1836	Mar. 3, 1837	89	King	
25th	1	Sept. 4, 1837	Oct. 16, 1837	43	King	Polk
	2	Dec. 4, 1837	July 9, 1838	218	King	
	3	Dec. 3, 1838	Mar. 3, 1839	91	King	
26th	1	Dec. 2, 1839	July 21, 1840	233	King	Robert M. T. Hunter of Virginia
	2	Dec. 7, 1840	Mar. 3, 1841	87		
27th	1	May 31, 1841	Sept. 13, 1841	106	Samuel L. Southard of New Jersey	John White of Kentucky
	2	Dec. 6, 1841	Aug. 31, 1842	269	Willie P. Mangum of North Carolina	
	3	Dec. 5, 1842	Mar. 3, 1843	89	Mangum	

(Footnotes, p. 179)

Congress	Session	Date of beginning[1]	Date of adjournment[2]	Length in days	President pro tempore of the Senate[3]	Speaker of the House of Representatives
28th	1	Dec. 4, 1843	June 17, 1844	196	Mangum	John W. Jones of Virginia
	2	Dec. 2, 1844	Mar. 3, 1845	92	Mangum	
29th	1	Dec. 1, 1845	Aug. 10, 1846	253	David R. Atchison of Missouri	John W. Davis of Indiana
	2	Dec. 7, 1846	Mar. 3, 1847	87	Atchison	
30th	1	Dec. 6, 1847	Aug. 14, 1848	254	Atchison	Robert C. Winthrop of Massachusetts
	2	Dec. 4, 1848	Mar. 3, 1849	90	Atchison	
31st	1	Dec. 3, 1849	Sept. 30, 1850	302	William R. King of Alabama	Howell Cobb of Georgia
	2	Dec. 2, 1850	Mar. 3, 1851	92	King	
32nd	1	Dec. 1, 1851	Aug. 31, 1852	275	King	Linn Boyd of Kentucky
	2	Dec. 6, 1852	Mar. 3, 1853	88	David R. Atchison of Missouri	
33rd	1	Dec. 5, 1853	Aug. 7, 1854	246	Atchison	Boyd
	2	Dec. 4, 1854	Mar. 3, 1855	90	Jesse D. Bright of Indiana	
					Lewis Cass of Michigan	
34th	1	Dec. 3, 1855	Aug. 18, 1856	260	Jesse D. Bright of Indiana	Nathaniel P. Banks of Massachusetts
	2	Aug. 21, 1856	Aug. 30, 1856	10	Bright	
	3	Dec. 1, 1856	Mar. 3, 1857	93	James M. Mason of Virginia	
					Thomas J. Rusk of Texas	
35th	1	Dec. 7, 1857	June 14, 1858	189	Benjamin Fitzpatrick of Alabama	James L. Orr of South Carolina
	2	Dec. 6, 1858	Mar. 3, 1859	88	Fitzpatrick	
36th	1	Dec. 5, 1859	June 25, 1860	202	Fitzpatrick	William Pennington of New Jersey
					Jesse D. Bright of Indiana	
	2	Dec. 3, 1860	Mar. 3, 1861	93	Solomon Foot of Vermont	
37th	1	July 4, 1861	Aug. 6, 1861	34	Foot	Galusha A. Grow of Pennsylvania
	2	Dec. 2, 1861	July 17, 1862	228	Foot	
	3	Dec. 1, 1862	Mar. 3, 1863	93	Foot	
38th	1	Dec. 7, 1863	July 4, 1864	209	Foot	Schuyler Colfax of Indiana
					Daniel Clark of New Hampshire	
	2	Dec. 5, 1864	Mar. 3, 1865	89	Clark	
39th	1	Dec. 4, 1865	July 28, 1866	237	Lafayette S. Foster of Connecticut	Colfax
	2	Dec. 3, 1866	Mar. 3, 1867	91	Benjamin F. Wade of Ohio	
40th	1	Mar. 4, 1867[9]	Dec. 2, 1867	274	Wade	Colfax
	2	Dec. 2, 1867[10]	Nov. 10, 1868	345	Wade	
	3	Dec. 7, 1868	Mar. 3, 1869	87	Wade	Theodore M. Pomeroy of New York
41st	1	Mar. 4, 1869	Apr. 10, 1869	38	Henry B. Anthony of Rhode Island	James G. Blaine of Maine
	2	Dec. 6, 1869	July 15, 1870	222	Anthony	
	3	Dec. 5, 1870	Mar. 3, 1871	89	Anthony	
42nd	1	Mar. 4, 1871	Apr. 20, 1871	48	Anthony	Blaine
	2	Dec. 4, 1871	June 10, 1872	190	Anthony	
	3	Dec. 2, 1872	Mar. 3, 1873	92	Anthony	
43rd	1	Dec. 1, 1873	June 23, 1874	204	Matthew H. Carpenter of Wisconsin	Blaine
	2	Dec. 7, 1874	Mar. 3, 1875	87	Carpenter	
					Henry B. Anthony of Rhode Island	

(Footnotes, p. 179)

Sessions of Congress

Congress	Session	Date of beginning[1]	Date of adjournment[2]	Length in days	President pro tempore of the Senate[3]	Speaker of the House of Representatives
44th	1	Dec. 6, 1875	Aug. 15, 1876	254	Thomas W. Ferry of Michican	Michael C. Kerr of Indiana[12]
						Samuel S. Cox of New York, pro tempore[12]
						Milton Sayler of Ohio, pro tempore
	2	Dec. 4, 1876	Mar. 3, 1877	90	Ferry	Samuel J. Randall of Pennsylvania
45th	1	Oct. 15, 1877	Dec. 3, 1877	50	Ferry	Randall
	2	Dec. 3, 1877	June 20, 1878	200	Ferry	
	3	Dec. 2, 1878	Mar. 3, 1879	92	Ferry	
46th	1	Mar. 18, 1879	July 1, 1879	106	Allen G. Thurman of Ohio	Randall
	2	Dec. 1, 1879	June 16, 1880	199	Thurman	
	3	Dec. 6, 1880	Mar. 3, 1881	88	Thurman	
47th	1	Dec. 5, 1881	Aug. 8, 1882	247	Thomas F. Bayard of Delaware	J. Warren Keifer of Ohio
					David Davis of Illinois	
	2	Dec. 4, 1882	Mar. 3, 1883	90	George F. Edmunds of Vermont	
48th	1	Dec. 3, 1883	July 7, 1884	218	Edmunds	John G. Carlisle of Kentucky
	2	Dec. 1, 1884	Mar. 3, 1885	93	Edmunds	
49th	1	Dec. 7, 1885	Aug. 5, 1886	242	John Sherman of Ohio	Carlisle
	2	Dec. 6, 1886	Mar. 3, 1887	88	John J. Ingalls of Kansas	
50th	1	Dec. 5, 1887	Oct. 20, 1888	321	Ingalls	Carlisle
	2	Dec. 3, 1888	Mar. 3, 1889	91	Ingalls	
51st	1	Dec. 2, 1889	Oct. 1, 1890	304	Ingalls	Thomas B. Reed of Maine
	2	Dec. 1, 1890	Mar. 3, 1891	93	Charles F. Manderson of Nebraska	
52nd	1	Dec. 7, 1891	Aug. 5, 1892	251	Manderson	Charles F. Crisp of Georgia
	2	Dec. 5, 1892	Mar. 3, 1893	89	Isham G. Harris of Tennessee	
53rd	1	Aug. 7, 1893	Nov. 3, 1893	89	Harris	Crisp
	2	Dec. 4, 1893	Aug. 28, 1894	268	Harris	
	3	Dec. 3, 1894	Mar. 3, 1895	97	Matt W. Ransom of North Carolina	
					Isham G. Harris of Tennessee	
54th	1	Dec. 2, 1895	June 11, 1896	193	William P. Frye of Maine	Thomas B. Reed of Maine
	2	Dec. 7, 1896	Mar. 3, 1897	87	Frye	
55th	1	Mar. 15, 1897	July 24, 1897	131	Frye	Reed
	2	Dec. 6, 1897	July 8, 1898	215	Frye	
	3	Dec. 5, 1898	Mar. 3, 1899	89	Frye	
56th	1	Dec. 4, 1899	June 7, 1900	186	Frye	David B. Henderson of Iowa
	2	Dec. 3, 1900	Mar. 3, 1901	91	Frye	
57th	1	Dec. 2, 1901	July 1, 1902	212	Frye	Henderson
	2	Dec. 1, 1902	Mar. 3, 1903	93	Frye	
58th	1	Nov. 9, 1903	Dec. 7, 1903	29	Frye	Joseph G. Cannon of Illinois
	2	Dec. 7, 1903	Apr. 28, 1904	144	Frye	
	3	Dec. 5, 1904	Mar. 3, 1905	89	Frye	
59th	1	Dec. 4, 1905	June 30, 1906	209	Frye	Cannon
	2	Dec. 3, 1906	Mar. 3, 1907	91	Frye	
60th	1	Dec. 2, 1907	May 30, 1908	181	Frye	Cannon
	2	Dec. 7, 1908	Mar. 3, 1909	87	Frye	

(Footnotes, p. 179)

Congress	Session	Date of beginning[1]	Date of adjournment[2]	Length in days	President pro tempore of the Senate[3]	Speaker of the House of Representatives
61st	1	Mar. 15, 1909	Aug. 5, 1909	144	Frye	Cannon
	2	Dec. 6, 1909	June 25, 1910	202	Frye	
	3	Dec. 5, 1910	Mar. 3, 1911	89	Frye	
62nd	1	Apr. 4, 1911	Aug. 22, 1911	141	Frye[15]	Champ Clark of Missouri
	2	Dec. 4, 1911	Aug. 26, 1912	267	Augustus O. Bacon of Georgia[16]; Frank B. Brandegee of Connecticut[17]; Charles Curtis of Kansas[18]; Jacob H. Gallinger of New Hampshire[19]; Henry Cabot Lodge of Mass.[20]	
	3	Dec. 2, 1912	Mar. 3, 1913	92	Bacon[21]; Gallinger[22]	
63rd	1	Apr. 7, 1913	Dec. 1, 1913	239	James P. Clarke of Arkansas	Clark
	2	Dec. 1, 1913	Oct. 24, 1914	328	Clarke	
	3	Dec. 7, 1914	Mar. 3, 1915	87	Clarke	
64th	1	Dec. 6, 1915	Sept. 8, 1916	278	Clarke[23]	Clark
	2	Dec. 4, 1916	Mar. 3, 1917	90	Willard Saulsbury of Delaware	
65th	1	Apr. 2, 1917	Oct. 6, 1917	188	Saulsbury	Clark
	2	Dec. 3, 1917	Nov. 21, 1918	354	Saulsbury	
	3	Dec. 2, 1918	Mar. 3, 1919	92	Saulsbury	
66th	1	May 19, 1919	Nov. 19, 1919	185	Albert B. Cummins of Iowa	Frederick H. Gillett of Massachusetts
	2	Dec. 1, 1919	June 5, 1920	188	Cummins	
	3	Dec. 6, 1920	Mar. 3, 1921	88	Cummins	
67th	1	Apr. 11, 1921	Nov. 23, 1921	227	Cummins	Gillett
	2	Dec. 5, 1921	Sept. 22, 1922	292	Cummins	
	3	Nov. 20, 1922	Dec. 4, 1922	15	Cummins	
	4	Dec. 4, 1922	Mar. 3, 1923	90	Cummins	
68th	1	Dec. 3, 1923	June 7, 1924	188	Cummins	Gillett
	2	Dec. 1, 1924	Mar. 3, 1925	93	Cummins	
69th	1	Dec. 7, 1925	July 3, 1926	209	George H. Moses of New Hampshire	Nicholas Longworth of Ohio
	2	Dec. 6, 1926	Mar. 3, 1927	88	Moses	
70th	1	Dec. 5, 1927	May 29, 1928	177	Moses	Longworth
	2	Dec. 3, 1928	Mar. 3, 1929	91	Moses	
71st	1	Apr. 15, 1929	Nov. 22, 1929	222	Moses	Longworth
	2	Dec. 2, 1929	July 3, 1930	214	Moses	
	3	Dec. 1, 1930	Mar. 3, 1931	93	Moses	
72nd	1	Dec. 7, 1931	July 16, 1932	223	Moses	John N. Garner of Texas
	2	Dec. 5, 1932	Mar. 3, 1933	89	Moses	
73rd	1	Mar. 9, 1933	June 15, 1933	99	Key Pittman of Nevada	Henry T. Rainey of Illinois[24]
	2	Jan. 3, 1934	June 18, 1934	167	Pittman	
74th	1	Jan. 3, 1935	Aug. 26, 1935	236	Pittman	Joseph W. Byrns of Tennessee[25]
	2	Jan. 3, 1936	June 20, 1936	170	Pittman	William B. Bankhead of Alabama[26]
75th	1	Jan. 5, 1937	Aug. 21, 1937	229	Pitman	Bankhead
	2	Nov. 15, 1937	Dec. 21, 1937	37	Pittman	
	3	Jan. 3, 1938	June 16, 1938	165	Pittman	
76th	1	Jan. 3, 1939	Aug. 5, 1939	215	Pittman	Bankhead[27]
	2	Sept. 21, 1939	Nov. 3, 1939	44	Pittman	
	3	Jan. 3, 1940	Jan. 3, 1941	366	Pittman[28] William H. King of Utah[30]	Sam Rayburn of Texas[29]

(Footnotes, p. 179)

Sessions of Congress

Congress	Session	Date of beginning[1]	Date of adjournment[2]	Length in days	President pro tempore of the Senate[3]	Speaker of the House of Representatives
77th	1	Jan. 3, 1941	Jan. 2, 1942	365	Pat Harrison of Mississippi[31]; Carter Glass of Virginia[32]	Rayburn
	2	Jan. 5, 1942	Dec. 16, 1942	346	Carter Glass of Virginia	
78th	1	Jan. 6, 1943[33]	Dec. 21, 1943	350	Glass	Rayburn
	2	Jan. 10, 1944[34]	Dec. 19, 1944	345	Glass	
79th	1	Jan. 3, 1945[35]	Dec. 21, 1945	353	Kenneth McKellar of Tennessee	Rayburn
	2	Jan. 14, 1946[36]	Aug. 2, 1946	201	McKellar	
80th	1	Jan. 3, 1947[37]	Dec. 19, 1947	351	Arthur H. Vandenberg of Michigan	Joseph W. Martin Jr. of Massachusetts
	2	Jan. 6, 1948[38]	Dec. 31, 1948	361	Vandenberg	
81st	1	Jan. 3, 1949	Oct. 19, 1949	290	Kenneth McKellar of Tennessee	Sam Rayburn of Texas
	2	Jan. 3, 1950[39]	Jan. 2, 1951	365	McKellar	
82nd	1	Jan. 3, 1951[40]	Oct. 20, 1951	291	McKellar	Rayburn
	2	Jan. 8, 1952[41]	July 7, 1952	182	McKellar	
83rd	1	Jan. 3, 1953[42]	Aug. 3, 1953	213	Styles Bridges of New Hampshire	Joseph W. Martin Jr. of Massachusetts
	2	Jan. 6, 1954[43]	Dec. 2, 1954	331	Bridges	
84th	1	Jan. 5, 1955[44]	Aug. 2, 1955	210	Walter F. George of Georgia	Sam Rayburn of Texas
	2	Jan. 3, 1956[45]	July 27, 1956	207	George	
85th	1	Jan. 3, 1957[46]	Aug. 30, 1957	239	Carl Hayden of Arizona	Rayburn
	2	Jan. 7, 1958[47]	Aug. 24, 1958	230	Hayden	
86th	1	Jan. 7, 1959[47]	Sept. 15, 1959	252	Hayden	Rayburn
	2	Jan. 6, 1960[49]	Sept. 1, 1960	240	Hayden	
87th	1	Jan. 3, 1961[50]	Sept. 27, 1961	268	Hayden	Rayburn[51]
	2	Jan. 10, 1962[52]	Oct. 13, 1962	277	Hayden	John W. McCormack of Massachusetts[53]
88th	1	Jan. 9, 1963[54]	Dec. 30, 1963	356	Hayden	McCormack
	2	Jan. 7, 1964[55]	Oct. 3, 1964	270	Hayden	
89th	1	Jan. 4, 1965	Oct. 23, 1965	293	Hayden	McCormack
	2	Jan. 10, 1966[56]	Oct. 22, 1966	286	Hayden	
90th	1	Jan. 10, 1967[57]	Dec. 15, 1967	340	Hayden	McCormack
	2	Jan. 15, 1968[58]	Oct. 14, 1968	274	Hayden	
91st	1	Jan. 3, 1969[59]	Dec. 23, 1969	355	Richard B. Russell of Georgia	McCormack
	2	Jan. 19, 1970[60]	Jan. 2, 1971	349	Russell	
92nd	1	Jan. 21, 1971[61]	Dec. 17, 1971	331	Russell[62]; Allen J. Ellender of Louisiana[63]	Carl Albert of Oklahoma
	2	Jan. 18, 1972[64]	Oct. 18, 1972	275	Ellender[65]; James O. Eastland of Mississippi[66]	
93rd	1	Jan. 3, 1973[67]	Dec. 22, 1973	354	Eastland	Albert
	2	Jan. 21, 1974[68]	Dec. 20, 1974	334	Eastland	
94th	1	Jan. 14, 1975[69]	Dec. 19, 1975	340	Eastland	Albert
	2	Jan. 19, 1976[70]	Oct. 2, 1976	258	Eastland	
95th	1	Jan. 4, 1977[71]	Dec. 15, 1977	346	Eastland	Thomas P. O'Neill Jr. of Massachusetts
	2	Jan. 19, 1978[72]	Oct. 15, 1978	270	Eastland	
96th	1	Jan. 15, 1979[73]	Jan. 3, 1980	354	Warren G. Magnuson of Washington	O'Neill
	2	Jan. 3, 1980[74]	Dec. 16, 1980	349	Magnuson	
97th	1	Jan. 5, 1981[75]	Dec. 16, 1981	347	Strom Thurmond of of South Carolina	O'Neill
	2	Jan. 25, 1982[76]	Dec. 23, 1982	333	Thurmond	
98th	1	Jan. 3, 1983[77]	Nov. 18, 1983	320	Thurmond	O'Neill
	2	Jan. 23, 1984[78]	Oct. 12, 1984	264	Thurmond	
99th	1	Jan. 3, 1985			Thurmond	O'Neill

(Footnotes, p. 179)

1. The Constitution (art I, sec. 4) provided that "The Congress shall assemble at least once in every year ... on the first Monday in December, unless they shall by law appoint a different day." Pursuant to a resolution of the Continental Congress, the first session of the First Congress convened March 4, 1789. Up to and including May 20, 1820, 18 acts were passed providing for the meeting of Congress on other days in the year. After 1820 Congress met regularly on the first Monday in December until 1934, when the 20th Amendment to the Constitution became effective changing the meeting date to Jan. 3. [Until then, brief special sessions of the Senate only were held at the beginning of each presidential term to confirm Cabinet and other nominations—and occasionally at other times for other purposes. The Senate last met in special session from March 4 to March 6, 1933.]

The first and second sessions of the First Congress were held in New York City; subsequently, including the first session of the Sixth Congress, Philadelphia was the meeting place; since then, Congress has convened in Washington.

2. Until adoption of the 20th Amendment, the deadline for adjournment of Congress in odd-numbered years was March 3. However, the expiring Congress often extended the "legislative day" of March 3 up to noon of March 4, when the new Congress came officially into being. After ratification of the 20th Amendment, the deadline for adjournment of Congress in odd-numbered years was noon on Jan. 3.

3. Until recent years the appointment or election of a President pro tempore was considered by the Senate to be for the occasion only, so that more than one appears in several sessions and in others none was chosen. Since March 12, 1890, they have served until "the Senate otherwise ordered."

4. Elected to count the vote for President and Vice President, which was done April 6, 1789, because there was a quorum of the Senate for the first time. John Adams, Vice President, appeared April 21, 1789, and took his seat as president of the Senate.

5. Elected Speaker pro tempore for April 20, 1798, and again for May 28, 1798.

6. Elected Speaker Jan. 19, 1814, to succeed Henry Clay, who resigned Jan. 19, 1814.

7. Elected Speaker Nov. 15, 1820, to succeed Henry Clay, who resigned Oct. 28, 1820.

8. Elected Speaker June 2, 1834, to succeed Andrew Stevenson of Virginia, who resigned.

9. There were recesses in this session from Saturday, Mar. 30, to Wednesday, July 1, and from Saturday, July 20, to Thursday, Nov. 21.

10. There were recesses in this session from Monday, July 27, to Monday, Sept. 21, to Friday, Oct. 16, and to Tuesday, Nov. 10. No business was transacted subsequent to July 27.

11. Elected Speaker Mar. 3, 1869, and served one day.

12. Died Aug. 19, 1876.

13. Appointed Speaker pro tempore Feb. 17, May 12, June 19.

14. Appointed Speaker pro tempore June 4.

15. Resigned as President pro tempore Apr. 27, 1911.

16. Elected to serve Jan. 11-17, Mar. 11-12, Apr. 8, May 10, May 30 to June 1 and 3, June 13 to July 5, Aug. 1-10, and Aug. 27 to Dec. 15, 1912.

17. Elected to serve May 25, 1912.

18. Elected to serve Dec. 4-12, 1911.

19. Elected to serve Feb. 12-14, Apr. 26-27, May 7, July 6-31, Aug. 12-26, 1912.

20. Elected to serve Mar. 25-26, 1912.

21. Elected to serve Aug. 27 to Dec. 15, 1912, Jan. 5-18, and Feb. 2-15, 1913.

22. Elected to serve Dec. 16, 1912, to Jan. 4, 1913, Jan. 19 to Feb. 1, and Feb. 16 to Mar. 3, 1913.

23. Died Oct. 1, 1916.

24. Died Aug. 19, 1934.

25. Died June 4, 1936.

26. Elected June 4, 1936.

27. Died Sept. 15, 1940.

28. Died Nov. 10, 1940.

29. Elected Sept. 16, 1940.

30. Elected Nov. 19, 1940.

31. Elected Jan. 6, 1941; died June 22, 1941.

32. Elected July 10, 1941.

33. There was a recess in this session from Thursday, July 8, to Tuesday, Sept. 14.

34. There were recesses in this session from Saturday, Apr. 1, to Wednesday, Apr. 12; from Friday, June 23, to Tuesday, Aug. 1; and from Thursday, Sept. 21, to Tuesday, Nov. 14.

35. The House was in recess in this session from Saturday, July 21, 1945, to Wednesday, Sept. 5, 1945, and the Senate from Wednesday, Aug. 1, 1945, to Wednesday, Sept. 5, 1945.

36. The House was in recess in this session from Thursday, Apr. 18, 1946, to Tuesday, Apr. 30, 1946.

37. There was a recess in this session from Sunday, July 27, 1947, to Monday, Nov. 17, 1947.

38. There were recesses in this session from Sunday, June 20, 1948, to Monday, July 26, 1948, and from Saturday, Aug. 7, 1948, to Friday, Dec. 31, 1948.

39. The House was in recess in this session from Thursday, Apr. 6, 1950, to Tuesday, Apr. 18, 1950, and both the Senate and the House were in recess from Saturday, Sept. 23, 1950, to Monday, Nov. 27, 1950.

40. The House was in recess in this session from Thursday, Mar. 22, 1951, to Monday, Apr. 2, 1951, and from Thursday, Aug. 23, 1951, to Wednesday, Sept. 12, 1951.

41. The House was in recess in this session from Thursday, Apr. 10, 1952, to Tuesday, Apr. 22, 1952.

42. The House was in recess in this session from Thursday, Apr. 2, 1953, to Monday, Apr. 13, 1953.

43. The House was in recess in this session from Thursday, Apr. 15, 1954, to Monday, Apr. 26, 1954, and adjourned sine die Aug. 20, 1954. The Senate was in recess in this session from Friday, Aug. 20, 1954, to Monday, Nov. 8, 1954; from Thursday, Nov. 18, 1954, to Monday, Nov. 29, 1954, and adjourned sine die Dec. 2, 1954.

44. There was a recess in this session from Monday, Apr. 4, 1955, to Wednesday, Apr. 13, 1955.

45. There was a recess in this session from Thursday, Mar. 29, 1956, to Monday, Apr. 9, 1956.

46. There was a recess in this session from Thursday, Apr. 18, 1957, to Monday, Apr. 29, 1957.

47. There was a recess in this session from Thursday, Apr. 3, 1958, to Monday, Apr. 14, 1958.

48. There was a recess in this session from Thursday, Mar. 26, 1959, to Tuesday, Apr. 7, 1959.

49. The Senate was in recess in this session from Thursday, Apr. 14, 1960, to Monday, Apr. 18, 1960; from Friday, May 27, 1960, to Tuesday, May 31, 1960, and from Sunday, July 3, 1960, to Monday, Aug. 8, 1960. The House was in recess in this session from Thursday, Apr. 14, 1960, to Monday, Apr. 18, 1960; from Friday, May 27, 1960, to Tuesday, May 31, 1960, and from Sunday, July 3, 1960, to Monday, Aug. 15, 1960.

50. The House was in recess in this session from Thursday, Mar. 30, 1961, to Monday, Apr. 10, 1961.

51. Died Nov. 16, 1961.

52. The House was in recess in this session from Thursday, Apr. 19, 1962, to Monday, Apr. 30, 1962.

53. Elected Jan. 10, 1962.

54. The House was in recess in this session from Thursday, Apr. 11, 1963, to Monday, Apr. 22, 1963.

55. The House was in recess in this session from Thursday, Mar. 26, 1964, to Monday, Apr. 6, 1964; from Thursday, July 2, 1964, to Monday, July 20, 1964; from Friday, Aug. 21, 1964, to Monday, Aug. 31, 1964. The Senate was in recess in this session from Friday, July 10, 1964, to Monday, July 20, 1964; from Friday, Aug. 21, 1964, to Monday, Aug. 31, 1964.

56. The House was in recess in this session from Thursday, Apr. 7, 1966, to Monday, Apr. 18, 1966; from Thursday, June 30, 1966, to Monday, July 11, 1966. The Senate was in recess in this session from Thursday, Apr. 7, 1966, to Wednesday, Apr. 13, 1966; from Thursday, June 30, 1966, to Monday, July 11, 1966.

57. There was a recess in this session from Thursday, Mar. 23, 1967, to Monday, Apr. 3, 1967; from Thursday, June 29, 1967, to Monday, July 10, 1967; from Thursday, Aug. 31, 1967, to Monday, Sept. 11, 1967; and from Wednesday, Nov. 22, 1967, to Monday, Nov. 27, 1967.

58. The House was in recess this session from Thursday, Apr. 11, 1968, to Monday, Apr. 22, 1968; from Wednesday, May 29, 1968, to Monday, June 3, 1968; from Wednesday, July 3, 1968, to Monday, July 8, 1968; from Friday, Aug. 2, 1968, to Wednesday, Sept. 4, 1968. The Senate was in recess this session from Thursday, Apr. 11, 1968, to Wednesday, Apr. 17, 1968; from Wednesday, May 29, 1968, to Monday, June 3, 1968; from Wednesday, July 3, 1968, to Monday, July 8, 1968; from Friday, Aug. 2, 1968, to Wednesday, Sept. 4, 1968.

59. The House was in recess this session from Friday, Feb. 7, 1969, to Monday, Feb. 17, 1969; from Thursday, Apr. 3, 1969, to Monday, Apr. 14, 1969; from Wednesday, May 28, 1969, to Monday, June 2, 1969; from Wednesday, July 2, 1969, to Monday, July 7, 1969; from Wednesday, Aug. 13, 1969, to Wednesday, Sept. 3, 1969; from Thursday, Nov. 6, 1969, to Wednesday, Nov. 12, 1969; from Wednesday, Nov. 26, 1969, to Monday, Dec. 1, 1969. The Senate was in recess this session from Friday, Feb. 7, 1969, to Monday, Feb. 17, 1969; from Thursday, Apr. 3, 1969, to Monday, Apr. 14, 1969; from Wednesday, July 2, 1969, to Monday, July 7, 1969; from Wednesday, Aug. 13, 1969, to Wednesday, Sept. 3, 1969; from Wednesday, Nov. 26, 1969, to Monday, Dec. 1, 1969.

60. The House was in recess this session from Tuesday, Feb. 10, 1970, to Monday, Feb. 16, 1970; from Thursday, Mar. 26, 1970, to Tuesday, Mar. 31, 1970; from Wednesday, May 27, 1970, to Monday, June 1, 1970; from Wednesday, July 1, 1970, to Monday, July 6, 1970; from Friday, Aug. 14, 1970, to Wednesday, Sept. 9, 1970; from Wednesday, Oct. 14, 1970, to Monday, Nov. 16, 1970; from Wednesday, Nov. 25, 1970, to Monday, Nov. 30, 1970; from Tuesday, Dec. 22, 1970, to Tuesday, Dec. 29, 1970. The Senate was in recess this session from Tuesday, Feb. 10, 1970, to Monday, Feb. 16, 1970; from Thursday, Mar. 26, 1970, to Tuesday, Mar. 31, 1970; from Wednesday, Sept. 2, 1970, to Tuesday, Sept. 8, 1970; from Wednesday, Oct. 14, 1970, to Monday, Nov. 16, 1970; from Wednesday, Nov. 25, 1970, to Monday, Nov. 30, 1970; from Tuesday, Dec. 22, 1970, to Monday, Dec. 28, 1970.

61. The House was in recess this session from Wednesday, Feb. 10, 1971, to Wednesday, Feb. 17, 1971; from Wednesday, Apr. 7, 1971, to Monday, Apr. 19, 1971; from Thursday, May 27, 1971, to Tuesday, June 1, 1971; from Thursday, July 1, 1971, to Tuesday, July 6, 1971; from Friday, Aug. 6, 1971, to Wednesday, Sept. 8, 1971; from Thursday, Oct. 7, 1971, to Tuesday, Oct. 12, 1971; from Thursday, Oct. 21, 1971, to Tuesday, Oct. 26, 1971; from Friday, Nov. 19, 1971, to Monday, Nov. 29, 1971. The Senate was in recess this session from Thursday, Feb. 11, 1971, to Wednesday, Feb. 17, 1971; from Wednesday, Apr. 7, 1971, to Wednesday, Apr. 14, 1971; from Wednesday, May 26, 1971, to Tuesday, June 1, 1971; from Wednesday, June 30, 1971, to Tuesday, July 6, 1971; from Friday, Aug. 6, 1971, to Wednesday, Sept. 8, 1971; from Thursday, Oct. 21, 1971, to Tuesday, Oct. 26, 1971; from Wednesday, Nov. 24, 1971, to Monday, Nov. 29, 1971.

62. Died Jan. 21, 1971.

63. Elected Jan. 22, 1971.

64. The House was in recess this session from Wednesday, Feb. 9, 1972, to Wednesday, Feb. 16, 1972; from Wednesday, Mar. 29, 1972, to Monday, Apr. 10, 1972; from Wednesday, May 24, 1972, to Tuesday, May 30, 1972; from Friday, June 30, 1972, to Monday, July 17, 1972; from Friday, Aug. 18, 1972, to Tuesday, Sept. 5, 1972. The Senate was in recess this session from Wednesday, Feb. 9, 1972, to Monday, Feb. 14, 1972; from Thursday, Mar. 30, 1972, to Tuesday, Apr. 4, 1972; from Thursday, May 25, 1972, to Monday, May 30, 1972; from Friday, June 30, 1972, to Monday, July 17, 1972; from Friday, Aug. 18, 1972, to Tuesday, Sept. 5, 1972.

65. Died July 27, 1972.

66. Elected July 28, 1972.

67. The House was in recess this session from Thursday, Feb. 8, 1973, to Monday, Feb. 19, 1973; from Thursday, Apr. 19, 1973, to Monday, Apr. 30, 1973; from Thursday, May 24, 1973, to Tuesday, May 29, 1973; from Saturday, June 30, 1973, to Tuesday, July 10, 1973; from Friday, Aug. 3, 1973, to Wednesday, Sept. 5, 1973; from Thursday, Oct. 4, 1973, to Tuesday, Oct. 9, 1973; from Thursday, Oct. 18, 1973, to Tuesday, Oct. 23, 1973; from Thursday, Nov. 15, 1973 to Monday, Nov. 26, 1973. The Senate was in recess this session from Thursday, Feb. 8, 1973, to Thursday, Feb. 15, 1973;

from Wednesday, Apr. 18, 1973, to Monday, Apr. 30, 1973; from Wednesday, May 23, 1973, to Tuesday, May 29, 1973; from Saturday, June 30, 1973, to Monday, July 9, 1973; from Friday, Aug. 3, 1973, to Wednesday, Sept. 5, 1973; from Thursday, Oct. 18, 1973, to Tuesday, Oct. 23, 1973; from Wednesday, Nov. 21, 1973, to Monday, Nov. 26, 1973.

68. The House was in recess this session from Thursday, Feb. 7, 1974, to Wednesday, Feb. 13, 1974; from Thursday, Apr. 11, 1974, to Monday, Apr. 22, 1974; from Thursday, May 23, 1974, to Tuesday, May 28, 1974; from Thursday, Aug. 22, 1974, to Wednesday, Sept. 11, 1974; from Thursday, Oct. 17, 1974, to Monday, Nov. 18, 1974; from Tuesday, Nov. 26, 1974, to Tuesday, Dec. 3, 1974. The Senate was in recess this session from Friday, Feb. 8, 1974, to Monday, Feb. 18, 1974; from Wednesday, Mar. 13, 1974, to Tuesday, Mar. 19, 1974; from Thursday, Apr. 11, 1974, to Monday, Apr. 22, 1974; from Wednesday, May 23, 1974, to Tuesday, May 28, 1974; from Thursday, Aug. 22, 1974, to Wednesday, Sept. 4, 1974; from Thursday, Oct. 17, 1974, to Monday, Nov. 18, 1974; from Tuesday, Nov. 26, 1974, to Monday, Dec. 2, 1974.

69. The House was in recess this session from Wednesday, Mar. 26, 1975, to Monday, Apr. 7, 1975; from Thursday, May 22, 1975, to Monday, June 2, 1975; from Thursday, June 26, 1975, to Tuesday, July 8, 1975; from Friday, Aug. 1, 1975, to Wednesday, Sept. 3, 1975; from Thursday, Oct. 9, 1975, to Monday, Oct. 20, 1975; from Thursday, Oct. 23, 1975, to Tuesday, Oct. 28, 1975; from Thursday, Nov. 20, 1975, to Monday, Dec. 1, 1975. The Senate was in recess this session from Wednesday, Mar. 26, 1975, to Monday, Apr. 7, 1975; from Thursday, May 22, 1975, to Monday, June 2, 1975; from Friday, June 27, 1975, to Monday, July 7, 1975; from Friday, Aug. 1, 1975, to Wednesday, Sept. 3, 1975; from Thursday, Oct. 9, 1975, to Monday, Oct. 20, 1975; from Thursday, Oct. 23, 1975, to Tuesday, Oct. 28, 1975; from Thursday, Nov. 20, 1975, to Monday, Dec. 1, 1975.

70. The House was in recess this session from Wednesday, Feb. 11, 1976, to Monday, Feb. 16, 1976; from Wednesday, Apr. 14, 1976, to Monday, Apr. 26, 1976; from Thursday, May 27, 1976, to Tuesday, June 1, 1976; from Friday, July 2, 1976, to Monday, July 19, 1976; from Tuesday, Aug. 10, 1976, to Monday, Aug. 23, 1976; from Thursday, Sept. 2, 1976, to Wednesday, Sept. 8, 1976. The Senate was in recess this session from Friday, Feb. 6, 1976, to Monday, Feb. 16, 1976; from Wednesday, Apr. 14, 1976, to Monday, Apr. 26, 1976; from Friday, May 28, 1976, to Wednesday, June 2, 1976; from Friday, July 2, 1976, to Monday, July 19, 1976; from Tuesday, Aug. 10, 1976, to Monday, Aug. 23, 1976; from Wednesday, Sept. 1, 1976, to Tuesday, Sept. 7, 1976.

71. The House was in recess this session from Wednesday, Feb. 9, 1977, to Wednesday, Feb. 16, 1977; from Wednesday, Apr. 6, 1977, to Monday, Apr. 18, 1977; from Thursday, May 26, 1977, to Wednesday, June 1, 1977; from Thursday, June 30, 1977, to Monday, July 11, 1977; from Friday, Aug. 5, 1977, to Wednesday, Sept. 7, 1977; from Thursday, Oct. 6, 1977, to Tuesday, Oct. 11, 1977. The Senate was in recess this session from Friday, Feb. 11, 1977, to Monday, Feb. 21, 1977; from Thursday, Apr. 7, 1977, to Monday, Apr. 18, 1977; from Friday, May 27, 1977, to Monday, June 6, 1977; from Friday, July 1, 1977, to Monday, July 11, 1977; from Saturday, Aug. 6, 1977, to Wednesday, Sept. 7, 1977.

72. The House was in recess this session from Thursday, Feb. 9, 1978, to Tuesday, Feb. 14, 1978; from Wednesday, Mar. 22, 1978, to Monday, Apr. 3, 1978; from Thursday, May 25, 1978, to Wednesday, May 31, 1978; from Thursday, June 29, 1978, to Monday, July 10, 1978; from Thursday, Aug. 17, 1978, to Wednesday, Sept. 6, 1978. The Senate was in recess this session from Friday, Feb. 10, 1978, to Monday, Feb. 20, 1978; from Thursday, Mar. 23, 1978, to Monday, Apr. 3, 1978; from Friday, May 26, 1978, to Monday, June 5, 1978; from Thursday, June 29, 1978, to Monday, July 10, 1978; from Friday, Aug. 25, 1978, to Wednesday, Sept. 6, 1978.

73. The House was in recess this session from Thursday, Feb. 8, 1979, to Tuesday, Feb. 13, 1979; from Tuesday, Apr. 10, 1979, to Monday, Apr. 23, 1979; from Thursday, May 24, 1979, to Wednesday, May 30, 1979; from Friday, June 29, 1979, to Monday, July 9, 1979; from Thursday, Aug. 2, 1979, to Wednesday, Sept. 5, 1979; from Tuesday, Nov. 20, 1979, to Monday, Nov. 26, 1979. The Senate was in recess this session from Friday, Feb. 9, 1979, to

Monday, Feb. 19, 1979; from Tuesday, Apr. 10, 1979, to Monday, Apr. 23, 1979; from Friday, May 25, 1979, to Monday, June 4, 1979; from Friday, Aug. 3, 1979, to Wednesday, Sept. 5, 1979; from Tuesday, Nov. 20, 1979, to Monday, Nov. 26, 1979.

74. The House was in recess this session from Wednesday, Feb. 13, 1980, to Tuesday, Feb. 19, 1980; from Wednesday, Apr. 2, 1980, to Tuesday, Apr. 15, 1980; from Thursday, May 22, 1980, to Wednesday, May 28, 1980; from Wednesday, July 2, 1980, to Monday, July 21, 1980; from Friday, Aug. 1, 1980, to Monday, Aug. 18, 1980; from Thursday, Aug. 28, 1980, to Wednesday, Sept. 13, 1980. The Senate was in recess this session from Monday, Feb. 11, 1980, to Thursday, Feb. 14, 1980; from Thursday, Apr. 3, 1980, to Tuesday, Apr. 15, 1980; from Thursday, May 22, 1980, to Wednesday, May 28, 1980; from Wednesday, July 2, 1980, to Monday, July 21, 1980; from Wednesday, Aug. 6, 1980, to Monday, Aug. 18, 1980; from Wednesday, Aug. 27, 1980, to Wednesday, Sept. 3, 1980; from Wednesday, Oct. 1, 1980, to Wednesday, Nov. 12, 1980; from Monday, Nov. 24, 1980, to Monday, Dec. 1, 1980.

75. The House was in recess this session from Friday, Feb. 6, 1981 to Tuesday, Feb. 17, 1981; from Friday, Apr. 10, 1981, to Monday, Apr. 27, 1981; from Friday, June 26, 1981, to Wednesday, July 8, 1981; from Tuesday, Aug. 4, 1981, to Wednesday, Sept. 9, 1981; from Wednesday, Oct. 7, 1981, to Tuesday, Oct. 13, 1981; from Monday, Nov. 23, 1981, to Monday, Nov. 30, 1981. The Senate was in recess this session from Friday, Feb. 6, 1981, to Monday, Feb. 16, 1981; from Friday, Apr. 10, 1981, to Monday, Apr. 27, 1981; from Thursday, June 25, 1981, to Wednesday, July 8, 1981; from Monday, Aug. 3, 1981, to Wednesday, Sept. 9, 1981; from Wednesday, Oct. 7, 1981, to Wednesday, Oct. 14, 1981; from Tuesday, Nov. 24, 1981, to Monday, Nov. 30, 1981.

76. The House was in recess this session from Wednesday, Feb. 10, 1982, to Monday, Feb. 22, 1982; from Tuesday, Apr. 6, 1982, to Tuesday, Apr. 20, 1982; from Thursday, May 27, 1982, to Wednesday, June 2, 1982; from Thursday, July 1, 1982, to Monday, July 12, 1982; from Friday, Aug. 20, 1982, to Wednesday, Sept. 8, 1982; from Friday, Oct. 1, 1982, to Monday, Nov. 29, 1982. The Senate was in recess this session Thursday, Feb. 11, 1982, to Monday, Feb. 22, 1982; from Thursday, Apr. 1, 1982, to Tuesday, Apr. 13, 1982; from Thursday, May 27, 1982, to Tuesday, June 8, 1982; from Thursday, July 1, 1982, to Monday, July 12, 1982; from Friday, Aug. 20, 1982, to Wednesday, Sept. 8, 1982; from Friday, Oct. 1, 1982, to Monday, Nov. 29, 1982.

77. The House was in recess this session Friday, Jan. 7, 1983, to Tuesday, Jan. 25, 1983; Thursday, Feb. 17, 1983, to Tuesday, Feb. 22, 1983; from Thursday, March 24, 1983, to Tuesday, Apr. 5, 1983; from Thursday, May 26, 1983, to Wednesday, June 1, 1983; from Thursday, June 30, 1983, to Monday, July 11, 1983; from Friday, Aug. 5, 1983, to Monday, Sept. 12, 1983; from Friday, Oct. 7, 1983, to Monday, Oct. 17, 1983. The Senate was in recess this session Monday, Jan. 3, 1983, to Tuesday, Jan. 25, 1983; Friday, Feb. 4, 1983, to Monday, Feb. 14, 1983; from Friday, March 25, 1983, to Tuesday, Apr. 5, 1983; from Friday, May 27, 1983, to Monday, June 6, 1983; from Friday, July 1, 1983, to Monday, July 11, 1983; from Friday, Aug. 5, 1983, to Monday, Sept. 12, 1983; from Monday Oct. 10, 1983, to Monday, Oct. 17, 1983.

78. The House was in recess this session Thursday, Feb. 9, 1984, to Tuesday, Feb. 21, 1984; from Friday, Apr. 13, 1984, to Tuesday, Apr. 24, 1984; from Friday, May 25, 1984, to Wednesday, May 30, 1984; from Friday, June 29, 1984, to Monday, July 23, 1984; Friday, Aug. 10, 1984, to Wednesday, Sept. 5, 1984. The Senate was in recess this session Friday, Feb. 10, 1984, to Monday, Feb. 20, 1984; from Friday, Apr. 13, 1984, to Tuesday, Apr. 24, 1984; from Friday, May 25, 1984, to Thursday, May 31, 1984; from Friday, June 29, 1984, to Monday, July 23, 1984; from Friday, Aug. 10, 1984, to Wednesday, Sept. 5, 1984.

Political Party Affiliations in Congress...

(Letter symbols for political parties: Ad—Administration; AM—Anti-Masonic; C—Coalition; D—Democratic; DR—Democratic-Republican; F—Federalist; J—Jacksonian; NR—National Republican; Op—Opposition; R—Republican; U—Unionist; W—Whig. Figures are for the beginning of the first session of each Congress.)

Year	Congress	HOUSE Majority party	HOUSE Principal minority party	HOUSE Other (except vacancies)	SENATE Majority party	SENATE Principal minority party	SENATE Other (except vacancies)	President
1985-1987	99th	D-252	R-182	-	R-53	D-47	-	R (Reagan)
1983-1985	98th	D-268	R-166	-	R-55	D-45	-	R (Reagan)
1981-1983	97th	D-243	R-192	-	R-53	D-46	1	R (Reagan)
1979-1981	96th	D-276	R-157	-	D-58	R-41	1	D (Carter)
1977-1979	95th	D-292	R-143	-	D-61	R-38	1	D (Carter)
1975-1977	94th	D-291	R-144	-	D-60	R-37	2	R (Ford)
1973-1975	93rd	D-239	R-192	1	D-56	R-42	2	R (Nixon-Ford)
1971-1973	92nd	D-254	R-180	-	D-54	R-44	2	R (Nixon)
1969-1971	91st	D-243	R-192	-	D-57	R-43	-	R (Nixon)
1967-1969	90th	D-247	R-187	-	D-64	R-36	-	D (L. Johnson)
1965-1967	89th	D-295	R-140	-	D-68	R-32	-	D (L. Johnson)
1963-1965	88th	D-258	R-177	-	D-67	R-33	-	D (L. Johnson)
								D (Kennedy)
1961-1963	87th	D-263	R-174	-	D-65	R-35	-	D (Kennedy)
1959-1961	86th	D-283	R-153	-	D-64	R-34	-	R (Eisenhower)
1957-1959	85th	D-233	R-200	-	D-49	R-47	-	R (Eisenhower)
1955-1957	84th	D-232	R-203	-	D-48	R-47	1	R (Eisenhower)
1953-1955	83rd	R-221	D-211	1	R-48	D-47	1	R (Eisenhower)
1951-1953	82nd	D-234	R-199	1	D-49	R-47	-	D (Truman)
1949-1951	81st	D-263	R-171	1	D-54	R-42	-	D (Truman)
1947-1949	80th	R-245	D-188	1	R-51	D-45	-	D (Truman)
1945-1947	79th	D-242	R-190	2	D-56	R-38	1	D (Truman)
1943-1945	78th	D-218	R-208	4	D-58	R-37	1	D (F. Roosevelt)
1941-1943	77th	D-268	R-162	5	D-66	R-28	2	D (F. Roosevelt)
1939-1941	76th	D-261	R-164	4	D-69	R-23	4	D (F. Roosevelt)
1937-1939	75th	D-331	R-89	13	D-76	R-16	4	D (F. Roosevelt)
1935-1937	74th	D-319	R-103	10	D-69	R-25	2	D (F. Roosevelt)
1933-1935	73rd	D-310	R-117	5	D-60	R-35	1	D (F. Roosevelt)
1931-1933	72nd	D-220	R-214	1	R-48	D-47	1	R (Hoover)
1929-1931	71st	R-267	D-167	1	R-56	D-39	1	R (Hoover)
1927-1929	70th	R-237	D-195	3	R-49	D-46	1	R (Coolidge)
1925-1927	69th	R-247	D-183	4	R-56	D-39	1	R (Coolidge)
1923-1925	68th	R-225	D-205	5	R-51	D-43	2	R (Coolidge)
1921-1923	67th	R-301	D-131	1	R-59	D-37	-	R (Harding)
1919-1921	66th	R-240	D-190	3	R-49	D-47	-	D (Wilson)
1917-1919	65th	D-216	R-210	6	D-53	R-42	-	D (Wilson)
1915-1917	64th	D-230	R-196	9	D-56	R-40	-	D (Wilson)
1913-1915	63rd	D-291	R-127	17	D-51	R-44	1	D (Wilson)
1911-1913	62nd	D-228	R-161	1	R-51	D-41	-	R (Taft)
1909-1911	61st	R-219	D-172	-	R-61	D-32	-	R (Taft)
1907-1909	60th	R-222	D-164	-	R-61	D-31	-	R (T. Roosevelt)
1905-1907	59th	R-250	D-136	-	R-57	D-33	-	R (T. Roosevelt)
1903-1905	58th	R-208	D-178	-	R-57	D-33	-	R (T. Roosevelt)
1901-1903	57th	R-197	D-151	9	R-55	D-31	4	R (T. Roosevelt)
								R (McKinley)
1899-1901	56th	R-185	D-163	9	R-53	D-26	8	R (McKinley)
1897-1899	55th	R-204	D-113	40	R-47	D-34	7	R (McKinley)
1895-1897	54th	R-244	D-105	7	R-43	D-39	6	D (Cleveland)
1893-1895	53rd	D-218	R-127	11	D-44	R-38	3	D (Cleveland)
1891-1893	52nd	D-235	R-88	9	R-47	D-39	2	R (B. Harrison)
1889-1891	51st	R-166	D-159	-	R-39	D-37	-	R (B. Harrison)
1887-1889	50th	D-169	R-152	4	R-39	D-37	-	D (Cleveland)
1885-1887	49th	D-183	R-140	2	R-43	D-34	-	D (Cleveland)
1883-1885	48th	D-197	R-118	10	R-38	D-36	2	R (Arthur)
1881-1883	47th	R-147	D-135	11	R-37	D-37	1	R (Arthur)
								R (Garfield)

...and the Presidency: 1789 to 1985

(Letter symbols for political parties: Ad—Administration; AM—Anti-Masonic; C—Coalition; D—Democratic; DR—Democratic-Republican; F—Federalist; J—Jacksonian; NR—National Republican; Op—Opposition; R—Republican; U—Unionist; W—Whig. Figures are for the beginning of the first session of each Congress.)

Year	Congress	HOUSE Majority party	HOUSE Principal minority party	HOUSE Other (except vacancies)	SENATE Majority party	SENATE Principal minority party	SENATE Other (except vacancies)	President
1879-1881	46th	D-149	R-130	14	D-42	R-33	1	R (Hayes)
1877-1879	45th	D-153	R-140	-	R-39	D-36	1	R (Hayes)
1875-1877	44th	D-169	R-109	14	R-45	D-29	2	R (Grant)
1873-1875	43rd	R-194	D-92	14	R-49	D-19	5	R (Grant)
1871-1873	42nd	R-134	D-104	5	R-52	D-17	5	R (Grant)
1869-1871	41st	R-149	D-63	-	R-56	D-11	-	R (Grant)
1867-1869	40th	R-143	D-49	-	R-42	D-11	-	R (A. Johnson)
1865-1867	39th	U-149	D-42	-	U-42	D-10	-	R (A. Johnson)
								R (Lincoln)
1863-1865	38th	R-102	D-75	9	R-36	D-9	5	R (Lincoln)
1861-1863	37th	R-105	D-43	30	R-31	D-10	8	R (Lincoln)
1859-1861	36th	R-114	D-92	31	D-36	R-26	4	D (Buchanan)
1857-1859	35th	D-118	R-92	26	D-36	R-20	8	D (Buchanan)
1855-1857	34th	R-108	D-83	43	D-40	R-15	5	D (Pierce)
1853-1855	33rd	D-159	W-71	4	D-38	W-22	2	D (Pierce)
1851-1853	32nd	D-140	W-88	5	D-35	W-24	3	W (Fillmore)
1849-1851	31st	D-112	W-109	9	D-35	W-25	2	W (Fillmore)
								W (Taylor)
1847-1849	30th	W-115	D-108	4	D-36	W-21	1	D (Polk)
1845-1847	29th	D-143	W-77	6	D-31	W-25	-	D (Polk)
1843-1845	28th	D-142	W-79	1	W-28	D-25	1	W (Tyler)
1841-1843	27th	W-133	D-102	6	W-28	D-22	2	W (Tyler)
								W (W. Harrison)
1839-1841	26th	D-124	W-118	-	D-28	W-22	-	D (Van Buren)
1837-1839	25th	D-108	W-107	24	D-30	W-18	4	D (Van Buren)
1835-1837	24th	D-145	W-98	-	D-27	W-25	-	D (Jackson)
1833-1835	23rd	D-147	AM-53	60	D-20	NR-20	8	D (Jackson)
1831-1833	22nd	D-141	NR-58	14	D-25	NR-21	2	D (Jackson)
1829-1831	21st	D-139	NR-74	-	D-26	NR-22	-	D (Jackson)
1827-1829	20th	J-119	Ad-94	-	J-28	Ad-20	-	C (John Q. Adams)
1825-1827	19th	Ad-105	J-97	-	Ad-26	J-20	-	C (John Q. Adams)
1823-1825	18th	DR-187	F-26	-	DR-44	F-4	-	DR (Monroe)
1821-1823	17th	DR-158	F-25	-	DR-44	F-4	-	DR (Monroe)
1819-1821	16th	DR-156	F-27	-	DR-35	F-7	-	DR (Monroe)
1817-1819	15th	DR-141	F-42	-	DR-34	F-10	-	DR (Monroe)
1815-1817	14th	DR-117	F-65	-	DR-25	F-11	-	DR (Madison)
1813-1815	13th	DR-112	F-68	-	DR-27	F-9	-	DR (Madison)
1811-1813	12th	DR-108	F-36	-	DR-30	F-6	-	DR (Madison)
1809-1811	11th	DR-94	F-48	-	DR-28	F-6	-	DR (Madison)
1807-1809	10th	DR-118	F-24	-	DR-28	F-6	-	DR (Jefferson)
1805-1807	9th	DR-116	F-25	-	DR-27	F-7	-	DR (Jefferson)
1803-1805	8th	DR-102	F-39	-	DR-25	F-9	-	DR (Jefferson)
1801-1803	7th	DR-69	F-36	-	DR-18	F-13	-	DR (Jefferson)
1799-1801	6th	F-64	DR-42	-	F-19	DR-13	-	F (John Adams)
1797-1799	5th	F-58	DR-48	-	F-20	DR-12	-	F (John Adams)
1795-1797	4th	F-54	DR-52	-	F-19	DR-13	-	F (Washington)
1793-1795	3rd	DR-57	F-48	-	F-17	DR-13	-	F (Washington)
1791-1793	2nd	F-37	DR-33	-	F-16	DR-13	-	F (Washington)
1789-1791	1st	Ad-38	Op-26	-	Ad-17	Op-9	-	F (Washington)

Sources: U.S. Bureau of the Census. *Historical Statistics of the United States, Colonial Times to 1970.* Washington, D.C: Government Printing Office, 1975; U.S. Bureau of the Census. *Statistical Abstract of the United States, 1985.* Washington, D.C.: Government Printing Office, 1984; U.S. Congress. Joint Committee on Printing. *Official Congressional Directory.* Washington, D.C.: Government Printing Office, 1967-—.

Leaders of the Senate and House

(For Presidents pro tempore of the Senate and Speakers of the House, see p. 173)

Congress	Senate Floor Leaders Majority	Minority	Senate Whips Majority	Minority
62nd (1911-1913)	Shelby M. Cullom (R Ill.)	Thomas S. Martin (D Va.)	None	None
63rd (1913-1915)	John W. Kern (D Ind.)	Jacob H. Gallinger (R N.H.)	J. Hamilton Lewis (D Ill.)	None
64th (1915-1917)	Kern	Gallinger	Lewis	James W. Wadsworth Jr. (R N.Y.) Charles Curtis (R Kan.)[8]
65th (1917-1919)	Thomas S. Martin (D Va.)	Gallinger/Henry Cabot Lodge (R Mass.)[1]	Lewis	Curtis
66th (1919-1921)	Henry Cabot Lodge (R Mass.)	Martin/Oscar W. Underwood (D Ala.)[2]	Charles Curtis (R Kan.)	Peter G. Gerry (D R.I.)
67th (1921-1923)	Lodge	Underwood	Curtis	Gerry
68th (1923-1925)	Lodge/Charles Curtis (R Kan.)[3]	Joseph T. Robinson (D Ark.)	Curtis/Wesley L. Jones (R Wash.)[9]	Gerry
69th (1925-1927)	Curtis	Robinson	Jones	Gerry
70th (1927-1929)	Curtis	Robinson	Jones	Morris Sheppard (D Texas)
71st (1929-1931)	James E. Watson (R Ind.)	Robinson	Simeon D. Fess (R Ohio)	Sheppard
72nd (1931-1933)	Watson	Robinson	Fess	Felix Hebert (R R.I.)
73rd (1933-1935)	Joseph T. Robinson (D Ark.)	Charles L. McNary (R Ore.)	Lewis	None
74th (1935-1937)	Robinson	McNary	Lewis	None
75th (1937-1939)	Robinson/Alben W. Barkley (D Ky.)[4]	McNary	Lewis	None
76th (1939-1941)	Barkley	McNary	Sherman Minton (D Ind.)	None
77th (1941-1943)	Barkley	McNary	Lister Hill (D Ala.)	Kenneth Wherry (R Neb.)
78th (1943-1945)	Barkley	McNary	Hill	Wherry
79th (1945-1947)	Barkley	Wallace H. White Jr. (R Maine)	Hill	Scott Lucas (D Ill.)
80th (1947-1949)	Wallace H. White Jr. (R Maine)	Alben W. Barkley (D Ky.)	Kenneth Wherry (R Neb.)	Leverett Saltonstall (R Mass.)
81st (1949-1951)	Scott W. Lucas (D Ill.)	Kenneth S. Wherry (R Neb.)	Francis Myers (D Pa.)	Saltonstall
82nd (1951-1953)	Ernest W. McFarland (D Ariz.)	Wherry/Styles Bridges (R N.H.)[5]	Lyndon B. Johnson (D Texas)	Earle Clements (D Ky.)
83rd (1953-1955)	Robert A. Taft (R Ohio)/ William F. Knowland (R Calif.)[6]	Lyndon B. Johnson (D Texas)	Leverett Saltonstall (R Mass.)	
84th (1955-1957)	Lyndon B. Johnson (D Texas)	William F. Knowland (R Calif.)	Earle Clements (D Ky.)	Saltonstall
85th (1957-1959)	Johnson	Knowland	Mike Mansfield (D Mont.)	Everett McKinley Dirksen (R Ill.)
86th (1959-1961)	Johnson	Everett McKinley Dirksen (R Ill.)	Mansfield	Thomas H. Kuchel (R Calif.)
87th (1961-1963)	Mike Mansfield (D Mont.)	Dirksen	Hubert H. Humphrey (D Minn.)	Kuchel
88th (1963-1965)	Mansfield	Dirksen	Humphrey	Kuchel
89th (1965-1967)	Mansfield	Dirksen	Russell Long (D La.)	Kuchel
90th (1967-1969)	Mansfield	Dirksen	Long	Kuchel
91st (1969-1971)	Mansfield	Dirksen/Hugh Scott (R Pa.)[7]	Edward M. Kennedy (D Mass.)	Hugh Scott (R Pa.)/ Robert P. Griffin (R Mich.)[10]
92nd (1971-1973)	Mansfield	Scott	Robert C. Byrd (D W.Va.)	Griffin
93rd (1973-1975)	Mansfield	Scott	Byrd	Griffin
94th (1975-1977)	Mansfield	Scott	Byrd	Griffin
95th (1977-1979)	Robert C. Byrd (D W.Va.)	Howard H. Baker Jr. (R Tenn.)	Alan Cranston (D Calif.)	Ted Stevens (R Alaska)
96th (1979-1981)	Byrd	Baker	Cranston	Stevens
97th (1981-1983)	Howard H. Baker Jr. (R Tenn.)	Robert C. Byrd (D W.Va.)	Ted Stevens (R Alaska)	Alan Cranston (D Calif.)
98th (1983-1985)	Baker	Byrd	Stevens	Cranston
99th (1985-1987)	Robert J. Dole (R Kan.)	Byrd	Alan K. Simpson (R Wyo.)	Cranston

---

Senate Footnotes

1. Lodge became minority leader on Aug. 24, 1918, filling the vacancy caused by the death of Gallinger on Aug. 17, 1918.

2. Underwood became minority leader on April 27, 1920, filling the vacancy caused by the death of Martin on Nov. 12, 1919. Gilbert M. Hitchcock (D Neb.) served as acting minority leader in the interim.

3. Curtis became majority leader on Nov. 28, 1924, filling the vacancy caused by the death of Lodge on Nov. 9, 1924.

4. Barkley became majority leader on July 22, 1937, filling the vacancy caused by the death of Robinson on July 14, 1937.

5. Bridges became minority leader on Jan. 8, 1952, filling the vacancy caused by the death of Wherry on Nov. 29, 1951.

6. Knowland became majority leader on Aug. 4, 1953, filling the vacancy caused by the death of Taft on July 31, 1953. Taft's vacant seat was filled by a Democrat, Thomas Burke, on Nov. 10, 1953. The division of the Senate changed to 48 Democrats, 47 Republicans and 1 Independent, thus giving control of the Senate to the Democrats. However, Knowland remained as majority leader until the end of the 83rd Congress.

7. Scott became minority leader on Sept. 24, 1969, filling the vacancy caused by the death of Dirksen on Sept. 7, 1969.

8. Wadsworth served as minority whip for only one week, from Dec. 6 to Dec. 13, 1915.

9. Jones became majority whip filling the vacancy caused by the elevation of Curtis to the post of majority leader. *(Footnote 3)*

10. Griffin became minority whip on Sept. 24, 1969, filling the vacancy caused by the elevation of Scott to the post of minority leader. *(Footnote 7)*

House Floor Leaders / House Whips

Congress	House Floor Leaders — Majority	House Floor Leaders — Minority	House Whips — Majority	House Whips — Minority
56th (1899-1901)	Sereno E. Payne (R N.Y.)	James D. Richardson (D Tenn.)	James A. Tawney (R Minn.)	Oscar W. Underwood (D Ala.)[6]
57th (1901-1903)	Payne	Richardson	Tawney	James T. Lloyd (D Mo.)
58th (1903-1905)	Payne	John Sharp Williams (D Miss.)	Tawney	Lloyd
59th (1905-1907)	Payne	Williams	James E. Watson (R Ind.)	Lloyd
60th (1907-1909)	Payne	Williams/Champ Clark (D Mo.)[1]	Watson	Lloyd[7]
61st (1909-1911)	Payne	Clark	John W. Dwight (R N.Y.)	None
62nd (1911-1913)	Oscar W. Underwood (D Ala.)	James R. Mann (R Ill.)	None	John W. Dwight (R N.Y.)
63rd (1913-1915)	Underwood	Mann	Thomas M. Bell (D Ga.)	Charles H. Burke (R S.D.)
64th (1915-1917)	Claude Kitchin (D N.C.)	Mann	None	Charles M. Hamilton (R N.Y.)
65th (1917-1919)	Kitchin	Mann	None	Hamilton
66th (1919-1921)	Franklin W. Mondell (R Wyo.)	Clark	Harold Knutson (R Minn.)	None
67th (1921-1923)	Mondell	Claude Kitchin (D N.C.)	Knutson	William A. Oldfield (D Ark.)
68th (1923-1925)	Nicholas Longworth (R Ohio)	Finis J. Garrett (D Tenn.)	Albert H. Vetal (R Ind.)	Oldfield
69th (1925-1927)	John Q. Tilson (R Conn.)	Garrett	Vestal	Oldfield
70th (1927-1929)	Tilson	Garrett	Vestal	Oldfield/John McDuffie (D Ala.)[8]
71st (1929-1931)	Tilson	John N. Garner (D Texas)	Vestal	McDuffie
72nd (1931-1933)	Henry T. Rainey (D Ill.)	Bertrand H. Snell (R N.Y.)	John McDuffie (D Ala.)	Carl G. Bachmann (R W.Va.)
73rd (1933-1935)	Joseph W. Byrns (D Tenn.)	Snell	Arthur H. Greenwood (D Ind.)	Hary L. Englebright (R Calif.)
74th (1935-1937)	William B. Bankhead (D Ala.)[2]	Snell	Patrick J. Boland (D Pa.)	Englebright
75th (1937-1939)	Sam Rayburn (D Texas)	Snell	Boland	Englebright
76th (1939-1941)	Rayburn/John W. McCormack (D Mass.)[3]	Joseph W. Martin Jr. (R Mass.)	Boland	Englebright
77th (1941-1943)	McCormack	Martin	Boland/Robert Ramspeck (D Ga.)[9]	Englebright
78th (1943-1945)	McCormack	Martin	Ramspeck	Leslie C. Arends (R Ill.)
79th (1945-1947)	McCormack	Martin	Ramspeck/John J. Sparkman (D Ala.)[10]	Arends
80th (1947-1949)	Charles A. Halleck (R Ind.)	Sam Rayburn (D Texas)	Leslie C. Arends (R Ill.)	John W. Mccormack (D Mass.)
81st (1949-1951)	McCormack	Martin	J. Percy Priest (D Tenn.)	Arends
82nd (1951-1953)	McCormack	Martin	Priest	Arends
83rd (1953-1955)	Halleck	Rayburn	Arends	McCormack
84th (1955-1957)	McCormack	Martin	Carl Albert (D Okla.)	Arends
85th (1957-1959)	McCormack	Martin	Albert	Arends
86th (1959-1961)	McCormack	Charles A. Halleck (R Ind.)	Albert	Arends
87th (1961-1963)	McCormack/Carl Albert (D Okla.)[4]	Halleck	Albert/Hale Boggs (D La.)[11]	Arends
88th (1963-1965)	Albert	Halleck	Boggs	Arends
89th (1965-1967)	Albert	Gerald R. Ford (R Mich.)	Boggs	Arends
90th (1967-1969)	Albert	Ford	Boggs	Arends
91st (1969-1971)	Albert	Ford	Boggs	Arends
92nd (1971-1973)	Hale Boggs (D La.)	Ford	Thomas P. O'Neill Jr. (D Mass.)	Arends
93rd (1973-1975)	Thomas P. O'Neill Jr. (D Mass.)	Ford/John J. Rhodes (R Ariz.)[5]	John J. McFall (D Calif.)	Arends
94th (1975-1977)	O'Neill	Rhodes	McFall	Robert H. Michel (R Ill.)
95th (1977-1979)	Jim Wright (D Texas)	Rhodes	John Brademas (D Ind.)	Michel
96th (1979-1981)	Wright	Rhodes	Brademas	Michel
97th (1981-1983)	Wright	Robert H. Michel (R Ill.)	Thomas S. Foley (D Wash.)	Trent Lott (R Miss.)
98th (1983-1985)	Wright	Michel	Foley	Lott
99th (1985-1987)	Wright	Michel	Foley	Lott

House Footnotes

1. Clark became minority leader in 1908.
2. Bankhead became Speaker of the House on June 4, 1936. The post of majority leader remained vacant until the next Congress.
3. McCormack became majority leader on Sept. 26, 1940, filling the vacancy caused by the elevation of Rayburn to the post of Speaker of the House on Sept. 16, 1940.
4. Albert became majority leader on Jan. 10, 1962, filling the vacancy caused by the elevation of McCormack to the post of Speaker of the House on Jan. 10, 1962.
5. Rhodes became minority leader on Dec. 7, 1973, filling the vacancy caused by the resignation of Ford on Dec. 6, 1973, to become Vice President.

6. Underwood did not become minority whip until 1901.
7. Lloyd resigned to become chairman of the Democratic Congressional Campaign Committee in 1908. The post of minority whip remained vacant until the beginning of the 62nd Congress.
8. John McDuffie became minority whip after the death of William Oldfield on Nov. 19, 1928.
9. Ramspeck became majority whip on June 8, 1942, filling the vacancy caused by the death of Boland on May 18, 1942.
10. Sparkman became majority whip on Jan. 14, 1946, filling the vacancy caused by the resignation of Ramspeck on Dec. 31, 1945.
11. Boggs became majority whip on Jan. 10, 1962, filling the vacancy caused by the elevation of Albert to the post of majority leader on Jan. 10, 1962.

Sources: Oleszek, Walter J. "Party Whips in the United States Senate." *Journal of Politics* 33 (November 1971): 955-979; Ripley, Randall B. *Party Leaders in the House of Representatives.* Washington, D.C.: Brookings Institution, 1967; U.S. Congress. Joint Committee on Printing. *Official Congressional Directory.* Washington, D.C.: Government Printing Office, 1967- . U.S. Congress. Senate. *Biographical Directory of the American Congress, 1774-1971.* Compiled by Lawrence F. Kennedy. 92d Cong, 1st sess., 1971. S Doc. 8; U.S. Congress. Senate. *Majority and Minority Leaders of the Senate.* Compiled by Floyd M. Riddick. 94th Cong., 1st sess., 1975. S Doc. 66.

Selected Bibliography

Books

Bibby, John F., and Roger H. Davidson. *On Capitol Hill.* 2nd ed. Hinsdale, Ill.: Dryden, 1972.

Christopher, Maurine. *Black Americans in Congress.* New York: Crowell, 1976.

Deckard, Barbara S. *Majority Leadership in the U.S. House.* Baltimore: Johns Hopkins, 1983.

Engelbarts, Rudolph. *Women in the United States Congress, 1917-1972: Their Accomplishments with Biographies.* Littleton, Colo.: Libraries Unlimited, 1974.

Fenno, Richard F., Jr. *Home Style.* Boston: Little, Brown, 1978.

—. *United States Senate: A Bicameral Perspective.* Washington, D.C.: American Enterprise Institute, 1982.

Gertzog, Irwin N. *Congressional Women: Their Recruitment, Treatment and Behavior.* New York: Praeger, 1983.

Goehlert, Robert, and John Sayre. *The United States Congress.* New York: Free Press, 1981.

Hibbing, John R. *Choosing to Leave: Voluntary Retirement from the House of Representatives.* Lanham, Md.: University Press of America, 1982.

Hoopes, Roy. *What a U.S. Senator Does.* New York: Harper and Row, 1975.

Lanham, Charles. *Dictionary of the U.S. Congress, and the General Government.* 6th ed. Hartford, Conn.: T. Belknap and H.E. Goodwin, 1869.

Mann, Thomas E. *Unsafe at Any Margin: Interpreting Congressional Elections.* Washington, D.C.: American Enterprise Institute, 1978.

—, and Norman J. Ornstein, ed. *The American Elections of 1982.* Washington, D.C.: American Enterprise Institute, 1983.

Mayhew, David R. *Congress: The Electoral Connection.* New Haven, Conn.: Yale University Press, 1974.

Scammon, Richard M., and Alice V. McGillivray. *America Votes: A Handbook of Contemporary American Election Statistics.* Washington, D.C.: Congressional Quarterly, 1983.

Smith, William Henry. *Speakers of the House of Representatives of the United States.* 1928 reprint. New York: AMS Press, 1971.

Sobel, Robert, ed. *Biographical Directory of the United States Executive Branch, 1774-1977.* Westport, Conn.: Greenwood Press, 1977.

Stineman, Esther. *American Political Women: Contemporary and Historical Profiles.* Littleton, Colo.: Libraries Unlimited, 1980.

Articles

Alford, John, and John Hibbing. "Increased Incumbency Advantage in the House." *Journal of American Politics* (November 1981): 1042-1061.

Brunk, Gregory. "Turnover and Voting Stability in the Senate." *American Politics Quarterly* (July 1982): 363-374.

Bullock, Charles S. III. "Congressional Voting and the Mobilization of a Black Electorate in the South." *Journal of Politics* (August 1981): 662-682.

—."House Careerists: Changing Patterns of Longevity and Attrition." *American Political Science Review* 66 (1972): 1295-1305.

Burnham, Walter Dean. "Insulation and Responsiveness in Congressional Elections." *Political Science Quarterly* 90 (1975): 411-435.

Campbell, James E. "The Return of the Incumbents: The Nature of the Incumbency Advantage." *Western Political Quarterly* (September 1983): 434-443.

Cooper, Joseph, and William West. "Voluntary Retirement, Incumbency, and the Modern House." *Political Science Quarterly* (Summer 1981): 279-300.

"Democrats Have Net Gain of Two Senate Seats." *Congressional Quarterly Weekly Report,* Nov. 10, 1984, 2901-2906.

"GOP Disappointed with Gains in the House." *Congressional Quarterly Weekly Report,* Nov. 10, 1984, 2897-2899.

"GOP Wins Senate Control for First Time in 28 Years." *Congressional Quarterly Weekly Report,* Nov. 8, 1980, 3300-3303.

Fiorina, Morris P., David W. Rohde, and Peter Wissel. "Historical Change in House Turnover." In *Congress in Change,* ed. Norman J. Ornstein. New York: Praeger, 1975.

Hibbing, John R. "Voluntary Retirements in the House in the Twentieth Century." *Journal of Politics* (November 1982): 1020-1034.

Hinckley, Barbara. "The American Voter in Congressional Elections." *American Political Science Review* 74 (1980): 641-650.

Krehbiel, Keith, and John Wright. "The Incumbency Effect in Congressional Elections: A Test of Two Explanations." *American Journal of Political Science* (February 1983): 140-157.

Mann, Thomas E., and Raymond E. Wolfinger. "Candidates and Parties in Congressional Elections." *American Political Science Review* 74 (1980): 617-632.

Meyer, Mary. "Black Congressmen and How They Grew: One Hundred Years in Congress." *Black Politician* (April 1970): 3-11.

Paulin, Charles O. "The First Elections Under the Constitution." *Iowa Journal of History and Politics* (January 1904): 28.

Peters, John G., and Susan Welch. "The Effects of Charges of Corruption on Voting Behavior in Congressional Elections." *American Political Science Review* 74 (1980): 697-708.

Ragsdale, Lyn. "The Fiction of Congressional Elections as Presidential Events."*American Politics Quarterly* 8 (1980): 395-398.

Government Publications

Baker, Richard A. *The United States Senate: A Historical Bibliography.* Compiled by the U.S. Senate Historical Office. Washington, D.C.: Government Printing Office, 1977.

U.S. Congress. *Black Americans in Congress 1870-1976.* Washington, D.C.: Government Printing Office, 1976.

—. Clerk of the House of Representatives. *Statistics of the Presidential and Congressional Election.* Washington, D.C.: Government Printing Office, 19—.

U.S. Library of Congress. Congressional Research Service. *Election Law Guidebook: Summary of Federal and State Laws Regulating the Nomination and Election of U.S. Senators.* Washington, D.C.: Government Printing Office, 1952—.

—. *Members of Congress Who Choose Not to Run for Reelection to the Seats They Occupy, 1930-1978.* Washington, D.C.: Government Printing Office, 1978.

Tansill, William R. *Members of Congress Who Have Served in Both Houses.* Prepared for U.S. Library of Congress, Legislative Reference Service. Washington, D.C.: Government Printing Office, 1965.

Van Helden, Morrigene. *Women in the Congress of the United States.* Prepared for U.S. Library of Congress, Legislative Reference Service. Washington, D.C.: Government Printing Office, 1968.